VW
Owners
Workshop
Manual

I M Coomber

Models covered
All VW Golf & Jetta 'Mk 2' models with petrol engines, including fuel injection, Formel E and 16-valve models 1043 cc, 1272 cc, 1595 cc & 1781 cc

Covers mechanical features of Van
Does not cover Convertible, Diesel engine, four-wheel-drive, 'Mk 1' models or low-emission models introduced September 1988

(1081-6P4)   ABCDE
                             FGHIJ
                             KL

Haynes

THE BOOK ®

Haynes Publishing Group
Sparkford Nr Yeovil
Somerset BA22 7JJ England

Haynes Publications, Inc
861 Lawrence Drive
Newbury Park
California 91320 USA

Acknowledgements

Thanks are due to the Champion Sparking Plug Company Limited who supplied the illustrations showing the spark plug conditions and Duckhams Oils who supplied lubrication data. Certain other illust-rations are the copyright of Volkswagenwerk Aktiengesellschaft, and are used with their permission. Thanks are also due to Sykes-Pickavant who supplied some of the workshop tools, and all those people at Sparkford who assisted in the production of this Manual.

A book in the **Haynes Owners Workshop Manual Series**

Printed by J. H. Haynes & Co. Ltd, Sparkford, Nr Yeovil, Somerset BA22 7JJ, England

ISBN 1 85010 523 5

British Library Cataloguing in Publication Data
Coomber, Ian, *1943–*
    VW Golf & Jetta ('84 to '88) owners workshop manual.
    1. Cars. Maintenance & repair – Amateurs' manuals
    I. Title   II. Series
    629.28'722
    ISBN 1-85010-523-5

Contents

VW Jetta GLX

VW Golf GL

About this manual

Its aim

The aim of this manual is to help you get the best value from your vehicle. It can do so in several ways. It can help you decide what work must be done (even should you choose to get it done by a garage), provide information on routine maintenance and servicing, and give a logical course of action and diagnosis when random faults occur. However, it is hoped that you will use the manual by tackling the work yourself. On simpler jobs it may even be quicker than booking the car into a garage and going there twice, to leave and collect it. Perhaps most important, a lot of money can be saved by avoiding the costs a garage must charge to cover its labour and overheads.

The manual has drawings and descriptions to show the function of the various components so that their layout can be understood. Then the tasks are described and photographed in a step-by-step sequence so that even a novice can do the work.

Its arrangement

The manual is divided into twelve Chapters, each covering a logical sub-division of the vehicle. The Chapters are each divided into Sections, numbered with single figures, eg 5; and the Sections into paragraphs (or sub-sections), with decimal numbers following on from the Section they are in, eg 5.1, 5.2, 5.3 etc.

It is freely illustrated, especially in those parts where there is a detailed sequence of operations to be carried out. There are two forms of illustration: figures and photographs. The figures are numbered in sequence with decimal numbers, according to their position in the Chapter – eg Fig. 6.4 is the fourth drawing/illustration in Chapter 6. Photographs carry the same number (either individually or in related groups) as the Section or sub-section to which they relate.

There is an alphabetical index at the back of the manual as well as a contents list at the front. Each Chapter is also preceded by its own individual contents list.

References to the 'left' or 'right' of the vehicle are in the sense of a person in the driver's seat facing forwards.

Unless otherwise stated, nuts and bolts are removed by turning anti-clockwise, and tightened by turning clockwise.

Vehicle manufacturers continually make changes to specifications and recommendations, and these, when notified, are incorporated into our manuals at the earliest opportunity.

Whilst every care is taken to ensure that the information in this manual is correct, no liability can be accepted by the authors or publishers for loss, damage or injury caused by any errors in, or omissions from, the information given.

Introduction to the Volkswagen Golf and Jetta

The 'new' Volkswagen Golf and Jetta range of models was introduced in March 1984, a revised body and trim features being the main visual difference to the earlier range of models.

The engine and transmission are mounted transversely at the front, and drive is through the front wheels. Detailed improvements have been made to the mechanics to improve the power output and economy.

As with earlier models the new range is proving popular, giving economy, reliability, comfort and, if previous models can be used as a yardstick, long life.

General dimensions, weights and capacities

Dimensions
Overall length:
    Golf .... 3985 mm (157 in)
    Jetta .... 4315 mm (170 in)
Overall width:
    Golf .... 1665 mm (66 in)
    Jetta .... 1665 mm (66 in)
Overall height:
    Golf .... 1415 mm (56 in)
    Golf GTI .... 1405 mm (55 in)
    Jetta .... 1415 mm (56 in)
Wheelbase:
    All models .... 2475 mm (98 in)
Turning circle:
    All models .... 10.5 m (34.4 ft)

Weights
Kerb weight:
    Golf Base model .... 837 kg (1845 lb)
    Golf C and C Formel E:
        Manual .... 847 kg (1867 lb)
        Automatic .... 867 kg (1911 lb)
    Golf GL:
        Manual .... 892 kg (1966 lb)
        Automatic .... 912 kg (2011 lb)
    Golf GTI .... 1003 kg (2211 lb)
    Jetta C .... 897 kg (1978 lb)
    Jetta CL Formel E .... 897 kg (1978 lb)
    Jetta GL:
        Manual .... 922 kg (2033 lb)
        Automatic .... 952 kg (2099 lb)
Trailer load (max) – with brakes:
    1.05 litre .... 800 kg (1764 lb)
    1.3 litre .... 1000 kg (2205 lb)
    1.6 and 1.8 litre .... 1200 kg (2646 lb)
Roof rack load (max):
    All models .... 75 kg (165 lb)

Capacities
Engine oil:
    1.05 and 1.3 litre:
        Rocker finger engine:
            With filter change .... 3.0 litre (5.3 Imp pints)
            Without filter change .... 2.5 litre (4.4 Imp pints)
        Hydraulic tappet engine:
            With filter change .... 3.5 litre (6.2 Imp pints)
            Without filter change .... 3.0 litre (5.3 Imp pints)
    1.6 and 1.8 litre:
        Pre-August 1985:
            With filter change .... 3.5 litre (6.2 Imp pints)
            Without filter change .... 3.0 litre (5.3 Imp pints)
        August 1985-on:
            With filter change .... 4.0 litre (7.0 Imp pints)
            Without filter change .... 3.5 litre (6.2 Imp pints)
Manual gearbox and final drive:
    4-speed (084 gearbox) .... 2.2 litre (3.9 Imp pints)
    4-speed (020 gearbox) .... 1.5 litre (2.6 Imp pints)
    5-speed (085 gearbox) .... 3.1 litre (5.5 Imp pints)
    5-speed (020 gearbox) .... 2.0 litre (3.5 Imp pints)
Automatic transmission fluid:
    Total from dry .... 6.0 litre (10.6 Imp pints)
    Service (drain and refill) .... 3.0 litre (5.3 Imp pints)
    Final drive capacity .... 0.75 litre (1.3 Imp pints)
Cooling system:
    Total capacity (approx) .... 6.3 litre (11.1 Imp pints)
Fuel tank:
    Total capacity (all models) .... 55 litre (12 gal)

Jacking and towing

Jacking

The jack supplied in the vehicle tool kit by the manufacturer should only be used for emergency roadside wheel changing unless it is supplemented by safety stands.

The jack supplied is of the half scissors type. Check that the handbrake is fully applied before using the jack, and only jack the vehicle up on firm level ground. If the ground is not firm you will need to position a large flat packing piece under the jack base to provide additional support.

Chock the wheel diagonally opposite the one to be changed. Using the tools provided remove the hub cap where necessary, then loosen the the wheel bolts half a turn. Locate the lifting arm of the jack beneath the reinforced seam of the side sill panel (photo) directly beneath the wedge shaped depression nearest to the wheel to be removed. Turn the jack

handle until the base of the jack contacts the ground directly beneath the sill then continue to turn the handle until the wheel is free of the ground. Unscrew the wheel bolts and remove the wheel. On light alloy wheels prise off the centre trim cap and press it into the spare wheel (photo).

Locate the spare wheel on the hub, then insert and tighten the bolts in diagonal sequence. Lower the jack and fully tighten the bolts. Refit the hub cap where necessary, remove the chock and relocate the tool kit, jack and wheel in the luggage compartment.

When jacking up the car with a pillar or trolley jack, position the jack beneath the reinforced plate behind the front wheel (see illustration) or beneath the reinforced seam at the rear of the side sill panel. Use the same positions when supporting the car with axle stands. *Never jack up the car beneath the suspension or axle components, the sump, or the gearbox*

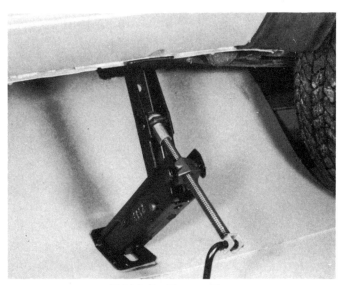

Vehicle jacking position

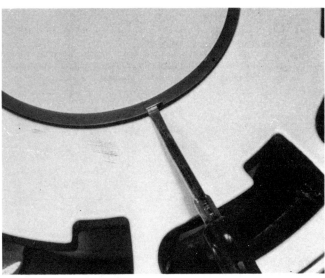

Removing the wheel centre trim

Alternative jack location point at front (A) and rear (B)

Towing

Towing eyes are fitted to the front and rear of the vehicle (photos), the front towing eye being covered by a plastic flap. Compress the flap and pivot it downwards to expose the towing eye. A tow line should not be attached to any other points. It is preferable to use a slightly elastic tow line, to reduce the strain on both vehicles, either by having a tow line manufactured from synthetic fibre, or one which is fitted with an elastic link.

When towing, the following important precautions must be observed:

(a) Turn the ignition key of the vehicle being towed, so that the steering wheel is free (unlocked)

(b) Remember that when the engine is not running the brake servo will not operate, so that additional pressure will be required on the brake pedal after the first few applications

(c) On vehicles with automatic transmission, ensure that the gear selector lever is at N. Do not tow faster than 30 mph (45 kph), or further than 30 miles (45 km) unless the front wheels are lifted clear of the ground.

(d) On models fitted with power steering additional force will be required to turn the steering wheel when the engine is not running.

Towing eye – front

Towing eye – rear

Buying spare parts and vehicle identification numbers

Buying spare parts

Spare parts are available from many sources, for example: VW garages, other garages and accessory shops, and motor factors. Our advice regarding spare parts is as follows:

Officially appointed VW garages – This is the best source of parts which are peculiar to your car and otherwise not generally available (eg complete cylinder heads, internal gearbox components, badges, interior trim etc). It is also the only place at which you should buy parts if your vehicle is still under warranty – non-VW components may invalidate the warranty. To be sure of obtaining the correct parts it will always be necessary to give the storeman your car's engine and chassis number, and if possible, to take the 'old' part along for positive identification. Remember that many parts are available on a factory exchange scheme – any parts returned should always be clean! It obviously makes good sense to go straight to the specialists on your car for this type of part for they are best equipped to supply you.

Other garages and accessory shops – These are often very good places to buy material and components needed for the maintenance of your car (eg oil filters, spark plugs, bulbs, drivebelts, oils and grease, touch-up paint, filler paste etc). They also sell general accessories, usually have convenient opening hours, charge lower prices and can often be found not far from home.

Motor factors – Good factors stock all of the more important components which wear out relatively quickly (eg clutch components, pistons, valves, exhaust systems, brake cylinders/pipes/hoses/seals/shoes and pads etc). Motor factors will often provide new or reconditioned components on a part exchange basis – this can save a considerable amount of money.

Vehicle identification numbers

It is most important to identify the vehicle accurately when ordering spare parts or asking for information. There have been many modifications to this range already.

The vehicle identification plate is located within the engine compartment on the right-hand side panel.

The chassis number is in the engine compartment on the bulkhead.

The engine number on 1.05 and 1.3 litre models is located on the cylinder block next to the alternator bracket.

The engine number on 1.6 and 1.8 litre models is located on the left-hand side of the cylinder block.

These numbers should be identified and recorded by the owner; they are required when ordering spares, going through the customers, and by the police if the vehicle is stolen.

When ordering spares remember that VW output is such that inevitably spares vary, are duplicated, and are held on a usage basis. If the storeman does not have the correct identification, he cannot produce the correct item. It is a good idea to take the old part if possible to compare it with a new one.

When fitting accessories it is best to fit VW recommended ones. They are designed specifically for the vehicle.

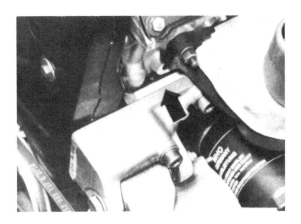

Engine number location – 1.05 and 1.3 litre

Identification number locations in the engine compartment

1 *Vehicle identification plate* 3 *Chassis number*
2 *Engine number*

Engine number location – 1.6 and 1.8 litre

General repair procedures

Whenever servicing, repair or overhaul work is carried out on the car or its components, it is necessary to observe the following procedures and instructions. This will assist in carrying out the operation efficiently and to a professional standard of workmanship.

Joint mating faces and gaskets

Where a gasket is used between the mating faces of two components, ensure that it is renewed on reassembly, and fit it dry unless otherwise stated in the repair procedure. Make sure that the mating faces are clean and dry with all traces of old gasket removed. When cleaning a joint face, use a tool which is not likely to score or damage the face, and remove any burrs or nicks with an oilstone or fine file.

Make sure that tapped holes are cleaned with a pipe cleaner, and keep them free of jointing compound if this is being used unless specifically instructed otherwise.

Ensure that all orifices, channels or pipes are clear and blow through them, preferably using compressed air.

Oil seals

Whenever an oil seal is removed from its working location, either individually or as part of an assembly, it should be renewed.

The very fine sealing lip of the seal is easily damaged and will not seal if the surface it contacts is not completely clean and free from scratches, nicks or grooves. If the original sealing surface of the component cannot be restored, the component should be renewed.

Protect the lips of the seal from any surface which may damage them in the course of fitting. Use tape or a conical sleeve where possible. Lubricate the seal lips with oil before fitting and, on dual lipped seals, fill the space between the lips with grease.

Unless otherwise stated, oil seals must be fitted with their sealing lips toward the lubricant to be sealed.

Use a tubular drift or block of wood of the appropriate size to install the seal and, if the seal housing is shouldered, drive the seal down to the shoulder. If the seal housing is unshouldered, the seal should be fitted with its face flush with the housing top face.

Screw threads and fastenings

Always ensure that a blind tapped hole is completely free from oil, grease, water or other fluid before installing the bolt or stud. Failure to do this could cause the housing to crack due to the hydraulic action of the bolt or stud as it is screwed in.

When tightening a castellated nut to accept a split pin, tighten the nut to the specified torque, where applicable, and then tighten further to the next split pin hole. Never slacken the nut to align a split pin hole unless stated in the repair procedure.

When checking or retightening a nut or bolt to a specified torque setting, slacken the nut or bolt by a quarter of a turn, and then retighten to the specified setting.

Locknuts, locktabs and washers

Any fastening which will rotate against a component or housing in the course of tightening should always have a washer between it and the relevant component or housing.

Spring or split washers should always be renewed when they are used to lock a critical component such as a big-end bearing retaining nut or bolt.

Locktabs which are folded over to retain a nut or bolt should always be renewed.

VW recommend that all self-locking nuts be renewed once they are removed.

Split pins must always be replaced with new ones of the correct size for the hole.

Special tools

Some repair procedures in this manual entail the use of special tools such as a press, two or three-legged pullers, spring compressors etc. Wherever possible, suitable readily available alternatives to the manufacturer's special tools are described, and are shown in use. In some instances, where no alternative is possible, it has been necessary to resort to the use of a manufacturer's tool and this has been done for reasons of safety as well as the efficient completion of the repair operation. Unless you are highly skilled and have a thorough understanding of the procedure described, never attempt to bypass the use of any special tool when the procedure described specifies its use. Not only is there a very great risk of personal injury, but expensive damage could be caused to the components involved.

Tools and working facilities

Introduction

A selection of good tools is a fundamental requirement for anyone contemplating the maintenance and repair of a motor vehicle. For the owner who does not possess any, their purchase will prove a considerable expense, offsetting some of the savings made by doing-it-yourself. However, provided that the tools purchased are of good quality, they will last for many years and prove an extremely worthwhile investment.

To help the average owner to decide which tools are needed to carry out the various tasks detailed in this manual, we have compiled three lists of tools under the following headings: *Maintenance and minor repair, Repair and overhaul,* and *Special.* The newcomer to practical mechanics should start off with the *Maintenance and minor repair* tool kit and confine himself to the simpler jobs around the vehicle. Then, as his confidence and experience grow, he can undertake more difficult tasks, buying extra tools as, and when, they are needed. In this way, a *Maintenance and minor repair* tool kit can be built-up into a *Repair and overhaul* tool kit over a considerable period of time without any major cash outlays. The experienced do-it-yourselfer will have a tool kit good enough for most repair and overhaul procedures and will add tools from the *Special* category when he feels the expense is justified by the amount of use to which these tools will be put.

It is obviously not possible to cover the subject of tools fully here. For those who wish to learn more about tools and their use there is a book entitled *How to Choose and Use Car Tools* available from the publishers of this manual.

Maintenance and minor repair tool kit

The tools given in this list should be considered as a minimum requirement if routine maintenance, servicing and minor repair operations are to be undertaken. We recommend the purchase of combination spanners (ring one end, open-ended the other); although more expensive than open-ended ones, they do give the advantages of both types of spanner.

> *Combination spanners - 8, 9, 10, 11, 12, 13, 14, 17 & 19 mm*
> *Adjustable spanner - 9 inch*
> *Gearbox drain plug key*
> *Spark plug spanner (with rubber insert)*
> *Spark plug gap adjustment tool*
> *Set of feeler gauges*
> *Brake bleed nipple spanner*
> *Screwdriver - 4 in long x $^1/4$ in dia (flat blade)*
> *Screwdriver - 4 in long x $^1/4$ in dia (cross blade)*
> *Combination pliers - 6 inch*
> *Hacksaw (junior)*
> *Tyre pump*
> *Tyre pressure gauge*
> *Oil can*
> *Fine emery cloth (1 sheet)*
> *Wire brush (small)*
> *Funnel (medium size)*

Repair and overhaul tool kit

These tools are virtually essential for anyone undertaking any major repairs to a motor vehicle, and are additional to those given in the *Maintenance and minor repair* list. Included in this list is a comprehensive set of sockets. Although these are expensive they will be found invaluable as they are so versatile - particularly if various drives are included in the set. We recommend the $^1/2$ in square-drive type, as this can be used with most proprietary torque wrenches. If you cannot afford a socket set, even bought piecemeal, then inexpensive tubular box spanners are a useful alternative.

The tools in this list will occasionally need to be supplemented by tools from the *Special* list.

> *Sockets (or box spanners) to cover range in previous list*
> *Reversible ratchet drive (for use with sockets)*
> *Extension piece, 10 inch (for use with sockets)*
> *Universal joint (for use with sockets)*
> *Torque wrench (for use with sockets)*
> *'Mole' wrench - 8 inch*
> *Ball pein hammer*
> *Soft-faced hammer, plastic or rubber*
> *Screwdriver - 6 in long x $^5/16$ in dia (flat blade)*
> *Screwdriver - 2 in long x $^5/16$ in square (flat blade)*
> *Screwdriver - $1^1/2$ in long x $^1/4$ in dia (cross blade)*
> *Screwdriver - 3 in long x $^1/8$ in dia (electricians)*
> *Pliers - electricians side cutters*
> *Pliers - needle nosed*
> *Pliers - circlip (internal and external)*
> *Cold chisel - $^1/2$ inch*
> *Scriber*
> *Scraper*
> *Centre punch*
> *Pin punch*
> *Hacksaw*
> *Valve grinding tool*
> *Steel rule/straight-edge*
> *Allen keys*
> *Selection of files*
> *Wire brush (large)*
> *Axle-stands*
> *Jack (strong trolley or hydraulic type)*

Special tools

The tools in this list are those which are not used regularly, are expensive to buy, or which need to be used in accordance with their manufacturers' instructions. Unless relatively difficult mechanical jobs are undertaken frequently, it will not be economic to buy many of these tools. Where this is the case, you could consider clubbing together with friends (or joining a motorists' club) to make a joint purchase, or borrowing the tools against a deposit from a local garage or tool hire specialist.

The following list contains only those tools and instruments freely available to the public, and not those special tools produced by the vehicle manufacturer specifically for its dealer network. You will find occasional references to these manufacturers' special tools in the text of this manual. Generally, an alternative method of doing the job without the vehicle manufacturers' special tool is given. However, sometimes, there is no alternative to using them. Where this is the case and the relevant tool cannot be bought or borrowed, you will have to entrust the work to a franchised garage.

Set of splined keys
Valve spring compressor
Piston ring compressor
Balljoint separator
Universal hub/bearing puller or slide hammer
Impact screwdriver
Micrometer and/or vernier gauge
Dial gauge
Stroboscopic timing light
Dwell angle meter/tachometer
Universal electrical multi-meter
Cylinder compression gauge
Lifting tackle
Trolley jack
Light with extension lead

Buying tools

For practically all tools, a tool factor is the best source since he will have a very comprehensive range compared with the average garage or accessory shop. Having said that, accessory shops often offer excellent quality tools at discount prices, so it pays to shop around.

Remember, you don't have to buy the most expensive items on the shelf, but it is always advisable to steer clear of the very cheap tools. There are plenty of good tools around at reasonable prices, so ask the proprietor or manager of the shop for advice before making a purchase.

Care and maintenance of tools

Having purchased a reasonable tool kit, it is necessary to keep the tools in a clean serviceable condition. After use, always wipe off any dirt, grease and metal particles using a clean, dry cloth, before putting the tools away. Never leave them lying around after they have been used. A simple tool rack on the garage or workshop wall, for items such as screwdrivers and pliers is a good idea. Store all normal wrenches and sockets in a metal box. Any measuring instruments, gauges, meters, etc, must be carefully stored where they cannot be damaged or become rusty.

Take a little care when tools are used. Hammer heads inevitably become marked and screwdrivers lose the keen edge on their blades from time to time. A little timely attention with emery cloth or a file will soon restore items like this to a good serviceable finish.

Working facilities

Not to be forgotten when discussing tools, is the workshop itself. If anything more than routine maintenance is to be carried out, some form of suitable working area becomes essential.

It is appreciated that many an owner mechanic is forced by circumstances to remove an engine or similar item, without the benefit of a garage or workshop. Having done this, any repairs should always be done under the cover of a roof.

Wherever possible, any dismantling should be done on a clean, flat workbench or table at a suitable working height.

Any workbench needs a vice: one with a jaw opening of 4 in (100 mm) is suitable for most jobs. As mentioned previously, some clean dry storage space is also required for tools, as well as for lubricants, cleaning fluids, touch-up paints and so on, which become necessary.

Another item which may be required, and which has a much more general usage, is an electric drill with a chuck capacity of at least 5/16 in (8 mm). This, together with a good range of twist drills, is virtually essential for fitting accessories such as mirrors and reversing lights.

Last, but not least, always keep a supply of old newspapers and clean, lint-free rags available, and try to keep any working area as clean as possible.

Spanner jaw gap comparison table

Jaw gap (in)	Spanner size
0.250	$\frac{1}{4}$ in AF
0.276	7 mm
0.313	$\frac{5}{16}$ in AF
0.315	8 mm
0.344	$\frac{11}{32}$ in AF; $\frac{1}{8}$ in Whitworth
0.354	9 mm
0.375	$\frac{3}{8}$ in AF
0.394	10 mm
0.433	11 mm
0.438	$\frac{7}{16}$ in AF
0.445	$\frac{3}{16}$ in Whitworth; $\frac{1}{4}$ in BSF
0.472	12 mm
0.500	$\frac{1}{2}$ in AF
0.512	13 mm
0.525	$\frac{1}{4}$ in Whitworth; $\frac{5}{16}$ in BSF
0.551	14 mm
0.563	$\frac{9}{16}$ in AF
0.591	15 mm
0.600	$\frac{5}{16}$ in Whitworth; $\frac{3}{8}$ in BSF
0.625	$\frac{5}{8}$ in AF
0.630	16 mm
0.669	17 mm
0.686	$\frac{11}{16}$ in AF
0.709	18 mm
0.710	$\frac{3}{8}$ in Whitworth; $\frac{7}{16}$ in BSF
0.748	19 mm
0.750	$\frac{3}{4}$ in AF
0.813	$\frac{13}{16}$ in AF
0.820	$\frac{7}{16}$ in Whitworth; $\frac{1}{2}$ in BSF
0.866	22 mm
0.875	$\frac{7}{8}$ in AF
0.920	$\frac{1}{2}$ in Whitworth; $\frac{9}{16}$ in BSF
0.938	$\frac{15}{16}$ in AF
0.945	24 mm
1.000	1 in AF
1.010	$\frac{9}{16}$ in Whitworth; $\frac{5}{8}$ in BSF
1.024	26 mm
1.063	$1\frac{1}{16}$ in AF; 27 mm
1.100	$\frac{5}{8}$ in Whitworth; $\frac{11}{16}$ in BSF
1.125	$1\frac{1}{8}$ in AF
1.181	30 mm
1.200	$\frac{11}{16}$ in Whitworth; $\frac{3}{4}$ in BSF
1.250	$1\frac{1}{4}$ in AF
1.260	32 mm
1.300	$\frac{3}{4}$ in Whitworth; $\frac{7}{8}$ in BSF
1.313	$1\frac{5}{16}$ in AF
1.390	$\frac{13}{16}$ in Whitworth; $\frac{15}{16}$ in BSF
1.417	36 mm
1.438	$1\frac{7}{16}$ in AF
1.480	$\frac{7}{8}$ in Whitworth; 1 in BSF
1.500	$1\frac{1}{2}$ in AF
1.575	40 mm; $\frac{15}{16}$ in Whitworth
1.614	41 mm
1.625	$1\frac{5}{8}$ in AF
1.670	1 in Whitworth; $1\frac{1}{8}$ in BSF
1.688	$1\frac{11}{16}$ in AF
1.811	46 mm
1.813	$1\frac{13}{16}$ in AF
1.860	$1\frac{1}{8}$ in Whitworth; $1\frac{1}{4}$ in BSF
1.875	$1\frac{7}{8}$ in AF
1.969	50 mm
2.000	2 in AF
2.050	$1\frac{1}{4}$ in Whitworth; $1\frac{3}{8}$ in BSF
2.165	55 mm
2.362	60 mm

Conversion factors

Length (distance)

Inches (in)	X	25.4	= Millimetres (mm)	X 0.0394	= Inches (in)
Feet (ft)	X	0.305	= Metres (m)	X 3.281	= Feet (ft)
Miles	X	1.609	= Kilometres (km)	X 0.621	= Miles

Volume (capacity)

Cubic inches (cu in; in³)	X	16.387	= Cubic centimetres (cc; cm³)	X 0.061	= Cubic inches (cu in; in³)
Imperial pints (Imp pt)	X	0.568	= Litres (l)	X 1.76	= Imperial pints (Imp pt)
Imperial quarts (Imp qt)	X	1.137	= Litres (l)	X 0.88	= Imperial quarts (Imp qt)
Imperial quarts (Imp qt)	X	1.201	= US quarts (US qt)	X 0.833	= Imperial quarts (Imp qt)
US quarts (US qt)	X	0.946	= Litres (l)	X 1.057	= US quarts (US qt)
Imperial gallons (Imp gal)	X	4.546	= Litres (l)	X 0.22	= Imperial gallons (Imp gal)
Imperial gallons (Imp gal)	X	1.201	= US gallons (US gal)	X 0.833	= Imperial gallons (Imp gal)
US gallons (US gal)	X	3.785	= Litres (l)	X 0.264	= US gallons (US gal)

Mass (weight)

Ounces (oz)	X	28.35	= Grams (g)	X 0.035	= Ounces (oz)
Pounds (lb)	X	0.454	= Kilograms (kg)	X 2.205	= Pounds (lb)

Force

Ounces-force (ozf; oz)	X	0.278	= Newtons (N)	X 3.6	= Ounces-force (ozf; oz)
Pounds-force (lbf; lb)	X	4.448	= Newtons (N)	X 0.225	= Pounds-force (lbf; lb)
Newtons (N)	X	0.1	= Kilograms-force (kgf; kg)	X 9.81	= Newtons (N)

Pressure

Pounds-force per square inch (psi; lbf/in²; lb/in²)	X	0.070	= Kilograms-force per square centimetre (kgf/cm²; kg/cm²)	X 14.223	= Pounds-force per square inch (psi; lbf/in²; lb/in²)
Pounds-force per square inch (psi; lbf/in²; lb/in²)	X	0.068	= Atmospheres (atm)	X 14.696	= Pounds-force per square inch (psi; lbf/in²; lb/in²)
Pounds-force per square inch (psi; lbf/in²; lb/in²)	X	0.069	= Bars	X 14.5	= Pounds-force per square inch (psi; lbf/in²; lb/in²)
Pounds-force per square inch (psi; lbf/in²; lb/in²)	X	6.895	= Kilopascals (kPa)	X 0.145	= Pounds-force per square inch (psi; lbf/in²; lb/in²)
Kilopascals (kPa)	X	0.01	= Kilograms-force per square centimetre (kgf/cm²; kg/cm²)	X 98.1	= Kilopascals (kPa)
Millibar (mbar)	X	100	= Pascals (Pa)	X 0.01	= Millibar (mbar)
Millibar (mbar)	X	0.0145	= Pounds-force per square inch (psi; lbf/in²; lb/in²)	X 68.947	= Millibar (mbar)
Millibar (mbar)	X	0.75	= Millimetres of mercury (mmHg)	X 1.333	= Millibar (mbar)
Millibar (mbar)	X	0.401	= Inches of water (inH₂O)	X 2.491	= Millibar (mbar)
Millimetres of mercury (mmHg)	X	0.535	= Inches of water (inH₂O)	X 1.868	= Millimetres of mercury (mmHg)
Inches of water (inH₂O)	X	0.036	= Pounds-force per square inch (psi; lbf/in²; lb/in²)	X 27.68	= Inches of water (inH₂O)

Torque (moment of force)

Pounds-force inches (lbf in; lb in)	X	1.152	= Kilograms-force centimetre (kgf cm; kg cm)	X 0.868	= Pounds-force inches (lbf in; lb in)
Pounds-force inches (lbf in; lb in)	X	0.113	= Newton metres (Nm)	X 8.85	= Pounds-force inches (lbf in; lb in)
Pounds-force inches (lbf in; lb in)	X	0.083	= Pounds-force feet (lbf ft; lb ft)	X 12	= Pounds-force inches (lbf in; lb in)
Pounds-force feet (lbf ft; lb ft)	X	0.138	= Kilograms-force metres (kgf m; kg m)	X 7.233	= Pounds-force feet (lbf ft; lb ft)
Pounds-force feet (lbf ft; lb ft)	X	1.356	= Newton metres (Nm)	X 0.738	= Pounds-force feet (lbf ft; lb ft)
Newton metres (Nm)	X	0.102	= Kilograms-force metres (kgf m; kg m)	X 9.804	= Newton metres (Nm)

Power

Horsepower (hp)	X	745.7	= Watts (W)	X 0.0013	= Horsepower (hp)

Velocity (speed)

Miles per hour (miles/hr; mph)	X	1.609	= Kilometres per hour (km/hr; kph)	X 0.621	= Miles per hour (miles/hr; mph)

Fuel consumption*

Miles per gallon, Imperial (mpg)	X	0.354	= Kilometres per litre (km/l)	X 2.825	= Miles per gallon, Imperial (mpg)
Miles per gallon, US (mpg)	X	0.425	= Kilometres per litre (km/l)	X 2.352	= Miles per gallon, US (mpg)

Temperature

Degrees Fahrenheit = (°C x 1.8) + 32   Degrees Celsius (Degrees Centigrade; °C) = (°F - 32) x 0.56

It is common practice to convert from miles per gallon (mpg) to litres/100 kilometres (l/100km), where mpg (Imperial) x l/100 km = 282 and mpg (US) x l/100 km = 235

Safety first!

Professional motor mechanics are trained in safe working procedures. However enthusiastic you may be about getting on with the job in hand, do take the time to ensure that your safety is not put at risk. A moment's lack of attention can result in an accident, as can failure to observe certain elementary precautions.

There will always be new ways of having accidents, and the following points do not pretend to be a comprehensive list of all dangers; they are intended rather to make you aware of the risks and to encourage a safety-conscious approach to all work you carry out on your vehicle.

Essential DOs and DON'Ts

DON'T rely on a single jack when working underneath the vehicle. Always use reliable additional means of support, such as axle stands, securely placed under a part of the vehicle that you know will not give way.

DON'T attempt to loosen or tighten high-torque nuts (e.g. wheel hub nuts) while the vehicle is on a jack; it may be pulled off.

DON'T start the engine without first ascertaining that the transmission is in neutral (or 'Park' where applicable) and the parking brake applied.

DON'T suddenly remove the filler cap from a hot cooling system – cover it with a cloth and release the pressure gradually first, or you may get scalded by escaping coolant.

DON'T attempt to drain oil until you are sure it has cooled sufficiently to avoid scalding you.

DON'T grasp any part of the engine, exhaust or catalytic converter without first ascertaining that it is sufficiently cool to avoid burning you.

DON'T allow brake fluid or antifreeze to contact vehicle paintwork.

DON'T syphon toxic liquids such as fuel, brake fluid or antifreeze by mouth, or allow them to remain on your skin.

DON'T inhale dust – it may be injurious to health (see *Asbestos* below).

DON'T allow any spilt oil or grease to remain on the floor – wipe it up straight away, before someone slips on it.

DON'T use ill-fitting spanners or other tools which may slip and cause injury.

DON'T attempt to lift a heavy component which may be beyond your capability – get assistance.

DON'T rush to finish a job, or take unverified short cuts.

DON'T allow children or animals in or around an unattended vehicle.

DO wear eye protection when using power tools such as drill, sander, bench grinder etc, and when working under the vehicle.

DO use a barrier cream on your hands prior to undertaking dirty jobs – it will protect your skin from infection as well as making the dirt easier to remove afterwards; but make sure your hands aren't left slippery. Note that long-term contact with used engine oil can be a health hazard.

DO keep loose clothing (cuffs, tie etc) and long hair well out of the way of moving mechanical parts.

DO remove rings, wristwatch etc, before working on the vehicle – especially the electrical system.

DO ensure that any lifting tackle used has a safe working load rating adequate for the job.

DO keep your work area tidy – it is only too easy to fall over articles left lying around.

DO get someone to check periodically that all is well, when working alone on the vehicle.

DO carry out work in a logical sequence and check that everything is correctly assembled and tightened afterwards.

DO remember that your vehicle's safety affects that of yourself and others. If in doubt on any point, get specialist advice.

IF, in spite of following these precautions, you are unfortunate enough to injure yourself, seek medical attention as soon as possible.

Asbestos

Certain friction, insulating, sealing, and other products – such as brake linings, brake bands, clutch linings, torque converters, gaskets, etc – contain asbestos. *Extreme care must be taken to avoid inhalation of dust from such products since it is hazardous to health.* If in doubt, assume that they *do* contain asbestos.

Fire

Remember at all times that petrol (gasoline) is highly flammable. Never smoke, or have any kind of naked flame around, when working on the vehicle. But the risk does not end there – a spark caused by an electrical short-circuit, by two metal surfaces contacting each other, by careless use of tools, or even by static electricity built up in your body under certain conditions, can ignite petrol vapour, which in a confined space is highly explosive.

Always disconnect the battery earth (ground) terminal before working on any part of the fuel or electrical system, and never risk spilling fuel on to a hot engine or exhaust.

It is recommended that a fire extinguisher of a type suitable for fuel and electrical fires is kept handy in the garage or workplace at all times. Never try to extinguish a fuel or electrical fire with water.

Note: *Any reference to a 'torch' appearing in this manual should always be taken to mean a hand-held battery-operated electric lamp or flashlight. It does NOT mean a welding/gas torch or blowlamp.*

Fumes

Certain fumes are highly toxic and can quickly cause unconsciousness and even death if inhaled to any extent. Petrol (gasoline) vapour comes into this category, as do the vapours from certain solvents such as trichloroethylene. Any draining or pouring of such volatile fluids should be done in a well ventilated area.

When using cleaning fluids and solvents, read the instructions carefully. Never use materials from unmarked containers – they may give off poisonous vapours.

Never run the engine of a motor vehicle in an enclosed space such as a garage. Exhaust fumes contain carbon monoxide which is extremely poisonous; if you need to run the engine, always do so in the open air or at least have the rear of the vehicle outside the workplace.

If you are fortunate enough to have the use of an inspection pit, never drain or pour petrol, and never run the engine, while the vehicle is standing over it; the fumes, being heavier than air, will concentrate in the pit with possibly lethal results.

The battery

Never cause a spark, or allow a naked light, near the vehicle's battery. It will normally be giving off a certain amount of hydrogen gas, which is highly explosive.

Always disconnect the battery earth (ground) terminal before working on the fuel or electrical systems.

If possible, loosen the filler plugs or cover when charging the battery from an external source. Do not charge at an excessive rate or the battery may burst.

Take care when topping up and when carrying the battery. The acid electrolyte, even when diluted, is very corrosive and should not be allowed to contact the eyes or skin.

If you ever need to prepare electrolyte yourself, always add the acid slowly to the water, and never the other way round. Protect against splashes by wearing rubber gloves and goggles.

When jump starting a car using a booster battery, for negative earth (ground) vehicles, connect the jump leads in the following sequence: First connect one jump lead between the positive (+) terminals of the two batteries. Then connect the other jump lead first to the negative (–) terminal of the booster battery, and then to a good earthing (ground) point on the vehicle to be started, at least 18 in (45 cm) from the battery if possible. Ensure that hands and jump leads are clear of any moving parts, and that the two vehicles do not touch. Disconnect the leads in the reverse order.

Mains electricity

When using an electric power tool, inspection light etc, which works from the mains, always ensure that the appliance is correctly connected to its plug and that, where necessary, it is properly earthed (grounded). Do not use such appliances in damp conditions and, again, beware of creating a spark or applying excessive heat in the vicinity of fuel or fuel vapour.

Ignition HT voltage

A severe electric shock can result from touching certain parts of the ignition system, such as the HT leads, when the engine is running or being cranked, particularly if components are damp or the insulation is defective. Where an electronic ignition system is fitted, the HT voltage is much higher and could prove fatal.

Routine maintenance

For modifications, and information applicable to later models, see Supplement at end of manual

Maintenance is essential for ensuring safety and desirable for the purpose of getting the best in terms of performance and economy from your car. Over the years the need for periodic lubrication has been greatly reduced, if not totally eliminated. This has unfortunately tended to lead some owners to think that because no such action is required,

the items either no longer exist, or will last forever. This is certainly not the case; it is essential to carry out regular visual examination as comprehensively as possible in order to spot any possible defects at an early stage, before they develop into major expensive repairs.

Engine compartment (1.3 litre) – air cleaner removed

1	Engine oil dipstick	4	Carburettor
2	Fuel line filter	5	Ignition coil
3	Brake master cylinder reservoir	6	Cooling system expansion tank

7	Windscreen/headlight washer reservoir	9	Battery
8	Ignition distributor	10	Cooling fan
		11	Engine oil filler cap

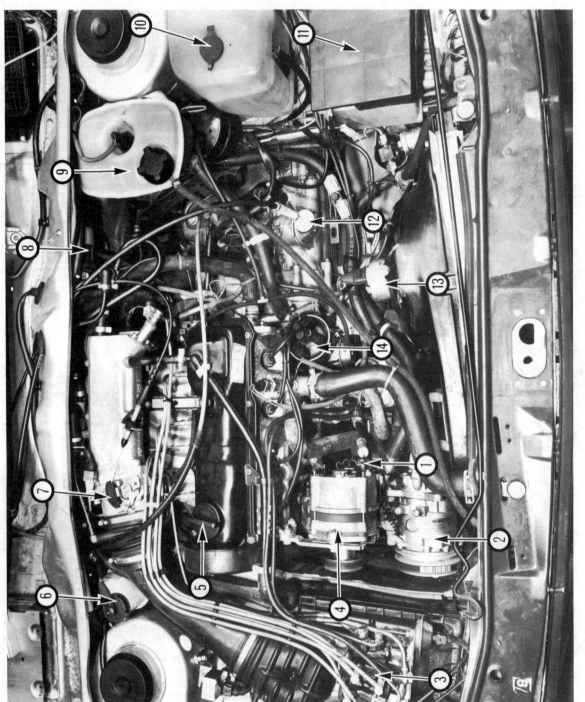

Engine compartment – fuel injection model

1 Engine oil dipstick
2 Compressor (air
   conditioning)
3 Fuel distributor

4 Alternator
5 Engine oil filler cap
6 Brake master cylinder
   reservoir

7 Throttle housing
8 Ignition coil
9 Cooling system expansion
   tank

10 Windscreen/headlamp
    washer reservoir
11 Battery

12 Clutch cable
13 Cooling fan
14 Ignition distributor

View from beneath front of 1.3 litre model

1 Alternator
2 Oil filter
3 Driveshaft
4 Front mounting
5 Cooling system bottom hose
6 Gearbox
7 Track control arm
8 Tie-rod
9 Exhaust
10 Engine sump

18

View from beneath front of fuel injected model

1 Driveshaft
2 Front mounting
3 Starter motor
4 Gearbox
5 Track control arm
6 Tie-rod
7 Anti-roll bar
8 Exhaust system
9 Engine sump

View from beneath rear of 1.3 litre model

1 Exhaust
2 Fuel tank
3 Rear shock absorber lower
   mounting
4 Axle beam
5 Handbrake cable
   (right-hand)
6 Handbrake cable (left-hand)
7 Rear drum brake

View from beneath rear of fuel injected model

1 Exhaust
2 Fuel tank
3 Rear shock absorber lower
   mounting
4 Axle beam
5 Fuel pump and associated
   fittings
6 Brake pressure regulator
7 Rear disc brake

Every 250 miles (400 km) or weekly – whichever comes first

Engine
Check the level of the oil and top up if necessary
Check the coolant level and top up if necessary
Check the level of electrolyte in the battery and top up if necessary

Tyres
Check the tyre pressures (photo)
Visually examine the tyres for wear and damage

Lights and wipers
Check that all the lights work
Clean the headlamps
Check the windscreen/tailgate washer fluid levels and top up if necessary

Brakes
Check the level of fluid in the brake master cylinder reservoir – if topping-up is required, check for leaks

Checking a tyre pressure

Every 10 000 (15 000 km) or 12 months – whichever comes first

Engine
Check and if necessary adjust the clutch (Chapter 5)
Check for oil, fuel and coolant leaks
Check antifreeze concentration and adjust if necessary
Check valve clearances and adjust if necessary (Chapter 1)
Check the condition and adjustment of the alternator, power steering pump and air conditioner compressor drivebelt(s) as applicable
Renew the belt(s) or adjust tension, as necessary
Renew the spark plugs
Renew the contact points and adjust dwell angle (Chapter 4)
Adjust ignition timing (Chapter 4)
Change engine oil and renew oil filter (Chapter 1)
Check exhaust system for leaks and damage
Adjust the slow running (Chapter 3)

Gearbox (Chapter 6)
Check oil level and top up if necessary
Check for oil leaks
Check automatic transmission fluid level and top up if necessary

Driveshafts (Chapter 7)
Check the CV joint boots for leaks and damage

Braking system (Chapter 8)
Check the brake lines, hoses and unions for leaks and damage
Check the disc pads and rear brake shoe linings for wear
Check the brake fluid level and top up if necessary

Electrical system (Chapter 9)
Check the operation of all electrical components, light bulbs, etc
Check the windscreen/rear window washer fluid level and top up if necessary
Check the battery electrolyte level and top up with distilled water if necessary
Check headlight beam alignment and adjust if necessary

Steering (Chapter 10)
Check steering gear bellows for leaks and damage
Check steering tie-rod ends for wear and condition of boots
Check power-assisted steering fluid level and top up if necessary

Tyres (Chapter 10)
Check tread depth and condition of tyres (photo)

Bodywork (Chapter 11)
Lubricate all hinges and catches
Check the underbody for corrosion and damage and reseal as necessary

Checking tyre tread depth

Every 20 000 miles (30 000 km) or 24 months – whichever comes first

Engine
Renew the air cleaner element (Chapter 3)
Renew the fuel filter (Chapter 3)

Every 2 years

Braking system
Renew the brake fluid and check the condition of the visible rubber components of the brake system

Every 40 000 miles (60 000 km)

Engine
Renew the timing belt (Chapter 1)

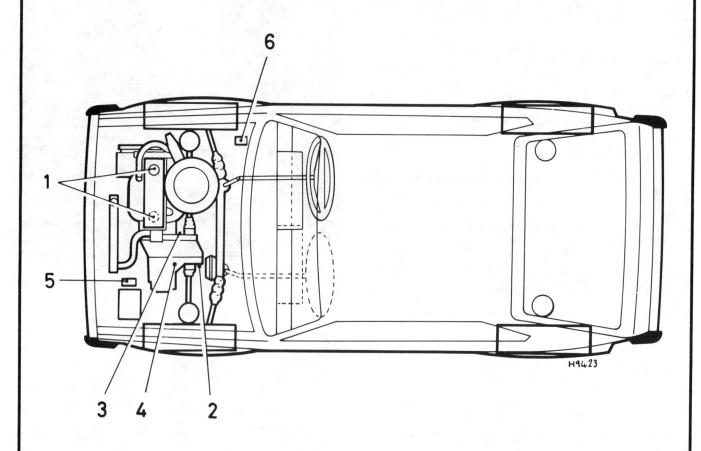

H9423

Recommended lubricants and fluids

Component or system	Lubricant type/specification	Duckhams recommendation
1 Engine	Multigrade engine oil, viscosity SAE 15W/50 or 20W/50	Duckhams QXR or Hypergrade
2 Manual gearbox/final drive	Gear oil, viscosity SAE 80	Duckhams Hypoid 80
3 Final drive (automatic transmission)	Hypoid gear oil, viscosity SAE 90EP	Duckhams Hypoid 90S
4 Automatic transmission	Dexron type ATF	Duckhams D-Matic
5 Power steering	Dexron type ATF	Duckhams D-Matic
6 Braking system	Hydraulic fluid to FMVSS 116 DOT 4	Duckhams Universal Brake and Clutch Fluid

Fault diagnosis

Introduction

The vehicle owner who does his or her own maintenance according to the recommended schedules should not have to use this section of the manual very often. Modern component reliability is such that, provided those items subject to wear or deterioration are inspected or renewed at the specified intervals, sudden failure is comparatively rare. Faults do not usually just happen as a result of sudden failure, but develop over a period of time. Major mechanical failures in particular are usually preceded by characteristic symptoms over hundreds or even thousands of miles. Those components which do occasionally fail without warning are often small and easily carried in the vehicle.

With any fault finding, the first step is to decide where to begin investigations. Sometimes this is obvious, but on other occasions a little detective work will be necessary. The owner who makes half a dozen haphazard adjustments or replacements may be successful in curing a fault (or its symptoms), but he will be none the wiser if the fault recurs and he may well have spent more time and money than was necessary. A calm and logical approach will be found to be more satisfactory in the long run. Always take into account any warning signs or abnormalities that may have been noticed in the period preceding the fault – power loss, high or low gauge readings, unusual noises or smells, etc – and remember that failure of components such as fuses or spark plugs may only be pointers to some underlying fault.

The pages which follow here are intended to help in cases of failure to start or breakdown on the road. There is also a Fault Diagnosis Section at the end of each Chapter which should be consulted if the preliminary checks prove unfruitful. Whatever the fault, certain basic principles apply. These are as follows:

Verify the fault. This is simply a matter of being sure that you know what the symptoms are before starting work. This is particularly important if you are investigating a fault for someone else who may not have described it very accurately.

Don't overlook the obvious. For example, if the vehicle won't start, is there petrol in the tank? (Don't take anyone else's word on this particular point, and don't trust the fuel gauge either!) If an electrical fault is indicated, look for loose or broken wires before digging out the test gear.

Cure the disease, not the symptom. Substituting a flat battery with a fully charged one will get you off the hard shoulder, but if the underlying cause is not attended to, the new battery will go the same way. Similarly, changing oil-fouled spark plugs for a new set will get you moving again, but remember that the reason for the fouling (if it wasn't simply an incorrect grade of plug) will have to be established and corrected.

Don't take anything for granted. Particularly, don't forget that a 'new' component may itself be defective (especially if it's been rattling round in the boot for months), and don't leave components out of a fault diagnosis sequence just because they are new or recently fitted. When you do finally diagnose a difficult fault, you'll probably realise that all the evidence was there from the start.

Electrical faults

Electrical faults can be more puzzling than straightforward mechanical failures, but they are no less susceptible to logical analysis if the basic principles of operation are understood. Vehicle electrical wiring exists in extremely unfavourable conditions – heat, vibration and chemical attack – and the first things to look for are loose or corroded connections and broken or chafed wires, especially where the wires pass through holes in the bodywork or are subject to vibration.

All metal-bodied vehicles in current production have one pole of the battery 'earthed', ie connected to the vehicle bodywork, and in nearly all modern vehicles it is the negative (–) terminal. The various electrical components – motors, bulb holders etc – are also connected to earth, either by means of a lead or directly by their mountings. Electric current flows through the component and then back to the battery via the bodywork. If the component mounting is loose or corroded, or if a good path back to the battery is not available, the circuit will be incomplete and malfunction will result. The engine and/or gearbox are also earthed by means of flexible metal straps to the body or subframe; if these straps are loose or missing, starter motor, generator and ignition trouble may result.

Assuming the earth return to be satisfactory, electrical faults will be due either to component malfunction or to defects in the current supply. Individual components are dealt with in Chapter 9. If supply wires are broken or cracked internally this results in an open-circuit, and the easiest way to check for this is to bypass the suspect wire temporarily with a length of wire having a crocodile clip or suitable connector at each end. Alternatively, a 12V test lamp can be used to verify the presence of supply voltage at various points along the wire and the break can be thus isolated.

If a bare portion of a live wire touches the bodywork or other earthed metal part, the electricity will take the low-resistance path thus formed back to the battery: this is known as a short-circuit. Hopefully a short-circuit will blow a fuse, but otherwise it may cause burning of the insulation (and possibly further short-circuits) or even a fire. This is why it is inadvisable to bypass persistently blowing fuses with silver foil or wire.

Spares and tool kit

Most vehicles are supplied with sufficient tools for wheel changing only; the *Maintenance and minor repair* tool kit detailed in *Tools and working facilities,* with the addition of a hammer, is probably sufficient for those repairs that most motorists would consider attempting at the roadside. In addition a few items which can be fitted without too much trouble in the event of a breakdown should be carried. Experience and

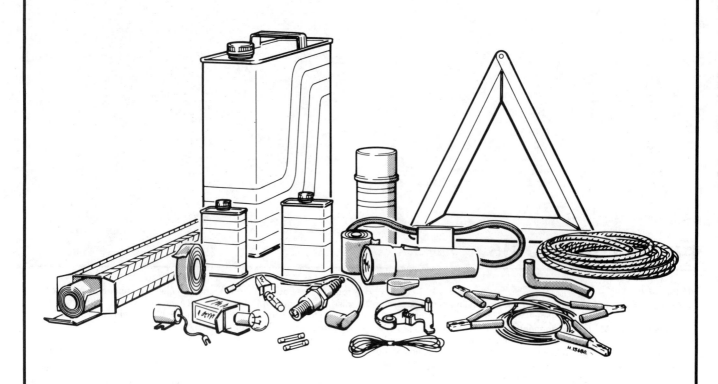

Carrying a few spares may save you a long walk!

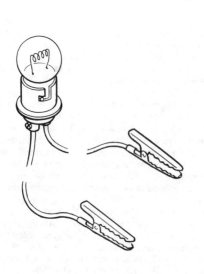

A simple test lamp is useful for investigating electrical faults

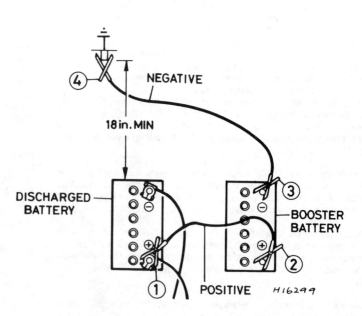

Jump start lead connections for negative earth – connect leads in order shown

available space will modify the list below, but the following may save having to call on professional assistance:

Spark plugs, clean and correctly gapped
HT lead and plug cap – long enough to reach the plug furthest from the distributor
Distributor rotor, condenser and contact breaker points (where applicable)
Drivebelt(s) – emergency type may suffice
Spare fuses
Set of principal light bulbs
Tin of radiator sealer and hose bandage
Exhaust bandage
Roll of insulating tape
Length of soft iron wire
Length of electrical flex
Torch or inspection lamp (can double as test lamp)
Battery jump leads
Tow-rope
Ignition waterproofing aerosol
Litre of engine oil
Sealed can of hydraulic fluid
Emergency windscreen
Worm drive clips
Tube of filler paste

If spare fuel is carried, a can designed for the purpose should be used to minimise risks of leakage and collision damage. A first aid kit and a warning triangle, whilst not at present compulsory in the UK, are obviously sensible items to carry in addition to the above.

When touring abroad it may be advisable to carry additional spares which, even if you cannot fit them yourself, could save having to wait while parts are obtained. The items below may be worth considering:

Clutch and throttle cables
Cylinder head gasket
Alternator brushes
Tyre valve core

One of the motoring organisations will be able to advise on availability of fuel etc in foreign countries.

Engine will not start

Engine fails to turn when starter operated

Flat battery (recharge, use jump leads, or push start)
Battery terminals loose or corroded
Battery earth to body defective
Engine earth strap loose or broken
Starter motor (or solenoid) wiring loose or broken
Automatic transmission selector in wrong position, or inhibitor switch faulty
Ignition/starter switch faulty
Major mechanical failure (seizure)
Starter or solenoid internal fault (see Chapter 9)
Faulty stop-start system (where fitted)

Starter motor turns engine slowly

Partially discharged battery (recharge, use jump leads, or push start)
Battery terminals loose or corroded
Battery earth to body defective
Engine earth strap loose
Starter motor (or solenoid) wiring loose
Starter motor internal fault (see Chapter 9)

Starter motor spins without turning engine

Flat battery
Starter motor pinion sticking on sleeve
Flywheel gear teeth damaged or worn
Starter motor mounting bolts loose

Engine turns normally but fails to start

Damp or dirty HT leads and distributor cap (crank engine and check for spark) – photo
Dirty or incorrectly gapped distributor points (if applicable)
No fuel in tank (check for delivery)

Using a spark plug to check for HT spark – do not remove plug from engine otherwise fuel/air mixture may ignite causing fire

Excessive choke (hot engine) or insufficient choke (cold engine)
Fouled or incorrectly gapped spark plugs (remove, clean and regap)
Other ignition system fault (see Chapter 4)
Other fuel system fault (see Chapter 3)
Poor compression
Major mechanical failure (eg camshaft drive)

Engine fires but will not run

Insufficient choke (cold engine)
Air leaks at carburettor or inlet manifold
Fuel starvation (see Chapter 3)
Ballast resistor defective, or other ignition fault (see Chapter 4)

Engine cuts out and will not restart

Engine cuts out suddenly – ignition fault

Loose or disconnected LT wires
Wet HT leads or distributor cap (after traversing water splash)
Coil or condenser failure (check for spark)
Other ignition fault (see Chapter 4)

Engine misfires before cutting out – fuel fault

Fuel tank empty
Fuel pump defective or filter blocked (check for delivery)
Fuel tank filler vent blocked (suction will be evident on releasing cap)
Carburettor needle valve sticking
Carburettor jets blocked (fuel contaminated)
Other fuel system fault (see Chapter 3)

Engine cuts out – other causes

Serious overheating
Major mechanical failure (eg camshaft drive)

Engine overheats

Ignition (no-charge) warning light illuminated

Slack or broken drivebelt – retension or renew (Chapter 9)

Ignition warning light not illuminated

Coolant loss due to internal or external leakage (see Chapter 2)
Thermostat defective

Low oil level
Brakes binding
Radiator clogged externally or internally
Electric cooling fan not operating correctly
Engine waterways clogged
Ignition timing incorrect or automatic advance malfunctioning
Mixture too weak

Note: *Do not add cold water to an overheated engine or damage may result*

Low engine oil pressure

Gauge reads low or warning light illuminated with engine running

Oil level low or incorrect grade
Defective gauge or sender unit
Wire to sender unit earthed
Engine overheating
Oil filter clogged or bypass valve defective
Oil pressure relief valve defective
Oil pick-up strainer clogged
Oil pump worn or mountings loose
Worn main or big-end bearings

Note: *Low oil pressure in a high-mileage engine at tickover is not necessarily a cause for concern. Sudden pressure loss at speed is far more significant. In any event, check the gauge or warning light sender before condemning the engine.*

Engine noises

Pre-ignition (pinking) on acceleration

Incorrect grade of fuel
Ignition timing incorrect
Distributor faulty or worn
Worn or maladjusted carburettor
Excessive carbon build-up in engine

Whistling or wheezing noises

Leaking vacuum hose
Leaking carburettor or manifold gasket
Blowing head gasket

Tapping or rattling

Incorrect valve clearances
Worn valve gear
Worn timing belt
Broken piston ring (ticking noise)

Knocking or thumping

Unintentional mechanical contact (eg fan blades)
Worn fanbelt
Peripheral component fault (generator, water pump etc)
Worn big-end bearings (regular heavy knocking, perhaps less under load)
Worn main bearings (rumbling and knocking, perhaps worsening under load)
Piston slap (most noticeable when cold)

Chapter 1 Engine

For modifications, and information applicable to later models, see Supplement at end of manual

Contents

Specifications

General

Type	Four-cylinder in-line, water cooled, overhead camshaft
Firing order	1-3-4-2 (No 1 at camshaft sprocket end)
Bore:	
1043 cc	75 mm (2.955 in)
1272 cc	75 mm (2.955 in)
1595 cc	81 mm (3.191 in)
1781 cc	81 mm (3.191 in)

Stroke:

1043 cc	59.0 mm (2.325 in)
1272 cc	72.0 mm (2.837 in)
1595 cc	77.4 mm (3.050 in)
1781 cc	86.4 mm (3.404 in)

Compression ratio:

1043 cc (engine code GN)	9.5 to 1
1272 cc (engine code HK)	9.5 to 1
1595 cc (engine code EZ)	9.0 to 1
1781 cc (engine code EV Jetronic – fuel injection and GU – carburettor)	10.0 to 1

Compression pressure:

	bar	lbf/in²
1.05 and 1.3 litre (new)	8 to 10	116 to 145
1.05 to 1.3 litre (minimum)	7	102
1.6 litre (new)	9 to 12	131 to 174
1.6 litre (minimum)	7.5	109
1.8 litre (new)	10 to 13	145 to 189
1.8 litre (minimum)	7.5	109
Maximum permissible difference between any two cylinders	3	44

Crankshaft

Main journal diameter (standard)	54.0 mm (2.128 in)
Main journal undersizes	53.75, 53.50 and 53.25 mm (2.118, 2.108 and 2.098 in)

Crankpin diameter (standard):

1.05 and 1.3 litre	42 mm (1.655 in)
1.6 and 1.8 litre	47.80 mm (1.883 in)

Crankpin journal undersizes:

1.05 and 1.3 litre	41.75, 41.50 and 41.25 mm (1.645, 1.635 and 1.625 in)
1.6 and 1.8 litre	47.55, 47.30 and 47.05 mm (1.873, 1.864 and 1.854 in)

Crankshaft endfloat (maximum):

1.05 and 1.3 litre	0.20 mm (0.0079 in)
1.6 and 1.8 litre	0.25 mm (0.0099 in)
Crankshaft endfloat (minimum)	0.07 mm (0.0028 in)
Main bearing running clearance (maximum)	0.17 mm (0.0067 in)

Connecting rods

Big-end running clearance (maximum):

1.05 and 1.3 litre	0.095 mm (0.0037 in)
1.6 and 1.8 litre	0.012 mm (0.0005 in)

Big-end endfloat (maximum):

1.05 and 1.3 litre	0.40 mm (0.0158 in)
1.6 and 1.8 litre	0.37 mm (0.0146 in)

Pistons

Piston clearance in bore (maximum)	0.07 mm (0.0028 in)
Piston clearance in bore (minimum)	0.03 mm (0.0012 in)

Piston diameter (standard):

1.05 and 1.3 litre	74.98 mm (2.954 in)
1.6 and 1.8 litre	80.98 mm (3.191 in)

Piston oversize diameters – 1.05 and 1.3 litre:

1st oversize	75.23 mm (2.964 in)
2nd oversize	75.48 mm (2.974 in)
3rd oversize	75.98 mm (2.994 in)

Piston oversize diameters – 1.6 and 1.8 litre:

1st oversize	81.23 mm (3.200 in)
2nd oversize	81.48 mm (3.210 in)
Piston wear limit (measured 10 mm from base at right angles to gudgeon pin)	0.04 mm (0.0016 in)

Piston rings

Clearance in grooves (maximum)	0.15 mm (0.006 in)
End gap – compression rings	0.30 to 0.45 mm (0.012 to 0.018 in)
End gap – oil scraper ring	0.25 to 0.40 mm (0.010 to 0.016 in)

Gudgeon pin

Fit in piston	Push fit at 60°C (140°F)

Intermediate shaft (1.6 and 1.8 litre)

Endfloat (maximum)	0.25 mm (0.010 in)

Cylinder head

Maximum allowable face distortion	0.1 mm (0.004 in)

Camshaft
Run-out at centre bearing:
    1.05 and 1.3 .... 0.02 mm (0.0008 in)
    1.6 and 1.8 .... 0.01 mm (0.0004 in)
Endfloat .... 0.15 mm (0.006 in)

Valves
Seat angle .... 45°

	1.05 and 1.3	1.6 and 1.8
Head diameter:		
Inlet	34.0 mm (1.340 in)	38.0 mm (1.497 in)
Exhaust	28.1 mm (1.107 in)	33.0 mm (1.300 in)
Stem diameter:		
Inlet	7.97 mm (0.314 in)	7.97 mm (0.314 in)
Exhaust	7.95 mm (0.313 in)	7.95 mm (0.313 in)
Overall length (standard):		
Inlet	110.5 mm (4.354 in)	98.70 mm (3.889 in)
Exhaust	110.5 mm (4.354 in)	98.50 mm (3.881 in)

Valve guides
Maximum valve rock (valve stem flush with guide):
    Inlet valve .... 1.0 mm (0.039 in)
    Exhaust valve .... 1.3 mm (0.051 in)

Valve timing (nil valve clearance, at 1 mm valve lift)
1.05 litre:
    Inlet opens .... 9° ATDC
    Inlet closes .... 13° ABDC
    Exhaust opens .... 15° BBDC
    Exhaust closes .... 11° BTDC
1.3 litre:
    Inlet opens .... 3° BTDC
    Inlet closes .... 38° ABDC
    Exhaust opens .... 41° BBDC
    Exhaust closes .... 3° BTDC
1.6 litre:
    Inlet opens .... 5° BTDC
    Inlet closes .... 21° ABDC
    Exhaust opens .... 41° BBDC
    Exhaust closes .... 3° BTDC
1.8 litre (engine code GU)
    Inlet opens .... 1° BTDC
    Inlet closes .... 37° ABDC
    Exhaust opens .... 42° BBDC
    Exhaust closes .... 2° ATDC
1.8 litre (engine code EV):
    Inlet opens .... 2° BTDC
    Inlet closes .... 45° ABDC
    Exhaust opens .... 45° BBDC
    Exhaust closes .... 8° BTDC

Valve clearances

	1.05 and 1.3 litre	1.6 and 1.8 litre
Warm:		
Inlet	0.15 to 0.20 mm (0.006 to 0.008 in)	0.20 to 0.30 mm (0.008 to 0.012 in)
Exhaust	0.25 to 0.30 mm (0.010 to 0.019 in)	0.40 to 0.50 mm (0.016 to 0.020 in)
Cold:		
Inlet	0.10 to 0.15 mm (0.004 to 0.006 in)	0.15 to 0.25 (0.006 to 0.010 in)
Exhaust	0.20 to 0.25 mm (0.008 to 0.010 in)	0.35 to 0.45 mm (0.014 to 0.018 in)

Lubrication
Oil type/specification .... Multigrade engine oil, viscosity SAE 15W/50 or 20W/50 (Duckhams QXR or Hypergrade)
1.05 and 1.3 litre:
    Oil pump type .... Eccentric gear driven by crankshaft
    Oil pressure at 2000 rpm, with oil temperature 80°C/176°F .... 2.0 bar (29 lbf/in²) minimum
    Oil capacity:
        With filter change .... 3.0 litre (5.3 lmp pint)
        Without filter change .... 2.5 litre (4.4 lmp pint)
1.6 and 1.8 litre:
    Oil pump type .... Twin gear, driven by intermediate shaft together with distributor
    Oil pressure at 2000 rpm, with oil temperature 80°C/176°F .... 2.0 bar (29 lbf/in²) minimum
    Oil capacity:
        With filter change .... 3.5 litre (6.2 lmp pint)
        Without filter change .... 3.0 litre (5.3 lmp pint)

Torque wrench settings

1.05 and 1.3 litre

	Nm	lbf ft
Engine to gearbox	55	41
Exhaust pipe to manifold	25	18
Flywheel bolts	75	55
Clutch bolts	25	18
Sump bolts	20	15
Sump drain plug	30	22
Main bearing cap bolts	65	48
Oil pump bolts	10	7
Connecting rod cap (big-end) nuts (oiled):		
Stage 1	30	22
Stage 2*	Tighten further ¹/₄ turn (90°)	Tighten further ¹/₄ turn (90°)
Oil suction pipe to pump	10	7
Oil relief valve plug	25	18
Oil pressure sender switch	25	18
Timing cover	10	7
Valve cover	10	7
Camshaft sprocket bolt	80	59
Crankshaft sprocket/pulley nut	80	59
Coolant pump bolts	10	7
Distributor flange bolts	20	15
Cylinder head bolts (engine cold):		
Stage 1	40	30
Stage 2	60	44
Stage 3	Turn further ¹/₂ turn (180°)	Turn further ¹/₂ turn (180°)

1.6 and 1.8 litre

	Nm	lbf ft
Engine to gearbox:		
M10	45	33
M12	75	55
Exhaust manifold nuts	25	18
Exhaust pipe to manifold	10	7
Flywheel/driveplate bolts	20	15
Clutch pressure plate/washer bolts (renew)	100	74
Sump bolts	20	15
Sump drain plug	30	22
Main bearing cap bolts	65	48
Connecting rod big-end cap nuts:		
Stage 1	30	22
Stage 2*	Further tighten ¹/₄ turn (90°)	Further tighten ¹/₄ turn (90°)
Oil pump bolts	10	7
Oil pressure switch	25	18
Oil filter flange bolts	25	18
Front seal flange bolts:		
Small	20	15
Large	10	7
Intermediate shaft flange bolts	25	18
Camshaft bearing cap nuts (in sequence)	20	15
Camshaft sprocket bolt	80	59
Valve cover nuts	10	7
Belt tensioner pulley	45	33
Crankshaft sprocket bolt (oiled)	200	148
Intermediate shaft sprocket bolt	80	59
V-belt pulley	20	15
Timing cover	10	7
Rear cover lower bolts	30	22
Rear cover top bolt	10	7
Coolant pump bolts	20	15
Fuel pump bolts	20	15
Distributor clamp bolt	25	18
Cylinder head bolts (engine cold)	As for 1.05 and 1.3 litre engines	

* When checking the connecting rod-to-crankshaft journal radial clearance using Plastigage, tighten only to 30 Nm (22 lbf ft).

All models (see Figs. 1.1, 1.2 and 12.7)

	Nm	lbf ft
Engine mountings (with oiled threads):		
(a) M8 – 105 and 1.3 litre	25	18
(a) M10 – 1.05 and 1.3 litre	45	33
(a) 1.6 and 1.8 litre	25	18
(b) all models	35	26
(c) all models	45	33
(d) all models	50	37
(e) all models	60	44
(f) all models	70	52
(g) all models	80	59

2.2 Topping-up engine oil

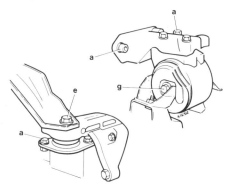

Fig. 1.1 Engine mounting bolts identification – see
Specifications for torque settings

Fig. 1.2 Engine/transmission mounting bolts identification –
see Specifications for torque settings

PART A: 1.05 AND 1.3 LITRE

1 General description

The engine is of four-cylinder, in-line, overhead camshaft type,
mounted transversely at the front of the car. The transmission is
attached to the left-hand side of the engine.

The crankshaft is of five bearing type and separate thrust washers
are fitted to the central main bearing to control the crankshaft endfloat.

The camshaft is driven by a toothed belt which also drives the water

pump – the toothed belt is tensioned by moving the water pump in its
eccentric mounting. The valves are operated from the camshaft by
rocker fingers which pivot on ball-head studs. The distributor is driven
by the camshaft and is located on the left-hand end of the cylinder
head.

The oil pump is of the eccentric gear type driven from the end of the
crankshaft.

The cylinder head is of crossflow design, with the inlet manifold at
the rear and the exhaust manifold at the front.

2 Routine maintenance – engine

The following routine maintenance procedures should be
undertaken at the specified intervals given at the start of this manual.
The intervals given are those for a vehicle used in normal driving
conditions. Where the vehicle is subject to more severe daily use, such
as city driving or in a hot dusty climate, then it is advisable to shorten
the maintenance intervals accordingly.

Engine oil check: Check the engine oil with the vehicle parked on
level ground, the engine switched off and having been stationary for a
short period. This will allow oil in the lubrication circuits to return to
the sump to provide a true level reading. The dipstick should be
withdrawn, wiped clean, fully inserted then withdrawn again to take
the oil level reading. The oil level must be kept between the maximum
and minimum markings on the dipstick at all times. If the oil level is
down to the minimum mark, it will need a litre (1.7 Imp pint) to raise
the oil level to the maximum mark. Do not overfill the engine. Top up
through the oil filler neck in the cylinder head cover (photo). Check
that the cover is firmly refitted and wipe clean any oil spillage. Recheck
the oil level on completion.

Engine oil change: With the vehicle standing on level ground,
remove the drain plug from the sump and drain the old engine oil into a
container of suitable capacity. Draining is best undertaken directly after
the vehicle has been used when the engine oil will be hot and will flow
more freely. When draining is complete, refit the drain plug (on 1.6 and
1.8 litre models, renew the O-ring) and top up the engine oil to the
correct level with the specified grade and quantity of engine oil

Engine oil filter: The oil filter must be renewed at the specified
intervals. The filter is best removed whilst waiting for the engine oil to
drain. Renewing the oil filter is described in Section 20 of this Chapter.

Engine general checks: Inspect the engine regularly for any signs of
oil, coolant or fuel leaks and if found attend to them without delay.

Fig. 1.3 Engine oil level dipstick and markings 1.05 and 1.3
litre (Sec 2)

3 Major operation possible with engine in car

The following operations can be carried out without having to
remove the engine from the car:

(a) *Removal and servicing of the cylinder head, camshaft and
timing belt*
(b) *Removal of the flywheel and crankshaft rear oil seal (after
removal of the gearbox)*

(c) *Removal of the sump*
(d) *Removal of the piston/connecting rod assemblies (after removal of the cylinder head and sump)*
(e) *Renewal of the crankshaft front and rear oil seals and the camshaft front oil seal*
(f) *Renewal of the engine mountings*
(g) *Removal of the oil pump*

4 Major operation only possible after removal of engine from car

The following operation can only be carried out after removal of the engine from the car:

Renewal of crankshaft main bearings

5 Method of engine removal

1   The engine, together with the gearbox, must be lifted from the engine compartment and the engine separated from the gearbox on the bench. Two people will be needed.
2   A hoist, capacity 150 kg (3 cwt), will be needed and the engine must be lifted approximately 1 metre (three feet). If the hoist is not portable, then sufficient room must be left behind the car to push the car back out of the way so that the power unit may be lowered. Blocks will be needed to support the engine after removal.
3   Ideally the car should be over a pit. If this is not possible then the body must be supported on axle stands so that the front wheels may be turned to undo the driveshaft nuts. The left one is accessible from above but the right-hand shaft must be undone from underneath. There are other jobs best done from below. Removal of the shift linkage can only be done from underneath, as can the removal of the exhaust pipe bracket. When all the jobs are done under the car, lower the car back to its wheels.
4   A set of splined keys will be required to remove and refit the socket-head bolts used to secure certain items in the engine, such as the cylinder head bolts (photo).

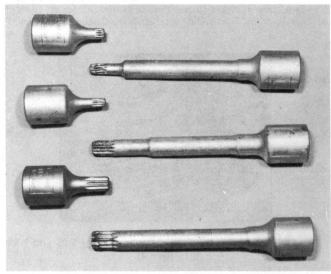

5.4 A splined key set will be required for various overhaul procedures on the car

5   Draining of oil and coolant is best done away from the working area if possible. This saves the mess made by spilled oil in the place where you must work.
6   If an air conditioning system is fitted, observe the cautionary notes in Section 48 of this Chapter.

6 Engine – removal

1   Disconnect the battery negative lead.
2   Remove the bonnet, as described in Chapter 11, and put it in a safe place.
3   Drain the engine coolant and remove the radiator, complete with the cooling fan unit, as described in Chapter 2.
4   Remove the air cleaner unit, as described in Chapter 3.
5   Loosen the clip and disconnect the top hose from the thermostat housing.
6   Place a suitable container beneath the engine then unscrew the sump drain plug and drain the oil (photo). When completed, clean the drain plug and washer and tighten it into the sump.

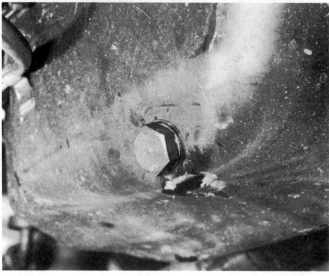

6.6 Sump drain plug

7   Identify the fuel supply and return hoses then disconnect them from the fuel pump (photo) and fuel reservoir/carburettor. Plug the hoses to prevent fuel leakage.
8   Loosen the clip and disconnect the bottom hose from the coolant pipe at the rear of the engine.
9   Disconnect the accelerator cable and, where applicable, the choke cable; with reference to Chapter 3.
10 Disconnect the heater hoses from the thermostat housing and rear coolant pipe.
11 Detach the following connections, but identify each lead as it is disconnected to avoid confusion on reassembly:

(a) *The oil pressure switches on the rear (carburettor side) of the cylinder head*
(b) *Inlet manifold preheating element line connector*
(c) *Thermo-switch leads (coolant hose intermediate piece)*
(d) *Distributor HT and LT leads*
(e) *Starter motor*
(f) *Temperature sender unit (thermostat housing)*
(g) *Fuel cut-off solenoid valve on carburettor*
(h) *Earth strap to the gearbox*

12 Detach the wiring loom from the location clip on the bottom hose and fold back out of the way.
13 Disconnect and unclip the vacuum hoses from the distributor and inlet manifold as necessary.
14 Disconnect the clutch cable, with reference to Chapter 5 (photo).
15 Disconnect the exhaust downpipe from the exhaust manifold, with reference to Chapter 3.
16 Disconnect the speedometer cable from the gearbox and place it on one side.
17 Apply the handbrake then jack up the front of the car and support it on axle stands.

6.7 Detach hoses from fuel pump

6.14 Earth lead (A) and clutch cable (B)

6.18 Shift rod coupling screw

18 Remove the screw from the shift rod coupling and ease the coupling from the rod (photo). The screw threads are coated with a liquid locking agent, and if difficulty is experienced it may be necessary to heat up the coupling with a blowlamp; *however, take the necessary fire precautions*. Note that once removed this screw should be renewed.
19 Note its orientation then withdraw the shift rod coupling.
20 Unbolt the exhaust steady bracket from the downpipe and clutch housing/starter motor.
21 Detach the reversing light switch lead (photo).
22 Unbolt the driveshafts from the drive flanges, with reference to Chapter 7, and tie them to one side with wire.
23 Attach a suitable hoist to the engine lifting eye brackets (one at each end of the cylinder head on the carburettor side) (photo). Take the weight of the engine and gearbox.
24 Working from above, undo the three engine mounting/bearer

retaining bolts (underneath the carburettor) (photo).
25 Undo and remove the gearbox mounting bolt (rear left side of engine compartment).
26 Undo and remove the front engine mounting bolt and then remove the bolts securing the bracket to the engine. Withdraw the mounting (photos).
27 Before lifting out the engine and gearbox assembly, get an assistant to hold the engine steady and help guide it clear of surrounding components as it is removed.
28 Raise the engine and gearbox assembly from the engine compartment (photo) while turning it as necessary to clear the internally mounted components. Make sure that all wires, cables and hoses have been disconnected.
29 Lower the assembly onto a workbench or large piece of wood placed on the floor.

6.21 Reversing light switch

6.23 Engine lifting eye

6.24 Engine mounting/bearer – right-hand rear

6.26A Undo the front mounting through-bolt

6.26B Unbolt and remove the mounting unit

6.28 Lifting out the engine and gearbox

7 Engine and gearbox – separation

1   The engine must be supported so that the gearbox can be eased away from it. Either support the engine on blocks so that the gearbox overhangs the bench, or do the job while the engine and gearbox are on the hoist.

2   Detach the lead from the alternator then unclip the lead from the locating clips on the sump side walls.

3   Because the rear bearing of the starter armature is in the bellhousing, it is necessary to remove the starter before separating the engine and gearbox. If not already removed, when unbolting the starter motor, also detach the exhaust pipe support bracket (photo).

4   Detach the coolant pipe at its flange on the rear side of the water pump and at the clutch housing.

5   Undo the clutch housing belly plate bolt and withdraw the plate.

6   Undo and remove the remaining engine-to-gearbox securing bolts then pull the gearbox free. **Do not insert wedges, or you will damage the facing;** tap the gearbox gently and wriggle it off the two dowels which locate it. The intermediate plate will remain in position (photos).

7   Reconnection is a reversal of the separating procedure.

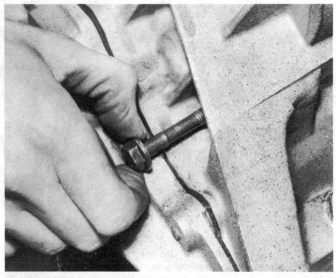

7.6B ... not forgetting the recessed bolt ...

7.3 Starter motor and exhaust support bracket

7.6C ... then separate the engine and transmission

8 Engine dismantling – general

1   If possible, mount the engine on a stand for the dismantling procedure, but failing this, support it in an upright position with blocks of wood.

2   Cleanliness is most important, and if the engine is dirty, it should be cleaned with paraffin while keeping it in an upright position.

3   Avoid working with the engine directly on a concrete floor, as grit presents a real source of trouble.

4   As parts are removed, clean them in a paraffin bath. However, do not immerse parts with internal oilways in paraffin as it is difficult to remove, usually requiring a high pressure hose. Clean oilways with nylon pipe cleaners.

5   It is advisable to have suitable containers to hold small items according to their use, as this will help when reassembling the engine and also prevent possible losses.

6   Always obtain complete sets of gaskets when the engine is being dismantled, but retain the old gaskets with a view to using them as a pattern to make a replacement if a new one is not available.

7   When possible, refit nuts, bolts and washers in their location after being removed, as this helps to protect the threads and will also be helpful when reassembling the engine.

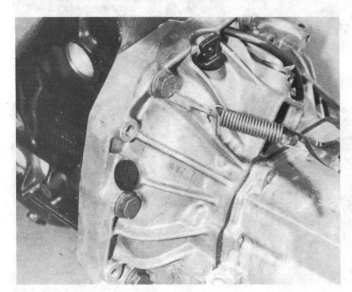

7.6A Undo the engine/transmission securing bolts ...

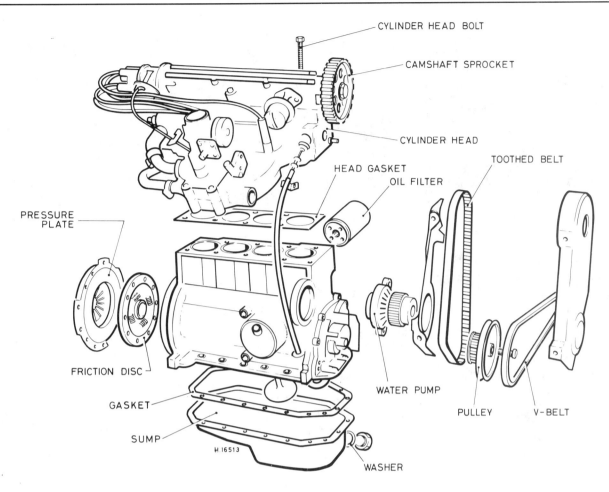

CYLINDER HEAD BOLT
CAMSHAFT SPROCKET
CYLINDER HEAD
HEAD GASKET
OIL FILTER
TOOTHED BELT
PRESSURE PLATE
FRICTION DISC
GASKET
SUMP
WASHER
WATER PUMP
PULLEY
V-BELT

H.16513

Fig. 1.4 Exploded view of engine main components (Sec 8)

8 Retain unserviceable components in order to compare them with the new parts supplied.

9 Engine ancillary components – removal

With the engine removed from the car and separated from the gearbox, the externally mounted ancillary components should now be removed before dismantling begins. The removal sequence need not necessarily follow the order given:

Alternator and drivebelt (Chapter 9)
Inlet manifold and carburettor (Chapter 3)

Exhaust manifold (Chapter 3)
Distributor (Chapter 4)
Fuel pump (Chapter 3)
Thermostat (Chapter 2)
Clutch (Chapter 5)
Crankcase ventilation hose (Section 21 of this Chapter)
Distributor cap and spark plugs (Chapter 4)
Oil filter (Section 20 of this Chapter)
Engine mountings (photos)
Dipstick (photo)
Oil pressure switches
Water temperature thermo-switch (Chapter 2)
Alternator mounting bracket and engine earth lead
Engine rear coolant pipe (photos)

9.1A Undo the two bolts (arrowed) ...

9.1B ... then lift the mounting away

9.1C Right-hand rear mounting viewed from above

9.1D Engine dipstick and tube

9.1E Unscrew the nuts ...

9.1F ... and remove the engine rear coolant pipe

10.1A Unscrew the nuts and bolts ...

10.1B ... and remove the valve cover ...

10.1C ... and gasket

10 Cylinder head – removal

If the engine is still in the car, first carry out the following operations:

(a) Disconnect the battery negative lead
(b) Remove the air cleaner and fuel pump (Chapter 3)
(c) Drain the cooling system and remove the top hose and thermostat (Chapter 2)
(d) Remove the distributor and spark plugs (Chapter 4)
(e) Remove the inlet and exhaust manifolds (Chapter 3) although if necessary this can be carried out with the cylinder head on the bench
(f) Disconnect the wiring from the coolant temperature sender and oil pressure switch

1   Unscrew the nuts and bolts from the valve cover and remove the cover together with the gasket and reinforcement strips (photos).
2   Turn the engine until the indentation in the camshaft sprocket appears in the TDC hole in the timing cover, and the notch in the crankshaft pulley is aligned with the TDC pointer on the front of the oil pump (photos). Now turn the crankshaft one quarter of a turn anti-clockwise so that none of the pistons are at TDC.
3   Unbolt and remove the timing cover (photo), noting that the dipstick tube and earth lead are fitted to the upper bolts. Pull the dipstick tube from the cylinder block.
4   Using a socket through the hole in the camshaft sprocket, unscrew the timing cover plate upper retaining bolt.
5   Loosen the water pump retaining bolts, then turn the pump body clockwise to release the tension from the timing belt. Remove the timing belt from the camshaft sprocket.
6   Remove the bolts and withdraw the timing cover plate, followed by the water pump if required.
7   Using a splined key, unscrew the cylinder head bolts half a turn at a time in the reverse order to that shown in Fig. 1.11. Note the location of the engine lifting hooks.
8   Lift the cylinder head from the block (photo). If it is stuck, tap it free with a wooden mallet. **Do not** insert a lever, as damage will occur to the joint faces.
9   Remove the gasket from the cylinder block (photo).

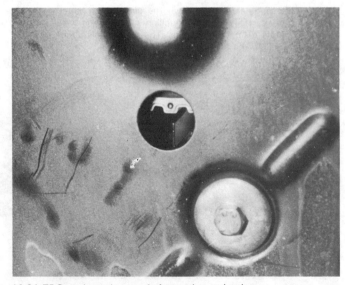
10.2A TDC mark on the camshaft sprocket and pointer

10.2B Crankshaft pulley notch aligned with the TDC pointer

10.9 ... and cylinder head gasket

10.3 Removing the timing cover

11 Camshaft – removal

If the engine is still in the car, first carry out the following operations:

    (a) *Disconnect the battery negative lead*
    (b) *Remove the air cleaner and fuel pump (Chapter 3)*
    (c) *Remove the distributor and spark plugs (Chapter 4)*

If the cylinder head is still fitted to the engine, first carry out the procedure described in paragraphs 1 to 4 inclusive.

1   Unscrew the nuts and bolts from the valve cover and remove the cover, together with the gasket and reinforcement strips.

2   Turn the engine until the indentation in the camshaft sprocket appears in the TDC hole in the timing cover, and the notch in the crankshaft pulley is aligned with the TDC pointer on the front of the oil pump. Now turn the crankshaft one quarter of a turn anti-clockwise so that none of the pistons are at TDC.

3   Unbolt and remove the timing cover, noting that the dipstick tube and earth lead are fitted to the upper bolts.

4   Loosen the water pump retaining bolts, then turn the pump body clockwise to release the tension from the timing belt. Remove the timing belt from the camshaft sprocket.

5   Prise the oil spray tube from the top of the cylinder head (photo).

10.8 Removing the cylinder head ...

11.5 Removing the oil spray tube

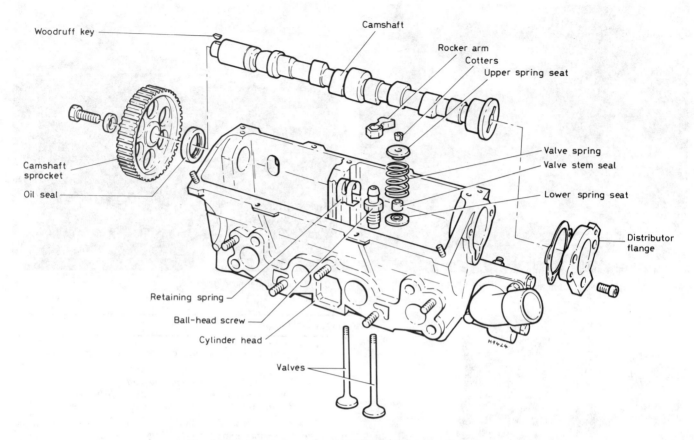

Fig. 1.5 Exploded view of cylinder head components (Sec 11)

6   Note how the cam follower clips are fitted then prise them from the ball-studs (photo).

7   Identify each cam follower for location then remove each one by levering with a screwdriver, but make sure that the peak of the relevant cam is pointing away from the follower first by turning the camshaft as necessary (photo).

8   Unscrew the camshaft sprocket bolt and remove the spacer (photo). The sprocket can be held stationary using a metal bar with two bolts, with one bolt inserted in a hole and the other bolt resting on the outer rim of the sprocket.

9   Tap the sprocket from the camshaft with a wooden mallet and prise out the Woodruff key (photo).

10   Using feeler blades, check the camshaft endfloat by inserting the blade between the end of the camshaft and distributor flanges (photo). If it is more than the amount given in the Specifications the components will have to be checked for wear and renewed as necessary.

11   Using an Allen key, unscrew the bolts and remove the distributor flange (photo). Remove the gasket.

12   Carefully slide the camshaft from the cylinder head, taking care not to damage the three bearing surfaces as the lobes of the cams pass through them (photo).

13   Prise the camshaft oil seal from the cylinder head (photo).

12 Cylinder head – dismantling, inspection and overhaul

1   Remove the cylinder head and camshaft, as described in the previous Sections.

2   Using a valve spring compressor, compress each valve spring in turn until the split collets can be removed. Release the compressor and remove the retainers and springs (photos). If the retainers are difficult to remove do not continue to tighten the compressor, but gently tap

11.6 Removing a cam follower clip

11.7 Removing a cam follower

11.8 Unscrew the bolt ...

11.9 ... and remove the camshaft sprocket (early type sprocket shown)

11.10 Checking the camshaft endfloat

11.11 Removing the distributor flange

11.12 Withdrawing the camshaft

11.13 Removing the camshaft oil seal

12.2A Compressing a valve spring to remove the split collets

12.2B Remove valve springs and retainers ...

12.4 ... and the valve spring lower seats

the top of the tool with a hammer. Always make sure that the compressor is held firmly over the retainer.

3   Remove each valve from the cylinder head, keeping them identified for location.

4   Prise the valve seals from the valve guides and remove the lower spring seats (photo).

5   Do not remove the cam follower ball-studs unless they are unserviceable, as they are likely to be seized in the head.

6   Decarbonising will normally only be required at comparatively high mileages. However, if performance has deteriorated even though engine adjustments are correct, decarbonising may be required; although this may be attributable to worn pistons and rings.

7   With the cylinder head removed, use a scraper to remove the

carbon. Remove all traces of gasket then wash the cylinder head thoroughly in paraffin and wipe dry.

8   Use a straight-edge and feeler blade to check that the cylinder head surface is not distorted. If it is, it must be resurfaced by a suitably equipped engineering works. If the cylinder head face is to be resurfaced, this will necessitate the valve seats being recut so that they are recessed deeper by an equivalent amount to that machined from the cylinder head. This is necessary to avoid the possibility of the valves coming into contact with the pistons and causing serious damage and is a task to be entrusted to a suitably equipped engine reconditioner.

9   Examine the heads of the valves for pitting and burning, especially the exhaust valve heads. Renew any valve which is badly burnt.

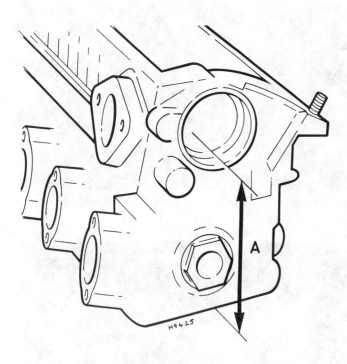

Fig. 1.6 Measure cylinder head depth between the points indicated (Sec 12)

Minimum allowable depth a = 119.3 mm (4.7 in)

Examine the valve seats at the same time. If the pitting is very slight, it can be removed by grinding the valve heads and seats together with coarse, then fine, grinding paste. Note that the exhaust valves should not be recut, therefore they should be renewed if the sealing face is excessively grooved as a result of regrinding.

10 Where excessive pitting has occurred, the valve seats must be recut or renewed by a suitably equipped engine reconditioner.

11 Valve grinding is carried out as follows. Place the cylinder head upside down on a bench with a block of wood at each end.

12 Smear a trace of coarse carborundum paste on the seat face and press a suction grinding tool onto the valve head. With a semi-rotary action, grind the valve head to its seat, lifting the valve occasionally to redistribute the grinding paste. When a dull matt even surface is produced on both the valve seat and the valve, wipe off the paste and repeat the process with fine carborundum paste as before. A light spring placed under the valve head will greatly ease this operation. When a smooth unbroken ring of light grey matt finish is produced on both the valve and seat, the grinding operation is complete.

13 Scrape away all carbon from the valve head stem, and clean away all traces of grinding compound. Clean the valves and seats with a paraffin-soaked rag, then wipe with a clean rag.

14 Check for wear in the valve guides. This may be detected by fitting a new valve in the guide and checking the amount that the rim of the valve will move sideways, when the top of the valve stem is flush with the top of the valve guide. The rock limit for the inlet valve is 1 mm (0.04 in) and 1.3 mm (0.05 in) for the exhaust valve. This can be measured with feeler gauges if you use a clamp as a datum, but it must be with a new valve. If the rock is at or below this limit with your old valve than this indicates that the existing guide(s) do not need renewal. Check each valve guide in turn, but note that the inlet and exhaust valve stem dimensions differ so do not get them confused. If the rock exceeds the limit with a new valve this will indicate the need for new valve guides as well. The removal and refitting of new guides is a task which must be entrusted to a suitably equipped engine reconditioner.

15 If possible, compare the length of the valve springs with new ones, and renew them as a set if any are shorter.

16 If the engine is still in the car, clean the piston crowns and cylinder bore upper edges, but make sure that no carbon drops between the

pistons and bores. To do this, locate two of the pistons at the top of their bores and seal off the remaining bores with paper and masking tape. Press a little grease between the two pistons and their bores to collect any carbon dust; this can be wiped away when the piston is lowered. To prevent carbon build-up, polish the piston crown with metal polish, but remove all traces of the polish afterwards.

13 Timing belt and sprockets – removal

If the engine is still in the car, first carry out the following operations:

(a) *Disconnect the battery negative lead*
(b) *Remove the air cleaner (Chapter 3)*
(c) *Remove the alternator drivebelt (Chapter 9)*

1 Turn the engine until the indentation in the camshaft sprocket appears in the TDC hole in the timing cover, and the notch in the crankshaft pulley is aligned with the TDC pointer on the front of the oil pump.

2 Unbolt and remove the timing cover, noting that the dipstick tube and earth lead are fitted to the upper bolts.

3 Loosen the water pump retaining bolts, then turn the pump body clockwise to release the tension from the timing belt. Remove the timing belt from the camshaft sprocket (photo).

13.3 Releasing the timing belt from the camshaft sprocket

4 Using an Allen key, unbolt the pulley from the crankshaft sprocket, then remove the timing belt.

5 To remove the camshaft sprocket, unscrew the bolt and remove the spacer. Then tap off the sprocket and remove the Woodruff key. Do not turn the camshaft. The sprocket can be held stationary using a metal bar with two bolts, with one bolt inserted through a sprocket hole and the other bolt resting on the outer rim.

6 To remove the crankshaft sprocket, unscrew the bolt and lever the sprocket from the crankshaft (photo). Do not turn the crankshaft otherwise the pistons may touch the valve heads. Hold the crankshaft stationary with a lever inserted in the starter ring gear (remove the starter as applicable). Remove the Woodruff key.

14 Flywheel – removal

1 Remove the clutch, as described in Chapter 5.

2 Hold the flywheel stationary with a lever or angle iron (photo) engaged with the starter ring gear.

3 Unscrew the bolts and lift the flywheel from the crankshaft (photo).

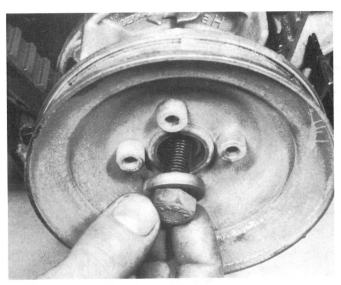

13.6 Crankshaft sprocket bolt and washer removal

14.2 One method of holding the flywheel stationary

14.3 Removing the flywheel

14.4 Removing the engine plate

4   Remove the engine plate from the cylinder block (photo).
5   The flywheel bolts must be renewed once they are removed.

15 Crankshaft oil seals – renewal

Front oil seal

1   Remove the crankshaft sprocket with reference to Section 13.
2   If available use VW tool 2085 to remove the oil seal from the oil pump housing. Removal of the seal with the engine and oil pump in position in the car can prove difficult without the special tool. In this instance, an alternative method is to drill two holes, diagonally opposed to each other in the oil seal, insert two self-tapping screws and then pull on the screws using grips to withdraw the seal. If using this method care must be taken not to drill into the housing.
3   If the oil pump is removed from the engine the seal can be prised out and a new seal fitted (photos 33.1A and 33.1B).
4   Clean the recess in the oil pump.
5   Smear a little engine oil on the lip and outer edge of the new oil seal, then fit it with VW tool 10-203 or by tapping it in with a suitable metal tube.
6   Refit the crankshaft sprocket with reference to Section 39.

Rear oil seal

7   Remove the flywheel, as described in Section 14.
Method 1
8   Drill two diagonally opposite holes in the oil seal, insert two self-tapping screws, and pull out the seal with grips.
9   Clean the recess in the housing.
10 Smear a little engine oil on the lip and outer edge of the new oil seal then tap it into the housing using a suitable metal tube.
11 Refit the flywheel, as described in Section 35.
Method 2
12 Remove the sump as described in Section 16.
13 Unscrew the bolts and withdraw the housing from the dowels on the cylinder block. Remove the gasket (photos).
14 Support the housing and drive out the oil seal (photo).
15 Clean the recess in the housing.
16 Smear a little engine oil on the lip and outer edge of the new oil seal then tap it into the housing using a block of wood (photo).
17 Clean the mating faces then refit the housing, together with a new gasket, and tighten the bolts evenly in diagonal sequence.
18 Refit the sump and flywheel, as described in Sections 34 and 35 respectively.

15.13A Crankshaft rear oil seal and housing

15.13B Withdraw the crankshaft rear oil seal housing ...

15.13C ... and remove the gasket

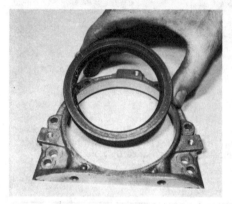

15.14 Remove the crankshaft rear oil seal from the housing

15.16 Installing the new crankshaft rear oil seal

16.1 Alternator wire clip on sump

16 Sump – removal

If the engine is still in the car, first carry out the following operations:

(a) Jack up the front of the car and support it on axle stands. Apply the handbrake

(b) Disconnect the right-hand side driveshaft (Chapter 7) and the exhaust system (Chapter 3)

(c) Unclip the alternator wire from the sump (photo)

(d) Drain the engine oil into a suitable container. Clean the drain plug and washer and refit it, tightening it to the specified torque

2   Unscrew the bolts and withdraw the sump from the cylinder block

(photo). If it is stuck, lever it away or cut through the gasket with a knife.

3   Scrape the gasket from the sump and cylinder block.

17 Oil pump – removal

1   Remove the timing belt and crankshaft sprocket, as described in Section 13.

2   Remove the sump, as described in Section 16.

3   Unbolt and remove the pick-up tube and strainer from the oil pump and cylinder block. Remove the flange gasket (photos).

4   Unscrew the bolts and withdraw the oil pump from the dowels on the front of the cylinder block. Note that the timing pointed bracket is

16.2 Removing the sump

17.3A Remove the stay bolts ...

17.3B ... flange bolts ...

17.3C ... and remove the oil pump pick-up
tube and strainer

17.4A Removing the oil pump ...

17.4B ... and gasket

located on the two upper central bolts, and the timing belt guard on the
two left-hand side bolts. Remove the gasket (photos).

18 Pistons and connecting rods – removal

1   Remove the cylinder head, as described in Section 10.
2   Remove the sump, as described in Section 16.
3   Unbolt and remove the pick-up tube and strainer from the oil pump
and cylinder block. Remove the flange gasket.
4   Using a feeler gauge, check that the connecting rod big-end
endfloat on each crankpin is within the limits given in the
Specifications (photo). If not, the components must be checked for
wear and renewed as necessary.
5   Check the big-end caps and connecting rods for identification

marks, and if necessary use a centre punch to mark them for location
and position. Note that the cut-outs in the connecting rods and caps
face the timing belt end of the engine. The arrows on the piston crown
also face the timing belt end of the engine (photo).
6   Turn the crankshaft so that No 1 crankpin is at its lowest point.
7   Unscrew the big-end nuts and tap free the cap, together with its
bearing shell (photo).
8   Using the handle of a hammer tap the piston and connecting rod
from the bore and withdraw it from the top of the cylinder block
(photo).
9   Loosely refit the cap to the connecting rod (photo).
10 Repeat the procedure given in paragraphs 7 to 9 on No 4 piston
and connecting rod, then turn the crankshaft through half a turn and
repeat the procedure on No 2 and 3 pistons.
11 Note that during reassembly, the connecting rod bolts must be
renewed.

18.4 Checking the connecting rod endfloat

18.5 Piston crown showing arrow which
points to the timing belt end of the engine

18.7 Withdrawing a big-end cap

18.8 Removing a piston

18.9 Big-end bearing components

19 Crankshaft and main bearings – removal

1 Disconnect the connecting rods from the crankshaft with reference to Section 18. However, it is not essential to remove the pistons or, therefore, to remove the cylinder head.
2 Remove the oil pump, as described in Section 17, and the rear oil seal housing as described in Section 15.
3 Using a feeler gauge check that the crankshaft endfloat is within the limits given in the Specifications (photo). Insert the feeler gauge between the centre crankshaft web and the thrust washers. This will indicate whether new thrust washers are required or not.
4 Check that the main bearing caps are identified for location and position – there should be a cast number in the crankcase ventilation pipe/water coolant pipe side of the caps, numbered from the timing belt end of the engine (photo).
5 Unscrew the bolts and tap the main bearing caps free. Keep the bearing shells and, where fitted, the thrust washers identified for position.
6 Lift the crankshaft from the crankcase and remove the remaining bearing shells and thrust washers, but keep them identified for position (photo).

20 Oil filter – renewal

1 The oil filter is located on the front of the engine beside the alternator (photo).
2 Place a suitable container beneath the filter then, using a suitable tool, unscrew the filter and discard it (photo).
3 Wipe clean the sealing face on the cylinder block.
4 Smear the sealing rubber on the new filter with engine oil, then fit and tighten the filter by hand only.

5 On completion top up the engine oil level as necessary then wipe clean the filter body. When the engine is restarted check around the filter joint for any signs of an oil leak.

21 Crankcase ventilation system – description

The crankcase ventilation system is of the positive type and consists of an oil separator on the rear (coolant pipe side) of the cylinder block, connected to the air cleaner by a rubber hose. Vacuum from the air cleaner provides a partial vacuum in the crankcase, and the piston blow-by gases are drawn through the oil separator and into the engine combustion chambers.
Periodically the hose should be examined for security and condition. Cleaning will not normally be necessary except when the engine is well worn.

22 Examination and renovation – general

With the engine completely stripped, clean all the components and examine them for wear. Each part should be checked and where necessary renewed or renovated, as described in the following Sections. Renew main and big-end shell bearings as a matter of course, unless you know that they have had little wear and are in perfect condition.

23 Crankshaft and bearings – examination and renovation

1 Examine the bearing surfaces of the crankshaft for scratches or scoring, and using a micrometer, check each journal and crankpin for

19.3 Checking the crankshaft endfloat

19.4 Crankshaft main bearing cap numbering

19.6 Removing the crankshaft

20.1 Oil filter location

20.2 Removing the oil filter using a chain wrench

ovality. Where this is found to be in excess of 0.17 mm (0.0066 in), the crankshaft will have to be reground and undersize bearings fitted.

2 Crankshaft regrinding should be carried out by a suitable engineering works, who will normally supply the matching undersize main and big-end shell bearings.

3 If the crankshaft endfloat is more than the maximum specified amount, new centre main bearing shells with side flanges will have to be fitted to replace the thrust washers. These are usually supplied together with the main and big-end bearings on a reground crankshaft.

24 Cylinder block/crankcase – examination and renovation

1 The cylinder bores must be examined for taper, ovality, scoring and scratches. Start by examining the top of the bores; if these are worn, a slight ridge will be found which marks the top of the piston ring travel. If the wear is excessive, the engine will have had a high oil consumption rate accompanied by blue smoke from the exhaust.

2 If available, use an inside dial gauge to measure the bore diameter just below the ridge and compare it with the diameter at the bottom of the bore, which is not subject to wear. If the difference is more than 0.15 mm (0.006 in) the cylinders will normally require reboring with new oversize pistons fitted.

3 Provided the cylinder bore wear does not exceed 0.20 mm (0.008 in), however, special oil control rings and pistons can be fitted to restore compression and stop the engine burning oil.

4 If new pistons are being fitted to old bores, it is essential to roughen the bore walls slightly with fine glasspaper to enable the new piston rings to bed in properly.

5 Thoroughly examine the crankcase and cylinder block for cracks and damage and use a piece of wire to probe all oilways and waterways to ensure they are unobstructed.

6 Check the core plugs for leaks and security (photo).

25 Pistons and connecting rods – examination and renovation

1 Examine the pistons for ovality, scoring and scratches. Check the connecting rods for wear and damage.

2 To remove the pistons from the connecting rods, first mark the two components in relation to each other – the indentation on the bearing end of the connecting rod faces the same way as the arrow on the piston crown.

3 Prise out the circlips then dip the piston in hot water (approximately 60°C), press out the gudgeon pin, and separate the piston from the connecting rod.

4 Assemble the pistons in reverse order.

5 If new rings are to be fitted to the original pistons, expand the old rings over the top of the pistons using two or three old feeler blades to prevent the rings dropping into empty grooves.

6 Before fitting the new rings insert each of them into the cylinder bore approximately 15.0 mm (0.6 in) from the bottom and check that the end gaps are as given in the Specifications (photo).

24.6 The core plugs in the cylinder block

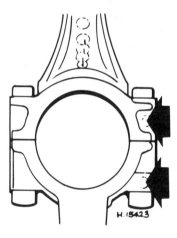
Fig. 1.7 The indentations on the big-end bearings (arrows) must face the same way as the arrow on the piston crown (Sec 25)

7 When fitting the rings to the pistons make sure that the TOP markings face towards the piston crown, and arrange the end gaps at 120° intervals (photo). Using a feeler gauge check that the clearance of each ring in its groove is within the limits given in Specifications (photo).

25.6 Checking the piston ring gaps

25.7A Space the ring gaps at 120° intervals

25.7B Checking the piston ring-to-groove wall clearance

26.1A Unscrew the relief valve plug ...

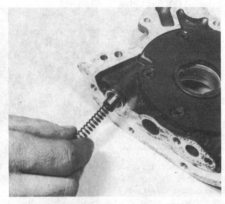

26.1B ... and remove the spring and plunger

26.2A Use an impact screwdriver to remove the screws ...

26.2B ... then remove the oil pump cover ...

26.3A ... and rotors

26.3B The outer rotor indentation (arrowed) must face the cover

26 Oil pump – examination and renovation

The manufacturer does not supply any clearances for checking the wear of the oil pump gears, so the pump must be assumed to be in good order provided that the oil pressure is as given in the Specifications. This can only be checked with the engine assembled and, as a pressure gauge will not be available to the home mechanic, the work should be entrusted to a VW garage. However, a visual examination of the oil pump can be made if required as follows.

1   Using an Allen key unscrew the relief valve plug and extract the spring and plunger (photos).
2   Using an impact screwdriver, remove the cross-head screws and withdraw the cover from the pump (photos).
3   Remove the rotors, noting that the indentation on the outer rotor faces the cover (photos).
4   Clean the components in paraffin and wipe dry, then examine them for wear and damage. If evident, renew the oil pump complete, but if in good order reassemble the pump in reverse order and tighten the screws and plug.

27 Flywheel – examination and renovation

1   There is not much you can do about the flywheel if it is damaged except renew it.
2   Inspect the starter ring teeth. If these are chipped or worn it is possible to renew the starter ring. This means heating the ring until it may be withdrawn from the flywheel, or alternatively splitting it. A new one must then be shrunk on. If you know how to do this, and you can get a new ring, then the job can be done, but it is beyond the capacity of most owners.
3   Serious scoring on the flywheel clutch facing again requires a new flywheel. **Do not** attempt to clean the scoring off with a scraper or emery.

28 Timing belt and sprockets – examination and renovation

1   The timing belt should be renewed as a matter of course if it has completed more than 20 000 miles (30 000 km) at the time of its removal. Otherwise renew it at 40 000 miles (60 000 km).
2   The camshaft and crankshaft sprockets do not normally require renewal as wear takes place very slowly.

29 Camshaft – examination and renovation

1   Examine the camshaft bearing surfaces, cam lobes, and followers for wear. If excessive renew the shaft and followers.
2   Check the camshaft run-out by turning it between fixed centres with a dial gauge on the centre journal. If the run-out exceeds the amount given in Specifications, renew the shaft.

30 Engine reassembly – general

1   To ensure maximum life with minimum trouble from a rebuilt engine, not only must everything be correctly assembled, but it must also be spotlessly clean. All oilways must be clear, and locking washers and spring washers must be fitted where indicated. Oil all bearings and other working surfaces thoroughly with engine oil during assembly.
2   Before assembly begins, renew any bolts or studs with damaged threads.
3   Gather together a torque wrench, oil can, clean rag, and a set of engine gaskets and oil seals, together with a new oil filter.

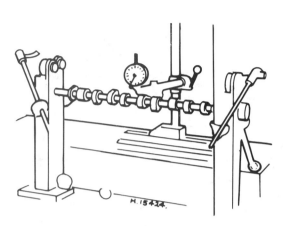

Fig. 1.8 Checking the camshaft run-out (Sec 29)

31.2B Oiling the main bearing shells

31 Crankshaft and main bearings – refitting

1 Clean the backs of the bearing shells and the bearing recesses in the cylinder block and main bearing caps.
2 Press the main bearing shells into the cylinder block and caps and oil them liberally (photo).
3 Where thrust washers are being refitted (instead of a shouldered type number three main bearing shell, a plain shell is used), smear the thrust washers with grease and stick them into position on the side of the centre main bearing and its cap (photo). The washers must be fitted so that their oilways face away from the bearings in the block and cap (photo).
4 Lower the crankshaft into position, then fit the main bearing caps in their previously noted positions (photo). Note that the bearing shell lugs are adjacent to each other.
5 Insert the bolts and tighten them evenly to the specified torque (photo). Check that the crankshaft rotates freely then check that the endfloat is within the limits given in the Specifications by inserting a feeler gauge between the centre crankshaft web and the thrust washers or bearing shoulder, as applicable.
6 Refit the rear oil seal bearing (Section 15) and oil pump (Section 33) and reconnect the connecting rods (Section 32).

31.3 Thrust washer location on the centre main bearing

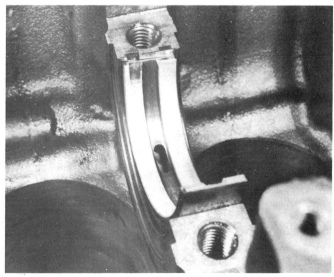

31.2A Fitting the centre main bearing shell

31.4 Fitting the centre main bearing cap

31.5 Tightening the main bearing cap bolts

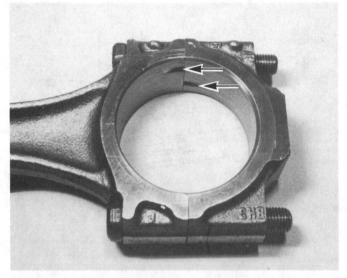

32.3B Correct location of tabs on big-end bearings – arrows

32 Pistons and connecting rods – refitting

1   As mentioned during removal, the manufacturers recommend that the connecting rod bolts be renewed, so assemble the new bolts to the rods.

2   Clean the backs of the bearing shells and the recesses in the connecting rods and big-end caps.

3   Press the big-end bearing shells into the connecting rods and caps in their correct positions and oil them liberally (photos).

4   Fit a ring compressor to No 1 piston then insert the piston and connecting rod into No 1 cylinder (photo). With No 1 crankpin at its lowest point, drive the piston carefully into the cylinder with the wooden handle of a hammer, and at the same time guide the connecting rod into the crankpin. Make sure that the arrow on the piston crown faces the timing belt end of the engine.

5   Fit the big-end bearing cap in its previously noted position then fit the nuts and tighten them evenly to the specified torque (photo).

32.4 Using a ring compressor to fit the pistons (No 2 piston shown)

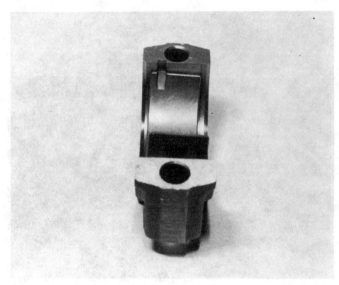

32.3A Fitting a big-end bearing shell

32.5 Tightening the big-end bearing nuts

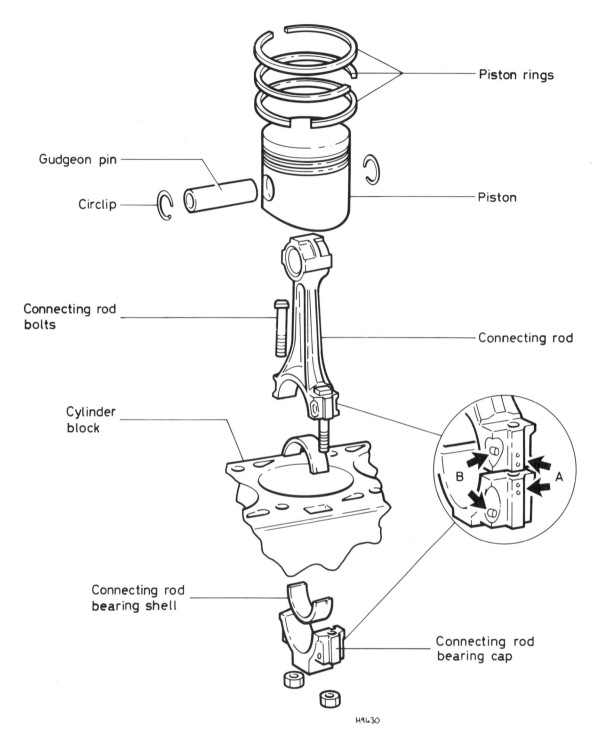

Fig. 1.9 Piston and connecting rod components (Sec 32)

Inset shows cylinder bore number markings (A) and fitting position (B)

6 Check that the crankshaft turns freely and use a feeler gauge to check that the connecting rod endfloat is within the limits given in the Specifications.

7 Repeat the procedure given in paragraphs 3 to 5 for No 4 piston and connecting rod, then turn the crankshaft through half a turn and repeat the procedure for No 2 and 3 pistons.

8 If the engine is in the car, refit the oil pump pick-up tube and strainer (Section 33), sump (Section 34), and cylinder head (Section 38).

33 Oil pump – refitting

1 Renew the oil seal in the oil pump housing with reference to Section 15 (photos).

2 Locate a new gasket on the dowels on the front of the cylinder block.

3 Locate the oil pump on the block, making sure that the inner rotor engages the flats on the crankshaft. Do not damage the oil seal.

33.1A Prising out the oil pump oil seal

33.1B Fitting the new oil seal to the oil pump

33.4 Fitted location of oil pump

4   Insert bolts, together with the timing pointer bracket and timing belt guard, and tighten them evenly to the specified torque (photo).
5   Locate a new gasket on the flange face then fit the pick-up tube and strainer, insert the bolts, and tighten them to the specified torque.
6   Refit the sump (Section 34) and timing belt and sprocket (Section 39).

34 Sump – refitting

1   If applicable (ie engine has been dismantled), refit the crankshaft rear oil seal and housing, with reference to Section 15.
2   Clean the mating faces of the sump and cylinder block.
3   Locate the new gasket either on the sump or block, then fit the sump, insert the bolts and tighten them evenly in diagonal sequence to the specified torque (photo). If required the two bolts at the flywheel end of the sump can be replaced by socket-headed bolts to facilitate their removal with the engine in the car.
4   If the engine is in the car refill the engine with oil, fasten the alternator wire to the sump clip, and lower the car to the ground.

35 Flywheel – refitting

1   Locate the engine plate on the dowels on the cylinder block.
2   Clean the mating faces of the flywheel and crankshaft, then locate the flywheel in position. Note that the bolt holes only align in one position, as they are offset.
3   Apply liquid locking fluid to the threads of new bolts, then insert them and tighten them in diagonal sequence to the specified torque while holding the flywheel stationary (photos).
4   Refit the clutch, as described in Chapter 5.

36 Cylinder head – reassembly

1   Fit the valves in their correct locations in the cylinder head.
2   Working on each valve at a time first locate the valve spring lower seat in position.
3   Before fitting the valve seal, locate the special plastic sleeve provided in the gasket set over the valve stem in order to prevent damage to the seal (photo).
4   Slide the new seal over the valve stem and press it firmly onto the guide using a metal tube (photo). Remove the plastic sleeve.
5   Fit the spring and retainer over the valve stem, then compress the spring with the compressor and insert the split collets. Release the compressor and remove it.
6   Repeat the procedure given in paragraphs 2 to 5 on the remaining valves. Tap the end of each valve stem with a non-metallic mallet to settle the collets.
7   Refit the camshaft, as described in Section 37.

37 Camshaft – refitting

1   Smear a little engine oil on the lip and outer edge of the camshaft oil seal, then drive it squarely into the cylinder head with a block of wood.
2   Oil the camshaft bearing surfaces then slide the camshaft into position, taking care not to damage the oil seal (photo).
3   Fit the distributor flange, together with a new gasket, and tighten the socket-head bolts.
4   Using a feeler gauge, check that the camshaft endfloat is as specified.
5   Fit the Woodruff key then fit the sprocket to the camshaft followed by the spacer and bolt. Tighten the bolt while holding the sprocket stationary with a metal bar and two bolts (photo).

34.3 Fitting the sump gasket

35.3A Apply liquid locking fluid to the flywheel bolts

35.3B Tightening the flywheel bolts

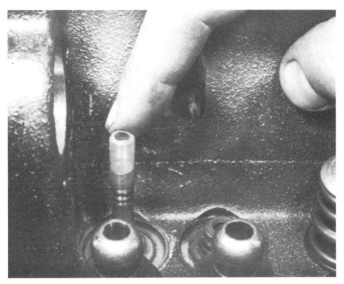
36.3 Locate the plastic sleeve on the valve stem ...

37.5 Method of tightening the camshaft sprocket bolt

36.4 ... then fit the new oil seal

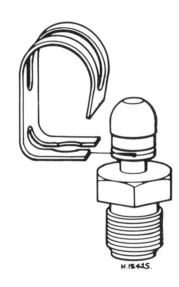
H.15425.

Fig. 1.10 Cam follower clip and groove in ball-stud (Sec 37)

6 Fit the cam followers by turning the camshaft so that the relevant cam lobe peak is pointing away from the valve, then tap the follower between the valve stem and cam, and onto the ball-stud.
7 Slide the cam follower clips into the grooves on the ball studs and locate the upper ends on the cam followers.
8 Adjust the valve clearances, as described in Section 40.
9 Turn the camshaft so that the indentation in the sprocket is pointing downwards and in line with the pointer on the timing cover plate (photo).
10 Turn the crankshaft a quarter of a turn clockwise so that the notch in the crankshaft pulley is aligned with the TDC pointer on the front of the oil pump.
11 Fit the timing belt to the camshaft sprocket and water pump.
12 Using a screwdriver in the water pump, turn the pump anti-clockwise and tension the timing belt until it can just be turned through 90° with the thumb and forefinger midway between the camshaft sprocket and water pump.
13 Tighten the water pump bolts when the belt tension is correct, and check the timing marks are still aligned.
14 Fit the dipstick tube to the cylinder block.

37.2 Oiling the camshaft bearing surfaces

37.9 Camshaft sprocket (later type) with index mark aligned with the timing cover TDC pointer

38.2 Correct fitting of the cylinder head gasket

15 Fit the timing cover, insert the bolts with the earth lead and dipstick tube bracket, and tighten the bolts.
16 Press the oil spray tube into the top of the cylinder head.
17 Refit the valve cover with a new gasket, locate the reinforcement strips, and tighten the nuts and bolts.
18 If the engine is in the car reverse the preliminary procedures given in Section 11.

38 Cylinder head – refitting

1   Position Nos 1 and 4 pistons at TDC then turn the crankshaft a quarter of a turn anti-clockwise so that neither of the pistons is at TDC.
2   Make sure that the faces of the cylinder head and block are perfectly clean then locate the new gasket on the block, making sure that all oil and water holes are visible – the gasket part number should be uppermost (photo).
3   Lower the cylinder head onto the gasket, then insert the bolts together with the engine lifting hooks.
4   Using a splined key tighten the bolts in the stages given in the Specifications, using the sequence shown in Fig. 1.11 (photo).
5   Refit the water pump, if applicable (Chapter 2).
6   Fit the timing cover plate and insert the water pump bolts loosely.
7   If required, refit the camshaft with reference to Section 37.
8   Refit and tighten the timing cover plate upper retaining bolt.
9   If applicable, refit the crankshaft sprocket and timing belt to the crankshaft as described in Section 39 (photo).
10 Turn the camshaft so that the indentation in the sprocket is aligned with the pointer on the timing cover plate.
11 Turn the crankshaft a quarter of a turn clockwise so that the notch in the crankshaft pulley (temporarily refit if necessary) is aligned with the TDC pointer on the front of the oil pump.
12 Fit the timing belt to the camshaft sprocket and water pump.
13 Using a screwdriver in the water pump, turn the pump anti-clockwise and tension the timing belt until it can just be turned through 90° with the thumb and forefinger midway between the camshaft sprocket and water pump (photo).
14 Tighten the water pump bolts when the tension is correct, and check that the timing marks are still aligned.
15 Fit the dipstick tube to the cylinder block.
16 Fit the timing cover, insert the bolts with the earth lead and dipstick tube bracket, and tighten the bolts.
17 Refit the valve cover with a new gasket, locate the reinforcement strips, and tighten the nuts and bolts.
18 If the engine is in the car reverse the preliminary procedures given in Section 10.

38.4 Tightening the cylinder head bolts

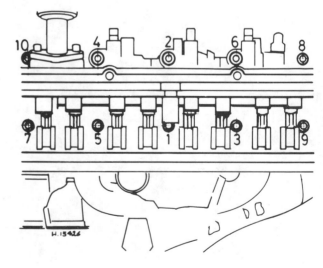

Fig. 1.11 Cylinder head bolt tightening sequence (Sec 38)

38.9 Fitting the crankshaft sprocket and timing belt

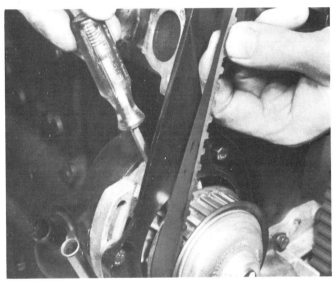
38.13 Tensioning the timing belt

through 90° with the thumb and forefinger midway between the camshaft sprocket and water pump (photo 38.13).

8 Tighten the water pump bolts when the tension is correct, and check that the timing marks are still aligned.

9 Fit the timing cover, insert the bolts with the earth lead and dipstick tube bracket, and tighten the bolts.

10 If the engine is in the car, reverse the preliminary procedures given in Section 13.

40 Valve clearances – checking and adjustment

1 The valve clearances can be checked and adjusted with the cylinder head removed (prior to refitting after overhaul) or in the normal manner such as during a routine service check.

2 Reference to the specifications will show that there are two clearance settings, these being for a cold or warm (coolant temperature above 35°C) engine condition. When the clearances are to be checked with the engine in the vehicle, run the engine up to its normal operating temperature, then switch off and remove the valve cover.

3 With the valve cover removed, turn the engine or camshaft (ie if head removed) until both cam peaks for No 1 cylinder are pointing upwards.

4 Insert a feeler blade of the correct thickness between the cam and cam follower. If the blade is not a firm sliding fit turn the adjustable ball-stud as necessary using an Allen key (photo). The valves from the timing belt end of the engine are in the following order: Inlet – Exhaust – Inlet – Exhaust – Inlet – Exhaust – Inlet – Exhaust.

40.4 Adjusting the valve clearances

39 Timing belt and sprockets – refitting

1 Fit the Woodruff key in the crankshaft and tap the sprocket into position.

2 Insert the bolt and tighten it to the specified torque while holding the crankshaft stationary with a lever in the starter ring gear.

3 Fit the Woodruff key to the camshaft then fit the sprocket followed by the spacer and bolt. Tighten the bolt while holding the sprocket stationary with a metal bar and two bolts.

4 Locate the timing belt on the crankshaft sprocket then fit the pulley, insert the bolts, and tighten them with an Allen key.

5 Turn the camshaft so that the indentation in the sprocket is aligned with the pointer on the timing cover plate. Check that the notch in the crankshaft pulley is aligned with the TDC pointer on the front of the oil pump.

6 Fit the timing belt to the camshaft sprocket and water pump.

7 Using a screwdriver in the water pump, turn the pump anti-clockwise and tension the timing belt until it can just be turned

5 Repeat the procedure given in paragraphs 3 and 4 for the remaining valves. If the engine is rotated in its normal direction, adjust the valves of No 3 cylinder followed by No 4 cylinder and No 2 cylinder.

6 Refit the valve cover, together with a new gasket.

7 If the clearances have been adjusted with the engine cold, recheck the clearances again after 600 miles (900 km) with the engine at its normal operating temperature.

41 Engine ancillary components and gearbox – refitting

1 Refer to Section 9, and refit the listed ancillary components with reference to the Sections or Chapters as applicable.

2 Refit the gearbox to the engine reversing the procedures described in Section 7.

42 Engine – refitting

Reverse the removal procedure given in Section 6, but note the following additional points:

(a) *When lowering the assembly into the engine compartment ensure that the driveshafts are aligned with the flanges*
(b) *Assemble the engine mountings loosely initially and tighten them only after the assembly is central without straining the mountings*
(c) *Adjust the clutch, as described in Chapter 5*
(d) *Adjust the accelerator cable and, where applicable, the choke cable, as described in Chapter 3*
(e) *Refill the engine with oil and water*

43 Engine – adjustments after major overhaul

1   With the engine refitted to the car, make a final check to ensure that everything has been reconnected and that no rags or tools have been left in the engine compartment.
2   If new pistons or crankshaft bearings have been fitted, turn the carburettor engine speed screw in about half a turn to compensate for the initial tightness of the new components.
3   Fully pull out the choke (manual choke models) and start the engine. This may take a little longer than usual as the fuel pump and carburettor float chamber may be empty.
4   As soon as the engine starts, push in the choke to the detent. Check that the oil pressure light goes out.
5   Check the oil filter, fuel hoses and water hoses for leaks.
6   Run the engine to normal operating temperature, then adjust the slow running (idle), as described in Chapter 3.
7   If new pistons or crankshaft bearings have been fitted, the engine must be run-in for the first 500 miles (750 km). Do not operate the engine at full throttle or allow the engine to labour in any gear.
8   Although not strictly essential, it is a good practice to change the engine oil and filter after the initial running-in period. This will get rid of the small metallic particles which are produced by new components bedding in to each other.

PART B: 1.6 AND 1.8 LITRE

44   General description

The engine is of four-cylinder, in-line, overhead camshaft type, mounted transversely at the front of the car. The gearbox (manual or automatic) is attached to the flywheel/driveplate end of the engine.
The crankshaft is of five main bearing type and the endfloat is controlled by a shouldered centre bearing or by half thrust washers located each side of the centre bearing.
The camshaft is driven by a toothed belt which is tensioned by a tensioner on an eccentric bearing. The valves are operated by bucket type cam followers in direct contact with the camshaft.
An intermediate shaft, which is also driven by the toothed timing belt, drives the distributor and oil pump, and on carburettor engines the fuel pump.
The oil pump is of the twin gear type, driven from the immediate shaft, and it incorporates a pressure relief valve.
The aluminium cylinder head is of conventional design with the inlet and exhaust manifolds mounted on the rear side (as viewed with the engine in the car).

45   Routine maintenance – engine

The procedure is the same as that described for the 1.05 and 1.3 litre variants given in Section 2 of this Chapter.

46 Major operations possible with engine in car

The following operations can be carried out without having to remove the engine from the car:

(a) *Removal and servicing of the cylinder head, camshaft, and timing belt*
(b) *Renewal of the crankshaft rear oil seal (after removal of the gearbox/transmission, driveplate or clutch as applicable)*
(c) *Removal of the sump and oil pump*
(d) *Removal of the piston/connecting rod assemblies (after removal of the cylinder head and sump*
(e) *Renewal of the crankshaft front oil seal, intermediate shaft front oil seal, and camshaft front oil seal*
(f) *Renewal of the engine mountings*

47 Major operations only possible after removal of engine from car

The following operations can only be carried out after removal of the engine from the car:

(a) *Renewal of crankshaft main bearings*
(b) *Removal and refitting of the crankshaft*
(c) *Removal and refitting of the intermediate shaft*

48 Method of engine removal

1   The engine, together with the gearbox/transmission, must be lifted from the engine compartment, then the engine separated from the gearbox/transmission on the bench. Two people will be needed for some of the time.
2   A hoist, capacity 150 kg (3 cwt) will be needed and the engine must be lifted approximately 1 metre (three feet). If the hoist is not portable and the engine is lifted, then sufficient room must be left behind the car to push the car back out of the way so that the power unit may be lowered. Blocks will be needed to support the engine after removal.
3   Ideally the car should be over a pit. If this is not possible then the body must be supported on axle stands so that the front wheels may be turned to undo the driveshaft nuts. The left one is accessible from above but the right-hand shaft must be undone from underneath. There are other jobs best done from below. Removal of the shift linkage can only be done from underneath, as can the exhaust downpipe-to-manifold detachment.
4   The exhaust downpipe-to-manifold flange connection is secured by special spring clips rather than bolts or studs and nuts. When disconnecting and reconnecting the joint it will be necessary to use the special VW tool designed for this task, its number being 3049A. Without this tool detachment and certainly reconnection of the joint and clips is virtually impossible, so make arrangements to borrow or hire this tool in advance. Refer to Chapter 3 for further details.
5   The only other special tools that will be required will be a set of splined key wrenches which will be needed to remove and refit the socket-head bolts used to secure certain items such as the cylinder head bolts (photo 5.4).
6   Draining of oil and coolant is best done away from the working area if possible. This saves the mess made by spilled oil in the place where you must work.
7   Although not listed as an optional fitting on UK market models, an air conditioning system may have been fitted to some models and, where this is the case, the following special precautions must be taken when handling the refrigerant lines of the system or the system components.

(a) *Do not stress or bend the flexible hose lines to a radius of less than 101 mm (4 inches)*
(b) *The flexible hose lines must be correctly located, must not chafe against adjacent components and must be kept well clear of the exhaust manifold and downpipe.*
(c) *All metal tubing lines must be kept free of kinks and must be handled with care*
(d) *Do not disconnect any of the air conditioning supply lines*

(e) *Do not weld or apply heat in the vicinity of the air conditioning lines or equipment*

(f) *If any part of the air conditioning system is to be detached and/or removed for any reason it must first be depressurised by your VW dealer or a competent air conditioning systems engineer. The only exception to this rule is the removal, refitting and renewal of the compressor drivebelt. This can be achieved in the same manner as that for the alternator drivebelt (refer to Chapter 9)*

49 Engine (carburettor) – removal

1   Disconnect the battery negative lead.
2   Remove the bonnet, as described in Chapter 11, and store it in a safe place.
3   Drain the engine coolant, as described in Chapter 2.
4   Position a suitable container beneath the engine then undo the sump drain plug and drain the engine oil (photo). On completion clean the drain plug and refit it. Renew the O-ring.

49.7A 0.3 bar oil pressure switch location in rear of cylinder head

49.4 Sump drain plug

49.7B 1.8 oil pressure switch location in filter mounting

5   Remove the radiator, together with the cooling fan unit, as described in Chapter 2.
6   On carburettor models remove the air cleaner unit, then disconnect the throttle cable at the carburettor (refer to Chapter 3). Place the cable out of the way.
7   Disconnect the following wiring connections, but identify each lead as it is detached to avoid confusion on reassembly.

   (a) *Alternator lead*
   (b) *Oil pressure switch lead(s) at cylinder head (photos) and oil filter bracket*
   (c) *Inlet manifold preheater thermo-switch lead*
   (d) *Choke cover thermo-switch lead (where applicable)*
   (e) *Ignition HT and LT leads*
   (f) *Choke cover lead separate connector*
   (g) *Coolant temperature sender unit lead*
   (h) *Earth strap to gearbox (photo) and multi-function switch to gearbox*
   (i) *Starter motor leads*

8   Disconnect the fuel supply hose from the fuel pump and the fuel return hose (to the fuel tank). Plug the hoses to prevent fuel leakage.
9   Disconnect the coolant and heater hoses from the engine.
10 On manual transmission models, disconnect the clutch cable; with reference to Chapter 5.

49.7C Earth strap to gearbox

11 Disconnect the following items from around the carburettor. Identify the connections where necessary to avoid confusion on reassembly:

    (a) *Thermotime valve*
    (b) *Idle/overrun cut-off valve*
    (c) *Inlet manifold preheater separator connector*
    (d) *Part throttle channel heater separate connector*

12 Disconnect the speedometer cable from the transmission.
13 Disconnect and remove the vacuum reservoir.
14 Disconnect the brake vacuum servo hoses and the vacuum hoses from the inlet manifold.
15 Undo and remove the gearbox mounting bolt.
16 Raise and support the vehicle on axle stands, allowing sufficient clearance to work underneath.
17 Disconnect the gearbox linkage, referring to Chapter 6 (manual gearbox).
18 On automatic transmission models select P (Park) then disconnect the throttle and selector cables from the transmission, with reference to Chapter 6.
19 Disconnect the driveshafts from the gearbox/transmission with reference to Chapter 7, and tie them up out of the way.
20 To disconnect the exhaust manifold to downpipe connection VW special tool number 3049A will be required. Although it may be possible to prise the clips free to separate this joint the special tool will definitely be required to refit the springs; see Chapter 3 for further details.

21 The car can now be lowered again; the remaining removal operations being from above.
22 Attach a suitable sling and hoist to the engine and gearbox/transmission unit and take its weight.
23 Disconnect the rear engine bearer by undoing the three bolts (photo 6.24).
24 The engine/gearbox front mounting must now be detached by unscrewing and removing the single through-bolt. It may be necessary to further lift, lower or twist the engine/gearbox unit to allow the through-bolt to be withdrawn (photo 6.26A).
25 The engine/gearbox unit is now ready for lifting out, but first make a final check that all cables, wiring and hoses are clear.
26 Have an assistant at hand to help guide the engine and gearbox unit clear of the surrounding components in the engine compartment as the unit is lifted out. The unit will have to be twisted slightly as it is raised and, once clear of the car, lower it to the ground or to the work area.

50 Engine (fuel injection) – removal

    On the fuel injection models, the engine removal procedure closely follows that described in the previous Section, but disregard those items concerning detachment of the carburettor and associated items. The following fuel injection equipment items will need to be

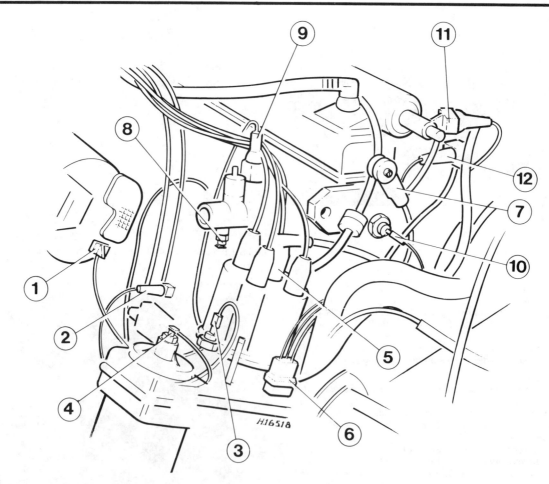

Fig. 1.12 Wiring connections to be detached – fuel injection models (Sec 50)

1 Alternator	5 Distributor HT cable	7 Vacuum switch	10 0.3 bar oil pressure switch
2 Warm-up valve	(terminal 4)	8 Coolant temperature sender	11 Cold start valve
3 1.8 bar oil pressure switch	6 Hall sender (distributor)	9 Thermotime switch	12 Auxiliary air valve
4 Oil temperature sender			

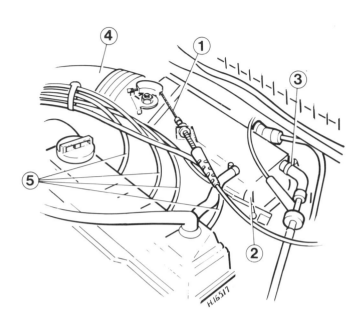

Fig. 1.13 Fuel injection components to be detached (Sec 50)

1 Throttle cable
2 Cold start valve
3 Vacuum hoses
4 Air intake pipe
5 Injectors

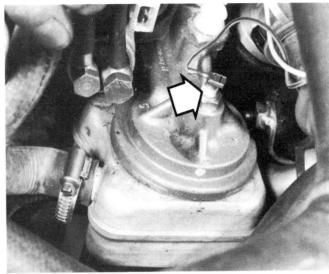

50.11 Oil temperature sender – arrowed (fuel injection models)

disconnected instead. Refer to Chapter 3 for further details concerning the detachment or removal where necessary of the respective fuel injection items.
1 Disconnect the wires from the warm-up valve (green connector).
2 Disconnect the wiring to the cold start valve (blue connector).
3 Disconnect the wiring to the auxiliary air valve.
4 Disconnect the throttle cable at the fast idle cam and bracket, but do not remove the securing clip.
5 Remove the cold start valve, but leave the fuel lines connected. Place out of the way.
6 Disconnect the air intake pipe at the flexible ducting attached to the throttle housing.
7 Disconnect the vacuum hoses from the inlet manifold and vacuum booster.
8 Leaving the fuel lines connected, undo the retaining bolts and withdraw the warm-up valve from the cylinder block. Position out of the way.
9 Detach the injectors from the cylinder head and plug the holes. Disconnect the injector lines from the locating bracket on the throttle housing and fold them back out of the way.
10 Detach the vacuum hoses to the throttle housing T-piece connector location clip at the bulkhead. Fold the hoses back out of the way.
11 Disconnect the oil temperature switch sender lead (photo).
12 When lifting out the engine and gearbox, greater care will have to be taken in manoeuvring the combined unit from the engine compartment due to the close proximity of the air inlet manifold to the bulkhead. The unit will need to be pulled forwards first then twisted and lifted.

51 Engine and gearbox – separation and reconnection

The procedure is fully described in Chapter 6, Section 10 (manual gearbox) or Section 22 (automatic transmission). However, it is only necessary to refer to those paragraphs pertinent to the particular method being used. The engine must be supported on blocks, or alternatively the gearbox/transmission can be withdrawn with the engine still on the hoist.

52 Engine dismantling – general

Refer to Section 8 of this Chapter.

53 Engine ancillary components – removal

1 With the engine removed from the car and separated from the transmission, the externally mounted ancillary components can be removed prior to engine dismantling. The removal sequence need not necessarily follow the order given.
2 Remove the alternator and drivebelt (refer to Chapter 9).
3 Unbolt and remove the inlet manifold and carburettor or inlet manifold and throttle housing (fuel injection models). Refer to Chapter 3 as required.
4 Remove the exhaust manifold (Chapter 3).
5 Remove the fuel pump (Chapter 3).
6 If still attached, remove the warm-up valve on fuel injection models (Chapter 3).
7 Remove the distributor, referring to Chapter 4.
8 Remove the oil filter with oil cooler (where applicable) and the oil filter mounting (Section 62).
9 Remove the oil pressure and coolant temperature and sensor switches, noting their locations.
10 Remove the water pump and coolant hose connectors from the cylinder block and cylinder head (Chapter 2). Note that new O-ring seals will be required when they are refitted.
11 Remove the clutch, as described in Chapter 5, on manual gearbox models, then unbolt the intermediate plate. On automatic transmission models unbolt the driveplate from the crankshaft, noting the location of the spacer and shim(s).

54 Timing belt and sprockets – removal

If the engine is still in the car, first carry out the following operations:

(a) Disconnect the battery earth lead
(b) Remove the alternator drivebelt (Chapter 9)
(c) Unbolt and remove the water pump pulley

1 Unbolt and remove the timing belt upper cover.
2 Unscrew the nuts and bolts from the valve cover and remove the cover, together with the gasket and reinforcement strips. Detach the crankcase emission hose(s) from the rocker cover.

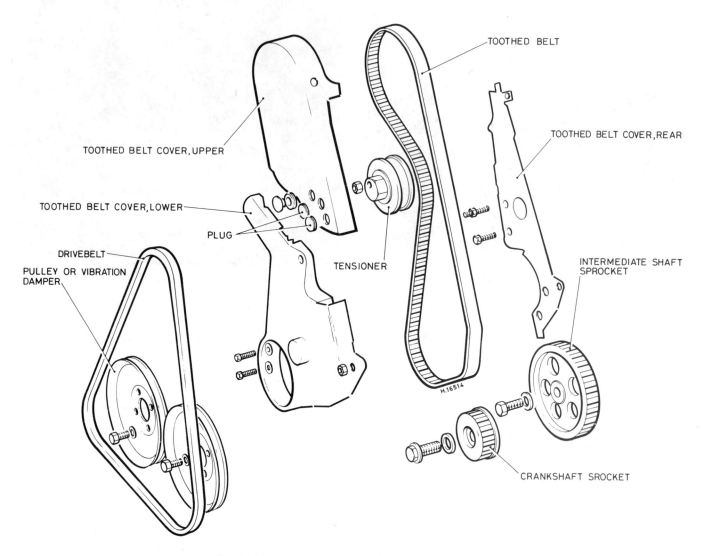

TOOTHED BELT

TOOTHED BELT COVER,REAR

TOOTHED BELT COVER,UPPER

TOOTHED BELT COVER,LOWER

PLUG

DRIVEBELT

PULLEY OR VIBRATION
DAMPER

TENSIONER

INTERMEDIATE SHAFT
SPROCKET

H.16514

CRANKSHAFT SROCKET

Fig. 1.14 Timing belt and cover components (Sec 54)

3   Mark the relative positions of the crankshaft pulley and crankshaft
sprocket, then undo the four socket-head bolts and withdraw the
pulley.
4   Unbolt and withdraw the lower timing cover.
5   The engine must now be set for timing. Temporarily refit the
crankshaft pulley. On the intermediate sprocket for the timing belt one
tooth has a centre-punch mark. Turn the engine until this mates with a
notch on the V-belt pulley bolted to the crankshaft sprocket (photo).
To turn the engine over, remove the spark plugs then fit a suitable
spanner onto the crankshaft sprocket retaining bolt and turn it in the
direction of engine rotation.
6   When these marks match, look at the sprocket on the camshaft.
One tooth of this has a centre-punch mark. This should be level with
the valve cover flange (Figure 1.15). Having turned the engine until
these marks agree now look at the cams for No 1 cylinder, the one
nearest the timing belt. They will both be in the 'valve closed' position
(photo). Now look through the hole in which the TDC sensor goes
where the timing marks show on the periphery of the flywheel and note
the reading.
7   Before removing the timing drivebelt, check its correct tension. If
held between the finger and thumb halfway between the intermediate
shaft and the camshaft it should be just possible to twist it through 90°.
If it is too slack, adjust it by slackening the bolt holding the eccentric
cam on the tensioner wheel. If you are satisfied it can be adjusted to
the correct tension remove it and examine it for wear. Now is the time
to order a new one if necessary.

54.5 Intermediate sprocket timing mark (arrowed) aligned with the
notch in the crankshaft pulley

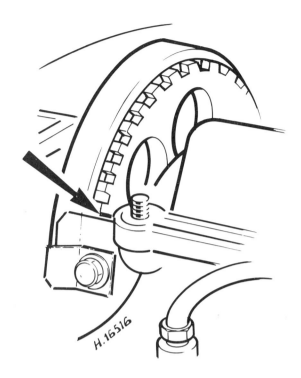

Fig. 1.15 Camshaft sprocket timing mark (arrowed) with No 1 cylinder at TDC on compression (Sec 54)

54.6 No 1 cylinder cam lobes in valve closed position

8 Loosen the tensioner then withdraw the timing belt from the camshaft, intermediate and crankshaft sprockets.

9 Each of the timing belt sprockets is secured by a central bolt and washer. The intermediate, camshaft and crankshaft sprocket (the latter in particular) securing bolts are tightened to a substantial torque and the sprockets will therefore need to be firmly held when undoing the bolts.

10 To remove the camshaft sprocket, unscrew the bolt with the sprocket held stationary by inserting a suitable metal bar through a sprocket hole and resting on the valve cover face of the cylinder head,

but take care not to damage the face. Remove the bolt and spacer washer then withdraw the sprocket, tapping it free if necessary. Check the fit of the Woodruff key in the camshaft and if loose in the groove it must be renewed. Lever out the Woodruff key and keep it with the sprocket.

11 To remove the crankshaft sprocket, hold the crankshaft stationary with a lever jammed in the starter ring gear (remove the starter motor as applicable). **Do not** allow the crankshaft to turn, or the pistons may touch the valve heads. Unscrew the retaining bolt and remove it, together with the spacer washer, then lever the sprocket free from the crankshaft. Check the fit of the Woodruff key (if fitted) in the crankshaft and if loose in its groove it must be renewed. Lever out the Woodruff key and keep it with the crankshaft sprocket.

12 The intermediate shaft sprocket is removed in a similar manner to that for the camshaft sprocket.

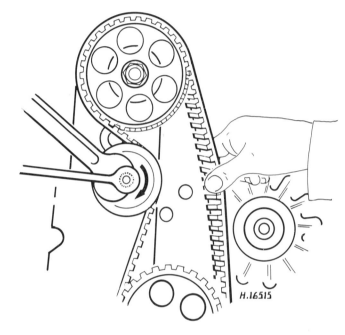

Fig. 1.16 Timing belt tension check method (Secs 54 and 79)

55 Camshaft – removal and refitting

To remove the camshaft with the engine in the car, first carry out the following operations:

    (a) Remove the timing cover and valve cover, then disconnect the timing belt from the camshaft sprocket, as described in Section 54

    (b) If the camshaft oil seal is to be renewed then the camshaft timing sprocket must also be removed

1 Refer to Fig. 1.17 or 1.18. Remove the camshaft bearing caps. These have to go back the same way in the same place. They are numbered (photo), but put a centre-punch on the side nearest the front of the head (where the sprocket was). No 1 is the one with a small oil seal on it.

2 Remove bearing caps 5, 1 and 3 in that order. Now undo the nuts holding 2 and 4 in a diagonal pattern and the camshaft will lift them up as the pressure of the valve springs is exerted. When they are free, lift the caps off and the camshaft may be lifted out as well. The oil seal on the front end will come with it.

3 The tappet buckets are now exposed and may be lifted out (photo). Take each one out in turn, prise the little disc out of the bucket by inserting a small screwdriver either side and lift the disc away. On the reverse the disc is engraved with a size (eg 3.75). This is its thickness number. Note the number and then clean the disc and refit it, number

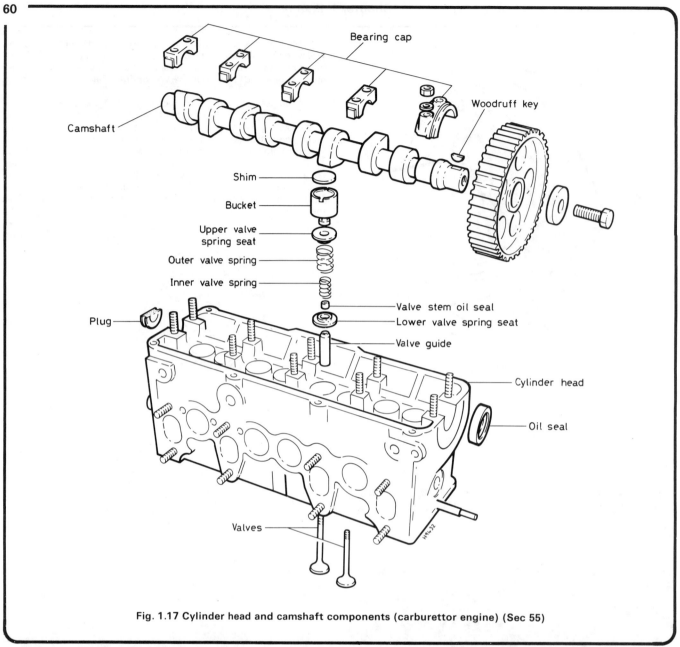

Bearing cap

Camshaft

Woodruff key

Shim

Bucket

Upper valve spring seat

Outer valve spring

Inner valve spring

Valve stem oil seal

Lower valve spring seat

Plug

Valve guide

Cylinder head

Oil seal

Valves

Fig. 1.17 Cylinder head and camshaft components (carburettor engine) (Sec 55)

55.1 Removing a camshaft bearing cap

55.3 Tappet bucket and shim

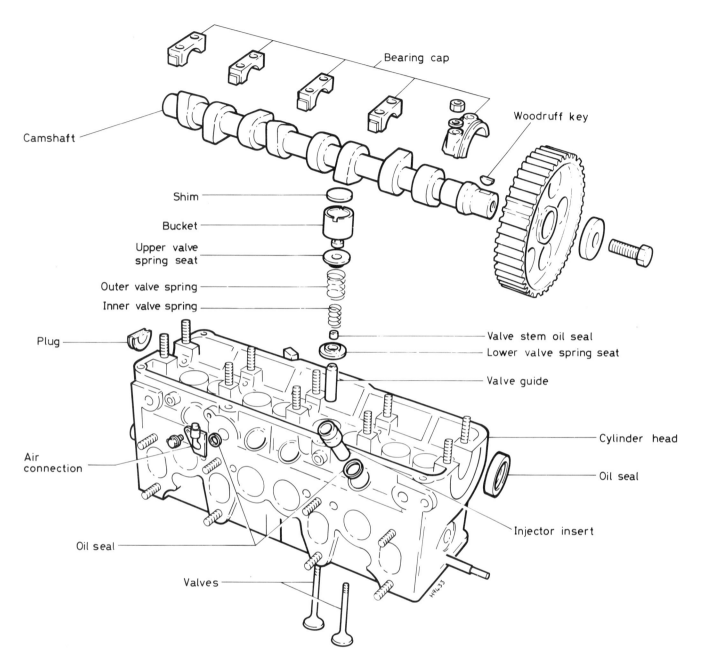

Fig. 1.18 Cylinder head and camshaft components (fuel injection engine) (Sec 55)

side down. There are eight of these and they must not be mixed. On assembly they must go back into the bore from which they came. This problem exists also for the valves, so a container for each valve assembly and tappet is required. Label them 1 to 8, 1 and 2 will be No 1 cylinder exhaust and inlet respectively. No 3 will be No 2 cylinder exhaust and No 4 its inlet valve. No 5 will be the inlet valve for No 3 cylinder and No 6 its exhaust valve. No 7 will be the inlet valve for No 4 cylinder and No 8 its exhaust valve. Note the thickness of all the tappet clearance discs from No 1 valve to No 8 valve for use on reassembly.

4   To check the camshaft, refer to Section 29 of this Chapter.

5   The refitting procedure is given in Section 57 of this Chapter.

56 Cylinder head – removal

1   If the cylinder head is being removed with the engine out of the car, proceed from paragraph 17. If the cylinder head is being removed with the engine in the car, it is best removed with the inlet and exhaust manifolds. They can then be detached after removal of the cylinder head, but note that a special tool is required to release (and subsequently reconnect) the exhaust downpipe-to-manifold flange retaining clips (refer to Chapter 3, Section 24). A special splined key will also be required to undo/tighten the cylinder head bolts.

2   Disconnect the battery earth lead. Drain the cooling system, then disconnect the cooling and heater hoses from the cylinder head (Chapter 2).

3   Disconnect the thermoswitch and oil pressure lead connections.

4   On carburettor models remove the air cleaner unit (Chapter 3).

5   Disconnect the alternator from the cylinder head attachment brackets and remove the V-belt (Chapter 9).

6   Disconnect/remove the inlet and exhaust manifolds as required although, as mentioned, it is possible to detach them after removing the cylinder head if the exhaust downpipe can be disconnected. If removing the manifolds with the cylinder head, disconnect the vacuum

hose from the inlet manifold, and the accelerator cable (and choke cable if applicable) from the carburettor.

7 Disconnect the HT leads from the spark plugs.

Fuel injection models

8 On models fitted with fuel injection, the following additional items must be disconnected.

9 Detach the injector lines from the cylinder head and their location clips and fold them back out of the way (see Chapter 3).

10 Disconnect the inlet duct at the flexible hose connection to the throttle valve housing.

11 Detach the vacuum hoses to the throttle valve housing and at the three-way connector on the bulkhead side of the cylinder head. Fold back and secure the hoses out of the way.

12 Disconnect the auxiliary air valve lead from the underside of the inlet manifold and the auxiliary air valve hose to the flexible hose on the throttle valve housing.

13 Disconnect the servo vacuum hose from the green connector on the flexible hose on the throttle housing.

14 If air conditioning is fitted, detach the hoses from the auxiliary air valve and tube connections.

15 Detach the MFI hose at the servo hose valve connection.

16 Detach the wiring connector from the cold start valve.

All models

17 Remove the timing cover and valve cover, then disconnect the timing belt from the camshaft sprocket, as described in Section 54.

18 Remove the camshaft, as described in Section 55.

19 The next job is to remove the cylinder head bolts. These are recessed in the well of the cylinder head and are socket-head bolts. These must be removed using the correct special splined tool. If an Allen key is used it is likely to strip the socket-head in the bolt and bolt removal will then be virtually impossible without major surgery.

20 The cylinder head bolts must be unscrewed in a progressive manner and in the reverse sequence to that shown in Fig. 1.25.

21 When all ten bolts have been removed, lift the head from the cylinder block. It may need a little tapping to loosen it, but do not try to prise it loose by hammering in wedges. Lift off the gasket and, if the engine is not being dismantled, clean the piston crowns and block face.

---

57 Cylinder head – dismantling, inspection and overhaul

1 Take the cylinder head away from the clean area and, with a wire brush, blunt screwdriver and steel wool, clean off all the carbon from the combustion chambers, valve faces and exhaust ports. When the head is clean and shining, wash your hands and take it back to the work area. Remove the spark plugs for cleaning.

2 The valves are not easy to get out unless a suitable valve spring compressor is available. Because the collets and spring caps are set so far down in the head a long claw is necessary on the compressor, and it must be split sufficiently to enable the collets to be removed and inserted. If such a tool is not to hand then find a piece of steel tube about 25 mm (1 in) inside diameter which will fit over the valve stem and press down the spring cover (see Fig. 1.19). The length will depend on the size of the compressor so fit the compressor over the head fully extended, measure the distance between the claw and the valve spring seat and cut the tube to a suitable length.

3 The next step is to cut two windows of suitable size, say 25 mm (1 in) long and 16 mm (0.6 in) wide, in opposite sides of the tube. The tube may then be used with the compressor to extract the collets from each valve stem in turn and the valve, springs, collets and seats may join the tappet in the appropriate receptacle, keeping them strictly together for refitting in the same valve guide from which they were taken (photo).

4 The valve springs must be renewed if they are damaged, distorted or known to have covered a high mileage. If in doubt as to their condition have your VW Dealer check them for compression efficiency using a calibrated valve spring compressor.

5 The valves should be be cleaned and checked for signs of wear or burring. Where this has occurred, the inlet valve may be reground on a machine at a dealer, but exhaust valves must not be reground on the machine but ground in by hand. Wear in the valve guides may be detected by fitting a new valve in the guide and checking the amount that the rim of the valve will move sideways, when the top of the valve

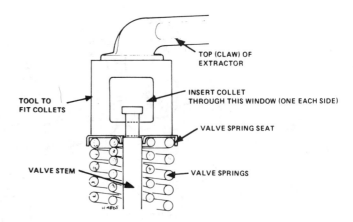

Fig. 1.19 Improvised tool used to remove and refit collets to valve stems (Sec 57)

stem is flush with the top of the valve guide. The valve rock limits are given in the Specifications. New valve guides must be fitted and reamed by your VW dealer.

6 Do not labour away too long grinding in the valves. If the valve seat and valve are not satisfactory after fifteen minutes hard work then you will probably do more harm than good by going on. Make sure both surfaces are clean, smear the grinding paste onto the valve evenly and using a suction type cup work the valve with an oscillating motion lifting the valve away from the seat occasionally to stop ridging. Clean the seat and valve frequently and carry on until there is an even band, grey in colour on both seat and valve then wipe off all the paste.

7 The surface of the head must be checked with a straight-edge and feeler gauge. Place the straight-edge along the centre of the machined face of the head. Make sure there are no ridges at the extreme ends and measure the clearance with feelers between each combustion chamber head. This is the area where the narrowest part of the cylinder head gasket comes – and where the gasket is most likely to fail. If the straight-edge is firmly in place and feelers in excess of 0.1 mm (0.004 in) can be put between the head and the straight-edge then the head should be taken to a dealer for servicing or, more probably, a new one.

8 If the cylinder head shows any signs of cracking anywhere have it inspected by your VW dealer to assess its condition for reuse. It may have to be renewed.

9 VW recommend that the valve stem oil seals should **always** be renewed to prevent possible high oil consumption. Pulling off the old seal is simple with pliers. With a packet of new oil seals is a small plastic sleeve. This is fitted over the valve stem and lubricated, and then the seal should be pushed on over the plastic sleeve until it seats on the guide. This should be done with a special tool (VW 10 204) which fits snugly round the outside of the seal and pushes it on squarely. If the seal is assembled without the plastic sleeve the seal will be damaged and oil consumption will become excessive. If you cannot pull them on properly then ask a dealer to do it for you.

10 Before reassembling the cylinder head, check the condition of the camshaft, as described in Section 29.

11 When all the parts, head, valve, seats, springs, guides, seals and camshaft have been pronounced satisfactory then assembly of the head may commence. Insert the valve in the correct guide (photo), fit the inner seat, valve springs and outer cap (photo), assemble the valve spring compressor and possibly the small tube and compress the valve spring until the collets may be assembled to the valve stem (photo). If your fingers are too big, put a blob of grease on the collet and pick it up with a small screwdriver, then insert it into the slot on the valve stem, assemble the second collet and holding them carefully together in place ease off the compressor until the spring seats the collets home. Remove the compressor, put a rag over the valve stem and tap the stem with a hammer. This is to ensure that the collets are seated correctly. If they are they will not come out. Repeat until all eight valves are in position in the cylinder head.

12 Refit the tappets in the bores from which they came (photo), then lubricate the camshaft bearing surfaces with oil and fit the camshaft, positioned so that No 1 cylinder cams point upwards.

57.3 Valve, springs, cap and collets

57.11A Inserting a valve into the cylinder head

57.11B Locate the valve springs and cap ...

57.11C ... and valve collets

57.12 Fit the tappet buckets

57.13 Fit the bearing caps

58.5 Refitting the oil pump

58.6 Refitting the sump

13 Fit a new oil seal at the sprocket end, lubricate the bearings, set the shaft in position, and install bearing caps (photo) Nos 2 and 4, tightening the nuts in a diagonal pattern until the shaft is in place. Now install the other bearing caps, making sure they are the right way round (centre-punch marks towards the drive pulley) and tighten the caps down using a diagonal pattern to the specified torque. Install a new rubber seal at the opposite end to the sprocket.

14 Adjust the valve clearances, with reference to Section 77.

15 To refit the cylinder head, refer to Section 78.

58 Sump and oil pump – removal and refitting

1 If the engine is in the car, first position a suitable container underneath the sump drain plug, undo the plug and drain the engine oil. Note that the plug has an O-ring seal fitted which must be renewed when refitting.

2 Undo the sump retaining bolts and remove the sump from the lower face of the crankcase. Remove the sump gasket. This must also be renewed when refitting the sump.

3 To remove the oil pump, undo the two retaining bolts and lower the pump unit, complete with the oil pick-up pipe and strainer.

4 Dismantling and inspection of the oil pump is dealt with in Section 69.

5 To refit the pump, ensure that the mating faces are clean, locate it into position, fit and tighten the securing bolts to the specified torque (photo).

6 Locate the new sump gasket, but **do not** apply an adhesive sealant. Refit the sump and tighten the retaining bolts evenly to the specified torque (photo).

7 Refit the oil drain plug fitted with a new O-ring seal and tighten it to the specified torque.

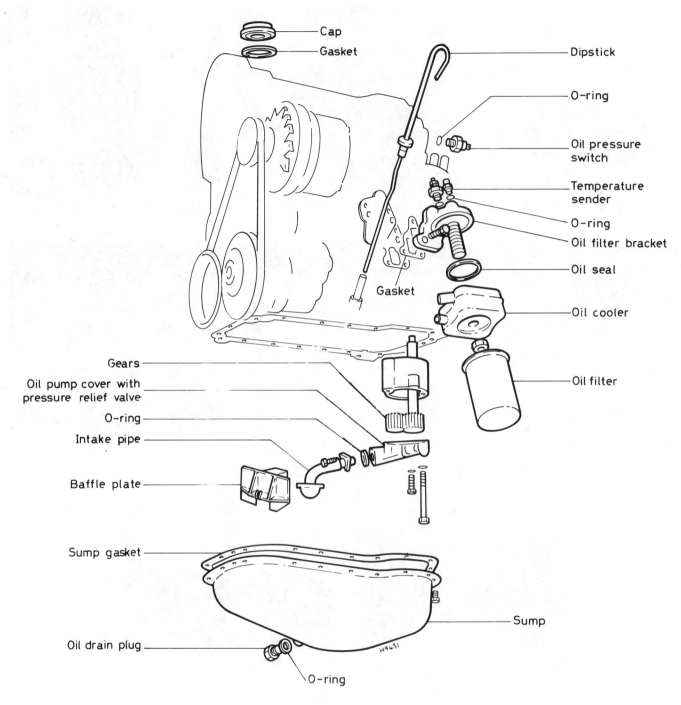

Cap
Gasket
Dipstick
O-ring
Oil pressure switch
Temperature sender
O-ring
Oil filter bracket
Oil seal
Gasket
Oil cooler
Gears
Oil pump cover with pressure relief valve
O-ring
Intake pipe
Oil filter
Baffle plate
Sump gasket
Sump
Oil drain plug
O-ring

Fig. 1.20 Sump, oil pump and oil filter components (Sec 58)

Fuel injection model shown

59 Pistons and connecting rods – removal

1   Remove the cylinder head, as described in Section 56.
2   Remove the sump, as described in Section 58.
3   Unscrew the two oil pump unit retaining bolts then lower and remove the pump unit, complete with oil pick-up pipe from the crankcase. Place it on one side for cleaning and inspection.
4   The piston and connecting rod removal procedure now follows that given for the smaller engine variants in Section 18.

60 Crankshaft and main bearings – removal

1   Disconnect the pistons and connecting rods from the crankshaft, as described in the previous Section. Note that, although the engine has to be removed to remove the crankshaft, the cylinder head, pistons and connecting rods can be left in position.
2   At the flywheel end, undo and remove the six bolts securing the oil seal flange to the crankcase. Withdraw the flange, seal and gasket.
3   Now examine the main bearing caps. It will be seen that the caps

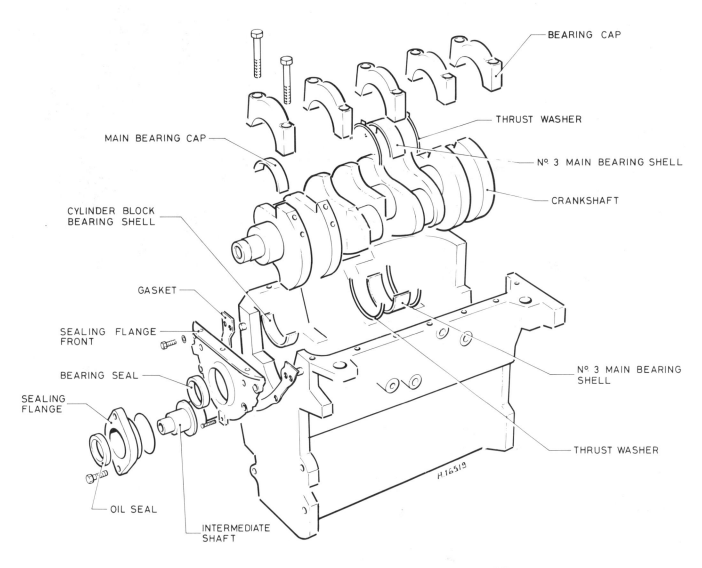

Fig. 1.21 Crankshaft and cylinder block components (Sec 60)

are numbered one to five and that the number is on the side of the engine opposite the oil pump position. Identify these numbers. If they are obscured then mark the caps in the same way as the connecting rod caps. Before removing the caps, push the crankshaft to the rear and check the endfloat using a feeler gauge between the thrust washer flanges on No 3 main bearing and the crankshaft web (photo). It must not exceed the specified maximum.

4   Remove the bearing cap retaining bolts, remove the bearing caps and lift out the thrust washers from each side of the centre main bearing.

5   Lift out the crankshaft and then remove the top half bearing shells. If the main bearings are not being renewed make sure the shells are identified so that they go back into the same bearing cap the same way round.

61 Intermediate shaft – removal

1   The intermediate shaft can only be withdrawn from the crankcase with the engine removed from the car (Section 49 or 50, as applicable).

2   Remove the timing belt, as described in Section 54.

3   Remove the fuel pump on carburettor models (Chapter 3) and the ignition distributor (Chapter 4).

60.3 Checking the crankshaft endfloat at No 3 main bearing

4   Before removing the intermediate shaft, check that the endfloat does not exceed the maximum allowable amount (see Specifications).
5   Undo the two sealing flange retaining bolts then withdraw the intermediate shaft, complete with sealing flange (photos).
6   Withdraw the sealing flange from the intermediate shaft. The oil seal within the flange and the O-ring must be renewed on reassembly (see Section 70).

61.5A Intermediate shaft retaining flange bolts (arrowed)

61.5B Withdrawing the intermediate shaft

62 Oil filter – renewal

1   The oil filter is located on the side of the crankcase beneath the distributor (photo), the filter being a disposable cartridge type which is screwed onto a mounting bracket which is attached to the crankcase. On fuel injection models an oil cooler is fitted between the mounting bracket and the filter cartridge.
2   The filter must be renewed at the specified intervals given in Routine Maintenance at the start of this Manual.
3   Place a suitable container beneath the filter then, using a strap wrench, unscrew the filter and discard it. For better access either jack up the front of the car or position the car on ramps.

62.1 Oil filter location viewed from underneath

4   Wipe clean the sealing faces of the filter and mounting/oil cooler.
5   If the oil cooler is being removed (fuel injection models), drain the cooling system (Chapter 2) and disconnect the coolant hoses from the cooler. The O-ring between the oil cooler and the mounting must be renewed.
6   If the oil filter mounting is to be removed, disconnect the oil pressure switch lead, undo the securing bolts and withdraw the mounting and gasket. The oil pressure switch can be unscrewed from the top face of the mounting if required. Remove and renew the switch O-ring.
7   Refitting is a reversal of the removal procedure. Renew the mounting gasket and O-ring(s) as necessary.
8   Smear the sealing rubber on the new filter with engine oil, then fit and tighten the filter by hand (or as directed on the filter cartridge).
9   Top up the engine oil and coolant (if applicable) levels. Start the engine and check for any signs of oil (or coolant) leaks.

63 Crankshaft, camshaft and intermediate shaft oil seals – renewal (engine in car)

Crankshaft oil seal (flywheel/driveplate end)
1   On manual gearbox models, remove the clutch and pressure plate, as described in Chapter 5. On automatic transmission models, remove the transmission, as described in Chapter 6, then unbolt the driveplate from the crankshaft, noting the location of the spacer and shim(s).
2   On all models, carefully prise out the oil seal with a screwdriver or strong wire and wipe clean the recess.
3   Fill the space between the lips of the new seal with multi-purpose grease, then drive it squarely into the housing using a block of wood or suitable metal tubing. If at all possible, use VW fitting sleeve No 2003 to avoid damage to the oil seal lip.
4   Refit the driveplate or clutch using a reversal of the removal procedure, with reference to Chapters 5 and 6 as necessary.

Crankshaft oil seal (timing belt end)
5   Remove the alternator as described in Chapter 9, together with the drivebelt.
6   Remove the timing belt cover and timing belt, as described in Section 54, making sure that the timing marks are correctly aligned.
7   Unscrew the bolt from the front of the crankshaft, withdraw the pulley and the sprocket and remove the Woodruff key. If the belt is difficult to loosen, have an assistant engage top gear and apply the brakes on manual gearbox models. On automatic transmission models remove the starter model and restrain the driveplate ring gear with a suitable lever.

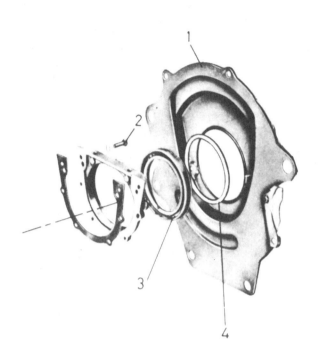

**Fig. 1.22 Flywheel end crankshaft oil seal components
(Sec 63)**

1 Intermediate plate
2 Bolt
3 Oil seal

4 Sealing ring (not fitted to all
models)

**Fig. 1.23 VW Tool 2085 for removing crankshaft oil seal
(timing belt end) and camshaft oil seal (Sec 63)**

8 Prise out the oil seal or extract it with VW tool No 2085, then wipe clean the recess.
9 Fill the space between the lips of the new seal with multi-purpose grease, then drive it squarely into the housing using a block of wood or suitable metal tubing. If available use VW fitting sleeve No 3083.
10 The remaining refitting procedure is a reversal of removal, but ensure that the timing marks are aligned before refitting the timing belt, and tension it with reference to Section 79.

Camshaft front oil seal
11 Remove the alternator, as described in Chapter 9, together with the drivebelt.
12 Remove the timing belt cover and timing belt, as described in Section 54, making sure that the timing marks are correctly aligned.
13 Hold the camshaft sprocket stationary with a screwdriver inserted through one of the holes, then unscrew the bolt and remove the washer, sprocket and Woodruff key.
14 Prise out the oil seal or alternatively extract it with VW tool No 2085, then wipe clean the recess.
15 Fill the space between the lips of the new seal with multi-purpose grease, then drive it squarely into the cylinder head using a block of wood or suitable metal tubing. If available use VW fitting sleeve No 10-203.
16 The remaining refitting procedure is a reversal of removal, but ensure that the timing marks are aligned before refitting the timing belt and tension it with reference to Section 79.

Intermediate shaft oil seal
17 Remove the alternator, as described in Chapter 9, together with the drivebelt.
18 Remove the timing belt cover and timing belt, as described in Section 54 making sure that the timing marks are correctly aligned.
19 Hold the intermediate shaft sprocket stationary with a screwdriver inserted through one of the holes, then unscrew the bolt and remove the washer, sprocket and Woodruff key.
20 Renew the oil seal, as described in Section 70.
21 The remaining refitting procedure is a reversal of removal, but ensure that the timing marks are aligned before refitting the timing belt and tension it with reference to Section 79.

64 Crankcase ventilation system – description

The crankcase ventilation system comprises a hose from the flywheel end of the valve cover to the side of the air cleaner.
On fuel injection models there is a hose to the air inlet manifold and a hose to the air cleaner from a three-way connector on the valve cover.
Periodically the hose(s) should be examined for security and condition. Cleaning will not normally be necessary except when the engine is well worn and sludge has accumulated.

65 Examination and renovation – general

Refer to Section 22 of this Chapter.

66 Crankshaft and main bearings – examination and renovation

Refer to Section 23 of this Chapter.

67 Cylinder block/crankcase – examination and renovation

Refer to Section 24 of this Chapter.

68 Pistons and connecting rods – examination and renovation

Refer to Section 25 of this Chapter.

69 Oil pump – examination and renovation

1 With the oil pump on the bench, prise off the cap with a screwdriver and clean the strainer gauze in fuel. Refit the gauze and press on the cap.
2 Remove the two small bolts and take the cover away from the body. Examine the face of the cover (photo). As will be seen in the

69.2 Examine the face of the oil pump cover for scoring

69.3 Checking the oil pump gear backlash

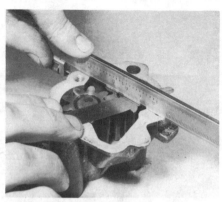

69.4 Checking the oil pump gear endfloat

photograph the gears have marked the cover. If the depth of this marking is significant then the face of the cover must be machined flat again.

3   Remove the gears and wash the body and gears in clean paraffin. Dry them and reassemble the gears, lubricating them with clean engine oil. Measure the backlash between the gears with a feeler gauge (photo). This should be 0.05 to 0.20 mm (0.002 to 0.008 in).

4   Now place a straight-edge over the pump body along the line joining the centre of the two gears and measure with a feeler gauge the axial clearance between the gears and the straight-edge (photo). This must not be more than 0.15 mm (0.006 in).

5   If all is well, check that the shaft is not slack in its bearings, and reassemble the pump for fitting to the engine.

6   If there is any doubt about the pump it is recommended strongly that a replacement be obtained. Once wear starts in a pump it progresses rapidly. In view of the damage that may follow a loss of oil pressure, skimping the oil pump repair is a false economy.

70 Intermediate shaft – examination and renovation

1   Check the fit of the intermediate shaft in its bearing. If there is excessive play, the shaft must be compared with a new one. If the shaft is in good order, but the bearings in the block are worn, this job is beyond your scope; you may even need a new block, so seek expert advice.

2   Check the surface of the cam which drives the fuel pump (where applicable). If serious ridging is present a new shaft is indicated.

3   Check the teeth of the distributor drivegear for scuffing or chipping. Check the condition of the timing belt sprocket.

4   It is unlikely that damage to this shaft has happened, but if it has, seek advice from the VW agent.

5   There is an oil seal in the flange for the intermediate shaft. This may need renewal if there are signs of leakage. To do this remove the timing belt sprocket and withdraw the flange from the shaft. The oil seal may now be prised out and a new one pressed in. Always fit a new O-ring on the flange before assembling it to the cylinder block.

71 Flywheel/driveplate – examination and renovation

1   There is not much you can do about the flywheel if it is damaged.

2   Inspect the starter ring teeth. If these are chipped or worn it is possible to renew the starter ring. This means heating the ring until it may be withdrawn from the flywheel, or alternatively splitting it. A new one must then be shrunk on. If you know how to do this and you can get a new ring then the job can be done but it is beyond the capacity of most owners.

3   Serious scoring on the flywheel clutch facing requires a new flywheel. Do not attempt to clean the scoring off with a scraper or emery. The face must be machined.

4   If it is necessary to fit a new flywheel, the ignition timing mark must be made by the owner. The new flywheel has only the TDC mark as an

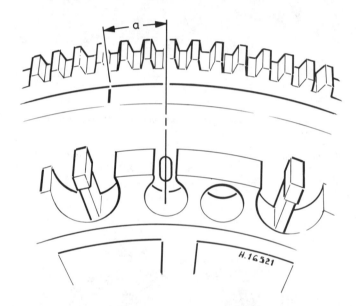

Fig. 1.24 Flywheel/driveplate ignition timing marks (Sec 71)

Engine code EZ (1.6) – flywheel: a = 37.0 mm (1.46 in) 18° BTDC
Engine code EZ (1.6) – driveplate: a = 42.0 mm (1.65 in) 18° BTDC
Engine code EV (1.8) – flywheel: a = 12.5 mm (0.49 in) 6° BTDC
Engine code GU (1.8) – flywheel: a = 37.0 mm (1.46 in) 18° BTDC
Engine code GU (1.8) – driveplate: a = 42.0 mm (1.65 in) 18° BTDC

O on the outer face, therefore punch or scribe the appropriate timing mark for your model (see Chapter 4), to the left of the TDC mark at the appropriate distance (see Fig. 1.24).

5   On automatic transmission models, check the driveplate as described for the flywheel; it will also be necessary to mark a new driveplate for ignition timing.

72 Timing belt and sprockets – examination and renovation

Refer to Section 28 of this Chapter. The information given also applies to the intermediate shaft sprocket.

73 Engine reassembly – general

Refer to Section 30 of this Chapter.

74 Crankshaft and main bearings – refitting

1   If a new crankshaft is being fitted to automatic transmission models the needle roller bearing supplied and fitted by the manufacturers will need to be removed from its aperture in the rear end of the crankshaft. It may already have been removed by the supplier, but check anyway.

2   Clean the crankcase recesses and bearing caps thoroughly and fit the bearing shells so that the tang on the bearing engages in the recess in the crankcase or bearing cap. Make sure that the shells fitted to the crankcase have oil grooves and holes, and that these line up with the drillings in the bearing housings. When fitting the bearing shells to the caps, note that bearing numbers 1, 2 and 5 are plain shells whilst bearing number 4 has an oil groove. The bearing shells of the centre bearing (No 3) may either be flanged to act as thrust washers, or may have separate thrust washers. These should be fitted oil groove outwards (photos). Fit the bearing shells so that the ends of the bearing are flush with the joint face (photo).

3   Oil the bearings and journals (photo) then locate the crankshaft in the crankcase.

4   Fit the main bearing caps (with centre main bearing thrust washers if applicable) in their correct positions (photo).

5   Fit the bolts to the bearing caps and tighten the bolts of the centre cap to the specified torque (photo), then check that the crankshaft rotates freely. If it is difficult to rotate the crankshaft, check that the bearing shells are seated properly and that the bearing cap is in the correct way round. Rotation will only be difficult if something is incorrect, and the fault must be found. Dirt on the back of a bearing shell is sometimes the cause of a tight main bearing.

6   Working out from the centre, tighten the remaining bearing caps in turn, checking that the crankshaft rotates freely after each bearing has been tightened.

74.2A Fitting the flanged type centre main bearing into the crankcase

74.2B Fitting the alternative type centre main bearing into the crankcase ...

74.2C ... together with its thrust washers

74.2D Fitting the flanged type centre main bearing to the cap

74.2E Fitting the centre bearing and separate thrust washers to the cap

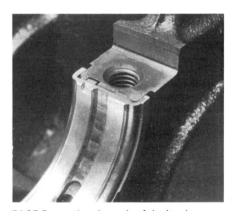

74.2F Ensure that the ends of the bearing are flush with the joint face

74.3 Lubricate the main bearing shells

74.4 Fit the main bearing caps ...

74.5 ... and tighten the retaining bolts

7   Check that the endfloat of the crankshaft is within specification, by inserting feeler gauges between the crankshaft and the centre bearing thrust face/washer while levering the crankshaft first in one direction and then in the other.
8   Lubricate the rear of the crankshaft and, using a new gasket, install the rear oil seal and flange. Tighten the six bolts.
9   Lubricate the front of the crankshaft and fit the front oil seal and flange with a new gasket. Tighten the bolts to the correct torque.

77.4 Checking the valve clerances with a feeler blade

74.8 Crankshaft rear oil seal

75 Intermediate shaft – refitting

Lubricate the intermediate shaft, then install it in the block. Fit the O-ring and flange, together with the oil seal, then tighten the bolts. Note that the oil hole must be at the bottom of the flange.

76 Pistons and connecting rods – refitting

1   Proceed as described in Section 32 of this Chapter, paragraphs 2 to 7 inclusive. When refitting the big-end nuts oil the threads.
2   On completion, check the endfloat of each connecting rod in a similar manner to that described for checking the crankshaft enfloat.
3   The oil pump and sump can be refitted, as described in Section 58.

77 Valve clearances – checking and adjustment

1   If a new or reconditioned cylinder head, complete with camshaft, is being fitted, the valve clearances will have been preset.
2   The valve clearances can be checked and if necessary adjusted during a normal routine service check or with the cylinder head removed (prior to refitting after overhaul).
3   Reference to the Specifications will show different clearance requirements for a cold or warm (coolant temperature above 35°C) engine. When the engine is in the vehicle, run it up to its normal operating temperature then switch off and remove the valve cover.
4   Check each valve clearance in turn by rotating the engine so that the valve to be checked has the cam lobe facing upwards. In this position the valve in question is fully closed and a feeler gauge inserted between the heel of the cam lobe and the valve tappet shim within the tappet bucket will give the clearance present. If possible, use a set of metric feeler gauges to avoid the complication of metric/Imperial conversions during subsequent operations. If the engine is fully assembled it will rotate more easily if the plugs are removed, but do not rotate the engine by turning the camshaft sprocket, this will stretch the timing belt. Use the alternator drivebelt (V-belt) or jack up one front wheel and with the engine in gear rotate the roadwheel. **Note:** *Do not turn the engine with any of the shims removed, otherwise the camshaft may foul the rim at the top of the bucket.*
5   Repeat this measurement for all the valves in turn and then compare the measurements with the Specifications.
6   Make a table of the actual clearances and then calculate the error from those specified. Suppose on No 1 exhaust valve the measured clearance is 0.15 mm. It is 0.3 mm too small so it must be adjusted and a shim 0.3 mm thinner fitted instead of the present one. As the shims are in steps of 0.05 mm variation the required shim can be selected once the size of the shim at present installed is known. If you have dismantled and reassembled the head then you know the size etched on the back of the shim, but if you do not then the shim must be removed to find out. Ideally VW tools 2078 and 10.208 should be used but we managed quite well with the tools shown (photo). They were a small electrician's screwdriver and a C-spanner which was just the right size to push the bucket down without pushing the tappet shim (ie pushing the rim down). With the cam turned to give maximum

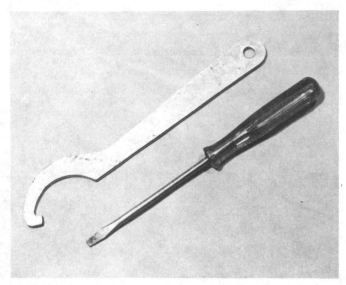

77.6A Tools required to remove and fit tappet bucket shims

77.6B Removing a tappet bucket shim

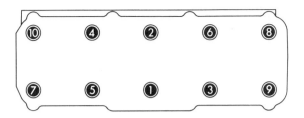

Fig. 1.25 Cylinder head bolt tightening sequence (Sec 78)

clearance the tappet is pushed down against the valve springs while the shim is levered out and removed by the VW tool or a screwdriver. Be careful; if the spanner slips when the shim is halfway out, the shim will fly out sharply (photo).
7   Once all the shim sizes are known a table may be constructed and the sizes of the new shims required may be calculated. Going back to the example, if the present shim is marked 3.60 then one marked 3.30 is required. Bucket shims are available in 26 different thicknesses which increase in increments of 0.05 mm from 3.00 mm to 4.25 mm.
8   As it is unlikely that you will have the required shims readily available it will be necessary to wait until they have been obtained before the tappets can be adjusted.
9   When inserting the shims ensure that the face with the thickness etching faces downwards.
10 If adjustment is made when the engine is cold then it must be checked again when the engine is hot (coolant above 35°C). If the cylinder head has been overhauled it should be checked again, hot, after 600 miles (900 km). The valve clearances should otherwise normally only need checking at the Routine Maintenance intervals given at the start of this Manual.
11 Once the correct clearances have been achieved, refit the spark plugs and the valve cover (engine in car).
12 One final suggestion. If you have done the job and know the sizes of all the shims this information should be kept in a safe place. It will save a lot of time during the next overhaul.

78 Cylinder head – refitting

1   Clean the top face of the block. Make a final inspection of the bores and lubricate them. Turn the crankshaft so that the pistons are in the mid cylinder position.
2   If you look at the edge of the block between No 3 and No 4 cylinders on the side above the distributor, the engine number is stamped on an inclined surface. Using this as a datum, install a new cylinder head gasket so that the word 'OBEN' engraved on the gasket is over this datum point and on the top side of the gasket (photo).
3   Lower the cylinder head into position, locating onto the centering pins where fitted. If the cylinder block does not have centering pins, initially refit No 8 and No 10 cylinder head bolts. Do not use jointing compound. Check that the gasket is seating correctly and fit the remainder of the bolts. Now following the sequence in Fig. 1.25 tighten the bolts until the head is firmly held. Using the torque wrench, tighten the bolts in stages to the specified torque following the same sequence (see Specifications).
4   Once the cylinder head has been tightened in stages to the specified torque wrench setting it will not need further tightening.

79 Timing belt and sprockets – refitting

1   Fit the Woodruff key into its groove in the intermediate shaft then refit the sprocket to the front of the shaft. Locate the spacer washer onto the bolt then fit and tighten the bolt to the specified torque wrench setting. Hold the sprocket stationary when tightening by inserting a screwdriver through one of its holes and jam it against the cylinder block.
2   Locate the Woodruff key (if applicable) to the groove at the front of the crankshaft then refit the timing belt sprocket onto the shaft. Lubricate the retaining bolt with oil, locate the spacer washer onto the bolt then fit and tighten it to the specified torque wrench setting. When tightening the bolt, prevent the crankshaft from turning by using the same method as that for its removal.

78.2 Cylinder head gasket on the block

78.3A Lowering the cylinder head onto the block

78.3B Tightening the cylinder head bolts

3   Locate the Woodruff key into its groove on the front of the camshaft then refit the camshaft sprocket. Refit the retaining bolt, together with the spacer washer, and tighten to the specified torque wrench setting. Hold the sprocket stationary when tightening by inserting a screwdriver through one of its holes and jam it against the cylinder block or head.
4   If removed, refit the timing belt rear cover (apply locking compound to the stud thread).
5   Locate the crankshaft pulley onto the sprocket (aligning the marks made previously) using one bolt to secure it temporarily.
6   Turn the camshaft sprocket so that both cams for No 1 cylinder are in the open position and the dot on the camshaft gear tooth is in line with the valve cover.
7   Rotate the crankshaft sprocket and the intermediate shaft sprocket until the dot on the intermediate sprocket and the mark on the V-belt pulley coincide. Install the timing belt tensioner loosely and then the timing belt. Making sure the marks are still in place, put a spanner on the adjuster and tighten the belt until it will twist only 90 degrees when held between the finger and thumb halfway between the camshaft and intermediate shaft sprockets. Tighten the eccentric adjuster nut to the specified torque (Fig. 1.16).
8   Unbolt and remove the crankshaft V-belt pulley.
9   Fit the lower timing cover then refit the crankshaft V-belt pulley and tighten its retaining bolts to the specified torque.
10 Locate the new valve cover gasket into position on the cylinder head, the seal to the No 1 camshaft bearing cap and the half round grommet into its location at the rear end of the cylinder head.
11 Fit the valve cover into position, locate the reinforcement strips then refit and tighten the retaining nuts evenly to the specified torque.
12 Refit the upper timing belt cover.

80 Engine ancillary components – refitting

1   On automatic transmission models refit the driveplate, together with shim(s) and spacer. Tighten the new bolts on the crankshaft to the specified torque. Using vernier calipers, check the distance from the driveplate to the cylinder block as shown in Fig. 1.26. If it is not between 30.5 mm and 32.1 mm (1.20 and 1.26 in) remove the driveplate and fit alternative shims as necessary. Note that the chamfer on the washer must face the driveplate. When the dimension is correct, remove the bolts, coat the threads with liquid locking agent and tighten again to the specified torque. **Note:** *If the engine is a new or reconditioned short block replacement, check that the bore in the rear end does not contain a needle roller bearing. If it does then remove the bearing as this is for manual transmission models only.*
2   On manual gearbox models refit the clutch, as described in Chapter 5, together with the intermediate plate.
3   Refit the inlet and exhaust manifolds, as described in Chapter 3.
4   Refit the water pump and all hoses to the engine, as described in Chapter 2.
5   Refit the alternator and drivebelt as described in Chapter 9.
6   Refit the oil pressure switch to the cylinder head or filter mounting as applicable using a new washer or O-ring seal. Tighten to the specified torque.
7   Fit the oil filter mounting to the cylinder block, together with a new gasket and tighten the bolts. On models fitted with an oil cooler, refit the supply and return hoses to their correct unions.
8   Fit the oil filter, as described in Section 62.
9   Refer to Chapter 4 and refit the distributor.
10 On carburettor models, refit the fuel pump, as described in Chapter 3.
11 On fuel injection models refit the warm-up valve (if the hoses were disconnected).
12 Refit the coolant temperature sender unit and the thermotime switch with new O-ring seals.

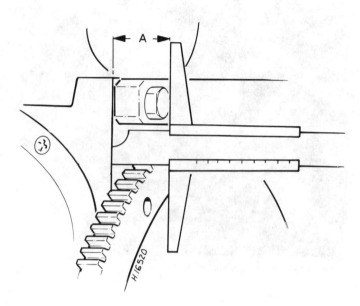

Fig. 1.26 Checking the driveplate-to-cylinder block dimension (A) using vernier calipers (Sec 80)

13 Refit the spark plugs if not already done and tighten them to the specified torque given in Chapter 4.
14 Refit the gearbox/transmission to the engine with reference to Section 51.

81 Engine – refitting

To refit the engine and gearbox/transmission, reverse the removal procedures given earlier in Section 49 or 50 (as applicable) of this Chapter, but note the following points:

(a) When lowering the assembly into the engine compartment, align the driveshafts with the flanges prior to attaching the respective mountings
(b) Assemble the engine mountings loosely initially and tighten them only after the assembly is central without straining the mountings
(c) Adjust the clutch cable (manual transmission) as described in Chapter 5
(d) On models with automatic transmission adjust the throttle and selector cables, as described in Chapter 6
(e) Reconnect and, if necessary, adjust the gear selector linkages on manual transmission models (Chapter 6)
(f) Adjust the throttle cable and, where applicable, the choke cable, with reference to Chapter 3
(g) Refill the cooling system, with reference to Chapter 2
(h) Refill the engine with the correct grade and quantity of oil

82 Engine – adjustments after major overhaul

Refer to Section 43 of this Chapter.

PART C: ALL MODELS

83 Fault diagnosis – engine

Symptom	Reason(s)
Engine fails to start	Discharged battery Loose battery connection Ignition system fault Fuel system fault Low cylinder compressions
Engine idles erratically	Inlet manifold air leak Leaking cylinder head gasket Worn camshaft lobes Faulty fuel pump Incorrect valve clearances Mixture adjustment incorrect Uneven cylinder compressions
Engine misfires	Ignition system fault Fuel system fault Burnt valve or valve seating Leaking cylinder head gasket Incorrect valve clearances Uneven cylinder compressions
Engine stalls	Mixture adjustment incorrect Inlet manifold air leak Ignition timing incorrect
Excessive oil consumption	Worn pistons and cylinder bores Valve guides and seals worn Oil leak (fuel pump vent hole is common)
Engine backfires	Mixture adjustment incorrect Ignition timing incorrect Incorrect valve clearances Exhaust manifold air leak Sticking or burnt valve

Chapter 2 Cooling system

For modifications, and information applicable to later models, see Supplement at end of manual

Contents

Specifications

General

System type	Pressurised with pump driven by timing or V-belt, front mounted radiator with internal or external expansion tank, electric cooling fan
System capacity (approx)	6.3 litre (11.1 Imp pint)

Radiator/expansion tank cap

Operating pressure	1.2 to 1.5 bar (17.4 to 21.8 lbf/in²)

Thermostat

	1.05 and 1.3 litre	1.6 and 1.8 litre
Opening temperature	92°C (198°F)	85°C (185°F)
Fully open temperature	108°C (226°F)	105°C (221°F)
Minimum stroke	7.0 mm (0.28 in)	7.0 mm (0.28 in)

Cooling fan thermo-switch

Switch-on temperature	93° to 98°C (199° to 208°F)
Switch-off temperature	88° to 93°C (190° to 199°F)

Antifreeze

Concentration:	Protection down to
40%	−25°C (−13°F)
50%	−35°C (−31°F)

Torque wrench settings

	Nm	lbf ft
Temperature sender unit	10	7
Thermo-switch (intake manifold preheater):		
1.6 and 1.8 carburettor models	10	7
1.8 fuel injection models	30	22
Water pump housing (1.6 and 1.8 litre)	20	14
Water pump cover (1.6 and 1.8 litre)	10	7
Water pump pulley bolts (1.6 and 1.8 litre)	20	14
Cooling fan thermo-switch	25	18
Thermostat housing through-bolts (1.05 and 1.3 litre)	20	14
Thermostat housing-to-pipe bolts (1.05 and 1.3 litre)	10	7
Thermostat housing to water pump (1.6 and 1.8 litre)	10	7
Water pump unit (1.05 and 1.3 litre)	10	7

1 General description

The cooling system is of pressurised type and includes a front mounted radiator, water pump, and a thermostatically operated electric cooling fan. Circulation through the radiator is controlled by a thermostat, the location of which differs according to engine. On the 1.05 and 1.3 litre models it is located in a housing on the rear end of the cylinder head (left side of car) below the distributor. On the 1.6 and 1.8 litre models the thermostat is located in the base of the water pump housing which is mounted low down on the front of the engine (timing case end).

The radiator is of aluminium construction and the expansion tank is located separately within the engine compartment.

The fuel injected engine incorporates a water-cooled oil cooler unit which is located between the oil filter and the filter mounting bracket.

The system functions as follows. Cold water from the bottom of the radiator circulates through the bottom hose to the water pump, where the pump impeller forces the water around the cylinder block and head passages. After cooling the cylinder bores, combustion surfaces and valve seats, the water reaches the cylinder head outlet and is returned to the water pump via the bypass hoses when the thermostat is closed. A further cylinder head outlet allows water to circulate through the inlet manifold and heater matrix (with heater control on) and it is then returned to the water pump.

When the coolant reaches the predetermined temperature (see Specifications), the thermostat opens and the water then circulates through the top hose to the top of the radiator. As the water circulates down through the radiator, it is cooled by the inrush of air when the car is in forward motion, supplemented by the action of the electric cooling fan when necessary. Having reached the bottom of the radiator, the water is now cooled and the cycle is repeated.

The electric cooling fan is controlled by a thermo-switch located in the left-hand side of the radiator.

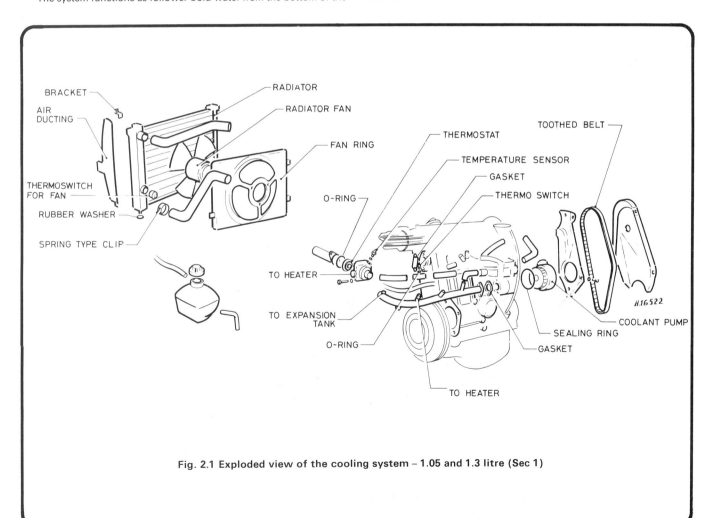

Fig. 2.1 Exploded view of the cooling system – 1.05 and 1.3 litre (Sec 1)

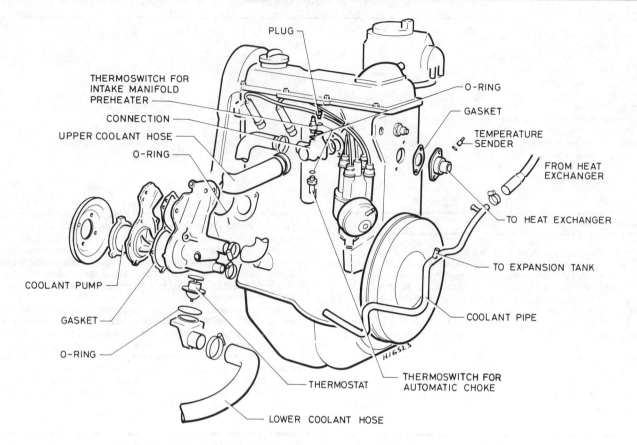

PLUG

THERMOSWITCH FOR
INTAKE MANIFOLD
PREHEATER

CONNECTION

UPPER COOLANT HOSE

O-RING

O-RING

GASKET

TEMPERATURE
SENDER

FROM HEAT
EXCHANGER

TO HEAT EXCHANGER

TO EXPANSION TANK

COOLANT PIPE

COOLANT PUMP

GASKET

O-RING

THERMOSTAT

THERMOSWITCH FOR
AUTOMATIC CHOKE

LOWER COOLANT HOSE

Fig. 2.2 Engine cooling system components – 1.6 and 1.8 litre carburettor (Sec 1)

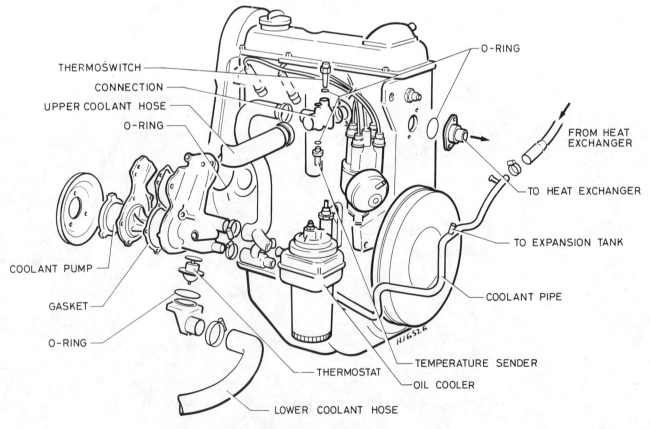

THERMOSWITCH

CONNECTION

UPPER COOLANT HOSE

O-RING

O-RING

FROM HEAT
EXCHANGER

TO HEAT EXCHANGER

TO EXPANSION TANK

COOLANT PIPE

COOLANT PUMP

GASKET

O-RING

THERMOSTAT

TEMPERATURE SENDER

OIL COOLER

LOWER COOLANT HOSE

Fig. 2.3 Engine cooling system components – 1.8 litre fuel injection (Sec 1)

2 Routine maintenance – cooling system

1   The cooling system must be regularly checked as part of the vehicle's routine maintenance.
2   A weekly check must be made to ensure that the coolant level is correct in the cooling system expansion tank. When the engine is cold the level of coolant within the expansion tank must be between the MAX and MIN marks. When the coolant level is checked with the engine hot the level of coolant in the expansion tank should be level with, or just above the MAX marking.
3   If a sudden drop in the coolant level should occur, investigate the cause without delay.
4   Periodically check the system hoses and connections for signs of leakage, deterioration and for security.
5   When topping-up the cooling system, use an antifreeze mixture wherever possible to maintain the strength of the antifreeze/corrosion inhibitor within the system (Section 6).
6   Periodically check the wiring connections to the temperature sender units and thermo-switch units are secure. **Note:** *the electric cooling fan will operate when the temperature of the coolant in the radiator reaches the predetermined level even if the ignition is switched off. Therefore extreme caution should be exercised when working in the vicinity of the fan blades.*

3 Cooling system – draining

1   It is preferable to drain the cooling system when the engine has cooled. If this is not possible, place a cloth over the expansion tank filler cap and turn it *slowly* in an anti-clockwise direction until the pressure starts to escape.
2   When all the pressure has escaped, remove the filler cap.
3   Set the heater controls to maximum heat, then place a suitable container beneath the left-hand side of the radiator.
4   Loosen the clip and ease the bottom hose away from the radiator outlet. Drain the coolant into the container (photos).

4 Cooling system – flushing

1   After some time the radiator and engine waterways may become restricted or even blocked with scale or sediment which can reduce the efficiency of the cooling system. When this occurs, the coolant will appear rusty and dark in colour and the system should then be flushed. In severe cases, reverse flushing may be required, although if a reputable antifreeze/corrosion inhibitor has been in constant use this is unlikely.
2   With the coolant drained, disconnect the top hose from the radiator. Insert a garden hose and allow the water to circulate through the radiator until it runs clear from the bottom outlet.
3   Disconnect the heater hose from the cylinder head outlet and insert a garden hose in the heater hose. With the heater controls set at maximum heat, allow water to circulate through the heater and out through the bottom hose until it runs clear.
4   In severe cases of contamination the system should be reverse flushed. To do this, remove the radiator, invert it and insert a garden hose in the outlet. Continue flushing until clear water runs from the inlet.
5   The engine should also be reverse flushed. To do this, disconnect the heater hose from the cylinder head outlet and insert a garden hose in the outlet. Continue flushing until clear water runs from the bottom hose.
6   The use of chemical cleaners should only be necessary as a last resort. Regular checking of the antifreeze/corrosion inhibitor concentration at the 10 000 mile (15 000 km) service should prevent the contamination of the system.

5 Cooling system – filling

1   Reconnect all the hoses and check that the heater controls are set to maximum heat.
2   Pour the recommended coolant into the expansion tank until it reaches the maximum mark.

3.4A Radiator bottom hose connection (1.3 litre)

3.4B Radiator bottom hose connection (1.8 litre)

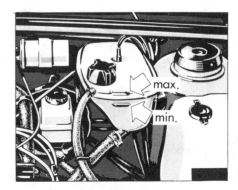

Fig. 2.4 Engine coolant level marks in the expansion tank
(Sec 5)

3   Refit and tighten the filler cap then run the engine at a fast idling speed for a few minutes, but keep an eye on the coolant level.
4   Stop the engine and top up the coolant level, as necessary, to the maximum mark (photo). Refit the filler cap.
5   After running the engine to normal operating temperature (ie until the electric cooling fan operates), the coolant level should be rechecked with the engine cold.

6   Antifreeze/corrosion inhibitor mixture – general

1   The manufacturers install G10 antifreeze/corrosion inhibitor mixture in the cooling system when the car is new. Every 10 000 miles (15 000 km) or 12 months the concentration of the coolant should be checked by a VW garage and if necessary topped up with fresh mixture.
2   The mixture must remain in the cooling system at all times as it prevents the formation of scale and also provides a higher boiling point than plain water – this maintains the efficiency of the coolant, particularly when the engine is operating at full load.
3   The concentration of the mixture can be calculated according to the lowest ambient temperature likely to be encountered as given in the Specifications. However it should never be less than 40%.
4   Before adding new mixture, check all hose connections for tightness.

7   Radiator – removal, inspection, cleaning and refitting

1   Disconnect the battery negative lead.
2   Drain the cooling system, as described in Section 3.
3   Disconnect the wiring from the thermo-switch and cooling fan motor (photos).
4   Disconnect the top hose and expansion tank hose from the radiator (photo).
5   Undo the two retaining bolts (photo) and remove the insulators and L brackets from the top of the radiator. Note that the longer bracket is the centre one.
6   Remove the front grille (see Chapter 11).
7   Remove the two bolts each side at the front and remove the left and right-hand air ducts.
8   The radiator can now be lifted from the engine compartment, but take care not to damage the matrix (photo).
9   Remove the screws and withdraw the cowling and fan from the radiator.
10 It is not possible to repair this radiator without special equipment, although minor leaks can be sealed using a proprietary coolant additive.

5.4 Topping-up coolant

7.3A Radiator thermo-switch (1.8 litre)

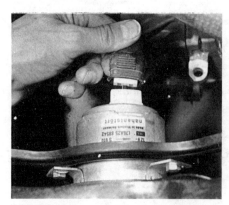
7.3B Detach the cooling fan lead connector

7.4 Radiator securing bolt (A), expansion tank hose connection (B) and top hose connection (C)

7.5 Radiator central retaining bolt and bracket

7.8 Lifting out the radiator and cooling fan assembly

7.12 Radiator lower mounting rubber

7.13 Secure the fan lead with a plastic clip (arrow)

11 Clean the radiator matrix of flies and small leaves with a soft brush or by hosing, then reverse flush the radiator, as described in Section 4. Renew the hoses and clips if they are damaged or deteriorated.
12 Refitting is a reversal of removal, but if necessary renew the radiator lower mounting rubbers (photo). Fill the cooling system, as described in Section 5.
13 When reconnecting the cooling fan motor wiring, secure the lead to the cowling web (photo).

8 Cooling fan and motor – removal and refitting

1 Disconnect the battery negative lead.
2 Disconnect the wiring from the cooling fan motor and cowling.
3 Remove the bolts and screws and lift the cowling, together with the cooling fan and motor, from the radiator.
4 Remove the nuts and withdraw the cooling fan and motor from the cowling (photo).

8.4 Cooling fan motor retaining nuts (arrowed)

5 If necessary the fan can be separated from the motor by prising off the clamp washer. On AEG motors drive out the roll pin, and on Bosch motors remove the shake-proof washer. Assemble the components in reverse order using a new clamp washer.
6 Refitting is a reversal of removal.

9 Cooling fan motor thermo-switch – removal, testing and refitting

1 Disconnect the battery negative lead.
2 Drain the cooling system, as described in Section 3.
3 Unscrew the thermo-switch from the left-hand side of the radiator and remove the sealing ring (photo).
4 To test the thermo-switch, suspend it with a piece of string so that its element is immersed in a container of water. Connect the thermo-switch in series with a 12 volt test lamp and battery. Gradually heat the water and note the temperature with a thermometer. The test lamp should light up at the specified switch-on temperature and go out at the specified switch-off temperature. If not, renew the thermo-switch.
5 Refitting is a reversal of removal, but fit a new sealing ring and tighten the thermo-switch to the specified torque. Fill the cooling system, as described in Section 5.

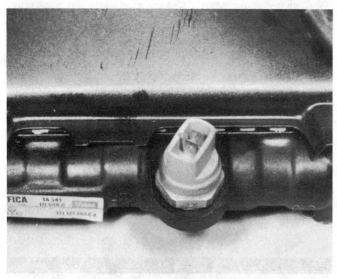

9.3 Cooling fan thermo-switch

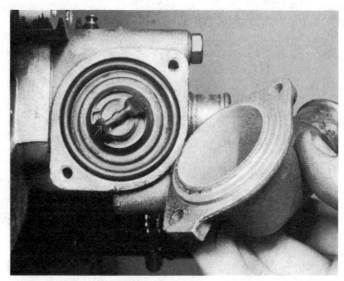

10.2B ... and remove the thermostat cover

10 Thermostat (1.05 and 1.3 litre) – removal, testing and refitting

1   The thermostat is located in the outlet housing on the left-hand (rear) end of the cylinder head. To remove it, first drain the cooling system, as described in Section 3.
2   Unscrew the bolts and remove the thermostat cover (photos). Place the cover with top hose still attached to one side.
3   Remove the sealing ring (photo).
4   Extract the thermostat from the outlet housing.
5   To test whether the unit is serviceable, suspend it with a piece of string in a container of water. Gradually heat the water and note the temperature at which the thermostat starts to open. Continue heating the water to the specified fully open temperature then check that the thermostat has opened by at least the minimum amount given in the Specifications. Remove the thermostat from the water and check that it is fully closed when cold.

10.3 Removing the thermostat sealing ring

6   Renew the thermostat if it fails to operate correctly.
7   Clean the thermostat seating and the mating faces of the outlet housing and cover.
8   Refitting is a reversal of removal, but fit a new sealing ring and tighten the cover bolts to the specified torque – the breather hole in the thermostat should face upwards. Fill the cooling system, as described in Section 5.

11 Thermostat (1.6 and 1.8 litre) – removal, testing and refitting

1   The thermostat is located in the bottom of the water pump behind the inlet elbow. To remove it, first drain the cooling system with reference to Section 3.
2   Unbolt the inlet elbow from the water pump and remove the seal and thermostat (photos).
3   Clean the water pump and elbow of any scale or corrosion.

10.2A Unscrew the socket-head bolts ...

11.2A Thermostat inlet elbow – undo the retaining bolts ...

4 To test the thermostat proceed as described in paragraphs 5 and 6 in the previous Section.
5 Refitting is a reversal of removal procedure, but always fit a new seal. Fill the cooling system, as described in Section 5.

12 Water pump (1.05 and 1.3 litre) – removal and refitting

1 Drain the cooling system, as described in Section 3.
2 Remove the air cleaner and air ducting, as described in Chapter 3, and disconnect the battery negative lead.
3 Unbolt and remove the timing belt cover.
4 Turn the engine with a spanner on the crankshaft pulley until the timing cover plate upper retaining bolt is visible through the camshaft sprocket hole. Unscrew and remove the bolt.
5 Align the timing marks and release the timing belt from the water pump and camshaft sprocket (photo), with reference to Chapter 1.
6 Remove the bolts and withdraw the timing cover plate followed by the water pump (photo). Remove the sealing ring.
7 It is not possible to repair the water pump, and if faulty it must be renewed. Clean the mating faces of the water pump and cylinder block.
8 Refitting is a reversal of removal, but fit a new sealing ring and refer to Chapter 1 when fitting and tensioning the timing belt. Fill the cooling system, as described in Section 5.

11.2B ... withdraw the elbow and thermostat ...

12.5 Disengage the timing belt from the water pump sprocket

11.2C ... then extract the thermostat and seal

12.6 Withdraw the water pump

13 Water pump (1.6 and 1.8 litre) – removal and refitting

1   Drain the cooling system, as described in Section 3.
2   Remove the alternator, as described in Chapter 9. On models fitted with power steering it will be necessary to remove the pump unit and mounting bracket for access to the water pump, whilst on models equipped with air conditioning, it will be necessary to remove the compressor unit and its mounting. Refer to Chapters 10 and 11 respectively for details, as required. **Do not** detach the air conditioning system hoses.
3   Disconnect the three coolant hoses from the pump, then remove the four bolts holding the pump to the cylinder block (photo). The pump will probably be stuck to the block but will come off if tapped gently. Remove the O-ring with the pump.
4   Remove the pulley and then take out the eight bolts which secure the bearing housing and impeller to the water pump housing. The two halves may now be separated (photo). **Do not** drive a wedge in to break the joint. Clean off the old gasket.
5   Remove the thermostat, with reference to Section 11.

6   The impeller housing and impeller complete with bearings are serviced as one part, so that if the coolant is leaking through the bearing, or the impeller is damaged, the complete assembly must be renewed.
7   Fit a new gasket using jointing compound, then fit the two halves together and tighten the bolts evenly. Fit the thermostat with reference to Section 11. The refitting procedure is a reversal of the removal procedure, but always fit a new O-ring. Fill the cooling system, as described in Section 5, and tension the drivebelt(s), as described in Chapters 9, 10 and 11, as applicable.

14 Temperature sender unit/thermo-switches – removal and refitting

1   It is not necessary to drain the cooling system if some form of plug such as an old sender unit or rubber plug is available. First release any pressure in the system by unscrewing the pressure cap – *if the system is still hot, observe the precaution in Section 3.* With all pressure released, tighten the cap again.
2   The location of the sender unit or thermo-switch is dependent on model but in general they are as follows:

1.05 and 1.3 litre
3   **Thermo-switch**: Located in the intermediate piece in the hoses between the intake manifold and the thermostat housing (photo).
4   **Temperature sensor**: Located in the thermostat housing (photo).

1.6 and 1.8 litre carburettor
5   **Temperature sender unit**: Located in the heat exchanger hose connecting flange on the rear of the cylinder head.
6   **Thermo-switch** (intake manifold preheater): Located on the top face of the hose connector on the spark plug side of the cylinder head.
7   **Thermo-switch (automatic choke)**: Located in the base of the hose connector on the spark plug side of the cylinder head.

1.8 litre fuel injection
8   **Temperature sender unit**: Located in the hose connector on the spark plug side of the cylinder head.
9   **Thermo-switch**: Located on the top face of the hose connector on the spark plug side of the cylinder head.

All models
10 Disconnect the wiring lead from the sender unit/switch concerned.
11 Unscrew and remove the sender unit/switch and plug the aperture.
12 Refitting is the reversal of the removal procedure, but tighten the sender unit/thermo-switch to the specified torque. Check and if necessary top up the cooling system, with reference to Section 5.

13.3 1.6 and 1.8 litre engine water pump location (engine removed from car)

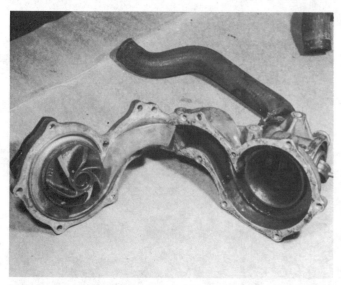

13.4 The two halves of the water pump (1.6 and 1.8 litre)

14.3 Thermo-switch location (1.05 and 1.3 litre)

14.4 Temperature sensor – arrowed (1.05 and 1.3 litre)

14.8 Temperature sender unit (A) and thermo-switch (B) (1.8 litre fuel injection)

15 Fault diagnosis – cooling system

Symptom	Reason(s)
Overheating	Low coolant level
	Faulty pressure cap
	Thermostat sticking shut
	Open-circuit thermo-switch
	Faulty electric cooling fan
	Clogged radiator matrix
	Retarded ignition timing
Slow warm-up	Thermostat sticking open
	Incorrect thermostat
Coolant loss	Damaged or deteriorated hose
	Leaking water pump or cylinder head outlet joint
	Blown cylinder head gasket
	Leaking radiator
	Defective core plug
	Defective filler cap

Chapter 3 Fuel and exhaust systems

For modifications, and information applicable to later models, see Supplement at end of manual

Contents

Specifications

General
Air cleaner
Type .... Renewable paper element, automatic air temperature control

Fuel system
Fuel pump (carburettor engines):

Type .... Mechanical, diaphragm, operated by plunger from camshaft (1.05 and 1.3 litre) or eccentric on intermediate shaft (1.6 and 1.8 litre)

Operating pressure at 4000 rpm (return line clamped):

1.05 and 1.3 litre	0.35 to 0.40 bar (5.1 to 5.8 lbf/in²)
1.6 and 1.8 litre	0.2 to 0.25 bar (2.9 to 3.6 lbf/in²)
Fuel tank capacity (approx)	55 litre (12 gal)

Fuel octane rating (minimum):

1.05 litre	97 RON (4 star)
1.3 and 1.6 litre	91 RON (2 star)
1.8 litre	98 RON (4 star)

Part A: Carburettor system
Carburettor – 1.05 litre

Type	Downdraught with manual or automatic choke
Code	31 PIC-7
Venturi	23
Main jet	X117.5
Air correction jet with emulsion tube	115 Z
Idling fuel jet	45
Idling air jet	135
Auxiliary fuel jet	32.5
Auxiliary air jet	130
Enrichment (primary/secondary)	70/70
Injection capacity (cc/stroke)	0.85 to 1.15
Float needle valve	1.5
Float needle valve washer thickness (mm)	2.0
Fast idle speed (rpm)	2500 to 2700
Choke valve gap (mm)	1.6 to 2.0
Throttle valve gap smooth running detent (mm)	2.2 to 2.8
Idle speed (rpm)	900 to 1000
CO content %	0.5 to 1.5

Carburettor – 1.3 litre

Type	Twin progressive choke downdraught, automatic choke	
Code	2E3	
Jets and settings:	**Stage I**	**Stage II**
Venturi	19	23
Main jet	X95	X110
Air correction jet with emulsion tube	120	130
Idling fuel/air jet	45/130	–
Full throttle enrichment	–	95
Pump injection tube diameter (mm)	0.35	–
Choke cover code	276	
Injection capacity (cc/stroke)	0.85 to 1.15	
Locking lever clearance (mm)	0.25 to 0.55	
Full throttle enrichment – height above atomizer (mm)	12	
Choke valve gap (mm)	1.9 to 2.1	
Fast idle speed (rpm)	1900 to 2100	
Idle speed (rpm)	750 to 850	
CO content %	1.5 to 2.5	

Carburettor – 1.6 litre

Type	Twin progressive choke, downdraught with automatic choke	
Type number	2E2	
Jets and settings:	**Stage I**	**Stage II**
Venturi diameter (mm)	22	26
Main jet	X110	X127
Air correction jet with emulsion tube (mm)	0.75/1.05	1.05
Idle fuel/air jet	42.5	–
Full throttle enrichment	–	0.7
Pump injection tube	0.5	–
Injection capacity (cc/stroke)	0.85 to 1.15	
Choke valve gap (mm) with primary throttle open 45°	6.3 + 0.3	
Fast idle speed (rpm)	2800 to 3200	
Idle speed (rpm)	900 to 1000	
Increased idle speed (rpm):		
Automatic transmission	800	
Air conditioner	900 to 1000	
CO content %	0.5 to 1.5	

Carburettor – 1.8 litre

Type	Twin progressive choke, downdraught with automatic choke	
Type number	2E2	
Jets and settings:	**Stage I**	**Stage II**
Venturi diameter	22	26
Main jet	X105	X120
Air correction jet with emulsion tube (mm)	105	100
Idle fuel/air jet	42.5	–
Full throttle enrichment	–	0.9
Pump injection tube:		
Carburettor part number type 027 129 015	0.35	–
Carburettor part number type 027 129 015 Q	0.5	–
Injection capacity (cc/stroke)	.95 to 1.25	
Choke valve gap (mm) – measured at lower edge:		
Initial setting	2.15 to 2.45	
Final setting	4.55 to 4.85	
Fast idle speed (rpm)	2800 to 3200	
Idle speed (rpm)	900 to 1000	
Increased idle speed (rpm):		
Automatic transmission	800	
Air conditioner	900 to 1000	
CO content %	0.5 to 1.5	

Part B: Fuel injection system
General

Type	K-Jetronic, continuous injection system (CIS)
System pressure	4.7 to 5.4 bar (68 to 78 lbf/in²)
Idle speed	900 to 1000 rpm
Idle speed – air conditioned models	850 to 1000 rpm
CO content %	0.5 to 1.5

All systems
Torque wrench settings

	Nm	lbf ft
1.05 and 1.3 litre		
Carburettor	10	7
Intermediate flange	10	7
Inlet manifold	25	18
Inlet manifold preheater	10	7
Fuel tank strap bolts	25	18
Exhaust manifold	25	18
Exhaust manifold to downpipe	25	18
Exhaust pipe clamp bolts	25	18
1.6 and 1.8 litre (carburettor engines)		
Carburettor	7	5
Fuel pump	20	15
Inlet manifold	25	18
Inlet manifold preheater	10	7
Fuel tank strap bolts	25	18
Exhaust manifold	25	18
Exhaust pipe clip:		
8 mm	25	18
10 mm	40	30
Fuel injection system		
Injector line to injector	25	18
Injector line to fuel metering distributor	10	7
System pressure relief valve	20	15
Cold start valve	10	7
Throttle valve housing to manifold	20	15
Inlet manifold	25	18
Fuel filter clamp	10	7
Union bolt at filter (from fuel accumulator)	25	18
Union nut at accumulator (to filter)	20	15
Union bolt at filter (to metering distributor)	20	15
Fuel pump reservoir mounting	10	7
Fuel pump non-return valve	20	15
Fuel pump damper unit	20	15
Exhaust manifold	25	18
Exhaust heat shield	10	7
Exhaust pipe clamp bolts	40	30

PART A: CARBURETTOR AND ASSOCIATED FUEL SYSTEM COMPONENTS

1 General description

The fuel system consists of a rear-mounted fuel tank, a mechanical diaphragm fuel pump and a downdraught carburettor. The carburettor type is dependent on model; see Specifications.

The fuel pump on 1.05 and 1.3 litre models is operated by means of a plunger activated by the camshaft, whilst on 1.6 and 1.8 litre models the fuel pump is operated direct by an eccentric on the intermediate shaft.

The air cleaner unit contains a renewable paper element and incorporates an automatic temperature control.

A conventional exhaust system is used on all models, being in sections for ease of replacement.

2 Routine maintenance – fuel and exhaust system

1 The following routine maintenance procedures are required for the fuel and exhaust system and must be carried out at the specified intervals given at the start of this Manual. It should be noted that the intervals quoted are those for a vehicle used in normal operating conditions. If a vehicle is used in adverse conditions, such as continuous city driving or in a hot dusty climate, then it is advisable to shorten the maintenance intervals accordingly.
2 **Fuel system, general:** Inspect the fuel system lines, hoses and connections at regular intervals for security and condition. In addition also check the associated vacuum hoses and connections. Occasionally lubricate the accelerator control linkages.
3 **Fuel system adjustments:** Check and if necessary adjust the engine idling speed and, where possible, the exhaust CO content (having first checked ignition timing, as described in Chapter 4).
4 **Air cleaner:** renew air cleaner element, as described in Section 3.
5 **Fuel filter:** The in-line filter should be renewed every 20 000 miles (30 000 km). To do this, remove the lips and extract the filter (photo). If necessary renew the crimped type clips with screw type ones. Fit the new filter in a horizontal position with its arrow facing the flow of fuel towards the fuel pump.
6 **Exhaust system:** Inspect the exhaust system for signs of joint leaks, excessive corrosion and general security. repair if necessary (Section 24).

3 Air cleaner element – renewal

1 A dirty air cleaner element will cause a loss of performance and an increase in fuel consumption. A new element should be fitted at the specified intervals and the element should be cleaned every twelve months or more frequently under dusty conditions.

1.05 and 1.3 litre
2 Release the spring clips securing the air cleaner lid and remove the lid (photo).
3 Cover the carburettor entry port to prevent any dirt entering it when the element is lifted out, and remove the element (photo). Wipe the inside of the air cleaner with a moist rag to remove all dust and dirt and then remove the covering from the entry port.
4 If cleaning the element, place well away from the vehicle, then tap the air cleaner element to remove dust and dirt. If necessary use a soft brush to clean the outside or blow air at very low pressure from the inside surface towards the outside.
5 Refit the element, clean the cover and put it in place, then clip the cover down, ensuring that the two arrows are aligned.

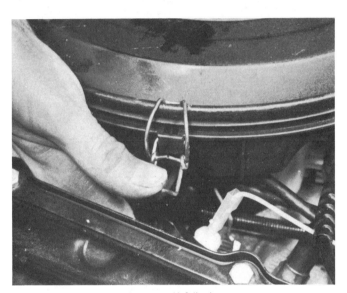

3.2 Removing the air cleaner cover (1.3 litre)

2.5 Typical fuel system in-line filter

3.3 Removing the air cleaner element (1.3 litre)

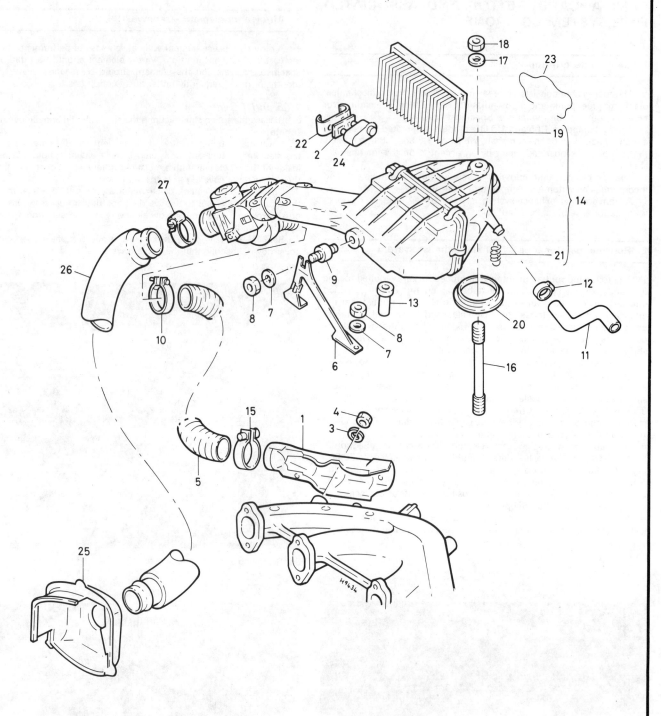

Fig. 3.1 Air cleaner components – 1.6 and 1.8 litre carburettor (Sec 3)

1	Warm air deflector plate	10	Clip	19	Filter element
2	Gasket	11	Air hose	20	Sealing washer
3	Spring washer	12	Clip	21	Spring
4	Nut	13	Spacer tube	22	Lockplate
5	Air hose	14	Air cleaner	23	Retaining clip
6	Bracket	15	Clip	24	Dual thermostat
7	Washer	16	Stud	25	Union
8	Nut	17	Washer	26	Air hose
9	Bonded rubber mounting	18	Self-locking nut	27	Clip

1.6 and 1.8 litre

6   To remove the element, unclip and remove the cover and withdraw the element. Note that on some models it is necessary to first loosen the front mounting nut (photos). Clean the interior of the air cleaner with a fuel-moistened cloth, then wipe it dry (photos).

7   Refer to paragraph 4 for cleaning the element.

8   Refit in the reverse order of removal.

4   Air cleaner unit – removal and refitting

1.05 and 1.3 litre

1   Remove the element, as described in Section 3.

2   Unscrew the nut(s) securing the air cleaner body and remove the adaptor or retaining ring (photo).

3   Note the location of all hoses and tubes then disconnect them and withdraw the air cleaner body from the carburettor. Remove the sealing ring (photos).

4   Refit in the reverse order of removal, ensuring that all hose connections are securely made.

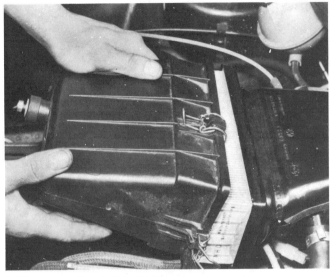

3.6C ... remove the air cleaner cover ...

3.6A Release the retaining clips ...

3.6D ... and withdraw the element (1.6 litre)

3.6B ... loosen the front mounting nut ...

4.2 Remove the air cleaner body retaining ring (1.3 litre)

4.3A Disconnect the temperature sensor hoses ...

5.1 Air cleaner vacuum unit

4.3B ... and the crankcase emission hose (1.3 litre)

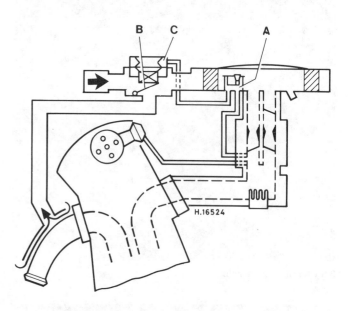

**Fig. 3.2 Air cleaner load and temperature control diagram –
1.05 and 1.3 litre (Sec 5)**

A   Temperature regulator   C   Vacuum unit
B   Intake pipe with thermostat

1.6 and 1.8 litre

5   Remove the element, as described in Section 3.
6   Unclip and detach the air hose at the side of the cleaner body.
7   Undo the retaining nut at the top and lift the cleaner unit clear, disconnecting the remaining hoses.
8   Refit in the reverse order of removal. Fit a new sealing washer if the old one has perished or distorted.

5   Automatic air cleaner temperature control – checking

1   Unclip and remove the vacuum unit and intake pipe, but leave the vacuum pipe connected (photo).
2   Suspend a thermometer in the flow of air through the inlet duct then start the engine. Between -20°C (4°F) and 17 to 20°C (63 to 68°F) the control flap in the unit should be a maximum of 2/3rds open to admit hot air from the exhaust manifold. Above 17 to 20°C (63 to 68°F) the control flap must close the hot air supply.
3   The control flap movement can be checked by sucking on the vacuum inlet.

4   With the engine running and inlet air temperature above 17 to 20°C (63 to 58°F), disconnect the vacuum hose from the vacuum unit. The control flap should fully open within a maximum of 20 seconds.
5   If the control unit does not operate correctly, renew it, together with the temperature sensor (photo).
6   Refit the vacuum unit and intake pipe.

6   Fuel pump – testing, removal and refitting

1   The location of the fuel pump is dependent on the engine type. On the 1.05 and 1.3 litre models the pump is located on the right-hand side of the engine, forward of the carburettor (photo). Mounted on the cylinder head, it is driven indirectly from the camshaft.

5.5 Upper view of the air temperature sensor (1.3 litre)

6.1 Fuel pump location (1.3 litre)

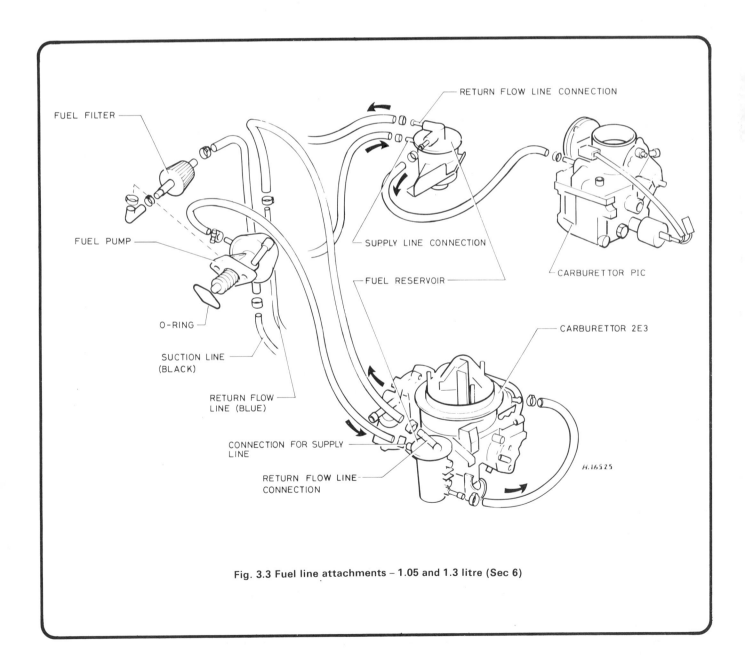

FUEL FILTER

FUEL PUMP

O-RING

SUCTION LINE
(BLACK)

RETURN FLOW
LINE (BLUE)

CONNECTION FOR SUPPLY
LINE

RETURN FLOW LINE
CONNECTION

RETURN FLOW LINE CONNECTION

SUPPLY LINE CONNECTION

FUEL RESERVOIR

CARBURETTOR PIC

CARBURETTOR 2E3

H.16525

Fig. 3.3 Fuel line attachments – 1.05 and 1.3 litre (Sec 6)

2 On the 1.6 and 1.8 litre models the fuel pump is located on the side of the cylinder block, next to the oil filter mounting bracket; the pump being driven direct from the intermediate shaft.

3 If the fuel pump is suspected of malfunctioning, disconnect the delivery pipe to the fuel reservoir and connect up a pressure gauge to the delivery pipe/connection from the pump. With the engine running at the specified speed check that the operating pressure of the pump is as given in the Specifications.

4 Alternatively, a less accurate method is to disconnect the supply pipe from the carburettor (air cleaner removed) and also disconnect the LT lead from the coil positive terminal. Spin the engine on the starter while to holding a wad of rag near the fuel pipe. Well defined spurts of fuel should be ejected from the pipe if the fuel pump is operating correctly, provided there is fuel in the fuel tank.

5 If the above test indicates that the pump is malfunctioning then it must be renewed, as it is not possible to service or repair it. However, prior to removal of the fuel pump, check the in-line filter for blockage.

6 The in-line filter should either be renewed at the intervals specified in the Routine Maintenance Section (Section 2) or if it becomes blocked beforehand.

7 To remove the fuel pump, first identify the hoses for position, then disconnect them from the pump.

8 Using a suitable splined or Allen key, unscrew the pump retaining bolts and withdraw the unit from the cylinder head or cylinder block (as applicable). Remove the sealing ring and, if applicable, note the earth lead location.

9 Clean the mating faces of the pump and cylinder head or cylinder block/seal flange.

10 Refitting is a reversal of the removal procedure. Renew the seal ring and, where crimped type hose clips were used, change them to screw type clips.

11 On completion check all hose connections, with the engine running, and look for any sign of fuel leaks.

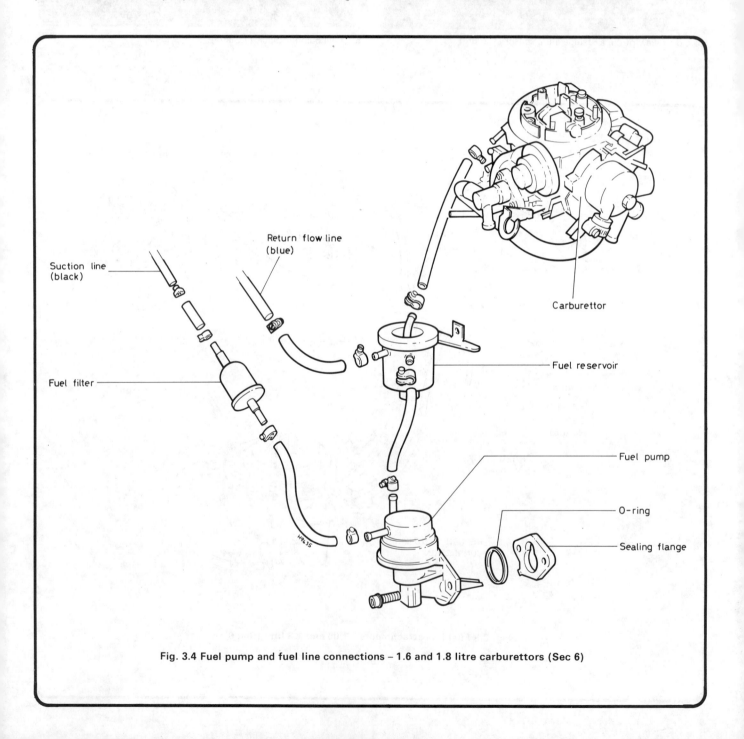

Fig. 3.4 Fuel pump and fuel line connections – 1.6 and 1.8 litre carburettors (Sec 6)

7 Fuel reservoir – removal and refitting

1 The fuel reservoir is located between the fuel pump and the carburettor (photo). The reservoir has three hose connections. These being from the fuel pump (arrow marked), to the carburettor (not marked) and to the fuel return line (marked R).
2 To remove the reservoir, disconnect the three line hoses and plug them to prevent leakage.

7.1 Fuel reservoir location (1.3 litre)

7.3 Fuel reservoir retaining screws (arrowed). Note the earth lead connection to the lower screw

3 Remove the support bracket retaining screws and lift away the reservoir. Note the earth lead connection (photo).
4 Refit in the reverse order to removal and then check for any aigns of leakage on completion.

8 Fuel tank – removal and refitting

For safety reasons the fuel tank must always be removed in a well ventilated area, never over a pit.
1 Disconnect the battery negative lead.
2 Siphon or pump all the fuel from the fuel tank (there is no drain plug).

3 Lift the floor covering from the luggage compartment then remove the circular sender unit cover.
4 Disconnect the wiring plug from the top of the sender unit, also the fuel feed (to pump) and return (from fuel reservoir) hoses.
5 Jack up the rear of the car and support it on axle stands. Chock the front wheels. remove the right-hand side rear wheel.
6 Disconnect the breather hose from the filler neck (photo).
7 Disconnect the expansion tank-to-filler neck hose and breather pipe.
8 Disconnect the filler neck funnel which is secured by a large C-clip.
9 Support the fuel tank with a trolley jack and length of wood, then unscrew the retaining nuts and bolts, detach the straps (photo) and lower the tank to the ground. On GTI models it will also be necessary to detach the side protector plate.
10 If the expansion reservoir is to be removed, undo the retaining bolt and lower it from the wheel arch.
11 If the tank is contaminated with sediment or water, remove the gauge sender unit, as described in Section 9, and swill the tank out with clean fuel. If the tank is damaged or leaks, it should be repaired professionally or alternatively renewed.
12 Refitting is a reversal of removal. Make sure that the rubber packing strips are fitted to the retaining straps. Refit the hoses free of any kinks.

8.6 Fuel filler breather valve and hose

8.9 Fuel tank tensioning (retaining) strap-to-floor bolts

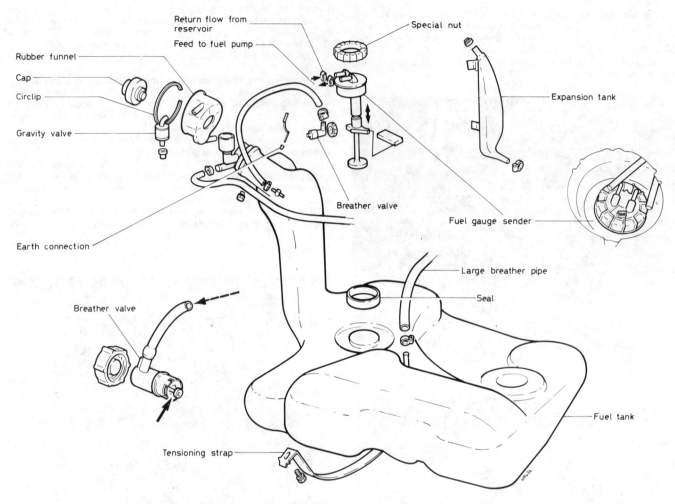

Fig. 3.5 Fuel tank and associated components – carburettor engines (Sec 8)

9 Fuel gauge sender unit – removal and refitting

For safety reasons the fuel gauge sender unit must always be removed in a well ventilated area, never over a pit.
1   Disconnect the battery negative lead.
2   Lift the luggage compartment floor covering and remove the circular sender unit cover.
3   Disconnect the wiring connector from the top of the sender unit then detach the fuel supply and return hoses.
4   Undo the retaining nut and lift out the sender unit, noting its orientation alignment marking. A suitable wrench may be necessary to loosen the securing nut.
5   Remove and renew the sender unit seal.
6   Refit in the reverse order to removal. Check that the unit is correctly aligned with the markings in register. Renew the crimped supply and return line clips with screw type clips. Check that the wiring connection is secure.

10 Fuel filter gravity valve – removal, checking and refitting

1   The gravity valve is located in the fuel filler neck and is accessible from within the right-hand rear wheel arch.
2   To remove the gravity valve, pull it upwards from the fuel filler neck and unclip it.
3   When the valve is held vertically the valve must be open, but when

the valve is angled at 45° it must shut. Renew the valve unit if found to be defective.
4   Refit in the reverse order of removal.

11 Accelerator cable (manual gearbox models) – removal, refitting and adjustment

1   Disconnect the battery earth lead.
2   Remove the air cleaner unit, as described in Section 4.
3   Prise free and release the inner cable securing clip(s) at the carburettor throttle control, noting how the clip(s) are located (photo).
4   Release the cable grommet from the support bracket (photo).
5   Working inside the car, remove the lower facia panel then unclip the inner cable from the accelerator pedal (photo).
6   Withdraw the complete cable into the engine compartment, together with the rubber grommets.
7   Refitting is a reversal of removal, but make sure that it is free of any kinks and correctly aligned. Finally adjust it as follows before refitting the air cleaner.

Adjustment
8   Before adjusting the cable, check that it is correctly aligned over its full length.
9   Have an assistant fully depress the accelerator pedal. Remove the air cleaner.

11.3 Accelerator cable to carburettor throttle control

11.4 Release the cable grommet from the support bracket

11.5 Accelerator cable-to-pedal attachment

10 Check that the clearance between the throttle lever at the carburettor and the fully open stop is a maximum of 1.0 mm (0.040 in). Note that the throttle lever must not be hard against the fully open stop (ie there must be a small clearance).

11 There are different cable adjustment arrangements. Where locknuts are provided at the engine end of the outer cable, loosen them, then adjust the cable position and tighten the locknuts. Where a ferrule and circlip are provided, extract the circlip, adjust the cable position then refit the circlip so that it is abutting the ferrule guide. On some models it is necessary to adjust the inner cable by loosening the clamp screw, repositioning the lever while holding the cable taut, then tightening the screw.

12 After adjustment refit the air cleaner.

12 Accelerator and throttle cable (automatic transmission models) – removal, refitting and adjustment

1 On automatic transmission models the accelerator pedal activates the accelerator cable which is attached to the operating lever of the

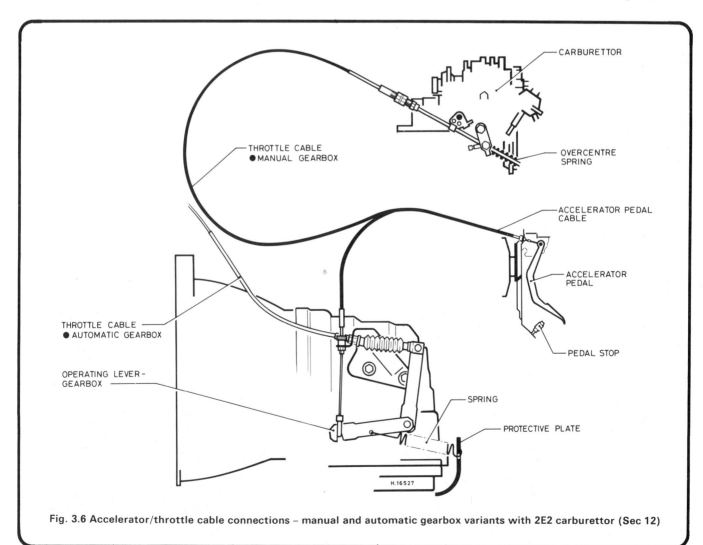

Fig. 3.6 Accelerator/throttle cable connections – manual and automatic gearbox variants with 2E2 carburettor (Sec 12)

gearbox shift control. This simultaneously operates the throttle cable fitted between the shift mechanism and the carburettor.

2   Before removing either cable, select P (Park).

3   To remove the accelerator pedal cable, first loosen the cable adjusting nut, then detach the inner cable from the operating lever clevis and the outer cable from its location bracket. The cable can then be disconnected from the pedal and removed in the same manner as that for manual gearbox models (see previous Section).

4   To remove the throttle cable, loosen the adjuster and locknut at the carburettor support bracket, remove the inner cable retaining clip and then disconnect the cable from the carburettor.

5   At the transmission end, prise free the securing clip and detach the cable from the operating lever and the cable support bracket.

6   Refitting of both cables is a reversal of the removal procedure, but each cable must be adjusted, and this procedure is described in Chapter 6.

13 Accelerator pedal – removal and refitting

1   Remove the lower facia panel.

2   Disconnect the accelerator cable from the pedal.

3   Prise out the clip and remove the pivot pin.

4   Remove the accelerator pedal. If necessary press out the pivot pin bushes.

5   Refitting is a reversal of removal, but lubricate the bushes with a little grease. Check the cable adjustment, with reference to Section 12.

14 Choke cable (1.05 litre) – removal, refitting and adjustment

1   Disconnect the battery negative lead.

2   Remove the air cleaner, as described in Section 4.

3   Using a screwdriver, loosen the inner and outer cable clamps and disconnect the cable from the carburettor (photo).

4   Working inside the car, remove the lower facia panel.

5   Pull out the clip and remove the choke knob.

6   Unscrew the ring and withdraw the cable from the facia.

7   Disconnect the wiring and withdraw the complete cable from inside the car.

8   Refitting is a reversal of removal, but make sure that the cable is correctly aligned, and that the grommets are firmly fitted in the bulkhead. Finally adjust it as follows before refitting the air cleaner.

9   Locate the outer cable in the clamp so that its end protrudes approximately 12.0 mm (0.47 in). Tighten the clamp with the outer cable in this position.

10 Push the choke knob fully in then pull it out 3.0 mm (0.12 in) – switch on the ignition and check that the warning lamp is not lit.

11 Insert the inner cable into the choke lever clamp and fully open the choke lever by hand. Tighten the inner cable clamp screw in this position.

12 Refit the air cleaner.

15 Carburettor – removal and refitting

1   Disconnect the battery earth lead.

2   Remove the air cleaner unit, as described in Section 4.

3   Disconnect the accelerator cable from the carburettor (Section 11 or 12 as applicable). Disconnect the wiring from the fuel cut-off solenoid, the bypass air cut-off valve, the part throttle channel heater, automatic choke control unit and the earth lead, as applicable.

4   Referring to Chapter 2, drain off half the engine coolant then disconnect the coolant hoses from the automatic choke unit and the expansion element (where applicable).

5   Disconnect the fuel supply and return hoses at the carburettor/fuel reservoir, as necessary, and plug or clamp the hoses to prevent fuel leakage. Note the connections in case of confusion when refitting.

6   Disconnect the vacuum hoses and note their connections.

7   Unscrew the through-bolts or retaining nuts, as applicable, and carefully remove the carburettor from the inlet manifold (photos).

15.7A Carburettor securing bolts (arrowed) – 2E3 carburettor

Fig. 3.7 Choke cable adjustment setting – 1.05 litre (Sec 14)

A   Outer cable projection   C   Choke inner cable
B   Cam and stop   connection

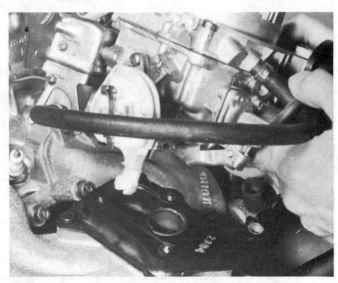

15.7B Carburettor removal from the intermediate flange/manifold – 2E3 carburettor

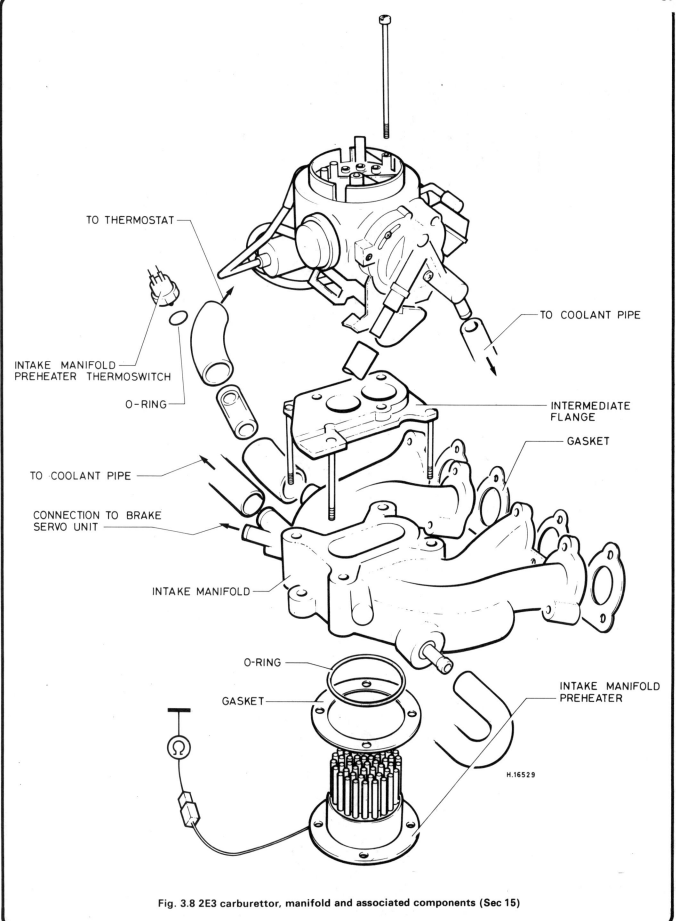

Fig. 3.8 2E3 carburettor, manifold and associated components (Sec 15)

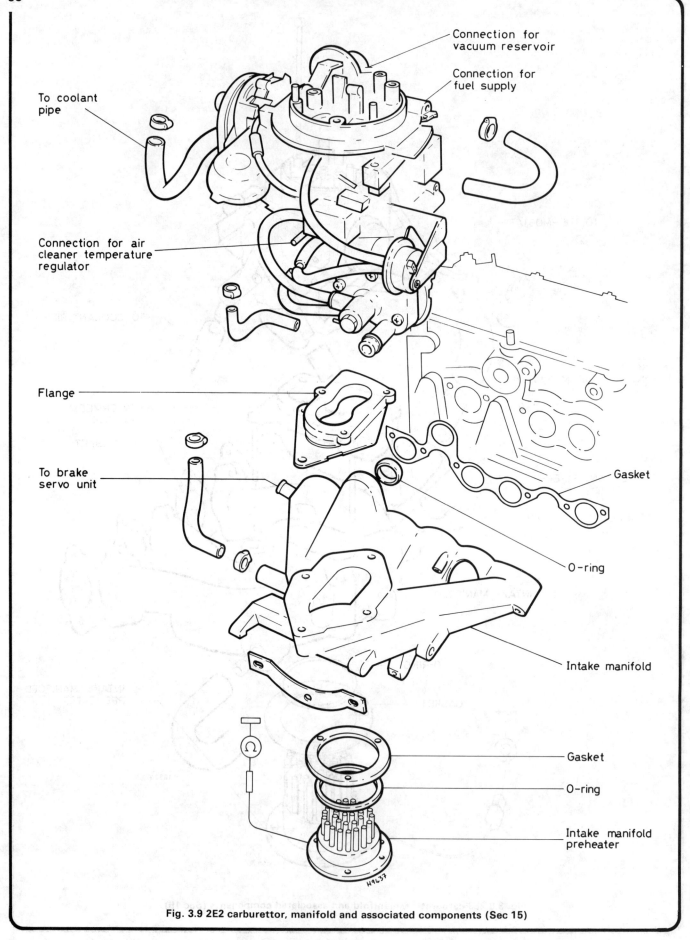

Connection for
vacuum reservoir

Connection for
fuel supply

To coolant
pipe

Connection for air
cleaner temperature
regulator

Flange

To brake
servo unit

Gasket

O-ring

Intake manifold

Gasket

O-ring

Intake manifold
preheater

Fig. 3.9 2E2 carburettor, manifold and associated components (Sec 15)

8   To remove the intermediate flange from the manifold, undo the four nuts on the manifold underside and lift the flange clear.

9   Refitting is a reversal of the removal procedure. Ensure that the inlet manifold, intermediate flange and carburettor mating faces are clean, and use new gaskets.

10 On completion, top up the cooling system (Chapter 2), restart the engine and check for fuel and coolant leaks. Adjust the carburettor as necessary.

16 Carburettor (31 PIC7) – dismantling, reassembly and adjustment

1   With the carburettor removed from the engine, clean the external surfaces with paraffin and wipe dry.

2   Remove the screws from the cover, noting the location of the earth lead (photo).

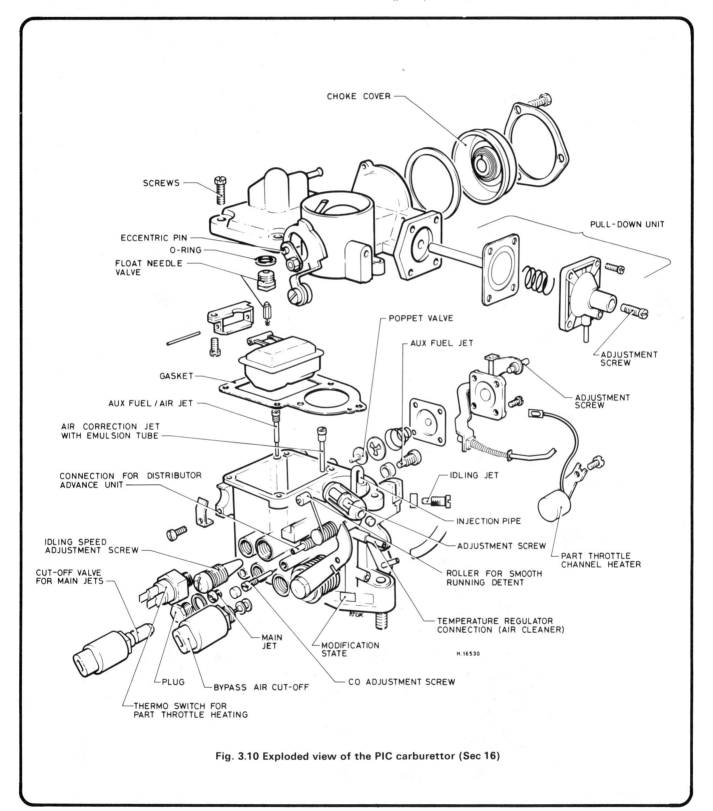

Fig. 3.10 Exploded view of the PIC carburettor (Sec 16)

3   Lift off the cover and remove the gasket (photo).
4   Prise out the retainer and remove the float from the carburettor (photos).
5   Clean out the float chamber with clean fuel (photo).
6   If necessary further dismantle the carburettor with reference to Fig. 3.10.
7   To check the bypass air cut-off valve when removed, depress the pin approximately 3 to 4 mm (0.12 to 0.16 in) then energise it with battery voltage. A click should be heard and the pin should move out.
8   To check the cut-off valve for the main jets (where fitted), apply battery voltage. It must be heard to click when the voltage is applied.
9   Reassembly is a reversal of dismantling, but renew all gaskets and rubber rings. Finally make the following adjustments.
10 To adjust the choke valve gap operate the choke lever fully then return it to the smooth running detent and hold it there. With the choke spindle lever against the cam check that the clearance between the choke valve and barrel is as given in the Specification. Use a twist drill to make the check and if necessary adjust the clearance by turning the adjusting screw as required (photos).
11 Although the choke valve gap smooth running detent position is preset during manufacture its setting can be checked and if necessary

16.4B ... and remove the float – PIC carburettor

16.3 Removing the carburettor cover – PIC carburettor

16.5 View of carburettor with cover removed – PIC carburettor

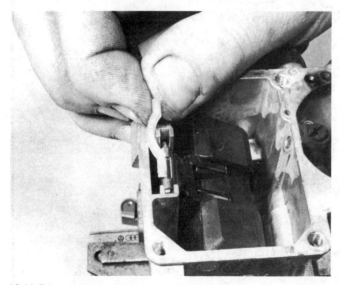

16.4A Prise out the retainer ...

16.10A Checking the choke valve gap with a twist drill – PIC carburettor

16.10B Adjusting screw location for the choke valve gap (A) and choke valve gap smooth running detent eccentric pin (B) – PIC carburettor

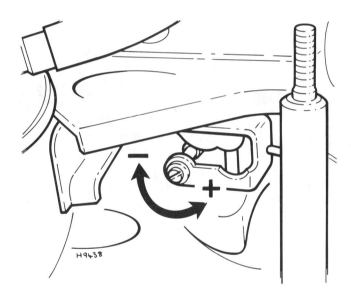

Fig. 3.11 Accelerator pump adjuster screw – PIC carburettor (Sec 16)

adjusted. Pull the choke out fully, then push it onto the smooth running detent. Press the choke lever against the cam and check the choke valve gap with a twist drill, as in the previous paragraph. If the gap is not as specified adjust by turning the eccentric pin on the choke spindle lever.

12 The accelerator pump injection capacity may be checked with the carburettor fitted or removed, however the air cleaner must be removed and the float chamber must be full. Open the choke valve and retain in the open position with a piece of wire, then push a length of close fitting plastic tube over the injection pipe. Operate the throttle until fuel emerges then place the tube in a measuring glass. Operate the throttle fully five times allowing at least three seconds per stroke. Divide the final quantity by five to determine the amount per stroke and compare with the amount given in the Specifications. If necessary reposition the adjusting screw on the accelerator pump lever. Note that the fuel must be injected into the throttle valve gap – if necessary bend the injection pipe.

17 Carburettor (31 PIC7) – slow running and fast idle speed adjustments

Accurate adjustment of the carburettor is only possible after adjustment of the ignition timing, dwell angle, and spark plug gaps. Incorrect valve clearances can also effect carburettor adjustment. Note that tamperproof caps may be fitted to the slow running adjustment screws and the removal of the caps may be prohibited by legislation in certain countries.

1 Run the engine to normal operating temperature then stop it. Connect a tachometer and, if available, an exhaust gas analyser.
2 Check that all electrical accessories are switched off and note that slow running adjustments should not be made while the radiator cooling fan is running.
3 Disconnect the crankcase ventilation hose from the air cleaner body and plug the air cleaner outlet.
4 Start the engine and let it idle. Check that the engine speed and CO content are as given in the Specification. If not, turn the two screws located above the cut-off solenoid alternately as necessary (photo).

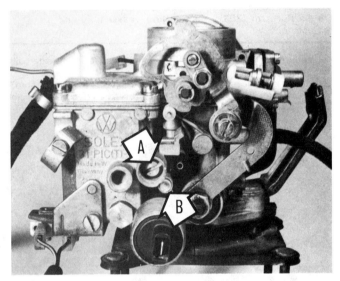

17.4 Idle speed (A) and mixture (B) adjusting screw locations – PIC carburettor

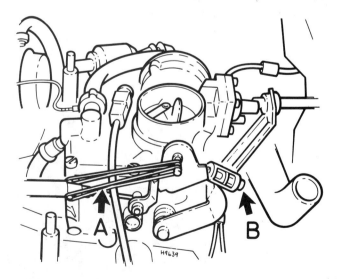

Fig. 3.12 Fast idle speed setting – PIC carburettor (Sec 17)

A   Choke valve held open with   B   Adjustment screw
    rubber band

5   If an exhaust gas analyser is not immediately available, an approximate mixture setting can be made by turning the mixture screw to give the highest engine speed.

6   Reconnect the crankcase ventilation hose. If this results in an increase in the CO content, the engine oil is diluted with fuel and should be renewed. Alternatively, if an oil change is not due, a long fast drive will reduce the amount of fuel in the oil.

7   Stop the engine and remove the tachometer and exhaust gas analyser.

8   To adjust the fast idle speed, first check that the engine is still at normal operating temperature. Remove the air cleaner.

9   With the engine stopped, pull the choke control knob fully out then push it in to the smooth running detent.

10 Retain the choke valve in its open position using an elastic band.

11 Connect a tachometer then start the engine and check that the fast idling speed is as given in the Specification. If not turn the adjustment screw on the side of the choke lever cam. Note that this screw may also have a tamperproof cap (Fig. 3.12).

12 Stop the engine, disconnect the tachometer and elastic band, and refit the air cleaner. Push the choke control knob fully in.

18 Carburettor (2E3) – dismantling, reassembly and adjustment

1   With the carburettor removed from the engine, clean it externally with paraffin and wipe/blow dry.

2   Undo and remove the cover screws then lift off the cover (photo), taking care not to break the gasket just in case a replacement is not readily available.

3   The respective components can now be removed from the cover and main body of the carburettor as required (photos), also referring to Fig. 3.13. Do not alter or remove the full throttle stop or the Stage II throttle valve adjustment screw settings.

4   Clean the internal components but do not probe jets and orifices with wire or similar to remove dirt, blow them through using an air line.

5   If the part throttle enrichment valve is removed it must be renewed.

6   To check the cut-off valve, apply battery voltage. It must be heard to click when the voltage is applied.

7   Reassembly is a reversal of the dismantling procedure, but renew all gaskets and rubber rings. Make the following checks and adjustments.

8   To check the choke valve gap the choke cover must be removed. Move the throttle valve and the fast idle cam so that the adjustment screw is against the highest cam stop. Now push the choke valve operating rod fully towards the adjustment screw (and pull-down unit), then check the choke valve-to-barrel clearance using a twist drill as a gauge. If necessary turn the adjuster screw as required to provide the specified choke valve gap (Figs. 3.14 and 3.15).

9   The accelerator pump injection capacity can be checked in the same manner as that described in Section 16, paragraph 12, but allow 1 second per stroke and 3 seconds between strokes (Fig. 3.16).

10 Ensure that the automatic choke cover and the choke housing alignment marks correspond. To check the choke, connect up a test lamp between a battery positive terminal and the choke lead. The test lamp should illuminate, if it doesn't then the choke unit is defective and must be renewed.

11 The choke pulldown unit can be checked whilst it is removed but, as this requires the use of a vacuum pump and gauge, it is a check best entrusted to your VW dealer. The pulldown unit can also be tested

18.2 Top cover securing screws (arrowed) – 2E3 carburttor

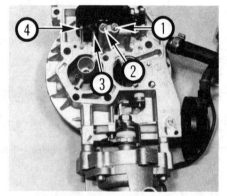

18.3A Underside view of the 2E3 carburettor
1   Stage I main jet
2   Stage II main jet
3   Full throttle enrichment lift pipe
4   Stage II progression lift pipe

18.3B 2E3 carburettor showing the fast idle cam (1), fast idle adjuster screw (2) and Stage II vacuum unit (3)

18.9 Acceleration injection pipe must align with recess (arrows) – 2E3 carburettor

18.10 Choke housing and cover must be correctly aligned – 2E3 carburettor

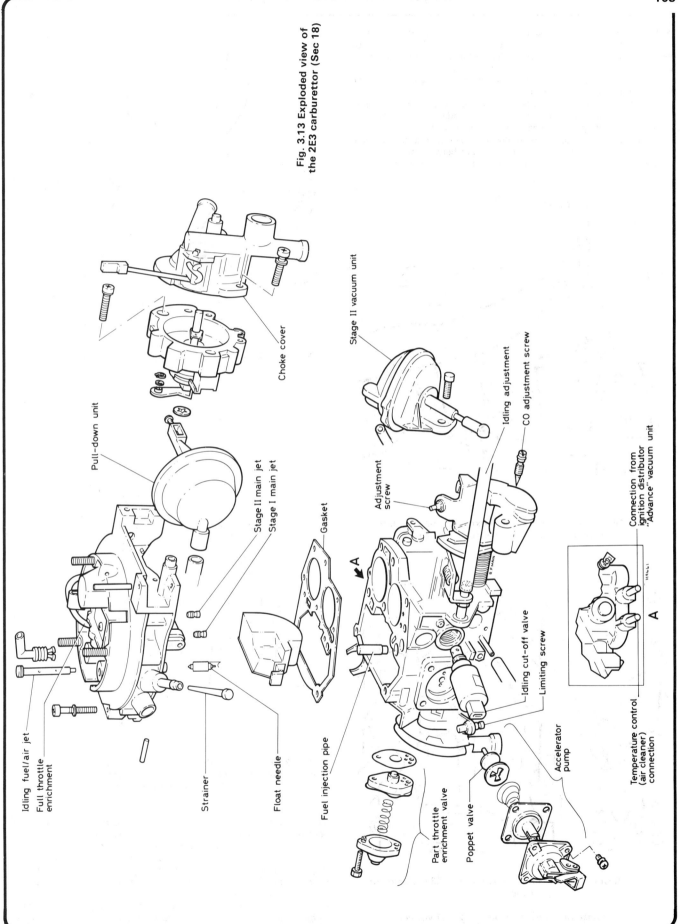

Fig. 3.13 Exploded view of the 2E3 carburettor (Sec 18)

when the carburettor is in position in the car. The air cleaner unit must be removed. Run the engine at idle speed then close the choke valve by hand and check that a resistance is felt over the final 3 mm (0.12 in) of travel. If no resistance is felt, there may be a leak in the vacuum connections, or the pulldown unit diaphragm to be broken, in which case the unit must be renewed.

12 The basic Stage II throttle valve adjustment is made during manufacture and should not require further adjustment. If, for any reason, the limiting screw has been removed or its setting altered, readjust it as follows. Open the throttle valve and hold in this position by inserting wooden rod or similar implement between the valve and venturi. Using a rubber band, pretension the Stage II throttle valve

Fig. 3.16 Accelerator pump adjustment – 2E3 carburettor (Sec 18)

1 Fast idle cam clamp screw   A Increase capacity
2 Fast idle cam   B Decrease capacity

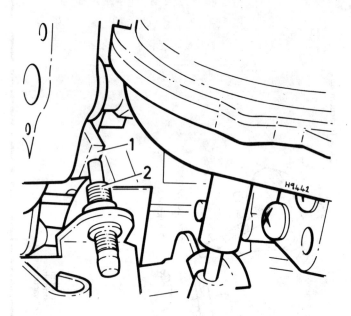

Fig. 3.14 Fast idle cam (1) and choke valve gap adjusting screw (2) – 2E3 carburettor (Sec 18)

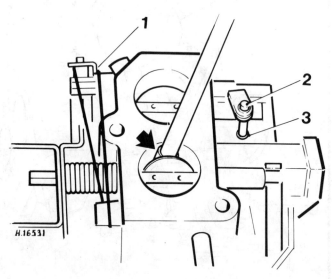

Fig. 3.17 Throttle valve basic setting showing rod to hold valve open (arrowed), lock lever (1), limiting screw (2) and stop (3) – 2E3 carburettor (Sec 18)

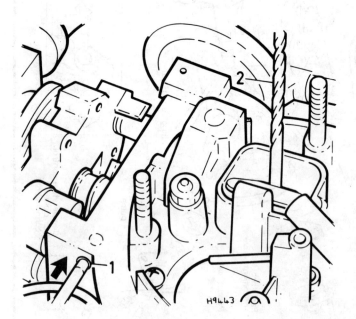

Fig. 3.15 Checking the choke valve gap – 2E3 carburettor (Sec 18)

1 Choke valve operating rod   2 Twist drill
(push in direction of arrow)

locking lever then unscrew the limiting screw to provide a clearance between the stop and the limiting screw. Now turn the limiting screw in so that it is just in contact with the stop. The limiting screw stop point can be assessed by inserting a thin piece of paper between the stop and screw. When the paper starts to get pinched between the two the stop point is reached, and from this point tighten the limiting screw a further quarter turn then secure it with locking compound. Close both throttle valves then measure the locking lever clearances (arrowed in Figure 3.18). If the clearances are not as specified bend them, as necessary.

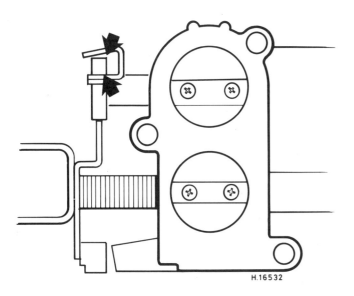

H.16532

Fig. 3.18 Locking lever clearance with throttle valves closed – 2E3 carburettor (Sec 18)

Clearance to equal 0.25 to 0.55 mm (each side)

Fig. 3.19 Fast idle speed adjustment screw (2) – 2E3 carburettor (Sec 19)

speed should be as specified. If the setting is incorrect, turn the adjustment screw in the required direction until it is correct – Fig. 3.19. (Note that the screw may have a tamperproof cap fitted).
4   On completion unplug the temperature control connector and refit the air cleaner.

19 Carburettor (2E3) – slow running and fast idle speed adjustment

1   To check and adjust the slow running setting refer to Section 17 and proceed as described in paragraphs 1 to 7 inclusive (photo).
2   To check and adjust the fast idle adjustment, first check that the engine is still at normal operating temperature. The air cleaner must be removed and the other provisional conditions must apply as for the slow running adjustment. Plug the air cleaner temperature control hose.
3   Restart the engine and open the throttle to give an engine speed of 2500 rpm (approximately). Press down the fast idle cam to its stop then move the throttle valve back so that the adjuster screw is on the second highest stop on the fast idle cam. In this position the fast idle

20 Carburettor (2E2) – dismantling, reassembling and adjustment

1   The dismantling and overhaul procedures for the 2E2 carburettor closely follow those described for the 2E3 carburettor in Section 18. The following checks and adjustments are additional to, or differ from, those given in that Section.
2   **Part throttle channel heater unit:** To check this unit, connect a test lamp between the unit wiring plug and a battery positive terminal. Earth the unit. If the test bulb fails to light the unit is defective and must be renewed. When fitting the unit ensure that it has a good carburettor earth connection.
3   **Choke pull down unit:** This can be checked in the same manner as that for the choke pull down unit on the 2E3 carburettor, but note that the resistance felt must be over the final 5 mm (0.20 in) of travel.
4   **Accelerator pump (carburettor removed):** To make this check, the carburettor must be removed and you will need a vacuum pump and an M8 x 20 mm bolt.
5   Detach the vacuum hoses from the three/four point unit then connect up the vacuum pump to the three/four point unit at A shown in Figure 3.21 and plug connection B (and C on four point unit). Apply vacuum with the pump to hold the diaphragm pushrod in the overrun/cut-off position and give a clearance between the fast idle speed and diaphragm pushrod.
6   Pivot up the warm-up lever to the point where the throttle valve control pin has clearance and insert the M8 x 20 mm bolt to hold the warm-up lever in this position (Figure 3.22).
7   Hold the carburettor over a funnel and measuring glass then slowly open the throttle valve lever fully five times allowing at least three seconds per stroke. Divide the total quantity by five and check the resultant injection capacity against that given in the Specifications.
8   If adjustment is necessary, refer to Figure 3.23, loosen screw A and rotate the cam plate B in the required direction to increase or decrease the injection capacity. On completion retighten the screw and seal in position with locking compound.
9   The accelerator pump injection capacity can also be checked with the carburettor in position in the vehicle, but as specialised equipment is required this is a task best entrusted to your VW dealer.
10   **Basic Stage II valve adjustment:** Proceed as described in paragraph 12 of Section 18, and refer to Figs. 3.17 and 3.24.

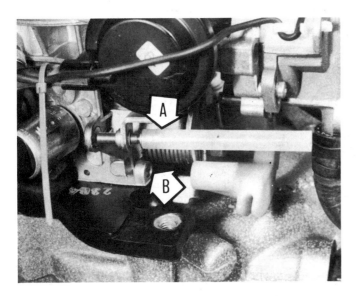

19.1 Idle speed adjustment screw and guide sleeve (A), mixture screw (B) – 2E3 carburettor

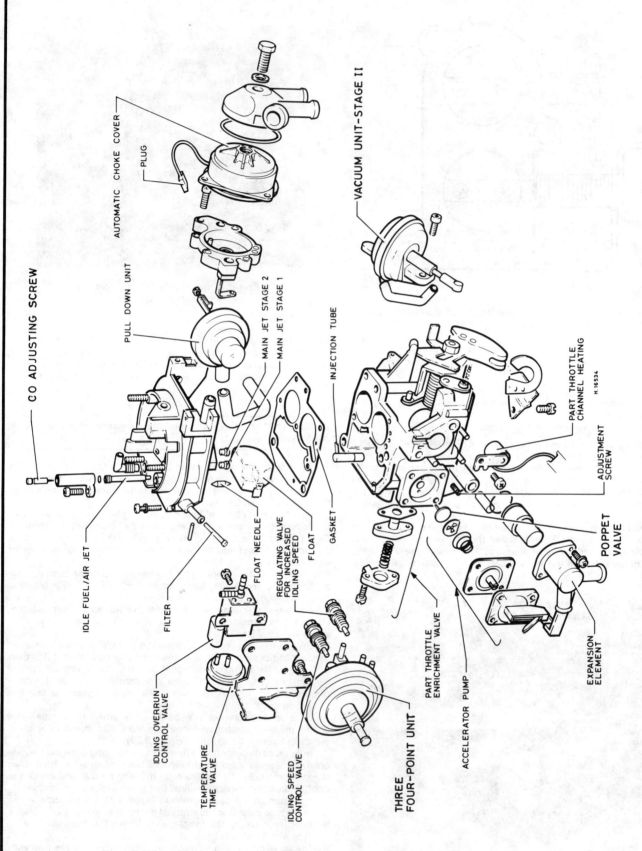

CO ADJUSTING SCREW

AUTOMATIC CHOKE COVER

PLUG

PULL DOWN UNIT

VACUUM UNIT-STAGE II

MAIN JET STAGE 2

MAIN JET STAGE 1

INJECTION TUBE

PART THROTTLE CHANNEL HEATING

H.16534

ADJUSTMENT SCREW

POPPET VALVE

IDLE FUEL/AIR JET

FILTER

FLOAT NEEDLE

REGULATING VALVE FOR INCREASED IDLING SPEED

FLOAT

GASKET

IDLING OVERRUN CONTROL VALVE

TEMPERATURE TIME VALVE

IDLING SPEED CONTROL VALVE

THREE FOUR-POINT UNIT

PART THROTTLE ENRICHMENT VALVE

ACCELERATOR PUMP

EXPANSION ELEMENT

Fig. 3.20 Exploded view of the 2E2 carburettor (Sec 20)

Fig. 3.21 2E2 carburettor ready for accelerator pump check
(Sec 20)

A   Vacuum pump connection
B   Plug vacuum connection (3-point unit)
C   Plug vacuum connection (4-point unit)

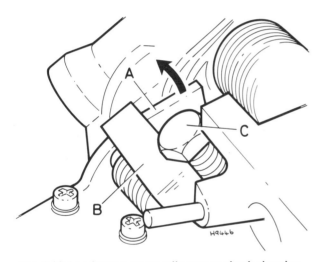

Fig. 3.22 Accelerator pump adjustment check showing
warm-up lever (A), lever (B) and bolt (C) – 2E2 carburettor
(Sec 20)

Fig. 3.23 Loosen screw (A) and turn cam plate (B) in
direction required to adjust accelerator pump injection
capacity – 2E2 carburettor (Sec 20)

Fig. 3.24 Lock lever clearance with throttle valves closed –
2E2 carburettor (Sec 20)

A = 0.3 to 0.5 mm   B = 0.9 to 1.1 mm

Fig. 3.25 2E2 carburettor ready for the 3- or 4-point unit
check (Sec 20)

Pushrod to idle point a = 8.5 mm
1 Vacuum connection   2 and 3 Plug these connections

11 **Three/four point unit**: To check this unit for satisfactory
operation you will need a vacuum pump.
12 Detach the vacuum hoses from the unit and attach the vacuum
pump to connection 1 in Fig. 3.25. Apply vacuum to pull the
diaphragm pushrod to the idle point and then measure the amount of
rod protrusion, which must be as specified.
13 To check the overrun cut-off point, plug off the vacuum
connection, 3 in Fig. 3.25, then apply increased vacuum with the
vacuum pump. This should cause the diaphragm pushrod to move to
the overrun/cut-off point. Measure the rod protrusion (a) which
should now be 1.0 mm (0.04 in). The pushrod should hold at this
position for one minute.
14 If the rod protrusion is incorrect, or it will not hold for the specified
period, then the diaphragm or three/four point unit probably leak and
are therefore in need of renewal.
15 **Stage II vacuum control unit**: This device is fitted to 1.6 litre
manual gearbox models and 1.8 automatic gearbox models from

August 1984 on. Its function is to delay the Stage II opening slightly whilst the coolant temperature is below 18°C (64°F). It achieves this by venting the vacuum hose via the thermo-pneumatic valve and the resistor (Fig. 3.26). Check that the straight hose at connection 3 on the thermo-pneumatic valve is not blocked and check the valve itself by blowing through it. It should be open at 18°C (64°F) and close when the temperature rises above 28°C (82°F).

16 The testing of other carburettor ancillary components such as the idle/overrun control valve and the temperature time valve should be entrusted to your VW dealer as specialised testing equipment is necessary.

Fig. 3.27 Three/four point unit with pushrod (A) and cold idling adjusting screw (B) in idling position – 2E2 carburettor (Sec 21)

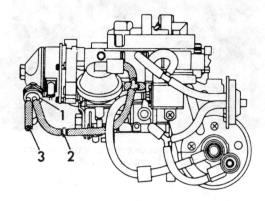

Fig. 3.26 Stage II vacuum unit control – 2E2 carburettor (Sec 20)

1 Thermo-pneumatic valve	3 Straight connection hose
2 Restrictor	

21 Carburettor (2E2) – slow running and fast idle speed adjustment

1   To check and adjust the slow running setting, refer to Section 17 and proceed as described in paragraphs 1 to 7 inclusive, but note the following differences:

(a) Before making any adjustments ensure that the three/four point unit pushrod is in the idling position with the cold idling adjusting screw touching the pushrod (Fig. 3.27)

(b) If adjustment is necessary turn the idling speed control valve (Fig. 3.28) and the CO adjustment screw (Fig. 3.29) as necessary. Access to the CO adjustment screw is gained by prising out the tamperproof plug. If the CO content is difficult to adjust, remove the adjustment screw and clean its point, then refit and adjust it

2   On automatic transmission models the increased idling speed can be checked and adjusted as follows. First, in addition to those preliminary requirements necessary when checking the idle speed slow running setting, the handbrake must be fully applied and chocks placed against the wheels.

3   When the engine is started, turn on the fresh air blower (fully), switch on the headlights (high beam) and the heated rear window. Get an assistant to sit in the vehicle and depress the footbrake then select D. Check that the four point unit diaphragm rod is in the increased idling position, the fast idle adjuster screw rests against the diaphragm rod and the engine increased idle speed is not under that specified. Adjust if necessary by altering the regulator valve setting (Figure 3.30).

4   On models fitted with air conditioning the procedure for checking the increased idling speed is similar to that for automatic transmission models except that it is also necessary to switch on the air conditioner and have the control set at maximum cooling at the highest blower speed. The increased idle speed must be as specified and if adjustment is required, alter the regulator valve setting accordingly.

5   With the slow/increased running idle speed adjustment complete the fast idle speed can be checked and, if necessary, adjusted. Check that the engine is still at its normal operating temperature.

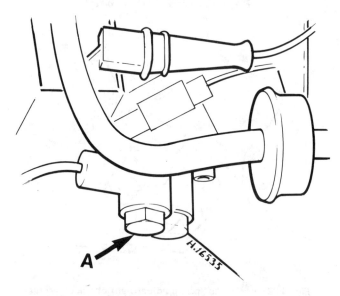

Fig. 3.28 Idling speed control valve (A) – 2E2 carburettor (Sec 21)

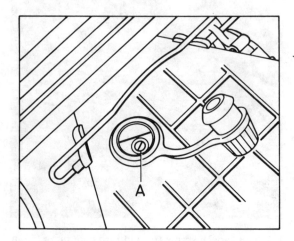

Fig. 3.29 Mixture (CO) adjustment screw (A) – 2E2 carburettor (Sec 21)

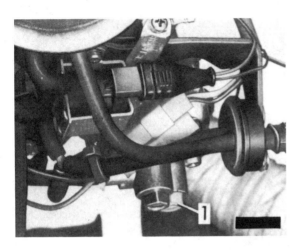

Fig. 3.30 Engine speed regulator valve (1) – 2E2 carburettor (Sec 21)

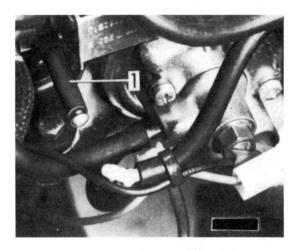

Fig. 3.31 Disconnect and plug vacuum hose (1) to check/adjust engine fast idle speed adjustment – 2E2 carburettor (Sec 21)

6 Detach the Y-piece from the vacuum hose and plug the hose (Fig. 3.31). Connect up a tachometer to the engine. Start and run the engine and check that the fast idle speed is as given in the Specifications, if not turn the adjustment screw on the linkage as necessary. On completion of adjustment apply sealant to the screw threads to lock it in position, unplug and reconnect the Y-piece to the vacuum hose and check that the slow running (idle) speed is as specified.

22 Inlet manifold preheating – description and testing

1 The inlet manifold is preheated by water from the cooling system and by a heater element located in the bottom of the inlet manifold.
2 To check the heater element, the engine should be cold. Disconnect the wire from the element at its inline connector, then attach an ohmmeter between the wire connector from the element and earth – 0.25 to 0.50 ohm should be recorded.
3 To remove the element disconnect the wire, then unscrew the bolts and withdraw the unit. Remove the sealing ring and gasket (photos). When refitting always renew the sealing ring and gasket.
4 The heater element is controlled by a thermo-switch located in the coolant supply hose to the inlet manifold (1.05 and 1.3 litre) or in the top of the coolant hose connecting piece mounted on the side of the cylinder head (1.6 litre).
5 Before removing the thermo-switch drain off some engine coolant to reduce spillage when the switch is removed (see Chapter 2).
6 To test the thermo-switch, detach the lead connector, unscrew and remove the switch from the housing and plug the hole to stop any leakage of coolant.

Fig. 3.32 Fast idle adjustment screw (A) – 2E2 carburettor (Sec 21)

22.3A Unscrew the bolts ...

22.3B ... and remove the heater element from the inlet manifold

22.3C Removing the sealing ring from the heater element

7 With an ohmmeter connected to the terminals, gradually heat the base of the switch unit in hot water. Below the following temperatures there should be zero resistance (ie internal contacts closed):

1.05 litre 65°C (149°F)
1.3, 1.6 and 1.8 litre 55°C (131°F)

8 Above the following temperatures there should be a maximum resistance (ie internal contacts open).

1.05 litre 75°C (167°F)
1.3, 1.6 and 1.8 litre 65°C (149°F)

If defective renew the switch.

23 Inlet and exhaust manifolds – removal and refitting

Inlet manifold
1 Remove the carburettor, as described in Section 15.
2 Disconnect the inlet manifold preheater wire at the in-line connector.
3 Drain the cooling system (Chapter 2) and disconnect the coolant hoses from the manifold.
4 Disconnect the manifold vacuum hoses as necessary (Fig. 3.33).
5 Where applicable, disconnect the stay rod between the base of the manifold and the crankcase (photo).
6 Undo the manifold retaining nuts and bolts (photo) noting their respective locations, and carefully withdraw the manifold from the cylinder head.
7 Remove the gasket and clean the mating faces of the manifold and cylinder head.
8 Refitting is a reversal of the removal procedure. Use a new manifold gasket and tighten the securing nuts and bolts to the specified torque setting.
9 Refit the carburettor, with reference to Section 15.

Exhaust manifold
10 Undo the retaining nut(s) and withdraw the warm air deflector plate from the exhaust manifold (photo).
11 On 1.05 and 1.3 litre models, unbolt and detach the exhaust downpipe from the manifold joint (photo).
12 On 1.6 and 1.8 litre models, refer to Section 24, paragraph 2.
13 Unscrew and remove the remaining manifold retaining bolts/nuts, then carefully withdraw the manifold from the cylinder head (photo). Remove the gasket.
14 Clean the mating faces of the manifold and cylinder head. Also the exhaust downpipe flange connections.
15 Refit in the reverse order of removal. Use a new gasket and tighten the securing nuts/bolts evenly to the specified torque wrench setting.
16 When reconnecting the downpipe to the manifold, smear a little exhaust jointing paste onto the flange prior to connection. This will ensure a good seal at the joint.

23.6 Inlet manifold-to-cylinder head securing nuts and bolts
Note the position of the earth lead spade connector – arrowed (1.3 litre)

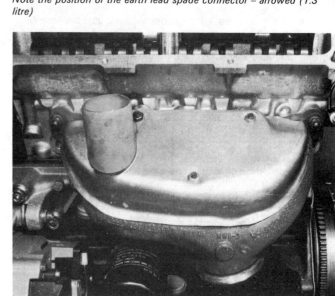

23.10 Warm air deflector plate (1.3 litre)

23.5 Inlet manifold support stay (1.3 litre)

23.11 Exhaust downpipe-to-manifold flange connection (1.3 litre)

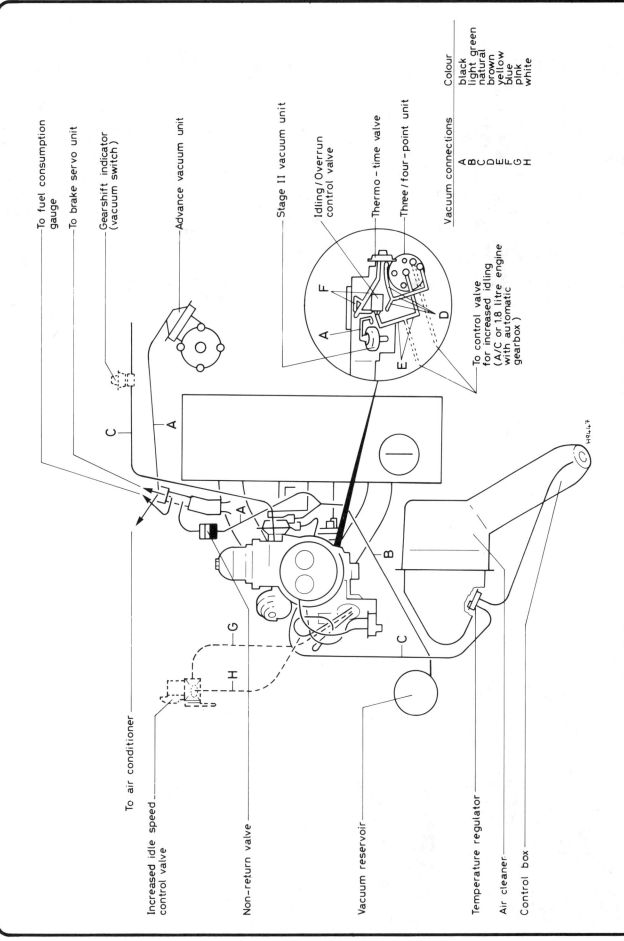

Fig. 3.33 Vacuum hose connections – 1.6 and 1.8 litre with the 2E2 carburettor (Sec 23)

23.13 Exhaust manifold (1.3 litre)

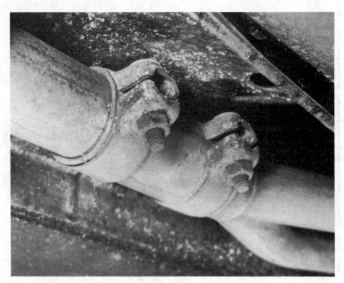

24.1B Check the exhaust system joints for leaks and security

24 Exhaust system – checking, removal and refitting

1   The exhaust system should be examined for leaks, damage, and security every 10 000 miles (15 000 km). To do this, apply the handbrake and allow the engine to idle. Check the full length of the exhaust system for leaks from each side of the car in turn while an assistant temporarily places a wad of cloth over the tailpipe. If a leak is evident, stop the engine and use a proprietary repair kit to seal it. If the leak is excessive or damage is evident, renew the section. Check the rubber mountings for deterioration, and renew them if necessary (photos).

2   On 1.6 and 1.8 litre models it should be noted that if the exhaust system is to be separated at the manifold/downpipe connection, a special VW tool will be necessary to release and subsequently refit the joint retaining clips. Without this tool (VW No 3049A) it is virtually impossible to separate and reassemble the joint without distorting the retaining clips. In view of this, removal and refitting of the system will necessitate detachment of the manifold and front pipe section, or manifold and system complete, and taking the assembly to your VW

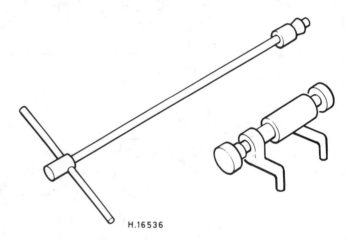

H.16536

Fig. 3.34 VW special tool number 3049A used to release/fit the exhaust downpipes to manifold clips on the 1.6 and 1.8 litre models (Sec 24)

dealer to separate/reassemble the front joint. If the complete system is in need of replacement it is probably best entrusted to your VW dealer.

3   The exhaust systems are shown in Figs. 3.35 and 3.36.

4   Before doing any dismantling work on the exhaust system, wait until the system has cooled down and then saturate the fixing bolts and joints with a proprietary anti-corrosion fluid.

5   When refitting the system, new nuts and bolts should be used, and it may be found easier to cut through the old bolts with a hacksaw, rather than unscrew them.

6   When removing any part of the exhaust system on 1.05 and 1.3 litre models it is usually easier to undo the manifold-to-front pipe joint and remove the complete system from the car, then separate the various pieces of the system, or cut out the defective part, using a hacksaw.

7   Refit the system a section at a time starting at the front. If the manifold has been removed its gasket must be renewed.

8   Smear all the joints with a proprietary exhaust sealing compound before assembly. This makes it easier to slide the pieces to align them and ensures that the joints will be gas tight. Leave all bolts loose.

9   Run the engine until the exhaust system is at normal temperature and then, with the engine running at idling speed, tighten all the mounting bolts and clips, starting at the manifold and working towards the rear silencer. *Take care to avoid touching any part of the system with bare hands because of the danger of painful burns.*

10 When the bolts and clips are tightened, it is important to ensure that there is no strain on any part of the system.

24.1A Check the exhaust system rubber mountings

113

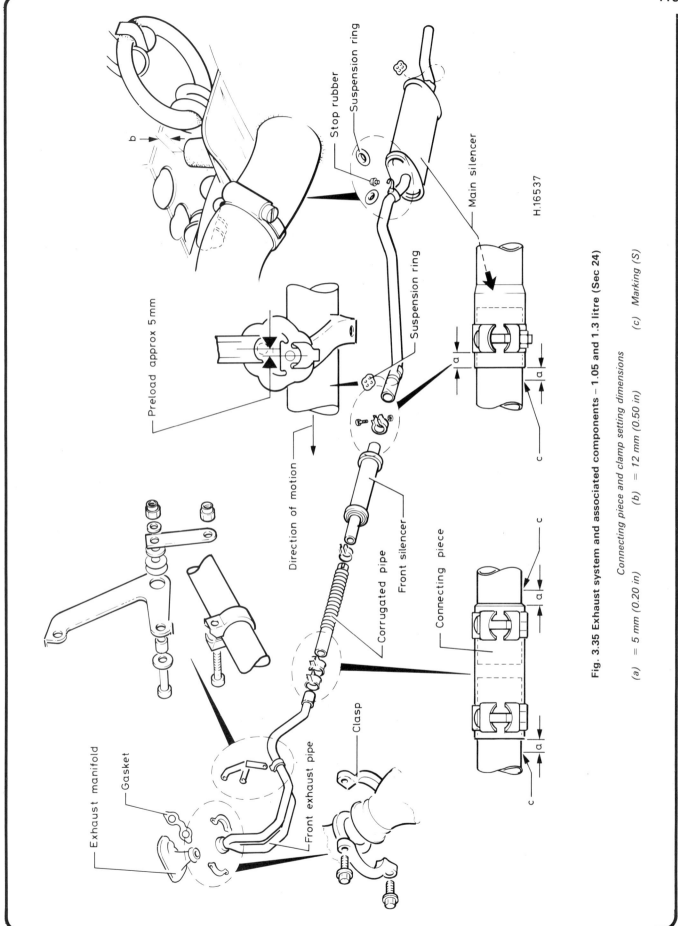

Fig. 3.35 Exhaust system and associated components – 1.05 and 1.3 litre (Sec 24)

Connecting piece and clamp setting dimensions

(a) = 5 mm (0.20 in)   (b) = 12 mm (0.50 in)   (c) Marking (S)

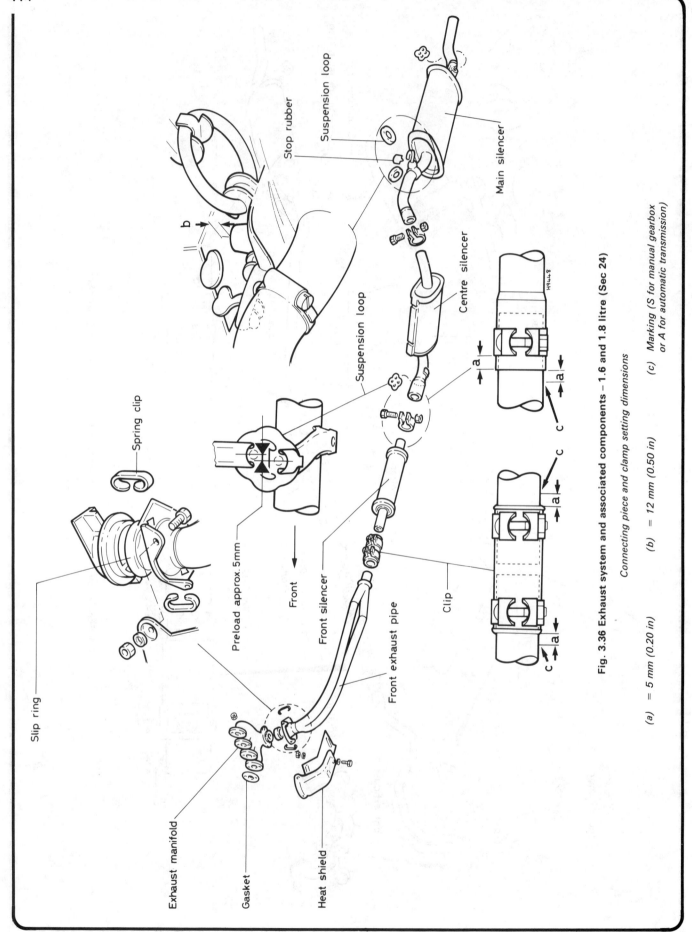

Spring clip

Slip ring

Exhaust manifold

Gasket

Heat shield

Preload approx. 5mm

Front

Front silencer

Front exhaust pipe

Clip

Suspension loop

Centre silencer

Stop rubber

Suspension loop

Suspension loop

Main silencer

b

a

a

c

c

c

a

a

c

H944 8

Fig. 3.36 Exhaust system and associated components – 1.6 and 1.8 litre (Sec 24)

Connecting piece and clamp setting dimensions

(a) = 5 mm (0.20 in)   (b) = 12 mm (0.50 in)   (c) Marking (S for manual gearbox or A for automatic transmission)

PART B: FUEL INJECTION SYSTEM

25 General description

1 The fuel injection system is known as the K-Jetronic. The principle of the system is very simple and there are no specialised electronic components. There is an electrically driven fuel pump and there are electrical sensors and switches, but these are no different from those in general use on cars.

2 The following paragraphs describe the system and its various elements. Later Sections describe the tests which can be carried out to ascertain whether a particular unit is functioning correctly, but dismantling and repair procedures of units are not generally given because repairs are not possible.

3 The system measures the amount of air entering the engine and determines the amount of fuel which needs to be mixed with the air to give the correct combustion mixture for the particular conditions of engine operation. The fuel is sprayed continuously by an injection nozzle to the inlet port of each cylinder. This fuel and air is drawn into the cylinder when the inlet valves open.

Airflow meter

4 This measures the volume of air entering the engine and relies on the principle that a circular disc, when placed in a funnel through which a current of air is passing, will rise until the weight of the disc is equal to the force on its lower surface which the air creates. If the volume of air is increased, and the plate were to remain in the same place, the rate of flow of air through the gap between the cone and the plate would increase and the force on the plate would increase.

5 If the plate is free to move, then, as the force on the plate increases, the plate rises in the cone and the area between the edge of the plate and the edge of the cone increases, until the rate of air flow and hence the force on the plate becomes the same as it was at the former lower flow rate and smaller cone area. Thus the height of the plate is a measure of the volume of air entering the engine.

6 The airflow meter consists of an air funnel with a sensor plate mounted on a lever which is supported at its fulcrum. The weight of the airflow sensor plate and its lever are balanced by a counterweight and the upward force on the sensor plate is opposed by a plunger. The plunger, which moves up and down as a result of the variations in air flow, is surrounded by a sleeve having vertical slots in it. The vertical movement of the plunger uncovers a greater or lesser length of the slots, which meters the fuel to the injection valves.

7 The sides of the air funnel are not a pure cone because optimum operation of the engine requires a different air/fuel ratio under different conditions such as idling, part load and full load. By making parts of the funnel steeper than the basic shape, a richer mixture can be provided for, at idling and full load. By making the funnel flatter than the basic shape, a leaner mixture can be provided.

Fuel supply

8 The rear-mounted fuel pump operates continuously while the engine is running, excess fuel being returned to the fuel tank. The fuel pump is operated when the ignition switch is in the START position, but once the starter is released a switch, connected to the air plate, prevents the pump from operating unless the engine is running.

9 The fuel line to the fuel supply valve incorporates a filter and also a fuel accumulator. The function of the accumulator is to maintain pressure in the fuel system after the engine has been switched off and so give good hot restarting.

10 Associated with the fuel accumulator is a pressure regulator which is an integral part of the fuel metering device. When the engine is switched off, the pressure regulator lets the pressure to the injection valves fall rapidly to cut off the fuel flow through them and so prevent the engine from 'dieseling' or 'running on'. The valve closes at just below the opening pressure of the injector valves and this pressure is then maintained by the pressure accumulator.

Fuel distributor

11 The fuel distributor is mounted on the air metering device and is controlled by the vertical movement of the airflow sensor plate. it consists of a spool valve which moves vertically in a sleeve, the sleeve having as many vertical slots around its circumference as there are cylinders on the engine.

12 The spool valve is adjusted to hydraulic pressure on the upper end and this balances the pressure on the air plate which is applied to the bottom of the valve by a plunger. As the spool valve rises and falls, it uncovers a greater or lesser length of metering slot and so controls the volume of fuel fed to each injector.

13 Each metering slot has a differential pressure valve, which ensures that the difference in pressure between the two sides of the slot is always the same. Because the drop in pressure across the metering slot is unaffected by the length of slot exposed, the amount of fuel flowing depends only on the exposed area of the slots.

Cold start valve

14 The cold start valve is mounted in the intake manifold and sprays additional fuel into the manifold during cold starting. The valve is solenoid operated and is controlled by a thermotime switch in the engine cooling system. The thermotime switch is actuated for a period which depends upon coolant temperature, the period decreasing with rise in coolant temperature. If the coolant temperature is high enough for the engine not to need additional fuel for starting, the switch does not operate.

Warm-up regulator (valve)

15 While warming up, the engine needs a richer mixture to compensate for fuel which condenses on the cold walls of the inlet manifold and cylinder walls. It also needs more fuel to compensate for power lost because of increased friction losses and increased oil drag in a cold engine. The mixture is made richer during warming up by the warm-up regulator. This is a pressure regulator which lowers the pressure applied to the control plunger of the fuel regulator during warm-up. This reduced pressure causes the airflow plate to rise higher than it would do otherwise, thus uncovering a greater length of metering slot and making the mixture richer.

16 The valve is operated by a bi-metallic strip which is heated by an electric heater. When the engine is cold the bi-metallic strip presses against the delivery valve spring to reduce the pressure on the diaphragm and enlarge the discharge cross-section. This increase in cross-section results in a lowering of the pressure fed to the control plunger.

Auxiliary air device

17 Compensation for power lost by greater friction is achieved by feeding a larger volume of fuel/air mixture to the engine than is supplied by the normal opening of the throttle. The auxiliary air device bypasses the throttle with a channel having a variable aperture valve in it. The aperture is varied by a pivoted plate controlled by a spring and a bi-metallic strip.

18 During cold starting the channel is open and increases the volume of air passing to the engine, but as the bi-metallic strip bends it allows a control spring to pull the plate over the aperture until at normal operating temperature the aperture is closed. The heating of the bi-metallic strip is similar to that of the warm-up regulator described above.

Cold acceleration enrichment

19 This system is fitted to later models and its description is given in Section 36.

26 Routine maintenance, adjustments and precautions – fuel injection system

1 Due to the complexity of the fuel injection system, any work should be limited to the operations described in this Chapter. Other adjustments and system checks are beyond the scope of most readers and should be left to your VW dealer.

2 The mixture setting is preset during production of the car and should not normally require adjustment. If new components of the system have been fitted, however, the mixture can be adjusted after reference to Section 31.

3 The only adjustment which may be needed is to vary the engine idle speed by means of the screw mounted in the throttle housing. Use the screw to set the engine speed to that specified when the engine is at the normal operating temperature.

4 Routine servicing of the fuel injection system consists of checking the system components for condition and security, and renewing the air cleaner element at the specified intervals (see Routine Maintenance).

116

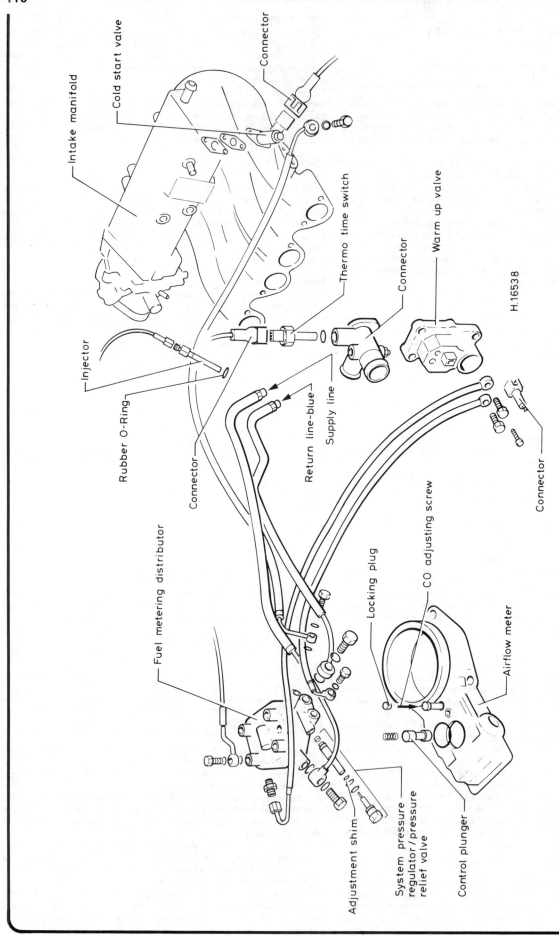

Intake manifold

Cold start valve

Connector

Thermo time switch

Connector

Warm up valve

H.16538

Injector

Rubber O-Ring

Connector

Return line–blue

Supply line

Connector

Fuel metering distributor

Locking plug

CO adjusting screw

Airflow meter

Adjustment shim

System pressure
regulator/pressure
relief valve

Control plunger

Fig. 3.37 Fuel injection system air intake components (Sec 27)

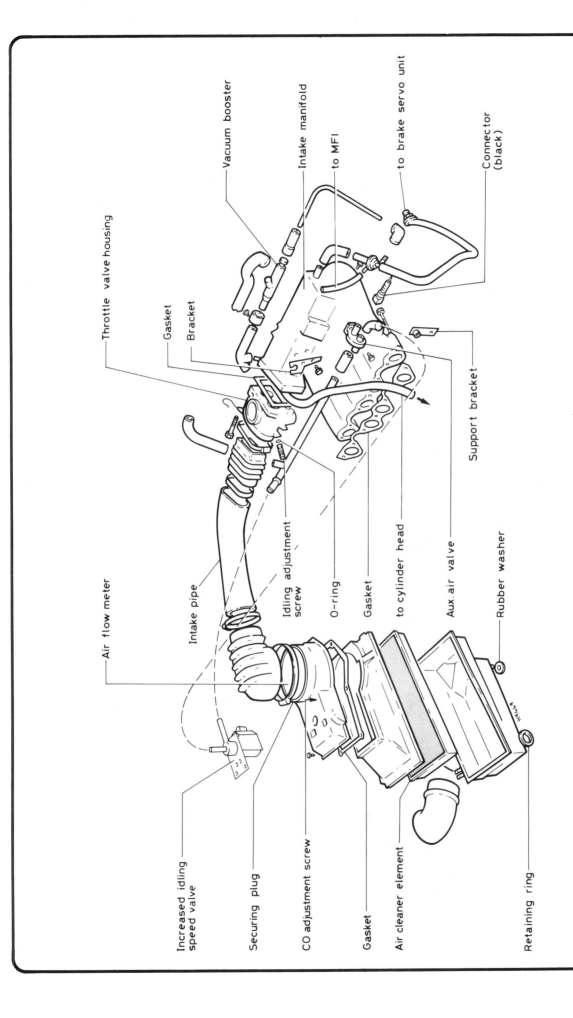

Vacuum booster

Intake manifold

to MFI

to brake servo unit

Connector (black)

Throttle valve housing

Gasket

Bracket

Support bracket

Air flow meter

Intake pipe

Idling adjustment screw

O-ring

Gasket

to cylinder head

Aux. air valve

Rubber washer

Increased idling speed valve

Securing plug

CO adjustment screw

Gasket

Air cleaner element

Retaining ring

Fig. 3.38 Air cleaner, inlet manifold and associated components – fuel injection system (Sec 27)

5   Check the system vacuum components for condition and security.

6   In the event of a malfunction in the system, reference should be made to the Fault Diagnosis Section at the end of this Chapter, but first make a basic check of the system hoses, connections, fuses and relays for any obvious and immediately visible defects.

7   If any part of the system has to be disconnected or removed for any reason, particular care must be taken to ensure that no dirt is allowed to enter the system.

8   The system is normally pressurised, irrespective of engine temperature, and care must therefore be taken when disconnecting fuel lines; the ignition must be off and the battery disconnected.

9   Before disconnecting any fuel lines, it is advisable to release the pressure in the system by slowly loosening the fuel feed pipe at the warm-up valve and absorb any fuel leakage in a cloth. Remember to retighten the feed pipe connection on completion.

27 Air cleaner element – removal, cleaning/renewal and refitting

1   Release the spring clips securing the air cleaner cover and separate the cover from the airflow meter (photo).

2   Withdraw the element from the housing (photo).

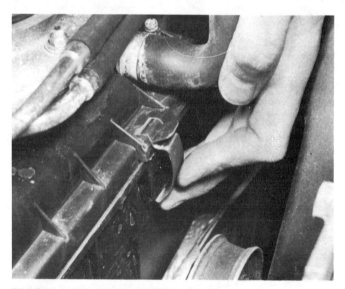

27.1 Release the air cleaner retaining clips

27.2 Air cleaner element withdrawal

3   If cleaning the element, place well away from the vehicle then tap the air cleaner element to remove dust and dirt. If necessary use a soft brush to clean the outside or blow air at a very low pressure from the inside surface towards the outside.

4   Wipe clean the inside of the cover.

5   Refit the element and secure the cover by pressing the clips.

28 Idle speed – adjustment

1   Run the engine until the oil temperature is at least 80°C (176°F), but do not let the engine coolant temperature rise above normal as the electric radiator fan will run and this should not be operating when checking or adjusting the idle speed.

2   Check the ignition timing and adjust if necessary, as described in Chapter 4.

3   The main headlights should be turned on (except air conditioned models). Disconnect and plug the crankcase breather hose from the valve cover.

4   Where air conditioning is fitted, the system must be switched off during checking and adjustment.

5   If the injector pipes have been disconnected, or possibly renewed, and reconnected just prior to checking and adjustment of the idle speed, run the engine speed up to 3000 rpm a few times and then let it idle for a minimum period of two minutes before checking/adjusting the idle speed.

6   If adjustment to the idle speed is necessary, remove the locking cap from the adjustment screw on the throttle assembly and turn the screw to achieve the idle speed given in the Specifications (photo). The adjustments should be made only when the electric radiator fan is stationary.

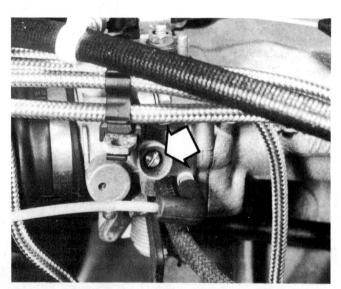

28.6 Idle speed adjustment screw location in the throttle valve housing (arrowed)

7   If an exhaust gas analyser is available, check the CO reading and compare it with the specified figure. If necessary adjust the idle mixture as described in Section 31.

8   Air conditioned models will also be fitted with an increased idle speed valve and, in some instances, a second idle speed boost valve as well. To check these, refer to Section 29 or 30 as applicable.

29 Increased idling speed valve (air conditioned models) – checking

1   Start and run the engine at its normal idle speed.

2   With the air conditioner switched off, pinch the hose at the increased idle speed valve (photo). The engine speed should not change.

29.2 Increased idling speed valve (air conditioned models)

3   Switch the air conditioning system on and then repeat the test. This time the engine speed should drop. If these tests prove the valve to be faulty it must be renewed.
4   Disconnect the hose, unclip and detach the wiring connector then unbolt and remove the valve from its support bracket.
5   Refit in the reverse order of removal.

30 Idle speed boost (air conditioned models) – description, checking and idle speed adjustment

1   The function of this device is to stabilize the engine speed when it drops below 700 rpm under certain operating conditions. This is achieved by increasing the air supply to the engine which raises the idling speed to approximately 1050 rpm. At this point the air supply valve is cut off and the idle speed then returns to normal. The two valves which control this system are attached to the right-hand front suspension mounting in the engine compartment (Fig. 3.39).
2   Valve number 1 (on the inboard side) increases the engine speed when it drops below 700 rpm, whilst valve number 2 (on the outboard side) increases the idle speed when the air conditioner is switched on.

Fig. 3.39 Idle speed boost valve check (Sec 30)

1	Valve No 1	3	Hose
2	Valve No 2		

Valve number 1 – checking and idle speed adjustment
3   Run the engine up to its normal operating temperature, switch off the air conditioner and allow the engine to idle. With the exception of the air conditioner, switch on all electrical consumers (lights etc), then adjust the idle speed to 700 rpm (see Section 28). When reaching the idle speed, the valve should open and the idle speed increase. Use a pair of pliers and pinch the air hose from the valve and check that the speed drops.
4   Switch off the electrical consumers, then pinch the air hose again and adjust the idle speed to that specified. When the correct idle speed is reached, unclamp the hose. The idle speed should then increase up to about 1050 rpm at which point the valve will close and the speed drop to the specified idle speed setting.

Valve number 2 – checking
5   Run the engine at its normal idle speed with the air conditioner switched off. Pinch the air hose and check that the engine speed remains the same.
6   Now switch the air conditioning on and repeat the test. When the hose is pinched the engine speed should drop.
7   If the air hose and/or valves number 1 or 2 are disconnected or removed for any reason it is important when refitting to note that the three-way hose connector large hole must go to valve number 2.

31 Idle mixture – adjustment

Note: *accurate idle mixture adjustment can only be made using an exhaust gas analyser*
1   The idle CO adjustment screw alters the height of the fuel metering distributor plunger relative to the air control plate of the air flow meter.
2   The screw is accessible by removing the locking plug from between the air duct scoop and the fuel metering distributor on the airflow meter casing (photo).

31.2 Idle CO adjustment screw location (arrowed)

3   Although a special tool is recommended for this adjustment, it can be made using a long, thin screwdriver.
4   Ensure that the engine is running under the same conditions as those necessary for adjusting the idling speed (see previous Sections, as applicable) and that the idling speed is correct.
5   Connect an exhaust gas analyser to the tailpipe, as directed by the equipment manufacturer, and read the CO level.
6   Turn the adjusting screw clockwise to raise the percentage of CO and anti-clockwise to lower it. It is important that the adjustment is made without pressing down on the adjusting screw, because this will move the airflow sensor plate and affect the adjustment.

7   Remove the tool, accelerate the engine briefly and re-check. If the tool is not removed before the engine is accelerated there is a danger of the tool becoming jammed and getting bent.

8   Recheck that the idle speed is correct and further adjust this if necessary (see previous Sections) to complete.

9   When reconnection of the crankcase ventilation hose results in an increase in the CO content, the engine oil is diluted with fuel and should be renewed. Alternatively, if an oil change is not due, a long fast drive will reduce the amount of fuel in the oil.

32 Accelerator cable – removal, refitting and adjustment

1   Disconnect the battery earth lead.

2   Prise free the inner cable retaining clip from the throttle valve control on the throttle valve housing (photo).

32.8 Accelerator cable adjuster and support bracket

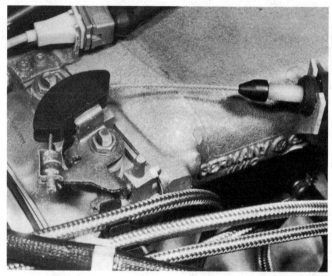

32.2 Accelerator cable connection to the throttle valve

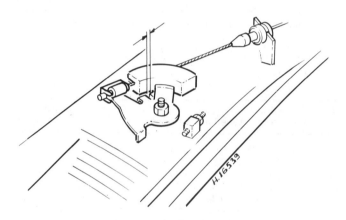

Fig. 3.40 Accelerator cable clearance (1 mm) at full throttle position (Sec 32)

3   Release the inner cable from the control quadrant and the outer cable from the location/adjustment bracket on top of the inlet manifold.

4   Prise free and remove the plastic cover from the top of the bulkhead trough.

5   Working inside the car, remove the lower facia panel on the driver's side.

6   Unclip the inner cable from the accelerator pedal, then withdraw the complete cable into the engine compartment, together with the rubber grommets.

7   Refitting is a reversal of removal, but ensure that the cable run is not kinked and is correctly aligned, then adjust the cable.

8   The accelerator cable is adjusted by getting an assistant to fully depress the accelerator pedal whilst the cable position is set at the throttle valve housing end. When the throttle valve is fully open there should be a 1.0 mm (0.040 in) clearance between the throttle valve lever and the stop (Fig. 3.40). Adjust by altering the cable retainer position at the location/adjustment bracket (photo).

33 Cold start valve and thermotime switch – checking

1   The thermotime switch energises the cold start valve for a short time on starting and the time for which the valve is switched on depends upon the engine temperature.

2   This check must only be carried out when the coolant temperature is below 30°C (86°F).

3   Pull the connector off the cold start valve and connect a test lamp across the contacts of the connector (Fig. 3.41).

4   Pull the high tension lead off the centre of the distributor and connect the lead to earth.

5   Pull the connector from the thermotime switch then connect an extension lead from earth to the thermotime switch W terminal (green and white wire). The red and black wire **must not** be earthed.

6   Operate the starter and check that the test lamp lights up. If it doesn't then there is an open circuit which must be located and repaired.

7   To check the cold start valve, leave the thermotime switch W terminal earthed, remove the cold start valve and reattach its connector. Take care not to break the gasket when withdrawing the cold start valve from the inlet manifold.

8   With fuel line and electrical connections connected to the valve, hold the valve over a glass jar and operate the starter for 10 seconds. The cold start valve should produce an even cone of spray during the time the thermotime switch is on.

9   Wipe dry the cold start valve nozzle with a clean non-fluffy cloth, then check that the valve does not drip or its body become damp over a period of one minute. If proved defective, renew the valve.

10 To check the thermotime switch, proceed as described in paragraphs 3 to 4 inclusive; the coolant should be at 30°C (86°F). If the

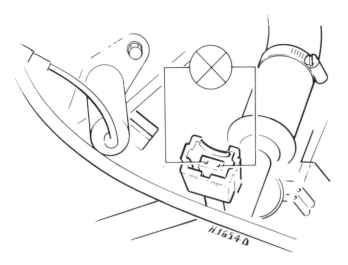

Fig. 3.41 Cold start valve check test lamp connections
(Sec 33)

switch needs to be cooled down to the temperature specified, remove it and immerse its base in cold water. When cooled, earth the switch to make the test.

11   Operate the starter for 10 seconds. The test lamp should light immediately and stay on for three seconds.

12   Refit the high tension lead onto the distributor, and reconnect the lead to the cold start valve.

34 Auxiliary air valve – checking

1   To carry out this test the engine coolant temperature must be below 30°C (86°F). Detach the distributor HT lead.

2   Detach the auxiliary air valve electrical plug and ensure that the contacts in the plug connector are in good condition (photo).

3   Connect up a voltmeter across the contacts of the plug connectors, start the engine and run at idle speed. The voltage reading must be a minimum of 11.6V. If a voltmeter is not available a test lamp check will suffice to check the voltage supply.

4   With the auxiliary air valve electrical plug still detached, leave the engine running at idle speed and pinch the air intake duct-to-auxiliary valve hose. The engine speed should drop.

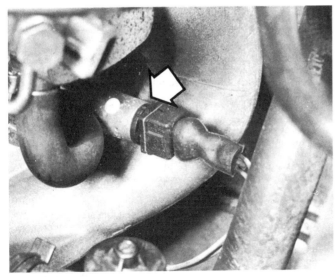

34.2 Auxiliary air valve (arrowed)

5   When the engine is warmed up to its normal operating temperature, reconnect the auxiliary valve plug then pinch the hose again. This time the engine speed should remain unaltered.

35 Warm-up valve – checking

1   Detach the distributor HT lead and earth it.

2   With the engine cold, detach the wiring connector from the warm-up valve (photo).

3   Connect a voltmeter across the terminals of the warm-up valve connector and operate the starter. The voltage across the terminals should be a minimum of 11.5 volts.

4   Switch the ignition off and connect an ohmmeter across the terminals of the warm-up valve (Fig. 3.42). If the meter does not indicate a resistance of about 20 to 26 ohm, the heater coil is defective and a new valve must be fitted.

35.2 Warm-up valve

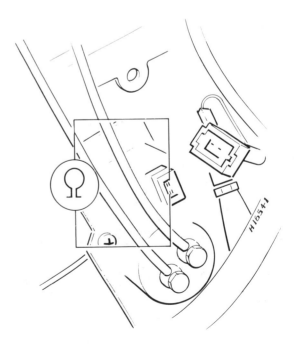

Fig. 3.42 Warm-up valve heater coil resistance test (Sec 35)

36 Cold acceleration enrichment system – description and checking

1   When the engine is cold (below 35°C/95°F), acceleration is improved by briefly richening the fuel mixture for a period of approximately 0.4 seconds. This cold acceleration enrichment will only operate if the thermotime switch, the diaphragm pressure switch and the throttle valve switch are shut off.

2   To check the system first check that the cold start valve is operational (Section 32).

3   Detach the wiring connector from the cold start valve and connect up a test lamp to its terminals.

4   Detach the wiring connector from the thermotime switch and connect a length of wire between an earth point and the connector number two terminal W (with the green and white wire). **Do not** earth the G terminal (red and black wire).

5   Run the engine and allow it to idle. The test lamp should not light up, but when the engine is quickly accelerated the test lamp should light up briefly (0.4 seconds) (Fig. 3.43).

6   If a fault is evident, check the wiring connections, the throttle valve switch and the diaphragm pressure switch.

7   The diaphragm pressure switch can be checked using an ohmmeter. Detach the wiring connector from the end of the diaphragm pressure switch, then start the engine and allow it to idle. Using the ohmmeter, check the resistance reading between the contacts. An infinity reading should· be given.

8   Accelerate the engine briefly and check that the resistance drops briefly and then returns to infinity. (Fig. 3.44).

9   To check the throttle valve switch, detach the switch lead connector and measure the resistance between the switch contacts. An infinity reading should be given.

10 Now slowly open the throttle valve to the point where the switch is heard to operate (it will click at this point). The ohmmeter should give a 0 ohm reading and the clearance between the throttle lever and the idle stop must be between 0.2 to 0.6 mm (0.008 to 0.024 in) – see Fig. 3.45.

11 If necessary adjust the switch by loosening the switch (underside of throttle housing) and positioning a feeler gauge blade of 0.4 mm (0.016 in) thickness between the lever and stop. Move the switch towards the lever until the point where the switch is heard to operate, then retighten the switch and check the adjustment.

12 If the throttle valve switch is being removed, prise the connector bracket apart to release the connector.

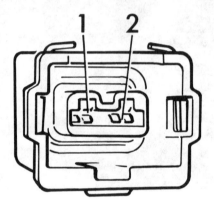

Fig. 3.43 Cold acceleration enrichment system check (Sec 36)

Cold start valve connector earth contact (2) (green/white wire to W terminal)
Do not earth contact 1

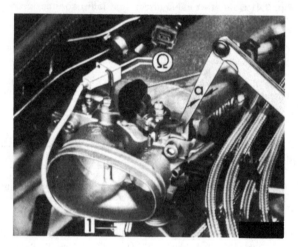

Fig. 3.45 Throttle valve switch check (Sec 36)

1   Throttle valve switch
(a) = 0.2 to 0.6 mm (0.008 to 0.024 in)

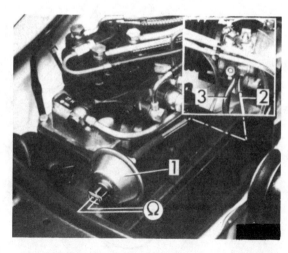

Fig. 3.44 Diaphragm pressure switch test (Sec 36)

1   Diaphragm pressure switch
2   Vacuum connection for switch (yellow)
3   Vacuum connection for spark control

37 Fuel injectors – checking

1   The injector may give trouble for one of four reasons. The spray may be irregular in shape; the nozzle may not close when the engine is shut down, causing flooding when restarting; the nozzle filter may be choked, giving less that the required ration of fuel; or the seal may be damaged, allowing an air leak.

2   To remove an injector for inspection, simply pull it free.

3   Inspect the rubber seal and, if it shows any signs of cracking, distortion or perishing, it must be renewed. If found to be defective, check the other injector seals, as they are likely to be in similar condition.

4   To check the performance of an injector, specialised tools are required for an accurate test. However, a basic check can be made as follows.

5   Hold the injector in a suitable measuring glass and plug up the injector location hole. Start the engine and let it idle on three cylinders and look at the shape of the spray. It should be of a symmetrical cone shape. If it is not the injector must be changed because the vibrator pin is damaged or the spring is broken. Shut off the engine and wait for 15 seconds. There must be no leak or dribble from the nozzle. If there is, the injector must be renewed, as dribble will cause flooding and difficult starting.

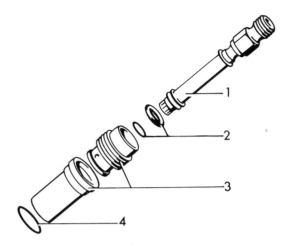

**Fig. 3.46 Air shrouded injector assembly (later models)
(Sec 37)**

1 Injector	3 Injector insert
2 Rubber rings	4 Washer

6 The injector cannot be dismantled for cleaning. If an injector is removed from the line the new one should be fitted and the union tightened to the specified torque.

7 When inserting the injector, lubricate the seal with petrol before fitting.

38 Airflow sensor plate and control plunger – checking

1 For the correct mixture to be supplied to the engine it is essential that the sensor plate is central in the venturi and that its height is correct. First run the engine for a period of about one minute.

2 Loosen the hose clips at each end of the air scoop and remove the scoop. If the sensor plate appears to be off-centre, loosen its centre screw and carefully run a 0.10 mm (0.004 in) feeler gauge round the edge of the plate to centralise it, then re-tighten the bolt (photo).

3 Raise the airflow sensor plate and then quickly move it to its rest position. No resistance should be felt on the downward movement; if there is resistance, the airflow meter is defective and a new one must be fitted.

4 If the sensor plate can be moved downwards easily, but has a strong resistance to upward movement, the control plunger is sticking. Remove the fuel distributor (Section 39) and clean the control plunger in fuel. If this does not cure the problem, a new fuel distributor must be fitted.

5 Release the pressure on the fuel distributor, as described in Section 39, and then check the rest position of the airflow sensor plate. The upper edge of the plate should be flush with the bottom edge of the air cone. It is permissible for the plate to be lower than the edge by not more than 0.5 mm (0.020 in), but if higher, or lower than the permissible limit, the plate must be adjusted.

6 Adjust the height of the plate by lifting it and bending the wire clips attaching the plate to the balance arm, but take care not to scratch or damage the surface of the air cone (photo).

7 After making the adjustment tighten the warm-up valve union and check the idle speed and CO content.

39 Fuel meter distributor – removal and refitting

1 Disconnect the battery terminals.

2 *Ensure that the vehicle is in a well ventilated space and that there are no naked flames or other possible sources of ignition.*

3 While holding a rag over the joint to prevent fuel from being sprayed out, loosen the control pressure line from the warm-up valve.

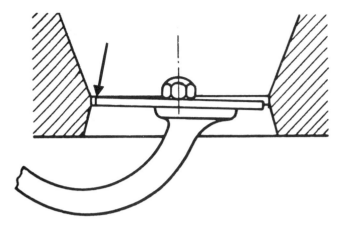

Fig. 3.47 Sensor plate position requirement (Sec 38)

Upper edge of plate (arrowed) must be flush with bottom of air cone

38.2 Top view of the airflow sensor plate

38.6 Airflow sensor plate adjustment clip (arrowed)

The control pressure line is the one connected to the large union of the valve.

4   Mark each fuel line, and its port on the fuel distributor. Carefully clean all dirt from around the fuel unions and distributor ports and then disconnect the fuel lines.

5   Unscrew and remove the connection of the pressure control line to the fuel metering distributor.

6   Remove the locking plug from the CO adjusting screw, then remove the three screws securing the fuel metering distributor (photo).

7   Lift off the fuel metering distributor, taking care that the metering plunger does not fall out. If the plunger does fall out accidentally, clean it in fuel and then re-insert it with its chamfered end downwards.

8   Before refitting the metering distributor, ensure that the plunger moves up and down freely. If the plunger sticks, the distributor must be renewed because the plunger cannot be repaired or replaced separately.

9   Refit the distributor, using a new sealing ring and after tightening the screws, lock them with paint.

10 Refit the fuel lines and the cap of the CO adjusting screw and tighten the union on the warm-up valve.

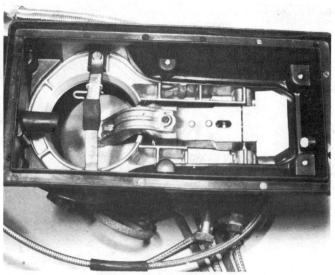

40.3 Airflow meter and fuel distributor unit (inverted)

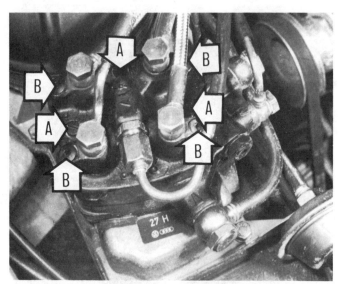

39.6 View showing the fuel distributor retaining screws (A)
Do not remove screws (B)

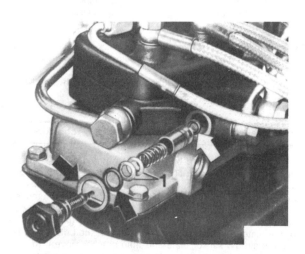

Fig. 3.48 Pressure relief valve components (Sec 41)

1   Shims   Arrows indicate O-rings

40 Airflow meter – removal and refitting

1   Remove the fuel lines from the distributor, as described in paragraphs 1 to 5 of the previous Section.

2   Loosen the clamps at the air cleaner and throttle assembly ends of the air scoop and take off the air scoop.

3   Remove the bolts securing the airflow meter to the air cleaner and lift off the airflow meter and fuel metering distributor (photo).

4   The fuel metering plunger should be prevented from falling out when the fuel metering distributor is removed from the airflow meter (see previous Section).

5   Refitting is the reverse of removing, but it is necessary to use a new gasket between the airflow meter and the air cleaner.

41 Pressure relief valve – removal, servicing and refitting

1   Release the pressure in the fuel system, as described in paragraphs 1 to 3 of Section 39.

2   Unscrew the non-return valve plug and remove the plug and its sealing washer.

3   Take out the O-ring, plunger and O-ring, in that order.

4   When refitting the assembly, use new O-rings and ensure that all

the shims which were removed are refitted. The number of shims fitted determine the system operating pressure. If for any reason the system pressure is suspect, it will be necessary to have a pressure check made by your VW dealer who should have the pressure gauge needed to check the pressure in the system. He will know the amount of shims required to correct the pressure should it be necessary.

42 Fuel lift pump – checking, removal and refitting

1   This is attached to the base of the fuel gauge sender unit fitted to the fuel tank (Fig. 3.49).

2   If this pump is suspected of malfunction, first check that pump wiring does not have an open circuit. Remove the luggage compartment floor covering and the circular cover in the floor for access to the sender unit and connections. Detach the wiring connector and make a continuity check between the centre wires and the outer (brown) wire of the connector (photo).

3   If the wiring proves correct, then check the pump relay and the pump fuse (number 5). Assuming the fuse to be in order, check the

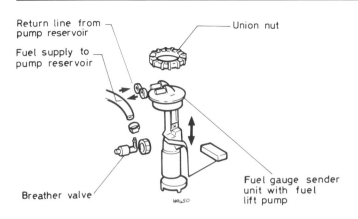

Return line from pump reservoir

Fuel supply to pump reservoir

Union nut

Breather valve

Fuel gauge sender unit with fuel lift pump

Fig. 3.49 Fuel tank sender unit – fuel injection system (Sec 42)

The tank and other associated components are identical to those used for carburettor engines (fig. 3.5)

the fuel tank on the right-hand side, the pump being housed in the pump reservoir (photo).
2   Disconnect the battery earth lead.
3   Raise the car at the rear and support it on axle stands.
4   Prise free the retaining clip and detach the pump wiring connector (photo).
5   Unscrew the damper unit from the rear end of the pump and detach the hose union, noting the washer each side of the union.
6   Undo the retaining nuts and washers and remove the adaptor.
7   Undo the three screws securing the pump retaining ring and withdraw the ring, followed by the pump unit.
8   Remove the O-ring and withdraw the strainer.
9   Refitting is a reversal of the removal procedure. Smear the O-ring with petrol when fitting and check that it does not get distorted when fitting.
10 When fitting the pump, position it so that its lug engages with the slot in the retaining ring.
11 If the pump non-return valve was removed from the rear end of the pump, refit it using a new seal washer. Also use a new seal washer each side of the hose union. Tighten the damper unit to the specified torque.
12 On completion check for any signs of leakage of fuel from the connections when the engine is running.

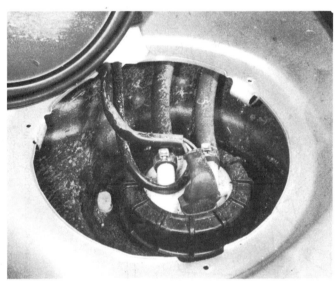

42.2 Fuel tank sender unit and connections

43.1 Fuel pump location and connections viewed from rear

relay by first detaching the Hall sender connector from the distributor (ignition).
4   Remove the fusebox and relay plate cover then pull free the pump relay from position 2.
5   Using a voltmeter, switch on the ignition and check the voltage reading between contact numbers 2 and earth, between contact numbers 2 and 1 and contacts 4 and 1. In each case battery voltage should show. Finally check the voltage between contacts 5 and 1; battery voltage should show.
6   Check that when the central connector wire is earthed briefly, there is a voltage drop. If the voltage does not drop on this test, check the ignition (TCI/H switch) unit. If the voltage does drop, renew the fuel pump relay. If the problem still persists, have the ignition Hall sender unit checked.
7   If after making the above checks and any repairs necessary the pump still malfunctions remove the sender unit, as described in Section 9 and detach the pump for renewal.
8   Refitting is a reversal of the removal procedure.

43 Fuel pump – removal and refitting

1   The fuel pump is located on the underside of the car, forwards of

43.4 Disconnect the wiring connector from the fuel pump

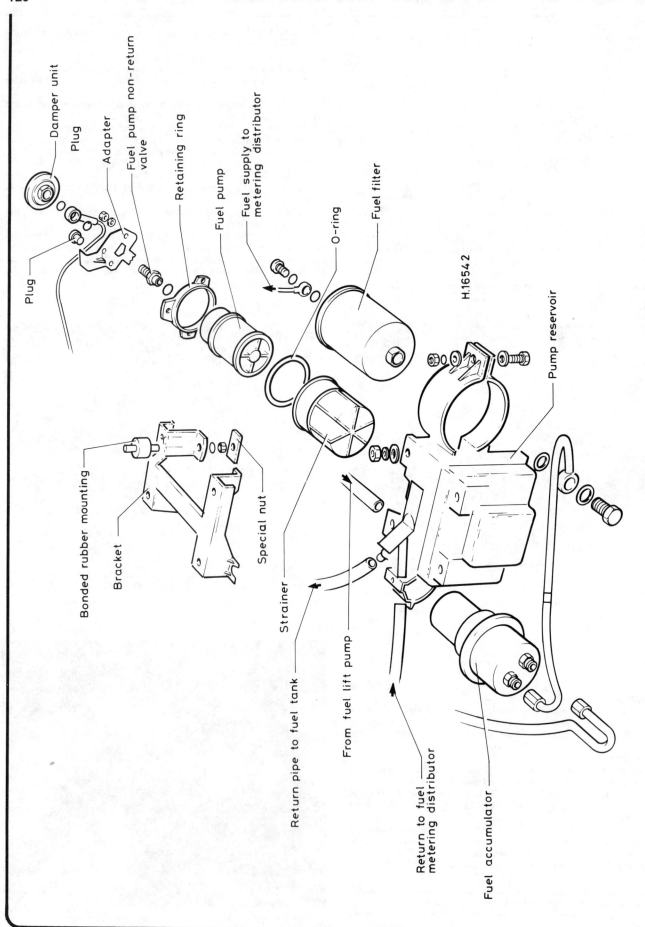

Fig. 3.50 Fuel pump and associated components – fuel injection system (Sec 43)

44 Fuel filter – removal and refitting

1 The fuel filter is mounted on the inboard side of the pump reservoir on the underside of the car at the rear just forward of the fuel tank (photo).
2 Disconnect the battery earth lead.
3 Raise the car at the rear and support it on axle stands.
4 At the forward end of the filter, undo the fuel accumulator hose union bolt and detach the union; collecting the washer each side of it.
5 At the rear end of the filter detach the fuel supply hose (to the metering distributor) by undoing the union bolt. Collect the washer each side of the union.
6 Loosen the filter retaining clamp and withdraw the filter.
7 Refitting is a reversal of the removal procedure. Renew the union washers and tighten the union bolts to the specified torque. Check that the arrow on the filter points in the direction of fuel flow.
8 On completion check for any signs of fuel leakage with the engine running.

44.1 Fuel filter unit clamp (A), hose to accumulator (B) and hose to metering valve (C)

45 Fuel accumulator – removal and refitting

1 The fuel accumulator is mounted on the outboard side of the fuel pump reservoir on the underside of the car at the rear, just forward of the fuel tank (photo).
2 Disconnect the battery earth lead.
3 Raise the car at the rear and support it on axle stands.
4 Disconnect the fuel pipes from their connections at the front end of the regulator.
5 Undo the clamp bolt and withdraw the accumulator.
6 Refit in the reverse order to removal. Check that the fuel line connections are clean before refitting. Check for fuel leaks on completion with the engine running.

46 Fuel tank and associated components – removal and refitting

1 The fuel tank and associated components can be removed and refitted in the same manner as that described for the carburettor models in Part A of this Chapter.
2 To check the breather valve blow through the hose (dotted arrow in Fig. 3.5) and push the lever in to see if the airflow opens, then shuts off as the lever is released. If defective renew the breather valve.

45.1 Fuel accumulator unit location

47 Inlet manifold – removal and refitting

Access to many of the fastenings and fittings of the manifold, on the bulkhead side in particular, is not good due to the restricted space and close proximity of associated adjacent components. It may therefore be found necessary to at least partially disconnect and remove the engine and gearbox units to gain access to certain items and allow clearance for the removal of the manifold. This being the case, refer to Chapter 1.
1 Disconnect the battery earth lead. Decompress the system as described in Section 39, paragraphs 2 and 3.
2 Disconnect the accelerator cable from the throttle valve and support/adjuster bracket on the manifold (Section 32).
3 Disconnect the wiring connector and the vacuum hose from the auxiliary air valve.
4 Disconnect the wiring and detach the warm-up valve.
5 Undo the hose clips and detach the vacuum hose from the connection on the end of the manifold (left side), and the rear side of the throttle valve housing (photo).

47.5 Vacuum hose-to-cylinder head connector

6 Disconnect the vacuum hoses from the front of the throttle housing, noting their connections.
7 Disconnect the injectors and hoses from the cylinder head, release them from the location clips and fold them back out of the way, where they will not get dirty.
8 Unclip and detach the intake ducting from the throttle housing.
9 Remove the bolts and disconnect the support bracket from the accelerator cable support/adjuster bracket and from the cam cover.
10 Disconnect the cam cover-to-inlet manifold breather hose.
11 Undo and remove the inlet manifold retaining bolts then carefully lift the manifold, together with the throttle housing, away from the cylinder head. Disconnect any wiring or hose connections still attached as it is withdrawn.
12 The throttle housing can be unbolted from the manifold and then withdrawn from it.
13 Refitting is a reversal of the removal procedure. Check that the mating faces are clean and use new gaskets. Tighten the securing bolts to the specified torque settings.
14 When reconnecting the accelerator cable, adjust it as decribed in Section 32.

15 Check that all connections are securely and correctly made before restarting the car.

48 Exhaust manifold – removal and refitting

Before starting to remove the manifold, refer to Section 24, paragraph 2 which concerns details on the special tool required to release and subsequently reconnect the exhaust manifold-to-downpipe securing clips. Unless this tool is available, the manifold is best removed and refitted by your VW dealer.
1 Remove the inlet manifold (Section 47).
2 Removal and refitting of the exhaust manifold is now similar to that described in Section 23 for carburettor variants.

49 Exhaust system

Refer to Section 24.

PART C: FAULT DIAGNOSIS

50 Fault diagnosis – fuel system (carburettor models)

Note: *High fuel consumption and poor performance are not necessarily due to carburettor faults. Make sure that the ignition system is properly adjusted, that the brakes are not binding and that the engine is in good mechanical condition before tampering with the carburettor.*

Symptom	Reason(s)
Fuel consumption excessive	Air cleaner choked, giving rich mixture
	Leak from tank, pump or fuel lines
	Float chamber flooding due to incorrect level or worn needle valve
	Carburettor incorrectly adjusted
	Idle speed too high
	Choke faulty (sticks on)
	Excessively worn carburettor
Lack of power, stalling or difficult starting	Faulty fuel pump
	Leak on suction side of pump or in fuel line
	Inlet manifold or carburettor flange gaskets leaking
	Carburettor incorrectly adjusted
	Faulty choke
Poor or erratic idling	Weak mixture (screw tampered with)
	Leak in inlet manifold
	Leak in distributor vacuum pipe
	Leak in crankcase extractor hose
	Leak in brake servo hose

51 Fault diagnosis – fuel system (fuel injection models)

Before assuming that a malfunction is caused by the fuel system, check the items mentioned in the special note at the start of the previous Section.

Symptom	Reason(s)
Engine will not start (cold)	Fuel pump faulty
	Auxiliary air device not opening
	Start valve not operating
	Start valve leak
	Sensor plate rest position incorrect
	Sensor plate and/or control plunger sticking
	Vacuum system leak
	Fuel system leak
	Thermotime switch remains open

Symptom	Reason(s)
Engine will not start (hot)	Faulty fuel pump Warm control pressure low Sensor plate rest position incorrect Sensor plate and/or control plunger sticking Vacuum system leak Fuel system leak Leaky injector valve(s) or low opening pressure Incorrect mixture adjustment
Engine difficult to start (cold)	Cold control pressure incorrect Auxiliary air device not opening Faulty start valve Sensor plate rest position faulty Sensor plate and/or control plunger sticking Fuel system leak Thermotime switch not closing
Engine difficult to start (hot)	Warm control pressure too high or too low Auxiliary air device faulty Sensor plate/control plunger faulty Fuel or vacuum leak in system Leaky injector valve(s) or low opening pressure Incorrect mixture adjustment
Rough idling (during warm-up period)	Incorrect cold control pressure Auxiliary air device not closing (or opening) Start valve leak Fuel or vacuum leak in system Leaky injector valve(s), or low opening pressure
Rough idling (engine warm)	Warm control pressure incorrect Auxiliary air device not closing Start valve leaking Sensor plate and/or control plunger sticking Fuel or vacuum leak in system Injector(s) leaking or low opening pressure Incorrect mixture adjustment
Engine backfiring into inlet manifold	Warm control pressure high Vacuum system leak
Engine backfiring into exhaust manifold	Warm control pressure high Start valve leak Fuel system leak Incorrect mixture adjustment
Engine misfires (on road)	Fuel system leak
Engine 'runs on'	Sensor plate and or control plunger sticking Injector valve(s) leaking or low opening pressure
Excessive petrol consumption	Fuel system leak Mixture adjustment incorrect Low warm control pressure
High CO level at idle	Low warm control pressure Mixture adjustment incorrect Fuel system leak Sensor plate and/or control plunger sticking Start valve leak
Low CO level at idle	High warm control pressure Mixture adjustment incorrect Start valve leak Vacuum system leak
Idle speed adjustment difficult (too high)	Auxiliary air device not closing

Chapter 4 Ignition system

For modifications, and information applicable to later models, see Supplement at end of manual

Contents

Specifications

General

System type .... 12 volt battery and coil, either contact breaker points or transistorized system

Firing order .... 1-3-4-2 (No 1 cylinder at crankshaft pulley end)

Coil

	Contact breaker ignition	Transistorized ignition
Primary winding resistance	1.7 to 2.1 ohm	0.52 to 0.76 ohm
Secondary winding resistance	7000 to 12 000 ohm	2400 to 3500 ohm

Distributor

Rotor rotation:
    1.05 and 1.3 litre .... Anti-clockwise
    1.6 and 1.8 litre .... Clockwise
Contact breaker gap (initial setting only) .... 0.4 mm (0.016 in)
Dwell angle (1.05, 1.3 and 1.6 litre):
    Setting .... 44 to 50° (50 to 56%)
    Wear limit .... 42 to 58° (47 to 64%)
Rotor cut-out speed:
    1.05 and 1.3 litre (if applicable) .... 6300 to 6700 rpm
    1.6 and 1.8 litre (carburettor engine) .... No figures available
    1.8 litre (injection engine) .... 6500 to 6900 rpm
Centrifugal advance:
    1.05 litre .... Begins at 1100 to 1500 rpm
    1.3 litre .... Begins at 1500 to 1900 rpm
    1.6 litre .... Begins at 1100 to 1300 rpm
    1.8 litre (carburettor engine) .... Begins at 900 to 1100 rpm
    1.8 litre (fuel injection engine) .... Begins at 1150 to 1450 rpm

Ignition timing (at idle)

1.05 and 1.3 litre .... 4 to 6° BTDC
1.6 and 1.8 litre (carburettor engine) .... 17 to 19° BTDC
1.8 litre (fuel injection engine) .... 5 to 7° BTDC

Spark plugs

Electrode gap:

1.05, 1.3 and 1.6 litre	0.6 to 0.8 mm (0.024 to 0.032 in)
1.8 litre	0.8 to 0.9 mm (0.032 to 0.035 in)

Type:

1.05 and 1.3 litre	Bosch W7D or W7DC
	Beru 14-7DU
	Champion N8Y
1.6 litre	Bosch W8D or W8DC
	Beru 14-8D, 14-8DU or RS33
	Champion N10Y
1.8 litre (carburettor engine)	Bosch W6DU
	Beru 14-6DU
	Champion N79Y
1.8 litre (fuel injection engine)	Bosch W6DO
	Beru 14-6DU
	Champion N79Y

Torque wrench settings

	Nm	lbf ft
Spark plugs	20	15
Distributor clamp bolt:		
1.05 and 1.3 litre	10	7
1.6 and 1.8 litre	25	18

1 General description

The ignition system may be of the conventional contact breaker type or the electronic transistorized type. On 1.05 and 1.3 litre engine variants the distributor is mounted on the left-hand (gearbox) end of the cylinder head and is driven direct from the camshaft. On 1.6 and 1.8 litre engine variants the distributor is mounted at the front (radiator) end of the engine and it is driven by a skew gear in mesh with the intermediate shaft of the engine.

To enable the engine to run correctly, it is necessary for an electrical spark to ignite the fuel/air mixture in the combustion chamber at

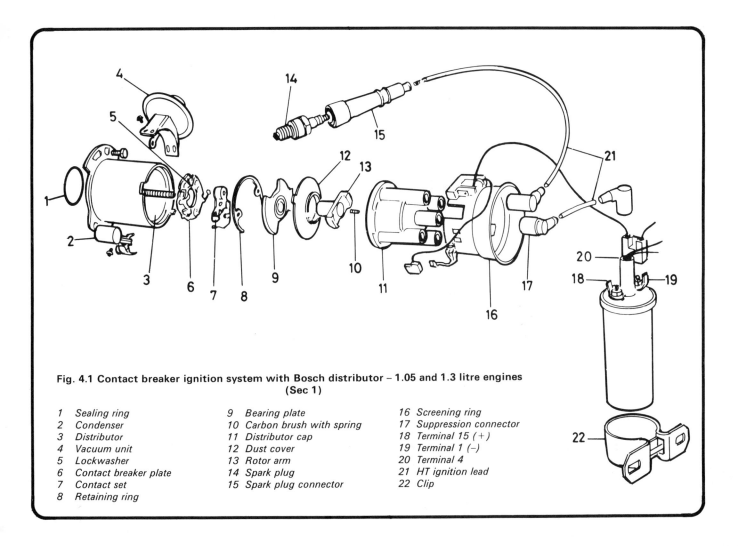

Fig. 4.1 Contact breaker ignition system with Bosch distributor – 1.05 and 1.3 litre engines
(Sec 1)

1	Sealing ring	9	Bearing plate	16	Screening ring
2	Condenser	10	Carbon brush with spring	17	Suppression connector
3	Distributor	11	Distributor cap	18	Terminal 15 (+)
4	Vacuum unit	12	Dust cover	19	Terminal 1 (–)
5	Lockwasher	13	Rotor arm	20	Terminal 4
6	Contact breaker plate	14	Spark plug	21	HT ignition lead
7	Contact set	15	Spark plug connector	22	Clip
8	Retaining ring				

exactly the right moment in relation to engine speed and load. The ignition system is based on feeding low tension voltage from the battery to the coil, where it is converted to high tension voltage. The high tension voltage is powerful enough to jump the spark plug gap in the cylinders many times a second under high compression, providing that the system is in good condition.

With the contact breaker type, the ignition system is divided into two circuits, the low tension circuit and the high tension circuit. The low tension (sometimes known as the primary) circuit consists of the battery, a lead to the ignition switch, a lead from the ignition switch to the low tension or primary coil windings (terminal +) and a lead from the low tension coil windings (coil terminal –) to the contact breaker points and condenser in the distributor. The high tension circuit consists of the high tension or secondary coil windings, the heavy ignition lead from the coil to the distributor cap, the rotor arm and the spark plug leads and spark plugs.

The system functions in the following manner. Low tension voltage is changed in the coil into high tension voltage by the opening and closing of the contact breaker points in the low tension circuit. High tension voltage is then fed via the carbon brush in the centre of the distributor cap to the rotor arm of the distributor, and each time it comes in line with one of the four metal segments in the cap, which are connected to the spark plug leads, the opening and closing of the contact breaker points causes the high tension voltage to build up, jump the gap from the rotor arm to the appropriate metal segment, and so via the spark plug lead to the spark plug, where it finally jumps the

spark plug gap before going to earth.

The transistorized ignition system functions in a similar manner, but an electronic sender unit replaces the contact points and condenser in the distributor, and a remotely-mounted electronic switch unit controls the coil primary circuit.

The ignition timing is advanced and retarded automatically, to ensure that the spark occurs at just the right instant for the particular load at the prevailing engine speed.

The ignition advance is controlled both mechanically and by a vacuum-operated system. The mechanical governor mechanism comprises two weights, which move out from the distributor shaft as the engine speed rises due to centrifugal force. As they move outwards they rotate the cam relative to the distributor shaft, and so advance the spark. The weights are held in position by two light springs, and it is the tension of the springs which is largely responsible for correct spark advancement.

The vacuum control consists of a diaphragm, one side of which is connected via a small bore pipe to the inlet manifold, and the other side to the contact breaker plate, or baseplate on transistorized distributors. Depression in the inlet manifold, which varies with engine speed and throttle opening, causes the diaphragm to move, so moving the contact breaker plate or baseplate, and advancing or retarding the spark. A fine degree of control is achieved by a spring in the vacuum assembly.

The contact breaker ignition system incorporates a ballast resistor or resistive wire in the low tension circuit, which is in circuit all the time

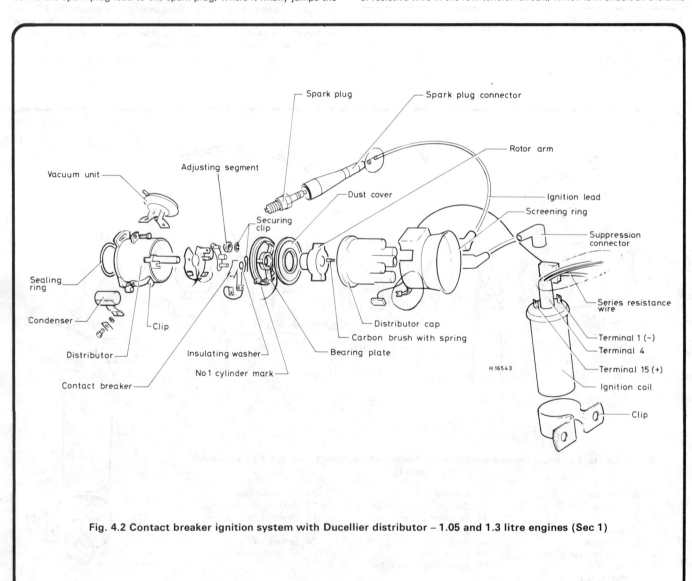

Fig. 4.2 Contact breaker ignition system with Ducellier distributor – 1.05 and 1.3 litre engines (Sec 1)

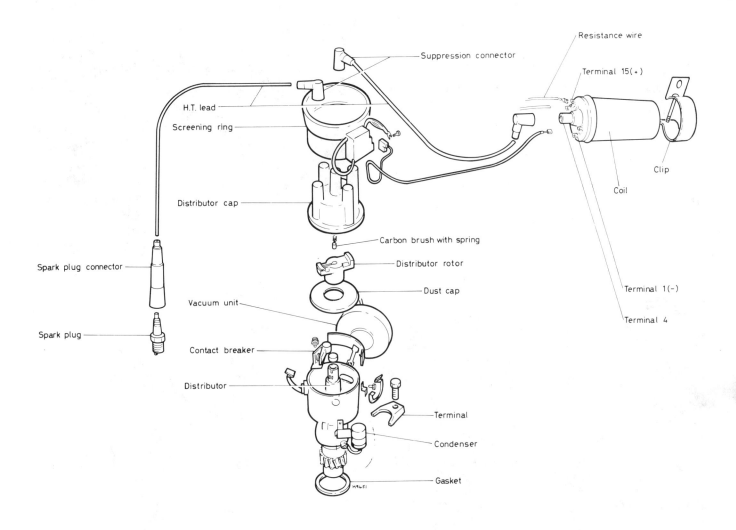

Fig. 4.3 Contact breaker ignition system – 1.6 litre engine (Sec 1)

that the engine is running. When the starter is operated, the resistance is bypassed to provide increased voltage at the spark plugs for easier starting.

2   Routine maintenance – ignition system

The following routine maintenance procedures must be carried out at the specified intervals given at the start of this manual.
1   Renew the spark plug. Set the electrode gap before fitting.
2   Clean and inspect the ignition system HT and LT lead connections. Renew if defective in any way.
3   Clean and inspect the contact breaker points midway between their specified renewal intervals. Check the adjustment of the contact breaker points and adjust if necessary, as described in Section 3.
4   Remove and renew the contact breaker points at the specified intervals (Section 4).
5   Check and, if necessary, adjust the ignition timing, as described in Section 12.

3   Contact breaker points – checking and adjustment

1   Disconnect the low tension lead from the terminal block on the

screening ring, and the earth strap spade connector on the distributor body. Release the two retaining clips and withdraw the distributor cap, complete with screen ring, from the distributor (photos).
2   Pull off the rotor arm and remove the dust cover (photo).
3   Using a screwdriver, prise open the points and check the condition of the faces (photo). If they are pitted and discoloured, remove them, as described in Section 4, and dress them using emery tape or a grindstone making sure that the surfaces are flat and parallel with each other. If the points are worn excessively, renew them. If the points are in good condition check their adjustment as follows.

Adjustment
4   Turn the engine with a spanner on the crankshaft pulley bolt until the moving contact point is fully open with the contact heel on the peak of one of the cam lobes.
5   Using a feeler blade, check that the gap between the two points is as given in the Specifications (photo). If not, loosen the fixed contact screw and reposition the fixed contact until the feeler blade is a firm sliding fit between the two points. In order to make a fine adjustment slightly loosen the screw then position the screwdriver in the fixed

contact notch and the two pips on the contact plate. With the gap adjusted tighten the screw (photos).

6   Using a dwell meter, check that the dwell angle of the contact points is as given in the Specifications while spinning the engine on the starter. If not, readjust the points gap as necessary – reduce the gap in order to increase the dwell angle, or increase the gap in order to reduce the dwell angle.

7   Clean the dust cover and rotor arm then refit them. Do not remove any metal from the rotor arm segment.

8   Wipe clean the distributor cap and make sure that the carbon brush moves freely against the tension of the spring. Clean the metal segments in the distributor cap, but do not scrape away any metal otherwise the HT spark at the spark plugs will be reduced. Also clean the HT leads and coil tower.

9   Refit the distributor cap and interference screen.

10 Start the engine and check that the dwell angle is as given in the Specifications both at idling and higher engine speeds. A decrease in dwell angle at high engine speeds indicates a weak spring on the moving contact points.

11 After making an adjustment to the contact points the ignition timing should be checked and adjusted as described in Section 12.

3.2 Remove the rotor arm

3.1A Detach the low tension lead (A), the earth strap (B) and release the securing clips (C)

3.3 Contact breaker points viewed through the window in the bearing plate – arrowed (Ducellier)

3.1B Withdraw the distributor cap and screen ring

3.5A Checking the contact breaker points gap with a feeler gauge

3.5B Adjusting the contact breaker points gap

4.2 Removing the bearing plate (1.05 and 1.3 litre)

3.5C Showing the two pips and notch for inserting a screwdriver when adjusting the contact breaker points gap

4 Contact breaker points – renewal

1 Proceed as described in paragraphs 1 and 2 in the previous Section.

2 Remove the screws and withdraw the bearing plate – 1.05 and 1.3 litre variants only (photo).

3 Disconnect the moving contact low tension lead from the terminal then remove the retaining screw and withdraw the contact breaker set from the distributor.

4 Wipe clean the contact breaker plate in the distributor and make sure that the contact surfaces of the new contact breaker set are clean. Lubricate the arm surface and moving contact pivot with a little multi-purpose grease. Use only a small amount, otherwise the contact points may become contaminated.

5 Fit the contact set on the baseplate and refit the retaining screw. Connect the low tension lead to the terminal.

6 Refit the bearing plate and tighten the screws (where applicable).

7 Adjust the contact breaker points as described in Section 3, paragraphs 4 to 11 inclusive.

5 Condenser – testing, removal and refitting

1 The condenser is fitted in parallel with the contact points and its purpose is to reduce arcing between the points and also to accelerate the collapse of the coil low tension magnetic field. A faulty condenser can cause the complete failure of the ignition system, as the point will be prevented from interrupting the low tension circuit.

2 To test the condenser, remove the distributor cap, rotor arm and dust cover and rotate the engine until the contact points are closed. Switch on the ignition and separate the points – if this is accompanied by a *strong* blue flash the condenser is faulty (a *weak* white spark is normal).

3 A further test can be made for short circuiting by removing the condenser and connecting a test lamp and leads to the supply lead and body (ie connecting the condenser in series with a 12 volt supply). If the test lamp lights, the condenser is faulty.

4 If the correct operation of the condenser is in doubt, substitute a new unit and check whether the fault persists.

5 To remove the condenser, unscrew the condenser retaining screw

5.5 Condenser location

and disconnect the low tension supply lead (at the coil on some models) (photo).
6   Withdraw the condenser far enough to disconnect the moving contact supply lead then withdraw the condenser. If the moving contact supply lead has insufficient length it will be necessary to remove the distributor cap, rotor arm, dust cover and bearing plate (if applicable) first.
7   Refitting is a reversal of removal.

6   Distributor (contact breaker type) – removal, overhaul and refitting

1   Disconnect the battery earth lead, then remove the distributor cap and screening ring (Section 3, paragraph 1).
2   Disconnect the vacuum hose.

1.05 and 1.3 litre engine
3   The distributor driveshaft is located in the end of the camshaft by an offset centre key and therefore the procedures described in paragraphs 4 and 5 are only necessary for checking purposes, such as when fitting a new distributor.
4   Turn the engine with a spanner on the crankshaft pulley bolt until the rotor arm points to the No 1 spark plug lead position. On some models a TDC groove is provided on the distributor body rim and the rotor arm must align with this. The mark on the crankshaft pulley should be aligned with the TDC pointer with No 1 piston (timing belt end) at TDC compression (photo).
5   Mark the distributor flange and cylinder head in relation to each other, then unscrew the bolts and withdraw the distributor (photo).

1.6 and 1.8 litre engine
6   Unscrew and remove the TDC sensor or blanking plug from the top of the gearbox (or automatic transmission) then turn the engine over so that TDC O mark on the flywheel or driveplate is visible and aligned with the timing pointer. The crankshaft pulley timing notch should be aligned with the TDC arrow mark on the timing case (Fig. 4.4). The rotor arm should be pointing to the timing mark on the top rim of the distributor body (Fig. 4.5).
7   Mark the distributor body in line with the tip of the rotor arm, and also mark the distributor body and cylinder block in relation to each other, then unscrew the clamp bolt and withdraw the clamp, followed by the distributor from the cylinder block. Note by how much the rotor turns clockwise. Remove the distributor body sealing washer (fit a new one on refitting).

6.5 Removing the distributor (1.05 and 1.3 litre)

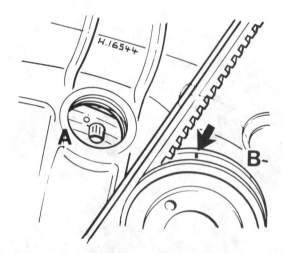
Fig. 4.4 TDC timing marks on the 1.6 and 1.8 litre engines (Secs 6 and 10)

A   Flywheel/driveplate   B   Crankshaft pulley

6.4 Crankshaft pulley mark at TDC (timing cover removed) – 1.3 litre

Fig. 4.5 Rotor arm aligned with TDC mark on the distributor body – 1.6 and 1.8 litre engines (Secs 6 and 12)

All models

8 The dismantling and overhaul of the distributor is similar on all models. The accompanying photos illustrate the distributor fitted to the 1.05 and 1.3 litre engine types.

9 Remove the contact breaker points (see Section 4).

10 On the Bosch distributor, mark the position of the guide pin then remove the bearing plate retaining ring (photos).

11 Before removing the vacuum unit on the Ducellier distributor, mark the adjustment segment position so that it can be correctly repositioned when reassembling.

12 Extract the circlip securing the vacuum unit arm to the contact breaker plate.

13 Remove the retaining screws, then unhook the arm and withdraw the vacuum unit. Note that the screws may also secure a suppression choke unit to the distributor body.

14 Remove the side screws, noting the location of the earth lead terminal, then remove the contact breaker plate by turning it anti-clockwise to align the lugs with the cut-outs (if applicable).

15 Wipe clean all the electrical components. Clean the distributor body assembly with paraffin then wipe dry.

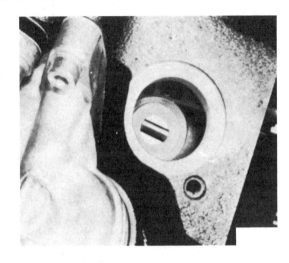

Fig. 4.6 Oil pump drive spigot position prior to refitting the distributor – 1.6 and 1.8 litre engines (Secs 6 and 12)

6.10A Correct fitted position of the bearing plate retaining ring (Bosch)

16 Check all components for wear and damage referring to Sections 3 and 5 for the contact breaker points, distributor cap, rotor and condenser.

17 Reassembly is a reversal of the dismantling procedure.

18 Realign the vacuum unit adjuster segment with the mark made when removing it (Ducellier).

19 On the Bosch distributor, locate the retaining ring guide pin as previously marked.

20 Lubricate the centrifugal mechanism and the contact breaker plate with a little multi-purpose grease. Adjust the contact breaker points, as described in Section 3.

21 To refit the 1.05 and 1.3 litre distributor reverse the removal procedure and align the timing marks made during removal before tightening the clamp bolts.

22 To refit the distributor on the 1.6 litre engine, first check that the oil pump drive spigot is correctly positioned with the spigot parallel to the crankshaft. This is visible through the distributor aperture (Fig. 4.6). Check that the TDC O mark is still aligned. Set the rotor arm to the position noted in paragraph 7, align the distributor body and cylinder block marks and insert the distributor. As the gears mesh, the rotor will turn anti-clockwise and point to the previously made mark. Refit the clamp and tighten the bolt. Reconnect the vacuum hose, and low tension lead or multi-plug (as applicable). Refit the TDC sensor or blanking plug.

23 Refit the distributor cap, then reconnect the battery negative terminal.

24 Check and if necessary adjust the ignition timing, as described in Section 12.

7 Transistorized ignition system (TCI-H) – precautions

1 On models equipped with transistorized ignition, certain precautions must be observed in order to prevent damage to the semi-conductor components and in order to prevent personal injury.

2 Before disconnecting wires from the system make sure that the ignition is switched off.

3 When turning the engine at starter speed without starting, the HT lead must be pulled from the centre of the distributor cap and kept earthed to a suitable part of the engine or bodywork.

4 Disconnect the battery leads before carrying out electric welding on any part of the car.

5 If the system develops a fault and it is necessary to tow the car with the ignition key switched on, the wiring must be disconnected from the TCI-H switch unit.

6 Do not under any circumstances connect a condenser to the coil terminals.

7 Take care to avoid receiving electric shocks from the HT system.

6.10B Removing the bearing plate retaining ring

138

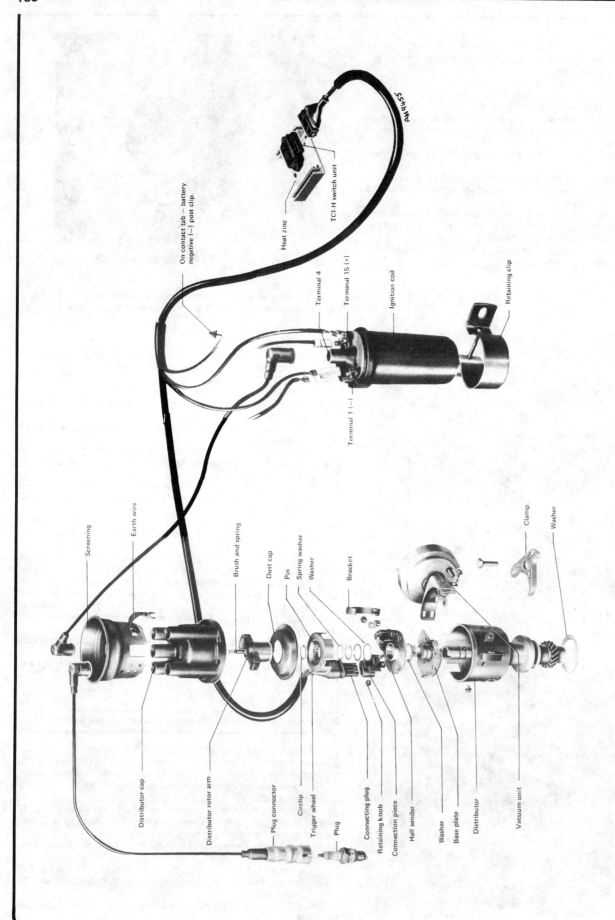

Fig. 4.7 Transistorized ignition system (TC1-H) – 1.6 litre (Sec 7)

The system for 1.8 litre engines is similar

8 Transistorized ignition switch unit – testing

1 When making this test the coil must be in good condition (Section 13).

2 Remove the plastic cover on the right-hand side of the plenum chamber for access to the switch unit (photos).

3 Disconnect the multi-plug from the switch unit and connect a voltmeter between terminals 4 and 2, as shown in Fig. 4.8.

4 Switch on the ignition and check that battery voltage, or slightly less, is available. If not, there is an open-circuit in the supply wires.

5 Switch off the ignition and reconnect the multi-plug to the switch unit.

6 Pull the multi-plug from the Hall sender on the side of the distributor (photo) then connect a voltmeter across the low tension terminals on the coil (Fig. 4.9).

7 Switch on the ignition and check that there is initially 2 volts, dropping to zero after 1 to 2 seconds. If this is not the case, renew the switch unit and coil.

8 Using a length of wire, earth the centre terminal of the distributor multi-plug briefly; the voltage should rise to at least 2 volts. If not, there is an open-circuit or the switch unit is faulty.

Fig. 4.8 Voltmeter connection when testing the transistorized ignition switch unit (Sec 8)

8.2A Carefully prise free the plastic cover ...

8.6 Multi-plug connection to the Hall sender on the side of the distributor

8.2B ... for access to the transistorized ignition switch

Fig. 4.9 Voltmeter connection to the coil when testing the transistorized ignition switch unit and coil (Sec 8)

9   Switch off the ignition and connect the voltmeter across the outer
terminals of the distributor multi-plug.
10 Switch on the ignition and check that 5 volts is registered on the
voltmeter.
11 If a fault still exists, renew the switch unit.
12 Switch off the ignition, remove the voltmeter, and reconnect the
distributor multi-plug.

9   Transistorized ignition Hall sender – testing

1   Check that the ignition system wiring and plugs are fitted correctly.
2   The coil must be known to be in good condition (Section 13), also
the TCI-H unit (see previous Section).
3   Pull the HT lead from the centre of the distributor cap, and earth the
lead to a suitable part of the engine or bodywork.
4   Pull back the rubber boot from the switch unit and connect a
voltmeter between terminals 6 and 3, as shown in Fig. 4.10.

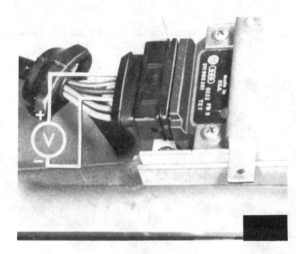

Fig. 4.10 Voltmeter connection when testing the
transistorized ignition Hall sender (Sec 9)

5   Switch on the ignition and turn the engine by hand in its normal
direction of rotation. The voltage should alternate from between 0 and
a minimum of 2 volts. If not, the Hall sender is faulty and must be
renewed.

10 Distributor (transistorized) – removal and refitting

1   Pull the high tension connection from the centre of the ignition coil
and remove the caps from the spark plugs.
2   Disconnect the screen (suppression) earth lead (photo) and
withdraw the screen, then release the clips and lift off the distributor
cap. Do not allow the cap retaining clips to fall inwards, as the rotor or
trigger wheel may be damaged.
3   Disconnect the control unit lead multi-plug by releasing the wire
retaining clip.
4   Unscrew and remove the TDC sensor or blanking plug from the top
of the gearbox or automatic transmission (photo) then turn the engine
over until the TDC O mark is aligned with the timing pointer (see Fig.
4.4). If not already marked, scribe an alignment mark on the distributor
body in line with the tip of the rotor arm. Also mark the distributor body
and cylinder block in relation to each other.
5   Pull the vacuum pipe(s) from the vacuum control unit, marking the
position of the pipes if there is more than one.
6   Remove the bolt and washer from the distributor clamp plate and
remove the clamp plate. Withdraw the distributor and remove the
gasket (this must be renewed) (photos).
7   Refitting is a reversal of the removal procedure. When the
distributor is in position, check that the rotor arm points to the No 1
cylinder mark before tightening the clamp plate bolt.
8   On completion check and if necessary adjust the ignition timing, as
described in Section 12.

10.2 Transistorized distributor earth lead connection to body (from
screen)

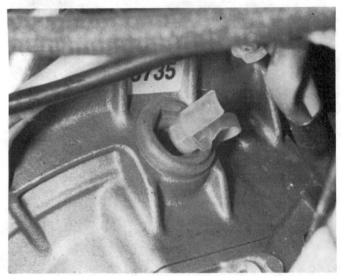

10.4 TDC blanking plug – manual gearbox

Fig. 4.11 Rotor arm position when at TDC – transistorized
ignition – 1.8 litre engine (Sec 10)

10.6A Transistorized distributor removal (1.8 litre)

11.2A Pull free the rotor ...

10.6B The gasket must be renewed

11.2B ... and lift off the dust cap

11 Distributor (transistorized) – dismantling, inspection and reassembly

Note: *Before commencing work, check that spare parts are available for this distributor. Specify whether the parts required will be for the 1.6 or 1.8 litre engine distributor.*

1 Wipe clean the exterior of the distributor.
2 Pull the rotor arm from the driveshaft then lift off the dust cover. Do not allow the cap retaining clips to touch the rotor during subsequent operations (photos).
3 Prise out the locking ring and withdraw the rotor up the shaft. Collect the locating pin (photos).
4 Undo the retaining screws securing the vacuum unit. Remove the vacuum unit, disengaging its operating arm (photo).
5 Remove the locking ring and collect the washers from the shaft.
6 Undo the cap clip and baseplate retaining screws from the body and lift out the Hall sender unit and the baseplate (photo).
7 Clean all the components and examine them for wear and damage.

11.3A Remove the locking ring and rotor ...

11.3B ... and the locating pin from the shaft groove (arrowed)

11.4 Vacuum unit removal

11.6 Hall sender unit, retaining ring and washers

8   Inspect the inside of the distributor cap for signs of burning, or tracking. Make sure that the small carbon brush in the centre of the distributor cap is in good condition and can move up and down freely under the influence of its spring.

9   Check that the rotor arm is not damaged. Use an ohmmeter to measure the resistance between the brass contact in the centre of the rotor arm and the brass contact at the edge of the arm. The measured value of resistance should be between 600 and 1400 ohm.

10 Suck on the pipe connection to the vacuum diaphragm and check that the operating rod of the diaphragm unit moves. Retain the diaphragm under vacuum to check that the diaphragm is not perforated.

11 Reassemble the distributor in reverse order of dismantling, but smear a little grease on the bearing surface of the baseplate and the Hall sender bearing surfaces.

12 Before fitting the rotor (trigger wheel) back over the shaft, locate the small engagement pin in the groove in the shaft. Smear the pin with grease to retain it in position. Align the indent in the rotor inner bore with the groove in the shaft and slide it down into position over the pin (photo).

13 On completion, rotate the distributor shaft by hand to ensure that it moves freely. If it doesn't then the rotor is possibly distorted and will need renewal.

11.12 Align the rotor indent with the groove in the shaft when refitting

12 Ignition timing – checking and adjustment

Note: *Accurate ignition timing is only possible using a stroboscopic timing light, although on some models a TDC sender unit is located on the top of the gearbox casing and may be used with a special VW tester to give an instant read-out. However, this tester will not normally be available to the home mechanic. For initial setting-up purposes of the conventional ignition system, the test bulb method can be used, but this must always be followed by the stroboscopic timing light method.*

Test bulb method (conventional ignition system only)

1   Remove the No 1 spark plug (crankshaft pulley end) and place the thumb over the aperture.

2   Turn the engine in the normal running direction (clockwise viewed from the crankshaft pulley end) until pressure is felt in No 1 cylinder, indicating that the piston is commencing its compression stroke. Use a spanner on the crankshaft pulley bolt, or engage top gear and pull the car forwards.

3   Continue turning the engine until the line on the crankshaft pulley is aligned with the pointer on the timing cover. If there are no marks on the timing cover, unscrew and remove the TDC sensor or blanking plug from the top of the gearbox or automatic transmission and align the timing

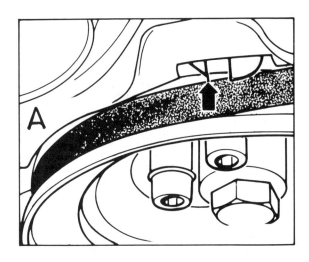

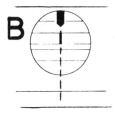

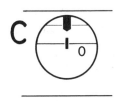

Fig. 4.12 Ignition timing marks (Sec 12)

A   1.05 and 1.3 litre
B   1.6 and 1.8 litre (carburettor models)
C   1.8 litre (fuel injection models)

mark (see Specifications) with the timing pointer. Refer to photo 6.4 or Fig. 4.5 and 4.6 as applicable.

4   Remove the distributor cap and check that the rotor arm is pointing toward the No 1 HT lead location in the cap.

5   Connect a 12 volt test bulb between the coil LT negative terminal and a suitable earthing point on the engine.

6   Loosen the distributor clamp retaining bolt.

7   Switch on the ignition. If the bulb is already lit, turn the distributor body slightly clockwise until the bulb goes out.

8   Turn the distributor body anti-clockwise until the bulb just lights up, indicating that the points have just opened. Tighten the clamp retaining bolt.

9   Switch off the ignition and remove the test bulb.

10   Refit the distributor cap and No 1 spark plug and HT lead. Once the engine has been started, check the timing stroboscopically, as follows, and adjust as necessary.

Stroboscopic timing light method

11   Run the engine until its normal operating temperature is reached.

12   On 1.05, 1.3 and 1.8 fuel injection engines disconnect and plug the distributor vacuum hose.

13   If there are no timing marks on the timing cover and crankshaft pulley, unscrew and remove the TDC sensor or blanking plug from the top of the gearbox or automatic transmission.

14   Connect the timing light to the engine in accordance with the manufacturer's instructions.

15   Connect a tachometer to the engine in accordance with the manufacturer's instructions.

16   Start the engine and run it at idling speed.

17   Point the timing light at the timing mark and pointer; they should appear to be stationary and aligned. If adjustment is necessary (ie the marks are not aligned), loosen the clamp retaining bolt and turn the distributor body to correct the ignition timing.

18   Gradually increase the engine speed while still pointing the timing light at the timing marks. The mark on the flywheel (or driveplate) or pulley should appear to move opposite to the direction of rotation, proving that the centrifugal weights are operating correctly. If not, the centrifugal mechanism is faulty and the distributor should be renewed.

19   Accurate checking of the vacuum advance (and retard where fitted) requires the use of a vacuum pump and gauge. However, providing that the diaphragm unit is serviceable, the vacuum hose(s) firmly fitted, and the internal mechanism not seized, the system should work correctly.

20   Switch off the engine, remove the timing light and tachometer, and refit the vacuum hose (where applicable).

13 Coil – description and testing

1   The coil is located on the bulkhead under the plenum chamber (photo). It should be periodically wiped clean to prevent high tension voltage loss through possible arcing.

13.1 Ignition coil location

2   To ensure the correct HT polarity at the spark plugs, the coil LT leads must always be connected correctly. The ignition lead from the fusebox must be connected to the positive (+) terminal 15, and the distributor lead (usually green) must be connected to the negative (−) terminal 1. Incorrect connections can cause bad starting, misfiring, and short spark plug life.

3   Complete testing of the coil requires special equipment. However, if an ohmmeter is available, the primary and secondary winding resistances can be checked and compared with those given in the Specifications. During testing the LT and HT wires must be disconnected from the coil. To test the primary winding, connect the ohmmeter between the two LT terminals. To test the secondary winding, connect the ohmmeter between the negative (−) terminal 1 and the HT terminal.

14 Spark plugs and HT leads – general

1   The correct functioning of the spark plugs is vital for the correct running and efficiency of the engine. The spark plugs should be renewed every 10 000 miles (15 000 km). However, if misfiring or bad starting is experienced before renewal is due, they must be removed, cleaned and regapped.

2   The condition of the spark plugs will also tell much about the overall condition of the engine.

3   If the insulator nose of the spark plug is clean and white, with no deposits, this is indicative of a weak mixture, or too hot a plug. (A hot plug transfers heat away from the electrode slowly – a cold plug transfers it away quickly.)

4   If the tip and insulator nose are covered with hard black-looking deposits, then this is indicative that the mixture is too rich. Should the plug be black and oily, then it is likely that the engine is fairly worn, as well as the mixture being too rich.

5   If the insulator nose is covered with light tan to greyish brown deposits, then the mixture is correct and it is likely that the engine is in good condition.

6   If there are any traces of long brown tapering stains on the outside of the white portion of the plug, then the plug will have to be renewed, as this shows that there is a faulty joint between the plug body and the insulator, and compression is being lost.

7   Plugs should be cleaned by a sand blasting machine, which will free them from carbon more thoroughly than cleaning by hand.

8   The spark plug gap is of considerable importance, as, if it is too large or too small, the size of the spark and its efficiency will be seriously impaired. The spark plug gap should be set to the figure given in the Specifications at the beginning of this Chapter.

9   To set it, measure the gap with a feeler gauge, and then bend open, or close, the *outer* plug electrode until the correct gap is achieved. The centre electrode should **never** be bent as this may crack the insulation and cause plug failure, if nothing worse.

10 Always tighten the spark plugs to the specified torque.

11 Periodically the spark plug leads should be wiped clean and checked for security.

15 Fault diagnosis – ignition system

By far the majority of breakdown and running troubles are caused by faults in the ignition system either in the low tension or high tension circuit. There are two main symptoms indicating ignition fault. Either the engine will not start or fire, or the engine is difficult to start and misfires. If it is a regular misfire, ie the engine is only running on two or three cylinders, the fault is almost sure to be in the secondary, or high tension circuit. If the misfiring is intermittent, the fault could be in either the high or low tension circuits. If the car stops suddenly or will not start at all it is likely that the fault is in the low tension circuit. Loss of power and overheating, apart from faulty carburation settings, are normally due to faults in the distributor or incorrect ignition timing.

Engine fails to start
Conventional and transistorized systems
1   If the engine fails to start and the car was running normally when it was last used, first check there is fuel in the petrol tank. If the engine turns over normally on the starter motor and the battery is evidently well charged, then the fault may be in either the high or low tension circuits. First check the HT circuit. If the battery is known to be fully charged, the ignition light comes on and the starter motor fails to turn the engine, check the tightness of the leads on the battery terminals and the security of the earth lead to its connection to the body. It is quite common for the leads to have worked loose, even if they look and feel secure. If one of the battery terminal posts gets very hot when trying to work the starter motor, this is a sure indication of a faulty connection to that terminal.

2   One of the most common reasons for bad starting is wet or damp spark plug leads and distributor. Remove the distributor cap. If condensation is visible internally dry the cap with a rag and wipe over the leads. Refit the cap.

3   If the engine on models fitted with conventional ignition still fails to start, check that current is reaching the plugs by disconnecting each plug lead in turn at the spark plug end. Hold the end of the cable with an insulated tool about 5 mm (0.2 in) away from the cylinder block, then spin the engine on the starter motor.

4   On engines with transistorized ignition remove each plug in turn and earth it to a suitable part of the engine with the HT cable connected. Spin the engine on the starter motor.

5   Sparking at the cables or plugs should be fairly strong, with a regular blue spark. If necessary remove the plugs for cleaning and regapping. The engine should now start.
Conventional system only
6   If there is no spark at the plug leads, take off the HT lead from the

centre of the distributor cap and hold it to the block as before. Spin the engine on the starter once more. A rapid succession of blue sparks between the end of the lead and the block indicates that the coil is in order and that the distributor cap is cracked, the rotor arm faulty or the carbon brush in the top of the distributor cap is not making good contact with the rotor arm.

7   If there are no sparks from the end of the lead from the coil, check the connections at the coil end of the lead. If this is in order start checking the low tension circuit. Commence by cleaning and gapping the points (Section 3).

8   Use a 12 volt voltmeter, or a 12 volt bulb and two lengths of wire. With the ignition switch on and the points open, test between the low tension wire to the coil (it is marked −) and earth. No reading indicates a break in the supply from the ignition switch. Check the connections at the switch to see if any are loose. Refit them, and the engine should run. A reading shows a faulty coil or condenser or broken lead between the coil and the distributor.

9   Remove the condenser from the distributor body, but leave the wiring connected. With the points open, test between the moving point and earth. If there now is a reading then the fault is in the condenser. Fit a new one and the fault is cleared.

10 With no reading from the moving point to earth, take a reading between earth and the negative (−) terminal of the coil. A reading here indicates a broken wire which must be renewed between the coil and distributor. No reading confirms that the coil has failed and must be renewed. For these tests it is sufficient to separate the contact breaker points with a piece of paper.

11 If the engine starts when the starter motor is operated, but stops as soon as the ignition key is returned to the normal running position the ballast resistor may have an open-circuit. Connect a temporary lead between the coil positive (+) terminal and the battery positive (+) terminal. If the engine now runs correctly, renew the resistor. Note that the ballast resistor or resistive wire must not be permanently bypassed otherwise the coil will overheat and be damaged.

Engine misfires
Conventional system only
12 If the engine misfires regularly, run it at a fast idling speed. Pull off each of the plug caps in turn and listen to the note of the engine. Hold the plug cap in a dry cloth or with a rubber glove as additional protection against a shock from the HT supply.

13 No difference in engine running will be noticed when the lead from the defective circuit is removed. Removing the lead from one of the good cylinders will accentuate the misfire.

14 Remove the plug lead from the end of the defective plug and hold it about 5 mm (0.2 in) away from the block. Restart the engine. If the sparking is fairly strong and regular, the fault must lie in the spark plug.
Conventional and transistorized systems
15 The plug may be loose, the insulation may be cracked, or the points may have burnt away, giving too wide a gap for the spark to jump. Worse still, one of the points may have broken off. Either renew the plug, or clean it, reset the gap and then test it.

16 Check the HT lead from the distributor to the plug. If the insulation is cracked or perished, renew the lead. Check the connections at the distributor cap.

17 Examine the distributor cap carefully for tracking. This can be recognised by a very thin black line running between two or more electrodes, or between an electrode and some other part of the distributor. These lines are paths which now conduct electricity across the cap, thus letting it run to earth. The only answer in this case is a new distributor cap.

18 Apart from the ignition timing being incorrect, other causes of misfiring have already been dealt with under the paragraphs dealing with the failure of the engine to start. To recap, these are that:

    (a) *The coil may be faulty giving an intermittent misfire*
    (b) *There may be a damaged wire or loose connection in the low tension circuit*
    (c) *The condenser may be short-circuiting (where applicable)*
    (d) *There may be a mechanical fault in the distributor (broken driving spindle or contact breaker spring where applicable).*

19 If the ignition timing is too far retarded it should be noted that the engine will tend to overheat, and there will be a quite noticeable drop in power. If the engine is overheating and the power is down, and the ignition timing is correct, then the carburettor should be checked as it is likely that this is where the fault lies.

Measuring plug gap. A feeler gauge of the correct size (see ignition system specifications) should have a slight 'drag' when slid between the electrodes. Adjust gap if necessary

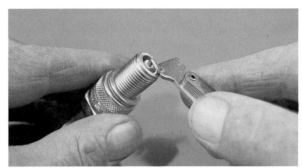

Adjusting plug gap. The plug gap is adjusted by bending the earth electrode inwards, or outwards, as necessary until the correct clearance is obtained. Note the use of the correct tool

Normal. Grey-brown deposits, lightly coated core nose. Gap increasing by around 0.001 in (0.025 mm) per 1000 miles (1600 km). Plugs ideally suited to engine, and engine in good condition

Carbon fouling. Dry, black, sooty deposits. Will cause weak spark and eventually misfire. Fault: over-rich fuel mixture. Check: carburettor mixture settings, float level and jet sizes; choke operation and cleanliness of air filter. Plugs can be re-used after cleaning

Oil fouling. Wet, oily deposits. Will cause weak spark and eventually misfire. Fault: worn bores/piston rings or valve guides; sometimes occurs (temporarily) during running-in period. Plugs can be re-used after thorough cleaning

Overheating. Electrodes have glazed appearance, core nose very white – few deposits. Fault: plug overheating. Check: plug value, ignition timing, fuel octane rating (too low) and fuel mixture (too weak). Discard plugs and cure fault immediately

Electrode damage. Electrodes burned away; core nose has burned, glazed appearance. Fault: pre-ignition. Check: as for 'Overheating' but may be more severe. Discard plugs and remedy fault before piston or valve damage occurs

Split core nose (may appear initially as a crack). Damage is self-evident, but cracks will only show after cleaning. Fault: pre-ignition or wrong gap-setting technique. Check: ignition timing, cooling system, fuel octane rating (too low) and fuel mixture (too weak). Discard plugs, rectify fault immediately

Chapter 5 Clutch

For modifications, and information applicable to later models, see Supplement at end of manual

Contents

Specifications

General

Type	Single dry plate, diaphragm spring pressure plate, cable operation. Automatic adjustment on 1.8 litre models
Free play at clutch pedal	15 to 20 mm (0.6 to 0.8 in)

Clutch friction disc diameter:

084 gearbox	180 mm (7.09 in)
020 4-speed gearbox	190 mm (7.49 in)
020 5-speed gearbox (4 + E)	200 mm (7.88 in)
020 5-speed gearbox (Sports)	210 mm (8.27 in)

Clutch components

Maximum inward taper:

084 gearbox	0.3 mm (0.012 in)
020, 4 and 5-speed gearbox	0.2 mm (0.008 in)

Maximum run-out allowance – measured 2.5 mm (0.099 in) from outer edge:

084 gearbox	0.4 mm (0.016 in)
020, 4 and 5-speed gearbox	0.3 mm (0.012 in)

Diaphragm spring finger scoring depth (maximum):

084 gearbox	0.3 mm (0.012 in)

Torque wrench settings

084 gearbox	Nm	lbf ft
Pressure plate	25	18
Flywheel	75	55
Guide sleeve	15	11

020, 4 and 5-speed gearbox		
Flywheel	20	15
Pressure plate:		
Bolt without shoulder	75	55
Bolt with shoulder	100	74

1 General description

The type of clutch fitted depends upon the gearbox; two distinct types of clutch type being used.

Clutch unit – 084 gearbox

With the gearbox, the clutch is of single dry plate type with a diaphragm spring pressure plate, and actuation is by cable. The pressure plate assembly is bolted to the flywheel and transmits drive to the friction disc which is splined to the gearbox input shaft. Friction linings are riveted to each side of the disc and radial damper springs are incorporated in the hub in order to cushion rotational shocks.

When the clutch pedal is depressed, the cable pulls the arm on the release shaft, and the release bearing is pushed along the guide sleeve against the diaphragm spring fingers. Further movement causes the diaphragm spring to withdraw the pressure plate from the friction disc which also moves along the splined input shaft away from the flywheel. Drive then ceases to be transmitted to the gearbox.

When the clutch pedal is released, the diaphragm spring forces the pressure plate back into contact with the friction disc which then moves along the input shaft into engagement with the flywheel. Drive is then transmitted directly through the clutch to the gearbox.

Wear of the friction disc linings causes the pressure plate to move closer to the flywheel and the cable free play to decrease. Cable adjustment must therefore be carried out as described in Section 2.

Clutch unit – 020, 4 and 5-speed gearbox

Unlike the more conventional clutch used on models with the 084 gearbox, on the 020 gearbox the clutch pressure plate is bolted to the crankshaft flange and the flywheel, which is dish shaped, is bolted to the pressure plate with the friction disc being held between them. This is in effect the reverse of the more conventional arrangement where the flywheel is bolted to the crankshaft flange and the clutch pressure plate bolted to the flywheel.

The release mechanism consists of a metal disc, called the release plate, which is clamped in the centre of the pressure plate by a retaining ring. In the centre of the release plate is a boss into which the clutch pushrod is fitted. The pushrod passes through the centre of the gearbox input shaft and is actuated by a release bearing located in the gearbox end housing. A single finger lever presses on this bearing when the shaft to which it is splined is turned by operation of the clutch pushrod, which in turn pushes the centre of the release plate inwards towards the crankshaft. The outer edge of the release plate presses on the pressure plate fingers forcing them back towards the engine and removing the pressure plate friction face from the friction disc, thus disconnecting the drive. When the clutch pedal is released the pressure plate reasserts itself, clamping the friction disc firmly against the flywheel and restoring the drive.

As the friction linings on the disc wear, the pressure plate will gradually move closer to the flywheel and the cable free play will decrease. Periodic adjustment must therefore be carried out as described in Section 2.

2 Clutch – adjustment

1 On some 1.6 and 1.8 litre models the clutch is automatically adjusted by means of a segment and pawl at the pedal end of the clutch cable. The only adjustment necessary with this type is when the cable has been disconnected for any reason or renewed; adjustment being made by depressing the clutch pedal several times once it is reconnected.

2 On all other models the clutch adjustment is made manually.

3 The clutch cable adjustment must be checked at the specified intervals given in Routine Maintenance at the front of this Manual. To do this, check the free play at the clutch pedal by measuring the distance it has to be moved in order to take up the slack in the cable. If the distance is not as given in the Specifications adjust the cable as follows.

084 gearbox

4 Locate the release arm on the gearbox clutch housing then turn the adjusting nut and half-round seating until the adjustment is correct (photo). Depress the arm if necessary to enable the nut to be turned

more easily, and if the nut is tight on its thread, hold the inner cable with a spanner.

5 Make sure that the adjusting nut is correctly seated in the release arm before finally checking the adjustment.

020 gearbox (manual adjustment)

6 Loosen the outer cable locknut at the gearbox bracket, then turn the serrated disc while holding the outer cable stationary until the pedal free play is correct (photo).

7 Fully depress the pedal several times and recheck the adjustment, then tighten the locknut. Lubricate the exposed part of the inner cable with a little multi-purpose grease.

2.6 Clutch cable adjuster (020 gearbox)

3 Clutch cable – renewal

1 Loosen the cable at the gearbox end, then disconnect the inner and outer cable from the release lever and support bracket (photo).

2 On models with an automatic adjustment clutch cable, pivot the segment forwards and retain it with the pawl, then disengage the cable from it. Withdraw the cable. On models with a manually adjusted clutch cable, unhook the inner cable from the clutch pedal, then withdraw the cable.

2.4 Clutch cable and release arm adjustment nut – arrowed (084 gearbox)

3.1 Inner cable to release lever viewed from underneath (020 gearbox)

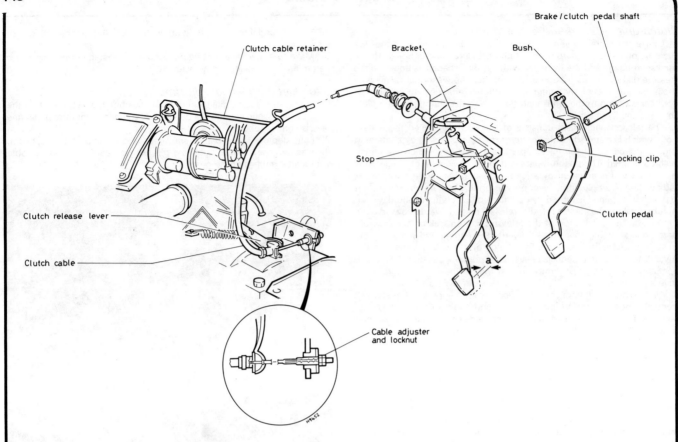

Fig. 5.1 Clutch pedal and cable components – 084 gearbox (Sec 3)

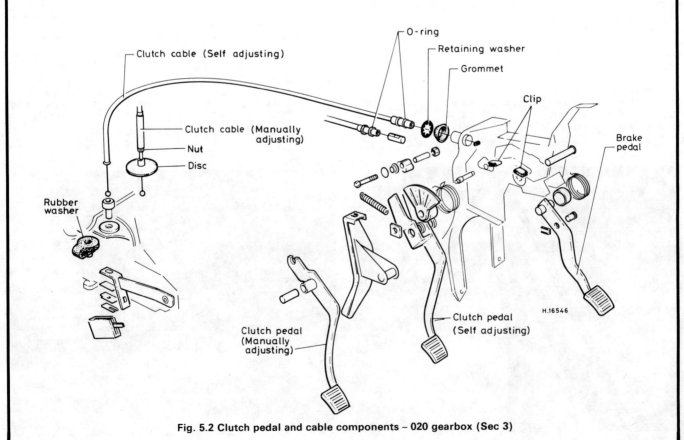

Fig. 5.2 Clutch pedal and cable components – 020 gearbox (Sec 3)

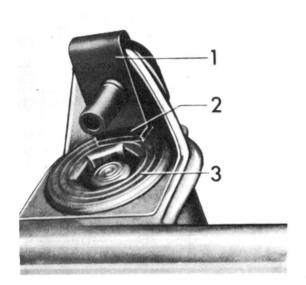

Fig. 5.3 Clutch cable guide rubber washer (1), sealing lip (2), and selector shaft end cap (3) – 020 gearbox (Sec 3)

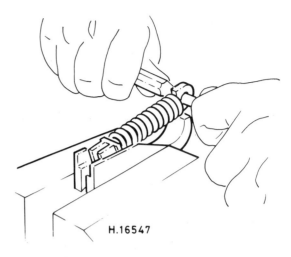

Fig. 5.4 Over-centre spring removal from retainer using VW tool 3113 (Sec 4)

3   If necessary, prise the guide sleeve from the rubber washer on the gearbox bracket, then remove the washer.

4   Check that the cable locating grommet and washer are secure in the bulkhead.

5   Fit the new cable using a reversal of the removal procedure. Check that the sealing ring is correctly located on the bulkhead end of the outer cable, and lightly lubricate the exposed parts of the inner cable with multi-purpose grease. Make sure that the inner sealing lip of the rubber washer on the gearbox bracket is parallel to the end cap, otherwise the gearbox breather may become blocked with foreign matter. Finally adjust the cable, as described in Section 2, or, on models with an automatic adjustment cable, simply depress the clutch pedal several times.

4   Clutch pedal – removal and refitting

1   Detach the clutch cable from the release arm on the gearbox clutch housing and then from the clutch pedal, as described in the previous Section.

2   On models with a manually adjusted clutch, prise free the clip from the end of the pedal shaft then carefully slide the pedal free from the shaft.

3   On models fitted with an automatic cable adjuster mechanism you will need to disconnect the steering column and move it to the left to allow pedal removal (refer to Chapter 10). When the steering column is moved to the left, you will then need to tension the over-centre spring and hold it under tension during its removal. A suitable spring retainer will therefore be required; if possible use VW special tool 3113.

4   With the over-centre spring held under tension, remove the clip, the over-centre spring and retainer. Now remove the circlip securing the pedal unit and withdraw the pedal, together with the segment and pawl.

5   Examine the shaft and pedal bush for wear and renew them if necessary. The bush is an interference fit in the pedal and can be removed or installed using a soft metal drift – make sure that the ends of the bush are flush with the ends of the pedal tube.

6   If dismantling the segment and panel on the automatic adjuster clutch type, note the orientation of the segment and pawl spring prior to dismantling. Check the pawl bush for excessive wear and renew any parts as necessary.

7   Refitting is a reversal of the removal procedure on both pedal types. Lubricate the pivot shaft with a little multi-purpose grease, also the pawl bush (automatic adjuster).

8   On manual cable adjuster models, recheck and adjust the cable, as described in Section 2. On models fitted with an automatic adjuster depress the pedal a few times to take up the adjustment.

5   Clutch (084 gearbox) – removal and refitting

1   Remove the gearbox, as described in Chapter 6.

2   Mark the pressure plate cover and flywheel in relation to each other.

3   Using an Allen key, unscrew the bolts securing the pressure plate cover to the flywheel in diagonal sequence one turn at a time (photo). If the key handle is pressed towards the centre of the flywheel it should be possible to loosen the bolts while holding the cover stationary by hand. If necessary hold the flywheel stationary using a screwdriver inserted in the starter ring gear teeth.

4   Withdraw the pressure plate assembly and the friction disc from the flywheel. Note that the friction disc hub extension containing the cushion springs faces the pressure plate.

5.3 Removing the pressure plate bolts (084 gearbox)

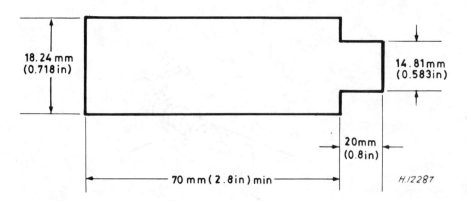

Fig. 5.5 Wooden mandrel dimensions for centralising the clutch friction disc – 084 gearbox (Sec 5)

5   Check the clutch components, as described in Section 6.

6   Before commencing the refitting procedure a tool must be obtained for centralising the friction disc, otherwise difficulty will be experienced when refitting the gearbox. Unlike the normal arrangement, the gearbox input shaft does not enter a bush or bearing in the rear of the crankshaft. If, however, the friction disc is not centralised the gearbox dowels will not be aligned correctly. If a centralising tool is not available a wooden mandrel may be made to the dimensions shown in Fig. 5.5.

7   Clean the friction faces of the flywheel and pressure plate, then fit the centralising tool to the crankshaft and locate the friction disc on it with the hub extension outwards (photo).

8   Fit the pressure plate assembly to the flywheel (in its original position if not renewed), then insert the bolts and tighten them evenly in diagonal sequence to the specified torque (photos).

9   Check the release bearing, as described in Section 7, before refitting the gearbox, as described in Chapter 6.

6   Clutch (084 gearbox) – inspection

1   Examine the surfaces of the pressure plate and flywheel for signs of scoring. Light scoring is normal, but if excessive the pressure plate must be renewed and the flywheel either machined or renewed.

2   Check the pressure plate diaphragm spring fingers for wear caused by the release bearing. If the scoring exceeds the maximum depth given in the Specifications, renew the assembly.

3   Using a straight-edge and feeler blade, check that the inward taper of the pressure plate does not exceed the maximum amount given in the Specifications (photo). Also check for loose riveted joints and for any cracks in the pressure plate components.

4   Check the friction disc linings for wear, and renew the disc if the linings are worn to within 1.0 mm (0.04 in) of the rivets.

5   Check that the friction disc damper springs and all rivets are secure, and that the linings are not contaminated with oil. Temporarily fit the

disc to the gearbox input shaft and check that the run-out does not exceed that given in the Specifications.

6   If the clutch components are contaminated with oil, the leak should be found and rectified. The procedure for renewing the crankshaft oil seal is described in Chapter 1, and the procedure for renewing the gearbox input shaft oil seal is described in Chapter 6.

7   Having checked the clutch disc and pressure plate, it is always worthwhile to check the release bearing with reference to Section 7.

7   Clutch release mechanism (084 gearbox) – removal, checking and refitting

1   With the gearbox removed, unhook the return spring from the release arm (photo).

2   Turn the release arm to move the release bearing up the guide sleeve, then disengage the two spring clips from the release fork and withdraw the bearing (photos).

3   Note how the springs and clips are fitted then prise the clips from the release bearing.

4   Spin the bearing by hand and check it for roughness, then attempt to move the outer race laterally against the inner race. If any excessive roughness or wear is evident, renew the bearing. Do not wash the bearing in solvent if it is to be re-used.

5   Using a splined key, unbolt and remove the guide sleeve from the clutch housing (photos).

6   Using a narrow drift, drive the release shaft outer bush from the clutch housing. Alternatively prise out the bush.

7   Pull the release shaft from the inner bearing then withdraw the shaft and arm from the housing (photo).

8   Check the bushes and bearing surfaces of the shaft for wear and also check the guide sleeve for scoring. The inner bush may be removed using a soft metal drift and the new bush driven in until flush.

9   Refitting is a reversal of removal, but lubricate all bearing surfaces with a little high melting-point grease. Make sure that the release shaft outer bush is correctly sealed with the tab located in the cut-out in the clutch housing (photo).

5.7 The friction disc and centralising tool (084 gearbox)

5.8A Fitting the pressure plate assembly (084 gearbox)

5.8B Clutch unit reassembled (084 gearbox)

6.3 Checking the pressure plate for taper

7.1 Clutch release arm return spring (084 gearbox)

7.2A The release bearing fitted to the arm (084 gearbox)

7.2B Release bearing and retaining clips (084 gearbox)

7.5A Unscrew the splined-head bolts (084 gearbox)

7.5B Withdraw the guide sleeve (084 gearbox)

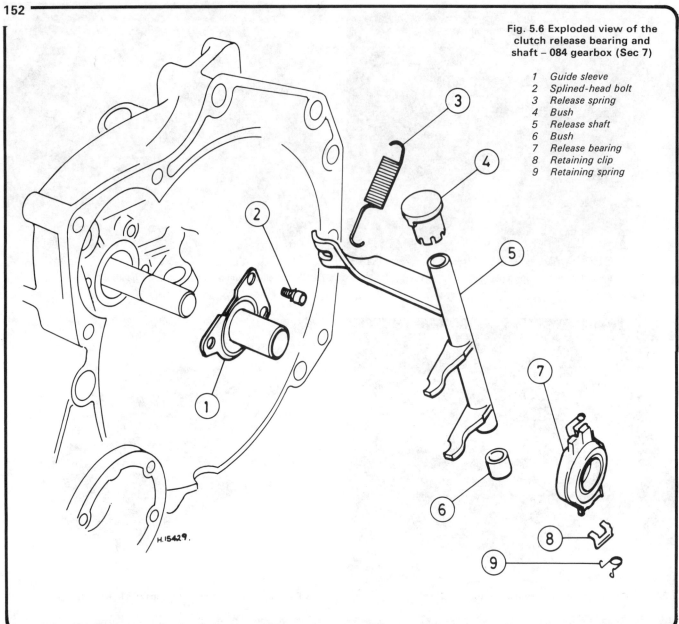

Fig. 5.6 Exploded view of the clutch release bearing and shaft – 084 gearbox (Sec 7)

1 Guide sleeve
2 Splined-head bolt
3 Release spring
4 Bush
5 Release shaft
6 Bush
7 Release bearing
8 Retaining clip
9 Retaining spring

H.15429.

7.7 Removing the release shaft (084 gearbox)

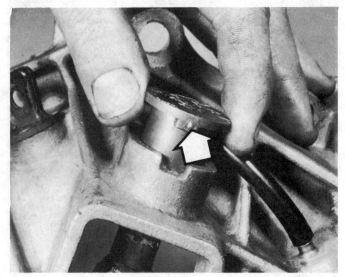

7.9 The location tab on the release shaft outer bush (084 gearbox)

8.2 Flywheel expanding peg for centering the pressure plate (020 gearbox)

8.4A Removing the clutch release plate (020 gearbox)

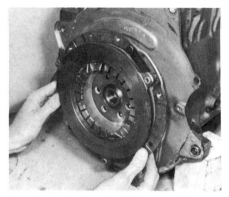

8.4B Removing the clutch pressure plate (020 gearbox)

8 Clutch (020 gearbox) – removal and refitting

1 Remove the gearbox, as described in Chapter 6.

2 Clamp the flywheel to prevent it turning, then undo the flywheel-to-pressure plate bolts in a progressive and diagonal sequence, releasing each one half a turn at a time until they are all slack and then take them out. The flywheel and the friction disc may now be removed, but note which way round the disc is fitted and also mark the flywheel and pressure plate in relation to each other, although centering pins are provided to ensure that the TDC mark on the flywheel is positioned correctly (photo).

3 Examine the pressure plate surface. If it is clean and free from scoring there is no reason to remove it unless the friction disc shows signs of oil contamination.

4 If the plate surface is defective then it must be removed. Note exactly where the ends of the retaining ring are located (the ring must be refitted this way later), and prise the ring out with a screwdriver. The release plate may now be removed (photo). The pressure plate is held to the crankshaft flange by six bolts fitted using a thread locking compound. These will be difficult to remove as they were tightened to a high torque before the locking fluid set, so the plate must be held with a clamp similar to that shown in Fig. 5.8 (photo). Once removed, these bolts must be renewed.

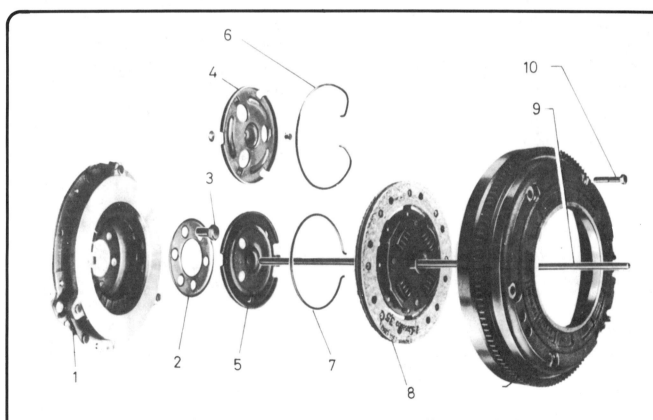

Fig. 5.7 Exploded view of the clutch components – 020 gearbox (Sec 8)

1 Pressure plate assembly	4 Release plate (200 and 210 mm diameter clutch)	6 Retaining ring (200 and 210 mm diameter clutch)	8 Friction disc
2 Packing plate			9 Pushrod
3 Bolt	5 Release plate (190 mm diameter clutch)	7 Retaining ring (190 mm diameter clutch)	10 Bolt

Fig. 5.8 Special VW tool for holding the pressure plate
stationary while unscrewing or tightening the retaining bolts
– 020 gearbox (Sec 8)

Fig. 5.9 Correct location of release plate retaining ring ends
(arrowed) on the 190 mm clutch – 020 gearbox (Sec 8)

8.5 Tightening the clutch pressure plate retaining bolts (020 gearbox)

Fig. 5.10 Correct location of the release plate retaining ring
ends (arrowed) on the 200 and 210 mm diameter clutch – 020
gearbox (Sec 8)

5   Refitting is a reversal of removal. Use thread locking compound on
the **new** bolts securing the pressure plate to the crankshaft flange (if
they were removed), and tighten them to the specified torque (photo).
Note that the bolt torque wrench setting differs according to bolt type,
which may or may not have a shoulder.
6   Make sure that the retaining ring is correctly seated (Figs. 5.9 and
5.10). Take care that no oil or grease is allowed to get onto the pressure
plate or friction surfaces. Where a new pressure plate is being fitted,
wipe the protective coating from the friction surfaces.
7   Lubricate the splines of the friction disc hub with a Moly paste or
spray lubricant, but do not get any lubricant onto the linings.
8   When refitting the friction disc, make sure the greater projecting
boss which incorporates the cushion springs is furthest from the
engine, then fit the flywheel over the pressure plate. Fit the securing
bolts and tighten them finger tight only.
9   The next operation is to centre the friction disc. If this is not done
accurately the gearbox mainshaft will not be able to locate in the
splines of the clutch disc hub, and it will be impossible to fit the
gearbox. The best centralising tool is VW 547 which fits in the flywheel
and has a spigot which fits exactly in the centre of the clutch disc hub
(Fig. 5.11). If you cannot borrow or hire tool VW 547 then we suggest

Fig. 5.11 Using VW tool 547 to centre the clutch friction disc
– 020 gearbox (Sec 8)

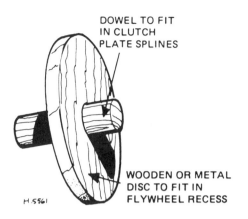

Fig. 5.12 Home-made tool for centralising the clutch friction disc – 020 gearbox (Sec 8)

DOWEL TO FIT IN CLUTCH PLATE SPLINES

WOODEN OR METAL DISC TO FIT IN FLYWHEEL RECESS

8.9 Using vernier calipers to check the friction disc centralisation

you make up a tool as shown in Fig. 5.12. Alternatively centre the disc using vernier calipers (photo). Once the friction disc is centred correctly, tighten the securing bolts in a diagonal sequence to the specified torque and check the centralisation again.

10 When refitting the transmission, put a smear of lithium based grease on the end of the clutch pushrod at the release plate end.

9 Clutch (020 gearbox) – inspection

1   The most probable part of the clutch to require attention is the friction disc. Normal wear will eventually reduce its thickness. The lining must stand proud of the rivets by not less than 0.6 mm (0.025 in). At this measurement the lining is at the end of its life and a new friction disc is needed.

2   The friction disc should be checked for run-out if possible. Mount the disc between the centres of a lathe and measure the run-out at the specified dimension from the outer edge, then compare the result with the Specifications. However, this requires a dial gauge and a mandrel. If the clutch has not shown signs of dragging then this test may be passed over, but if it has we suggest that expert help be sought to test the run-out.

3   Examine the pressure plate. There are three important things to

check. Put a straight-edge across the friction surface and measure any bow or taper with feeler gauges (see photo 6.3).

4   The rivets which hold the spring fingers in position must be tight. If any of them are loose the pressure plate must be scrapped. Finally, the condition of the friction surface. Ridges or scoring indicate undue wear and unless they can be removed by light application of emery paper it would be better to renew the plate.

5   The flywheel friction surface must be similarly checked.

6   So far the inspection has been for normal wear. Two other types of damage may be encountered. The first is overheating due to clutch slip. In extreme cases the pressure plate and flywheel may have radial cracks. Such faults mean that they require renewal. The second problem is contamination by oil or grease. This will cause clutch slip; but probably without the cracks. There will be shiny black patches on the friction disc which will have a glazed surface. There is no cure for this, a new friction disc is required. In addition it is **imperative** that the source of contamination be located and rectified. It will be either the crankshaft oil seal or the gearbox input shaft oil seal (or both!). Examine them and renew them as necessary – the procedures are given in Chapters 1 and 6.

7   Whilst the gearbox is removed, it is as well to check the release bearing for satisfactory condition – see Section 10.

10 Clutch release mechanism (020 gearbox) – removal and refitting

1   The clutch release mechanism is located in the gearbox end housing and is accessible after the removal of the end cover or plate (as applicable).

2   On 4-speed gearbox models, unbolt the end cover from the gearbox and remove the gasket (photo).

10.2 Removing the gearbox end cover (020 4-speed gearbox)

3   On 5-speed gearbox models, first support the engine/gearbox unit with a trolley jack, then disconnect the engine/gearbox front mounting and the gearbox rear mounting (see Chapter 1). Lower the jack a few inches to gain access to the end plate in the gearbox housing cover. Using a sharp instrument, pierce the endplate and lever it out from the gearbox. A new plate must be obtained (Fig. 5.13).

4   On both 4 and 5-speed gearboxes the release lever is located on the shaft by two circlips. Extract the circlips (photo).

5   With the clutch cable disconnected (see Section 3) withdraw the release arm and shaft from the gearbox and remove the lever and spring (photo).

6   Remove the release bearing (photo) and, on 4-speed models only, extract the guide sleeve. Removal of the pushrod on the 4-speed gearbox is not possible unless the unit is lowered.

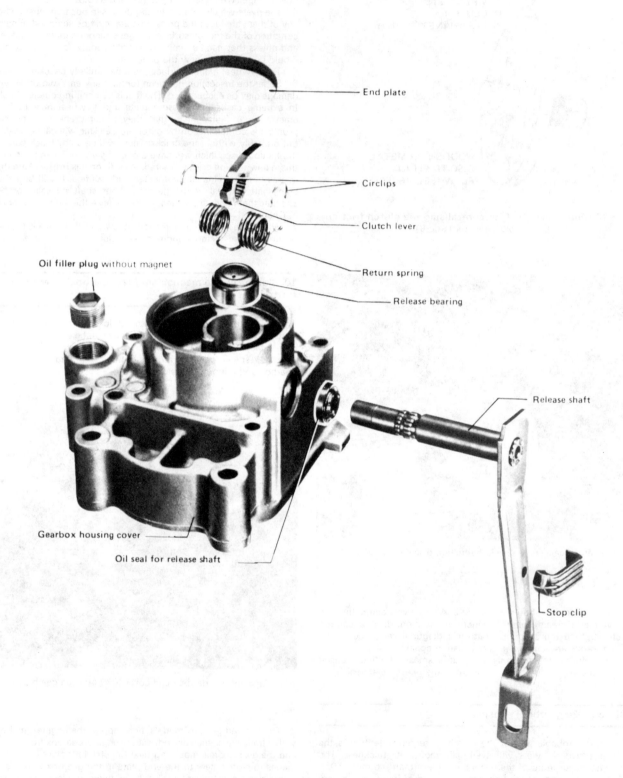

End plate

Circlips

Clutch lever

Return spring

Oil filler plug without magnet

Release bearing

Release shaft

Gearbox housing cover

Oil seal for release shaft

Stop clip

Fig. 5.13 Exploded view of the clutch release mechanism on the 020 5-speed gearbox (Sec 10)

10.4 Extracting the clutch release lever location circlips (020 4-speed gearbox)

10.5 Withdrawing the clutch release arm and shaft (020 4-speed gearbox)

10.6 Removing the clutch release bearing (020 4-speed gearbox)

7   Rotate the release bearing and check it for wear and roughness; renew it if necessary. Check the shaft oil seal for wear or deterioration, and if necessary prise it out and drive in a new seal squarely using a suitable length of metal tubing. Fill the space between the seal lips with multi-purpose grease.

8   Refitting is a reversal of removal. Note that the release lever and shaft have a master spline, and when fitting the return spring ensure that the bent ends bear against the casing with the centre part hooked over the release lever. Always fit a new gasket to the end cover on 4-speed models, and use a suitable length of metal tubing to drive the new endplate into the housing on 5-speed models.

11 Fault diagnosis – clutch

Symptom	Reason(s)
Judder when taking up drive	Loose engine/gearbox mountings Friction linings worn or contaminated with oil Worn splines on gearbox input shaft or friction disc
Clutch fails to disengage	Incorrect cable adjustment Friction disc sticking on input shaft splines (may be due to rust if car off road for long period) Faulty pressure plate assembly
Clutch slips	Incorrect cable adjustment Friction linings worn or contaminated with oil Faulty pressure plate assembly
Noise when depressing clutch pedal	Worn release bearing Worn splines on gearbox input shaft or friction disc
Noise when releasing clutch pedal	Distorted friction disc Broken or weak friction disc cushion springs

Chapter 6
Manual gearbox and automatic transmission

For modifications, and information applicable to later models, see Supplement at end of manual

Contents

Specifications

Manual gearbox

Type .... Four or five-speed (all synchromesh) and reverse. Drive to the front wheels by double CV jointed driveshafts

Gearbox identification codes
Four-speed (1.05 litre) 084 (6F)
Four-speed (1.3 litre) .... 084 (4F or 5F)
Four-speed (1.6 litre) 020 (4R)
Five-speed (1.6 litre) .... 020 (4T or 9A)
Five-speed (1.8 litre) 020 (8A)

Lubrication
Oil capacity:
    084 gearbox .... 2.2 litre (3.9 Imp pint)
    020 gearbox (four-speed) .... 1.5 litre (2.6 Imp pint)
    020 gearbox (five-speed) .... 2.0 litre (3.5 Imp pint)
Lubricant type .... Gear oil, viscosity SAE 80 (Duckhams Hypoid 80)

Ratios (:1)

	084 (All)	020 (4R)	020 (4T)	020 (9A)
1st	3.45	3.45	3.45	3.45
2nd	1.95	1.94	1.94	2.11
3rd	1.25	128	1.28	1.44
4th	0.89	0.90	0.90	1.12
5th	–	–	0.74	0.89
Reverse	3.38	3.16	3.16	3.16
Final drive	3.88 (4F)	3.66	3.66	3.66
	4.06 (5F)			
	4.57 (6F)			
Overall ratio in top gear	3.47 (4F)	3.33	2.73	3.27
	3.64 (5F)			
	3.82 (6F)			

Wear limits
084 gearbox:
Synchro ring gap clearance .... 0.5 mm (0.0197 in)
Input and output shaft maximum endfloat .... 0.5 mm (0.0197 in)
020, 4 and 5-speed gearbox:
Synchro-ring gap clearance .... 0.5 mm (0.0196 in)
3rd gear axial play circlips available:

	Thickness
Brown	2.5 mm (0.099 in)
Black	2.6 mm (0.102 in)
Bright	2.7 mm (0.106 in)
Copper	2.8 mm (0.110 in)
Brass	2.9 mm (0.114 in)
Blue	3.0 mm (0.118 in)

Automatic transmission
Type .... 3-speed epicyclic geartrain type, incorporating multi-plate clutches and brake, and one brake band. Drive from engine transmission by torque converter

Identification
Gearbox code number 010
Gearbox code letters:
1.6 litre .... TKA
1.8 litre .... TJA
Torque converter code letter:
1.6 litre .... M
1.8 litre .... K

Ratios (:1)
1st 2.71
2nd 1.50
3rd 1.00
Reverse 2.43
Final drive:
1.6 litre 3.41
1.8 litre 3.12

Lubrication
Lubricant type:
Gearbox .... Dexron type ATF (Duckhams D-Matic)
Final drive .... Hypoid gear oil viscosity SAE 90EP (Duckhams Hypoid 90S)
Capacity:
Total (from dry) .... 6.0 litre (10.6 Imp pint)
Service (drain and refill) .... 3.0 litre (5.3 Imp pint)
Final drive oil capacity .... 0.75 litre (1.3 Imp pint)

All transmissions

Torque wrench settings

	Nm	lbf ft
084 gearbox		
Clutch guide sleeve to gearbox	15	11
Gear lever stop plate nuts	10	7
Shift rod mounting coupling screw (new)	20	15
Shift rod clip nut	20	15
Gearshift housing bolts	15	11
Gearbox to engine:		
M12	75	55
M10	45	33
Driveshaft to gearbox	45	33
Bracket to engine	45	33
Gearbox mountings	60	44
Drive flange bolt	25	18
Clutch housing-to-gearbox bolts	25	18
Gearbox housing cover bolts	25	18
Relay lever bolt	35	26
Oil filler plug	25	18
Oil drain plug	25	18
Selector finger (to inner shift lever)	25	18

020 four-speed gearbox	Nm	lbf ft
Gearbox to engine (M12)	75	55
Starter motor to gearbox/engine	60	44
Driveshafts to flange	45	33
Left console to gearbox	35	26
Left console to subframe	60	44
Rear right console to engine	25	18
Gearbox to clutch housing	25	18
Peg bolt for selector shaft	20	15
Reverse shaft screw	20	15
Selector shaft end cap	50	37
Output shaft bearing plate bolts	40	30
Input shaft bearing clamp screw nut	15	11

020 five-speed gearbox		
Gear lever retaining plate nuts	10	7
Selector shaft lever nut	15	11
Gearbox housing cover bolts	25	18
Gearbox-to-clutch housing bolts	25	18
Selector shaft end cap	50	37
Reverse shaft securing bolt	20	15
Selector shaft securing bolt	20	15
First gear synchronizer screw	150	111
Bearing plate bolts	40	30
Oil filler plug	25	18

Automatic transmission		
Selector lever cable clamp nut	8	6
Driveshaft to flange	45	33
Converter to driveplate	35	26
Gearbox to engine	75	55
Left-hand gearbox mounting to gearbox	60	44
Left-hand gearbox mounting to console	35	26
Console (rear right) to engine	25	18
Oil pan bolts	20	15
Oil strainer (filter) cover bolts	3	2

1 Manual gearbox – general description

The manual gearbox is VW type 084 or 020, according to model. It incorporates four or five forward speeds and one reverse speed, with synchromesh engagement on all forward gears. The clutch withdrawal mechanism comprises a release arm and lever located at the outer end of the gearbox and a pushrod located in the input shaft.

Gearshift is by means of a floor-mounted lever connected by a remote control housing and shift rod to the gearbox selector shaft and relay lever.

The differential (final drive) unit is integral with the main gearbox and is located between the main casing and the bearing housing.

Drain and filler/level plugs are screwed into the main gearbox casing.

When overhauling the gearbox, due consideration should be given to the costs involved, since it is often more economical to obtain a service exchange or good secondhand gearbox rather than fit new parts to the existing gearbox.

2 Routine maintenance – manual gearbox

The manual gearbox requires the minimum amount of maintenance, only the following checks need be made at the specified intervals given at the front of this manual (see Routine Maintenance).

1 **Check gearbox for signs of oil leaks:** If possible run the vehicle over an inspection pit or raise and support it on axle stands to make this (and the following) check. Inspect the gearbox casing for any signs of serious oil leaks. Oil leakage from the transmission will necessitate further investigation and, if serious, must be remedied without delay. A very minor leak may be permissible providing regular checks are made to ensure that the leak does not get any worse and to ensure that the

gearbox oil level is maintained. Do not confuse gearbox oil leaks with engine oil leaks which may have sprayed onto the gearbox casing.

2 **Check the gearbox oil level.** The vehicle must be parked level for this check. Remove the oil level/filler plug from the gearbox (photo and Fig. 6.1) and check that the oil level is up to the base of the filler orifice. If not, top up with the specified grade of oil and refit the plug.

2.2 Using a key to remove the gearbox filler plug (020 5-speed gearbox)

Fig. 6.1 Gearbox filler plug location (arrowed) – 084 gearbox (Sec 2)

---

3 Manual gearbox (084) – removal and refitting

The following paragraphs describe how to remove the gearbox leaving the engine in situ. However, if work is necessary on the engine as well, the engine and gearbox can be removed as one unit then separated on the bench, as described in Chapter 1.

1   The gearbox is removed downwards, so the vehicle must be raised from the ground sufficiently to withdraw the box from underneath. The ideal is to work over a pit, but axle stands or similar support under the body can be arranged. However, note that you must be able to turn the wheels to disconnect the driveshafts. Do not raise it too much or you will be unable to get at the box through the opening in the engine compartment. About 600 mm (24 in) clearance is required.

2   Since the engine will be left unsupported at the rear it is necessary to make provision to take the weight of it. If you have a block and tackle or a garage crane this will be simple, but if not it is possible to make a simple support similar to that used in the VW agency. Fig. 6.2 shows a simple beam which is supported on either side of the vehicle in the channels which house the bonnet sides on the top of the wings. Alternatively the engine can be supported from underneath with blocks placed under the sump, but this method means that the car cannot be moved while the transmission is out of the car.

3   Remove the bonnet, as described in Chapter 11, and place it safely out of the way.

4   Having supported the engine, disconnect the battery negative lead.

5   For the purposes of this Section the front is the engine end of the gearbox, left and right are as if you are standing at the side of the car behnd the gearbox looking towards the engine.

6   Remove the left gearbox mounting complete and take it away. Drain the gearbox oil (photo).

7   Disconnect the clutch cable from the gearbox, with reference to Chapter 5.

8   Disconnect the earth strap at the gearbox support.

9   Unbolt and remove the starter motor, with reference to Chapter 9.

10 Disconnect the reversing light lead from the gearbox (photo).

11 Disconnect the speedometer drive cable from the gearbox by undoing the collar.

12 Unscrew and remove the upper engine-to-gearbox securing bolts.

13 Disconnect the inner ends of the driveshafts from the gearbox flanges, with reference to Chapter 7 and tie them out of the way.

14 Unbolt and remove the cover plate from the clutch housing (photo).

15 Unscrew and remove the remaining engine-to-gearbox bolts, noting the location of the rear mounting bracket.

16 Unscrew the rear mounting nut and remove the bracket, or leave the mounting on the bracket and remove the mounting bolts (photo).

17 Remove the screw from the shaft rod coupling and ease the coupling from the rod (photo). The screw threads are coated with a liquid locking agent and, if difficulty is experienced, it may be necessary to heat up the coupling with a blowlamp; *however, take the necessary fire precautions.* If required, remove the coupling ball from the adaptor.

18 Support the gearbox on a trolley jack (if available).

19 Now is the time to stop and think. Check round that nothing else

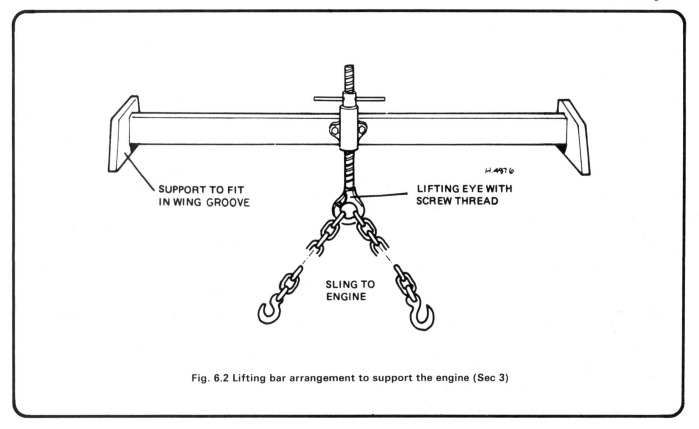

Fig. 6.2 Lifting bar arrangement to support the engine (Sec 3)

3.6 Gearbox drain plug (084 gearbox)

3.10 Disconnecting the reversing light switch wiring (084 gearbox)

3.14 Clutch housing cover plate (084 gearbox)

3.16 Gearbox rear mounting and securing bolt (084 gearbox)

3.17 Disconnect the shaft rod coupling (084 gearbox)

holds the box and assess just how it is to be lowered. Apart from the dowels the gearbox driveshaft splines are engaged in the friction disc of the clutch and the box must be pulled back to withdraw the shaft from the boss of the disc. This must be done carefully or there will be damage to the friction disc. In fact, if the box is not kept level the shaft will jam in the splines.

20 **Do not** try to separate the box from the engine by driving a wedge between the flanges, this will damage the castings. This box can be pulled backwards easily enough if it is kept level. The dowels are a tight fit and when they come out of the dowel holes the weight of the box will be felt suddenly. **Do not** let the box drop at all or you will damage the gear driveshaft splines, but move it away from the engine until you can see the shaft clear and then lower the box to the ground and remove it from under the car.

21 Refitting is a reversal of removal, but first smear a little molybdenum disulphide based grease on the splines of the input shaft, and make sure that the engine rear plate is correctly located on the dowels. Delay fully tightening the mounting nuts and bolts until the gearbox is in its normal position. Adjust the gearchange if necessary, as described in Section 9.

22 Adjust the clutch with reference to Chapter 5, and check that the gearshift mechanism operates correctly. Refill the gearbox with oil.

4 Manual gearbox (084) – dismantling and overhaul

Dismantling into major assemblies

1 Unscrew the drain and filler plug using a hexagon key and drain the remaining oil into a suitable container. Refit and tighten the plugs.

2 Remove the clutch release bearing and shaft, described in Chapter 5.

3 Unscrew and remove the reversing light switch (photo).

4 Temporarily screw two bolts into each drive flange, and, using a bar

to hold the flange stationary, unscrew each retaining bolt. Identify each flange left and right, then pull them from the differential (photos). Extract the coil spring thrust washer and taper ring from the drive flange location in the differential housing and keep them with their respective drive flanges.

5 The drive flange oil seals may be levered out and renewed, if necessary, either at this stage or later when servicing the differential unit. This job can also be done with the gearbox *in situ* once the drive flanges are removed, but note that the right and left-hand seals are dimensionally different.

6 Unscrew and remove the bolts securing the clutch housing to the gearbox housing. Make sure that all the bolts are removed from inside the clutch housing.

7 Support the gearbox with the clutch housing uppermost and, using a wooden mallet, tap the clutch housing from the gearbox housing and remove it (photo). If it is difficult to free the housing from the dowels, tap out the dowels first using a soft metal drift.

8 Remove the gasket, if applicable, and take the magnetic swarf collector from the slot in the bottom of the gearbox housing (photo).

9 Lift the differential from the gearbox housing (photo).

10 Support the gearbox housing with the end cover uppermost.

11 Unscrew and remove the bolts and remove the bearing end cover (photo). Identify the input and output bearing shims then remove them (photo). Do not interchange the shims otherwise the shaft endfloats will need adjusting on reassembly, Remove the gasket.

12 Using circlip pliers, extract the circlip from the end of the input shaft and remove the small shim.

13 Check that the selector rods are in the neutral position then, using an Allen key, unscrew the gear detent plugs with their washers, and extract the sleeves, springs and plungers (photos).

14 Unscrew the reverse relay cross-head bolt next to the detent holes (photo). The bolt is very tight and an impact driver will be required or, if not available, a cold chisel.

15 Invert the gearbox housing and remove the reverse selector rod and

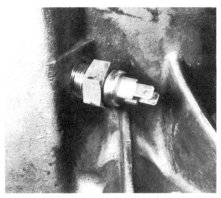

4.3 Removing the reversing light switch (084 gearbox)

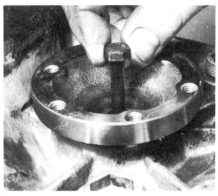

4.4A Remove the retaining bolt ...

4.4B ... and withdraw the drive flange (084 gearbox)

4.7 Clutch housing removal (084 gearbox)

4.8 Remove the magnetic swarf collector (084 gearbox)

4.9 Withdraw the differential unit (084 gearbox)

4.11A Removing the bearing end cover ...

4.11B ... and output bearing shim (084 gearbox)

4.13A Unscrew the gear detent plugs (084 gearbox)

4.13B Extract the sleeves, springs and plungers (084 gearbox)

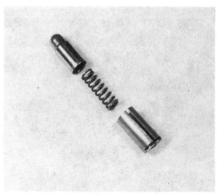

4.13C Detent sleeve, spring and plunger (084 gearbox)

4.14 Reverse relay pivot bolt

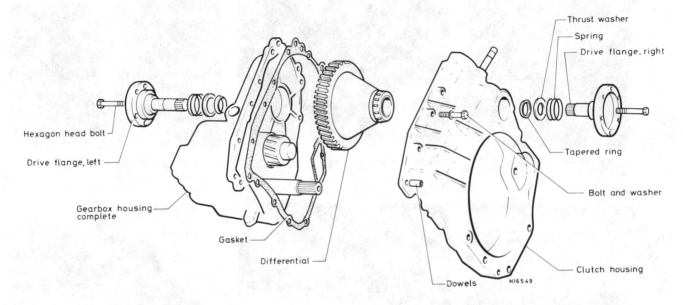

Hexagon head bolt

Drive flange, left

Gearbox housing complete

Gasket

Differential

Dowels

Thrust washer

Spring

Drive flange, right

Tapered ring

Bolt and washer

Clutch housing

H16549

Fig. 6.3 Gearbox, clutch housing and associated components – 084 gearbox (Sec 4)

relay lever (photos). The relay lever has slotted ends to engage the pin on the selector rod and the reverse gear.

16 The next stage is the removal of the input and output shafts, and the use of a bearing puller is described in the following paragraphs (photo). However, it is possible, with some difficulty, to remove the shafts simultaneously by tapping them through the end bearings without the use of a puller. This method is not recommended since damage to the housing may occur and also the synchromesh units can easily come apart causing further damage.

17 Make up a support plate and bolt it to the housing, together with packing washers, to hold the input shaft stationary (see Fig. 6.5). Locate an M16 hexagonal nut (arrowed) between the gearshift shaft and housing to jam the shaft.

18 Support the gearbox with the end bearings uppermost, then using a puller remove the input shaft bearing from the housing (photos).

19 Remove the support plate.

20 Using a large nut, or piece of wire, retain the selector relay shaft against the spring tension.

4.15 Remove the reverse selector rod

4.16 Suitable puller for removing the input shaft bearing

4.18A Fit the puller to the input shaft bearing ...

4.18B ... and withdraw the bearing (084 gearbox)

4.21 Input shaft and 3rd/4th selector rod removal (084 gearbox)

4.23A Extract the circlip from the output shaft ...

4.23B ... and remove the small shim (084 gearbox)

4.24A Pressing the output shaft from the bearing with a puller (084 gearbox)

4.24B Removing the output shaft and 1st/2nd selector rod (084 gearbox)

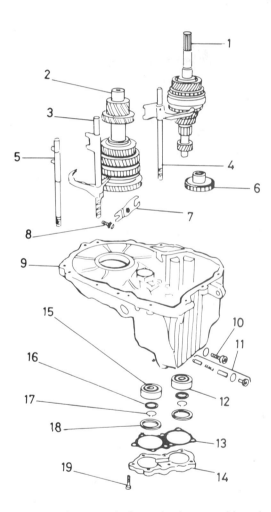

Fig. 6.4 Input and output shafts and selector rod locations in the gearbox housing – 084 gearbox (Sec 4)

1	Input shaft
2	Output shaft
3	Selector rod and fork, 1st and 2nd gears
4	Selector rod and fork, 3rd and 4th gears
5	Selector rod, reverse gear
6	Reverse gear
7	Relay lever
8	Pin for relay lever
9	Gearbox housing
10	Bolt – relay lever
11	Gear detent
12	Input shaft bearing
13	Gasket
14	Bearing cover
15	Output shaft bearing
16	Small shim
17	Circlip
18	Large shim
19	Hexagon bolt

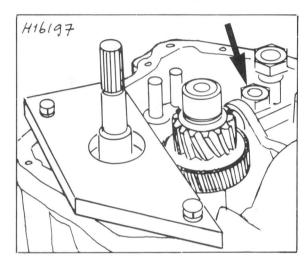

Fig. 6.5 Support plate location for removal of the input shaft bearing. Jam gearshift shaft with M16 hexagonal nut (arrowed) – 084 gearbox (Sec 4)

21 Move the input shaft away from the output shaft then lift it from the gearbox housing, together with the 3rd/4th selector rod and fork (photo). Lift the reverse gear slightly to allow the input shaft 1st gear to pass.

22 Remove the M16 nut or piece of wire used to jam the selector relay shaft.

23 Using circlip pliers, extract the circlip from the end of the output shaft and remove the small shim (photos).

24 Using the puller, press the output shaft from the end bearing and, at the same time, remove the 1st/2nd selector rod and fork, and the reverse gear (photos). Make sure that the selector rod and reverse gear do not become jammed.

25 Extract the interlock plungers from the gearbox housing.

26 Using a soft metal drift, drive the output shaft bearing from the gearbox housing. Keep both input and output shaft bearings identified.

Clutch housing – overhaul

27 Clean the housing and examine it for damage or cracks. If evident it will have to be renewed, but note that this will necessitate readjustment of the differential unit, as described in Section 7.

28 Prise the seal from the inner shift lever. If the lever is not being removed smear the lip of the new seal with grease then drive it squarely into the housing until flush with the rim of the bush. To remove the lever unscrew and remove the finger then slide out the lever (photos). Using a soft metal drift drive out the lever bush from the housing. Drive the new bush into position then smear the lever friction surfaces with molybdenum disulphide grease, slide it into the housing, fit the finger and tighten it to the specified torque. Fit the new seal as previously described.

4.28A Inner shift lever oil seal location (084 gearbox)

4.28B Inner shift lever location in the clutch housing (084 gearbox)

4.31 Output shaft needle roller bearing location in the clutch housing (084 gearbox)

4.32A Input shaft seal and bearing viewed from the engine side of the clutch housing (084 gearbox)

4.32B Input shaft bearing viewed from inside of clutch housing (084 gearbox)

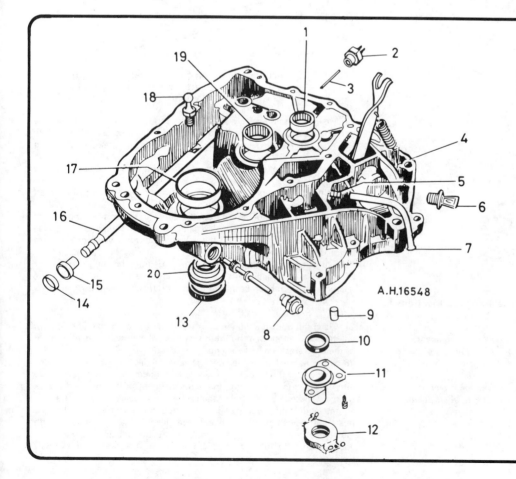

A.H.16548

Fig. 6.6 Exploded view of the clutch housing – 084 gearbox (Sec 4)

1   Needle bearing
2   Switch
3   Extension pin
4   Clutch housing
5   Breather connection
6   Plug
7   Breather pipe
8   Input shaft pinion
9   Starter bush
10 Input shaft seal
11 Guide sleeve
12 Release bearing
13 Driveshaft oil seal
14 Seal
15 Bush
16 Inner shift lever
17 Outer race taper roller bearing
18 Selector finger
19 Needle bearing
20 Seal sleeve

29 Unscrew the speedometer pinion bush and withdraw the pinion. Examine the components for wear and renew them if necessary. Insert the pinion then tighten the bush.
30 Check the starter bush in the housing. If necessary remove it with VW tools 228 b and 204 b, then drive in the new bush with a soft metal drift. Do not grease the bush.
31 Check the output shaft needle roller bearing and if necessary remove it with a puller. Support the housing and drive in the new bearing making sure that the end face with the lettering faces inside the gearbox (photo).
32 Check the input shaft needle roller bearing. To remove it, prise out the oil seal then use a soft metal drive from the outside of the gearbox to drive it out. Support the housing and drive in the new bearing flush, making sure that the end face with the lettering faces inside the gearbox (photos). Smear the lip of the new seal with grease then use a metal tube to drive it squarely into the housing as far as it will go. The fitted position of the seal is approximately 2.5 mm (0.098 in) below the housing surface.

Gearbox housing – overhaul

33 Clean the housing and examine it for damage or cracks. If evident the housing will have to be renewed, and will necessitate readjustment of the differential, and input and output shafts (Sections 7 and 8 respectively).
34 Check the selector relay shaft for excessive play in the bushes (photo). If evident unscrew the relay lever and withdraw the shaft from

4.34 Selector relay shaft location in the gearbox housing (084 gearbox)

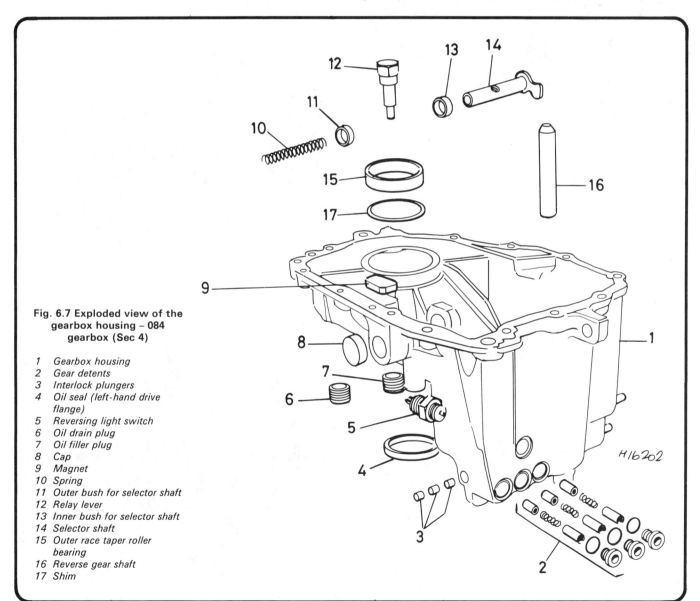

Fig. 6.7 Exploded view of the gearbox housing – 084 gearbox (Sec 4)

1 Gearbox housing
2 Gear detents
3 Interlock plungers
4 Oil seal (left-hand drive flange)
5 Reversing light switch
6 Oil drain plug
7 Oil filler plug
8 Cap
9 Magnet
10 Spring
11 Outer bush for selector shaft
12 Relay lever
13 Inner bush for selector shaft
14 Selector shaft
15 Outer race taper roller bearing
16 Reverse gear shaft
17 Shim

inside the housing. Remove the spring and use a soft metal drift to drive
out the cap. Also use a drift to drive out the bushes. Note that they are of
different lengths, the outer one being 9.5 mm long, the inner one 12 mm
long. Drive in the new bushes flush then fit the shaft, insert the relay
lever, and tighten it to the specified torque. Insert the spring and drive in
the retaining cap.

35 Check the reverse gear shaft and if worn excessively use a soft metal
drift to drive the shaft from the housing (photo) – heat the surrounding
housing with a blowlamp if difficulty is experienced. Apply a liquid
locking agent to the contact end of the shaft then heat up the housing
and drive in the shaft from the outside until the inner end is 83.3 mm
(3.280 in) from the mating face of the housing (Fig. 6.8).

5.1 Extracting the circlip from the input shaft (084 gearbox)

4.35 Reverse gear shaft location in the gearbox housing (084
gearbox)

5.2A Remove the 4th gear ...

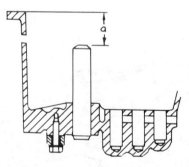

**Fig. 6.8 Reverse gear shaft fitting dimension – 084 gearbox
(Sec 4)**

$a = 83.3$ mm (3.280 in)

36 Check the input and output shaft bearings for wear by spinning
them, and renew them if there is excessive play or any roughness
evident. Also examine the end cover for condition.

37 Examine the selector rods and forks for damage and check the
reverse gear for bore wear and chipping or pitting of the teeth. Renew
the components as necessary.

5 Input and output shafts (084 gearbox) – servicing

Input shaft

1   Using circlip pliers extract the circlip from the splined end of the
input shaft (photo).

2   Withdraw the 4th gear and needle bearing (photos).

5.2B ... and needle bearing (084 gearbox)

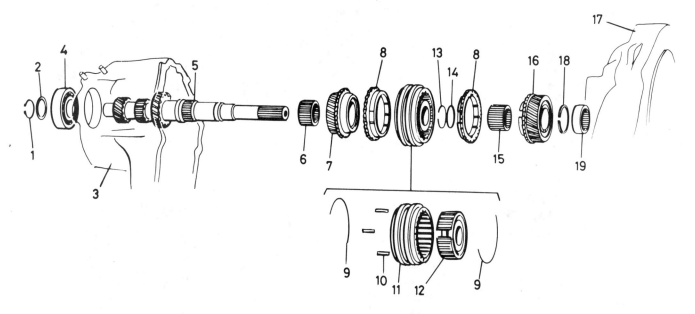

Fig. 6.9 Exploded view of the input shaft assembly – 084 gearbox (Sec 5)

1 Circlip	6 Needle bearing for 3rd gear	10 Key	15 Needle bearing for 4th gear
2 Shim	7 3rd speed gear	11 Sleeve	16 4th gear
3 Gearbox housing	8 Synchro-rings for 3rd and	12 Synchro-hub	17 Clutch housing
4 Grooved ball-bearing	4th gears	13 Circlip	18 Circlip
5 Input shaft	9 Spring	14 Thrust washer	19 Needle bearing

3 Remove the 4th synchro-ring (photo).
4 Remove the thrust washer (photo) then, using circlip pliers, remove the circlip from the 3rd/4th synchro unit (photo). Do not overstretch the circlip.
5 Using a puller beneath the 3rd gear, pull off the gear, together with the 3rd/4th synchro unit (photo). When removed, separate the components and remove the 3rd synchro-ring.
6 Remove the 3rd gear needle bearing (photos).
7 Clean the components in paraffin and examine them for wear and damage. Check the gearteeth for pitting, and similarly check the needle rollers. Renew the components as necessary.
8 Servicing of the synchro units is described in Section 6.
9 Commence reassembly by locating the 3rd gear needle bearing on the input shaft. Lubricate it with gear oil.
10 Fit the 3rd gear (photo).
11 Locate the 3rd synchro ring on the 3rd/4th synchro unit with the cutouts engaged with the keys. Then, using a puller, press the synchro

unit onto the splines (photos). Alternatively use a metal tube to drive it on. Make sure that the groove on the side of the hub will face the 4th gear position.
12 Fit the circlip in the groove followed by the thrust washer.
13 Locate the 4th synchro ring on the 3rd/4th synchro unit with the cutouts engaged with the keys.
14 Locate the 4th gear needle bearing on the shaft and lubricate it with gear oil, then fit the 4th gear.
15 Fit the circlip in the groove, making sure that it is correctly seated (photo).

Output shaft

16 Using circlip pliers, extract the circlip from the end of the output shaft, and remove the thrust washer (photos). Note that the circlip must be renewed on reassembly.
17 Remove the 1st gear and needle roller bearing (photos).

5.3 Removing the 4th synchro ring (084 gearbox)   5.4A Remove the thrust washer ...   5.4B ... and circlip (084 gearbox)

5.5 Pulling off the 3rd gear and 3rd/4th synchro unit (084 gearbox)

5.6A 3rd gear needle bearing location (084 gearbox)

5.6B Input shaft with gears removed (084 gearbox)

5.10 Fitting the 3rd gear on the input shaft (084 gearbox)

5.11 Fitting the 3rd gear synchro ring and 3rd/4th synchro unit to the input shaft (084 gearbox)

5.15 Circlip fitted to 4th gear

5.16A Remove the circlip ...

5.16B ... and thrust washer from the output shaft (084 gearbox)

5.17A Remove 1st gear ...

5.17B ... and needle roller bearing (084 gearbox)

5.18 Remove the 1st gear synchro ring (084 gearbox)

5.19A Remove the thrust washer ...

5.19B ... and circlip (084 gearbox)

5.21A Remove the 2nd gear needle bearing (084 gearbox)

5.21B Output shaft with gears removed (084 gearbox)

18 Remove the 1st synchro-ring (photo).

19 Remove the thrust washer then, using circlip pliers, remove the circlip from the 1st/2nd synchro unit (photos). Renew this circlip when reassembling.

20 Using a puller beneath the 2nd gear, pull off the gear, together with the 1st/2nd synchro unit. When removed, separate the components and remove the 2nd synchro-ring.

21 Remove the 2nd gear needle bearing (photos).

22 Clean the components in paraffin and examine them for wear and damage. Check the gearteeth for pitting, and similarly check the needle rollers. Renew the components as necessary. If the 3rd and/or 4th gears require renewal it is recommended that the output shaft is taken to a VW garage as a press is necessary and the new gears must be heated to 120°C (248°) before fitting. Note that the shoulders on the two gears are adjacent. The gear on the output shaft and the final drive crownwheel are not matched so, if necessary, the output shaft can be renewed separately, but it will be necessary to check and possibly adjust the output shaft endfloat adjustment, as described in Section 8. In addition,

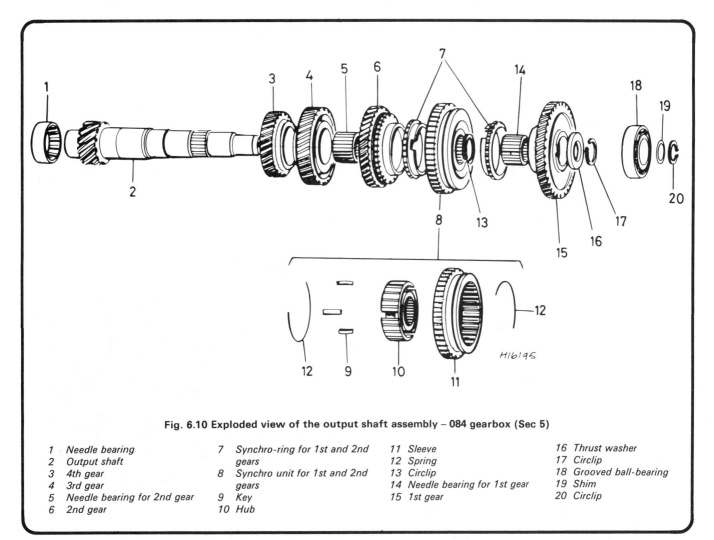

Fig. 6.10 Exploded view of the output shaft assembly – 084 gearbox (Sec 5)

1 Needle bearing	11 Sleeve
2 Output shaft	12 Spring
3 4th gear	13 Circlip
4 3rd gear	14 Needle bearing for 1st gear
5 Needle bearing for 2nd gear	15 1st gear
6 2nd gear	16 Thrust washer
7 Synchro-ring for 1st and 2nd gears	17 Circlip
8 Synchro unit for 1st and 2nd gears	18 Grooved ball-bearing
9 Key	19 Shim
10 Hub	20 Circlip

5.25 Fitting 2nd gear on the output shaft (084 gearbox)

5.26 Fitting the 2nd synchro-ring and 1st/2nd syncho unit to the output shaft (084 gearbox)

5.27 Using a puller to press on the 1st/2nd synchro unit (084 gearbox)

when fitting a new output shaft, ensure that the replacement has the correct number of final drive gearteeth by comparing with the old shaft. Further identification is shown in Fig. 6.11.

23 Check the synchro-rings and synchro units with reference to Section 6, paragraphs 3 and 4; however, there are no grooves or dot.

24 Commence reassembly by locating the 2nd gear needle bearing on the output shaft. Lubricate it with gear oil.

25 Fit the 2nd gear (photo).

26 Locate the 2nd synchro-ring on the 1st/2nd synchro unit with the cutouts engaged with the keys. The ring must be fitted on the reverse gear teeth end of the unit (photo).

27 Using a puller, press the synchro unit onto the splines (photo). Alternatively use a metal tube to drive it on. When fitted the selector groove must be on the 1st gear end of the unit.

28 Fit the **new** circlip in the groove, followed by the thrust washer.

29 Locate the 1st synchro-ring on the 1st/2nd synchro unit with the cutouts engaged with the keys.

30 Locate the 1st gear needle bearing on the shaft and lubricate it with gear oil, then fit the 1st gear.

31 Fit the thrust washer and a **new** circlip, making sure that it is correctly seated.

6 Synchro units (084 gearbox) – servicing

1 Unless the transmission is the victim of neglect or misuse, or has covered very high mileages, the synchro-hub assemblies do not normally need renewing. If they do, they must be renewed as a complete assembly. It is not practical to fit an inner hub or outer sleeve alone – even if you could buy one.

2 When synchro baulk rings are being renewed, it is advisable to fit new sliding keys (blocker bars) and retaining springs in the hubs, as this will ensure that full advantage is taken of the new, unworn cut-outs in the rings.

3 Check the synchro-rings by assembling them on their respective gears and using a feeler gauge to measure the gap between the dogs. If it is less than 0.5 mm (0.02 in), renew the rings (photo).

4 To dismantle the synchro unit, first mark the hub and sleeve in relation to each other, then press the hub out of the sleeve and remove the keys and springs.

5 Check the components then slide the sleeve onto the hub so that the marks are aligned. Note that the recesses in the inside of the sleeve

Fig. 6.11 Output shaft is identified for type by groove(s) – arrowed – and number of final drive teeth – 084 gearbox (Sec 5)

Ratio	Identification
4.27 (64 : 15)	No groove
3.88 (62 : 16)	One groove
4.06 (65 : 16)	Three grooves

6.3 Checking the synchro-rings for wear

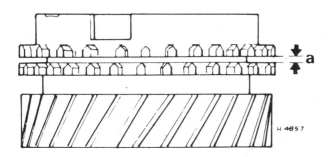

Fig. 6.12 Synchro-ring wear checking dimension (a) (Sec 6)

must be aligned with the key grooves in the hub, and the dot on the sleeve applied during manufacture (where applicable) must face the same way as the groove on the side of the hub. The groove is on the same side as the longer splines on the hub. Insert the keys and fit the springs with the angled ends located in the keys. Refer to Fig. 6.13 and note that the springs point in opposite directions with the angled ends 120° apart (photos).

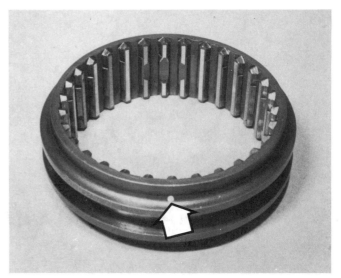

6.5C The dot on the synchro sleeve (arrowed) ...

6.5A Recess in synchro sleeve (arrowed) to align with key

6.5D ... must be on the long spline side of the hub (arrowed)

6.5B Assembling the synchro sleeve to the hub

6.5E Insert the keys ...

6.5F ... and fit the springs

6.5G The assembled synchro unit (084 gearbox)

7 Differential unit (084 gearbox) – servicing

1   Overhaul of the differential unit is not within the scope of the home mechanic as special instrumentation is required; including the use of thermo pencils to obtain extremely accurate temperatures. However, if the gearbox or clutch housings are renewed, the differential bearing preload must be adjusted, and this procedure is included in the following paragraphs for the renewal of the differential taper bearings.

2   Examine the taper bearing rollers and races for pitting and scoring, and if evident renew the bearings as follows. Note that the bearings and races are matched so the new bearings must be fitted with their corresponding races.

3   Using a puller, pull the inner races and rollers from each side of the differential.

4   Wipe clean the bearing surfaces on the differential then heat the new inner races and bearings in boiling water and immediately drive them onto the differential using a metal tube on the races only. Make sure that the narrow diameter of the rollers faces away from the differential.

5   Using a metal tube, drive the outer races from the clutch and gearbox housings after prising out the oil seals. Drive them out from the outside of the housings then remove the shims. Keep the shim from the gearbox housing. This shim is 1 mm (0.04 in) thick and must be fitted to the gearbox housing during assessment of the bearing preload and when refitting the bearing on final reassembly.

6   Clean the recesses in the housings. If necessary, the seal sleeve in the clutch housing can be removed by levering out with a suitable screwdriver, but take care not to damage the housing. Once removed, a new seal sleeve must be refitted and this can be pressed in using a suitable tube drift.

7   Fit the 1 mm (0.04 in) shim into the gearbox housing and drive the new outer bearing race into position whilst supporting the housing on a block of wood.

8   Similarly drive the new outer race into the clutch housing without a shim.

9   Locate the differential in the gearbox housing then clean the mating faces and fit the clutch housing (together with a new gasket if applicable). Insert the bolts and tighten them to the specified torque in diagonal sequence.

10   Attach a dial gauge to the gearbox and, without turning the differential, measure the endfloat by pushing the differential in and out – dimension A (Fig. 6.14).

11   The bearing preload is 0.30 mm (0.0118 in) – dimension B. Add

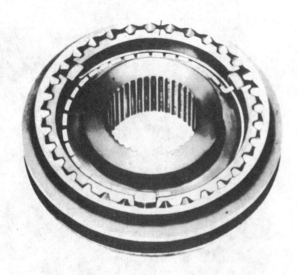

Fig. 6.13 Synchro sleeve and hub unit showing correct fitting positions for keys and spring (Sec 6)

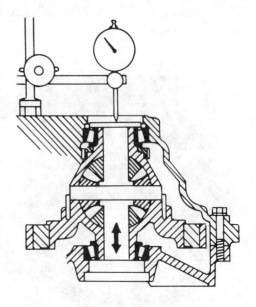

Fig. 6.14 Cross-section diagram showing method of checking differential bearing endfloat – 083 gearbox (Sec 7)

dimension A to dimension B to obtain the thickness of the shim to fit in the clutch housing.

Example:

Dimension A	=	1.50 mm (0.0591 in)
Dimension B	=	0.30 mm (0.0118 in)
Shim thickness	=	1.80 mm (0.0709 in)

12 Remove the clutch housing, drive out the outer race, then fit the correct shim and drive in the outer race.
13 Allow any water to dry from the taper roller bearings before the gearbox is reassembled, and fit new oil seals as described in Section 4.

8 Manual gearbox (084) – reassembly

Make sure that all components are clean and, during reassembly, lubricate all bearings and bearing surfaces with gear oil.
1 Using a metal tube, drive the output shaft bearing into the gearbox housing with the closed side of the bearing facing in the gearbox.
2 Grease the interlock plungers and locate them in the housing – use a pen magnet if necessary (photo).

8.3 Use a large nut to hold the selector relay shaft against the spring tension (084 gearbox)

3 Using a large nut or piece of wire, retain the selector relay shaft against the spring tension (photo).
4 Locate the 1st/2nd selector rod and fork in the groove of the synchro unit on the output shaft.
5 Locate the reverse gear on its shaft, but retain it in a slightly raised position with a piece of wire.
6 Lower the output shaft and selector rod into the gearbox housing and at the same time feed the reverse gear in after the 1st gear (photo).
7 With the output shaft entered fully in its bearing check that the selector rod is in neutral and the reverse gear is free to move.
8 If a new gearbox housing, bearing or output shaft has been fitted, determine and fit the bearing preload shims as follows. Fit the circlip and using a feeler gauge determine the clearance between the circlip and bearing inner race (photo). Select a small shim to set the clearance to between 0 and 0.05 mm (0 and 0.002 in) then fit the shim beneath the circlip. Using a dial gauge, or straight-edge and feeler gauge, determine the clearance between the housing face (without gasket) and bearing outer race. Add 0.27 to 0.31 mm (0.011 to 0.012 in) to the clearance for the thickness of the large shim to fit against the outer race. When assessing the large shim requirement, ensure that the

8.2 Using a pen magnet to insert the interlock plungers (084 gearbox)

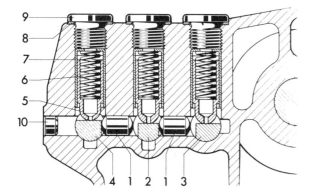

Fig. 6.15 Cross-section of gear selector detents – 084 gearbox (Sec 8)

1 Interlock plunger	6 Spring
2 Shift rod 1st/2nd gear	7 Sleeve
3 Shift rod 3rd/4th gear	8 Seal
4 Shift rod reverse gear	9 Threaded plug
5 Bush	10 Plug in interlock bore

8.8 Checking the output shaft bearing endfloat (084 gearbox)

Fig. 6.16 Using a dial gauge to determine the bearing preload shim thickness – 084 gearbox (Sec 8)

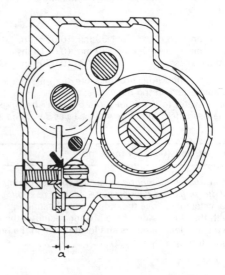

Fig. 6.17 Showing clearance between the reverse relay lever and the 1st/2nd selector rod – arrow shows roll pin flush – 084 gearbox – (Sec 8)

a = 1.3 to 2.8 mm (0.051 to 0.110 in)

bearing is fully seated in its housing and, if a dial gauge is used, it should be zeroed wth a 2 mm (0.079 in) preload.

9   Locate the 3rd/4th selector rod and fork in the groove of the synchro unit on the input shaft.

10 Lower the input shaft and selector rod into the gearbox housing and mesh the gears with those on the output shaft. Lift the reverse gear slightly to allow the input shaft 1st gear to pass.

11 Support the output shaft using the plate described in Section 4 then remove the wire from the reverse gear.

12 Using a metal tube, drive the input shaft bearing into the gearbox housing and onto the shaft. The closed side of the bearing must face into the gearbox (photo).

13 Refer to paragraph 8, and if necessary determine and fit the small and large shims to the end of the input shaft.

14 Remove the input shaft support plate.

15 Remove the nut or wire from the selector relay shaft.

16 Locate the relay lever on the reverse selector rod then lower them into the housing and engage the lever with the reverse gear. It will be necessary to lift the gears slightly.

17 Position the relay lever approximately 2.0 mm (0.08 in) away from

8.17 The fitted position of the reverse relay lever – arrowed (084 gearbox)

8.12 Fitting the input shaft bearing to the gearbox housing (084 gearbox)

the 1st/2nd selector rod. Make sure that the roll pin on the selector rod is flush with the fork (photo).

18 Screw in the cross-head bolt and washer, and tighten it to the specified torque. Check that the clearance between the relay lever and selector rod is 1.3 to 2.8 mm (0.051 to 0.110 in).

19 Insert the detent plungers, springs and sleeves in the housing apertures followed by the plugs and their washers. Tighten the plugs with an Allen key.

20 Move the relay shaft lever and check that each gear can be engaged easily. Also check that it is not possible to move two adjacent selector rods at the same time.

21 Locate the correct large shims on the input and output shaft bearings then fit the end cover, together with a new gasket (photo). Apply a liquid locking agent to the bolt thread then insert the bolts and tighten them to the specified torque in diagonal sequence (photos).

8.21A Bearing end cover gasket and large shims located on the bearings (084 gearbox)

8.22 Differential located in the gearbox housing (084 gearbox)

8.21B Apply a liquid locking agent to the bolt threads ...

22 Invert the gearbox and fit the differential unit into position in it (photo).

23 Clean the mating faces of the gearbox and clutch housings. If applicable fit a new gasket, otherwise apply sealing compound to the faces.

24 Locate the magnetic swarf collector in the gearbox housing slot.

25 Check that the selector rods are in neutral, then lower the clutch housing onto the gearbox housing making sure that the shift lever engages the relay shaft lever.

26 Tap in the dowels, then insert the bolts and tighten them evenly to the specified torque in diagonal sequence (photo).

27 Insert the drive flanges into the differential, together with the taper ring, thrust washer and spring. Insert the bolts and tighten them to the specified torque. Hold the flanges stationary with a bar between two bolts into adjacent holes (photo). Note that the left and right flanges are different.

28 Insert and tighten the reversing light switch.

29 Refit the clutch release shaft and bearing, described in Chapter 5.

30 Refill the gearbox with oil after fitting it to the engine.

8.21C ... then insert and tighten the bolts (084 gearbox)

8.26 Tightening the clutch housing-to-gearbox housing bolts

8.27 Method of tightening the drive flange bolts

9 Gearshift mechanism (084 gearbox) – removal, refitting and adjustment

1   Jack up the front of the car and support on axle stands. Apply the handbrake.
2   With neutral selected, mark the shift rod and coupling in relation to each other, then unscrew the coupling clamp and pull out the shift rod.
3   Working inside the car, unscrew the gear knob and remove the gaiter.
4   Unscrew the nuts from the ballhousing stop plate, and withdraw the complete gearchange mechanism upwards into the car (photo). Recover the spacers.
5   Dismantle the mechanism as necessary and examine the components for wear and damage. Renew as necessary.
6   Lubricate the joints and bearing surfaces with high melting-point grease then refit using a reversal of the removal procedure. If a new coupling has been fitted it will be necessary to adjust the coupling position – this is best carried out by a VW garage using tool 3069, but if necessary the following method can be used in an emergency. With the coupling disconnected and the gearbox in neutral have an assistant hold the gear lever in neutral position between 3rd and 4th gear positions (ie halfway between front and rear movement and to the right). Engage the shift rod and coupling fully and, with the gear lever in the same position, tighten the clamp bolt.

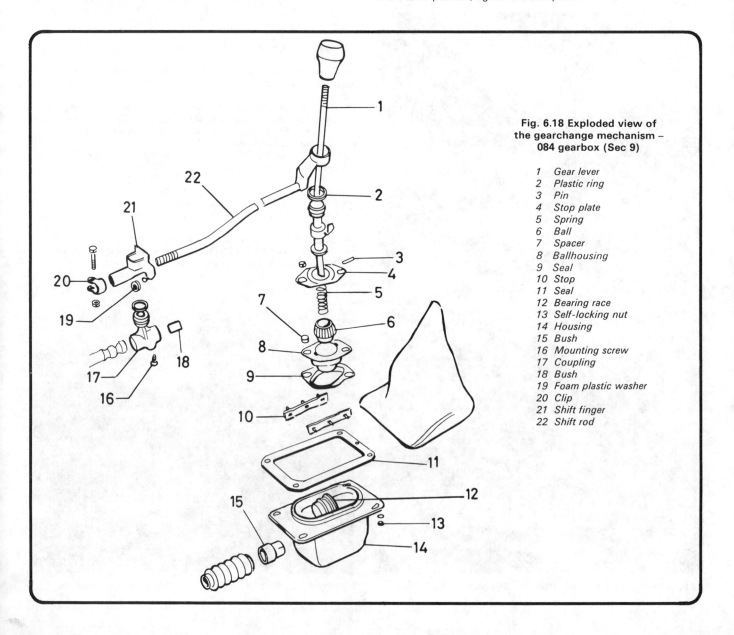

Fig. 6.18 Exploded view of the gearchange mechanism – 084 gearbox (Sec 9)

1   Gear lever
2   Plastic ring
3   Pin
4   Stop plate
5   Spring
6   Ball
7   Spacer
8   Ballhousing
9   Seal
10 Stop
11 Seal
12 Bearing race
13 Self-locking nut
14 Housing
15 Bush
16 Mounting screw
17 Coupling
18 Bush
19 Foam plastic washer
20 Clip
21 Shift finger
22 Shift rod

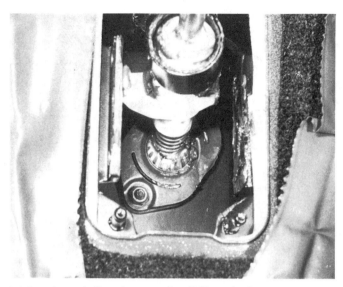

9.4 Gearchange ballhousing stop plate (084 gearbox)

10.3 Speedometer cable and retaining bolt (020 gearbox)

10 Manual gearbox (020, 4 and 5-speed) – removal and refitting

1   Proceed as described in Section 3, paragraphs 1 to 5 inclusive. Drain the oil from the gearbox (photo).
2   Disconnect the clutch cable from the release arm (Chapter 5).
3   Disconnect the speedometer cable from the gearbox by undoing the retaining bolt and withdrawing the cable (photo). Tie the clutch and speedometer cables back out of the way.
4   Disconnect the multi-function switch connector from the gearbox (photo).
5   Undo the retaining nut and detach the gearbox mounting support arm. Undo the nut and detach the earth strap.
6   Detach the gearchange selector rod by pressing back the clips on the plastic balljoint connectors (photo).
7   Detach the gearchange connecting link. If removing completely note that the link ends differ in angle and the end with the notched mark is at the selector shaft lever end.

10.4 Multi-function switch on 020 gearbox

10.1 Gearbox drain plug (020 gearbox)

10.6 Gearchange connecting rod links and plastic balljoint (020 gearbox)

8   Detach the heater hose support bracket (inboard of the starter motor).
9   Unbolt and remove the starter motor, leaving the leads attached. Position the starter motor out of the way.
10 Undo the single retaining bolt and withdraw it from the mounting to the rear of the left-hand driveshaft (right rear of gearbox looking from left side of car).
11 Unbolt and remove the engine/gearbox mounting on the left-hand side (front of car) – photo.
12 Unscrew and remove the engine-to-gearbox attachment bolts at the top.
13 Working underneath the vehicle, detach the right and left-hand driveshafts at their driveshaft flanges. Tie up the driveshafts to support them. Refer to Chapter 7 for further details.
14 Detach and remove the wheel arch cover on the left-hand side.
15 Unbolt and remove the clutch housing cover plate bolts (photo).
16 Unscrew and remove the lower engine-to-gearbox attachment bolt (under the right-hand drive flange) and the cover plate bolts.
17 Disconnect the exhaust downpipe from the manifold flange (see Chapter 3).

10.15 Clutch housing cover plate (020 gearbox)

10.11 Front engine/gearbox mounting viewed from underneath (1.8 litre)

10.18 Right-hand rear engine mounting viewed from underneath (1.8 litre gearbox)

Fig. 6.19 Remove cover plate from the driveshaft flange (arrowed) – 020 gearbox (Sec 10)

18 Unbolt and detach, but do not remove, the engine mounting unit (between the engine and the bulkhead) – photo. This will allow the engine to be pivoted to allow gearbox removal.
19 Lower the engine and gearbox a little and pull the gearbox to the front, but take care not to strain any of the engine ancillary attachments. An assistant will be useful here to check on this and to hold the engine at the angle required so that the gearbox will clear the wheel arch when being separated from the engine.
20 Pull the gearbox free and separate it from the engine, as described in Section 3, paragraphs 18, 19 and 20.
21 Refitting is a reversal of the removal procedure. Ensure that the joint surfaces are clean and smear a small amount of graphite powder, Moly paste or spray onto the input shaft splines. Line up the gearbox so that the input shaft will enter the clutch friction disc.
22 When the engine and gearbox are re-engaged, refit the attachment bolts and tighten them to the specified torque. Do not allow the weight of the gearbox to rest on the input shaft at any time.
23 When the engine and gearbox are located on the mountings check that they are not under any strain prior to retightening the mounting bolts.
24 Adjust the clutch, with reference to Chapter 5, and check that the gearshift mechanism operates correctly. Refill the gearbox with oil.

11 Manual gearbox (020, 4-speed) – dismantling and overhaul

1 Proceed as described in paragraphs 1 and 2 of Section 4.
2 Prise free and remove the release shaft circlips.
3 Undo and remove the selector shaft peg bolt.
4 Remove the switch unit from the gearbox.
5 Remove the clutch release shaft, clutch lever, return spring and release bearing and guide sleeve.
6 Prise free the plugs then undo and remove the three nuts (Fig. 6.21).

7 Using a spark plug spanner, unscrew and remove the selector shaft end cap. Engage neutral and pull out the selector shaft.
8 Undo and remove the reverse gear shaft retaining screw (photo).
9 Prise the plastic cap from the centre of the left-hand drive flange, remove the circlip and washer and withdraw the flange with a suitable puller (photos).
10 Unscrew the main casing-to-gear carrier (clutch housing) bolts then use a puller to draw the main casing away. Recover the bearing shim (if fitted) and remove the gasket and magnet from the gear carrier casing.
11 Withdraw the selector fork rod and remove the fork set sideways.
12 Remove the circlip securing 4th gear on the output shaft then

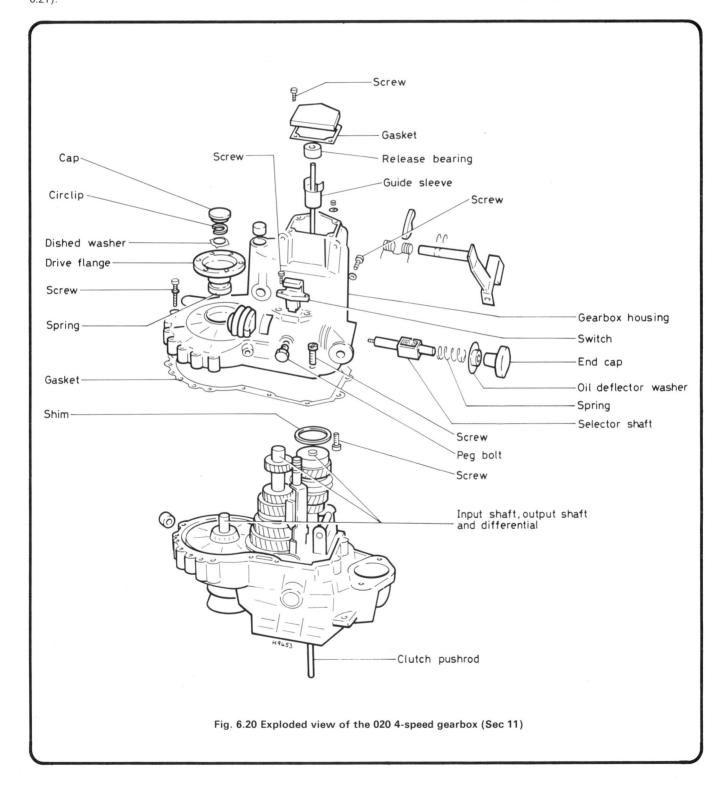

Fig. 6.20 Exploded view of the 020 4-speed gearbox (Sec 11)

Fig. 6.21 Undo the three nuts shown. Lever off the plugs
(arrowed) where necessary (Sec 11)

11.9B Drive flange circlip and washer

11.8 Removing the reverse gear shaft retaining screw (020 4-speed
gearbox)

11.9C Using a puller to withdraw a drive flange

11.9A Remove the drive flange plastic cap

withdraw the gear, using a puller if necessary.
13 The input shaft unit can now be withdrawn as a complete
assembly.
14 The remaining removal and overhaul procedures are now the same
as those described in paragraphs 17 and 25 inclusive in Section 14.
15 If the input shaft ball-bearing is to be removed from the main
casing, unscrew the clamping screws then press or drift out the bearing
and collect the shim (if fitted). When the new bearing is pressed into
position the wide shoulder on its inner race must face towards 4th
gear. If a shim was fitted, locate it into the housing before pressing the
bearing into position. Fit the bearing clamping screws and tighten the
nuts.
16 The input shaft and output shaft units can be serviced as described
in the following Section.
17 The inspection and servicing of the differential unit is as described
in Section 17.

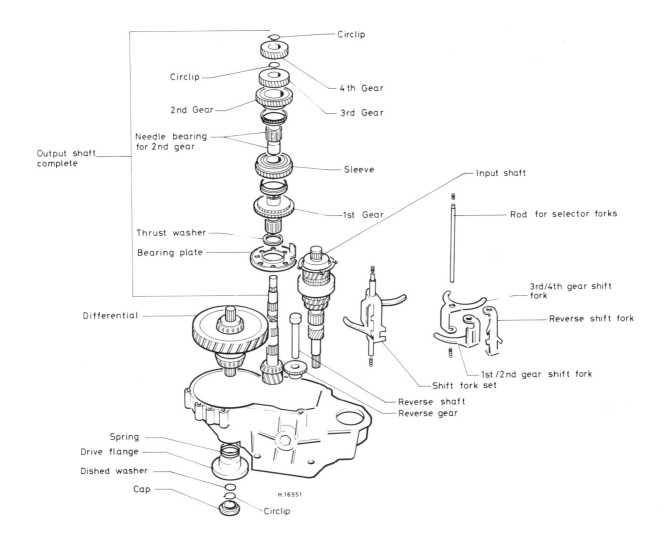

Fig. 6.22 Exploded view of the gear assemblies and clutch housing components – 020 4-speed gearbox (Sec 11)

12 Input and output shafts (020 4-speed) – servicing

Input shaft

1 Remove 4th gear with its synchro-ring and withdraw the needle bearing (photos).

2 The input shaft servicing procedure now follows that given for the 020 5-speed gearbox in Section 15, paragraphs 4 to 11 inclusive.

Output shaft

3 Refer to Section 14, paragraphs 16 to 19 inclusive, and Section 15, paragraphs 15 to 18.

12.1A Remove 4th gear with the synchro-ring ...

12.1B ... and the needle roller bearing from the input shaft (020 4-speed gearbox)

12.1C Input shaft (020 4-speed gearbox)

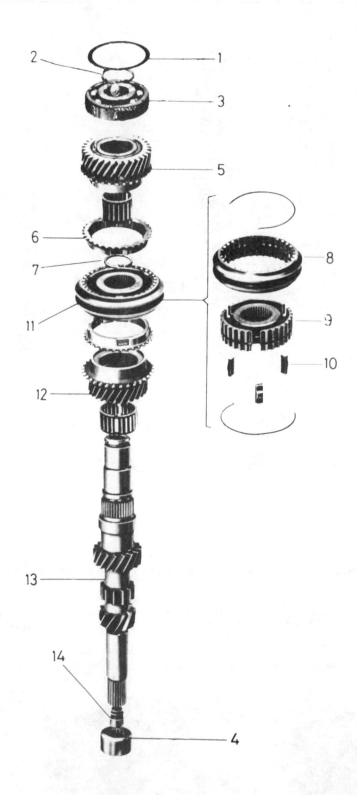

Fig. 6.23 Exploded view of the input shaft – 020 4-speed gearbox (Sec 12)

1	Shim	6	4th gear synchro-ring	11	3rd/4th synchronizer
2	Circlip	7	Circlip	12	3rd gear
3	Ball-bearing	8	Sleeve	13	Input shaft
4	Needle bearing	9	Hub	14	Clutch pushrod bush and seal
5	4th gear	10	Sliding key		

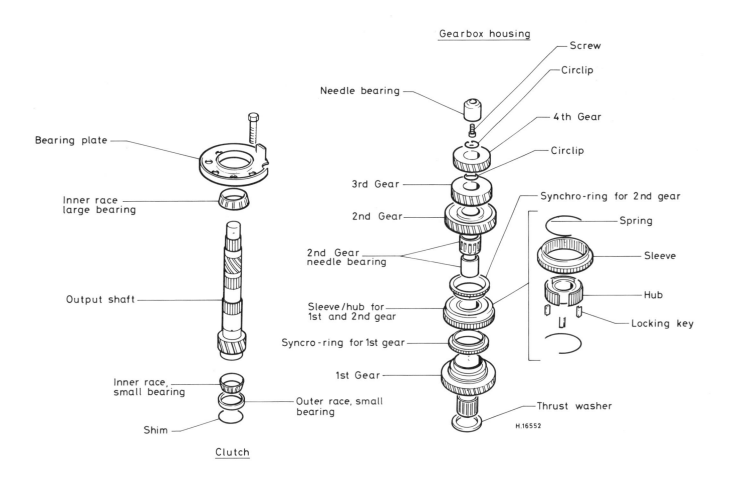

Gearbox housing — Screw

Needle bearing — Circlip

4th Gear

Circlip

Bearing plate

Inner race large bearing

3rd Gear

2nd Gear

Synchro-ring for 2nd gear

Spring

Sleeve

Output shaft

2nd Gear needle bearing

Hub

Locking key

Sleeve/hub for 1st and 2nd gear

Inner race, small bearing

Syncro-ring for 1st gear

Outer race, small bearing

Shim

1st Gear

Thrust washer

Clutch

H.16552

Fig. 6.24 Exploded view of the output shaft – 020 4-speed gearbox (Sec 12)

13 Manual gearbox (020, 4-speed) – reassembly

1 Proceed as described in Section 18, paragraphs 1 to 11 inclusive. Photos 13.1A to 13.1F show the assembly sequence of the input shaft and the shift fork assemblies for the 020 4-speed gearbox.
2 If not already fitted, locate the input shaft ball-bearing with its original shim (if fitted) into position in the main casing, as described in paragraph 15 of Section 11.

3 Now refer to Section 18 again and proceed as described in paragraphs 12 to 18 inclusive.
4 Fit the left-hand drive flange, followed by the spring washer, retaining clip and cap.
5 With the shift forks in neutral, insert the selector shaft, spring and oil deflector washer. Tighten the end cap to the specified torque.
6 Refit the reverse light/consumption indicator switch.
7 Locate and tighten the selector shaft peg bolt to the specified torque.

13.1A Fitting the input shaft assembly to the gear carrier housing (020 4-speed gearbox)

13.1B Fitting the shift forks ...

13.1C ... and shift fork shaft (020 4-speed gearbox)

13.1D Fitting the reverse shift fork pivot posts (020 4-speed gearbox)

13.1E Reverse shift fork assembly (020 4-speed gearbox)

13.1F Reverse shift fork location on reverse idler gear (020 4-speed gearbox)

8   Fit the circlip to the input shaft and check that it is fully engaged.

9   Refit the release bearing and guide sleeve. The release shaft, clutch lever and return spring can then be fitted, but ensure that the bent ends of the spring are in contact with the housing and with the centre bridge hooked to the clutch lever.

10 Refit the release shaft circlips.

11 Locate a new end cover gasket then refit the cover.

12 With the gearbox reassembled, select each gear in turn to ensure correct and satisfactory engagement.

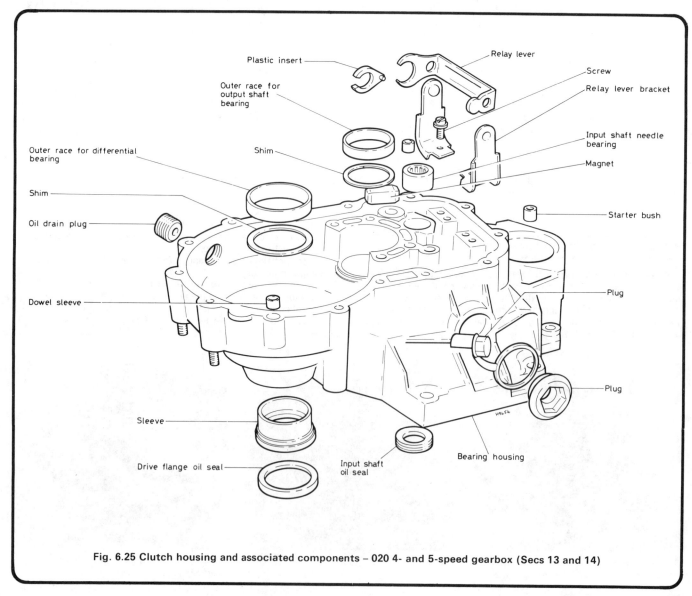

Fig. 6.25 Clutch housing and associated components – 020 4- and 5-speed gearbox (Secs 13 and 14)

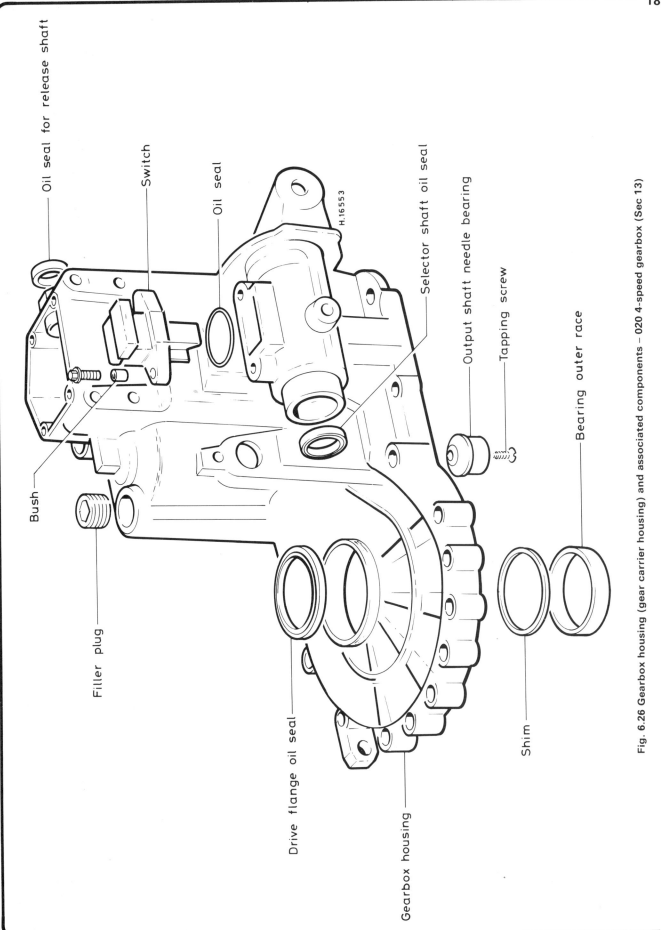

Oil seal for release shaft

Switch

Oil seal

H.16553

Selector shaft oil seal

Output shaft needle bearing

Tapping screw

Bearing outer race

Bush

Filler plug

Drive flange oil seal

Gearbox housing

Shim

Fig. 6.26 Gearbox housing (gear carrier housing) and associated components – 020 4-speed gearbox (Sec 13)

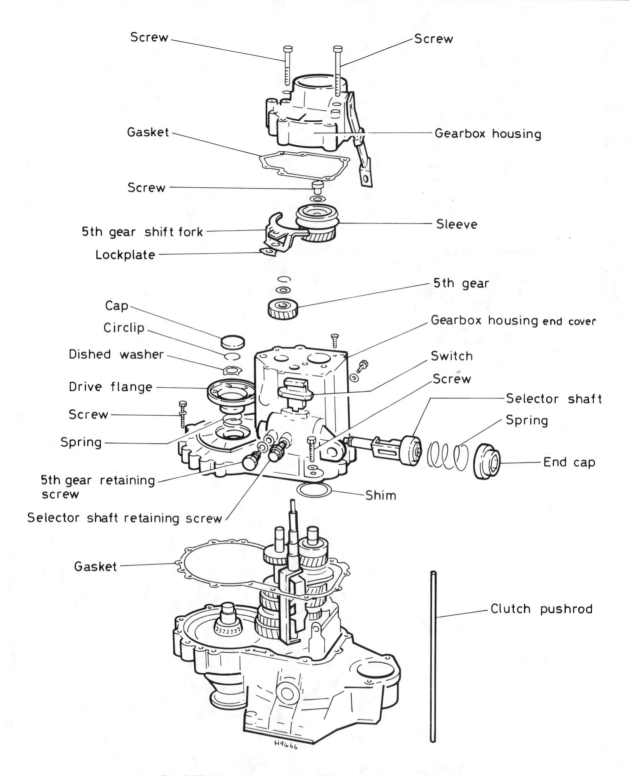

Fig. 6.27 Exploded view of the 020 5-speed gearbox (Sec 14)

14 Manual gearbox (020, 5-speed) – dismantling and overhaul

Before starting to dismantle the gearbox note the general overhaul information given in Section 4.

1   Remove the clutch pushrod from the input shaft.

2   Unbolt and remove the end cover from the main casing. Remove the gasket.

3   Remove the selector shaft detent plunger or peg bolt, the 5th gear retaining screw, and the gearbox switch.

4   Using a spark plug spanner, unscrew the selector shaft end cap and remove the spring.

5   Engage neutral and withdraw the selector shaft. If difficulty is experienced, extract the circlip and drive out the shaft. However, this may cause damage to the shaft components.

6   Unscrew the reverse gear shaft lockbolt.

7   Prise the plastic cap from the centre of the left-hand side drive

flange, remove the circlip and washer, and withdraw the flange with a suitable puller.

8   Engage 5th and reverse gears by removing the selector forks, then unscrew the 5th gear synchronizer retaining nut using a 12 mm Allen key. The bolt is very tight and an assistant will be required to hold the main casing.

9   Engage neutral, then unscrew the sleeve or prise out the locking plate from the end of the shift fork tube (Fig. 6.28).

10 Unscrew the selector tube anti-clockwise from the 5th gear selector fork, but do not remove the selector rod.

11 Withdraw the 5th gear, together with the synchronizer and selector fork from the input shaft.

12 Extract the circlip from the end of the output shaft, then remove the 5th gear with a suitable puller.

13 Using a 5 mm Allen key, unscrew the bolts securing the input shaft bearing retaining plate.

14 Unscrew the bolts attaching the main casing to the gear carrier (clutch) housing, then use a puller to draw the main casing from the input shaft. Recover the shim located against the bearing outer track. Remove the gasket and the magnet from the gear carrier housing.

15 Pull the selector fork rod from the gear carrier housing and withdraw the fork set sideways.

16 Extract the circlip from the end of the output shaft, then remove the input shaft assembly from the gear carrier housing while removing the 4th gear from the output shaft.

17 Extract the remaining circlip from the output shaft and remove 3rd gear, 2nd gear, 2nd synchro-ring and the needle bearing, using a puller if necessary (photos).

18 Remove the reverse gear and shaft from the gear carrier housing.

19 Using a suitable puller, remove the 1st gear and 1st/2nd synchronizer from the output shaft, together with the 2nd gear needle bearing inner race. Remove the 1st gear needle bearing and thrust washer.

20 Unbolt the bearing retaining plate and remove the output shaft from the gear carrier housing. Note that the retaining plate incorporates the reverse gear stop which locates beneath the reverse gear (photos).

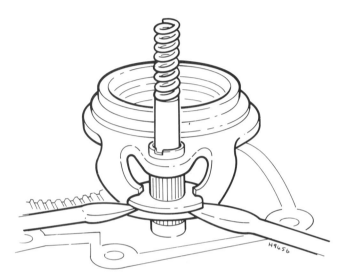

Fig. 6.28 Selector fork tube locking plate removal method –
020 5-speed gearbox (Sec 14)

14.17A Removing the 3rd gear retaining circlip (output shaft)

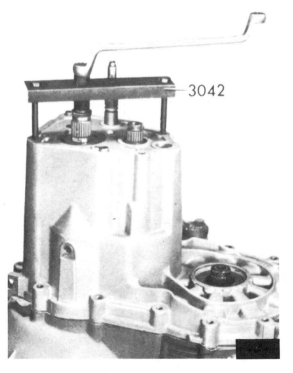

Fig. 6.29 Main casing removal using VW tool 3042 (Sec 14)

14.17B Removing 3rd gear from the output shaft

14.17C Removing 2nd gear from the output shaft

14.17D 2nd gear needle roller bearing location

14.19A 1st gear needle roller bearing location on the output shaft

14.19B Remove the 1st gear thrust washer ...

14.20A ... undo the retaining bolts ...

14.20B ... and withdraw the bearing retainer plate

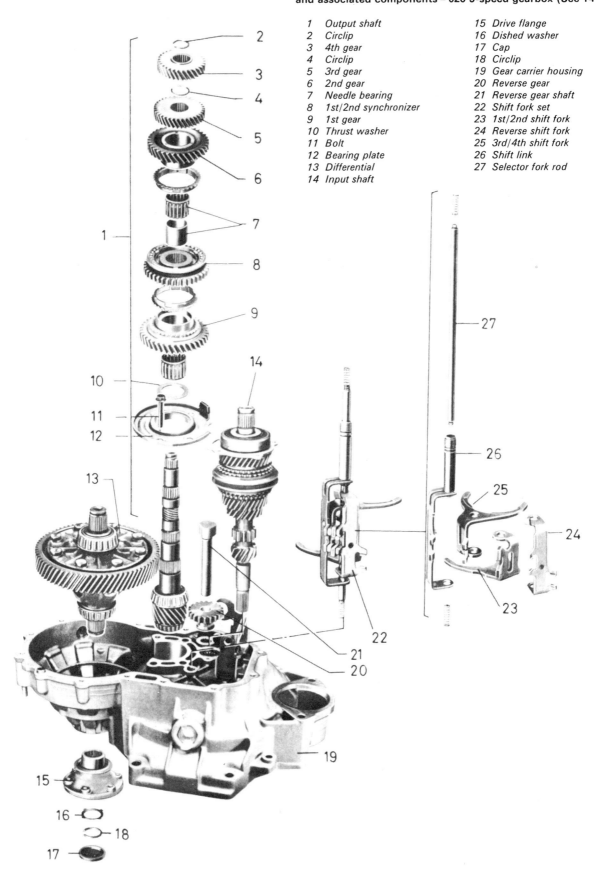

Fig. 6.30 Exploded view of the gear carrier (clutch) housing and associated components – 020 5-speed gearbox (Sec 14)

1	Output shaft	15	Drive flange
2	Circlip	16	Dished washer
3	4th gear	17	Cap
4	Circlip	18	Circlip
5	3rd gear	19	Gear carrier housing
6	2nd gear	20	Reverse gear
7	Needle bearing	21	Reverse gear shaft
8	1st/2nd synchronizer	22	Shift fork set
9	1st gear	23	1st/2nd shift fork
10	Thrust washer	24	Reverse shift fork
11	Bolt	25	3rd/4th shift fork
12	Bearing plate	26	Shift link
13	Differential	27	Selector fork rod
14	Input shaft		

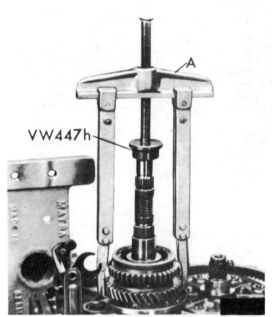

Fig. 6.31 Showing suitable two-arm puller (A) required to remove the 1st gear, synchro-hub and sleeve assembly – 020 5-speed gearbox (Sec 14)

21 Remove the remaining drive flange, as described in paragraph 7, then lift out the differential unit. Overhaul of the differential unit is best entrusted to a VW agent and should not be attempted by the home mechanic (see Section 7).

22 To overhaul the gear carrier housing, no special tools are necessary and the procedures are similar to those described in Section 4. The drive flange housing on the gear carrier side also has a sleeve fitted. This can be levered out using a screwdriver, but take care not to damage the housing. Once removed this sleeve must be renewed. Drive the new sleeve into position using a suitable tube drift.

23 The end cover retaining the clutch release components is separate from the main casing and is dealt with in Chapter 5. The main casing is otherwise serviced as described in Section 4.

24 If the output shaft bearings (and/or differential unit or gear carrier housing) are to be renewed note that the large and small bearings locate the output shaft relative to the crownwheel, adjustment being by shim which is selected by one of sixteen different thicknesses available. If either bearing is defective then both must be renewed. In the removal process the bearings are destroyed. New ones have to be shrunk on and the shim under the smaller bearing changed for one of the correct size.

25 This operation is quite complicated and requires special equipment for preloading of the shaft and measurement of the torque required to rotate the new bearings. In addition the shim at the top of the input shaft and the axial play at the circlip of the 3rd gear on the output shaft will be affected. This will mean selection of a new shim and circlip. There are six different thicknesses of circlip. Therefore it is recommended that if these bearings require renewal, the work should be left to your VW agent.

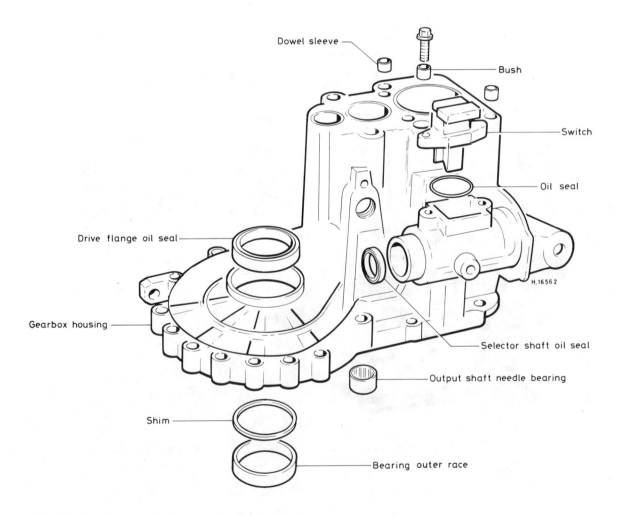

Fig. 6.32 Gearbox housing (gear carrier housing) and associated components – 020 5-speed gearbox (Sec 14)

15 Input and output shafts (020 5-speed) – servicing

Input shaft

1   Remove the 5th gear needle bearing.
2   Use a suitable puller and withdraw the ball-bearing from the input shaft. If a shim was fitted on the 5th gear side of this bearing, keep the shim with the bearing, as it was selected during manufacture and must be re-used.
3   Remove the clamping plate, 4th gear and needle bearing, and 4th gear synchro-ring.
4   Remove the circlip, then support 3rd gear and press the input shaft through the 3rd/4th synchro-hub. Tape the synchro unit together to prevent it from coming apart.
5   Remove the needle bearing to complete the dismantling of the shaft (photo).
6   Should the clutch pushrod be loose in the input shaft the bush may be driven out of the end of the shaft and a new bush and oil seal fitted. Press the new oil seal into position with the fitting plug supplied. When fitted, check that the oil seal depth in the shaft bore is 0.8 to 1.3 mm (0.032 to 0.051 in).
7   If gears on either shaft are to be renewed then the mating gear on the other shaft must be renewed as well. They are supplied in pairs only.
8   The inspection of the synchro units is dealt with in Section 16.
9   When reassembling the input shaft lightly oil all the parts.
10   Fit 3rd gear needle bearing and 3rd gear. Press on the 3rd/4th gear synchro-hub and fit a **new** retaining circlip. When pressing on the synchro-hub and sleeve, turn the rings so that the keys and grooves line up. The chamfer on the inner splines of the hub must face 3rd gear (photos).
11   Fit the 4th gear synchro-ring, the needle bearing and 4th gear.
12   Locate the shim (if fitted) in the main casing, then press in the bearing with the inner race wide shoulder facing 4th gear.

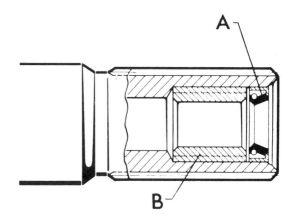

Fig. 6.33 Clutch pushrod seal (A) and bush (B) location in the input shaft (Sec 15)

13   Fit the plate to the main casing and tighten the bolts to the specified torque using a 5 mm Allen key.
14   Note that there is no adjustment for the input shaft endfloat and that the bearing shim remains constant.

Output shaft

15   Cleaning and examination of the output shaft components (dismantled during removal) will show which items are to be renewed.
16   The inspection of the synchro units is dealt with in Section 16.
17   Refer to paragraph 7 if renewing any of the gears.

15.5 3rd gear needle roller bearing location on the input shaft

15.10A Fit 3rd gear ...

15.10B ... and synchro-ring onto the input shaft

15.10C Fit the 3rd/4th gear synchro unit onto the input shaft ...

15.10D ... and retain in position with a circlip

194

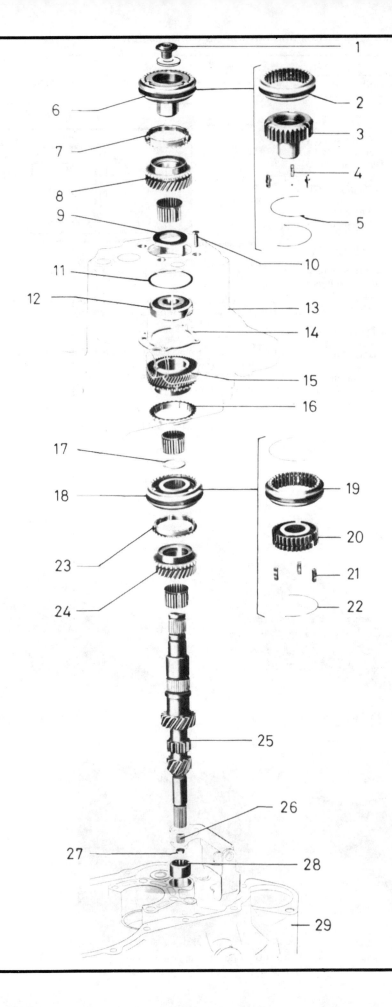

Fig. 6.34 Exploded view of the input shaft – 020 5-speed gearbox (Sec 15)

1 Screw
2 Sleeve
3 Hub
4 Locking key
5 Spring
6 5th gear synchronizer
7 Synchro-ring
8 5th gear
9 Thrust washer
10 Screw
11 Shim
12 Ball-bearing
13 Main casing
14 Clamping plate
15 4th gear
16 Synchro-ring
17 Circlip
18 3rd/4th synchronizer
19 Sleeve
20 Hub
21 Locking key
22 Spring
23 Synchro-ring
24 3rd gear
25 Input shaft
26 Bush
27 Seal
28 Needle bearing
29 Gear carrier housing

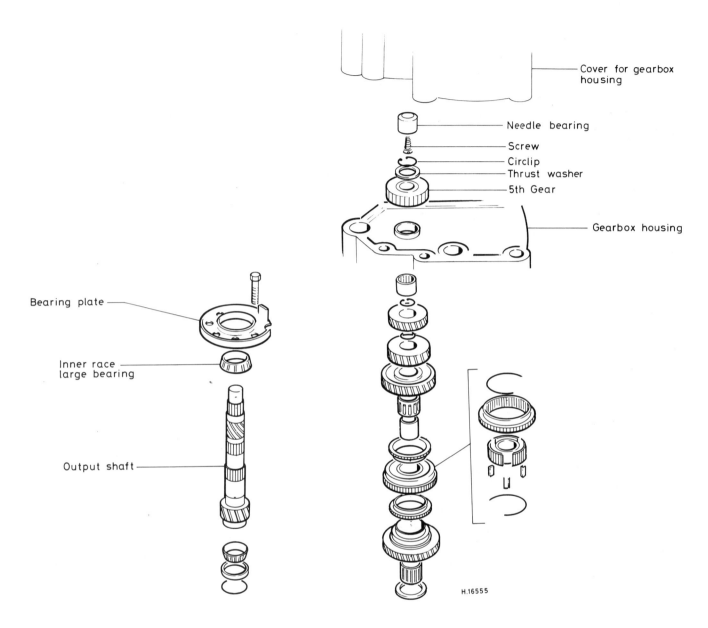

Cover for gearbox housing

Needle bearing

Screw

Circlip

Thrust washer

5th Gear

Gearbox housing

Bearing plate

Inner race large bearing

Output shaft

H.16555

Fig. 6.35 Exploded view of the output shaft – 020 5-speed gearbox (Sec 15)

18 If the output shaft is in need of renewal then the crownwheel must also be renewed as they are a matched pair. Crownwheel renewal, together with the differential overhaul, is a task best entrusted to your VW agent. He will be able to accurately reset the new output shaft and bearings at the same time (see paragraphs 24 and 25 in the previous Section).

16 Synchro units (020 4 and 5-speed) – servicing

1 Refer to Section 6, but note the following points which are applicable to the 020 gearbox types.
2 **1st/2nd synchro:** The 1st gear synchro-ring fitted during manufacture differs from the other synchro-rings in having a tooth missing. When refitting this synchro-ring ensure that it is only fitted to 1st gear. When the synchro-ring is renewed, a ring with full teeth will be supplied.
3 When assembling the hub and sleeve, the groove on the end face of

Fig. 6.36 1st gear synchronizer ring – early type with tooth missing – 020 gearbox (Sec 16)

the hub must face 1st gear, the assembly position is otherwise unimportant.

4 Assemble the keys and springs in the manner described in paragraph 5 of Section 6.

5 **3rd/4th synchro:** When assembling the hub and sleeve the chamfer on the hub inner splines must face towards 3rd gear with the outer groove on the end face towards 4th gear. The assembly position is otherwise unimportant.

6 Assemble the keys and springs in the manner described in paragraph 5 of Section 6.

7 **5th gear synchro:** Ensure when fitting that the chamfer on the splines of the synchro sleeve faces towards 5th gear.

17 Differential unit (020 4 and 5-speed) – servicing

Refer to Section 7 for details, but note that the following differences apply to the 020 gearbox:

(a) When assessing the preload allowance for the taper bearings, dimension B must be 0.40 mm (0.0157 in). A typical example will then be:

    Dimension A   =   0.90 mm (0.0354 in)
    Dimension B   =   0.40 mm (0.0157 in)
    Shim thickness =   1.30 mm (0.0511 in)

(b) The 1 mm (0.04 in) shim must be fitted to the gear carrier (clutch) housing side and the adjustment shims to the main casing (gearbox housing) side.

18 Manual gearbox (020 5-speed) – reassembly

1 Refit the differential unit in the gear carrier (clutch) housing (photo).

2 Fit the right-hand drive flange followed by the spring washer, retaining circlip, and cap.

3 Fit the output shaft, complete with taper bearings, into the gear carrier housing and mesh it with the differential gear.

4 Fit the bearing retaining plate and tighten the bolts (photo).

5 Locate the 1st gear thrust washer on the output shaft with its shoulder facing the bearing plate.

6 Fit the needle bearing and 1st gear, followed by the 1st synchro-ring. Press on the 1st/2nd synchronizer, making sure that the sliding keys locate in the synchro-ring cut-outs. Heat the synchronizer to 120°C (248°F) before fitting it (photos).

7 Insert the reverse gear shaft complete with the gear into the gear carrier housing, and at the same time engage the gear with the relay lever jaw.

8 Using a metal tube, drive on the 2nd gear needle bearing inner race, then fit the needle bearing. 2nd synchro-ring, and 2nd gear.

9 Heat the 3rd gear and press it on the output shaft with its shoulder facing 2nd gear. Select and fit a **new** circlip. The circlip selected should be the thickest one possible that will fully engage in the location groove on the shaft and take up any play of 3rd gear. The circlips available vary in thickness and are colour-coded (see Specifications).

10 Fit the input shaft into the gear carrier housing and mesh the gears with the output shaft.

11 Heat the 4th gear and press it on the output shaft with its shoulder facing away from the 3rd gear. Fit the circlip.

12 Locate the selector fork rod spring in the gear carrier housing, then install the fork set. To do this engage the 1st/2nd fork in the synchro sleeve groove, then rotate the fork set around the shaft and engage the 3rd/4th fork and the reverse fork with the relay lever.

13 Push the selector fork rod into the gear carrier housing, and align the slots in the forks to the neutral position.

14 The gear carrier housing and shafts are now ready for the assembly of the main casing.

15 Check that the reverse gear shaft is in the correct position (see Fig.

18.1 Locate the differential unit into the gear carrier (clutch) housing

18.4 Tightening the output shaft bearing retainer plate bolts

18.6A Fit 1st gear onto the output shaft ...

18.6B ... locate the synchro-ring ...

18.6C ... and synchro unit (1st/2nd)

18.6D Using a metal tube to drive the 1st/2nd synchro unit onto the output shaft

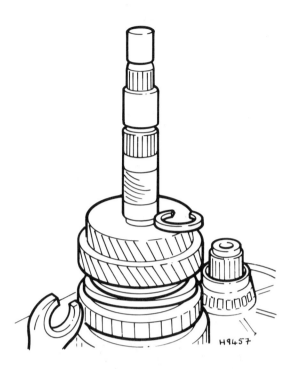

Fig. 6.37 Select suitable circlip to adjust play of 3rd gear – 020 gearbox (Sec 18)

Fig. 6.38 Reverse idle gear shaft alignment – 020 5-speed gearbox (Sec 18)

X = X

6.38) and set the geartrain in neutral. Make sure that the spring is located on the end of the selector fork rod.

16 Fit a new gasket on the gear carrier housing flange, and make sure that the magnet is in position.

17 Lower the main casing over the shafts and selector rod, then use metal tubing to drive the bearing inner race onto the input shaft while supporting the shaft on a block of wood.

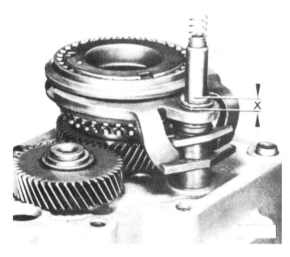

Fig. 6.39 Selector tube fitting dimension – 020 5-speed gearbox (Sec 18)

X = 5.0 mm (0.2 in)

18 Insert and tighten the reverse gear shaft lockbolt, then insert and tighten the bolts attaching the main casing to the gear carrier housing.

19 Check the input shaft bearing retaining plate bolts for tightness.

20 Fit the 5th gear thrust washer on the input shaft with the chamfer facing the bearing, followed by the needle bearing.

21 Heat the 5th gear to 100°C (212°F) and press it onto the output shaft with the groove facing away from the main casing.

22 Fit the thrust washer and a **new** circlip to the output shaft.

23 With the selector fork engaged with the groove in the 5th gear synchronizer, fit the 5th gear, synchro-ring, and synchronizer onto the mainshaft and selector fork extension together with the locking plate. Note that the locking plate should be renewed.

24 Without displacing the selector fork rod, screw the selector tube (clockwise) into the fork, then screw it out until it projects by 5.0 mm (0.2 in) (see Fig. 6.39). Take care not to pull the selector fork rod from the tube during this operation or the shift forks within the gearbox will be disengaged; in which case the gearbox will have to be partially dismantled again to re-engage them.

25 Coat the threads of a **new** 5th gear synchronizer retaining screw with locking compound then screw it into the mainshaft. Engage 5th and reverse gears by moving the selector forks (front fork slot down), then tighten the screw to the specified torque. In view of the high torque loading required, a 12 mm, 12-point socket-head screw wrench should be used if available, but failing this try using a 12 mm Allen key.

26 Engage neutral and insert the selector shaft. The gearbox is best positioned on its side for this operation so that the selector shaft can be lowered into position vertically.

27 Fit the spring and tighten the selector shaft cover (using a spark plug box spanner).

28 Insert and tighten the reverse light/consumption indicator switch unit.

29 Locate and tighten the selector shaft peg bolt to the specified torque.

30 Fit and adjust the 5th gear retaining screw. To do this first fit the shift linkage lever to the selector shaft. With the gears in neutral remove the cap and loosen the locknut. Tighten the sleeve until the central plunger just starts to move, then loosen the sleeve ¹/₂ a turn and tighten the locknut.

31 Adjust the 5th gear selector fork as follows, taking care not to allow gear disengagement. First check that the selector tube projection is as shown in Fig. 6.39. Engage 5th gear with the aid of a lever if necessary, then press the synchronizer sleeve away from the gearbox to eliminate any play and check that the sleeve overlaps the hub by 1.0 mm (0.039 in) (see Fig. 6.41). If not, turn the selector tube as necessary.

32 Fit the new locking plate into position. Support the shift fork with a pair of open-ended spanners (19 mm and 24 mm) or other suitable tool(s) about 12 mm (0.5 in) thick and knock the plate on.

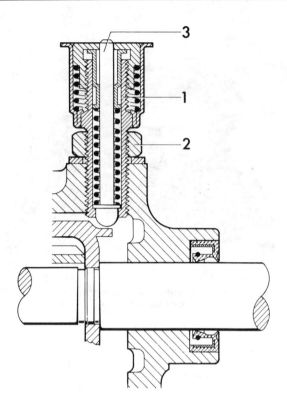

**Fig. 6.40 Sectional view showing 5th gear detent plunger –
020 gearbox (Sec 18)**

1 Adjusting sleeve   *3 Plunger*
2 Locknut

**Fig. 6.41 5th gear selector fork adjustment dimension (a) –
020 gearbox (Sec 18)**

33 Locate a new end cover gasket and then refit the end cover (with the release bearing) and tighten the retaining bolts.
34 Lubricate the clutch pushrod and insert it in the input shaft.
35 Fit the left-hand drive flange followed by the spring washer, retaining circlip and cap.
36 Gearbox reassembly is now complete. Select each gear in turn to ensure satisfactory and correct engagement.

**19 Gearshift mechanism (020 gearbox, 4 and 5-speed) –
removal, refitting and adjustment**

1   The layout of the gearshift mechanism is shown in Fig. 6.42.
2   The most likely items to require inspection and attention are those of the relay linkage assembly (photo). The shift rod bushes, relay links and lever pivots will wear and cause a progressive deterioration in the positive action of the gearchange.
3   If removing any parts of the linkage mechanism, first take note of its orientation to avoid possible confusion when refitting.
4   The selector rods (long and short) have balljoint linkages, and these can be detached by pressing back the clips on the plastic ends using a screwdriver.
5   When reassembling, lubricate the linkage pivot joints.

19.2 View showing the shift linkage connecting link (A), lever (B) and selector rod (C)

Gear lever and shift rod

6   Remove the gear lever knob and withdraw the rubber boot.
7   Undo the console retaining screw and withdraw the console.
8   Unbolt and remove the exhaust downpipe from the manifold and intermediate pipe section (Chapter 3). Disconnect the deflector plate and remove it by pulling it forwards.
9   Mark the relative positions of the shift rod and front clips, then loosen the clip bolt.
10   Undo the three retaining screws and detach the mounting from the steering and remove from the shift rod.
11   Disconnect the lever housing from the body, pull the housing forwards and, pressing it downwards, remove it.
12   Disconnect the retaining plate then press out the shift rod bush (inwards) and withdraw the rod from the housing.
13   Refitting is a reversal of the removal procedure. Align the shift rod and clip alignment marks to initially set the shift linkage adjustment. If, on completion, the respective gears cannot be positively engaged and further adjustment is necessary, try readjustment by loosening the shift rod clip and with the gears in neutral, centralise the gear lever in neutral and retighten the clip bolt. Accurate adjustment of the gear lever/shift linkage mechanism can only be made using a special VW tool and as this is not generally available, have the adjustment checked and set by your VW dealer.

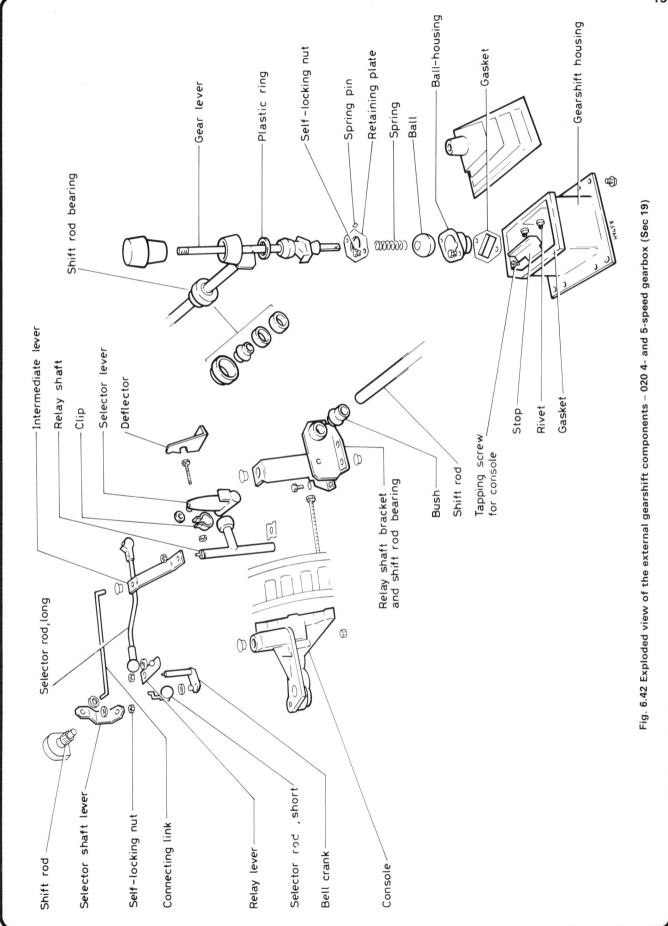

Fig. 6.42 Exploded view of the external gearshift components – 020 4- and 5-speed gearbox (Sec 19)

Shift rod bearing

Gear lever

Plastic ring

Self-locking nut

Spring pin

Retaining plate

Spring

Ball

Ball-housing

Gasket

Gearshift housing

Intermediate lever

Relay shaft

Clip

Selector lever

Deflector

Selector rod, long

Shift rod

Selector shaft lever

Self-locking nut

Connecting link

Relay lever

Selector rod, short

Bell crank

Console

Relay shaft bracket and shift rod bearing

Bush

Shift rod

Tapping screw for console

Stop

Rivet

Gasket

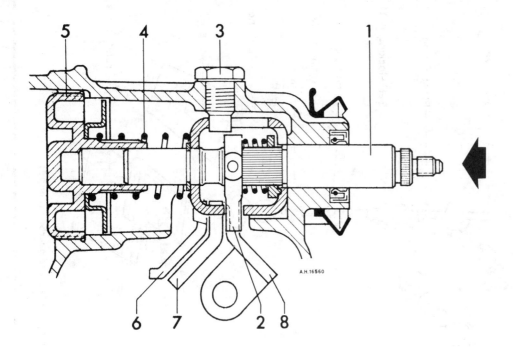

Fig. 6.43 Sectional view of gearshift internal linkage – 020 4-speed gearbox (Sec 19)

1   Selector shaft
2   Shift finger
3   Peg bolt
4   Spring
5   End cap
6   Reverse gear shift fork
7   1st/2nd gear shift fork
8   3rd/4th gear shift fork

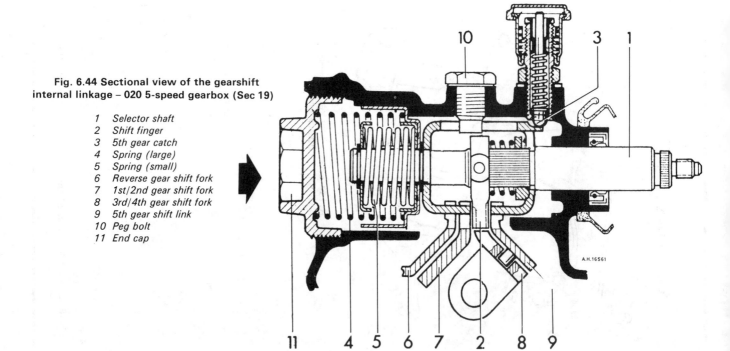

Fig. 6.44 Sectional view of the gearshift internal linkage – 020 5-speed gearbox (Sec 19)

1   Selector shaft
2   Shift finger
3   5th gear catch
4   Spring (large)
5   Spring (small)
6   Reverse gear shift fork
7   1st/2nd gear shift fork
8   3rd/4th gear shift fork
9   5th gear shift link
10 Peg bolt
11 End cap

20 Automatic transmission – general description

The automatic transmission is of the 3-speed epicyclic geartrain type incorporating two multi-plate clutches, one multi-plate brake, and one brake band. A fluid-filled torque converter transmits drive from the engine.

Three forward gears and one reverse are provided, with a kickdown facility for rapid acceleration during overtaking when an immediate change to a lower gear is required.

Due to the complex design of the automatic transmission, only the procedures described in the following Sections should be contemplated by the home mechanic. Further, if the unit develops a fault it

should be tested by a VW agent while still in the car in order to verify the fault.

If the vehicle is to be towed due to a malfunction in the automatic transmission, reference should first be made to the special precautionary notes in the *Jacking and towing* Section at the start of this manual.

21 Routine maintenance – automatic transmission

1   Every 10 000 miles (15 000 km) the automatic transmission fluid level should be checked and topped up if necessary. The check must be

made with the engine warm and idling, with the selector lever in position N (neutral) and the handbrake firmly applied.

2 With the car on a level surface, withdraw the dipstick and wipe it clean with a lint-free cloth. Reinsert it and withdraw it again; the level must be between the two marks on the dipstick. If not, top up the level through the dipstick tube using the specified fluid. Check for leaks if much topping-up is required. If, on inspection, no external leaks are visible check the final drive oil level. If this is found to be too high it is probable that the transmission fluid is leaking internally into the final drive casing and if this is the case it must be attended to without delay by your VW dealer.

3 The difference in quantity of fluid between the maximum and minimum marks on the fluid level dipstick is 0.4 litre (0.70 Imp pint).

4 Finally insert the dipstick and switch off the engine.

5 Every 30 000 miles (45 000 km) the automatic transmission fluid must be renewed, and the oil pan and strainer cleaned (where applicable). Under extreme operating conditions the fluid should be changed at more frequent intervals. First jack up the car and support it on axle stands.

6 Remove the drain plug and drain the fluid into a suitable container. If there is no drain plug, loosen the oil pan front bolts, then unscrew the rear bolts and lower the pan in order to drain the fluid. Take care to avoid scalding if the engine has just been run.

7 Unbolt and remove the pan from the transmission and remove the gasket. Clean the inside of the pan.

8 Unbolt the strainer cover and remove the strainer and gasket.

9 Clean the strainer and cover and dry thoroughly.

10 Refit the cover and strainer, together with a new gasket, and tighten the bolts to the specified torque.

11 Refit the pan, together with a new gasket, and tighten the securing bolts to the specified torque. Lower the vehicle.

12 Initially refill the transmission with 2.5 litre (4.4 Imp pint) of transmission fluid (see Specifications for type), then restart the engine. Check that the handbrake is still fully applied then move the gear selector lever through the full range of gears finishing at N. With the engine still idling, check the fluid level on the dipstick. The fluid level should at least be visible on the dipstick, but if it isn't add the minimum amount of fluid necessary to bring the level up to be visible on the tip of the dipstick.

13 Take the vehicle on a short drive to warm-up the fluid in the transmission then recheck the fluid level, as described in paragraph 2, and top up if necessary. Do not overfill with fluid or the excess will have to be drained off.

14 To check the oil level in the final drive unit (at the specified intervals given for the automatic transmission) the vehicle will need to be over an inspection pit or raised and supported on a level position on axle stands for access to the filler/level plug (Fig. 6.47).

15 Remove the plug (arrowed) and check that the oil is level with the bottom edge of the plug hole. If it isn't, top up the level through the plug hole with the specified lubricant type, then refit the plug. Lower the vehicle to ground to complete.

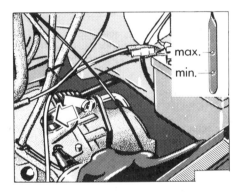

Fig. 6.45 Automatic transmission fluid level dipstick – remove in direction of arrow (Sec 21)

Fig. 6.47 Final drive oil level/filler plug location (arrowed) – automatic transmission (Sec 21)

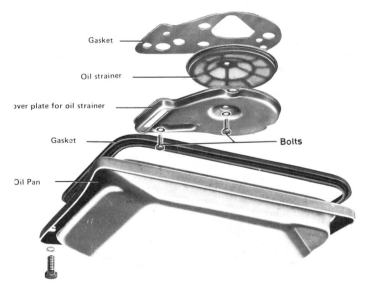

Fig. 6.46 Automatic transmission oil pan and strainer (Sec 21)

22 Automatic transmission – removal and refitting

1 Disconnect the battery earth lead.

2 Detach the speedometer drive cable connection from the transmission.

3 Unscrew and remove the upper engine-to-transmission securing bolts and the upper starter motor retaining bolt.

4 Referring to Section 3 in this Chapter, use a method suggested in paragraphs 1 and 2 to support the engine and transmission. Ultimately the transmission is lowered to the ground.

5 With the engine supported, undo the three engine mounting retaining bolts at the right-hand rear side of the engine.

6 Unbolt and remove the left rear engine/transmission mounting, complete with support.

7 Unbolt and remove the front engine/transmission mounting. Push the engine rearwards to withdraw the mounting.

8 Referring to Chapter 7, unbolt and detach the left-hand driveshaft from the transmission drive flange.

9 Undo the starter motor lower retaining bolts and withdraw the starter motor.

10 Unbolt and withdraw the engine sump protector plate.

11 Check that the selector lever is in the P position then detach the drive range selector cable (see Section 24).

12 Detach the cables support bracket from the transmission.
13 Disconnect the throttle and accelerator pedal cables, but do not alter their settings.
14 Working through the hole left by the starter, locate and undo the three bolts holding the torque converter to the driveplate. These can be seen also in the gap left when the bottom cover plate is removed.
15 Unbolt and detach the right-hand driveshaft (Chapter 7).
16 Detach the lower balljoint from the track control arm (wishbone) then support it at the outboard end (Fig. 6.48). Take care not to damage the driveshaft gaiter.

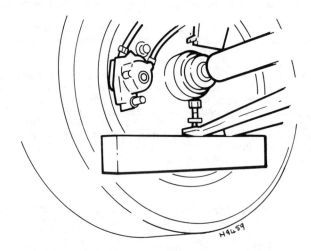

Fig. 6.48 Disconnect and support lower balljoint/track control arm with block of wood (Sec 22)

17 Now push the engine and transmission unit to the right as far as the stop then lift and tie up the left-hand drive shaft out of the way.
18 Locate a trolley jack under the transmission for support.
19 Undo and remove the remaining engine-to-transmission bolts at the bottom then check that all other transmission attachments are disconnected.
20 The transmission may now be removed. Lift a little and push the driveshaft up and out of the way. Pull the transmission off the dowels and lower it gently, at the same time supporting the torque converter, which will fall out if not held in place in the transmission. There are two shafts and two sets of splines; be careful not to bend either of them or you will have a leaking torque converter.
21 The transmission is too heavy for one person to lift so a sling and tackle must be used to support and lower the transmission if a suitable trolley jack is not available.
22 When the transmission is separated from the engine, it can be lowered and manoeuvred from beneath the vehicle.
23 Position a suitable support plate across the torque converter housing to retain the torque converter in position whilst the transmission is removed.
24 Refitting is the reversal of removal. Ensure that the torque converter remains fully engaged when attaching the engine and transmission.
25 Semi-tighten the respective mountings as they are attached then, when fully located, remove the engine/transmission supports and fully tighten the mounting bolts to the specified torque wrench settings.
26 If a new transmission unit has been fitted it will be necessary to readjust the throttle cable (Section 25).
27 Check the selector cable adjustment, as described in Section 24.
28 Refill the transmission with the correct quantity of fluid and recheck the fluid level, as described in Section 21.
29 Remove the final drive filler/level plug and check that the oil level is to the bottom of the hole. If necessary top up the level with the specified oil, then refit the plug.

23 Automatic transmission – stall test

1 The stall test is used to check the performance of the torque converter and the results can also indicate certain faults in the automatic transmission.

2 Connect a tachometer to the engine, then run the engine until warm.
3 Finally apply the handbrake and footbrake, and select position D,
4 Fully depress the accelerator pedal and record the engine speed, then release the pedal. **Do not** depress the pedal for any period longer than five seconds otherwise the torque converter will overheat. After a period of twenty seconds repeat the test. According to gearbox type the stall speeds should be as follows:

TJA	2390 to 2640 rpm
TKA	2340 to 2590 rpm

Note: Deduct 125 rpm per 1000 m (3200 feet) altitude.
5 If the stall speed is higher than the speed given above then the forward clutch or 1st gear one-way clutch may be slipping. Repeat the test in position 1; if the stall speed is now correct the 1st gear one-way clutch is faulty, but if the speed is still too high, the forward clutch is faulty.
6 A stall speed up to 200 rpm below the specified amount indicates poor engine performance, and the engine should therefore be tuned up as necessary.
7 If the stall speed is more than 200 rpm below the specified amount, the torque converter stator one-way clutch is faulty and the torque converter should be renewed, but first ensure that the engine is tuned correctly and, if adjustments are necessary, recheck the stall speed.
8 Switch off the engine and disconnect the tachometer.

24 Automatic transmission selector cable – removal, refitting and adjustment

1 At the transmission end of the cable, undo the cable clamp nut and detach the cable from the selector lever cable bracket.
2 Working inside the car, remove the retaining screws securing the selector lever cover to the console, lift the cover up the lever and turn it to one side.
3 Prise free the retaining clip (locking washer) securing the selector cable to the shift mechanism and detach the cable.
4 The cable can now be withdrawn and removed.
5 Refit the selector cable reversing the removal procedure. Lubricate the cable at each end with some light grease before connecting. Use a new locking washer to secure it to the selector mechanism. Before tightening the cable clamp nut at the gearbox operating lever adjustment must be made.
6 To adjust the selector cable, push the selector lever to the P position and move the selector lever at the gearbox rearwards against the stop to the corresponding P position. Check that the cable is not kinked or bent at any point through its run then tighten the clamp nut.

25 Automatic transmission throttle and accelerator pedal cables (2E2 carburettor) – adjustment

1 Start the engine and run it up until its normal operating temperature and idle speed is reached. This ensures that the throttle valve is in the overrun position which is essential for this adjustment.
2 With the selector lever at the P position, loosen the accelerator pedal adjustment nut and detach the cable (see Fig. 6.51).
3 Remove the air cleaner unit, as described in Chapter 3.
4 Loosen the throttle cable nut at the support bracket at the carburettor.
5 Referring to Fig. 6.52 rotate the warm-up lever A so that the throttle control pin is not touching it, then retain the lever in this position by moving lever C with a screwdriver.
6 Pull free and detach the respective vacuum hoses from the three/four point unit.
7 You will now need a vacuum pump with a connecting hose suitable for connecting to the lower vacuum hose connection (E) on the three/four point unit. Plug off connections F and G (Fig. 6.53).
8 Apply vacuum with the pump so that the diaphragm pushrod holds in the overrun position and a clearance exists between the cold idle adjustment screw and the diaphragm pushrod. Pull the throttle cable sleeve away from the carburettor to take up the play whilst ensuring that the throttle valve remains closed and the operating lever at the transmission remains against the overrun stop. Tighten the throttle

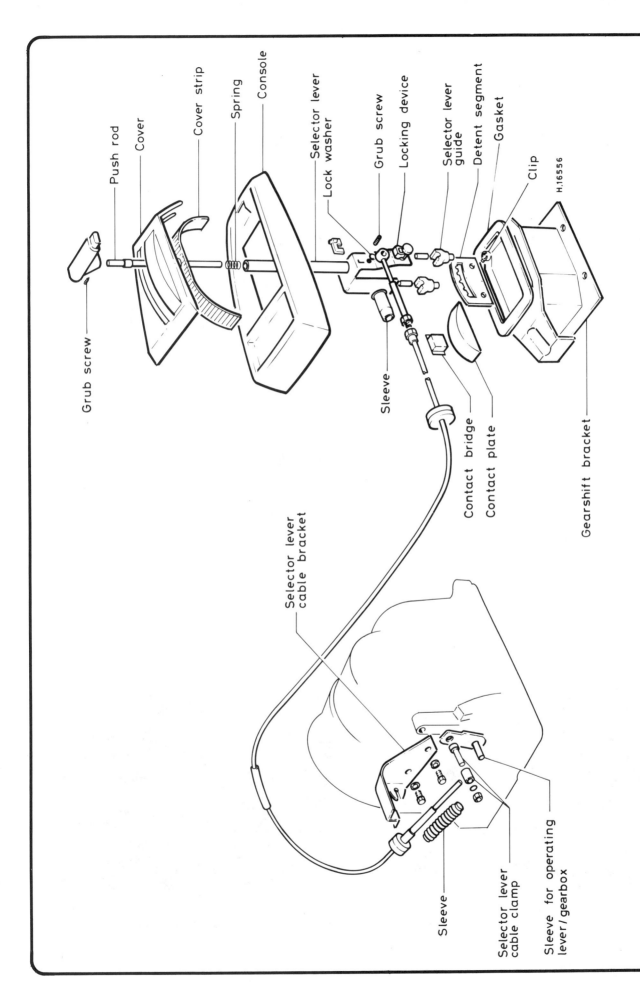

Grub screw

Push rod

Cover

Cover strip

Spring

Console

Selector lever

Lock washer

Grub screw

Locking device

Selector lever guide

Detent segment

Gasket

Clip

H.16556

Sleeve

Contact bridge

Contact plate

Gearshift bracket

Selector lever cable bracket

Sleeve

Selector lever cable clamp

Sleeve for operating lever / gearbox

Fig. 6.49 Automatic transmission selector cable and shift mechanism (Sec 24)

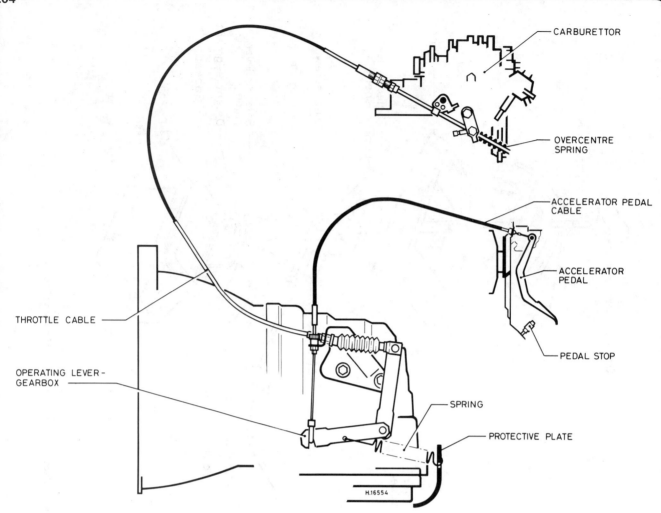

— CARBURETTOR

— OVERCENTRE SPRING

— ACCELERATOR PEDAL CABLE

— ACCELERATOR PEDAL

THROTTLE CABLE —

OPERATING LEVER - GEARBOX —

— PEDAL STOP

SPRING —

PROTECTIVE PLATE —

H.16554

Fig. 6.50 Automatic transmission throttle and accelerator pedal cables (Sec 25)

Fig. 6.51 Accelerator pedal cable adjusting nut and operating lever connection (arrowed) – automatic transmission (Sec 25)

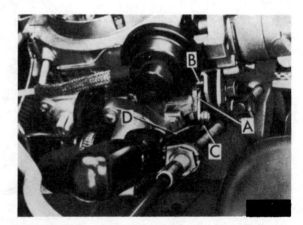

Fig. 6.52 View showing warm-up lever (A), throttle valve control pin (B), lever (C) and screwdriver location (D) (Sec 25)

Fig. 6.53 Vacuum pump connections to the three/four-point vacuum unit (Sec 25)

Fig. 6.54 Throttle cable adjuster nut (1) and locknut (2) (Sec 25)

Fig. 6.55 Throttle cable over-centre spring compression point (a) (Sec 25)

cable adjuster so that it contacts the support bracket and is stress-free, then retighten the locknut to secure (Fig. 6.54).

9 Reconnect the accelerator pedal cable then get an assistant to press the accelerator pedal down to the kickdown stop position. Rotate the accelerator pedal adjustment nut so that the gearbox operating lever is in contact with the kickdown stop, then tighten the locknut.

10 To check the adjustment is correctly made, the throttle must be in the overrun position and the gearbox operating lever must be in contact with the overrun stop. Get an assistant to depress the accelerator pedal until the full throttle pressure point is reached (not kickdown), then check that the throttle lever is resting against the full throttle stop and that the over-centre spring is not compressed.

11 Next depress the accelerator pedal past the full throttle position to the kickdown position and then check that the gearbox operating lever rests against the kickdown stop, and the over-centre spring is compressed approximately 8 mm (0.3 in) (Fig. 6.55).

12 On completion refit the air cleaner to the carburettor, with reference to Chapter 3.

Fault diagnosis overleaf

26 Fault diagnosis – manual gearbox and automatic transmission

Symptom	Reason(s)
Manual gearbox	
Gearbox noisy in neutral	Mainshaft (input shaft) bearings worn
Gearbox noisy only when moving (in all gears)	Pinion shaft (output shaft) bearings worn Differential bearings worn
Gearbox noisy in only one gear	Worn, damaged, or chipped gearteeth
Jumps out of gear	Worn synchro-hubs or baulk rings Worn selector shaft detent plunger or spring Worn selector forks
Ineffective synchromesh	Worn baulk rings or synchro-hubs
Difficulty in engaging gears	Clutch fault Gearshift mechanism out of adjustment Worn synchro-hubs or baulk rings
Automatic transmission	
Shift speeds too high or too low	Throttle and pedal cables out of adjustment
Loss of drive	Fluid level too low Driveplate-to-torque converter bolts fallen out Internal fault
Erratic drive	Fluid level too low Dirty oil pan filter
Gear selection jerky	Fluid level too low Idle speed too high
Poor acceleration	Faulty torque converter Throttle and pedal cables out of adjustment Brakes sticking on

Chapter 7 Driveshafts

Contents

Specifications

Type	Solid (left) and tubular (right) driveshafts with constant velocity (CV) joints at each end. Vibration damper fitted to right-hand driveshaft on 55 and 66 kW engine models

Length

	Left-hand	Right-hand
084 gearbox	465 mm (18.32 in)	677.2 mm (26.68 in)
020 gearbox:		
Not GTI models	443 mm (17.45 in)	677.2 mm (26.68 in)
GTI models	447 mm (17.61 in)	681.2 mm (26.84 in)
010 gearbox (automatic)	443 mm (17.45 in)	677.2 mm (26.68 in)

Torque wrench settings

	Nm	lbf ft
Driveshaft to flange	45	33
Driveshaft/hub nut	230	170
Drive flange retaining bolt (1.05 and 1.3 litre)	25	18

1 General description

Drive from the differential unit to the roadwheels is provided by two driveshafts. Each driveshaft has a constant velocity (CV) joint at each end, the inner end being flanged and secured to the final drive flange by bolts and the outer end being splined to the hub.

The left-hand driveshaft is of solid construction and is shorter than the tubular right-hand driveshaft.

The driveshaft joints are sealed and require no maintenance apart from checking the rubber boots at the specified routine maintenance intervals for any sign of leakage or damage, in which case they must be renewed (photo).

If the joints are suspected of excessive wear, noticeable when changing from acceleration to overrun and vice versa, the shafts should be removed and the joints dismantled to inspect for wear or damage, and overhauled or renewed as necessary.

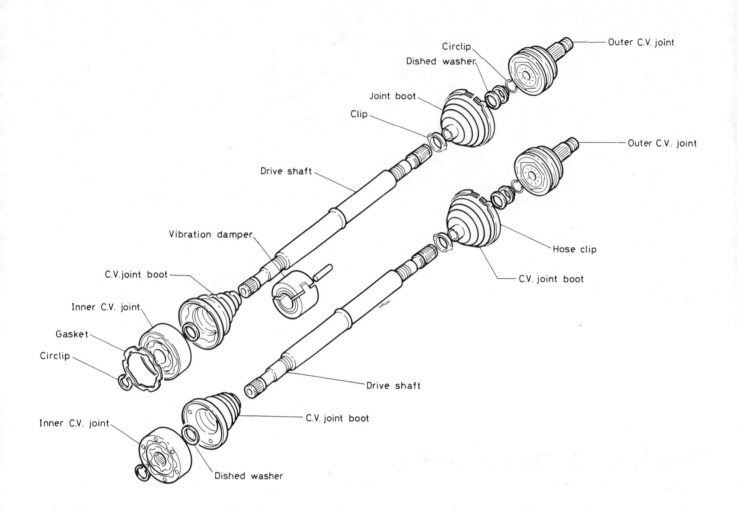

Fig. 7.1 Exploded view of the driveshaft (Sec 1)

Upper GTI models   *Lower Other models*

1.3 Check the condition of the driveshaft rubber boots

2 Driveshaft – removal and refitting

1   The driveshafts are secured to the drive flanges at the gearbox end by socket-head bolts, the removal of which will require the use of a special splined key. Whilst an Allen key may suffice, it is also likely to strip the socket in the bolts.

2   Remove the wheel trim from the relevant wheel. With the handbrake applied, loosen the driveshaft nut. The nut is tightened to a high torque and a socket extension may be required.

3   Jack up the front of the car and support it on axle stands. Remove the roadwheel.

4   Using a splined tool, remove the socket-head bolts holding the inner CV joint to the final drive flange. Be careful to use a proper key for if the socket head is damaged the result will be time consuming to say the least. These bolts are quite tight (photos).

5   Once all the bolts are removed the CV joint may be pulled away from the final drive and the shaft removed from the hub joint. If difficulty is experienced, separate the track control arm (wishbone) from the wheel bearing housing (see Chapter 11) and pivot the arm downwards. The suspension strut can then be pulled outwards and the driveshaft removed. Do not move the car on its wheels with either driveshaft removed, otherwise damage may occur to the wheel bearings.

6   If the driveshaft(s) are to be renewed complete, the vibration damper fitted to the right-hand driveshaft on 1.6 and 1.8 litre carburettor engine models will have to be transferred to the new shaft.

2.4A Driveshaft-to-final drive flange socket-head bolts

2.4B Removal of the socket-head bolts and spacer plates

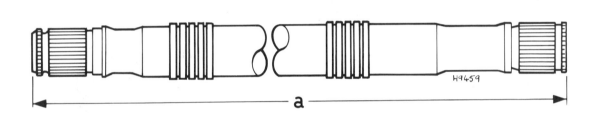

Fig. 7.2 Measure new driveshaft between points indicated (a) to ensure correct length for your model (Sec 2)

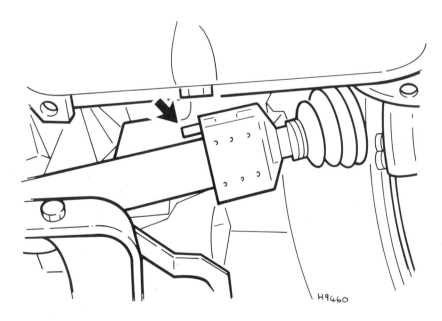

Fig. 7.3 Vibration damper and retaining pin (arrowed) – 1.6 and 1.8 litre carburettor models (Sec 2)

To remove the damper, use a pin punch and drive out one of the retaining spring pins. The damper can then be pivoted open and removed from the driveshaft. Note the position of the damper unit on the shaft as it must be refitted in the same position.

7   Before fitting the vibration damper, check that the adhesive tape on its inner diameter is still sticky. Renew the tape if necessary. It is also advisable to renew the spring pin when refitting the damper. When the damper is in position check it for security.

8   Refitting of the driveshaft is a reversal of the removal procedure. The hub and driveshaft splines must be clean and lubricated with a little molybdenum disulphide based grease. Check that the inner flange/CV joint mating faces are clean and, where applicable, renew the joint gasket on the joint face of the inner CV unit.

9   A new driveshaft/hub nut must be fitted, initially hand tightened, then fully tightened to the specified torque when the car is lowered to the ground. Also tighten the inner bolts to the specified torque setting.

3   Driveshaft – dismantling and reassembly

1   Having removed the shaft from the car it may be dismantled for the individual parts to be checked for wear.

2   The rubber boots, clips and thrust washers may be renewed if necessary but the CV joints may only be renewed as complete assemblies. It is not possible to fit new hubs, outer cases, ball cages or balls separately for they are mated to a tolerance on manufacture. A replacement CV joint assembly kit will include the rubber boot and a tube of special grease, but you will need to specify which car model you have as the CV joints differ.

Outer joint

3   Loosen the rubber boot clips and release the large diameter end of the boot from the joint.

4   Using a soft-faced mallet, drive the outer joint from the driveshaft.

5   Extract the circlip from the driveshaft and remove the spacer (if fitted) and dished washer; noting that the concave side faces the outboard end of the driveshaft.

6   Slide the rubber boot and clips from the driveshaft.

7   Mark the hub in relation to the cage and joint housing.

8   Swivel the hub and cage until the rectangular apertures are aligned with the housing then withdraw the cage and hub.

9   Turn the cage until the rectangular apertures are aligned with the housing then withdraw the cage and hub.

10 Turn the hub and insert one of the segments into one of the rectangular apertures, then swivel the hub from the cage.

11 Note that the joint components including the balls form a matched set and must only be fitted to the correct side.

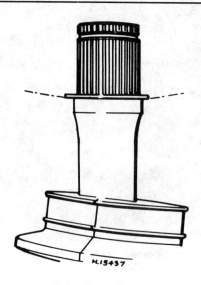

Fig. 7.5 Correct fitment of the dished washer (Sec 3)

Fig. 7.6 Removing the cage and hub from the outer joint housing (Sec 3)

Arrow shows rectangular aperture

Fig. 7.7 Removing the outer joint hub from the cage (Sec 3)

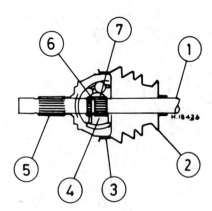

Fig. 7.4 Cross-section diagram of the driveshaft outer joint (Sec 3)

1	Driveshaft	*5*	Splined shaft
2	Rubber boot	*6*	Distance washer
3	Worm drive clip	*7*	Dished washer
4	Bearing race		

12 Clean the components in paraffin and examine them for wear and damage. Excessive wear will have been evident when driving the car, especially when changing from acceleration to overrun. Renew the components as necessary.

13 Commence reassembly by inserting half the amount of special grease (ie 45g) into the joint housing.

14 Fit the hub to the cage by inserting one of the segments into the rectangular aperture.

15 With the rectangular apertures aligned with the housing, fit the hub and cage to the housing in its original position.
16 Swivel the hub and cage and insert the balls from alternate sides.
17 Fit the rubber boot and clips on the driveshaft.
18 Fit the dished washer and spacer (if applicable) to the driveshaft and insert the circlip in the groove.
19 Locate the outer joint on the driveshaft and, using a soft-faced mallet, drive it fully into position until the circlip is engaged.
20 Insert the remaining grease in the joint then locate the boot and tighten the clips. On models fitted with the 90 mm (3.55 in) diameter CV joint, ventilate the joint briefly prior to tightening the small hose clip, to balance the pressure in the joint.

Inner joint – models except GTI
21 Extract the retaining clip (photo).
22 Where applicable, use a small drift to drive the plastic cap from the joint housing.
23 Mark the exact location of the rubber boot end face relative to the driveshaft. A length of insulation tape or quick-drying paint applied to the shaft will suffice. This will show the exact location for the rubber boot on the shaft when refitting (particularly important on the GTI model).
24 Loosen the clip and slide the rubber boot away from the joint.

3.21 Driveshaft inner joint retaining clip (arrowed) – 1.3 litre

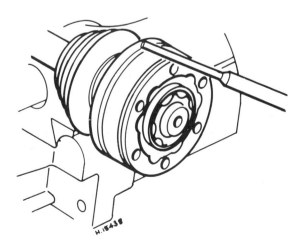

Fig. 7.8 Removing the plastic cap from the inner joint housing (Sec 3)

Fig. 7.9 Removing the inner joint hub from the cage (Sec 3)

Align the grooves – arrowed

25 Support the joint over the jaws of a vice and, using a soft metal drift, drive out the driveshaft.
26 Remove the dished washer from the driveshaft, noting that the concave side faces the end of the driveshaft.
27 Slide the rubber boot and clip from the driveshaft.
28 Mark the hub in relation to the cage and joint housing.
29 Turn the hub and cage 90° to the housing and press out the hub and cage.
30 Extract the balls then turn the hub so that one of the track grooves is located on the rim of the cage, and withdraw the hub.
31 Note that the joint components including the balls form a matched set and must only be fitted in the correct side.
32 Clean the components in paraffin and examine them for wear and damage. Excessive wear will have been evident when driving the car especially when changing from acceleration to overrun. Renew the components as necessary.
33 Commence reassembly by fitting the hub to the cage.
34 Insert the balls into position using the special grease to hold them in place.
35 Press the hub and cage into the housing, making sure that the wide track spacing on the housing will be adjacent to the narrow spacing on the hub (see Fig. 7.10) when fully assembled. Note also that the chamfer on the hub splines must face the large diameter side of the housing.
36 Swivel the cage ahead of the hub so that the balls enter their respective tracks then align the hub and cage with the housing.
37 Check that the hub can be moved freely through its operating arc.
38 Fit the rubber boot and clip to the driveshaft followed by the dished washer.

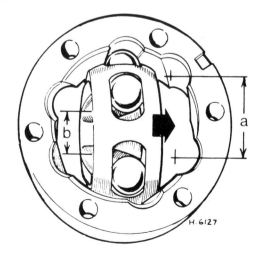

Fig. 7.10 Assembly of the inner joint cage and hub to the housing (Sec 3)

a must be aligned with b

39 Mount the driveshaft in a vice then drive the joint onto the driveshaft using a suitable metal tube on the hub.
40 Fit the returning circlip in its groove.
41 Insert the remaining grease in the joint then tap the plastic cap into position (where applicable).
42 Reposition the driveshaft boot, ensuring that when fitted it is not twisted or distorted abnormally and that the outer end aligns with the mark made during removal.

Inner joint – GTI

43 Proceed as described for other models, but note that a gasket is located on the drive flange end face of the inner joint. This gasket must be renewed. Wipe dry the mating face on the joint, peel the protective foil from the gasket and carefully locate it onto the inner face of the joint.
44 When refitting the driveshaft boot its fitting position is critical and is shown in Figs. 7.11 and 7.12.

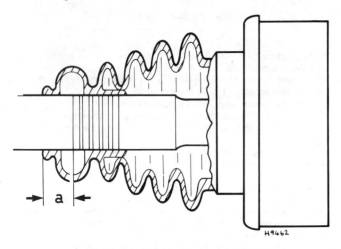

Fig. 7.11 Inner CV joint boot installation position – GTI models (Sec 3)

a = 17 mm (0.669 in) on left-hand shaft

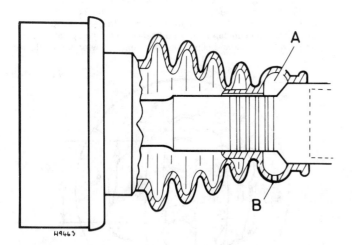

Fig. 7.12 Inner CV joint boot installation position on the right-hand driveshaft – GTI models (Sec 3)

    A Ventilation chamber   B Ventilation hole

4 Drive flange oil seals – renewal

1 Jack up the front of the car and support on axle stands. Apply the handbrake.

2 Detach the inner ends of the driveshafts from the drive flange with reference to Section 2, but note the following:

  (a) On 1.05 and 1.3 litre models detachment of the right-hand driveshaft will necessitate unbolting the anti-roll bar from its body mounting and disconnecting the track control arm from the suspension strut on that side (see Chapter 11 for details). Pivot the track control arm downwards

  (b) On automatic transmission models, detachment of the left-hand driveshaft will necessitate disconnecting the track control arm from the suspension strut on that side (see Chapter 11 for details). Pivot the track control arm downwards.

3 With the driveshaft disconnected from the drive flange tie it up out of the way.
4 On 1.05 and 1.3 litre models, unscrew the bolt from the centre of the drive flange using a bar and two temporarily inserted bolts to hold the flange stationary.
5 On other models, prise off the cap (where fitted) and extract the circlip and dished washer from the drive flange. Note which way round the dished washer is fitted.
6 Place a container beneath the gearbox then remove the drive flanges and lever out the old oil seals (photo). Identify the flanges side for side.

4.6 Prising out the drive flange oil seal from the gearbox housing

Fig. 7.13 Drive flange removal using VW tool (Sec 4)

Gearbox 020

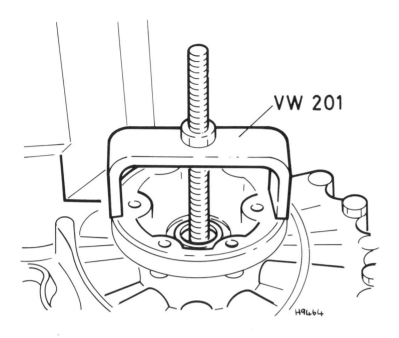

Fig. 7.14 Drive flange refitting using VW tool (Sec 4)

Gearbox 020

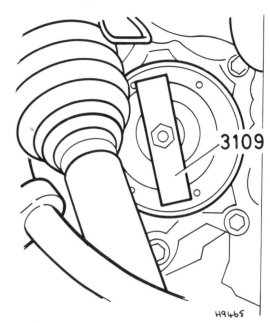

Fig. 7.15 Drive flange refitting using VW tool (Sec 4)

Automatic transmission

7   Clean and inspect the oil seal recesses. Where applicable, renew the sleeve in the recess if it is damaged.

8   Fill the space between the lips of the new seal with multi-purpose grease, then drive it fully into the housing using a suitable length of metal tube.

9   Refit the drive flange, taking care not to damage the oil seal lips. If available use VW special tool to fit the flange.

10 With the drive flange in position, refit and tighten the securing bolt to the specified torque wrench setting (1.05 and 1.3 litre) or locate the dished washer (ensuring correct orientation noted when removing) and the circlip on other models.

11 Refit the cap (where applicable) and the driveshaft with reference to Section 2. Reconnect the track control arm to the suspension strut and the anti-roll bar to the body mounting, where applicable, referring to Chapter 11.

12 With the car lowered to the ground, remove the final drive filler/level plug and check that the oil level is to the bottom of the hole. If necessary top up the level with the specified oil, then refit the plug.

5   Fault diagnosis – driveshafts

Symptom	Reason(s)
Vibrations and noise on turns	Worn driveshaft joints
Noise on taking up drive	Worn driveshaft joints Worn drive flange and/or driveshaft splines Loose driveshaft bolts or nut

Chapter 8 Braking system

Contents

Specifications

System type ....

Hydraulic, dual circuit, split diagonally, pressure regulator on some models. Cable-operated handbrake on rear wheels. Disc front brakes on all models, drum or disc rear brake according to model

Front brakes

Disc thickness (new):
1.05 and 1.3 litre	10 mm (0.394 in)
1.6 and 1.8 litre	12 mm (0.473 in)
1.8 litre with ventilated discs	20 mm (0.790 in)

Disc thickness (minimum):
1.05 and 1,3 litre	8 mm (0.315 in)
1.6 and 1.8 litre	10 mm (0.394 in)
1.8 litre with ventilated discs	18 mm (0.709 in)

Disc pad thickness – new (excluding backplate):
1.05 and 1.3 litre	12 mm (0.473 in)
1.6 and 1.8 litre	14 mm (0.552 in)
1.8 litre with ventilated discs	10 mm (0.394 in)

Disc pad thickness – minimum (including backplate):
All models	7 mm (0.276 in)

Rear brakes – drum

Drum internal diameter (new)	180.0 mm (7.092 in)
Drum internal diameter (maximum)	181.0 mm (7.131 in)

Maximum drum run-out:
Radial (at friction surface)	0.05 mm (0.002 in)
Lateral (wheel contact surface)	0.2 mm (0.008 in)

Lining thickness:
Minimum (including shoe)	5.00 mm (0.20 in)
Minimum (excluding shoe)	2.5 mm (0.10 in)

Rear brakes – disc

Disc thickness (new)	10.0 mm (0.394 in)
Disc thickness (minimum)	8.0 mm (0.315 in)
Maximum disc run-out	0.06 mm (0.002 in)
Disc pad thickness – new (including backplate)	12.0 mm (0.473 in)
Disc pad thickness – minimum (including backplate)	7.0 mm (0.28 in)

General

Master cylinder diameter	20.65 mm (0.814 in)
Brake wheel cylinder diameter	14.29 mm (0.563 in)
Brake servo unit diameter:	
Manual transmission	178 mm (7.0 in)
Automatic transmission	228 mm (9.0 in)
Brake fluid type	Hydraulic fluid to FMVSS 116 DOT 4 (Duckhams Universal Brake and Clutch Fluid)

Torque wrench settings

	Nm	lbf ft
Caliper upper securing bolt	25	19
Caliper lower securing bolt	25	19
Master cylinder securing nuts	20	15
Servo unit securing nuts	20	15
Splash guard to strut	10	7
Backplate to rear axle	60	44
Rear disc brake guide pin (self-locking)	35	26
Rear disc brake carrier bolts	65	48
Rear disc brake cover plate-to-axle bolts	60	44
Roadwheel bolt	110	81

1 General description

The braking system is of hydraulic, dual circuit type with discs at the front and drum or disc brakes (according to model) at the rear. The hydraulic circuit is split diagonally so that with the failure of one circuit, one front and one rear brake remain operative. A load-sensitive pressure regulator is incorporated in the rear hydraulic circuits on some models to prevent the rear wheels locking in advance of the front wheels during heavy application of the brakes. The regulator proportions the hydraulic pressure between the front and rear brakes according to the load being carried.

The handbrake operates on the rear wheels only and the lever incorporates a switch which illuminates a warning light on the instrument panel when the handbrake is applied. The same warning light is wired into the low hydraulic fluid switch circuit.

2 Routine maintenance – braking system

1   The brake fluid level should be checked every week – the reservoir is translucent and the fluid level should be between the MIN and MAX marks. If necessary, top up with the specified brake fluid (photo). However, additional fluid will only be necessary if the hydraulic system is leaking, therefore the source of the leak must first be traced and rectified. Note that the level will drop slightly as the front disc pads wear, but in this case it is not necessary to top up the level.

2   Every 10 000 miles (15 000 km) or 12 months, if this occurs sooner, the hydraulic pipes and unions should be checked for chafing, leakage, cracks and corrosion. At the same time check the operation of the brake pressure regulator and check the disc pads and rear brake linings for wear. Also check the servo vacuum hose for condition and security.

3   Check the brake warning device for correct operation by switching the ignition on and releasing the handbrake. Now press the contact on the reservoir filler cap down and get an assistant to check that the handbrake and dual circuit warning lamp light up (photo).

4   Renew the brake fluid every 2 years.

3 Front brake disc pads – inspection and renewal

1   The disc pad lining wear can be checked by viewing through a hole in the wheel rim and by using a mirror on the inside of the wheel (photo). The use of a torch may also be necessary. If the thickness of any disc pad is less than the minimum amount given in the Specifications, renew the front pads as a set. Where the thickness is more than the minumum amount, due consideration must be given to whether there is sufficient lining left until the next service: 1 mm (0.04 in) of lining will last for approximately 6000 miles (10 000 km).

2   To remove the disc pads, first jack up the front of the car and support it on axle stands. Apply the handbrake and remove both front wheels.

2.1 Topping-up brake fluid

2.3 Press contact (arrowed) to check the brake warning device

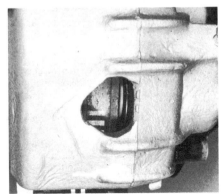
3.1 Front brake pad inspection aperture in caliper

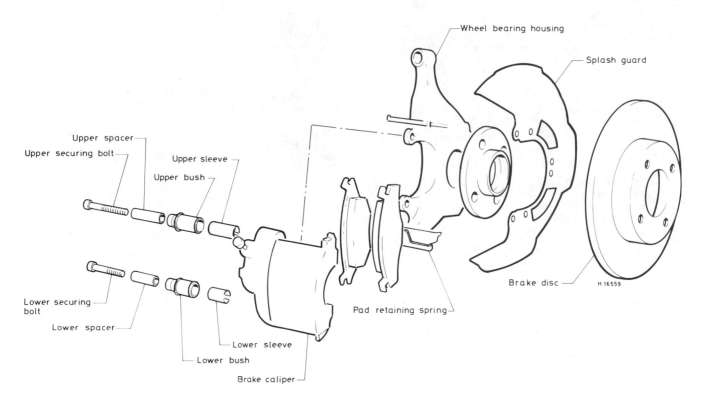

Fig. 8.1 Exploded view of a typical disc brake assembly (Sec 3)

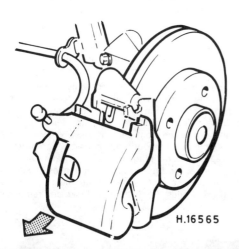

Fig. 8.2 Caliper removal – pivot outwards from the bottom
(Sec 3)

3   Use an Allen key and unscrew the upper and lower caliper securing bolts (photo). Withdraw the caliper and tie it up out of the way. Do not allow the weight of the caliper to stretch or distort the brake hose (photo).
4   Withdraw each pad by sliding it sideways from the wheel bearing housing, noting that the pads differ, the pad with the larger friction area being fitted to the outside.
5   The retaining spring can be detached from the wheel bearing housing, but note its orientation (photo). Replace the spring when renewing the pads.
6   Brush the dust and dirt from the caliper, piston, disc and pads, *but do not inhale it as it is injurious to health.* Scrape any scale or rust from the disc and pad backing plates.

7   If the pads are to be renewed, they must be replaced as a set on both sides at the front. If the original pads are to be re-used they must be refitted to their original positions each side.
8   Using a piece of wood, push the piston back into the caliper, but while doing this check the level of the fluid in the reservoir and if necessary draw off some with a pipette or release some from the caliper bleed screw. Tighten the screw immediately afterwards.
9   Relocate the retaining spring (photo).
10 Refit the inner pad (smaller friction area), followed by the outer pad. Locate the pad backing plate notches as shown (photo).
11 Refit the brake caliper, locating it at the top end first. Pivot the bottom end into position, align the upper and lower retaining bolt

3.3A Caliper securing bolt removal

3.3B Removing the caliper

3.10 Refitting the front brake disc pads

3.5 Removing the retaining spring

holes, then insert the bolts. Take care not to press the caliper in more than is necessary when fitting the bolts or the retainer springs may be distorted which, in turn, will give noisy braking. Tighten the bolts to the specified torque.

12 On completion, the brake pedal should be depressed firmly several times with the car stationary so that the brake pads take up their normal running positions. Also check the brake hydraulic fluid level in the master cylinder reservoir and top up if necessary.

4 Front brake disc caliper – removal, overhaul and refitting

1 Unbolt and remove the caliper from the wheel bearing housing, as described in the previous Section.

2 If available fit a hose clamp to the caliper flexible brake hose. Alternatively remove the fluid reservoir filler cap and tighten it down onto a piece of polythene sheet in order to reduce the loss of hydraulic fluid.

3 Loosen and detach the brake hose union at the caliper; allow for a certain amount of fluid spillage, and plug the hose union to prevent the ingress of dirt.

3.9 Pad retaining spring is located as shown

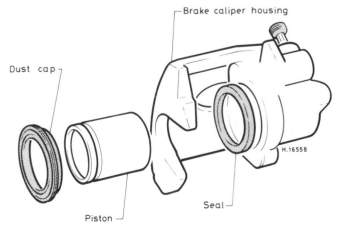

Fig. 8.3 Front disc brake caliper components (Sec 4)

4   Clean the external surfaces of the caliper with paraffin and wipe dry; plug the fluid inlet during this operation.
5   Prise free and remove the dust seal from the piston (photo).
6   Using air pressure from a foot pump in the fluid inlet blow the piston from the cylinder, but take care not to drop the piston. Prise the sealing ring from the cylinder bore. Take care not to scratch the cylinder bore.
7   Clean the components with methylated spirit and allow to dry. Inspect the surfaces of the piston, cylinder and frames for wear, damage and corrosion. If evident renew the caliper, but if the components are in good condition obtain a repair kit of seals.
8   Dip the new sealing ring in brake fluid and locate it in the cylinder bore groove using the fingers only to manipulate it.
9   Manipulate the new dust cap into position on the piston, the inner seal lip engaging in the piston groove. Use a suitable screwdriver to ease it into position, but take care not to damage the seal or scratch the piston.
10 Smear the piston with brake fluid and press it into position in the caliper bore.
11 Check that the brake hose union is clean, then unplug it and refit it to the caliper, but do not fully tighten it at this stage.
12 Refit the caliper to the wheel bearing housing, as described in the previous Section.
13 Tighten the brake hose union so that the hose is not twisted or in a position where it will chafe against surrounding components.
14 Remove the hose clamp or polythene sheet from the reservoir. Top up the brake fluid reservoir and bleed the brakes, described in Section 15.

Fig. 8.4 Dust seal location on the caliper piston (Sec 4)

4.5 Removing the dust seal (cap)

5   Front brake disc – examination, removal and refitting

1   Remove the disc pads and caliper, as described in Section 3, leaving the brake hose attached to the caliper. Support the caliper to prevent straining the hose.
2   Rotate the disc and examine it for deep scoring or grooving.
3   Using a micrometer, check that the disc thickness is not less than the minimum amount given in the Specifications.
4   Remove the cross-head screw and withdraw the brake disc from the hub (photo).
5   If necessary the splash guard can be removed from the wheel bearing housing by unscrewing the three bolts.
6   Refitting is a reversal of removal, but make sure that the mating faces of the disc and hub are clean. Refer to Section 3 when refitting the disc pads and caliper.

5.4 Front brake disc retaining screw (arrowed)

6   Rear brake disc pads – inspection and renewal

1   To check the rear brake disc pads for wear, refer to Section 3, paragraph 1.
2   To remove the disc pads, chock the front wheels, jack up the rear of the car and support it on axle stands. Remove both rear wheels.
3   Release the handbrake then detach the handbrake cable from the caliper (photo).
4   Undo and remove the caliper upper retaining bolt (photo). Renew this self-locking bolt on reassembly.
5   Pivot the caliper downwards (photo).
6   Before removing each brake pad, if they are to be re-used, mark them for identification to ensure that they are refitted to their original location, their positions must not be changed.
7   Brush the dust and dirt from the caliper, piston, disc and pads, *but do not inhale it as it is injurious to health.* Scrape any scale or rust from the disc and pad backing plates.
8   Using a piece of wood push the piston back into the caliper, but while doing this check the level of the fluid in the reservoir and if necessary draw off some with a pipette or release some from the caliper bleed screw. Tighten the screw immediately afterwards.
9   Locate the respective brake pads into position (photo).
10 Before refitting the caliper and retaining bolt, the piston position must be set to provide a 1 mm (0.04 in) clearance between the outer brake pad and the caliper. Check the adjustment by relocating the caliper and upper retaining bolt (use the old one) and insert a feeler gauge as shown (Fig. 8.6). If adjustment is necessary, remove the upper securing bolt, pivot the caliper down and rotate the piston in the required direction using an Allen key or socket head wrench (photo).

6.3 Release the handbrake cable (arrowed) from the caliper

6.4 Rear caliper bolt removal – prevent the guide pin from turning with open-ended spanner

6.5 Rear brake caliper removal

6.9 Locating the rear disc brake pads

6.10 Rotate the piston to adjust the outer brake pipe-to-caliper clearance

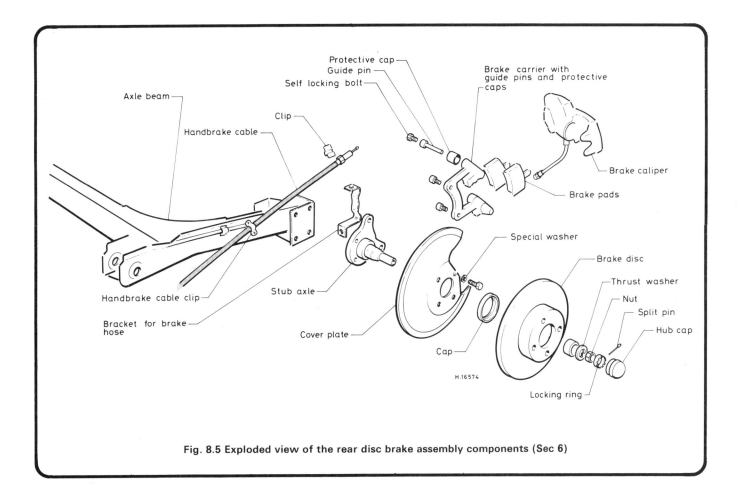

Fig. 8.5 Exploded view of the rear disc brake assembly components (Sec 6)

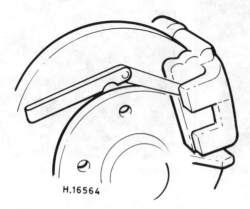

Fig. 8.6 Checking the outer brake pad-to-caliper clearance (Sec 6)

11 Refit the caliper and insert the new self-locking bolt when the adjustment is correct. Tighten the bolt to the specified torque setting.
12 If new brake pads and/or discs have been fitted it is necessary to carry out a basic rear wheel brake adjustment before reconnecting the handbrake cable. To do this apply a medium pressure to the brake pedal and depress it a total of 40 times (car stationary).
13 Reconnect the handbrake cable to the caliper.
14 On completion check the handbrake adjustment, as described in Section 17.

7 Rear brake disc caliper – removal, overhaul and refitting

1 Remove the brake disc pads, as described in the previous Section.

2 If available, fit a hose clamp to the caliper flexible brake hose. Alternatively remove the fluid reservoir filler cap and tighten it down onto a piece of polythene sheet in order to reduce the loss of hydraulic fluid.
3 Loosen and detach the brake hose union at the caliper. Allow for a certain amount of fluid spillage and plug the hose union to prevent the ingress of dirt.
4 Unscrew and remove the lower caliper retaining bolt and remove the caliper (photo). This self-locking bolt must be renewed.

7.4 Rear brake caliper removal

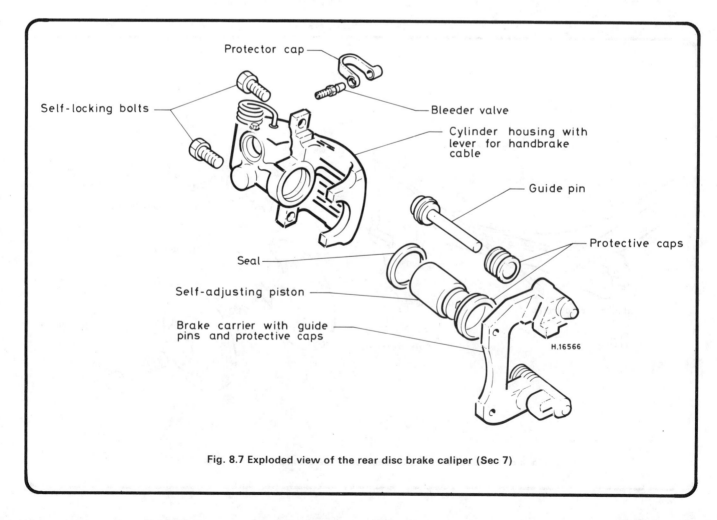

Fig. 8.7 Exploded view of the rear disc brake caliper (Sec 7)

5   Clean the external surfaces of the caliper with paraffin and wipe dry – plug the fluid inlet during this operation.
6   Secure the caliper in a soft-jawed vice and, using an Allen key, unscrew the piston from the cylinder (Fig. 8.8).
7   Using a suitable screwdriver, carefully ease out the O-ring seal from the cylinder bore.
8   Prise free the protective cap from the piston.

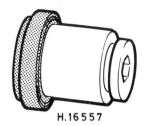

Fig. 8.10 Protective cap on piston (Sec 7)

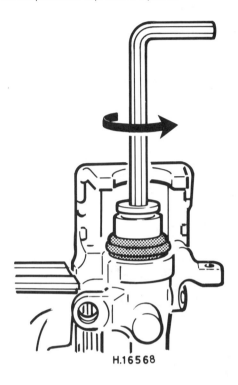

Fig. 8.8 Remove the piston from the cylinder (Sec 7)

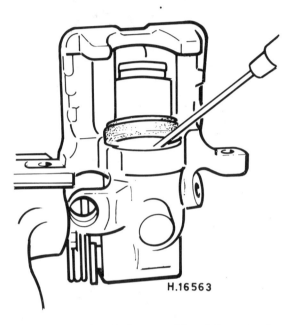

Fig. 8.11 Manipulating the inner seal lip of the protective cap into the cylinder bore groove (Sec 7)

9   Clean the components with methylated spirit and allow to dry. Inspect the surfaces of the piston, cylinder and frames for wear, damage and corrosion. If evident renew the caliper, but if the components are in good condition obtain a repair kit of seals.
10 Dip the new sealing ring in brake fluid and locate it in the cylinder bore groove using the fingers only to manipulate it.
11 Smear the piston with brake fluid then manipulate the new protective cap into position on the inner end of the piston with the outer seal lip on the piston (Fig. 8.10).
12 Hold the piston at the entrance to the cylinder housing and carefully manipulate the inner seal lip of the protective cap into the groove in the cylinder bore using a suitable screwdriver (Fig. 8.11).
13 Locate the Allen key into the piston and, pressing it firmly down, screw the piston fully home into the cylinder, so that the outer seal lip of the protective cap springs into the location groove in the piston.
14 Caliper reassembly is now complete, but before refitting it to the car it must be topped up with brake fluid and bled. To do this, unscrew the bleeder valve then support the caliper in the upright position. Connect a suitable union, hose and fluid supply applicator to the bleed valve connection in the caliper. Apply fluid and top up the caliper until fluid is seen to emerge from the brake hose connection without air bubbles. Tighten the bleed valve and plug the brake hose connection aperture.
15 The caliper can now be refitted to the car. Insert a new self-locking bolt into the lower end of the caliper then refit the caliper as described in Section 6, paragraphs 8 to 14 inclusive.

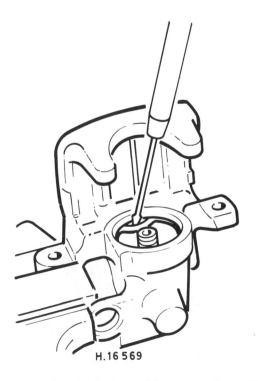

Fig. 8.9 Removing the O-ring seal from the cylinder (Sec 7)

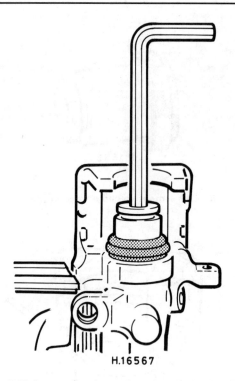

Fig. 8.12 Screw the piston downwards through the protective cap and into position in the cylinder (Sec 7)

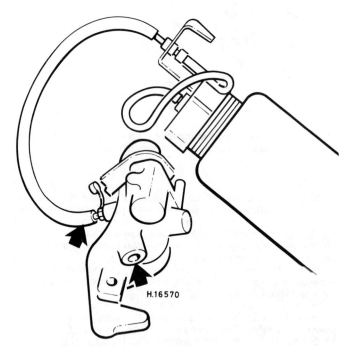

Fig. 8.13 Bleed the rear brake caliper unit prior to refitting (Sec 7)

Arrows indicate brake bleed valve and brake hose connection point

8 Rear brake disc and hub bearings – examination, removal and refitting

1   Proceed as described in Section 5, paragraphs 1 to 3 inclusive, but remove the caliper as described in the previous Section leaving the brake hydraulic hose attached. Support the caliper to prevent straining the hose.

2   Using a dial gauge or metal block and feeler gauges, check that the disc run-out measured on the friction surface does not exceed the maximum amount given in the Specifications.

3   Unbolt and remove the rear brake carrier. Use a screwdriver and prise free the hub cap (photo).

4   Straighten and extract the split pin, then withdraw the locking ring (photo).

5   Undo the hub nut and then withdraw the thrust washer and outer taper bearing race (photo).

6   Withdraw the disc from the stub axle.

7   The inner bearing can now be removed from the disc by levering free the cap then prising out the oil seal. The bearing can then be extracted.

8   The bearing outer races can be removed from the disc, by drifting them out using a soft drift whilst supporting the disc.

9   If required the brake cover plate can be unbolted, together with the stub axle, from the axle beam. Note that the retaining bolts have high tension spring washers fitted.

10 Unless a disc is being renewed after a fairly low mileage due to damage or other defect, both rear brake discs must be renewed at the same time (rather than one).

11 Commence reassembly by refitting the stub axle and splash guard. Tighten the securing bolts to the specified torque setting.

8.3 Prise free the hub cap (rear disc brake)

8.4 Remove the split pin and lock ring

8.5 Remove the outer washer and bearing

14 Lubricate the stub axle with grease then refit the rear brake disc over it, taking care not to damage the inner oil seal lips.

15 Lubricate the outer taper roller bearing with grease and then locate it onto the stub axle against its bearing outer race.

16 Refit the thrust washer, engaging the inner lug with the groove in the stub axle, then hand tighten the securing nut to the point where the thrust washer can just be moved with a screwdriver and finger pressure but **without** levering it. Check that the disc rotates freely without binding or excessive endfloat, then locate the locking ring over the nut and insert a new split pin to secure.

17 Half fill the hub cap with bearing grease and tap it carefully into position.

18 Before refitting the brake carrier, check that the protective caps and guide pins are not damaged. If they are then the carrier must be renewed. Locate and fit the carrier retaining bolts, tightening to the specified torque setting.

19 The disc caliper and pads can now be refitted, as described in Section 7, paragraph 15.

9 Rear drum brake shoes – inspection and renewal

1 Jack up the rear of the car and support it on axle stands. Chock the front wheels.

2 Working beneath the car remove the rubber plugs from the front of the backplates and check that the linings are not worn below the minimum thickness given in the Specifications. If necessary use a torch. Refit the plugs.

3 To remove the rear brake shoes first remove the wheels.

4 Prise off the hub cap then extract the split pin and remove the locking ring (photos).

5 Unscrew the hub nut and remove the thrust washer and outer wheel bearing (photos).

6 Check that the handbrake is fully released, then withdraw the brake drum. If difficulty is experienced, the brake shoes must be backed away from the drum first. To do this, insert a screwdriver through one of the

12 Check that the bearing recesses in the disc are clean, then support the disc and drive the new bearing outer races into position using a suitable tube drift. Ensure that they are fully home. If re-using the old bearings be sure to keep the original bearings and races together when assembling.

13 Lubricate the inner bearing with grease and locate it onto its outer race. The oil seal can now be driven into position. Lubricate its seal lip when fitted. Drive the dust cap into position using a suitable tube drift.

9.4A Remove the rear brake drum hub cap and ...

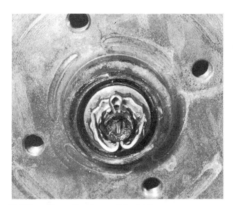

9.4B ... the split pin and lock ring

9.5A Undo the hub nut ...

9.5B ... remove the thrust washer ...

9.5C ... and outer bearing

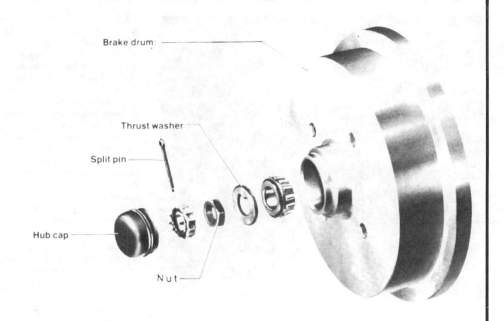

Brake drum:

Thrust washer

Split pin

Hub cap

Nut

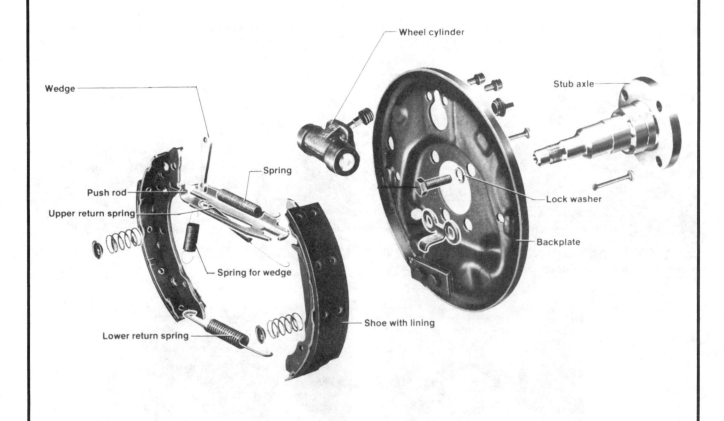

Wheel cylinder

Stub axle

Wedge

Spring

Push rod

Upper return spring

Spring for wedge

Lock washer

Backplate

Lower return spring

Shoe with lining

Fig. 8.14 Rear drum brake assembly components (Sec 9)

bolt holes and push the automatic adjuster wedge upwards against the spring tension. This will release the shoes from the drum.

7   Brush the dust from the brake drum, brake shoes and backplate, *but do not inhale it as it is injurious to health*. Scrape any scale or rust from the drum. Note that the rear brake shoes should be renewed as a set of four.

8   Using a pair of pliers depress the steady spring cups, turn them through 90° and remove the cups, springs and pins (photo).

9   Note the location of the return springs and strut on the brake shoes, then lever the shoes from the bottom anchor. Unhook and remove the lower return spring (photo).

10   Disengage the handbrake cable from the lever on the trailing brake shoe (photo).

11   Release the brake shoes from the wheel cylinder, unhook the wedge spring and upper return spring and withdraw the shoes (photo).

12   Grip the strut in a vice and release the shoe, then remove the wedge and spring. The backplate and stub axle may be removed, if necessary, by unscrewing the four bolts after removing the wheel cylinder (Section 10). Note the location of the handbrake cable bracket. If the wheel cylinder is being left in position, retain the pistons with an elastic band. Check that there are no signs of fluid leakage and, if necessary, repair or renew the wheel cylinder, as described in Section 10.

9.10 Handbrake cable attachment point to trailing brake shoe (arrowed)

9.8 Brake shoe steady spring and cup (arrowed)

9.11 View showing wheel cylinder, upper return spring and pushrod assembly

9.9 Lower return spring fixing points to the brake shoes

13   Fit the new brake shoes using a reversal of the removal procedure, but note that the lug on the wedge faces the backplate.

14   Check the brake drum for wear and damage, as described in Section 11.

15   Before refitting the brake drum, smear the lips of the oil seal with a little grease.

16   Refit the drum onto the stub axle, taking care not to damage the oil seal, then lubricate the outer taper roller bearing and fit it onto the stub axle.

17   Fit the thrust washer and hub nut, and tighten the nut hand tight.

18   Refit the wheel.

19   With the hub cap, split pin, and locking ring removed, tighten the hub nut firmly while turning the wheel in order to settle the bearings.

20   Back off the nut then tighten it until it is just possible to move the thrust washer laterally with a screwdriver under finger pressure. Do not twist the screwdriver or lever it.

21   Fit the locking ring, together with a new split pin, then tap the hub cap into the drum with a mallet.

22   Check that the brake drum rotates freely then refit the roadwheel(s) and lower the car to the ground. Finally, fully depress the brake pedal several times in order to set the shoes in their correct position.

10 Rear wheel cylinder – removal, overhaul and refitting

1   Remove the rear brake shoes, as described in Section 9.
2   If available, fit a hose clamp to the flexible brake hose. Alternatively remove the fluid reservoir filler cap and tighten it down onto a piece of polythene sheet in order to reduce the loss of hydraulic fluid.
3   Unscrew the hydraulic pipe union from the rear of the cylinder, and plug the end of the pipe.
4   Remove the two screws and withdraw the wheel cylinder from the backplate.
5   Prise off the dust caps then remove the pistons, keeping them, identified for location. If necessary, use air pressure from a foot pump in the fluid inlet.
6   Remove the internal spring and, if necessary, unscrew the bleed valve.
7   Clean all the components in methylated spirit and allow to dry. Examine the surfaces of the piston and cylinder bore for wear, scoring and corrosion. If evident, renew the complete wheel cylinder. If the components are in good condition, discard the seals and obtain a repair kit.
8   Dip the inner seals in clean brake fluid and fit them to the grooves on the pistons using the fingers only to manipulate them. Make sure that the larger diameter ends face the inner ends of the pistons.
9   Smear brake fluid on the pistons then insert the spring and press the pistons into the cylinder, taking care not to damage the seal lips.
10 Locate the dust caps on the pistons and in the grooves on the outside of the cylinder.
11 Insert and tighten the bleed valve.
12 Clean the mating faces then fit the wheel cylinder to the backplate and tighten the screws.
13 Refit the hydraulic pipe and tighten the union. Remove the hose clamp or polythene sheet.
14 Refit the rear brake shoes, as described in Section 9.
15 Top up the brake fluid reservoir and bleed the valves, as described in Section 15.

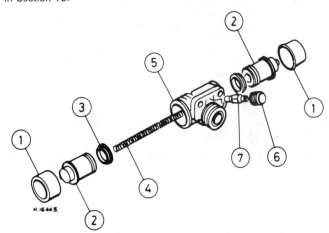

Fig. 8.15 Exploded view of the rear wheel cylinder (typical) (Sec 10)

1	Boot	5	Brake cylinder housing
2	Piston	6	Dust cap
3	Cap	7	Bleed valve
4	Spring		

11 Brake drum – examination and renovation

1   Whenever the brake drums are removed, they should be checked for wear and damage. Light scoring of the friction surface is normal, but if excessive the drums must either be renewed as a pair or reground provided that the maximum internal diameter given in the Specifications is not exceeded.
2   After a high mileage the drums may become warped and oval. The run-out can be checked with a dial gauge and, if in excess of the maximum amounts given in the Specifications, the drums should be renewed as a pair.

11.3 Prising out the brake drum oil seal

3   The inner oil seal should be checked for condition and if necessary removed and renewed. Prise out the old seal using a screwdriver (photo). Drive the new seal into position so that it is flush with the boss face.

12 Master cylinder – removal and refitting

1   Disconnect the battery negative lead.
2   Disconnect the wiring from the fluid level switches on the master cylinder and fluid reservoir filler cap.
3   On carburettor models, remove the air cleaner, as described in Chapter 3.
4   On fuel injection models detach the injection hoses from the retaining clips on the intake ducting then unclip and detach the intake duct between the fuel distributor unit and the throttle housing.
5   Place a suitable container beneath the master cylinder and place some cloth on the surrounding body to protect it from any spilled brake fluid.
6   Unscrew the unions and disconnect the hydraulic fluid pipes from the master cylinder (photo).
7   Unscrew the mounting nuts and withdraw the master cylinder from the servo unit. Remove the spacer and seal where applicable.
8   Remove the master cylinder from the engine compartment, taking care not to spill any hydraulic fluid on the body paintwork.
9   Clean the exterior of the master cylinder with paraffin and wipe dry.
10 If the master cylinder is defective it cannot be overhauled and must be renewed as a unit. This being the case, remove the reservoir by pulling it free from the rubber grommets, then prise free the grommets from the cylinder.
11 Commence reassembly by smearing the rubber grommets in brake fluid and press them into the cylinder, then press the reservoir into the grommets.
12 Refitting the master cylinder is otherwise a reversal of the removal procedure, but fit a new mounting seal between the cylinder and servo unit. On completion, bleed the brake hydraulic system, as described in Section 15.

13 Brake pressure regulator – general

1   A brake pressure regulator is fitted in the rear brake circuit of some models and its purpose is to prevent the rear wheels locking in advance of the front wheels during heavy application of the brakes. The regulator is also load sensitive in order to vary the pressure according to the load being carried.
2   The regulator is located on the under-body, in front of the left-hand rear wheel (photo).

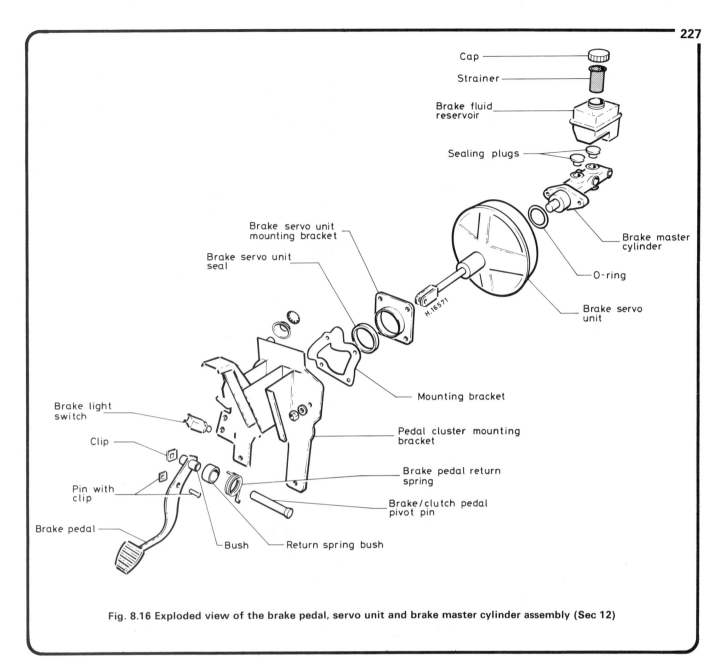

Cap

Strainer

Brake fluid reservoir

Sealing plugs

Brake master cylinder

O-ring

Brake servo unit

Brake servo unit mounting bracket

Brake servo unit seal

H.16571

Mounting bracket

Pedal cluster mounting bracket

Brake light switch

Clip

Pin with clip

Brake pedal

Bush

Return spring bush

Brake pedal return spring

Brake/clutch pedal pivot pin

Fig. 8.16 Exploded view of the brake pedal, servo unit and brake master cylinder assembly (Sec 12)

12.6 Master cylinder and brake line connections

13.2 Brake pressure regulator unit (fitted to some models)

3   Checking of the regulator is best left to a VW garage, as special pressure gauges and spring tensioning tools are required. Adjustment is made by varying the spring tension, but this must be carried out by the garage.

4   Removal and refitting are straightforward but, after fitting, bleed the hydraulic system, as described in Section 15, and have the regulator adjusted by a garage.

14 Hydraulic pipes and hoses – inspection and renewal

1   At the intervals given in Section 2 clean the rigid brake lines and flexible hoses and check them for damage, leakage, chafing and cracks. If the coating on the rigid pipes is damaged or if rusting is apparent they must be renewed. Check the retaining clips for security, and clean away any accumulations of dirt and debris (photos).

2   To remove a rigid brake pipe, unscrew the union nuts at each end and where necessary remove the line from the clips. Refitting is a reversal of removal.

3   To remove a flexible brake hose, unscrew the union nut securing the rigid brake pipe to the end of the flexible hose and remove the

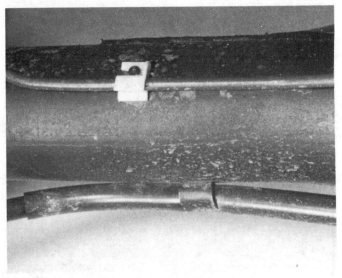

14.1C Rigid pipe retaining clip (to rear axle beam)

14.1A Bend flexible brake hose to check for signs of cracks

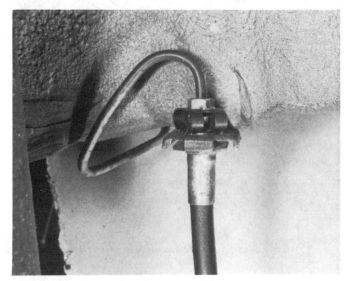

14.3 Rigid pipe-to-flexible hose connection

14.1B Flexible hose retaining clip (to front strut)

spring clip and hose end fitting from the bracket (photo). Unscrew the remaining end from the component or rigid pipe according to position. Refitting is a reversal of removal.

4   Bleed the complete hydraulic system, as described in Section 15, after fitting a rigid brake pipe or flexible brake hose.

15 Hydraulic system – bleeding

1   This is not a routine operation, but will be required after any component in the system has been removed and refitted or any part of the hydraulic system has been 'broken'. When an operation has only affected one circuit of the hydraulic system, then bleeding will normally only be required to that circuit (front and rear diagonally opposite). If the master cylinder or the pressure regulating valve have been disconnected and reconnected, then the complete system must be bled.

2   One of three methods can be used to bleed the system.

Bleeding – two-man method

3   Gather together a clean jar and a length of rubber or plastic bleed tubing which will fit the bleed valve tightly. The help of an assistant will be required.

4   Take great care not to spill brake fluid onto the paintwork as it will act as a paint stripper. If any is spilled, wash it off at once with cold water.

5   Clean around the bleed valve on the rear brake and attach the bleed tube to the valve (photo)

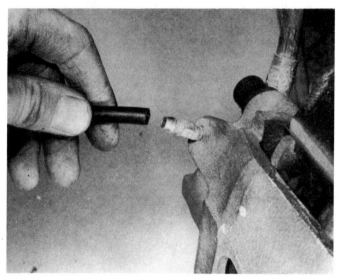

15.5 Connect the bleed tube to the bleed valve

6   Check that the master cylinder reservoir is topped up and then destroy the vacuum in the brake servo (where fitted) by giving several applications of the brake foot pedal.

7   Immerse the open end of the bleed tube in the jar, which should contain 50 to 76 mm (2 to 3 in) of hydraulic fluid. The jar should be positioned about 300 mm (12.0 in) above the bleed valve to prevent any possibility of air entering the system down the threads of the bleed valve when it is slackened.

8   Open the bleed valve half a turn and have your assistant depress the brake pedal slowly to the floor and then quickly remove his foot to allow the pedal to return unimpeded. Tighten the bleed valve at the end of each downstroke to prevent expelled air and fluid being drawn back into the system.

9   Observe the submerged end of the tube in the jar. When air bubbles cease to appear, fully tighten the bleed valve when the pedal is being held down by your assistant.

10 Top up the fluid reservoir. It must be kept topped up throughout the bleeding operations. If the connecting holes in the master cylinder are exposed at any time due to low fluid level, then air will be drawn into the system and work will have to start all over again.

11 Repeat the operation on the diagonally opposite front brake. If the whole system is being bled, follow the sequence given below.

12 On completion, remove the bleed tube. Discard the fluid which has been bled from the system unless it is required for bleed jar purposes, **never** use it for filling the system.

Bleeding – with one-way valve

13 There are a number of one-man brake bleeding kits currently available from motor accessory shops. It is recommended that one of these kits should be used whenever possible as they greatly simplify the bleeding operation and also reduce risk of expelled air or fluid being drawn back into the system. Refer to paragraph 4.

14 Connect the outlet tube of the bleeder device to the bleed valve and then open the valve half a turn. Depress the brake pedal to the floor and slowly release it. The one-way valve in the device will prevent expelled air from returning to the system at the completion of each stroke. Repeat this operation until clean hydraulic fluid, free from air bubbles, can be

seen coming through the tube. Tighten the bleed screw and remove the tube.

15 Repeat the procedure on the remaining bleed nipples in the order described in paragraph 11. Remember to keep the master cylinder reservoir full.

Bleeding – with pressure bleeding kits

16 These are available from motor accessory shops and are usually operated by air pressure from the spare tyre.

17 By connecting a pressurised container to the master cylinder fluid reservoir, bleeding is then carried out by simply opening each bleed valve in turn and allowing the fluid to run out, rather like turning on a tap, until no air bubbles are visible in the fluid being expelled. Refer to para 4.

18 Using this system, the large reserve of fluid provides a safeguard against air being drawn into the master cylinder during the bleeding operations.

19 This method is particularly effective when bleeding 'difficult' systems or when bleeding the entire system at routine fluid renewal.

All methods

20 If the entire system is being bled the procedures described above should now be repeated at each wheel, finishing at the wheel nearest to the master cylinder. The correct sequence is as follows:

> *Right-hand rear wheel*
> *Left-hand rear wheel*
> *Right-hand front wheel*
> *Left-hand front wheel*

Do not forget to recheck the fluid level in the master cylinder at regular intervals and top up as necessary.

21 When completed, recheck the fluid level in the master cylinder, top up if necessary and refit the cap. Check the 'feel' of the brake pedal which should be firm and free from any 'sponginess' which would indicate air still present in the system.

22 Discard any expelled hydraulic fluid as it is likely to be contaminated with moisture, air and dirt which makes it unsuitable for further use.

23 On completion refit the rubber protector caps over each bleed valve (photo).

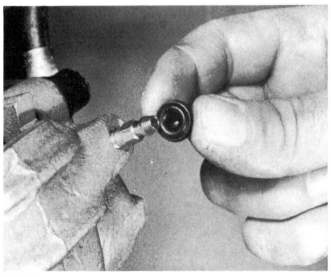

15.23 Fit the protector caps on completion

16 Handbrake lever – removal and refitting

1   Position a chock each side of the front wheels, then pull the cover from the lever (by prising open the bottom edges of the cover) then fully release the handbrake.

2   Undo each cable locknut and adjuster nut and disconnect the cables from the compensating lever (photo).

16.2 Handbrake lever and cables with adjuster and locknuts
*The handbrake lever ON switch retaining screw is just visible
underneath the lever*

3   Prise free the lever retaining clamp on the right-hand side, then
withdraw the pivot pin and remove the lever.
4   If required remove the screw from the lever switch, disconnect the
wiring, and remove the switch.
5   Refitting is a reversal of removal. Lubricate the pivot pin and, on
completion, adjust the handbrake cables, as described in Section 17.

17 Handbrake cables – removal, refitting and adjustment

1   Chock the front wheels, then jack up the rear of the car and support
it on axle stands. Release the handbrake.
2   Remove the cover from the handbrake lever then undo the locknut
and adjuster nut from the cable concerned.
3   Remove the rear roadwheel(s).
4   On drum brake models, remove the brake drum and disconnect the
cable from the shoe operating lever, as described in Section 9. Detach
the cable from the backplate.
5   On models fitted with disc brakes at the rear, disengage the cable
from the caliper lever, then prise free the outer cable retaining clip from
the caliper. Note how the clip is located.
6   Release the cable from its retaining clips and then carefully
withdraw it from under the car (photo).
7   Refitting is a reversal of removal, but adjust the cable as follows
before lowering the car.

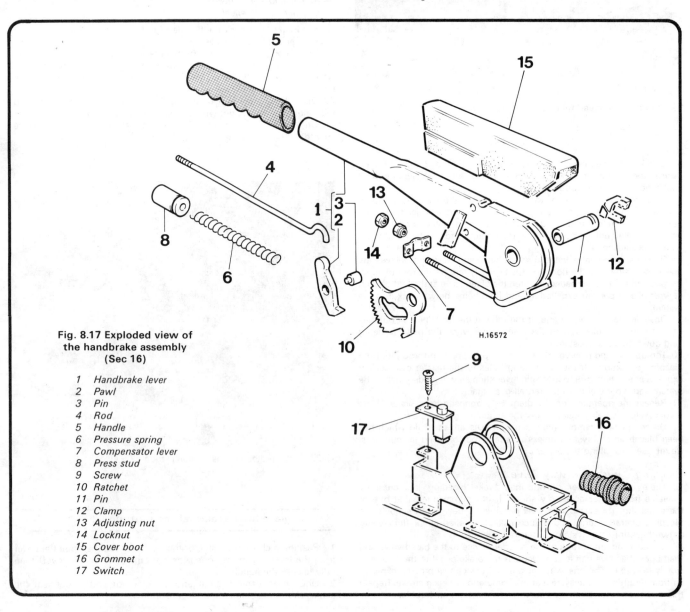

Fig. 8.17 Exploded view of
the handbrake assembly
(Sec 16)

H.16572

1   Handbrake lever
2   Pawl
3   Pin
4   Rod
5   Handle
6   Pressure spring
7   Compensator lever
8   Press stud
9   Screw
10 Ratchet
11 Pin
12 Clamp
13 Adjusting nut
14 Locknut
15 Cover boot
16 Grommet
17 Switch

17.6 Handbrake cable retaining clip (arrowed) at rear axle beam pivot

H.16573

Fig. 8.18 Handbrake adjustment on rear disc brakes – lever on caliper (arrowed) should be just clear of stop (Sec 17)

Cable adjustment – drum brakes

8 With the handbrake lever fully released, depress the footbrake, applying firm pressure, once only. Now pull the handbrake up onto its second notch position.

9 Tighten the adjuster nut on the cable concerned so that the rear roadwheel is just felt to bind when rotated. Fully release the handbrake lever, then check that the roadwheel spins freely without binding. Tighten the locknut against the adjuster nut, then apply the handbrake and check that the wheel is locked. Repeat the procedure with the other cable.

Cable adjustment – disc brakes

10 Before checking and adjusting the handbrake cables, first check the outer brake pad to caliper clearance, as described in Section 6.

11 Fully release the handbrake lever then tighten the cable adjuster nut

to the point where the caliper lever just separates from its stop (Fig. 8.18). An assistant is useful here to ensure that, as the nut is tightened, the lever-to-stop clearance does not exceed 1 mm (0.04 in). Tighten the locknut then fully release the handbrake and check that the roadwheel rotates freely then apply the handbrake and check that the roadwheel is locked.

12 Repeat the procedure on the other side.

18 Footbrake pedal – removal and refitting

1 The brake and clutch pedals share a common bracket assembly and pivot shaft.

2 Remove the clutch pedal, as described in Chapter 5.

3 Extract the clip and withdraw the clevis pin securing the servo pushrod.

4 Extract the clip from the pivot shaft, unhook the return spring, withdraw the pivot shaft and remove the pedal.

5 Check the pedal bushes for wear. If necessary drive them out from each side and press in new bushes using a soft-jawed vice.

6 Refitting is a reversal of removal, but lubricate the pivot shaft with a little multi-purpose grease.

19 Vacuum servo unit – description and testing

1 The vacuum servo unit is located between the brake pedal and the master cylinder and provides assistance to the driver when the brake pedal is depressed. The unit operates by vacuum from the inlet manifold.

2 The unit basically consists of a diaphragm and non-return valve. With the brake pedal released, vacuum is channelled to both sides of the diaphragm, but when the pedal is depressed, one side is opened to the atmosphere. The resultant unequal pressures are harnessed to assist in depressing the master cylinder pistons.

3 Normally, the vacuum servo unit is very reliable, but if the unit becomes faulty, it should be renewed. In the event of a failure, the hydraulic system is in no way affected, except that higher pedal pressures will be necessary.

4 To test the vacuum servo unit depress the brake pedal several times with the engine switched off to dissipate the vacuum. Apply moderate pressure to the brake pedal then start the engine. The pedal should move down slightly if the servo unit is operating correctly.

5 To test the check valve in the vacuum hose, disconnect it from the hose then blow through the valve in the direction of the arrow marking. Air should pass through the check valve. However, if air is supplied in the reverse direction through the valve it should not, as the valve must be closed to airflow in that direction. Renew the valve unit if found to be defective.

20 Vacuum servo unit – removal and refitting

1 Remove the brake master cylinder as described in Section 12.

2 Pull the vacuum hose free from the servo unit connector and, where applicable, the non-return valve.

3 Working inside the vehicle, detach the lower trim panel on the driver's side.

4 Disconnect the pushrod clevis from the brake pedal by releasing the clip and withdrawing the clevis pin.

5 Unscrew the mounting nuts and withdraw the servo unit from the bulkhead into the engine compartment.

6 Refitting is a reversal of removal. Lubricate the clevis pin with a little molybdenum disulphide based grease. The mounting nuts are self-locking and should always be renewed.

Fault diagnosis overleaf

21 Fault diagnosis – braking system

Symptom	Reason(s)
Excessive pedal travel	Brake fluid leak Air in hydraulic system Worn rear brake shoes
Uneven braking and pulling to one side	Contaminated linings Seized wheel cylinder or caliper Incorrect and unequal tyre pressures Loose suspension anchor point Different lining material at each wheel
Brake judder	Worn drums and/or discs Loose suspension anchor point Loose rear brake backplate
Brake pedal feels spongy	Air in hydraulic system Faulty master cylinder seals
Excessive effort to stop car	Seized wheel cylinders or calipers Incorrect lining material Contaminated linings New linings not yet bedded-in Excessively worn linings

Chapter 9 Electrical system

For modifications, and information applicable to later models, see Supplement at end of manual

Contents

Specifications

System type .... 12 volt, negative earth

Battery .... 36 amp hour or 45 amp hour
Minimum voltage (under load) .... 9.6 volts at 110 amps

Alternator
Type .... Bosch or Motorola
Maximum output (amps) .... 55, 65 or 90
Minimum allowable brush length .... 5 mm (0.2 in)

Rotor winding resistance (ohms):	Bosch	Motorola
55 amp	2.9 to 3.2	3.1 to 3.3
65 amp	2.8 to 3.1	3.9 to 4.1
90 amp	3.0 to 4.0	–

Starter motor
Type .... Pre-engaged

Model	VW part/type number
1.05 and 1.3 litre	036 911 023 G
1.3 litre	036 911 023 H
1.6 litre:	
Manual gearbox	055 911 023 G
Automatic transmission	055 911 023 A
1.8 litre	027 911 023

Fuses

Fuse number	Component	Rating (amps)
1	Radiator fan	30
2	Brake light	10
3	Cigarette lighter, radio, clock, interior light, central locking	15
4	Emergency light system	15
5	Fuel pump	15
6	Foglights (main current)	15
7	Tail and sidelights, left	10
8	Tail and sidelights, right	10
9	High beam right, high beam warning lamp	10
10	High beam, left	10
11	Windscreen wipers and washer, headlight washer	15
12	Rear wiper and washer, seat heater control, electric mirror control	15
13	Rear window heating, mirror heating	15
14	Blower, glovebox light	20
15	Reversing lights, shift pattern illumination (automatic gearbox)	10
16	Horn	15
17	Carburettor	10
18	Horn (dual tone), coolant level warning lamp	15
19	Turn signals, stop-start system, brake warning lamp	10
20	Number plate light, foglights (switch current)	10
21	Low beam, left, headlight range control, left	10
22	Low beam right, headlight range control, right	10

Additional fuses:

In separate holders above the fusebox	Rating (amps)
Rear foglight	10
Electric windows	30
Air conditioner	30

Relays

Relays .... See wiring diagrams at end of Manual

Bulbs

	Wattage
Headlamps (halogen)	60/55
Sidelight	4
Tail light	5
Stop-light	21
Direction indicators	21
Foglight (rear)	21
Reversing light	21
Instrument light	1.2

Torque wrench settings

	Nm	lbf ft
Starter motor:		
1.05 and 1.3 litre	20	15
1.6 and 1.8 litre (manual gearbox)	60	44
1.6 litre (automatic transmission)	20	15
Alternator:		
Pulley nut	40	30
Mounting (to engine) bolts	45	33
Mounting/alternator pivot bolt	45	33
Adjuster strap bolts	25	18

1 General description

The electrical system is of 12 volt negative earth type. The battery is charged by a belt-driven alternator which incorporates a voltage regulator. The starter motor is of pre-engaged type incorporating a solenoid which moves the drive pinion into engagement with the flywheel/driveplate ring gear before the motor is energised.

Although repair procedures are given in this Chapter, it may well be more economical to renew worn components as complete units.

2 Electrical system – maintenance

The following routine maintenance procedures should be undertaken at the specified intervals given at the start of this manual.

1 **Battery:** Refer to Section 4 in this Chapter.
2 **Alternator:** Refer to Section 7 in this Chapter.
3 **Alternator drivebelt:** Check condition and adjustment of the drivebelt, as described in Section 8 of this Chapter.
4 **Vehicle lighting:** Periodically check that all of the front and rear lights are functioning correctly. The headlights and (where applicable) the foglights should be checked for alignment, as described in Section 31. Renew any defective bulbs.
5 **Windscreen/rear window wipers:** Check their operation (having wet the glass first) and also the condition of the wiper blade rubbers. Renew if necessary. At the same time, check that the windscreen, rear window and headlamp washers (as applicable) operate in a satisfactory manner. Check and, when necessary, top up the fluid reservoirs.
6 **Wiring:** Periodically check the wiring and connections for condition and security.

3 Battery – removal and refitting

1 The battery is located in the engine compartment on the left-hand side.
2 Loosen the battery terminal clamp nuts and disconnect the negative lead followed by the positive lead (photo).

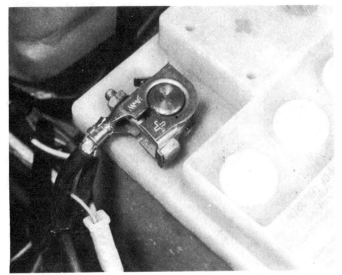

3.2 Battery positive terminal and lead connection

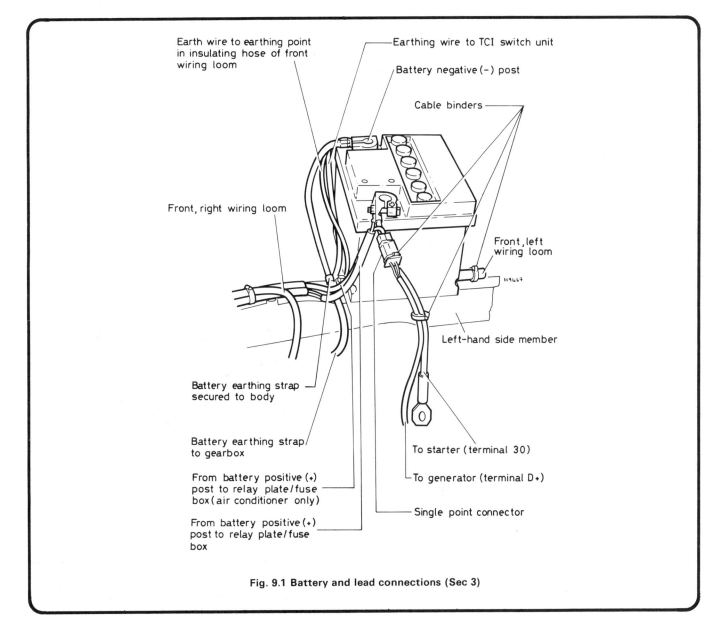

Fig. 9.1 Battery and lead connections (Sec 3)

3.3 Battery retaining clamp and bolt

3   Unscrew the bolt and remove the battery retaining clamp (photo).
4   Lift the battery from its platform; taking care not to spill any electrolyte on the bodywork.
5   Refitting is a reversal of removal, but make sure that the leads are fitted to their correct terminals, and do not overtighten the lead clamp nuts or the battery retaining clamp bolt. Finally smear a little petroleum jelly on the terminals and clamps.

4 Battery – maintenance

1   Where a conventional battery is fitted, the electrolyte level of each cell should be checked every month and, if necessary, topped up with distilled or de-ionized water until the separators are just covered. On some batteries the case is translucent and incorporates minimum and maximum level marks. The check should be made more often if the car is operated in high ambient temperature conditions.
2   Where a low maintenance battery is fitted it is not necessary to check the electrolyte level.
3   Every 10 000 miles (15 000 km) or 12 months, whichever occurs first, disconnect and clean the battery terminals and leads. After refitting them, smear the exposed metal with petroleum jelly.
4   At the same time, inspect the battery clamp and platform for corrosion. If evident, remove the battery and clean the deposits away, then treat the affected metal with a proprietary anti-rust liquid and paint with the original colour.
5   When the battery is removed, for whatever reason, it is worthwhile checking it for cracks and leakage. Cracks can be caused by topping-up the cells with distilled water in winter *after* instead of *before* a run. This gives the water no chance to mix with the electrolyte, so the former freezes and splits the battery case. If the battery case is fractured, it may be possible to repair it with a proprietary compound, but this depends on the material used for the case. If electrolyte has been lost from a cell, refer to Section 5 for details of adding a fresh solution.
6   If topping-up the battery becomes excessive and the case is not fractured, the battery is being over-charged and the voltage regulator will have to be checked.
7   If the car covers a very small annual mileage, it is worthwhile checking the specific gravity of the electrolyte every three months to determine the state of charge of the battery. Use a hydrometer to make the check, and compare the results with the following table.

	Normal climates	Tropics
Discharged	1.120	1.080
Half charged	1.200	1.160
Fully charged	1.280	1.230

8   If the battery condition is suspect, first check the specific gravity of electrolyte in each cell. A variation of 0.040 or more between any cells indicates loss ot electrolyte or deterioration of the internal plates.
9   A further test can be made using a battery heavy discharge meter. The battery should be discharged for a maximum of 15 seconds at a load of three times the ampere-hour capacity (at the 20 hour discharge rate). Alternatively connect a voltmeter across the battery terminals and spin the engine on the starter with the ignition disconnected (see Chapter 4), and the headlamps, heated rear window and heater blower switched on. If the voltmeter reading remains above 9.6 volts, the battery condition is satisfactory. If the voltmeter reading drops below 9.6 volts, and the battery has already been charged as described in Section 6, it is faulty and should be renewed.

5 Battery – electrolyte replenishment

Note: *This Section is not applicable to maintenance-free batteries.*
1   If the battery has been fully charged, but one cell has a specific gravity of 0.025 or more less than the others it is most likely that electrolyte has been lost from the cell at some time and the acid over-diluted with distilled water when topping-up.
2   In this case, remove some of the electrolyte with a hydrometer and top up with fresh electrolyte. It is best to get this done at a service station, for making your own electrolyte is messy, dangerous, and expensive for the small amount you need. If you must do it yourself add 1 part of sulphuric acid (concentrated) to 2.5 part of water. **Add the acid to the water,** not the other way round or the mixture will spit back as water is added to acid and you will be badly burnt. Add the acid a drop at a time to the water.
3   If topping-up is needed, the battery cap removal may necessitate piercing the cap notch with a screwdriver then turning the cap (with screwdriver still inserted) to the stop. The caps can then be unscrewed. Add distilled or de-ionized water to each cell as necessary then refit the caps.
4   Having added fresh electrolyte, recharge and recheck the readings. In all probability this will cure the problem. If it does not, then there is a short-circuit somewhere.
5   Electrolyte must always be stored away from other fluids and should be locked up, not left about. If you have children this is even more important.

Fig. 9.2 Where necessary, pierce the battery cap notch (arrowed) with a screwdriver when removing the caps (Sec 5)

6 Battery – charging

1   In winter time when heavy demand is placed upon the battery, such as starting from cold, and much electrical equipment is continually in use, it is a good idea occasionally to have the battery fully charged from an external source at the rate of 3.5 to 4 amps. Always disconnect it from the car electrical circuit when charging.

2   Continue to charge the battery at this rate until no further rise in specific gravity is noted over a four hour period.

3   Alternatively, a trickle charger, charging at the rate of 1.5 amps, can be safely used overnight. Disconnect the battery from the car electrical circuit before charging or you will damage the alternator.

4   Specially rapid 'boost' charges which are claimed to restore the power of the battery in 1 to 2 hours can cause damage to the battery plates through overheating. Maintenance-free batteries should not be rapid charged.

5   While charging the battery note that the temperature of the electrolyte should never exceed 37.8°C (100°F).

6   Make sure that your charging set and battery are set to the same voltage.

7   'Maintenance-free' batteries must **only** be trickle charged and may require twice the charging period of a normal battery.

7 Alternator – maintenance and special precautions

1   Periodically wipe away any dirt which has accumulated on the outside of the unit, and also check that the plug is pushed firmly on the terminals. At the same time check the tension of the drivebelt and adjust it if necessary as described in Section 8.

2   Take extreme care when making electrical circuit connections on the car, otherwise damage may occur to the alternator or other electrical components employing semiconductors. Always make sure that the battery leads are connected to the correct terminals. Before using electric arc welding equipment to repair any part of the car, disconnect the battery leads and alternator multi-plug. Disconnect the battery leads before using a mains charger. Never run the alternator with the multi-plug or a battery lead disconnected.

8 Alternator drivebelt – adjustment

1   The alternator drivebelt should be adjusted at the specified Routine Maintenance intervals. To check its tension, depress the belt firmly with a finger or thumb midway between the alternator and crankshaft pulleys (photo). The belt should deflect approximately 5 mm (0.2 in). If a new drivebelt has been fitted the initial adjustment should give a deflection of 2 mm (0.08 in) then, after a suitable running in period of about 500 miles (750 km), the belt adjustment should be rechecked and, if necessary, adjusted to deflect 5 mm (0.2 in).

2   If adjustment is necessary, loosen the nut on the adjusting link (photos) and pivot bolt, then lever the alternator away from the cylinder block until the belt is tensioned correctly, using a lever at the pulley end of the alternator.

3   Tighten the nut and bolt after adjusting the drivebelt.

8.2A Alternator adjustment link – 1.8 litre

8.2B Alternator adjustment link – 1.3 litre

8.1 Checking the alternator drivebelt tension

9 Alternator – testing

Accurate testing of the alternator is only possible using specialised instruments and is therefore best left to a qualified electrician. If, however, the alternator is faulty the home mechanic should dismantle it, with reference to Section 11 or 12, and check the condition of the brushes, soldered joints etc. If the fault cannot be found, refit the alternator and have it checked professionally.

10 Alternator – removal and refitting

1   Disconnect the battery negative lead.

2   Release the clip and pull the multi-plug from the rear of the alternator (photo).

3   Loosen the pivot and adjustment bolts (photo) then push the alternator in towards the engine and slip the drivebelt from the alternator.

10.2 Rear view of Bosch alternator showing lead multi-plug and retaining clip (arrowed)

11.2A Voltage regulator location (arrowed) – Bosch

10.3 Alternator pivot bolt and bracket – 1.3 litre

11.2B Removing the voltage regulator and brush assembly – Bosch

4   Remove the adjustment link nut and washer.
5   Support the alternator then remove the pivot bolt and withdraw the unit from the engine.
6   Refitting is a reversal of removal but, before fully tightening the pivot and adjustment bolts, tension the drivebelt, as described in Section 8.

11 Alternator (Bosch) – overhaul

1   Wipe clean the exterior surfaces of the alternator.
2   Remove the two screws and withdraw the voltage regulator and brush assembly from the rear of the alternator (photos).
3   Mark the end housings and stator in relation to each other, then unscrew the through-bolts and tap the drive end housing from the stator and end housing.
4   Grip the pulley in a soft-jawed vice and unscrew the nut. Tap the rotor shaft through the pulley and remove the spacers and fan; noting the direction or rotation arrow on the front of the fan.
5   Using a three-arm puller, press the rotor shaft out of the drive end housing. Note that the arms of the pulley must be located on the

bearing retainer otherwise damage may occur to the retainer screws.
6   Remove the screws and the retainer and use a soft metal drift to drive out the bearing.
7   Using a puller, remove the bearing from the end of the rotor shaft.
8   If necessary the stator and diode plate can be removed from the end housing after removing the retaining screws.
9   Clean all the components in paraffin or petrol and wipe them dry.
10   Check that the length of the carbon brushes is not less than the minimum amount given in the Specifications (photo). If necessary unsolder the leads and remove the old brushes then clean the housing, insert the new brushes, and solder the new leads into position.
11   The rotor bearings should be renewed as a matter of course.
12   To check the stator, first identify the wire positions then unsolder them using long-nosed pliers to dissipate heat from the diode plate. Check the windings for short circuits by connecting an ohmmeter between each of the four wires (ie between wires 1 and 2, wires 1 and 3, wires 1 and 4, then wires 2 and 3, wires 2 and 4 and wires 3 and 4). In each case a 0 ohm reading must be given. Check the windings for insulation by connecting a 12 volt test lamp and leads between each of the wires and the stator ring. If the lamp illuminates, the windings are faulty.

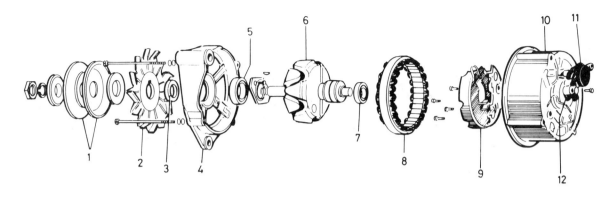

Fig. 9.3 Exploded view of the Bosch alternator (Sec 11)

1	Belt pulley	4	Drive housing	7	Bearing
2	Fan	5	Bearing	8	Stator
3	Spacer	6	Rotor	9	Diode plate

10	Housing
11	Regulator
12	Regulator brushes

11.10 Checking the length of the alternator brushes

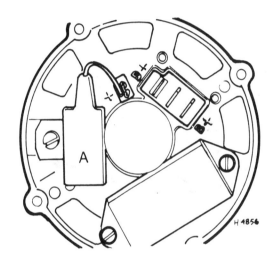

Fig. 9.4 Location of the suppression condenser (A) on the rear of the Bosch alternator (Sec 11)

13 Check the rotor windings for continuity by connecting an ohmmeter to the two slip rings. A reading of 2.9 to 3.2 ohms should be obtained for the 55 amp alternator or 2.8 to 3.1 ohms for the 65 amp alternator. Check the windings for insulation by connecting a 12 volt test lamp and leads between each of the slip rings and the winding core. If the lamp illuminates, the windings are faulty.

14 The diodes can be checked by connecting an ohmmeter across them. The reading should be between 50 and 80 ohms in one direction and at or near infinity in the other direction (ie with lead positions reversed).

15 Clean the slip rings with fine glass paper and wipe clean with a fuel-moistened cloth.

16 Reassemble the alternator using a reversal of the dismantling procedure. When fitting the bearing to the rotor shaft, drive it on with a metal tube located on the inner race. If the diode plate has been renewed, a suppression condenser should (if not already) be fitted to the rear of the alternator as shown in Fig. 9.4 – check this with your dealer.

12 Alternator (Motorola) – overhaul

1 The procedure is similar to that described in Section 11, and the exploded diagram of this alternator is shown in Fig. 9.5. Identify the regulator wires for position before disconnecting them (photo).

12.1 Voltage regulator/brush unit removal from the Motorola alternator

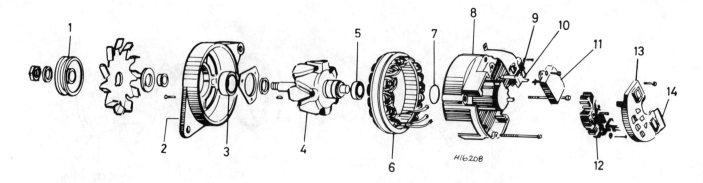

Fig. 9.5 Exploded view of the Motorola alternator (Sec 12)

1 Belt pulley	5 Bearing (slip ring end)	9 Brush holder	12 Diode plate
2 Drive-end housing	6 Stator	10 D + connecting plate	13 Cover
3 Bearing (drive end)	7 O-ring	11 Regulator	14 Wire clip
4 Rotor	8 Housing		

Fig. 9.6 The correct routing of the D+ wire on the Motorola
alternator (Sec 12)

2   The stator windings are checked in the same manner as that described for the Bosch alternator, but a 0 ohm reading should be given between each of the three leads (not four).
3   When checking the rotor windings for continuity, the 55 amp alternator should give a reading of 3.1 to 3.3 ohms and the 65 amp alternator a reading of 3.9 to 4.1 ohms.
4   On the 65 amp version the DT wire must be routed as shown in Fig. 9.6.

13 Starter motor – testing in the car

1   If the starter motor fails to operate, first check the condition of the battery by switching on the headlamps. If they glow brightly, then gradually dim after a few seconds, the battery is in an uncharged condition.
2   If the battery is in good condition, check the wiring connections on the starter for security and also check the earth wire between the gearbox and body.
3   If the starter still fails to turn, use a voltmeter or 12 volt test lamp and leads to check that current is reaching the main terminal (terminal 30) on the starter solenoid.
4   With the ignition switched on and the ignition key in the start position check that current is reaching the remaining terminals on the solenoid. Also check that an audible click is heard as the solenoid operates indicating that the internal contacts are closed and that current is available at the field windings terminal.

5   Failure to obtain current at terminal 50 indicates a faulty ignition switch.
6   If current at the correct voltage is available at the starter motor, yet it does not operate, the unit is faulty and should be removed for further investigation.

14 Starter motor – removal and refitting

1   Disconnect the earth lead from the battery.
2   Jack up the front of the car and support it on axle stands. Apply the handbrake.
3   Where a heat deflector plate is fitted, undo the retaining nuts and remove the plate.
4   Identify the wiring for position then disconnect it from the solenoid (photo).
5   Where applicable, unbolt and detach the support bracket.
6   Undo the retaining bolts and withdraw the starter motor. On 1.6 and 1.8 litre models, move the steering fully to the right and if

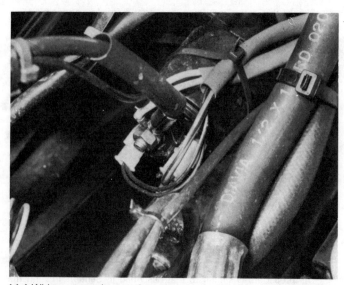

14.4 Wiring connections to the starter motor solenoid – 1.3 litre

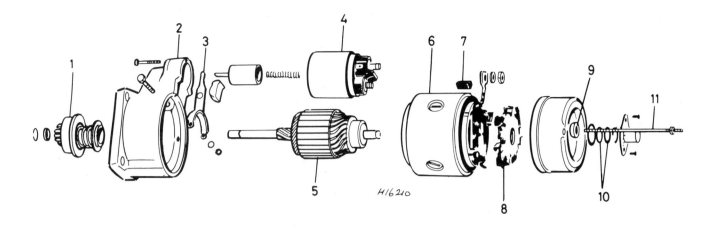

Fig. 9.7 Exploded view of the starter motor (typical) (Sec 15)

1 Pinion
2 Mounting bracket
3 Operating lever
4 Solenoid
5 Armature
6 Housing with windings
7 Carbon brushes
8 Brush plate
9 Bush
10 Spacers
11 Through-bolt

necessary detach the right-hand driveshaft at the gearbox drive flange to allow room for removal.

7 Refitting is a reversal of removal, but tighten the bolts to the specified torque. Where a support bracket is fitted, do not fully tighten the nuts and bolts until the bracket is correctly located and free of any tension.

15 Starter motor – overhaul

1 Wipe clean the exterior surfaces of the starter motor.
2 Unscrew the terminal nut and disconnect the field windings lead from the solenoid.
3 Unscrew the bolts and withdraw the solenoid from the housing, then unhook the solenoid core from the operating lever.
4 Remove the screws and lift off the end cap, then prise out the circlip and remove the shims.
5 Unscrew the through-bolts and remove the end cover.
6 Lift the springs and remove the carbon brushes from the brush holder, then withdraw the holder.
7 Remove the field coil housing from the end housing.
8 Using a metal tube drive the stop ring towards the pinion, then remove the circlip and stop ring.
9 Slide the armature from the pinion, and withdraw the pinion.
10 Prise the rubber pad from the end housing.
11 Unscrew and remove the pivot bolt and withdraw the operating lever.
12 Clean all the components in paraffin and wipe dry. Check the pinion teeth for wear and pitting and check that the one-way clutch only allows the pinion to turn in one direction. Clean the commutator with a fuel-moistened cloth and, if necessary, use fine glass paper to remove any carbon deposits. If the commutator is worn excessively it cannot be machined and renewal is necessary.
13 Check the brushes for excessive wear and if in any doubt renew them. To do this, crush the old brushes with a pair of pliers and clean the leads. Insert the leads into the new brushes and splay out the ends. Solder the wires in position but grip the wire next to the brush with long-nosed pliers in order to prevent the solder penetrating the flexible section of the wire. File off any surplus solder.
14 Check the bush in the end cover and if necessary drive it out with a soft metal drift. Soak the end cover in hot oil for five minutes before driving the new bush into it.
15 Assemble the starter motor in reversal of the dismantling procedure but note that the unit must be sealed with suitable sealant on the surfaces shown in Fig. 9.8. Lubricate the pinion drive with a little molybdenum disulphide grease. Make sure that the stop ring is fitted from the inside of the circlip with the annular groove facing outwards,

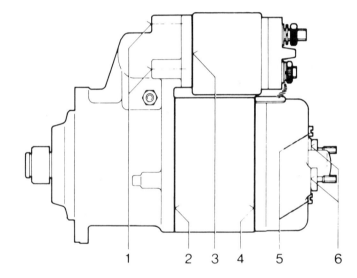

Fig. 9.8 Surfaces to be sealed when reassembling the starter motor (Sec 15)

1 Solenoid securing screws
2 Starter/mounting surface
3 Solenoid joint
4 Starter/end cap joint
5 Through-bolts
6 Shaft cover joint and screws

and also make sure that the stop ring turns freely on the shaft. Lubricate the solenoid and operating lever with a little molybdenum disulphide grease. When fitting the brush holder, the springs may be held in a raised position by using two lengths of bent wire.

16 Automatic stop-start system – general

This system is fitted as optional equipment to some models and is a fuel economy device. Activated by a control switch, the system automatically switches off the engine when the vehicle is stationary during traffic delays.

The system is switched on and off by means of a switch on the dash insert between the instrument panel and the heater/fresh air control panel. A warning light in the switch advises when the system is switched on.

The system should only be used when the vehicle has reached its normal operating temperature. When activated, the system will automatically stop the engine when the vehicle speed drops below 3.1 mph (5 kph) and has run at its normal idle speed for a period of at least 2 seconds. In addition the vehicle must previously have been driven at a speed in excess of 3.1 mph (5 kph). When the engine is stopped by the system, the rear window heater will automatically cut out.

When traffic conditions permit, the engine can be restarted by depressing the clutch pedal and moving the gear lever fully to the left in neutral. Once the engine has restarted, the gear engagement can be made in the normal manner. If for any reason the engine stalls or stops after restarting, the restart procedure should be repeated, but the gear lever must be moved back into neutral within 6 seconds.

The following safety precautions should be noted when using the system, these being:

(a) *Do not use the system when the engine temperature is below 55°C (131°F) or when the ambient temperature is very low as the engine will take longer to warm up*

(b) *Do not allow the vehicle to roll when the engine is switched off, check that the handbrake is fully applied*

(c) *During extended delays switch the engine off in the normal manner with the ignition key, as electrical accessories will otherwise be left on and the battery run down*

(d) *If leaving the vehicle for any length of time, switch off the system and always take the ignition key with you*

17 Gearchange and consumption gauge – general

1   When fitted, the gearchange and consumption gauge is fitted in the instrument panel in place of the coolant temperature gauge.
2   The gearchange indicator lights up in all gears except top gear when better economy without loss of power can be obtained by changing up to a higher gear. The indicator does not operate during acceleration or deceleration, or on carburettor engines when the engine is cold.
3   The gearchange indicator light goes out when a higher gear is engaged.
4   On automatic transmission models the gearchange indicator is non-operational since all forward gears are automatically changed in accordance with engine speed/output and vehicle speed.
5   The fuel consumption indicator operates only in top gear (D in automatic transmission models), and indicates the actual fuel consumption in mpg.
6   The gearchange and consumption gauge is operated by a switch

on the gearbox and a sender in the vacuum line to the distributor (photo).

18 Fuses and relays – general

1   The fuses and relays are located under the facia panel on the right-hand side (photo).
2   The fuses are numbered consecutively for identification. Always renew a fuse with one of identical rating and never renew it more than once without finding out the source of the trouble (usually a short circuit).
3   All relays are of the plug-in type and, again, they are numbered for identification, though not consecutively.
4   Relays cannot be repaired and, if at all suspect, should be removed and taken to an auto-electrical workshop for testing.
5   The fuse/relay unit holder complete can be removed by twisting the securing knob on the lower right-hand side and removing the knob. Twist the slotted retainer on the left-hand side and withdraw the fuse/relay box. The various connectors on the rear face of the unit are then accessible for detachment as required (photo).

18.1 General view of the fuse and relay box unit

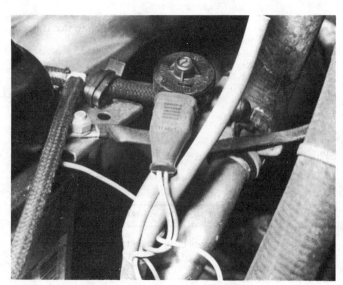

17.6 Fuel consumption gauge sender unit

18.5 Fuse/relay box removal, showing rear connections

18.6 Typical relay installation in the engine compartment

21.4 Combination switch retaining screws (arrowed)

6   In addition to those fuses and relays located at the main fuse/relay unit, some models will have in-line fuses and relays fitted to some circuits, these being shown in the wiring diagrams and photo 18.6.

19 Direction indicators and hazard flasher system – general

1   The direction indicators are controlled by the left-hand column switch.
2   A switch on the facia board operates all four flashers simultaneously, and although the direction indicators will not work when the ignition is switched off, the emergency switch overrides this and the flasher signals continue to operate.
3   All the circuits are routed through the relay on the console and its fuse.
4   If the indicators do not function correctly, a series of tests may be done to find which part of the circuit is at fault.
5   The most common fault is in the flasher lamps, defective bulbs, and dirty or corroded contacts or mountings. Check these first, then test the emergency switch. Remove it from the circuit and check its operation. If the switch is in good order, refit it and again turn on the emergency lights. If nothing happens then the relay is not functioning properly and it should be renewed. If the lights function on emergency but not on operation of the column switch then the wiring and column switch are suspect (see Section 21).

20 Ignition switch/steering column lock – removal and refitting

The procedure is described in Chapter 10 for the removal and refitting of the steering lock.

21 Combination switches – removal and refitting

1   Remove the steering wheel, as described in Chaper 10.
2   Disconnect the battery negative lead.
3   Remove the screws and withdraw the steering column lower shroud.
4   Remove the three screws securing the combination switch (photo).
5   Disconnect the multi-plugs (photo).
6   Rotate the indicator switch clockwise and withdraw it, noting location of the plastic retaining arms (photo).

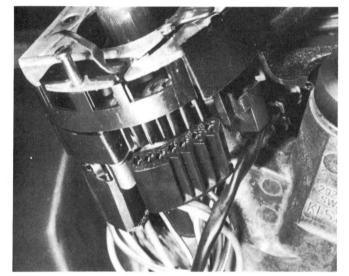

21.5 Combination switch multi-plug connections

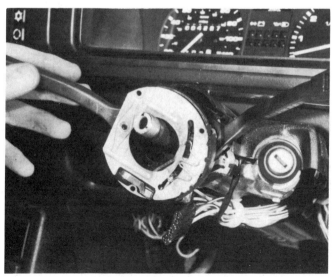

21.6 Removing the indicator switch ...

244

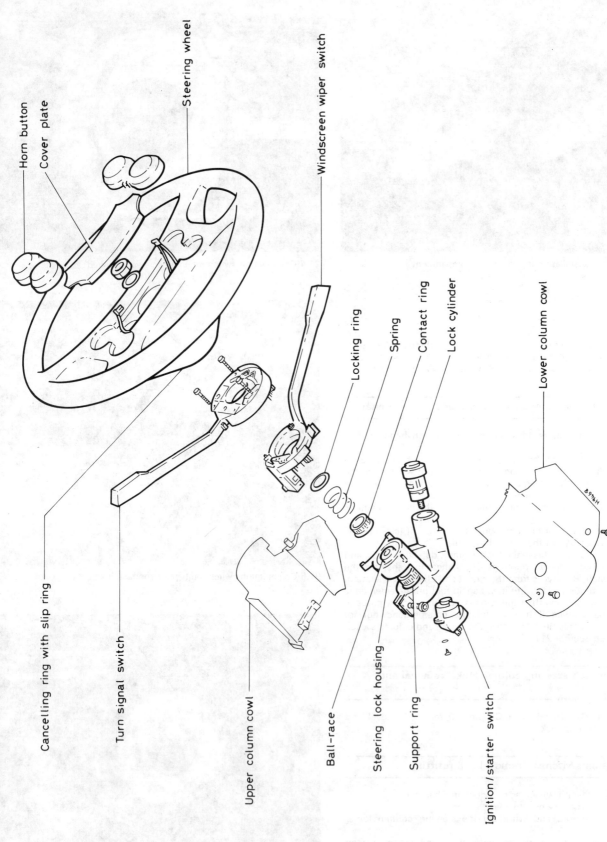

Horn button

Cover plate

Steering wheel

Windscreen wiper switch

Cancelling ring with slip ring

Turn signal switch

Locking ring

Spring

Contact ring

Lock cylinder

Lower column cowl

Upper column cowl

Ball-race

Steering lock housing

Support ring

Ignition/starter switch

Fig. 9.9 Steering column combination switches and associated components (Sec 21)

7 Withdraw the wiper control switch from the column. Full removal of the switch of GTI models will necessitate detaching the additional wire from its connector under the dash panel (photo).
8 Refitting is a reversal of the removal procedure. Check that the indicator switch is centralised before fitting the steering wheel otherwise the cancelling cams could be damaged.
9 Refit the steering wheel, with reference to Chapter 10.
10 On completion check the operation of the switches.

21.7A ... and wiper control switch

21.7B Additional under dash wiring connection and insulator – GTI

22 Facia switches – removal and refitting

1 Disconnect the battery earth lead.
2 To remove a rocker type switch such as the lighting switch, press the switch to the ON position then insert a suitable screwdriver blade into the notch at the base of the switch, and prise the switch free form the facia (photo).
3 On other switch types such as the heated rear seat switch, simply lever the switch free from the bottom edge, as shown in Fig. 9.10.
4 With the switch withdrawn, detach the wiring connector. Where

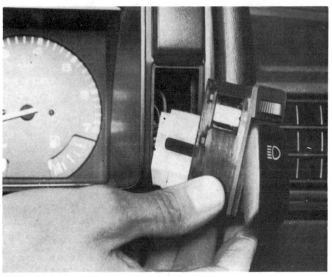

22.2 Facia switch removal

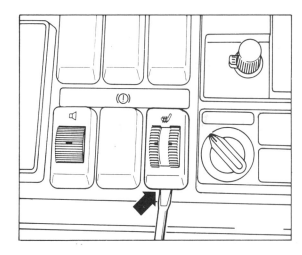

Fig. 9.10 Prise free the switch from the bottom edge (Sec 22)

applicable, warning light bulb holders can be withdrawn from the switch and the bulb removed.
5 Refitting is a reversal of the removal procedure. Check the switch for satisfactory operation on completion.

23 Warning lamp cluster – removal and refitting

1 Disconnect the battery earth lead.
2 Remove the facia control switches, as described in the previous Section, then, reaching through the vacant switch apertures in the facia, compress the retainers and push out the warning lamp cluster unit (photo).
3 Disconnect the multi-plug for full cluster removal.
4 Withdraw the warning light bulbholder from the cluster and pull free the bulb for inspection and, if necessary, renewal (photo). Where two or more warning lamp bulbs are contained in a single mounting plate, the plate unit complete must be renewed as it is not possible to renew a single bulb in this instance.
5 Refit in the reverse order of removal and, on completion, check the operation of the switches and warning light bulb(s).

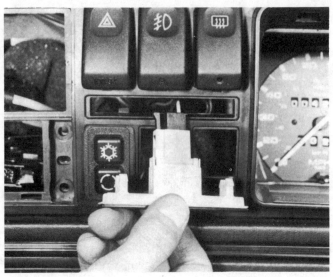

23.2 Warning lamp cluster removal

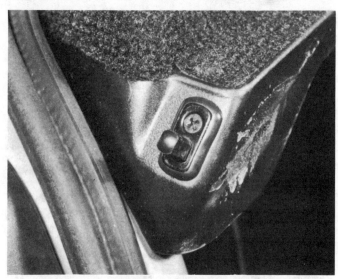

24.2 Tailgate actuated luggage compartment light switch

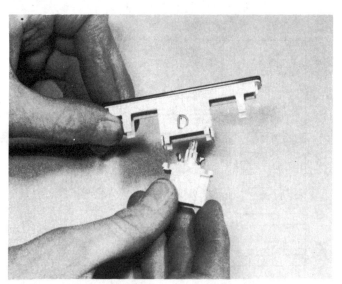

23.4 Warning lamp cluster bulbholder removal

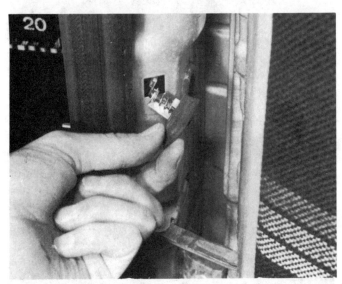

24.3 Door courtesy light switch removal

24 Courtesy and luggage compartment light switches – removal and refitting

1 Disconnect the battery negative lead.
2 Open the door, boot lid or tailgate (as applicable) and unscrew the cross-head screw from the switch (photo).
3 Withdraw the switch and disconnect the wiring. Tie a loose knot in the wire to prevent it from dropping into the door pillar (photo).
4 Check the switch seal for condition and renew it, if necessary.
5 Refitting is a reversal of removal.

25 Cigarette lighter – removal and refitting

1 Disconnect the battery negative lead.
2 Remove the lower facia panel then reach up and disconnect the wiring from the cigarette lighter.
3 Remove the retaining ring and withdraw the cigarette lighter from the facia.
4 Refitting is a reversal of removal.

26 Speedometer cable – removal and refitting

1 Open the bonnet and then reach down and unscrew the speedometer cable nut from the transmission.
2 Withdraw the instrument panel far enough to disconnect the cable; with reference to Section 27.
3 Remove the air cleaner, as described in Chapter 3.
4 Carefully unclip and detach the plastic cover from the top edge of the bulkhead. Pull the speedometer cable through the bulkhead and withdraw it from the engine compartment side.
5 Refitting is a reversal of removal. Make sure that the grommet is correctly fitted in the bulkhead and that there are no sharp bends in the cable. **Do not** grease the cable ends.

27 Instrument panel cluster – removal and refitting

1 Disconnect the battery earth lead.
2 Remove the facia panel, as described in Section 29.

3   Remove the instrument panel retaining screws – one each side at the top (photo).
4   Prise the panel away, tilting from the top edge. Reach behind the panel and disconnect the speedometer cable (photo) and, where applicable, the vacuum hose from the vacuum sender. Detach the wiring multi-connectors from the rear lower edge then lift the instrument panel out; taking care not to damage the printed circuit on its rear face (photo).
5   The individual circuits of the printed circuit foil can be checked for continuity using an ohmmeter. For circuit identification refer to the wiring diagram.
6   Refitting is a reversal of the removal sequence, but make sure that all connections are securely made. Check instruments for satisfactory operation on completion.

---

28 Instrument panel – dismantling, testing and reassembly

1   Remove the instrument panel cluster, as described in Section 27.
2   Remove the relevant instrument, with reference to Figs. 9.11 or 9.12, but take particular care not to damage the printed circuit foil.
3   To test the voltage stabilizer, connect a voltmeter between the terminals shown in Fig. 9.13 with a 12 volt supply to the remaining

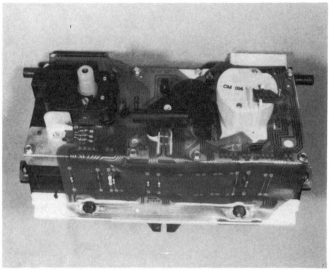

27.4B Rear view of the instrument panel unit

27.3 Instrument panel screws removal

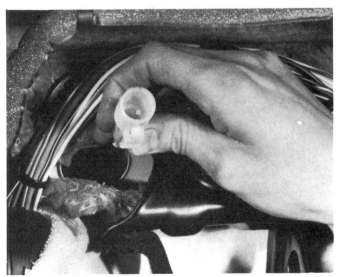

27.4A Disconnect the speedometer cable

terminal. A constant voltage of 10 volts must be registered. If the voltage is above 10.5 volts or below 9.5 volts renew the voltage stabilizer.
4   The accuracy of the fuel gauge can be checked by draining the fuel tank and then adding excactly 5 litres of fuel. After leaving the ignition switched on for at least two minutes the fuel gauge needle should be level with the upper edge of the red reserve zone. If not, either the fuel gauge or tank unit is faulty.
5   If renewing the gearchange/consumption indicator avoid touching the back of the gauge. Removal necessitates detaching the printed circuit and the vacuum sender unit then undoing the three securing screws (Fig. 9.14). Renew the diode (LED) or consumption indicator unit, as necessary.
6   When renewing the normal type clock (which incorporates the fuel gauge) it is important to ensure the correct printed circuit connections when refitting. The connections are shown in Fig. 9.15.
7   The digital type clock is secured by two retaining screws. When removing the clock take care not to allow the adjuster pins for the hours and minutes to fall out.
8   The warning lamp LED indicators in the lamp housing are positioned as shown in Fig. 9.16. When renewing the LEDs, each diode can be pulled free from the retainer plate, but note that one of the connector prongs is wider. This is the minus connection and it is important that it is correctly refitted. If necessary the diode holder unit can be removed by carefully levering it free from the warning lamp housing.
9   The individual circuits of the printed circuit foil can be checked for continuity using an ohmmeter and referring to the appropriate wiring diagram.
10 If renewing the printed circuit foil it should be noted that a common type may be supplied for all models. If fitting a new printed circuit foil to the dash insert on models with a normal type clock it may be necessary to cut off the connector pins used for the digital clock and vice versa for models with the digital clock. Check this with your supplier.
11 To remove the plug housing from the instrument panel insert, press the plastic rib on the housing (using a screwdriver) over the engagement lugs and pull the housing with printed circuit in the direction of the arrow (Fig. 9.17). The plug housing can be removed from the printed circuit by pressing free the engagement lugs and pulling the housing away from the printed circuit in the direction of the arrow shown in Fig. 9.18.
12 If removing the tachometer, first remove the gearshift and fuel consumption indicator (paragraph 5) then undo the two retaining screws and remove the tachometer, together with the multi-function indicator (printed circuit). The VDO type multi-function indicator can then be removed by undoing the retaining screws, pressing the

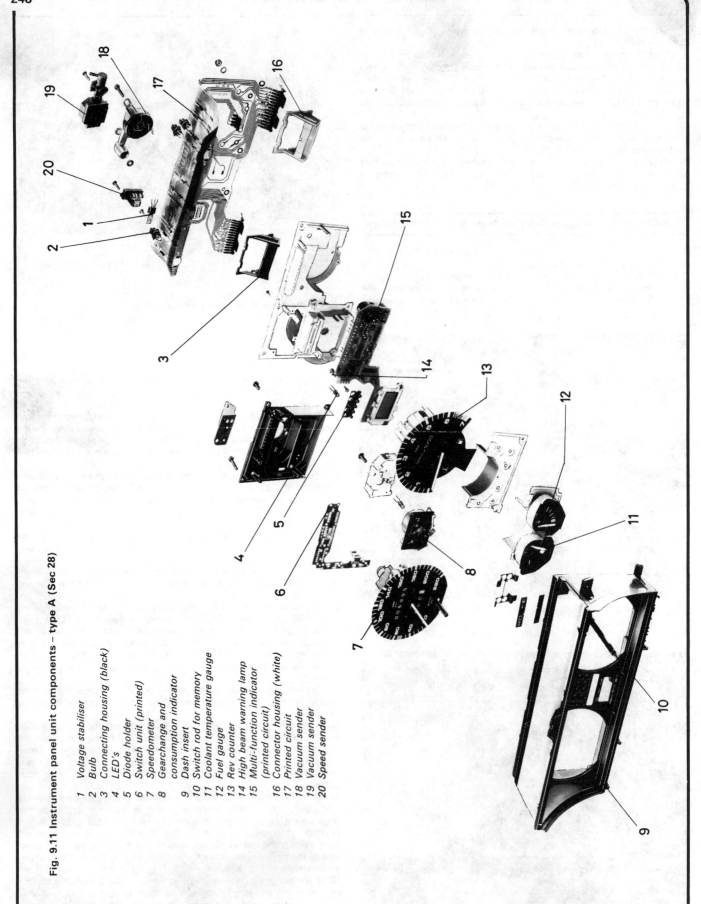

Fig. 9.11 Instrument panel unit components – type A (Sec 28)

1 Voltage stabiliser
2 Bulb
3 Connecting housing (black)
4 LED's
5 Diode holder
6 Switch unit (printed)
7 Speedometer
8 Gearchange and
  consumption indicator
9 Dash insert
10 Switch rod for memory
11 Coolant temperature gauge
12 Fuel gauge
13 Rev counter
14 High beam warning lamp
15 Multi-function indicator
  (printed circuit)
16 Connector housing (white)
17 Printed circuit
18 Vacuum sender
19 Vacuum sender
20 Speed sender

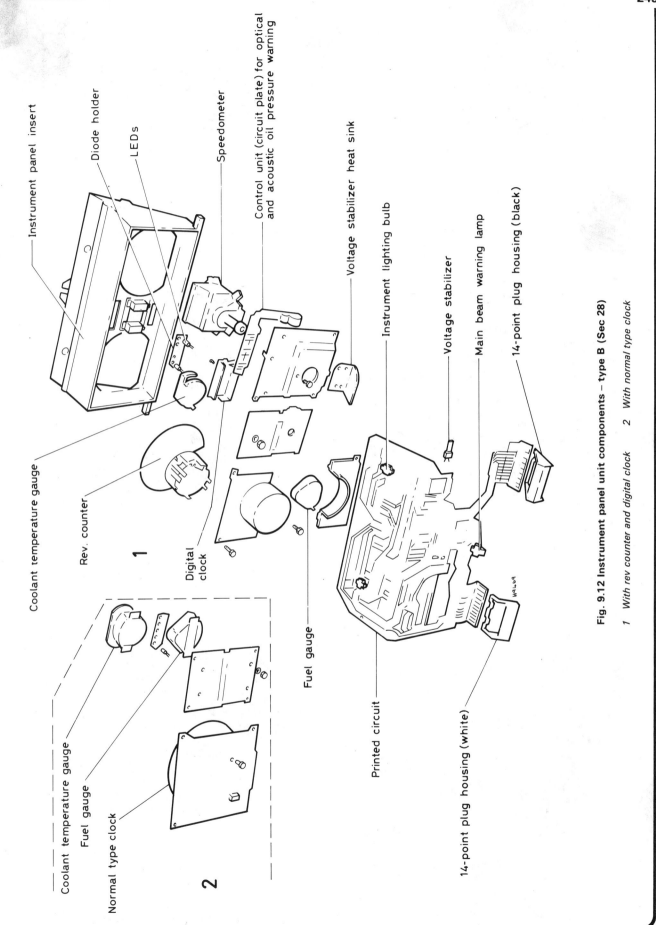

Coolant temperature gauge

Instrument panel insert

Diode holder

LEDs

Speedometer

Control unit (circuit plate) for optical and acoustic oil pressure warning

Voltage stabilizer heat sink

Instrument lighting bulb

Voltage stabilizer

Main beam warning lamp

14-point plug housing (black)

Rev. counter

Digital clock

Coolant temperature gauge

Fuel gauge

Normal type clock

Fuel gauge

Printed circuit

14-point plug housing (white)

1

2

Fig. 9.12 Instrument panel unit components – type B (Sec 28)

1 With rev counter and digital clock   2   With normal type clock

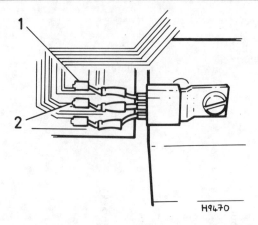

Fig. 9.13 Voltage stabilizer test terminals (Sec 28)

Connect a voltmeter between 1 and 2

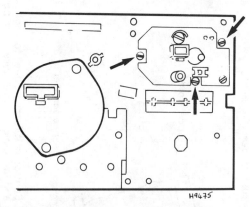

Fig. 9.14 Gearchange and fuel indicator unit retaining screws – arrowed (Sec 28)

Fig. 9.15 Normal type clock connections (Sec 28)

1   *Earth connection*   2   *Plus (+) live connection*

Fig. 9.16 LED connections in the warning lamp housing (Sec 28)

K1	*Main beam (blue)*	K5	*Indicators (green)*
K2	*Alternator (red)*	K48	*Gearchange indicator*
K3	*Oil pressure (red)*		*(yellow)*

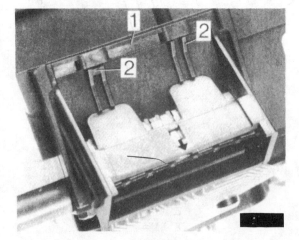

Fig. 9.17 Plug housing detachment from the instrument panel insert (Sec 28)

1   *Plastic rib*   2   *Engagement lugs*
Pull housing in direction of arrow

Fig. 9.18 Plug housing removal from the printed circuit (Sec 28)

1   *Engagement lugs*
Pull housing in direction of arrow

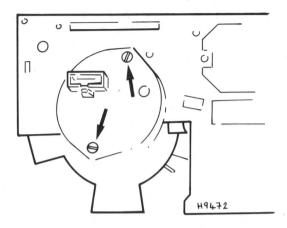

Fig. 9.19 Tachometer retaining screws (arrowed) (Sec 28)

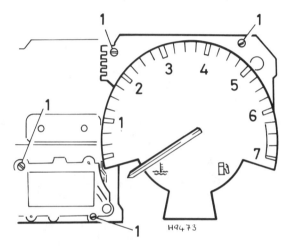

Fig. 9.20 Multi-function indicator (VDO type) and retaining screws (1) (Sec 28)

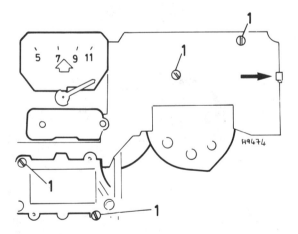

Fig. 9.21 Multi-function indicator (Motometer type) and retaining screws (1) (Sec 28)

retaining lugs from the printed circuit and withdrawing the indicator unit (Fig. 9.20). The Motometer type multi-function indicator is removed in a similar manner (see Fig. 9.21).

Reassembly
13 Reassembly of the instrument panel is a reversal of the dismantling procedure.

29 Facia panel – removal and refitting

1 Disconnect the battery earth lead.
2 To improve accessibility, remove the steering wheel, as described in Chapter 10.
3 Remove the radio, referring to Section 43 for details.
4 Pull free the heater/fresh air control lever knobs, then release the control panel retaining clips around the outer edge and pull the panel from the facia. Detach the wiring multi-connectors.
5 Remove the lower switches from the facia panel, referring to Section 22, and, where applicable, remove the blank pads by prising them free.
6 Unscrew the facia panel retaining screws from the following locations:

> (a) Light switch aperture
> (b) Top inner edge of radio aperture
> (c) Fader control (or blank) aperture (photo)
> (d) Heater control panel aperture
> (e) Top of the instrument panel (photo)
> (f) Top left side of panel

29.6A Facia panel retaining screw through fader control aperture

29.6B Remove the instrument panel retaining screws at the top

29.7 Facia panel removal

30.1B Detaching the headlamp bulb connector

7   Partially withdraw the panel and detach any remaining switch lead multi-connectors. Remove the facia panel (photo).
8   Refit in the reverse order of removal, ensuring that all wiring connections are securely made. Check operation of various switches and controls on completion.

30 Headlamp bulbs and headlamps – removal and refitting

1   To remove a headlamp bulb, first open the bonnet and pull the connector from the rear of the headlamp (photos).
2   Prise off the rubber cap.
3   Squeeze the bulb retaining spring clips together and release the clip from the bulb (photo).
4   Withdraw the bulb, but do not touch its glass with your fingers if it is to be re-used (photo).
5   To remove the headlamp unit, first remove the radiator grille, as described in Chapter 11.

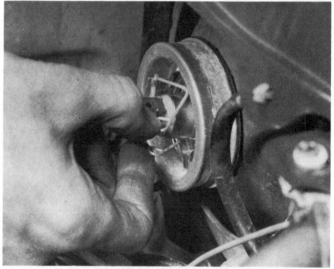

30.3 Squeeze the bulb retaining clips free ...

30.1A Rear view of headlight (round type) showing wiring connectors

30.4 ... withdraw the bulb

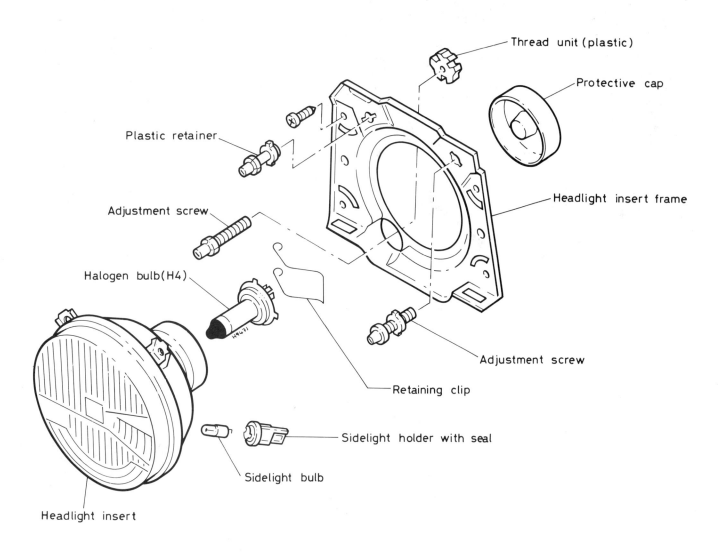

Thread unit (plastic)

Protective cap

Plastic retainer

Headlight insert frame

Adjustment screw

Halogen bulb (H4)

Adjustment screw

Retaining clip

Sidelight holder with seal

Sidelight bulb

Headlight insert

Fig. 9.22 Headlamp unit (round type) and associated components (Sec 30)

30.6 Front view of the round type headlamp unit

6 With the headlamp bulb removed, unscrew the screws securing the carrier plate to the front panel, and withdraw the unit (photo).
7 Refitting is a reversal of removal, but check and, if necessary, adjust the beam alignment, as described in Section 31.

31 Headlamps – alignment

1 The headlamp beam alignment should be checked and if necessary adjusted every 10 000 miles (15 000 km).
2 It is recommended that the alignment is carried out by a VW garage using modern beam setting equipment. However, in an emergency, the following procedure will provide an acceptable light pattern.
3 Position the car on a level surface with tyres correctly inflated, approximately 10 metres (33 feet) in front of, and at right-angles to, a wall or garage door.
4 Draw a horizontal line on the wall or door at headlamp centre height. Draw a vertical line corresponding to the centre line of the car, then measure off a point either side of this, on the horizontal line, corresponding with the headlamp centres.
5 Switch on the main beam and check that the areas of maximum illumination coincide with the headlamp centre marks on the wall. If not, turn the upper cross-head adjustment screw to adjust the beam laterally, and the lower screw to adjust the beam vertically (photo).

31.5 Headlamp alignment adjuster screw locations (arrowed)

32 Headlamp range control – removal and refitting

1   Where fitted, the system is designed to provide the driver with in-car headlamp adjustment to counteract the effects of heavy loading at the rear. The system operates on dipped headlamps only, and the light units are raised or lowered by means of an electrically-operated motor mounted at the rear of each unit. For safety reasons an integral height adjustment limit control is fitted.
2   The range control switch can be removed in the manner described in Section 22.
3   To remove a range control motor from the rear of a headlamp unit first disconnect the battery earth lead.
4   Pull free the plug connector from the rear of the motor unit.
5   On the round type headlamp unit, detach the motor from the frame by twisting it to the right (clockwise).
6   On rectangular headlamp units, the adjuster motor on the right-hand side is disconnected by turning it to the left, whilst on the left-hand unit it must be turned to the right.
7   Undo the headlamp adjustment screw from the front (Fig. 9.26) then pull the motor from the frame to the rear for removal.
8   Refit in the reverse order of removal. Check the range control operation on completion.

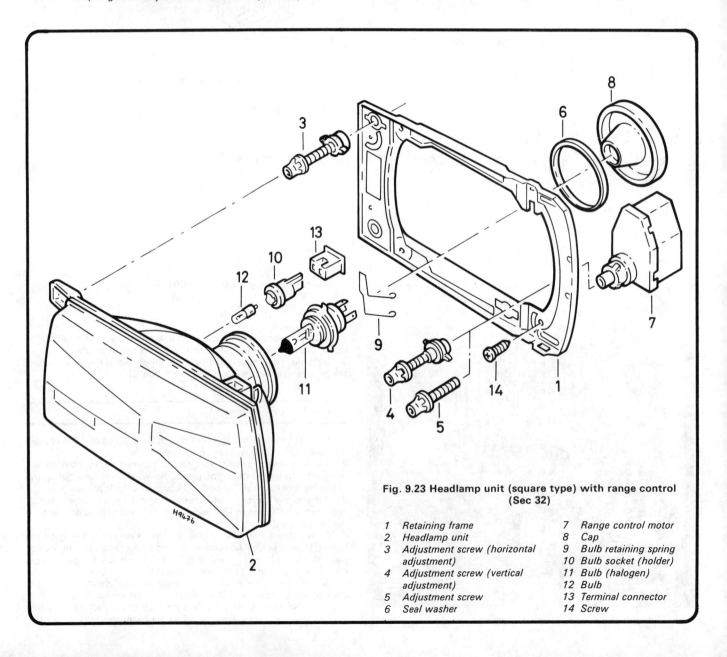

**Fig. 9.23 Headlamp unit (square type) with range control
(Sec 32)**

1 Retaining frame	7 Range control motor
2 Headlamp unit	8 Cap
3 Adjustment screw (horizontal adjustment)	9 Bulb retaining spring
	10 Bulb socket (holder)
4 Adjustment screw (vertical adjustment)	11 Bulb (halogen)
	12 Bulb
5 Adjustment screw	13 Terminal connector
6 Seal washer	14 Screw

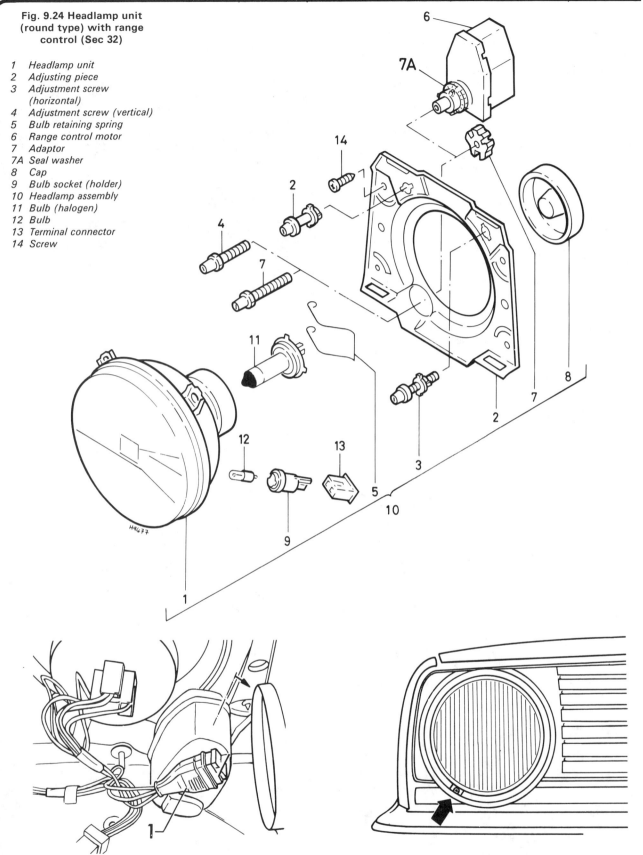

Fig. 9.24 Headlamp unit (round type) with range control (Sec 32)

1 Headlamp unit
2 Adjusting piece
3 Adjustment screw (horizontal)
4 Adjustment screw (vertical)
5 Bulb retaining spring
6 Range control motor
7 Adaptor
7A Seal washer
8 Cap
9 Bulb socket (holder)
10 Headlamp assembly
11 Bulb (halogen)
12 Bulb
13 Terminal connector
14 Screw

Fig. 9.25 Range control motor and terminal multi-connector (1) – round unit type (Sec 32)

Detach motor by rotating clockwise – arrowed

Fig. 9.26 Remove headlamp adjuster screw (arrowed) (Sec 32)

33 Foglight (front) bulb and unit – removal and refitting

1   To remove the bulb, pull back the rubber cover from the rear of the lamp unit, compress the bulb retaining spring clip and release it (photo).
2   The bulb can now be withdrawn, but do not handle its glass with the fingers (photo).
3   The foglight unit is removed in a similar manner to that described for the headlamps (Section 30).
4   Refit in the reverse order of removal and check operation of lamp on completion. If necessary adjust the lamp beam alignment by means of the adjustment screws (photo).
5   Foglight alignment should be carried out by a VW dealer with the proper beam setting equipment. In an emergency follow the procedure for headlamps given in Section 31.

34 Lamp bulbs – renewal

Note: *Lamp bulbs should always be renewed with ones of similar type and rating, as listed in the Specifications.*

Sidelights
1   Open the bonnet and pull the connector from the sidelight bulbholder located beneath the headlamp bulb.
2   Turn the bulbholder anti-clockwise and remove it from the reflector (photo).
3   Depress and twist the bulb to remove it.

Front indicator lights
4   Remove the cross-head screws and withdraw the lens (photo).
5   Depress and twist the bulb to remove it (photo).
6   If necessary the lamp unit can be withdrawn from the bumper and the wiring disconnected (photo).
7   When refitting the lens make sure that the gasket is correctly located.

33.1 Prise free the rubber cover from the rear of the foglight

Rear lights
8   Open the tailgate or bootlid, as applicable, and compress the bulb carrier securing tabs to release the bulb carrier, and withdraw it for bulb inspection/renewal.
9   Depress and twist the relevant bulb to remove it (photo).

Number plate light
10   Remove the cross-head screws and withdraw the lens and cover (photo).

33.2 Bulb and holder removal from foglight

33.4 Foglight beam alignment adjuster screws (arrowed)

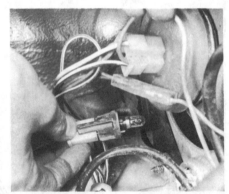

34.2 Sidelight bulb and holder removal

34.4 Front indicator lens removal

34.5 Front indicator lamp bulb

34.6 Front indicator lamp unit removal

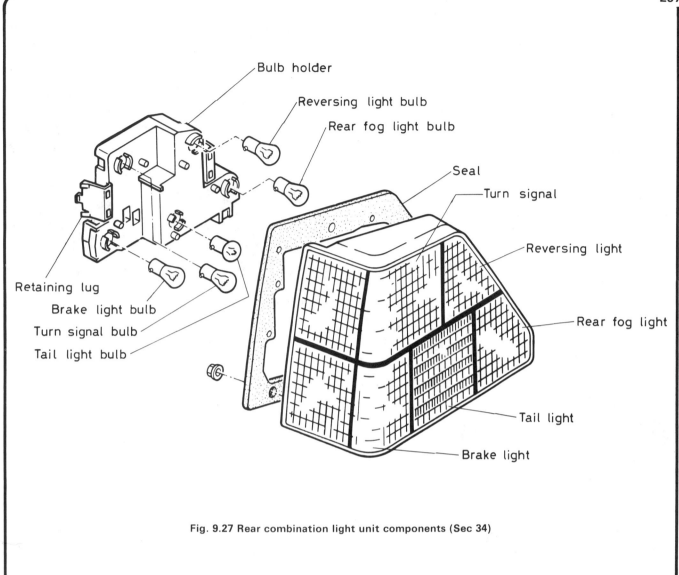

Bulb holder

Reversing light bulb

Rear fog light bulb

Seal

Turn signal

Reversing light

Rear fog light

Retaining lug

Brake light bulb

Turn signal bulb

Tail light bulb

Tail light

Brake light

Fig. 9.27 Rear combination light unit components (Sec 34)

34.9 Rear combination light unit and bulbs

34.10 Number plate lens removal

11 Depress and twist the bulb to remove it.
12 When refitting the lens and cover make sure that the lug is correctly located.

Interior light
13 Using a screwdriver, depress the spring clip then withdraw the light from the roof (photos).
14 Release the festoon type bulb from the spring terminals.
15 When fitting the new bulb make sure that the terminals are tensioned sufficiently to retain the bulb. The switch end of the light should be inserted into the roof first.

Luggage compartment light/glovebox light
16 Prise free and withdraw the lens. The bulb is retained in the lens and can be pulled free for renewal (photo). If renewing the lens detach the wiring spade connectors from the lens.

Instrument panel light
17 Remove the instrument panel, as described in Section 27.
18 Twist the bulbholder through 90° to withdraw it (photo), then pull out the bulb.

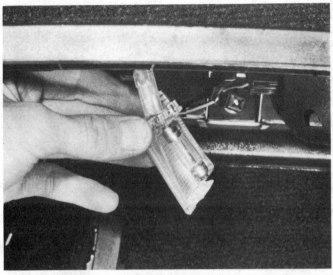

34.16 Luggage compartment lamp lens removal

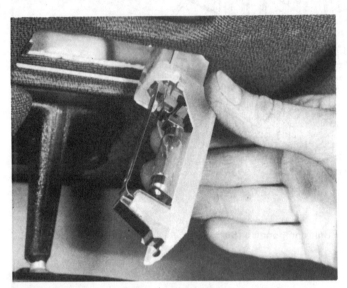

34.13A Interior light removal – 1.8 litre

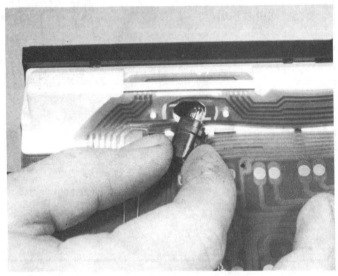

34.18 Instrument panel light bulb and holder removal

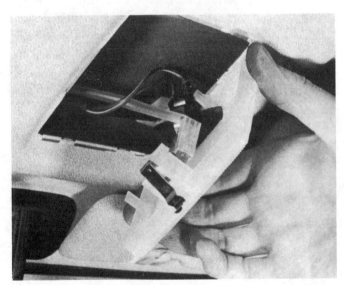

34.13B Interior light removal – 1.3 litre

Facia switch lights
19 Remove the relevant facia switch, as described in Section 22.
20 Remove the bulb from the switch or connector as applicable.

35 Electrically-operated door mirror motor – removal and refitting

1 Disconnect the battery earth lead.
2 Release the mirror glass by rotating the retainer anti-clockwise as shown in Fig. 9.28, using a suitable screwdriver.
3 Remove the mirror and disconnect the wiring.
4 Undo the four retaining screws and withdraw the mirror motor. Detach the wiring from the motor.
5 Carefully lever free the door mirror adjuster switch from the trim panel and withdraw it so that the multi-connector plug can be detached.
6 Further removal of the wiring will necessitate door trim removal; see Chapter 11.

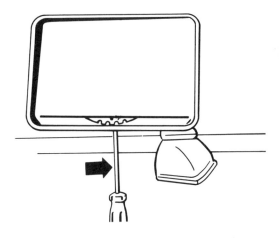

Fig. 9.28 Turn retainer anti-clockwise for electrically-operated door mirror removal (Sec 35)

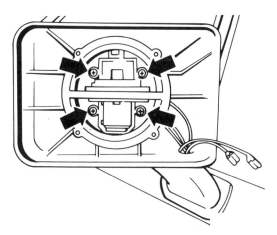

Fig. 9.29 Mirror motor retaining screws (arrowed) (Sec 35)

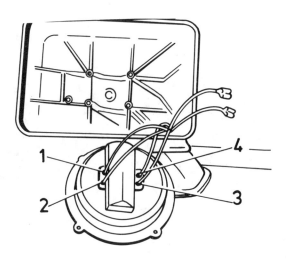

Fig. 9.30 Door mirror wiring identification (Sec 35)

1	Blue	3	White
2	Brown	4	Black

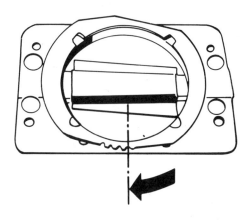

Fig. 9.31 Rotate retainer clockwise before fitting the glass (Sec 35)

7   Refitting is a reversal of the removal procedure. Note that the mirror motor wires are colour-coded for correct reconnection (Fig. 9.30).
8   When refitting the mirror glass, rotate the retainer in a clockwise direction to its full extent, then carefully insert the glass into its housing.

36 Wiper blades – renewal

1   To remove a wiper blade pull the arm from the windscreen/rear window as far as possible, then depress the plastic clip and slide the blade from the arm (photo).

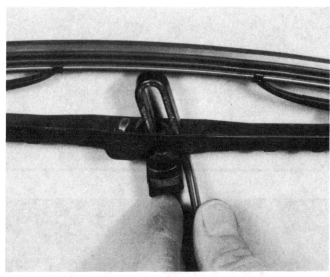

36.1 Wiper blade removal from arm

2   If necessary the wiper rubber may be renewed separately. To do this use pliers to compress the rubber so that it can be removed from the blade.
3   Refitting is a reversal of removal.

37 Wiper arms – removal and refitting

1   Make sure that the wiper arms are in their parked position then remove the wiper blade, as described in Section 36.
2   Lift the hinged cover and unscrew the nut (photo).
3   Ease the wiper arm from the spindle, taking care not to damage the paintwork (photo).

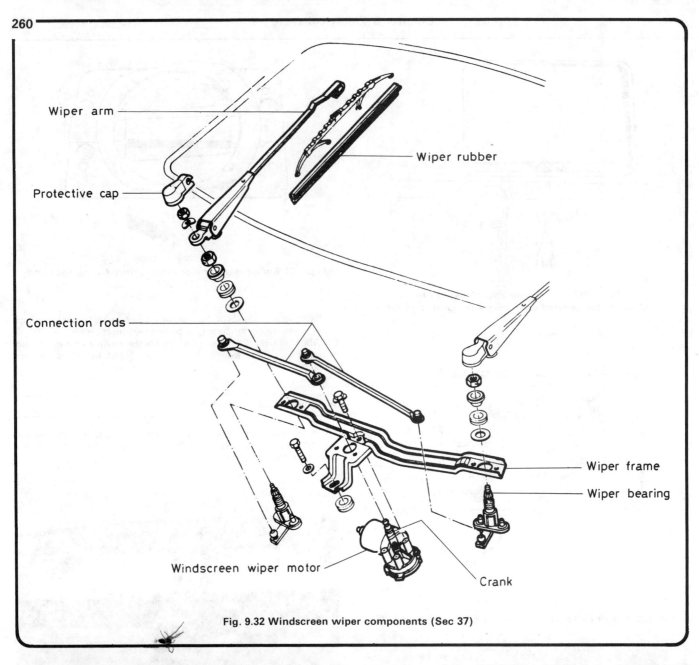

Wiper arm

Wiper rubber

Protective cap

Connection rods

Wiper frame

Wiper bearing

Windscreen wiper motor

Crank

Fig. 9.32 Windscreen wiper components (Sec 37)

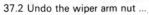

37.2 Undo the wiper arm nut ...

37.3 ... and withdraw the arm from the spindle

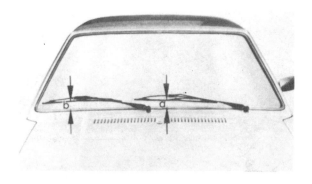

Fig. 9.33 Windscreen wiper blade setting positions (Sec 37)

a = 55 mm (2.16 in)   b = 59 mm (2.32 in)

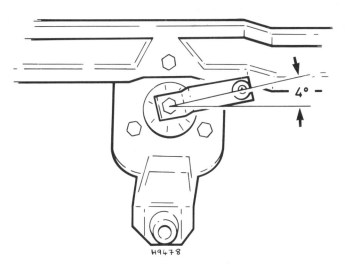

Fig. 9.34 Windscreen wiper motor bellcrank angle (with motor at rest) (Sec 37)

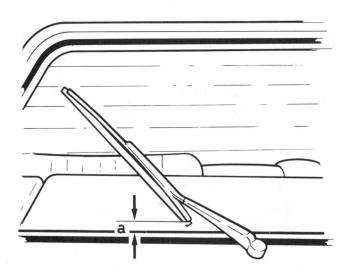

Fig. 9.35 Rear window wiper adjustment position (Sec 37)

a = 15 mm (0.60 in)

4   Refitting is a reversal of removal. In the parked position, the end of the wiper arm (ie middle of the blade), should be as shown in Fig. 9.33. On the rear window the dimension should be measured at the points shown in Fig. 9.35.

38 Windscreen wiper motor – removal and refitting

1   Open the bonnet and disconnect the battery negative lead.
2   Pull the weatherstrip from the front of the plenum chamber and remove the plastic cover.
3   Unscrew the nut and remove the crank from the motor spindle.
4   Disconnect the wiring multi-plug (photo).
5   Unscrew the bolts and withdraw the wiper motor from the frame.
6   Refitting is a reversal of removal, but when fitting the crank to the spindle (motor in parked position) make sure that the marks are aligned.

38.4 Windscreen wiper motor showing multi-plug connection and retaining bolts

39 Rear window wiper motor – removal and refitting

1   Disconnect the battery negative lead.
2   Open the tailgate and prise off the inner trim panel.
3   Remove the wiper arm, as described in Section 37, and unscrew the outer nut. Remove the spacers.
4   Undo the bearing retaining bolts and the motor mounting bolts. Withdraw the motor and disconnect the wiring plug (photos).
5   If detaching the crank and connecting rod from the wiper motor pivot, mark a corresponding alignment position across the crank arm and pivot end face. Undo the nut to detach the crank arm.
6   The wiper motor is secured to the mounting by three bolts.
7   Refitting is a reversal of the removal procedure. Correctly align the crank arm when refitting so that the wiper arm will park correctly (Fig. 9.37).

40 Windscreen wiper linkage – removal and refitting

1   Disconnect the battery negative lead.
2   Remove the wiper arms, as described in Section 37, then unscrew the bearing nuts and remove the spacers.
3   Pull the weatherstrips from the front of the plenum chamber and remove the plastic cover.
4   Disconnect the wiring multi-plug.
5   Unscrew the frame mounting bolt, then withdraw the assembly from the bulkhead.

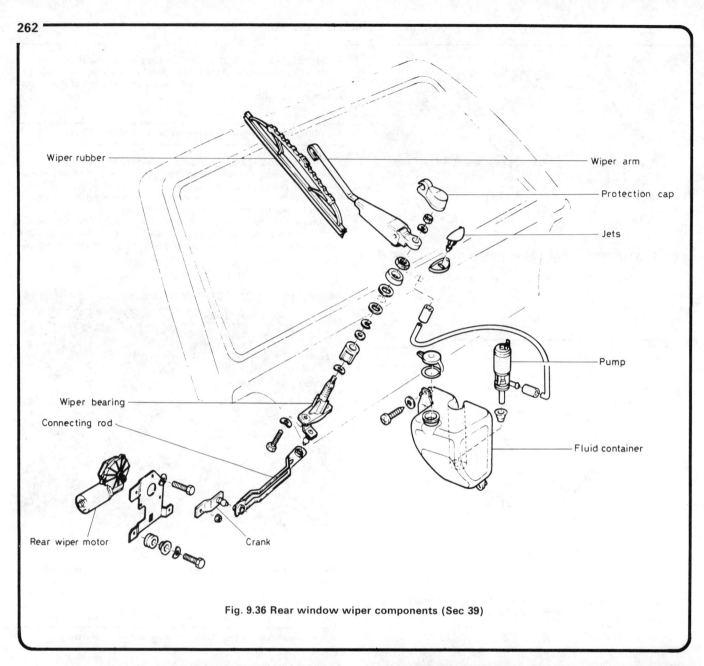

Wiper rubber

Wiper arm

Protection cap

Jets

Pump

Wiper bearing

Connecting rod

Fluid container

Rear wiper motor

Crank

Fig. 9.36 Rear window wiper components (Sec 39)

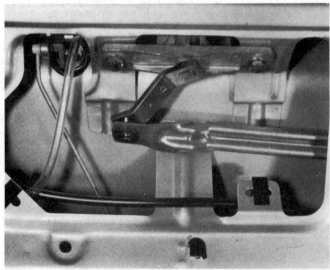

39.4A Rear wiper bearing mounting and connecting rod

39.4B Rear wiper motor mounting in tailgate

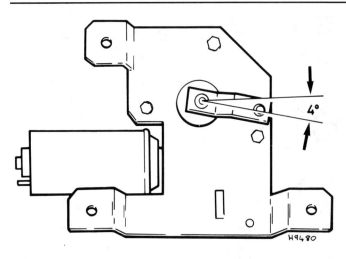

Fig. 9.37 Rear wiper motor bellcrank angle (Sec 39)

6 Prise the pullrods from the motor crank and bearing levers.
7 Unbolt the wiper motor from the frame.
8 Refitting is a reversal of removal, but lubricate the bearing units and pullrod joints with molybdenum disulphide grease.

41 Windscreen, headlamp and rear window washer system – general

1 The windscreen washer fluid reservoir is located on the left-hand side of the engine compartment, and the pump and motor are fitted to the side of the reservoir (photo).
2 The rear window washer reservoir is located on the right-hand side rear corner of the luggage compartment, the pump and motor being attached to the side of the reservoir (photo).
3 The reservoir should be regularly topped up with a suitable washer fluid.
4 To adjust the jets, use a needle to direct the spray into the centre of the wiped area (Fig. 9.38). A special tool (VW tool 3019A) is necessary to direct the headlight washer spray to the centre of the headlights although a needle may be used as an alternative.

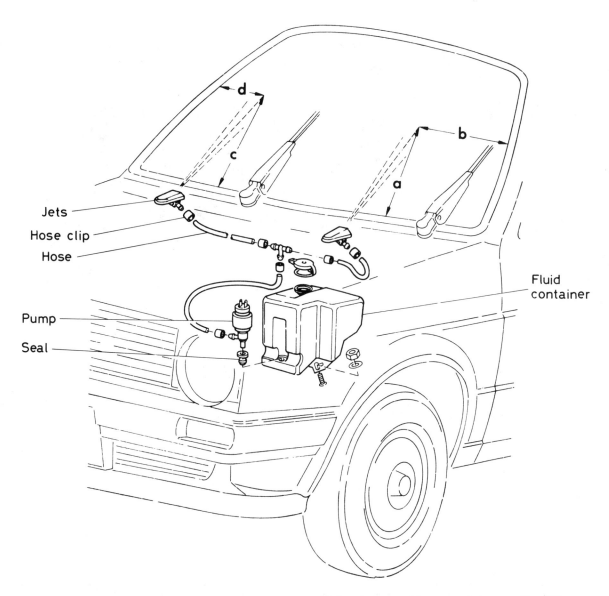

Fig. 9.38 Windscreen washer system components with jet aiming positions on windscreen (Sec 41)

a = 345 mm (13.5 in)   b = 300 mm (11.8 in)   c = 320 mm (12.5 in)   d = 420 mm (16.5 in)

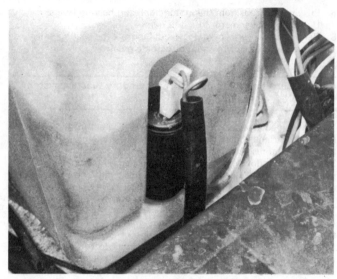

41.1 Windscreen washer pump and wire connector

42.1A Single horn location behind front grille

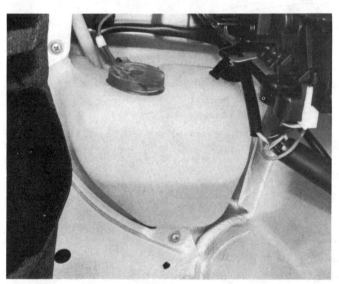

41.2 Rear window washer reservoir unit location

42.1B High tone horn location – twin horn installation

42 Horn – removal and refitting

1   If a single horn is fitted it will be located behind the radiator grille. On models with two horns the additional high tone horn is located under the forward section of the front left-hand wheel arch (photos).
2   To remove the horn first disconnect the battery negative lead.
3   Remove the radiator grille, as described in Chapter 11 (for access to the low tone horn).
4   Unscrew the mounting bolt, disconnect the wires, and withdraw the horn.
5   If the horn emits an unsatisfactory sound it may be possible to adjust it by removing the sealant from the adjusting screw and turning it one way or the other.
6   Refitting is a reversal of removal. Check that horn(s) operate in a satisfactory manner on completion.

43 Radio/cassette player – removal and refitting

1   Disconnect the battery earth lead.
2   To withdraw the radio/cassette unit from its aperture you will need

to fabricate the U-shaped extractor tool from wire rod of suitable gauge to insert into the withdrawal slots on each side of the unit (in the front face) (Fig. 9.39).
3   Insert the withdrawal tools then, pushing each outwards simultaneously, pull them evenly to withdraw the radio/cassette unit. It is important that an equal pressure is applied to each tool as the unit is withdrawn.
4   Once withdrawn from its aperture, disconnect the aerial cable, the power lead, the aerial feed, the speaker plugs, the earth lead and the light and memory feed (where applicable).
5   Push the retaining clips inwards to remove the removal tool from each side (Fig. 9.40).
6   The radio/cassette container box is secured by locking tabs. To remove the container box, bend back the tabs and withdraw the box (photo).
7   Refit in the reverse order of removal. The withdrawal tools do not have to be used, simply push the unit into its aperture until the securing clips engage in their slots.

44 Loudspeaker – removal and refitting

1   Disconnect the battery earth lead.

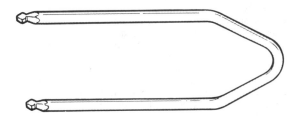

Fig. 9.39 Radio/cassette extractor tool (Sec 43)

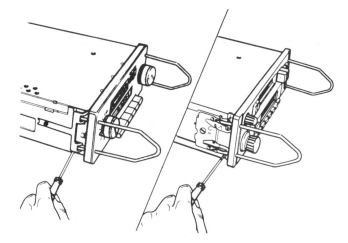

Fig. 9.40 Releasing the extractor tool (Sec 43)

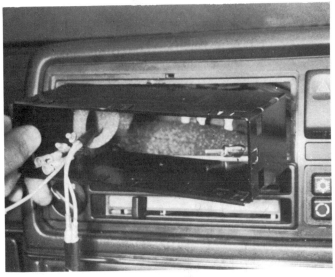

43.6 Radio/cassette container removal

Facia-mounted loudspeakers

2 Carefully prise free the small square plastic cap covering the screw head in the speaker grille then undo and remove the screw. Lift the speaker grille clear.
3 Undo the two screws securing the speaker unit and lift the speaker out far enough to enable the leads to be disconnected (photo).
4 Refit in the reverse order of removal.

44.3 Facia-mounted loudspeaker retaining screws (arrowed)

44.5 Luggage compartment loudspeaker retaining nuts (arrowed)

Luggage compartment loudspeakers

5 Undo the retaining nuts from underneath, withdraw the loudspeaker unit and detach the wiring connector (photo).
6 Refit in reverse order of removal.

45 Mobile radio equipment – interference-free installation

Aerials – selection and fitting

The choice of aerials is now very wide. It should be realised that the quality has a profound effect on radio performance, and a poor, inefficient aerial can make suppression difficult.

A wing-mounted aerial is regarded as probably the most efficient for signal collection, but a roof aerial is usually better for suppression purposes because it is away from most interference fields. Stick-on wire aerials are available for attachment to the inside of the windscreen, but are not always free from the interference field of the engine and some accessories.

Motorised automatic aerials rise when the equipment is switched on and retract at switch-off. They require more fitting space and supply leads, and can be a source of trouble.

There is no merit in choosing a very long aerial as, for example, the type about three metres in length which hooks or clips on to the rear of the car, since part of this aerial will inevitably be located in an interference field. For VHF/FM radios the best length of aerial is about one metre. Active aerials have a transistor amplifier mounted at the base and this serves to boost the received signal. The aerial rod is sometimes rather shorter than normal passive types.

A large loss of signal can occur in the aerial feeder cable, especially over the Very High Frequency (VHF) bands. The design of feeder cable is invariably in the co-axial form, ie a centre conductor surrounded by a flexible copper braid forming the outer (earth) conductor. Between the inner and outer conductors is an insulator material which can be in solid or stranded form. Apart from insulation, its purpose is to maintain the correct spacing and concentricity. Loss of signal occurs in this insulator, the loss usually being greater in a poor quality cable. The quality of cable used is reflected in the price of the aerial with the attached feeder cable.

The capacitance of the feeder should be within the range 65 to 75 picofarads (pF) approximately (95 to 100 pF for Japanese and American equipment), otherwise the adjustment of the car radio aerial trimmer may not be possible. An extension cable is necessary for a long run between aerial and receiver. If this adds capacitance in excess of the above limits, a connector containing a series capacitor will be required, or an extension which is labelled as 'capacity-compensated'.

Fitting the aerial will normally involve making a $7/8$ in (22 mm) diameter hole in the bodywork, but read the instructions that come with the aerial kit. Once the hole position has been selected, use a centre punch to guide the drill. Use sticky masking tape around the area for this helps with marking out and drill location, and gives protection to the paintwork should the drill slip. Three methods of making the hole are in use:

(a) Use a hole saw in the electric drill. This is, in effect, a circular hacksaw blade wrapped round a former with a centre pilot drill.
(b) Use a tank cutter which also has cutting teeth, but is made to shear the metal by tightening with an Allen key.
(c) The hard way of drilling out the circle is using a small drill, say $1/8$ in (3 mm), so that the holes overlap. The centre metal drops out and the hole is finished with round and half-round files.

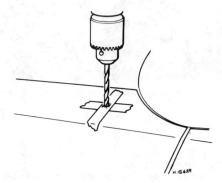

Fig. 9.41 Drilling the bodywork for aerial mounting (Sec 45)

Whichever method is used, the burr is removed from the body metal and paint removed from the underside. The aerial is fitted tightly ensuring that the earth fixing, usually a serrated washer, ring or clamp, is making a solid connection. *This earth connection is important in reducing interference.* Cover any bare metal with primer paint and topcoat, and follow by underseal if desired.

Aerial feeder cable routing should avoid the engine compartment and areas where stress might occur, eg under the carpet where feet will be located. Roof aerials require that the headlining be pulled back and that a path is available down the door pillar. It is wise to check with the vehicle dealer whether roof aerial fitting is recommended.

Loudspeakers

Speakers should be matched to the output stage of the equipment, particularly as regards the recommended impedance. Power transistors used for driving speakers are sensitive to the loading placed on them.

Before choosing a mounting position for speakers, check whether the vehicle manufacturer has provided a location for them. Generally door-mounted speakers give good stereophonic reproduction, but not all doors are able to accept them. The next best position is the rear parcel shelf, and in this case speaker apertures can be cut into the shelf, or pod units may be mounted.

For door mounting, first remove the trim, which is often held on by 'poppers' or press studs, and then select a suitable gap in the inside door assembly. Check that the speaker would not obstruct glass or winder mechanism by winding the window up and down. A template is often provided for marking out the trim panel hole, and then the four fixing holes must be drilled through. Mark out with chalk and cut cleanly with a sharp knife or keyhole saw. Speaker leads are then threaded through the door and door pillar, if necessary drilling 10 mm diameter holes. Fit grommets in the holes and connect to the radio or tape unit correctly. Do

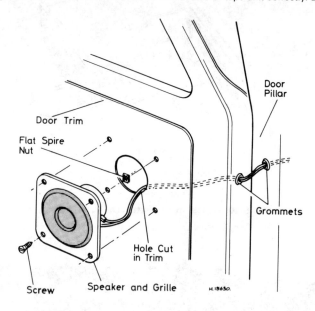

Fig. 9.42 Door mounted speaker installation (Sec 45)

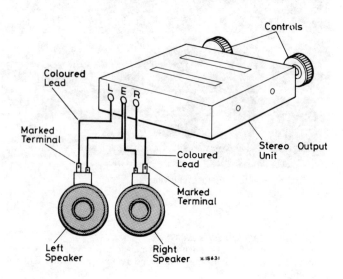

Fig. 9.43 Speaker connections must be correctly made as shown (Sec 45)

not omit a waterproofing cover, usually supplied with door speakers. If the speaker has to be fixed into the metal of the door itself, use self-tapping screws, and if the fixing is to the door trim use self-tapping screws and flat spire nuts.

Rear shelf mounting is somewhat simpler but it is necessary to find gaps in the metalwork underneath the parcel shelf. However, remember that the speakers should be as far apart as possible to give a good stereo effect. Pod-mounted speakers can be screwed into position through the parcel shelf material, but it is worth testing for the best position. Sometimes good results are found by reflecting sound off the rear window.

Unit installation

Many vehicles have a dash panel aperture to take a radio/audio unit, a recognised international standard being 189.5 mm x 60 mm. Alternatively a console may be a feature of the car interior design and this, mounted below the dashboard, gives more room. If neither facility is available a unit may be mounted on the underside of the parcel shelf; these are frequently non-metallic and an earth wire from the case to a good earth point is necessary. A three-sided cover in the form of a cradle is obtainable from car radio dealers and this gives a professional appearance to the installation; in this case choose a position where the controls can be reached by a driver with his seat belt on.

Installation of the radio/audio unit is basically the same in all cases, and consists of offering it into the aperture after removal of the knobs *(not push buttons)* and the trim plate. In some cases a special mounting plate is required to which the unit is attached. It is worthwhile supporting the rear end in cases where sag or strain may occur, and it is usually possible to use a length of perforated metal strip attached between the unit and a good support point nearby. In general it is recommended that tape equipment should be installed at or nearly horizontal.

Connections to the aerial socket are simply by the standard plug terminating the aerial downlead or its extension cable. Speakers for a stereo system must be matched and correctly connected, as outlined previously.

Note: *While all work is carried out on the power side, it is wise to disconnect the battery earth lead.* Before connection is made to the vehicle electrical system, check that the polarity of the unit is correct. Most vehicles use a negative earth system, but radio/audio units often have a reversible plug to convert the set to either + or – earth. *Incorrect connection may cause serious damage.*

The power lead is often permanently connected inside the unit and terminates with one half of an in-line fuse carrier. The other half is fitted with a suitable fuse (3 or 5 amperes) and a wire which should go to a power point in the electrical system. This may be the accessory terminal on the ignition switch, giving the advantage of power feed with ignition or with the ignition key at the 'accessory' position. Power to the unit stops when the ignition key is removed. Alternatively, the lead may be taken to a live point at the fusebox with the consequence of having to remember to switch off at the unit before leaving the vehicle.

Before switching on for initial test, be sure that the speaker connections have been made, for running without load can damage the output transistors. Switch on next and tune through the bands to ensure that all sections are working, and check the tape unit if applicable. The aerial trimmer should be adjusted to give the strongest reception on a weak signal in the medium wave band, at say 200 metres.

Interference

In general, when electric current changes abruptly, unwanted electrical noise is produced. The motor vehicle is filled with electrical devices which change electric current rapidly, the most obvious being the contact breaker.

When the spark plugs operate, the sudden pulse of spark current causes the associated wiring to radiate. Since early radio transmitters used sparks as a basis of operation, it is not surprising that the car radio will pick up ignition spark noise unless steps are taken to reduce it to acceptable levels.

Interference reaches the car radio in two ways:

(a) by conduction through the wiring.
(b) by radiation to the receiving aerial.

Initial checks presuppose that the bonnet is down and fastened, the radio unit has a good earth connection *(not through the aerial downlead outer)*, no fluorescent tubes are working near the car, the aerial trimmer has been adjusted, and the vehicle is in a position to receive radio signals, ie not in a metal-clad building.

Switch on the radio and tune it to the middle of the medium wave (MW) band off-station with the volume (gain) control set fairly high. Switch on the ignition (but do not start the engine) and wait to see if irregular clicks or hash noise occurs. Tapping the facia panel may also produce the effects. If so, this will be due to the voltage stabiliser, which is an on-off thermal switch to control instrument voltage. It is located usually on the back of the instrument panel, often attached to the speedometer. Correction is by attachment of a capacitor and, if still troublesome, chokes in the supply wires.

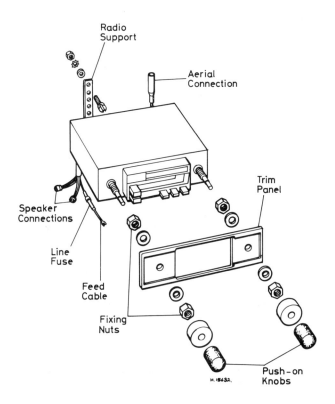

Fig. 9.44 Mounting component details for radio/cassette unit (Sec 45)

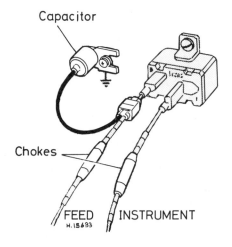

Fig. 9.45 Voltage stabilizer interference suppression (Sec 45)

Switch on the engine and listen for interference on the MW band. Depending on the type of interference, the indications are as follows.

A harsh crackle that drops out abruptly at low engine speed or when the headlights are switched on is probably due to a voltage regulator.

A whine varying with engine speed is due to the alternator. Try temporarily taking off the fan belt – if the noise goes this is confirmation.

Regular ticking or crackle that varies in rate with the engine speed is due to the ignition system. With this trouble in particular and others in general, check to see if the noise is entering the receiver from the wiring or by radiation. To do this, pull out the aerial plug, (preferably shorting out the input socket or connecting a 62 pF capacitor across it). If the noise disappears it is coming in through the aerial and is *radiation noise*. If the noise persists it is reaching the receiver through the wiring and is said to be *line-borne*.

Interference from wipers, washers, heater blowers, turn-indicators, stop lamps, etc is usually taken to the receiver by wiring, and simple treatment using capacitors and possibly chokes will solve the problem. Switch on each one in turn (wet the screen first for running wipers!) and listen for possible interference with the aerial plug in place and again when removed.

Note that if most of the vehicle accessories are found to be creating interference all together, the probability is that poor aerial earthing is to blame.

Component terminal markings

Throughout the following sub-sections reference will be found to various terminal markings. These will vary depending on the manufacturer of the relevant component. If terminal markings differ from those mentioned, reference should be made to the following table, where the most commonly encountered variations are listed.

Alternator	Alternator terminal (thick lead)	Exciting winding terminal
DIN/Bosch	B+	DF
Delco Remy	+	EXC
Ducellier	+	EXC
Ford (US)	+	DF
Lucas	+	F
Marelli	+B	F

Ignition coil	Ignition switch terminal	Contact breaker terminal
DIN/Bosch	15	1
Delco Remy	+	–
Ducellier	BAT	RUP
Ford (US)	B/+	CB/–
Lucas	SW/+	–
Marelli	BAT/+B	D

Voltage regulator	Voltage input terminal	Exciting winding terminal
DIN/Bosch	B+/D+	DF
Delco Remy	BAT/+	EXC
Ducellier	BOB/BAT	EXC
Ford (US)	BAT	DF
Lucas	+/A	F
Marelli		F

Suppression methods – ignition

Suppressed HT cables are supplied as original equipment by manufacturers and will meet regulations as far as interference to neighbouring equipment is concerned. It is illegal to remove such suppression unless an alternative is provided, and this may take the form of resistive spark plug caps in conjunction with plain copper HT cable. For VHF purposes, these and 'in-line' resistors may not be effective, and resistive HT cable is preferred. Check that suppressed cables are actually fitted by observing cable identity lettering, or measuring with an ohmmeter – the value of each plug lead should be 5000 to 10 000 ohms.

A 1 microfarad capacitor connected from the LT supply side of the ignition coil to a good nearby earth point will complete basic ignition interference treatment. *NEVER fit a capacitor to the coil terminal to the contact breaker – the result would be burnt out points in a short time.*

If ignition noise persists despite the treatment above, the following sequence should be followed:

(a) Check the earthing of the ignition coil; remove paint from fixing clamp.

(b) If this does not work, lift the bonnet. Should there be no change in interference level, this may indicate that the bonnet is not electrically connected to the car body. Use a proprietary braided strap across a bonnet hinge ensuring a first class electrical connection. If, however, lifting the bonnet increases the interference, then fit resistive HT cables of a higher ohms-per-metre value.

(c) If all these measures fail, it is probable that re-radiation from metallic components is taking place. Using a braided strap between metallic points, go round the vehicle systematically – try the following: engine to body, exhaust system to body, front suspension to engine and to body, steering column to body, gear lever to engine and to body, Bowden cable to body, metal parcel shelf to body. When an offending component is located it should be bonded with the strap permanently.

(d) As a next step, the fitting of distributor suppressors to each lead at the distributor end may help.

(e) Beyond this point is involved the possible screening of the distributor and fitting resistive spark plugs, but such advanced treatment is not usually required for vehicles with entertainment equipment.

Electronic ignition systems have built-in suppression components, but this does not relieve the need for using suppressed HT leads. In some cases it is permitted to connect a capacitor on the low tension supply side of the ignition coil, but not in every case. Makers' instructions should be followed carefully, otherwise damage to the ignition semiconductors may result.

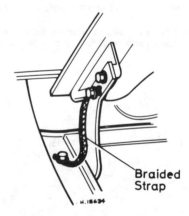

Fig. 9.46 Braided earth strap between bonnet and body (Sec 45)

Suppression methods – generators

Alternators should be fitted with a 3 microfarad capacitor from the B+ main output terminal (thick cable) to earth. Additional suppression may be obtained by the use of a filter in the supply line to the radio receiver.

It is most important that:

(a) *Capacitors are never connected to the field terminals of the alternator.*

(b) *Alternators must not be run without connection to the battery.*

Suppression methods – voltage regulator

Integral electronic voltage regulators such as those fitted to, and built into the alternators fitted to the models covered in this manual do not normally generate much interference, but when encountered this is in combination with alternator noise. A 1 microfarad or 2 microfarad capacitor from the warning lamp (IND) terminal to earth for Lucas ACR alternators and Femsa, Delco and Bosch equivalents should cure the problem.

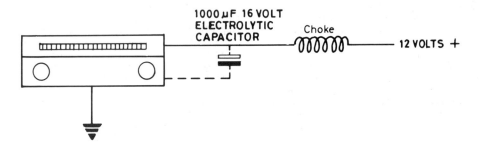

Fig. 9.47 Line-borne interference suppression (Sec 45)

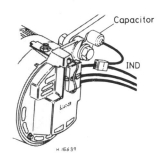

Fig. 9.48 Suppression of interference from electronic voltage
regulator when integral with alternator (Sec 45)

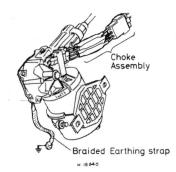

Fig. 9.49 Wiper motor suppression (Sec 45)

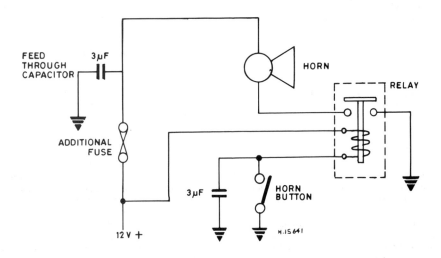

Fig. 9.50 Use of relay to reduce horn interference (Sec 45)

Suppression methods – other equipment

Wiper motors – Connect the wiper body to earth with a bonding strap. For all motors use a 7 ampere choke assembly inserted in the leads to the motor.

Heater motors – Fit 7 ampere line chokes in both leads, assisted if necessary by a 1 microfarad capacitor to earth from both leads.

Electronic tachometer – The tachometer is a possible source of ignition noise – check by disconnecting at the ignition coil CB terminal. It usually feeds from ignition coil LT pulses at the contact breaker terminal. A 3 ampere line choke should be fitted in the tachometer lead at the coil CB terminal.

Horn – A capacitor and choke combination is effective if the horn is directly connected to the 12 volt supply. The use of a relay is an alternative remedy, as this will reduce the length of the interference-carrying leads.

Electrostatic noise – Characteristics are erratic crackling at the receiver, with disappearance of symptoms in wet weather. Often shocks may be given when touching bodywork. Part of the problem is the build-up of static electricity in non-driven wheels and the acquisition of charge on the body shell. It is possible to fit spring-loaded contacts at the wheels to give good conduction between the rotary wheel parts and the vehicle frame. Changing a tyre sometimes helps – because of tyres' varying resistances. In difficult cases a trailing flex which touches the ground will cure the problem. If this is not acceptable it is worth trying conductive paint on the tyre walls.

Fuel pump – Suppression requires a 1 microfarad capacitor between the supply wire to the pump and a nearby earth point. If this is insufficient a 7 ampere line choke connected in the supply wire near the pump is required.

Fluorescent tubes – Vehicles used for camping/caravanning frequently have fluorescent tube lighting. These tubes require a relatively high voltage for operation and this is provided by an inverter (a form of oscillator) which steps up the vehicle supply voltage. This can give rise to serious interference to radio reception, and the tubes themselves can contribute to this interference by the pulsating nature of the lamp discharge. In such situations it is important to mount the aerial as far away from a fluorescent tube as possible. The interference problem may be alleviated by screening the tube with fine wire turns spaced an inch (25 mm) apart and earthed to the chassis. Suitable chokes should be fitted in both supply wires close to the inverter.

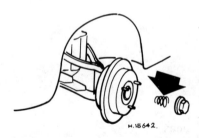

Fig. 9.51 Use of spring contacts at wheels (Sec 45)

Radio/cassette case breakthrough

Magnetic radiation from dashboard wiring may be sufficiently intense to break through the metal case of the radio/cassette player. Often this is due to a particular cable routed too close and shows up as ignition interference on AM and cassette play and/or alternator whine on cassette play.

The first point to check is that the clips and/or screws are fixing all parts of the radio/cassette case together properly. Assuming good earthing of the case, see if it is possible to re-route the offending cable – the chances of this are not good, however, in most cars.

Next release the radio/cassette player and locate it in different positions with temporary leads. If a point of low interference is found, then if possible fix the equipment in that area. This also confirms that local radiation is causing the trouble. If re-location is not feasible, fit the radio/cassette player back in the original position.

Alternator interference on cassette play is now caused by radiation

from the main charging cable which goes from the battery to the output terminal of the alternator, usually via the + terminal of the starter motor relay. In some vehicles this cable is routed under the dashboard, so the solution is to provide a direct cable route. Detach the original cable from the alternator output terminal and make up a new cable of at least 6 mm² cross-sectional area to go from alternator to battery with the shortest possible route. *Remember – do not run the engine with the alternator disconnected from the battery.*

Ignition breakthrough on AM and/or cassette play can be a difficult problem. It is worth wrapping earthed foil round the offending cable run near the equipment, or making up a deflector plate well screwed down to a good earth. Another possibility is the use of a suitable relay to switch on the ignition coil. The relay should be mounted close to the ignition coil; with this arrangement the ignition coil primary current is not taken into the dashboard area and does not flow through the ignition switch. A suitable diode should be used since it is possible that at ignition switch-off the output from the warning lamp alternator terminal could hold the relay on.

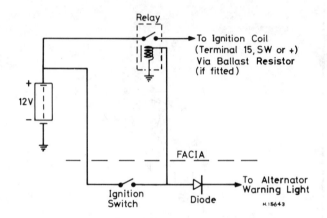

Fig. 9.52 Use of ignition coil relay to suppress case breakthrough (Sec 45)

Connectors for suppression components

Capacitors are usually supplied with tags on the end of the lead, while the capacitor body has a flange with a slot or hole to fit under a nut or screw with washer.

Connections to feed wires are best achieved by self-stripping connectors. These connectors employ a blade which, when squeezed down by pliers, cuts through cable insulation and makes connection to the copper conductors beneath.

Chokes sometimes come with bullet snap-in connectors fitted to the wires, and also with just bare copper wire. With connectors, suitable female cable connectors may be purchased from an auto-accessory shop together with any extra connectors required for the cable ends after being cut for the choke insertion. For chokes with bare wires, similar connectors may be employed together with insulation sleeving as required.

VHF/FM broadcasts

Reception of VHF/FM in an automobile is more prone to problems than the medium and long wavebands. Medium/long wave transmitters are capable of covering considerable distances, but VHF transmitters are restricted to line of sight, meaning ranges of 10 to 50 miles, depending upon the terrain, the effects of buildings and the transmitter power.

Because of the limited range it is necessary to retune on a long journey, and it may be better for those habitually travelling long distances or living in areas of poor provision of transmitters to use an AM radio working on medium/long wavebands.

When conditions are poor, interference can arise, and some of the suppression devices described previously fall off in performance at very high frequencies unless specifically designed for the VHF band. Available suppression devices include reactive HT cable, resistive distributor caps, screened plug caps, screened leads and resistive spark plugs.

For VHF/FM receiver installation the following points should be particularly noted:

(a) Earthing of the receiver chassis and the aerial mounting is important. Use a separate earthing wire at the radio, and scrape paint away at the aerial mounting.

(b) If possible, use a good quality roof aerial to obtain maximum height and distance from interference generating devices on the vehicle.

(c) Use of a high quality aerial downlead is important, since losses in cheap cable can be significant.

(d) The polarisation of FM transmissions may be horizontal, vertical, circular or slanted. Because of this the optimum mounting angle is at 45° to the vehicle roof.

Citizens' Band radio (CB)

In the UK, CB transmitter/receivers work within the 27 MHz and 934 MHz bands, using the FM mode. At present interest is concentrated on 27 MHz where the design and manufacture of equipment is less difficult. Maximum transmitted power is 4 watts, and 40 channels spaced 10 kHz apart within the range 27.60125 to 27.99125 MHz are available.

Aerials are the key to effective transmission and reception. Regulations limit the aerial length to 1.65 metres including the loading coil and any associated circuitry, so tuning the aerial is necessary to obtain optimum results. The choice of a CB aerial is dependent on whether it is to be permanently installed or removable, and the performance will hinge on correct tuning and the location point on the vehicle. Common practice is to clip the aerial to the roof gutter or to employ wing mounting where the aerial can be rapidly unscrewed. An alternative is to use the boot rim to render the aerial theftproof, but a popular solution is to use the 'magmount' – a type of mounting having a strong magnetic base clamping to the vehicle at any point, usually the roof.

Aerial location determines the signal distribution for both transmission and reception, but it is wise to choose a point away from the engine compartment to minimise interference from vehicle electrical equipment.

The aerial is subject to considerable wind and acceleration forces. Cheaper units will whip backwards and forwards and in so doing will alter the relationship with the metal surface of the vehicle with which it forms a ground plane aerial system. The radiation pattern will change correspondingly, giving rise to break-up of both incoming and outgoing signals.

Interference problems on the vehicle carrying CB equipment fall into two categories:

(a) Interference to nearby TV and radio receivers when transmitting.

(b) Interference to CB set reception due to electrical equipment on the vehicle.

Problems of break-through to TV and radio are not frequent, but can be difficult to solve. Mostly trouble is not detected or reported because the vehicle is moving and the symptoms rapidly disappear at the TV/radio receiver, but when the CB set is used as a base station any trouble with nearby receivers will soon result in a complaint.

It must not be assumed by the CB operator that his equipment is faultless, for much depends upon the design. Harmonics (that is, multiples) of 27 MHz may be transmitted unknowingly and these can fall into other user's bands. Where trouble of this nature occurs, low pass filters in the aerial or supply leads can help, and should be fitted in base station aerials as a matter of course. In stubborn cases it may be necessary to call for assistance from the licensing authority, or, if possible, to have the equipment checked by the manufacturers.

Interference received on the CB set from the vehicle equipment is, fortunately, not usually a severe problem. The precautions outlined previously for radio/cassette units apply, but there are some extra points worth noting.

It is common practice to use a slide-mount on CB equipment enabling the set to be easily removed for use as a base station, for example. Care must be taken that the slide mount fittings are properly earthed and that first class connection occurs between the set and slide-mount.

Vehicle manufacturers in the UK are required to provide suppression of electrical equipment to cover 40 to 250 MHz to protect TV and VHF radio bands. Such suppression appears to be adequately effective at 27 MHz, but suppression of individual items such as alternators, clocks, stabilisers, flashers, wiper motors, etc, may still be necessary. The suppression capacitors and chokes available from auto-electrical suppliers for entertainment receivers will usually give the required results with CB equipment.

Other vehicle radio transmitters

Besides CB radio already mentioned, a considerable increase in the use of transceivers (ie combined transmitter and receiver units) has taken place in the last decade. Previously this type of equipment was fitted mainly to military, fire, ambulance and police vehicles, but a large business radio and radio telephone usage has developed.

Generally the suppression techniques described previously will suffice, with only a few difficult cases arising. Suppression is carried out to satisfy the 'receive mode', but care must be taken to use heavy duty chokes in the equipment supply cables since the loading on 'transmit' is relatively high.

Fault diagnosis overleaf

46 Fault diagnosis – electrical system

Symptom	Reason(s)
Starter fails to turn engine	Battery discharged or defective Battery terminal and/or earth leads loose Starter motor connections loose Starter solenoid faulty Starter brushes worn or sticking Starter commutator dirty or worn Starter field coils earthed
Starter turns engine very slowly	Battery discharged Starter motor connections loose Starter brushes worn or sticking
Starter noisy	Pinion or flywheel ring gear badly worn Mounting bolts loose
Battery will not hold charge	Battery defective Electrolyte level too low Battery terminal leads loose Alternator drivebelt slipping Alternator or regulator faulty Short circuit in wiring
Ignition lights stays on	Alternator faulty Alternator drivebelt faulty
Ignition lights fails to come on	Warning bulb blown Alternator faulty
Fuel and temperature readings increase with engine speed	Voltage stabiliser faulty
Lights inoperative	Fuse blown Bulb blown Switch faulty Connections or wiring faulty
Failure of component motor	Commutator dirty or burnt Armature faulty Brushes sticking or worn Armature bearings seized Fuse blown
Failure of individual component	Wiring loose or broken Fuse blown Switch faulty Component faulty

Chapter 10 Suspension and steering

For modifications, and information applicable to later models, see Supplement at end of manual

Contents

Specifications

Front suspension

Type .... Independent with spring struts, lower track control arms (wishbones), anti-roll bar on some models. Telescopic shock absorbers incorporated in struts

Rear suspension

Type .... Semi-independent incorporating torsion axle beam, trailing arms and spring struts/shock absorbers. Anti-roll bar on some models

Steering

Type .... Rack and pinion with safety column. Power steering optional on Golf GL models

Turning circle (approx) .... 10.5 m (34.4 ft)
Steering roll radius .... Negative 8.2 mm (0.323 in)
Steering wheel turns lock to lock:
    Standard 3.83
    Power-assisted 3.17
Steering ratio:
    Standard 20.8
    Power-assisted 17.5
Power-assisted steering fluid type .... Dexron type ATF (Duckhams D-Matic)

Front wheel alignment

Total toe .... 0° ± 10'
Camber (in straight-ahead position) .... −30' ± 20'
Maximum difference – side to side .... 30'
Castor .... 1° 30' ± 30'
Maximum difference – side to side .... 1°
Note: *the camber and caster settings may differ on some variants – check with your VW dealer*

Rear wheel alignment

Total toe .... 25' ± 15'
Maximum deviation in adjustment .... 25'
Camber .... −1° 40' ± 20'
Maximum difference – side to side .... 25'

Wheels

Golf base, C, CL and C Formel E	5J x 13
Golf GL	5$\frac{1}{2}$J x 13
Golf GTI	5$\frac{1}{2}$ or 6J x 13
Jetta	5$\frac{1}{2}$J x 13

Tyres

Type	Radial ply	
Size:		
Golf base, C, GL and C Formel E	155 SR 13	
Golf GL	175/70 SR 13	
Golf GTI	185/60 HR 14	
Jetta	175/70 SR 13	
Tyre pressures – bar (lbf/in²):	**Front**	**Rear**
Golf and Jetta:		
1.05 and 1.3 litre:		
Half load	1.8 (26)	1.8 (26)
Full load	1.8 (26)	2.4 (35)
All other models:		
Half load	2.0 (29)	1.8 (26)
Full load	2.0 (29)	2.4 (35)
Temporary spare wheel (space saver)	4.2 (61)	
Normal spare wheel	2.4 (35)	

Torque wrench settings

Front suspension

	Nm	lbf ft
Strut to body	60	44
Strut to wheel bearing housing	80	59
Lower track control arm:		
Pivot bolt to subframe	130	96
Lower balljoint bolts	25	18
Track control arm/subframe bolts	130	96
Subframe rear mounting strut to body	80	59
Shock absorber slotted nut	40	30
Anti-roll bar eye bolt nut	25	18
Hub nut	230	170

Rear suspension

	Nm	lbf ft
Mounting bracket shouldered bolt	85	63
Shock absorber lower mounting nut	70	52
Stub axle	60	44
Axle beam/mounting bracket pivot bolt nut	60	44
Brake pressure regulator spring bracket	35	26
Shock absorber top cover nut	15	11
Shock absorber spacer retaining nut	15	11

Steering

	Nm	lbf ft
Steering wheel	40	30
Column tube mounting bracket	20	15
Tie-rod inner	35	26
Tie-rod balljoint	35	26
Tie-rod balljoint locknut	50	37
Rack mounting clip	30	22
Steering column joint	30	22
Power steering pressure and return hose unions	20	15
Power steering pump and swivel bracket bolts	20	15
Power steering pump tensioner/bracket	20	15
Power steering pump pulley	20	15
Power steering tie-rod to rack	70	52
Roadwheels	110	81

1 General description

The front suspension is of independent type, incorporating coil struts and lower wishbones. The struts are fitted with telescopic shock absorbers and both front suspension units are mounted on a subframe. An anti-roll bar is fitted to the track control arm (wishbone) on some models.

The rear suspension consists of a transverse torsion axle with trailing arms rubber-bushed to the body. The axle is attached to the lower ends of the shock absorbers, which act as struts, since they incorporate mountings for the coil springs (Figure 10.2).

The steering is of rack and pinion type mounted on the front subframe. The tie-rods are attached to a single coupling which is itself bolted to the steering rack. Power assistance is fitted to some models.

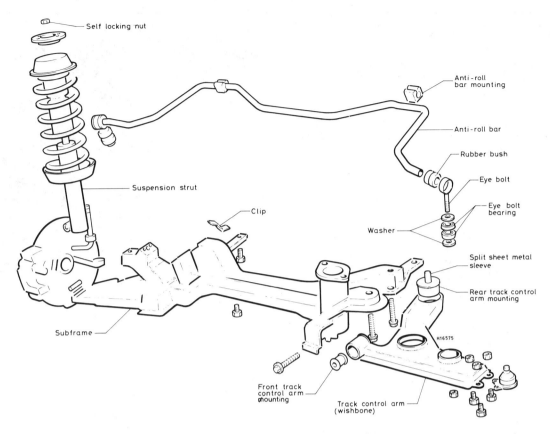

Self locking nut

Anti-roll
bar mounting

Anti-roll bar

Rubber bush

Eye bolt

Suspension strut

Eye bolt
bearing

Clip

Washer

Split sheet metal
sleeve

Rear track control
arm mounting

H16575

Subframe

Front track
control arm
mounting

Track control arm
(wishbone)

Fig. 10.1 Front suspension main components (Sec 1)

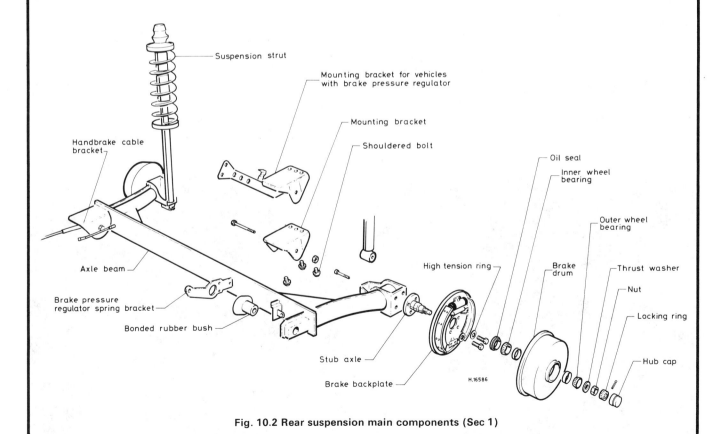

Suspension strut

Mounting bracket for vehicles
with brake pressure regulator

Mounting bracket

Shouldered bolt

Oil seal

Inner wheel
bearing

Handbrake cable
bracket

Outer wheel
bearing

High tension ring

Brake
drum

Thrust washer

Nut

Axle beam

Locking ring

Brake pressure
regulator spring bracket

Bonded rubber bush

Hub cap

Stub axle

Brake backplate

H.16586

Fig. 10.2 Rear suspension main components (Sec 1)

2   Maintenance – suspension and steering

The following routine maintenance procedures should be undertaken at the specified intervals given at the start of this manual.

Tyres
1   Check and if necessary adjust the tyre pressures. Check the condition and general wear characteristics of the tyres and, if wearing unevenly, have the steering and suspension alignment checked. Refer to Section 24 for further details on wheels and tyres.

Fig. 10.3 Tyre tread wear indicator strips show when tyres need renewal (Sec 2)

Suspension
2   Raise and support each end of the vehicle in turn and inspect the suspension and steering components for signs of excessive wear or damage. Inspect the suspension balljoints for wear and the dust covers for any signs of splits or deterioration. Renew if necessary. Check the track control arm (wishbone) and anti-roll bar mounting/pivot bushes for signs of excessive wear and/or deterioration and again renew if necessary. Check the shock absorbers for signs of leakage and the suspension to subframe and body mountings for signs of corrosion (photo).

2.3 Check the tie-rod end balljoint and dust caps regularly

Steering
3   Inspect the steering tie-rod end balljoints for signs of excessive wear and the dust covers for splits or deterioration and leakage (photo). Inspect the steering gear bellows for signs of leakage or splitting. Check that all steering joints and mountings are secure.

Power-assisted steering
4   Check the power steering reservoir fluid level and top up using the specified type of fluid if necessary. Check the power steering pump drivebelt. Adjust or, if necessary, renew it, as described in Section 22.

3   Front suspension strut – removal and refitting

1   Apply the handbrake then jack up and support the front of the car on axle stands. Remove the roadwheel on the side concerned.
2   Position a jack under the outer end of the track control arm for support.
3   In the engine compartment, prise the cap from the top of the strut (photo) and unscrew the self-locking nut whilst holding the piston rod

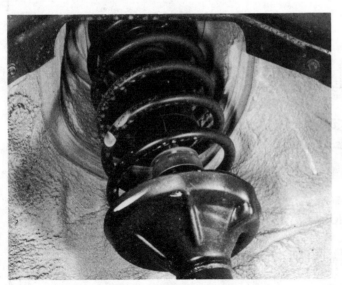

2.2 Check the shock absorbers for signs of leaking

3.3 Removing the front suspension strut top cap

stationary with an Allen key. Renew the self-locking nut once removed.

4   Undo and remove the anti-roll bar eye bolt nut (see Section 5).

5   Detach the steering tie-rod balljoint, as described in Section 16.

6   Remove the brake caliper, with reference to Chapter 8, and hang it up to one side. Detach the brake line from the strut.

7   Scribe an alignment mark around the periphery of the suspension strut-to-wheel bearing housing location lugs to ensure accurate positioning when refitting, then undo the two retaining nuts and withdraw the two bolts securing the strut at its bottom end to the wheel bearing housing (photo). Renew the self-locking nuts and special washers.

8   Lower the track control arm to disengage the strut from its top mounting, then prise it free from the wheel bearing housing.

9   Note that the lower balljoint must not be detached from the track control arm without first referring to Section 8.

10 Refitting is a reversal of the removal procedure. Refer to Chapter 8 when refitting the brake caliper and Sections 5 and 16 in this Chapter when refitting the balljoint and anti-roll bar. Tighten the retaining nuts to the specified torque. Use only new self-locking nuts with special washers to secure the strut-to-wheel bearing housing bolts.

3.7 Strut-to-front wheel bearing housing retaining nuts/bolts

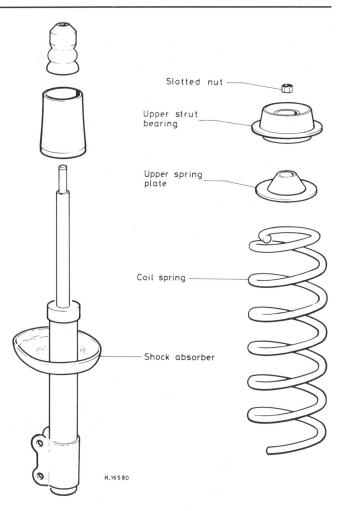

Fig. 10.4 Front suspension strut and coil spring components (Sec 4)

4 Front suspension strut and coil spring – separation and assembly

1   Remove the front suspension strut, as described in the previous Section.

2   Do not attempt to remove the coil spring from the strut unless a spring compressor is available. If a suitable compressor is not available, take the strut to a garage for dismantling and assembly.

3   Support the lower end of the strut in a vice then fit the coil spring compressor into position and check that it is securely located.

4   Compress the spring until the upper spring retainer is free of tension, then remove the slotted nut from the top of the piston rod. To do this, a special tool is available (Fig. 10.5). However, it is possible to hold the piston rod stationary with an Allen key, or spanner on the flats (as applicable) and use a peg spanner to unscrew the slotted nut.

5   Remove the strut bearing, followed by the spring retainer.

6   Lift the coil spring from the strut with the compressor still in position. Mark the top of the spring for reference.

7   Withdraw the bump stop components from the piston rod, noting their order of removal.

8   Move the shock absorber piston rod up and down through its complete stroke and check that the resistance is even and smooth. If there are any signs or seizing or lack of resistance, or if fluid has been leaking excessively, the shock absorber/strut unit should be renewed.

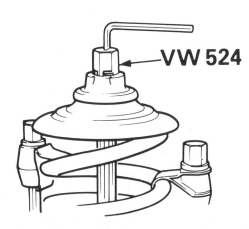

Fig. 10.5 Using the special tool to unscrew the slotted nut from the front suspension. A peg spanner and Allen key or suitable spanner will suffice if necessary – see text (Sec 4)

9   The coil springs are normally colour-coded and if the springs are to be renewed (it is advisable to renew the spring each side at the same time), be sure to get the correct replacement type with the identical colour code.

10 Reassembly is a reversal of removal. Tighten the slotted nut to the specified torque before releasing the spring compressor.

5 Front anti-roll bar – removal and refitting

1   Apply the handbrake then jack up the front of the car and support it on axle stands.
2   Undo and remove the anti-roll bar eye bolt nuts from the underside of the track control arm each side (photo).
3   Position a jack under the subframe and raise to support it.
4   Undo the subframe-to-body strut retaining bolt at the rear end, loosen the front bolt and swing the strut round to allow the anti-roll bar and bush clearance for removal. Repeat on the other side.
5   Lift the anti-roll bar eye bolts and disengage them from the anti-roll bar (photo). Note the location and orientation of the eye bolt bushes and washers. Remove the anti-roll bar.
6   Renew the anti-roll bar if it is damaged or distorted. Renew the bushes if they are perished or worn.
7   Refitting is a reversal of the removal procedure. Check that the eye bolt bushes are fitted with their conical face towards the washers, the cover faces of which must face away from the bush mountings.
8   Do not fully tighten the retaining nuts and bolts until the vehicle is free standing and has been bounced a few times to settle the mountings.

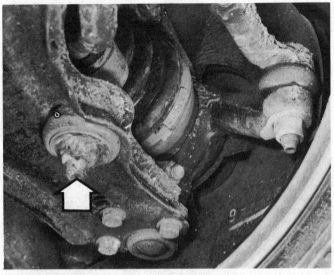

5.2 Anti-roll bar eye bolt nut (arrowed)

6 Front wheel bearing housing – removal and refitting

1   Refer to Chapter 7, Section 2 and proceed as described in paragraphs 1 to 5 inclusive to remove the driveshaft on the side concerned.
2   Refer to Section 16 in this Chapter and disconnect the tie-rod balljoint from the wheel bearing housing.
3   Refer to Chapter 8, Section 4 and remove the brake caliper. Leave the brake hydraulic line connected to the caliper and hang up the caliper to support it. Disconnect the hydraulic line location bracket from the strut.
4   Undo the retaining screw and remove the brake disc.
5   Scribe an alignment mark around the periphery of the suspension strut-to-wheel bearing housing location lugs, to ensure accurate positioning when refitting.
6   Undo the two suspension arm-to-wheel bearing retaining bolt nuts and remove them, together with their special washers. These nuts must be renewed when refitting. Withdraw the bolts and separate the wheel bearing housing from the suspension strut.
7   If the wheel bearing housing is to be renewed, remove the wheel bearing, as described in Section 7, then fit the bearing and hub to the new housing, with reference to the same Section.
8   Refitting is a reversal of the removal procedure. Renew all self-locking nuts.
9   When refitting the suspension strut to the wheel bearing housing check that they are correctly positioned according to the alignment scribe marks made during dismantling before tightening the securing bolts and nuts to the specified torque setting.
10 Refit the driveshaft, as described in Section 2 of Chapter 7.
11 Reconnect the tie-rod balljoint and the anti-roll bar (where applicable) to the track control arm with reference to Sections 5 and 8 respectively.
12 Refit the brake disc and caliper, with reference to the appropriate Sectons in Chapter 8.
13 On completion, lower the car to the ground and tighten the hub nut to the specified torque wrench setting.

5.5 Anti-roll bar location in eye bolt

7 Front wheel bearing – removal and refitting

1   Remove the wheel bearing housing, as described in the previous Section.
2   If still fitted, undo the cross-head screw and remove the brake disc.
3   Remove the screws and withdraw the splash guard.
4   Support the wheel bearing housing with the hub facing downward, and press or drive out the hub, using a suitable mandrel. The bearing inner race will remain on the hub, and therefore, once removed, it is not possible to re-use the bearing. Use a puller to remove the inner race from the hub.
5   Extract the circlips, then, while supporting the wheel bearing

housing, press or drive out the bearing, using a mandrel on the outer race.
6   Clean the recess in the housing, then smear it with a little general purpose grease. Where a new wheel bearing kit has been obtained, the kit will contain a sachet of Molypaste. Smear some Molypaste onto the bearing seat (not the bearing).
7   Fit the outer circlip, then support the wheel bearing housing and press or drive in the new bearing, using a metal tube *on the outer race only*.
8   Fit the inner circlip, making sure that it is correctly seated.
9   Position the hub with its bearing shoulder facing upward, then press or drive on the bearing and housing, using a metal tube *on the inner race only*.
10 Refit the splash guard and brake disc, then refit the wheel bearing housing, as described in the previous Section.
11 On completion, lower the car to the ground and tighten the hub nut to the specified torque setting. If the bearings have been renewed it is advisable to raise the car at the front again after the hub nut has been tightened and check that the front roadwheel and hub can be spun freely without excessive binding or lateral play.

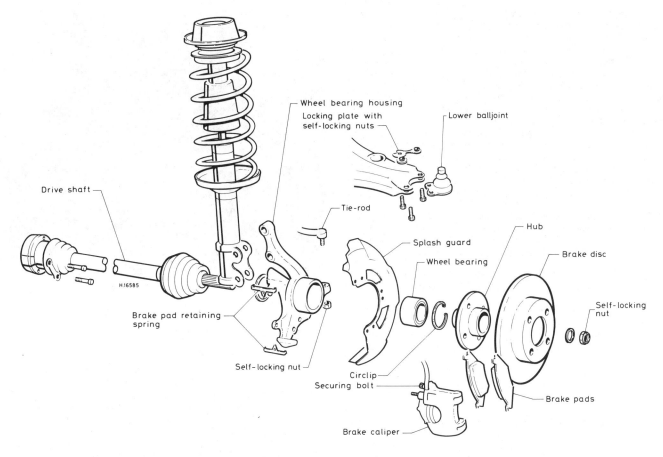

Fig. 10.6 Exploded view of the wheel bearing housing and associated components (Sec 6)

8 Track control arm (wishbone) – removal, overhaul and refitting

1 Loosen the front roadwheel bolts, jack up the front of the car and support on axle stands. Remove the roadwheel(s).
2 Where applicable remove the anti-roll bar (Section 5).
3 Unscrew and remove the track control arm balljoint clamp bolt at the wheel bearing housing (photo). Note that the bolt head faces forwards. Tap the control arm downwards to release the balljoint from the wheel bearing housing.
4 Unscrew and remove the pivot bolt from the front inboard end of the track control arm (to subframe) (photo).
5 Undo and remove the track control arm rear mounting bolt and remove the bolt, together with the strut. Withdraw the split sleeve from the bolt hole using suitable pliers.

8.3 Track control arm balljoint and clamp bolt

8.4 Track control arm pivot bolt

6 Pivot the track control arm downwards at the front and withdraw it from the subframe at the rear mounting, levering if necessary.
7 With the track control arm removed, clean it for inspection.
8 Check the balljoint for excessive wear, and check the pivot bushes for deterioration. Also examine the track control arm for damage and distortion. If necessary, the balljoint and bushes should be renewed.
9 To renew the balljoint, first outline its exact position on the track control arm. This is important as the relative positions of the track control arm and the balljoint are set during production and the new balljoint must be accurately positioned when fitting it. Unscrew the nuts and remove the balljoint and clamp plate. Fit the new balljoint in the exact outline, and tighten the nuts. If fitting a new track control arm locate the balljoint centrally in the elongated hole.
10 To renew the front pivot bush, use a long bolt, together with a metal tube and washers, to pull the bush from the track control arm. Fit the new bush using the same method but, to ease insertion, dip the bush into soapy water first.
11 The rear mounting bonded rubber bush can be removed by prising free but, failing this, you will need to carefully cut through its rubber and steel sections to split and release it by driving it out. The latter course of action should only be necessary if it is badly corroded into position.
12 Press or drive the new mounting bush into position from the top end of the control arm but ensure that it is positioned correctly, as shown in Fig. 10.7.
13 Refitting the track control arm is a reverse of removal, but delay tightening the pivot bolts until the weight of the car is on the suspension. Refer to Section 5 when refitting the anti-roll bar. Have the front wheel camber angle checked and, if necessary, adjusted by a VW dealer.

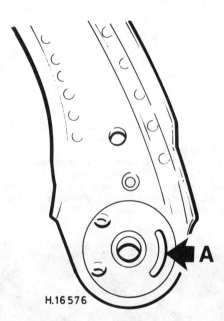

Fig. 10.7 Correct fitting position for mounting bush in the control arm (Sec 8)

Opening A to be located on inboard side of vehicle

9 Rear suspension strut and coil spring – removal and refitting

1 Detach the trim panel from the top of the rear suspension strut within the luggage compartment.
2 Chock the front roadwheels and then jack up the rear of the car and support on axle stands. Remove the roadwheel(s) at the rear for improved access.
3 Support the weight of the trailing arm with a trolley jack.

9.4 Removing the rear suspension strut top cap

4 Remove the cap from the top of the strut (photo), then unscrew the upper securing nut from the top of the strut, if necessary holding the rod stationary with a spanner.
5 Withdraw the dished washer then undo the second retaining nut and withdraw the thrust washer and upper bearing ring.
6 At the bottom end of the strut, engage a spanner on the self-locking nut retaining the mounting bolt; access being through the trailing arm tube (photo). Undo the bolt and withdraw it.
7 Lower the trailing arm as far as possible and withdraw the strut assembly (photo).
8 To remove the coil spring from the strut, undo the retaining nut then withdraw the spacer sleeve, lower bearing ring, upper spring seat and packing. Note how the packing is fitted for correct direction on reassembly.
9 Withdraw the coil spring, rubber stop and ring with protective tube, bottom cap, packing piece and lower spring seat.
10 If the shock absorber is faulty it will normally make a knocking noise as the car is driven over rough surfaces. However, with the unit

9.6 Rear suspension strut bottom mounting

9.7 Remove the rear suspension strut and coil spring downwards

removed, uneven resistance tight spots will be evident as the central rod is operated. Check the condition of the buffers, bump stop and associated components and renew them as necessary.

11 Coil springs should only be renewed as a pair at the rear and it is important to fit the correct replacements. The springs are colour-coded for identification.

12 Refitting is a reversal of removal, but make sure that the coil spring is correctly located in the seats. Delay tightening the lower mounting bolt until the full weight of the car is on the roadwheels.

13 If new coil springs have been fitted it is advisable to have a rear wheel alignment check made by your VW dealer after an initial distance of 1000 miles (1500 km) has been covered and the springs have settled.

10 Rear axle beam – removal and refitting

Note: *If the axle beam is suspected of being distorted it should be checked in position by a VW garage using an optical alignment instrument.*

1 Remove the rear stub axles, as described in Section 11.

2 Support the weight of the trailing arms with axle stands then disconnect the struts/shock absorbers by removing the lower mounting bolts.

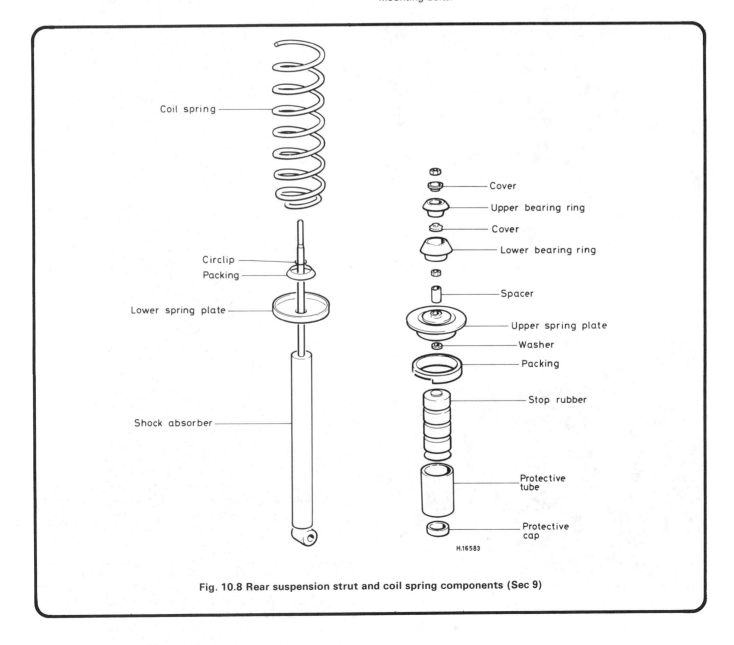

Fig. 10.8 Rear suspension strut and coil spring components (Sec 9)

3   On models fitted with a brake pressure regulator unit, unbolt the spring bracket from the axle beam (photo).
4   Disconnect the handbrake cables from the axle beam and from the left-hand side and underbody bracket with reference to Chapter 8.
5   Remove the brake fluid reservoir filler cap and tighten it down onto a piece of polythene sheet in order to reduce the loss of hydraulic fluid.
6   Lower the axle beam and disconnect the brake hydraulic hoses with reference to Chapter 8. Plug the hoses to prevent the ingress of dirt.
7   Support the weight of the axle beam with axle stands then unscrew and remove the pivot bolts and lower the axle beam to the ground. Note that the pivot bolt heads face as shown (photo).
8   If the bushes are worn renew them. Using a two-arm puller, force the bushes from the axle beam. Dip the new bushes in soapy water before pressing them in from the outside with the puller. Locate the bush so that the segments which protrude point in the direction of travel, see Fig. 10.9. When fitted, the cylindrical bush section should protrude by 8 mm (0.31 in).
9   If the mounting bracket is removed, note its fitted position relative to the axle. If the bolts shear when removing, the stud will have to be accurately drilled out and the resultant hole tapped for a 12 mm x 1.5 thread. Be careful to drill in the centre of the broken stud since

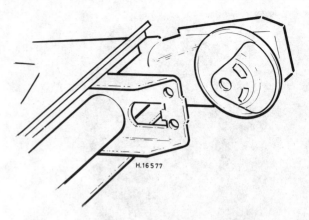

Fig. 10.9 Rear axle bonded rubber bush orientation – protruding segments to face forwards (Sec 10)

misalignment of the hole will in turn mean misalignment of the axle. Unless you have experience in this type of work it is best entrusted to a trained mechanic.
10 When the mounting bracket is refitted its inclination angle to the axle beam should be 12° ± 2°.
11 Refitting is a reversal of removal, but note the following. When the axle is fitted into position with the mountings under tension, locate the securing bolts then align the right side mounting so that the bolts are centralised in the slotted holes. Now on the left-hand side, use a couple of suitable levers and press the mounting to the rubber bush so

10.3 Brake pressure regulator unit showing spring bracket

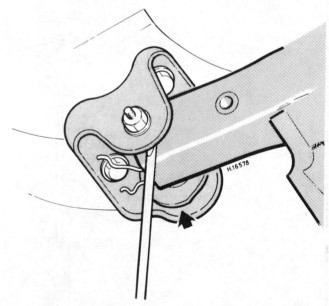

Fig. 10.10 Rear axle refitting – check that the clearance (arrowed) is minimal on the left-hand mounting inner side (Sec 10)

that a minimal gap exists on the inside (Fig. 10.10). The respective retaining bolts can now be tightened to the specified torque wrench setting.
12 On completion, bleed the brake hydraulic system, as described in Chapter 8.

11 Rear wheel hub bearings – removal and refitting

10.7 Axle beam pivot bolt heads to be as shown

1   On models fitted with rear disc brakes refer to Chapter 8, Section 8.
2   On models fitted with drum brakes at the rear, remove the brake

drum, as described in Section 9 of Chapter 8. The bearings and oil seal can be removed in the same manner as that given for the corresponding components in the rear brake disc in Section 8 of Chapter 8.

3   Refit the brake disc or drum, as applicable, and adjust the bearing as described in the appropriate Section (8 or 9) in Chapter 8.

12 Steering wheel – removal and refitting

1   Disconnect the battery earth lead.
2   Set the front roadwheels in the straight-ahead position.
3   Prise free the cover from the centre of the steering wheel. Where the cover is the horn push button, note the location of the wires and disconnect them from the terminals on the cover (photos).
4   Mark the steering wheel and inner column in relation to each other, then unscrew the nut and withdraw the steering wheel (photo). Remove the washer.
5   Refitting is a reversal of removal, but make sure that the turn signal lever is in its neutral position, otherwise damage may occur in the

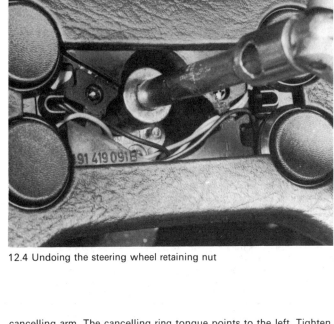

12.4 Undoing the steering wheel retaining nut

12.3A Removing the steering wheel centre cover – GTI

cancelling arm. The cancelling ring tongue points to the left. Tighten the retaining nut to the specified torque.
6   On completion reconnect the battery and check that the horn and column switches operate satisfactorily.

13 Steering column – removal, overhaul and refitting

1   Disconnect the battery negative lead.
2   Remove the steering wheel, as described in Section 12.
3   Remove the screws and withdraw the steering column lower shroud.
4   Remove the three screws and withdraw the combination switch. Disconnect the wiring multi-connectors (photo).
5   Remove the screws and withdraw the lower facia trim panel.
6   Remove the column mounting bolts. Where shear-head bolts have been fitted, it will be necessary to drill off the heads and unscrew the threaded portions, or use a centre punch to unscrew them. On some models one of the mounting bolts may be a socket-head type, in which case use an Allen key to unscrew it.

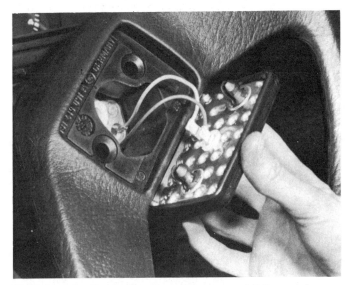

12.3B Removing the steering wheel centre cover – 1.3 litre

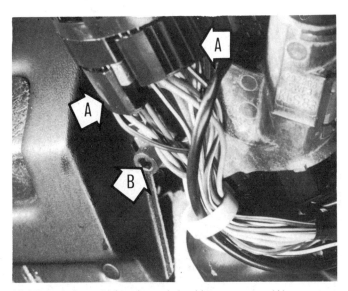

13.4 Detach the multi-function switch wiring connectors (A)
Steering column mounting bolt is also shown (B)

7 Undo and withdraw the universal joint-to-column clamp bolt (photo). Undo the lower mounting-to-column transverse bolt then withdraw the column from the universal joint, and collect the coil spring.

8 On early (pre-July 1984) models, a two section column is fitted. With this type push the two sections together to disengage the rectangular engagement pins within the housing, collect the rubber insulation caps and withdraw the lower section upwards through the housing tube.

9 Check the various components for excessive wear. If the column has been damaged in any way it must be renewed as a unit. If renewing the earlier type column as a unit the later telescopic type column unit may be fitted, in which case a new lower mounting must also be fitted as the earlier type is not compatible with the later type.

10 To dismantle the top housing (both types), prise free the lockwasher from the inner column and withdraw the spring and contact ring. (Renew the lockwasher.)

11 Check the condition of the flange tube bushes and if necessary renew them. Lever the old bushes out with a screwdriver then press in the new bushes after dipping them in soapy water. Unscrew the old shear bolt(s) and obtain new bolts.

12 Using an Allen key, unscrew the clamp bolt securing the steering lock and withdraw the lock. Note that the ignition key must be inserted and the lock released.

13 Withdraw the inner column from the outer columns and remove the support ring.

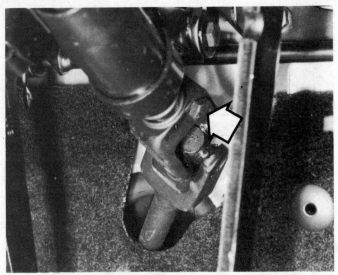

13.7 Steering column universal joint (upper). Clamp bolt is arrowed

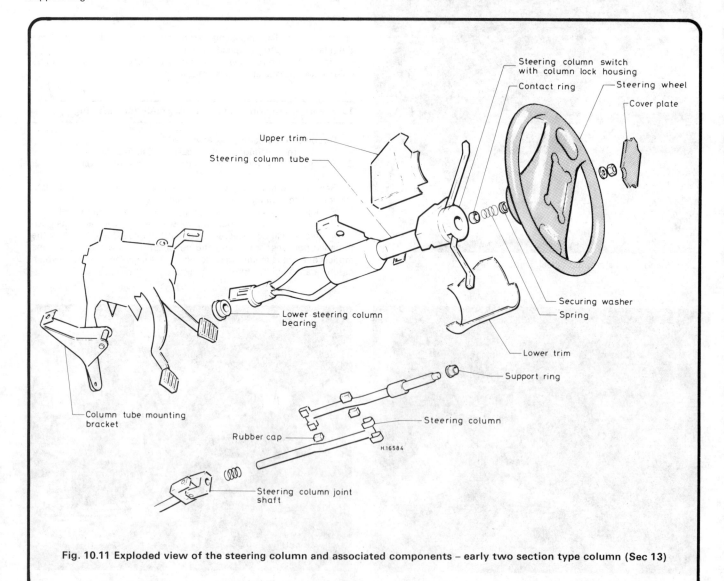

Fig. 10.11 Exploded view of the steering column and associated components – early two section type column (Sec 13)

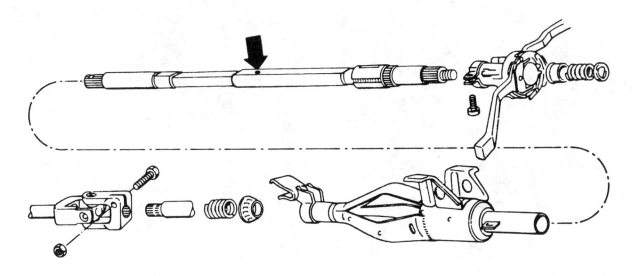

Fig. 10.12 Exploded view of the later steering column type (Sec 13)

Reassembly alignment hole arrowed

14 Clean the components and examine them for wear. Renew them as necessary.

15 Reassembly is a reversal of dismantling, but lubricate bearing surfaces with multi-purpose grease and renew the inner column lockwasher.

16 On later models with the telescopic single section column reassembly differs. Secure the lower end of the column in a vice (with soft jaws) so that the upper section rests on the jaws and the two halves of the column cannot be slid together. The small lug in the lower part must be visible through the hole in the upper part (arrowed in Fig. 10.12). Assemble the support ring with the column switch and lock housing, the contact ring, spring and locking washer.

17 On both steering column types the locking washer is fitted by driving it down the shaft until it is completely pressed on. On the earlier two section type column, compress the two columns together using a suitable pair of pliers as the washer is driven into position.

18 Check that the column alignment is correct when connecting it to the universal joint. Tighten the retaining nuts and bolts to the specified torque setting. Tighten the shear bolt(s) until their head(s) break off.

19 On completion check that the operation of the steering and various steering column switches and the horn are satisfactory.

14 Steering lock – removal and refitting

1 Disconnect the battery negative lead.

2 Remove the steering wheel, as described in Section 12.

3 Remove the screws and withdraw the steering column lower shroud.

4 Remove the three screws and withdraw the combination switch. Disconnect the wiring plug.

5 Using an Allen key, unscrew the clamp bolt securing the steering lock.

6 Prise the lockwasher from the inner column and remove the spring and contact ring.

7 Disconnect the wiring plug and withdraw the steering lock from the top of the column together with the upper shroud. Note that the ignition key must be inserted to ensure that the lock is in its released position.

8 Remove the screw and withdraw the switch from the lock housing.

9 To remove the lock cylinder, drill a 3.0 mm (0.118 in) diameter hole in the location shown in Fig. 10.13, depress the spring pin, and extract the cylinder.

10 Refitting is a reversal of removal, but renew the inner column

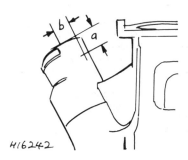

Fig. 10.13 Drilling position when removing steering lock cylinder (Sec 14)

a = 12 mm (0.473 in)   b = 10 mm (0.394 in)

lockwasher and press it fully onto the stop while supporting the lower end of the column.

15 Steering gear bellows – renewal

1 The steering gear bellows can be removed and refitted with the steering gear unit *in situ* or removed from the vehicle.

2 Remove the tie-rod outer balljoint or the tie-rod, as applicable, referring to Section 16. On power steering models the outer balljoint can be removed from the left and right-hand side tie-rods and there is therefore no need to remove the tie-rod.

3 Unscrew and remove the outer balljoint locknut nut from the tie-rod.

4 Release the retaining clips and withdraw the bellows from the steering gear and tie-rod (photo).

5 Refit in the reverse order of removal. Smear the inner bore of the bellows with lubricant prior to fitting to ease its assembly. Renew the balljoint locknuts.

6 On completion check the front wheel alignment, as described in Section 23.

15.4 Steering tie-rod bellows and retaining clip

16.4 Balljoint separator tool in position on left-hand balljoint (not adjustable)

16 Tie-rods and balljoints (manual steering) – removal and refitting

1   If the steering tie-rod and balljoints are worn, play will be evident as the roadwheel is rocked from side to side, and the balljoint must then be renewed. On RHD models the right-hand tie-rod is adjustable (photo) and the balljoint on this tie-rod can be renewed separately, however the left-hand tie-rod must be renewed complete. On LHD models the tie-rods are vice versa.
2   Jack up the front of the car and support on axle stands. Apply the handbrake and remove the front wheel(s).
3   If removing the tie-rod end balljoint, measure the distance of the exposed thread inboard of the locknut. Make a note of the distance then loosen the locknut.
4   Unscrew the balljoint nut on the side concerned then use a balljoint nut separator tool to release the joint from the wheel bearing housing (photo). With the tie-rod outer joint separated from the wheel bearing housing, the outer balljoint can be unscrewed from the tie-rod (where applicable).

5   To remove the tie-rod, release the retaining clips from the steering gear bellows then slide the bellows outwards along the tie-rod to expose the inner balljoint.
6   Loosen the inner joint locknut then unscrew the tie-rod from the steering rack. The steering gear bellows can then be withdrawn from the inboard end of the tie-rod. Renew the bellows if they are damaged or perished.
7   Refitting is a reversal of the removal procedure, but note the following special points.
8   Clean the old locking fluid from the steering rack, and from the old tie-rod if it is being refitted. Smear both threads with a locking solution prior to assembly.
9   Lubricate the inner bore of the gaiter ends before sliding it onto the tie-rod.
10 When reconnecting the tie-rod to the rack, screw it in to give the specified dimension 'b' as shown in Fig. 10.14. Where both tie-rods (left and right) are being refitted to the rack, centralise the rack so that dimension 'a' shown in Fig. 10.15 is equal on each side.
11 With the steering gear centralised, set the adjustable tie-rod to give the specified fixed distance of 379 mm (14.93 in) between the steering gear and the centre of the outer balljoint – see Fig. 10.16. Tighten the locknut to secure in this position.
12 Alternatively, screw on the balljoint to give the exposed thread dimension noted during removal, then tighten the locknut. Check that the steering gear-to-inner balljoint distance is as previously specified then lock the inner locknut. Refit the steering gear bellows and ensure that they are not distorted.

16.1 Right-hand balljoint (adjustable)

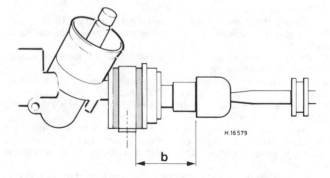

H.16579

Fig. 10.14 Tie-rod-to-rack dimension (b) to be as follows (Sec 16)

All models: b = 70.5 mm (2.78 in)

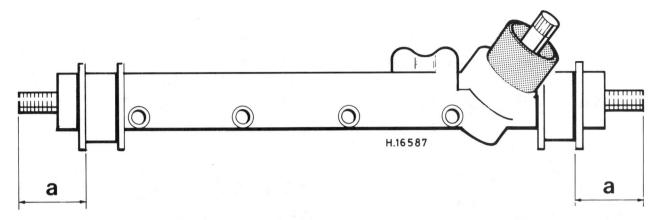

Fig. 10.15 Steering rack is centralised when dimension (a) is equal on each side (Sec 16)

Fig. 10.16 Adjustable outer joint tie-rod distance (c) to steering gear (Sec 16)

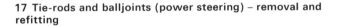

13 Reconnect the outer balljoints to the wheel bearing housing and tighten the locknuts to the specified torque wrench settings. Always fit new locknuts if refitting the old balljoints/tie-rod.
14 On completion check the front wheel alignment, as described in Section 23.

17 Tie-rods and balljoints (power steering) – removal and refitting

1 Remove the steering gear unit, together with the tie-rods from the car. This is necessary to avoid damaging the rack and pinion. Refer to Section 20 for removal details.
2 With the steering gear removed, clean it externally, then release the clips and slide the bellows outwards along the tie-rods away from the inner joints.
3 Support the steering gear in a soft jaw vice with the steering rack in the jaws. **Do not** clamp the rack into a vice not fitted with protective jaws.
4 Each tie-rod and the outer balljoint can be removed in a similar manner to that described for the manual steering gear unit type (see previous Section).
5 Refit the steering tie-rods to the rack, as described in the previous Section, and adjust the fitted lengths as given. Tighten the tie-rods to the specified torque when the settings are correct.
6 Refit the steering gear and tie-rods, as described in Section 20.
7 On completion check the front wheel alignment, as described in Section 23.

18 Steering gear (manual) – adjustment

1 If there is any undue slackness in the steering gear, resulting in noise or rattles, the steering gear should be adjusted as follows, with reference to the photo.

18.1 Manual steering gear adjustment screw (arrowed)

2 Raise and support the car at the front end on axle stands.
3 With the wheels in the straight-ahead position, tighten the self-locking adjustment screw by 20° (approximately).
4 Lower the vehicle to the ground then road test the car. If the steering fails to self-centre after cornering, loosen the adjustment screw a fraction at a time until it does.
5 If, when the correct self-centring point is reached, there is still excessive wear in the steering retighten the adjuster nut a fraction to take up the play.
6 If the adjustment procedures listed above do not provide satisfactory steering adjustment it is probable that the steering gear is worn beyond an acceptable level and it must be removed and overhauled.

19 Steering gear (power-assisted) – adjustment

1 Remove the steering gear unit, as described in Section 20.
2 Loosen the adjuster screw locknut then turn the adjustment screw in to the point where the rack can just be moved by hand without binding or sticking (see Fig. 10.17). Retighten the locknut.
3 Refit the steering gear to the car.

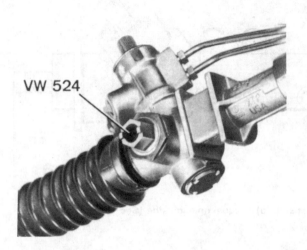

Fig. 10.17 Power steering gear adjustment – use VW special tool if available (Sec 19)

20 Steering gear unit – removal and refitting

1   Apply the handbrake, jack up the front of the car, and support it on axle stands. Remove the roadwheels.
2   Disconnect the inner ends of the tie-rods described in Section 16.
3   On power steering models, detach the fluid suction hose at the pump unit end by loosening the hose clip, withdrawing the hose from the pump and draining the fluid into a suitable container.
4   Disconnect the steering tie-rod outer balljoints, with reference to Section 16.

5   Where applicable, disconnect the gearshift securing bracket from the steering gear.
6   Undo and remove the steering gear pinion-to-lower column joint clamp bolt (photo). Prise free the joint shaft bellows and pull the bellows up the shaft for access to the clamp bolt.
7   Undo and remove the steering gear unit retaining clamp nuts and withdraw the clamps. Note that the retaining bolts remain in the subframe. If necessary the bolts can be removed by driving them out downwards using a soft metal drift.
8   On power steering models, disconnect the pressure and return flow fluid hoses at the union connections to the steering gear unit.

20.6 Steering gear pinion-to-lower column joint

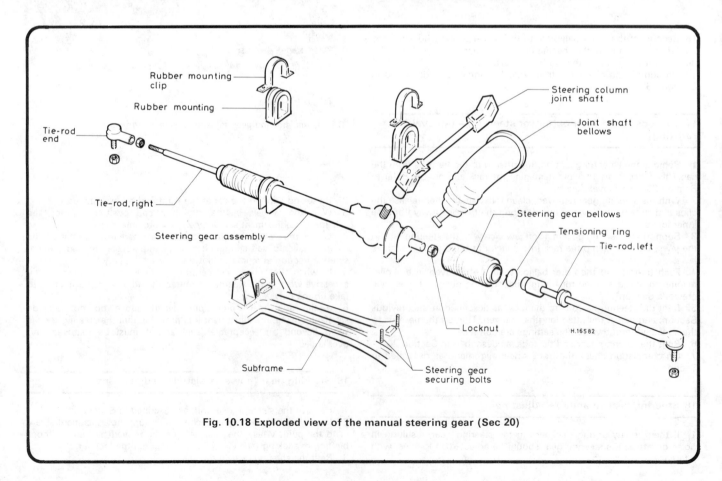

Fig. 10.18 Exploded view of the manual steering gear (Sec 20)

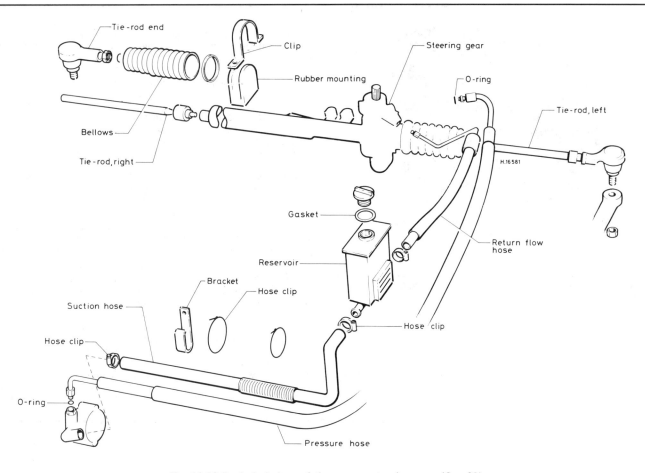

Fig. 10.19 Exploded view of the power steering gear (Sec 20)

9   To enable the steering unit to be withdrawn it may be necessary to detach and withdraw the steering column a sufficient amount to enable the pinion shaft to disengage from the lower column joint; in which case refer to Section 13. Before disengaging the pinion from the lower column joint it is advisable to make an index mark between the two to ensure correct alignment when refitting.

10 On power steering models support the weight of the engine and gearbox units using a hoist (see Chapter 1) then unscrew and remove the left-hand subframe bolt. Loosen but do not remove the right-hand subframe retaining bolt.

11 On manual steering models withdraw the steering gear unit through the aperture in the left-hand side wheel arch.

12 On power steering models remove the steering gear unit from the left side, guiding it past the partially lowered subframe. Plug the power steering fluid hoses whilst the steering gear is removed to prevent the ingress of dirt.

13 Remove the tie-rods from the steering gear, described in Section 16.

14 Refitting is a reversal of the removal procedure. All self-locking nuts must be renewed.

15 Lubricate the steering gear rack with steering gear grease before refitting the tie-rods. Adjust the tie-rods when fitting them to the rack, as described in Section 16.

16 Establish that the pinion shaft-to-lower column alignment is correctly made to ensure that the correct steering centralisation is made. If a new steering gear unit is being fitted, centralise the rack and the steering column before assembly.

17 Delay tightening all nuts and bolts until the weight of the car is on the suspension. Check and, if necessary, adjust the front wheel alignment, as described in Section 23.

18 On power steering models unplug the hoses and reservoir cap ventilation hole, connect the hoses taking care not to let dirt enter the system. Top up the system fluid, as described in Section 21, and check for any signs of leakage on completion.

21 Power steering fluid – level checks, draining and refitting

1   The power steering fluid level is checked with the roadwheel in the straight-ahead position and the engine running. Check that the fluid level in the reservoir is between the MAX and MIN marks. If necessary, top up the level using only the specified fluid through the reservoir filler neck.

2   If the system is in need of constant topping-up, check for signs of leakage at the pump, reservoir and steering gear unit hose unions and make repairs as necessary.

3   To drain the fluid from the system, detach the fluid suction hose at the pump unit and drain the fluid into a container for disposal. When draining, turn the steering wheel from lock to lock to expel as much fluid as possible.

4   After draining off the fluid, reconnect the suction hose to the pump unit then fill the reservoir to the top with new fluid. Restart the engine and switch off as soon as it fires, repeating the starting and stopping sequence several times; this will cause fluid to be drawn into the system quickly.

5   Watch the level of fluid and keep adding fluid so that the reservoir is never sucked dry. When the fluid ceases to drop as a result of the start/stop sequence, start the engine and allow it to run at idling speed.

6   Turn the steering from lock to lock several times, being careful not to leave the wheels on full lock because this will cause the pressure in the system to build up.

7   Watch the level of the fluid in the reservoir and add fluid if necessary to keep the level at the MAX mark.

8   When the level stops falling and no more air bubbles appear in the reservoir, switch the engine off and fit the reservoir cap. The level of fluid will rise slightly when the engine is switched off.

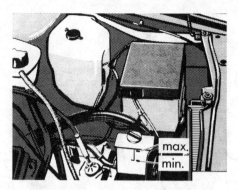

Fig. 10.20 Fluid level marks on the power steering fluid reservoir (Sec 21)

22 Power steering pump – removal, refitting and adjustment

1　If the power steering is suspected of malfunction have the supply and system pressure checked by your VW dealer. The pump unit cannot be overhauled or repaired and if defective it must be renewed as a unit.
2　To remove the pump unit, first drain the system fluid, as described in the previous Section.
3　Disconnect the pressure hose from the pump unit.

4　Loosen the pump unit retaining bolts and pivot the pump so that the drivebelt can be disconnected from the pulley.
5　Support the pump, withdraw the retaining bolts and withdraw the pump unit.
6　Refitting is a reversal of removal, but tension the drivebelt as described in paragraph 7 and top up with new fluid and bleed the system as described in the previous Section.

Adjusting the drivebelt tension
7　To adjust the drivebelt tension, the pump unit retaining nuts and bolts should be loosened. Also loosen the adjuster bolt locknut on the pump bracket. Turn the tensioning bolt until the belt can be depressed approximately 10.0 mm (0.4 in) under firm thumb pressure midway between the crankshaft and pump pulleys. Tighten the adjusting bolt locknut when the tension is correct. Also tighten the pump retaining nuts and bolts.

23 Wheel alignment – checking and adjustment

1　Accurate wheel alignment is essential for good steering and slow tyre wear. The alignment details are given in the Specifications and can be accurately checked by a suitably equipped garage. However, front wheel alignment gauges can be obtained from most motor accessory stores, and the method of using one is as follows.
2　Check that the car is only loaded to kerbside weight, with a full fuel tank and the tyres correctly inflated.
3　Position the car on level ground, with the wheels straight-ahead, then roll the car backwards 4 m (12 ft) and forwards again.
4　Using a wheel alignment gauge in accordance with the manufacturer's instructions, check that the front wheel toe dimension is as given in the Specifications. If adjustment is necessary, loosen the

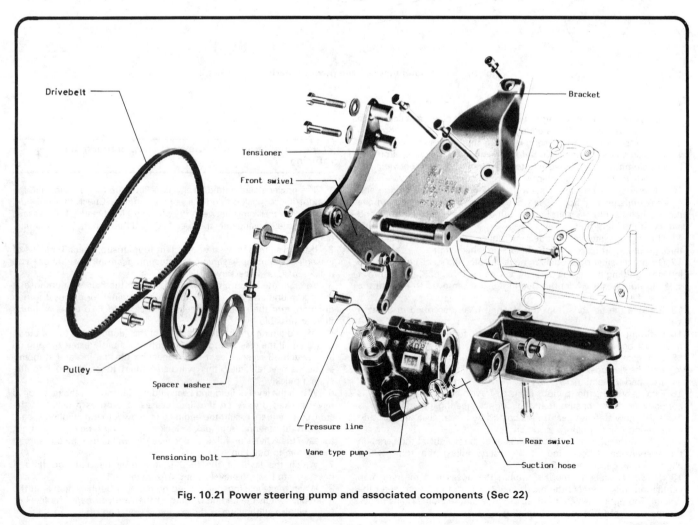

Fig. 10.21 Power steering pump and associated components (Sec 22)

balljoint-to-tie-rod locknut on the right-hand side and turn the tie-rod as required, then retighten the locknut.

5 Although the camber angle of the front wheels can be adjusted this is a task best entrusted to your VW dealer.

6 The castor angle is not adjustable but, as with the camber angle, is best checked by your VW dealer.

24 Roadwheels and tyres – general

1 Clean the insides of the roadwheels whenever they are removed. If necessary, remove any rust and repaint them, where applicable.

2 At the same time, remove any flints or stones which may have become embedded in the tyres. Examine the tyres for damage and splits. Where the depth of tread is almost down to the legal minimum renew them.

3 The wheels should be rebalanced half way through the life of the tyres to compensate for loss of rubber.

4 Check and adjust the tyre pressures regularly, and make sure that the dust caps are correctly fitted. Do not forget to check the spare tyre.

5 If interchanging steel or alloy roadwheels from other models in the range it may be necessary to change the retaining bolts. Check with your VW dealer.

6 The use of a temporary (space saver) spare wheel may contravene the law.

25 Fault diagnosis – suspension and steering

Symptom	Reason(s)
Excessive play in steering	Worn steering gear Worn tie-rod end balljoints Worn tie-rod bushes Incorrect rack adjustment Worn suspension balljoints
Wanders, or pulls to one side	Incorrect wheel alignment Worn tie-rod balljoints Worn suspension balljoints Uneven tyre pressures Weak shock absorbers Broken or weak coil spring
Heavy or stiff steering	Seized steering or suspension balljoint Incorrect wheel alignment Low tyre pressures Leak of lubricant in steering gear Power steering faulty (where applicable) Power steering pump drivebelt broken (where applicable)
Wheel wobble and vibration	Roadwheels out of balance Roadwheel damaged Weak shock absorbers Worn wheel bearings
Excessive tyre wear	Incorrect wheel alignment Weak shock absorbers Incorrect tyre pressures Roadwheels out of balance

Chapter 11 Bodywork and fittings

For modifications, and information applicable to later models, see Supplement at end of manual

Contents

Specifications

Torque wrench settings

	Nm	lbf ft
Front bumper bracket bolts	82	61
Rear bumper bracket bolts	70	52
Tailgate spider nut	6	4
Front seat cap nut	1.5	1.1
Seat belt anchor bolts	40	30

1 General description

The body is of all-steel unit construction with impact-absorbing front and rear crumple zones which take the brunt of any accident, leaving the passenger compartment with minimum distortion. The front crumple zones take the form of two corrugated box sections in the scuttle and firewall.

The Golf is available in two or four-door hatchback versions, and all models have a large tailgate which is propped open with a steel rod or a gas-filled telescopic strut.

The Jetta is only available as a four-door 'notchback' incorporating a conventional boot and lid.

On all models the front wings are bolted to the body and can easily be renewed in the event of damage.

2 Maintenance – bodywork and underframe

The general condition of a vehicle's bodywork is the one thing that significantly affects its value. Maintenance is easy but needs to be regular. Neglect, particularly after minor damage, can lead quickly to further deterioration and costly repair bills. It is important also to keep watch on those parts of the vehicle not immediately visible, for instance the underside, inside all the wheel arches and the lower part of the engine compartment.

The basic maintenance routine for the bodywork is washing – preferably with a lot of water, from a hose. This will remove all the loose solids which may have stuck to the vehicle. It is important to flush these off in such a way as to prevent grit from scratching the finish. The wheel arches and underframe need washing in the same way to remove any accumulated mud which will retain moisture and tend to encourage rust. Paradoxically enough, the best time to clean the underframe and wheel arches is in wet weather when the mud is thoroughly wet and soft. In very wet weather the underframe is usually cleaned of large accumulations automatically and this is a good time for inspection.

Periodically, except on vehicles with a wax-based underbody protective coating, it is a good idea to have the whole of the underframe of the vehicle steam cleaned, engine compartment included, so that a thorough inspection can be carried out to see what minor repairs and renovations are necessary. Steam cleaning is available at many garages and is necessary for removal of the accumulation of oily grime which sometimes is allowed to become thick in certain areas. If steam cleaning facilities are not available, there are one or two excellent grease solvents available which can be brush applied. The dirt can then be simply hosed off. Note that these methods should not be used on vehicles with wax-based underbody protective coating or the coating will be removed. Such vehicles should be inspected annually, preferably just prior to winter, when the underbody should be washed down and any damage to the wax coating repaired. Ideally, a completely fresh coat should be applied. It would also be worth considering the use of such wax-based protection for injection into door panels, sills, box sections, etc, as an additional safeguard against rust damage where such protection is not provided by the vehicle manufacturer.

After washing paintwork, wipe off with a chamois leather to give an unspotted clear finish. A coat of clear protective wax polish will give added protection against chemical pollutants in the air. If the paintwork sheen has dulled or oxidised, use a cleaner/polisher combination to restore the brilliance of the shine. This requires a little effort, but such dulling is usually caused because regular washing has been neglected. Care needs to be taken with metallic paintwork, as special non-abrasive cleaner/polisher is required to avoid damage to the finish. Always check that the door and ventilator opening drain holes and pipes are completely clear so that water can be drained out. Bright work should be treated in the same way as paint work. Windscreens and windows can be kept clear of the smeary film which often appears by the use of a proprietary glass cleaner. Never use any form of wax or other body or chromium polish on glass.

3 Maintenance – upholstery and carpets

Mats and carpets should be brushed or vacuum cleaned regularly to keep them free of grit. If they are badly stained remove them from the vehicle for scrubbing or sponging and make quite sure they are dry before refitting. Seats and interior trim panels can be kept clean by wiping with a damp cloth. If they do become stained (which can be more apparent on light coloured upholstery) use a little liquid detergent and a soft nail brush to scour the grime out of the grain of the material. Do not forget to keep the headlining clean in the same way as the upholstery. When using liquid cleaners inside the vehicle do not over-wet the surfaces being cleaned. Excessive damp could get into the seams and padded interior causing stains, offensive odours or even rot. If the inside of the vehicle gets wet accidentally it is worthwhile taking some trouble to dry it out properly, particularly where carpets are involved. *Do not leave oil or electric heaters inside the vehicle for this purpose.*

4 Minor body damage – repair

The photographic sequences on pages 294 and 295 illustrate the operations detailed in the following sub-sections.
Note: *For more detailed information about bodywork repair, the Haynes Publishing Group publish a book by Lindsay Porter called The Car Bodywork Repair Manual. This incorporates information on such aspects as rust treatment, painting and glass fibre repairs, as well as details on more ambitious repairs involving welding and panel beating.*

Repair of minor scratches in bodywork

If the scratch is very superficial, and does not penetrate to the metal of the bodywork, repair is very simple. Lightly rub the area of the scratch with a paintwork renovator, or a very fine cutting paste, to remove loose paint from the scratch and to clear the surrounding bodywork of wax polish. Rinse the area with clean water.

Apply touch-up paint to the scratch using a fine paint brush; continue to apply fine layers of paint until the surface of the paint in the scratch is level with the surrounding paintwork. Allow the new paint at least two weeks to harden: then blend it into the surrounding paintwork by rubbing the scratch area with a paintwork renovator or a very fine cutting paste. Finally, apply wax polish.

Where the scratch has penetrated right through to the metal of the bodywork, causing the metal to rust, a different repair technique is required. Remove any loose rust from the bottom of the scratch with a penknife, then apply rust inhibiting paint to prevent the formation of rust in the future. Using a rubber or nylon applicator fill the scratch with bodystopper paste. If required, this paste can be mixed with cellulose thinners to provide a very thin paste which is ideal for filling narrow scratches. Before the stopper-paste in the scratch hardens, wrap a piece of smooth cotton rag around the top of a finger. Dip the finger in cellulose thinners and then quickly sweep it across the surface of the stopper-paste in the scratch; this will ensure that the surface of the stopper-paste is slightly hollowed. The scratch can now be painted over as described earlier in this Section.

Repair of dents in bodywork

When deep denting of the vehicle's bodywork has taken place, the first task is to pull the dent out, until the affected bodywork almost attains its original shape. There is little point in trying to restore the original shape completely, as the metal in the damaged area will have stretched on impact and cannot be reshaped fully to its original contour. It is better to bring the level of the dent up to a point which is about ⅛ in (3 mm) below the level of the surrounding bodywork. In cases where the dent is very shallow anyway, it is not worth trying to pull it out at all. If the underside of the dent is accessible, it can be hammered out gently

from behind, using a mallet with a wooden or plastic head. Whilst doing this, hold a suitable block of wood firmly against the outside of the panel to absorb the impact from the hammer blows and thus prevent a large area of the bodywork from being 'belled-out'.

Should the dent be in a section of the bodywork which has a double skin or some other factor making it inaccessible from behind, a different technique is called for. Drill several small holes through the metal inside the area – particularly in the deeper section. Then screw long self-tapping screws into the holes just sufficiently for them to gain a good purchase in the metal. Now the dent can be pulled out by pulling on the protruding heads of the screws with a pair of pliers.

The next stage of the repair is the removal of the paint from the damaged area, and from an inch or so of the surrounding 'sound' bodywork. This is accomplished most easily by using a wire brush or abrasive pad on a power drill, although it can be done just as effectively by hand using sheets of abrasive paper. To complete the preparation for filling, score the surface of the bare metal with a screwdriver or the tang of a file, or alternatively, drill small holes in the affected area. This will provide a really good 'key' for the filler paste.

To complete the repair see the Section on filling and re-spraying.

Repair of rust holes or gashes in bodywork

Remove all paint from the affected area and from an inch or so of the surrounding 'sound' bodywork, using an abrasive pad or a wire brush on a power drill. If these are not available a few sheets of abrasive paper will do the job just as effectively. With the paint removed you will be able to gauge the severity of the corrosion and therefore decide whether to renew the whole panel (if this is possible) or to repair the affected area. New body panels are not as expensive as most people think and it is often quicker and more satisfactory to fit a new panel than to attempt to repair large areas of corrosion.

Remove all fittings from the affected area except those which will act as a guide to the original shape of the damaged bodywork (eg headlamp shells etc). Then, using tin snips or a hacksaw blade, remove all loose metal and any other metal badly affected by corrosion. Hammer the edges of the hole inwards in order to create a slight depression for the filler paste.

Wire brush the affected area to remove the powdery rust from the surface of the remaining metal. Paint the affected area with rust inhibiting paint; if the back of the rusted area is accessible treat this also.

Before filling can take place it will be necessary to block the hole in some way. This can be achieved by the use of aluminium or plastic mesh, or aluminium tape.

Aluminium or plastic mesh is probably the best material to use for a large hole. Cut a piece to the approximate size and shape of the hole to be filled, then position it in the hole so that its edges are below the level of the surrounding bodywork. It can be retained in position by several blobs of filler paste around its periphery.

Aluminium tape should be used for small or very narrow holes. Pull a piece off the roll and trim it to the approximate size and shape required, then pull off the backing paper (if used) and stick the tape over the hole; it can be overlapped if the thickness of one piece is insufficient. Burnish down the edges of the tape with the handle of a screwdriver or similar, to ensure that the tape is securely attached to the metal underneath.

Bodywork repairs – filling and re-spraying

Before using this Section, see the Sections on dent, deep scratch, rust holes and gash repairs.

Many types of bodyfiller are available, but generally speaking those proprietary kits which contain a tin of filler paste and a tube of resin hardener are best for this type of repair. A wide, flexible plastic or nylon applicator will be found invaluable for imparting a smooth and well contoured finish to the surface of the filler.

Mix up a little filler on a clean piece of card or board – measure the hardener carefully (follow the maker's instructions on the pack) otherwise the filler will set too rapidly or too slowly. Using the applicator apply the filler paste to the prepared area; draw the applicator across the surface of the filler to achieve the correct contour and to level the filler surface. As soon as a contour that approximates to the correct one is achieved, stop working the paste – if you carry on too long the paste will become sticky and begin to 'pick up' on the applicator. Continue to add thin layers of filler paste at twenty-minute intervals until the level of the filler is just proud of the surrounding bodywork.

Once the filler has hardened, excess can be removed using a metal plane or file. From then on, progressively finer grades of abrasive paper should be used, starting with a 40 grade production paper and finishing

This sequence of photographs deals with the repair of the dent and paintwork damage shown in this photo. The procedure will be similar for the repair of a hole. It should be noted that the procedures given here are simplified — more explicit instructions will be found in the text

In the case of a dent the first job — after removing surrounding trim — is to hammer out the dent where access is possible. This will minimise filling. Here, the large dent having been hammered out, the damaged area is being made slightly concave

Now all paint must be removed from the damaged area, by rubbing with coarse abrasive paper. Alternatively, a wire brush or abrasive pad can be used in a power drill. Where the repair area meets good paintwork, the edge of the paintwork should be 'feathered', using a finer grade of abrasive paper

In the case of a hole caused by rusting, all damaged sheet-metal should be cut away before proceeding to this stage. Here, the damaged area is being treated with rust remover and inhibitor before being filled

Mix the body filler according to its manufacturer's instructions. In the case of corrosion damage, it will be necessary to block off any large holes before filling — this can be done with aluminium or plastic mesh, or aluminium tape. Make sure the area is absolutely clean before ...

... applying the filler. Filler should be applied with a flexible applicator, as shown, for best results; the wooden spatula being used for confined areas. Apply thin layers of filler at 20-minute intervals, until the surface of the filler is slightly proud of the surrounding bodywork

Initial shaping can be done with a Surform plane or Dreadnought file. Then, using progressively finer grades of wet-and-dry paper, wrapped around a sanding block, and copious amounts of clean water, rub down the filler until really smooth and flat. Again, feather the edges of adjoining paintwork

The whole repair area can now be sprayed or brush-painted with primer. If spraying, ensure adjoining areas are protected from over-spray. Note that at least one inch of the surrounding sound paintwork should be coated with primer. Primer has a 'thick' consistency, so will find small imperfections

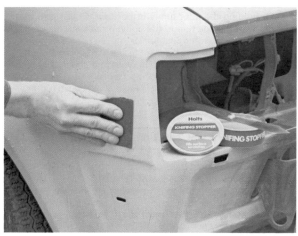

Again, using plenty of water, rub down the primer with a fine grade wet-and-dry paper (400 grade is probably best) until it is really smooth and well blended into the surrounding paintwork. Any remaining imperfections can now be filled by carefully applied knifing stopper paste

When the stopper has hardened, rub down the repair area again before applying the final coat of primer. Before rubbing down this last coat of primer, ensure the repair area is blemish-free – use more stopper if necessary. To ensure that the surface of the primer is really smooth use some finishing compound

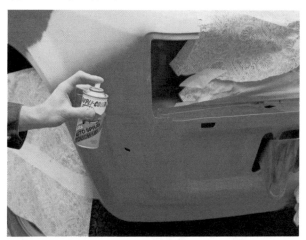

The top coat can now be applied. When working out of doors, pick a dry, warm and wind-free day. Ensure surrounding areas are protected from over-spray. Agitate the aerosol thoroughly, then spray the centre of the repair area, working outwards with a circular motion. Apply the paint as several thin coats

After a period of about two weeks, which the paint needs to harden fully, the surface of the repaired area can be 'cut' with a mild cutting compound prior to wax polishing. When carrying out bodywork repairs, remember that the quality of the finished job is proportional to the time and effort expended

with 400 grade wet-and-dry paper. Always wrap the abrasive paper around a flat rubber, cork, or wooden block – otherwise the surface of the filler will not be completely flat. During the smoothing of the filler surface the wet-and-dry paper should be periodically rinsed in water. This will ensure that a very smooth finish is imparted to the filler at the final stage.

At this stage the 'dent' should be surrounded by a ring of bare metal, which in turn should be encircled by the finely 'feathered' edge of the good paintwork. Rinse the repair area with clean water, until all of the dust produced by the rubbing-down operation has gone.

Spray the whole repair area with a light coat of primer – this will show up any imperfections in the surface of the filler. Repair these imperfections with fresh filler paste or bodystopper, and once more smooth the surface with abrasive paper. If bodystopper is used, it can be mixed with cellulose thinners to form a really thin paste which is ideal for filling small holes. Repeat this spray and repair procedure until you are satisfied that the surface of the filler, and the feathered edge of the paintwork are perfect. Clean the repair area with clean water and allow to dry fully.

The repair area is now ready for final spraying. Paint spraying must be carried out in a warm, dry, windless and dust free atmosphere. This condition can be created artificially if you have access to a large indoor working area, but if you are forced to work in the open, you will have to pick your day very carefully. If you are working indoors, dousing the floor in the work area with water will help to settle the dust which would otherwise be in the atmosphere. If the repair area is confined to one body panel, mask off the surrounding panels; this will help to minimise the effects of a slight mis-match in paint colours. Bodywork fittings (eg chrome strips, door handles etc) will also need to be masked off. Use genuine masking tape and several thicknesses of newspaper for the masking operations.

Before commencing to spray, agitate the aerosol can thoroughly, then spray a test area (an old tin, or similar) until the technique is mastered. Cover the repair area with a thick coat of primer; the thickness should be built up using several thin layers of paint rather than one thick one. Using 400 grade wet-and-dry paper, rub down the surface of the primer until it is really smooth. While doing this, the work area should be thoroughly doused with water, and the wet-and-dry paper periodically rinsed in water. Allow to dry before spraying on more paint.

Spray on the top coat, again building up the thickness by using several thin layers of paint. Start spraying in the centre of the repair area and then, using a circular motion, work outwards until the whole repair area and about 2 inches of the surrounding original paintwork is covered. Remove all masking material 10 to 15 minutes after spraying on the final coat of paint.

Allow the new paint at least two weeks to harden, then, using a paintwork renovator or a very fine cutting paste, blend the edges of the paint into the existing paintwork. Finally, apply wax polish.

5 Major body damage – repair

Where serious damage has occurred, or large areas need renewal due to neglect, it means that completely new sections or panels will need welding in, and this is best left to professionals. If the damage is due to impact, it will also be necessary to completely check the alignment of the bodyshell structure. Due to the principle of construction, the strength and shape of the whole car can be affected by damage to one part. In such instances the services of a VW agent with specialist checking jigs are essential. If a body is left misaligned, it is first of all dangerous, as the car will not handle properly, and secondly, uneven stresses will be imposed on the steering, engine and transmission, causing abnormal wear or complete failure. Tyre wear may also be excessive.

6 Maintenance – hinges and locks

1   At regular intervals (see Routine Maintenance) lubricate the door, bonnet and tailgate/boot lid hinges with a little oil. Similarly lubricate the bonnet release mechanism and door, bonnet and tailgate/boot lid locks.
2   At the same time lubricate the door check straps with a little multi-purpose grease.
3   Do not attempt to lubricate the steering lock.

7 Door rattles – tracing and rectification

1   Check first that the door is not loose at the hinges, and that the latch is holding the door firmly in position. Check also that the door lines up with the aperture in the body. If the door is out of alignment, adjust it as described in Section 19.
2   If the latch is holding the door in the correct position, but the latch still rattles, the lock mechanism is worn and should be renewed.
3   Other rattles from the door could be caused by wear in the window operating mechanism, interior lock mechanism, or loose glass channels.

8 Bonnet – removal, refitting and adjustment

1   Support the bonnet in its open position, and place some cardboard or rags beneath the corners by the hinges.
2   Mark the location of the hinges with a pencil then loosen the four retaining bolts (photo).
3   Where applicable, disconnect the windscreen washer tubes from the jets on the bonnet (photo).
4   With the help of an assistant, release the stay, remove the bolts, and withdraw the bonnet from the car.
5   Refitting is a reversal of removal, but adjust the hinges to their original positions and check that the bonnet is level with the surrounding bodywork. If necessary adjust the height of the bonnet front edge by screwing the rubber buffers in or out (photo).
6   Check that the bonnet lock operates in a satisfactory manner.

9 Bonnet lock and release cable – removal and refitting

1   The bonnet lock is not adjustable for position and is secured to the front cross panel by four pop-rivets (photo). To remove the lock,

8.2 Bonnet hinge

8.3 Disconnecting the windscreen washer tubes from the bonnet

8.5 Bonnet rubber buffer

disconnect the lock release cable, as described below, then carefully drill down through the rivets and withdraw the lock.

2   Refit the lock reversing the removal procedure. Ensure that the new pop-rivets secure the lock firmly.

3   To remove the bonnet lock release cable, raise and support the bonnet. See paragraph 8 if the cable has broken. Remove the radiator grille (Section 10).

4   Reaching through the aperture in the front, press the release to one side and disconnect the cable from it (photo). Release the cable from the retaining clip on the underside of the front panel.

5   Unclip the cable from the retainers in the engine compartment.

6   Detach the cable from the release handle inside the vehicle and pull the cable through the bulkhead grommet and remove it.

7   Refit in the reverse order to removal. Pull the release lever to operate and check the satisfactory operation of the catch before closing the bonnet.

8   If the cable should break with the bonnet shut it is possible to release the catch by hand. A largish screwdriver will just reach the lock release when inserted through the grille centre badge, and by pushing the screwdriver, or carefully using the badge as a pivot, the bonnet can be unlocked.

9.1 Bonnet lock and securing rivets

9.4 Bonnet release cable-to-lock attachment

10 Radiator grille – removal and refitting

1   Raise and support the bonnet.

2   Undo and remove the two grille retaining screws on the top front edge (photo).

3   Release the clips from the top of the grille (photo). Withdraw the grille lifting it upwards from the front valance.

4   Refit in the reverse order of removal.

10.2 Undoing the front grille retaining screws

10.3 Front grille securing clips

11 Tailgate support strut – removal and refitting

1   Open and support the tailgate.

2   Unhook the spring clip from the end of the strut attached to the body, pull up the ball-head and disconnect the strut from the ball-pin (photo).

3   Lever the spring clip from the other end of the strut, remove the washer, and withdraw the strut from the pivot pin.

4   Refit in the reverse order of removal.

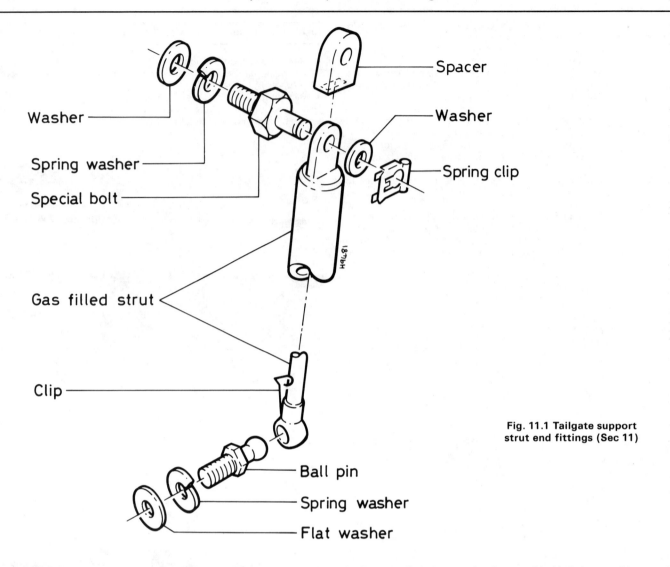

Washer

Spring washer

Special bolt

Gas filled strut

Clip

Spacer

Washer

Spring clip

Ball pin

Spring washer

Flat washer

Fig. 11.1 Tailgate support
strut end fittings (Sec 11)

11.2 Releasing the tailgate strut balljoint clip

12 Tailgate – removal and refitting

1   Open and support the tailgate. Disconnect the straps supporting
the rear shelf.

2   Remove the trim panel using a wide-bladed screwdriver, and
disconnect the wiring from the heated rear window and wiper motor.
Disconnect the washer tube and pull the wiring and tube from the
tailgate.
3   Pull the weatherseal from the body aperture by the hinge positions.
4   Carefully pull the headlining down to reveal the hinge bolts.
5   Lever the spring clips from the struts, remove the washers, and
disconnect the struts from the tailgate.
6   Unscrew the hinge bolts and withdraw the tailgate from the car.
7   Refitting is a reversal of removal, but before tightening the hinge
bolts make sure that the tailgate closes centrally within the body
aperture. If necessary adjust the lock as described in Section 13.

13 Tailgate lock, grip and lock cylinder – removal, refitting and adjustment

1   Open the tailgate and, using an Allen key, unscrew the two lock
retaining screws. Withdraw the lock (photo).
2   The striker plate can be removed by undoing the two retaining
screws.
3   To remove the tailgate grip and lock cylinder, undo the cross-head
screws on the outside, then compress the retaining lug each side of the
lock cylinder together (on the inside) and pull free the grip.
4   Fit the key to the lock cylinder, prise free the retaining clip and
withdraw the lock cylinder by pulling on the key.
5   To remove the cylinder housing, prise free the retaining ring and
withdraw the housing from the grip.
6   Refitting is a reversal of removal, but before fully tightening the
striker, close and open the tailgate two or three times to centralise it.

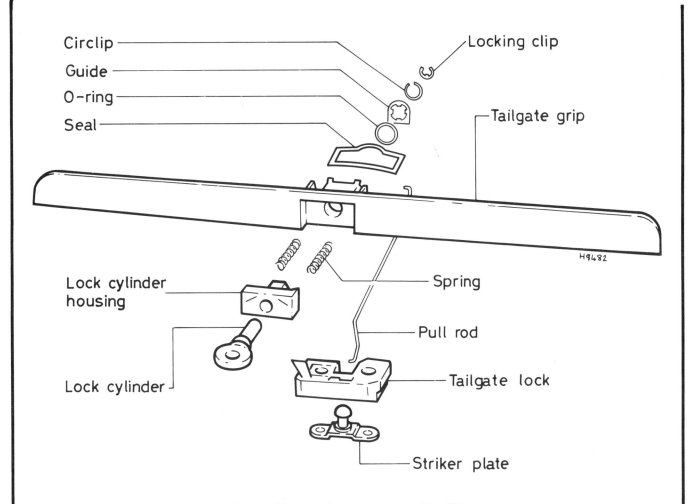

Circlip
Guide
O-ring
Seal

Locking clip

Tailgate grip

H9482

Lock cylinder housing

Spring

Pull rod

Lock cylinder

Tailgate lock

Striker plate

Fig. 11.2 Tailgate lock components (Sec 13)

13.1 Tailgate lock

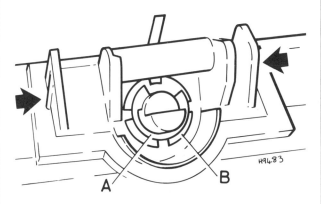

H9483

A   B

Fig. 11.3 Tailgate grip/lock cylinder retaining clip (A) and securing ring (B). Compress lugs (arrowed) in direction indicated (Sec 13)

14 Boot lid – removal, refitting and adjustment

1   Support the boot lid in its open position, and place some cardboard or rags beneath the corners by the hinges.
2   Disconnect the wiring loom and mark the location of the hinges with a pencil.
3   With the help of an assistant, unscrew the nuts and withdraw the boot lid from the car.
4   Refitting is a reversal of removal, but adjust the hinges to their original positions so that the boot lid is level with the surrounding bodywork.

15 Boot lid lock and lock cylinder – removal and refitting

The boot lid lock and lock cylinder are of similar design to the equivalent items on the tailgate fitted to Golf models. Therefore reference can be made to Section 13 for their removal and refitting details.

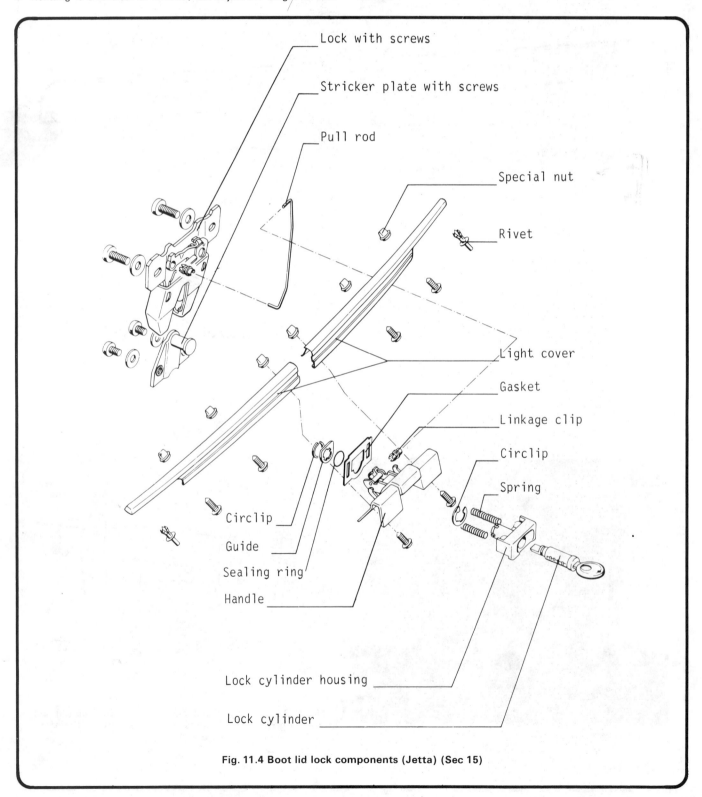

Fig. 11.4 Boot lid lock components (Jetta) (Sec 15)

16 Door trim panel – removal and refitting

1 Unscrew and remove the locking knob (photo).
2 Remove the inner handle surround by sliding it to the rear (photo).
3 Prise the cover from the door pull with a small screwdriver, remove the cross-head screws, and withdraw the door pull (photos).
4 Note the position of the window regulator handle with the window shut then prise off the cover, remove the cross-head screw and withdraw the handle and washer (photos).
5 Where applicable, prise free the door mirror adjuster knob and remove the gaiter (photo).
6 Remove the self-tapping screws and withdraw the storage compartment panel (where applicable).
7 Prise out the stoppers and remove the cross-head screws from the trim panel (photos).
8 Using a wide-bladed screwdriver, prise the trim panel clips from the door, taking care not to damage the panel. Remove the panel.
9 Remove the window regulator handle packing (where applicable).
10 Carefully prise free the plastic cover for access to the inner door components (photo).
11 Refitting is a reversal of removal. However, it is recommended that the window regulator handle retaining screw is locked by coating its threads with a liquid locking agent.

16.3A Remove the door pull cover

16.1 Unscrew the door locking knob

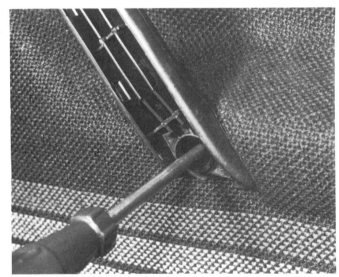
16.3B Remove the door pull retaining screws

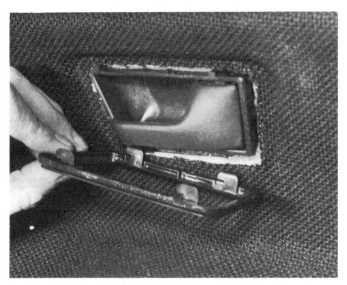
16.2 Removing the door inner handle surround

16.4A Remove the window regulator handle cover ...

16.4B ... and remove the handle retaining screw

16.7B Trim panel retaining screw removal (rear edge)

16.5 Removing the door mirror adjuster knob

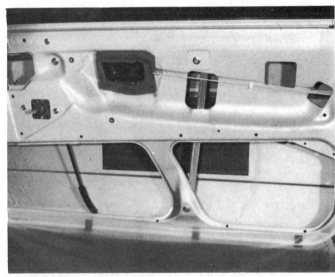

16.10 Plastic cover peeled back for access to door components

16.7A Remove stoppers (where necessary) for access to trim panel screws

17 Door handle (interior) – removal and refitting

1   Remove the trim panel, as described in Section 16.
2   Pull the foam seal away then prise the retainer from the bottom of the handle.
3   Press the fingerplate forwards out of the door and unhook it from the rod (photo).
4   Refitting is a reversal of removal.

18 Door handle (exterior) – removal and refitting

1   Remove the trim panel as described in Section 16.
2   Using a small screwdriver, lever the plastic strip from the exterior door handle.
3   Remove the cross-head screws from the handle grip and the end of the door.
4   Withdraw the handle and release it from the lock (photo). Remove the gaskets.
5   Refitting is a reversal of removal, but fit new gaskets if necessary.

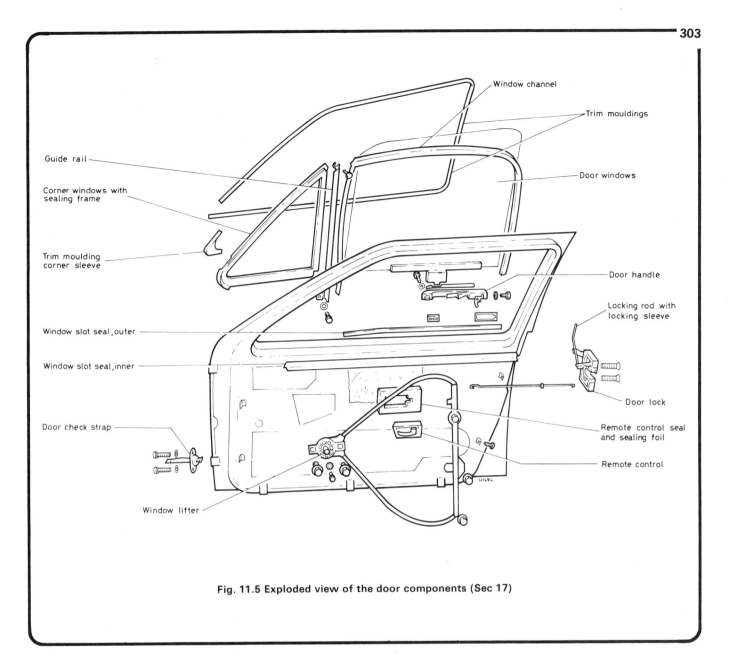

Window channel

Trim mouldings

Guide rail

Door windows

Corner windows with sealing frame

Trim moulding corner sleeve

Door handle

Locking rod with locking sleeve

Window slot seal, outer

Window slot seal, inner

Door lock

Door check strap

Remote control seal and sealing foil

Remote control

Window lifter

Fig. 11.5 Exploded view of the door components (Sec 17)

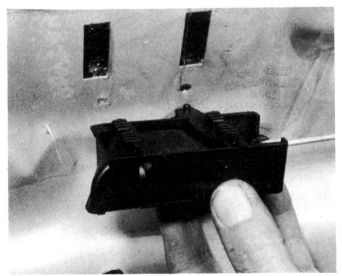

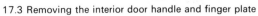
17.3 Removing the interior door handle and finger plate

18.4 View of exterior door handle from inside the door

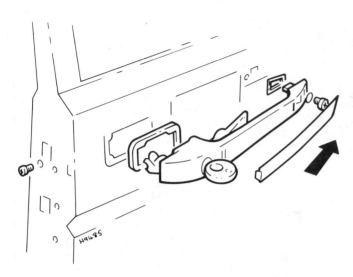

Fig. 11.6 Exterior door handle components. Remove handle in direction of arrow (Sec 18)

19.1 Door check strap and hinge

19 Door – removal and refitting

1   Open the door and use a punch to drive the pivot pin up from the check strap (photo).
2   Mark the position of the door on the hinges.
3   Support the door then unscrew and remove the lower hinge bolt followed by the upper hinge bolt, and withdraw the door from the car.
4   Refitting is a reversal of removal, but if necessary adjust the position of the door on the hinges so that, when closed, it is level with the surrounding bodywork and central within the body aperture. Lubricate the hinges with a little oil and the check strap with grease. If necessary adjust the door striker position (photo) – see Section 20.

20 Door striker – adjustment

1   Mark round the door striker with a pencil, or a fine ballpoint pen.
2   Fit a spanner to the hexagon on the striker and unscrew the striker about one turn so that the striker moves when tapped with a soft-headed hammer.
3   Tap the striker towards the inside of the car if the door rattles, or towards the outside of the car if the door fits too tightly, but be careful to keep the striker in the same horizontal line, unless it also requires vertical adjustment. Only move the striker a small amount at a time; the actual amount moved can be checked by reference to the pencil marks made before the striker was loosened.
4   When a position has been found in which the door closes firmly, but without difficulty, tighten the striker.

19.4 Door striker

21 Door lock – removal and refitting

1   It is not necessary to remove the trim panel. First open the door and set the lock in the locked position either by moving the interior knob or by turning the exterior key.
2   Using an Allen key, unscrew the retaining screws and withdraw the lock approximately 12 mm (0.5 in) to expose the operating lever (photo).
3   Retain the operating lever in the extended position by inserting a screwdriver through the hole in the bottom of the lock (Fig. 11.7).
4   Unhook the remote control rod from the operating lever and pull the upper lever from the sleeve. Withdraw the lock from the door.
5   Refitting is a reversal of removal, but remember to set the lock in the locked position first, and make sure that the lugs on the plastic sleeve are correctly seated.

21.2 Door lock

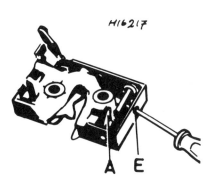

Fig. 11.7 Using a screwdriver through the door lock hole (E)
to retain the operating lever (A) in the extended position
(Sec 21)

22.3A Window regulator securing bolts

22.3B Lifting plate-to-window channel bolts

22 Window regulator (manual) – removal and refitting

1   Remove the trim panel, as described in Section 16.
2   Temporarily refit the window regulator handle and lower the
window until the lifting plate is visible.
3   Remove the bolts securing the regulator to the door and the bolts
securing the lifting plate to the window channel (photos).
4   Release the regulator from the door and remove it through the
aperture.
5   Refitting is a reversal of removal, but ensure that the inner cable is
adequately lubricated with grease and if necessary adjust the position
of the regulator so that the window moves smoothly.

23 Window regulator (electric) – removal and refitting

1   Disconnect the battery earth lead.
2   Remove the door trim panel, as described in Section 16.
3   Lower the window to enable the bolts securing the lifting plate to
the window channel to be unscrewed.
4   Disconnect the wiring connector.
5   Unscrew and remove the window regulator motor securing bolts
and the three bolts securing the guide rail (Fig. 11.8).
6   Withdraw the window regulator assembly, ie the motor, cables and
guide rails, from the aperture at the bottom end of the door.
7   Refit in the reverse order of removal. Ensure that the upper cable is
located underneath the guide rail securing bracket and, when refitting
the door trim panel, the plastic cover is crease free.

24 Windows – removal and refitting

Door windows

1   Remove the window regulator, as described in Section 22 or 23.
2   With the window fully lowered, unclip the inner and outer mouldings
from the window aperture.
3   Remove the bolt and screw and pull out the front window channel
abutting the corner window.
4   Withdraw the corner window and seal.
5   Lift the glass from the door.
6   Refitting is a reversal of removal. If the glass is being renewed, make
sure that the lift channel is located in the same position as in the old
glass.

Windscreen and fixed glass

7   Removal and refitting of the windscreen and fixed glass windows is
best left to a VW garage or windscreen specialist who will have the
necessary equipment and expertise to complete the work properly.

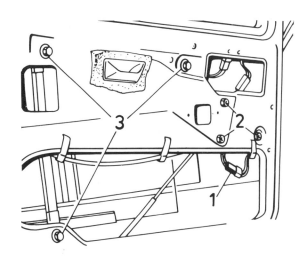

Fig. 11.8 Window regulator (electric) (Sec 23)

1   Wiring connector   *3   Guide rail bolts*
2   Motor securing bolts

25 Bumpers – removal and refitting

Front bumper

1   Working inside the engine compartment, first disconnect the battery negative lead, then disconnect the wiring to the direction indicator lights.
2   Raise the front of the car and support securely on axle stands.
3   Working underneath the front end of the car, undo and remove the bumper brackets from the longitudinal member on each side then withdraw the bumper (photo).
4   Refitting is a reversal of removal. Check that the indicators operate in a satisfactory manner on completion.

Rear bumper

5   Raise and support the car securely at the rear.
6   Working underneath the rear end of the car undo and remove the two bumper support bracket retaining bolts on each side (photo).
7   Withdraw the bumper by pulling it rearwards and disengaging it from the guide on each side quarter panel (Fig. 11.9).
8   Refitting is a reversal of removal.

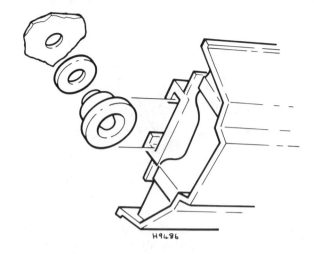

Fig. 11.9 Bumper side quarter panel location guide (Sec 25)

25.3 Front bumper bracket securing points to longitudinal member (arrowed)

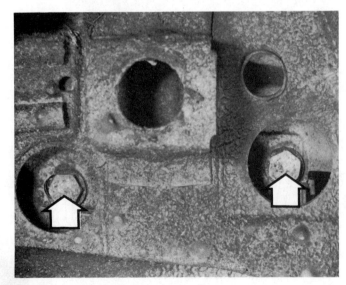

25.6 Rear bumper bracket bolts (arrowed)

26 Bumper trim covering – removal and renewal

1   Remove the bumper concerned, as described in the previous Section.
2   Use a suitable lever to carefully prise free the old covering from the bumper.
3   To fit the new covering, locate the covering on the bumper then support the covering and bumper with the covering underneath (bumper inverted). Use a firmly padded support if possible to protect the new covering.
4   Press or tap the bumper down onto the covering so that the securing clips engage in the bumper. Start from the centre and work progressively outwards, alternating from side to side.
5   Refit the bumper on completion.

27 Exterior mirrors – removal and refitting

Non remote control type

1   Prise the plastic cover from inside the door.
2   Unscrew the cross-head screws and remove the clips.
3   Withdraw the outer cover and mirror.
4   Refitting is a reversal of removal.

Remote control type

5   Pull off the adjusting knob and bellows from the inside of the door.
6   Remove the door trim panel, as described in Section 16.
7   Unscrew the locknut and remove the adjusting knob from the bracket.
8   Prise off the plastic cover then unscrew the cross-head screws and remove the clips.
9   Withdraw the mirror, together with the adjusting knob and gasket.
10 Refitting is a reversal of removal, but fit a new gasket if necessary.

28 Front wheel housing liner – removal and refitting

1   Raise the front of the car and support it on axle stands.
2   Remove the roadwheel from the side concerned.
3   Remove the two cross-head screws from the positions indicated in Fig. 11.11.
4   Swivel the liner 90° downwards and pull it free from the elongated hole.
5   Undo and remove the cross-head screws (with washers) from the points indicated in Fig. 11.12 then withdraw the liner after disengaging its location peg A from the leading lower edge.
6   Renew any retaining screw location rivets which are damaged.
7   Refit in the reverse order of removal.

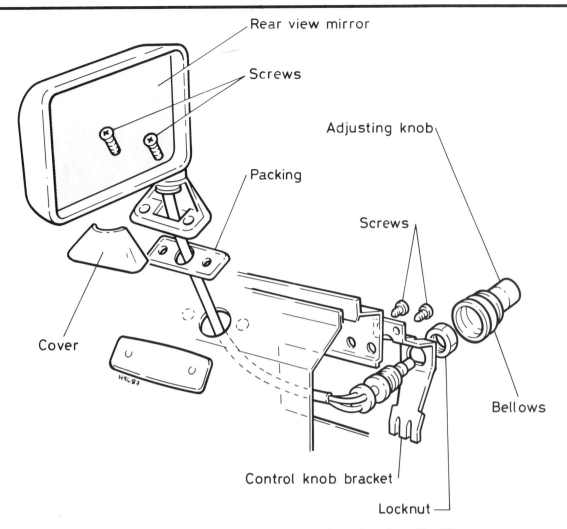

Rear view mirror

Screws

Adjusting knob

Packing

Screws

Cover

Control knob bracket

Bellows

Locknut

Fig. 11.10 Exploded view of remote control exterior mirror (Sec 27)

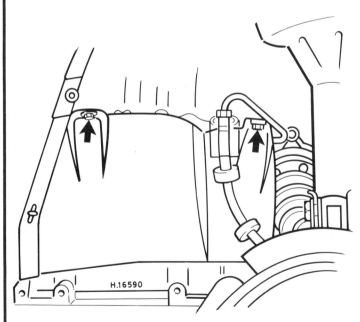

Fig. 11.11 Remove wheel housing liner retaining screws
(arrowed) (Sec 28)

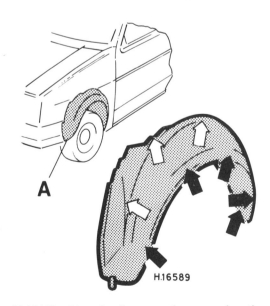

Fig. 11.12 Wheel housing liner securing screw locations –
arrowed (Sec 28)

A   Location peg

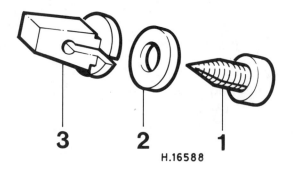

Fig. 11.13 Wheel housing liner securing screw (1), washer (2) and special rivet (3) (Sec 28)

29 Front wing – removal and refitting

1   A damaged front wing may be renewed complete. First remove the front bumper, as described in Section 25.
2   Remove the screws and withdraw the liner from inside the wing (see previous Section).
3   Where applicable disconnect/remove the wing-mounted radio aerial.
4   Remove all the screws and lever the wing from the guides. If necessary warm the sealing joints with a blowlamp to melt the adhesive underseal, *but be sure to take the necessary fire precautions.*
5   Clean the mating faces and treat with rust inhibitor if necessary.
6   Apply sealant along the line of the screws before fitting the wing. Once in place, apply underseal as necessary. Paint the wing then fit the liner and front bumper.

30 Body protective and decorative trim fittings – removal and refitting

Tailgate spoiler and foils – GTI

1   These are shown in Fig. 11.15.
2   The spoiler is secured by a nut, grommet and spacer sleeve. Access to the retaining nuts is gained by removing the inner trim panel and prising free the nut cap.
3   When refitting the spoiler, ensure that the body surface is clean.
4   The foils are stuck in position with adhesive and are best removed and refitted by a VW dealer. If refitting them yourself, the working temperature must be between 15 and 25°C (60 to 77°F) and it is essential that the body surface to which the foil is to be fitted is thoroughly cleaned and prepared (see paragraph 8).

Wheel and extensions

5   These are secured to the wing panels by pop-rivets. Drill out the rivet heads and remove the arch extensions. Refit in the reverse order, but make sure that the adjacent body sections are cleaned off and prepared.
6   Commence by riveting at the centre and work alternately down from it (side to side) when securing in position.

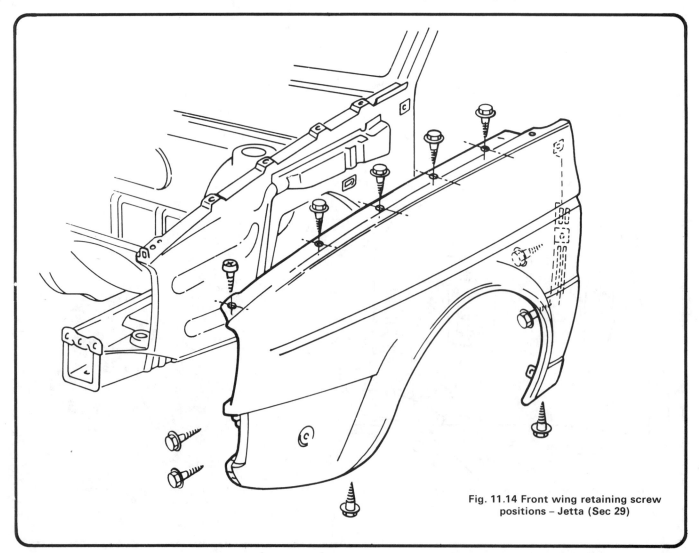

Fig. 11.14 Front wing retaining screw positions – Jetta (Sec 29)

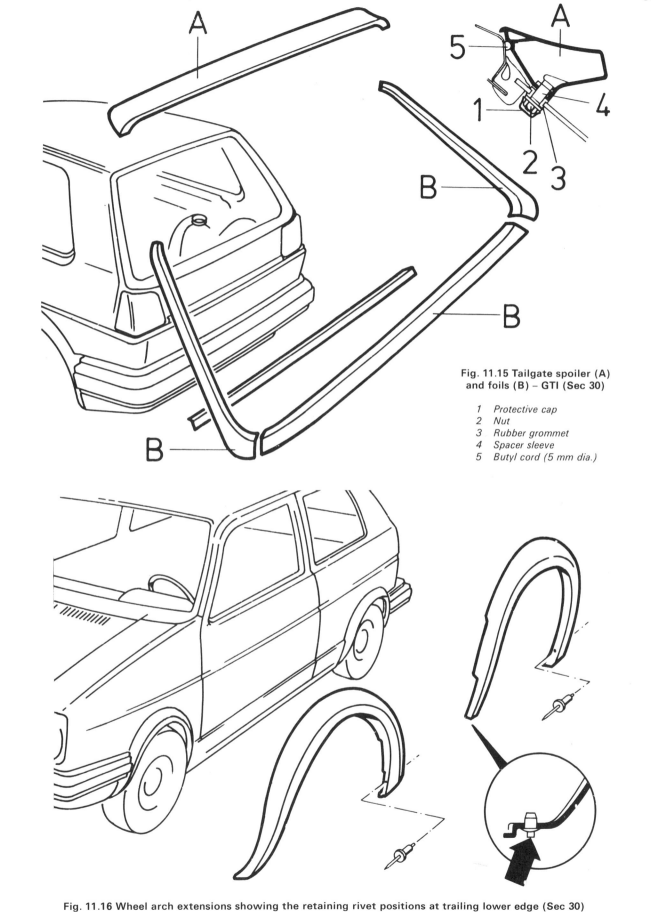

Fig. 11.15 Tailgate spoiler (A) and foils (B) – GTI (Sec 30)

1 Protective cap
2 Nut
3 Rubber grommet
4 Spacer sleeve
5 Butyl cord (5 mm dia.)

Fig. 11.16 Wheel arch extensions showing the retaining rivet positions at trailing lower edge (Sec 30)

309

Protective rubbing strips

7　To remove a rubbing strip you will need to heat the strip using a suitable hot air blower, but care must obviously be taken to protect the paintwork.

8　Clean off the adhesive and polish using white spirit and a suitable silicone remover.

9　Before fitting the new strip into position, check that the contact area on the body is dry and heat it up to a temperature of 35°C (95°F). Peel back the foil from the new strip and carefully locate it into position by pressing firmly home, particularly at each end.

31 Sunroof – removal, refitting and adjustment

1　Half open the sunroof then prise off the five steel trim clips.

2　Close the sunroof and push the trim to the rear.

3　Unscrew the guide screws from the front of the sunroof and remove the guides.

4　Disengage the leaf springs from the rear guides by pulling them inwards.

5　Remove the screws and withdraw the rear support plates.

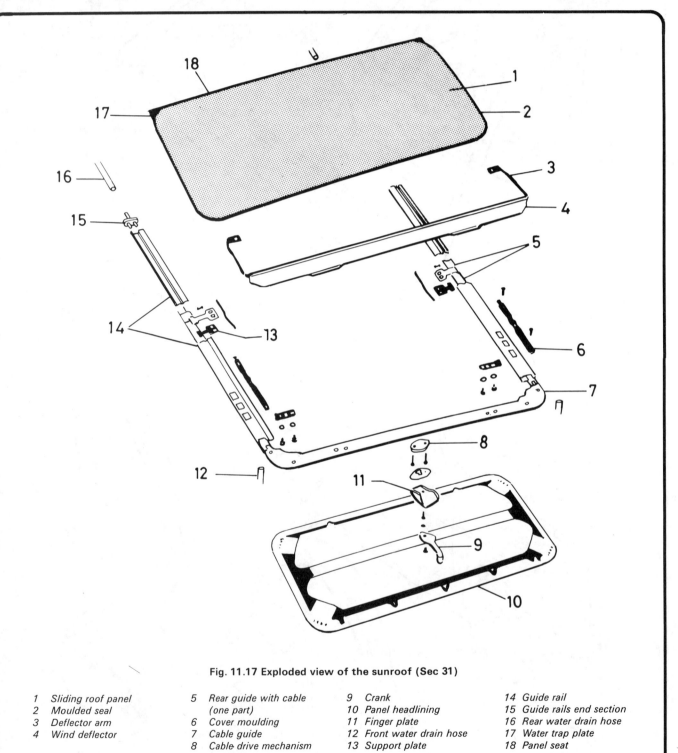

Fig. 11.17 Exploded view of the sunroof (Sec 31)

1	Sliding roof panel	5	Rear guide with cable (one part)	9	Crank	14	Guide rail
2	Moulded seal			10	Panel headlining	15	Guide rails end section
3	Deflector arm	6	Cover moulding	11	Finger plate	16	Rear water drain hose
4	Wind deflector	7	Cable guide	12	Front water drain hose	17	Water trap plate
		8	Cable drive mechanism	13	Support plate	18	Panel seat

6   Lift the sunroof from the car.
7   To refit the sunroof, locate it in the aperture and fit the front guides.
8   With the sunroof closed and correctly aligned, fit the rear guides and leaf springs.
9   The correct adjustment of the sunroof is shown in Fig. 11.18 – the front edge must be level with or a maximum of 1.0 mm (0.040 in) below the roof panel, and the rear edge must be level with or a maximum of 1.0 mm (0.040 in) above the roof panel.
10 To adjust the front edge of the sunroof, loosen the front guide screws and turn the adjustment screws as necessary, then tighten the guide screws.
11 To adjust the rear edge, detach the leaf springs, loosen the slotted screws and move the sunroof as necessary in the serrations. Tighten the screws and refit the leaf springs after making the adjustment.
12 Refit the trim with the clips.

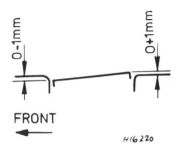

Fig. 11.18 Sunroof adjustment dimensions (Sec 31)

32 Centre console – removal and refitting

1   Disconnect the battery earth lead.
2   Unscrew and remove the gear lever knob then unclip and withdraw the boot.
3   Undo the retaining screws and then pull free the console from its guides at the rear. Disconnect any console switch lead connectors (Fig. 11.19).
4   Refit in the reverse order of removal. Check operation of the console switches (where fitted) on completion.

33 Instrument panel – removal and refitting

1   Remove the steering wheel, as described in Chapter 10.
2   Undo the retaining screws and withdraw the undertray on the driver and passenger sides (see Figs. 11.20 and 11.21).
3   Remove the centre console, as described in the previous Section.
4   Pull free the heater/fresh air control knobs then carefully unclip the control panel trim and detach the electrical connectors.
5   Referring to Chapter 9, remove the radio/cassette unit or cubby hole, the instrument panel surround and cluster, and the loudspeaker and grille.
6   Remove the air vent pivot grilles by carefully levering them free, then undo the screws securing the air vent housing and lever out the housing.
7   Referring to Fig. 11.22, undo and remove the instrument panel retaining screws from the points indicated. To remove the nuts/bolts at the front, access is from the plenum chamber in the engine compartment.
8   Check that the instrument panel is fully disconnected then carefully withdraw it from the car.
9   Refit in the reverse order of removal. When fitting the securing nuts in the plenum chamber use the correct type of sealing washers.
10 On completion, check the operation of the various instruments, switches and controls.

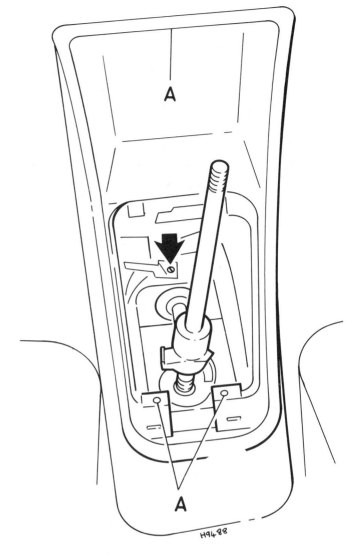

Fig. 11.19 Centre console retaining screw (arrowed) and guide locations (A) (Sec 32)

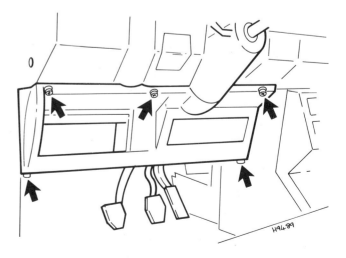

Fig. 11.20 Instrument panel lower shelf retaining screw locations – driver's side (left-hand drive shown) (Sec 33)

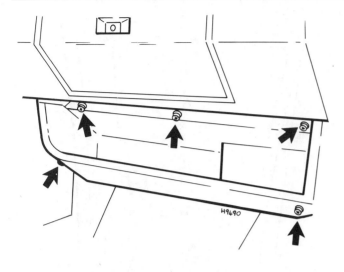

Fig. 11.21 Instrument panel lower shelf retaining screw locations – passenger side (left-hand drive shown) (Sec 33)

34 Front seats – removal and refitting

1   Prise free the lower runner cover and clip towards the rear of the seat.
2   Pull the cover from the runner and then pull the seat forwards.
3   Referring to Fig. 11.24 unscrew the cap nut, remove the washer and cheesehead screw. Then, after releasing the securing rod, remove the seat rearwards.
4   Difficulty in seat position adjustment longitudinally is probably due to worn front and rear slides, in which case renew them (Fig. 11.25).
5   Refitting is a reversal of the removal procedure, but the cap nut must be tightened to the manufacturer's recommended torque setting.

35 Rear seat – removal and refitting

1   Remove the seat cushion by pressing on the pressure points each side at the front lower edge of the cushion, and lift the cushion out (Fig. 11.26).
2   On the luggage compartment side, release the backrest retaining hooks whilst an assistant pushes the backrest downwards (Fig. 11.27).
3   Refitting is a reversal of the removal procedure, but ensure that the backrest retaining hooks fully engage.

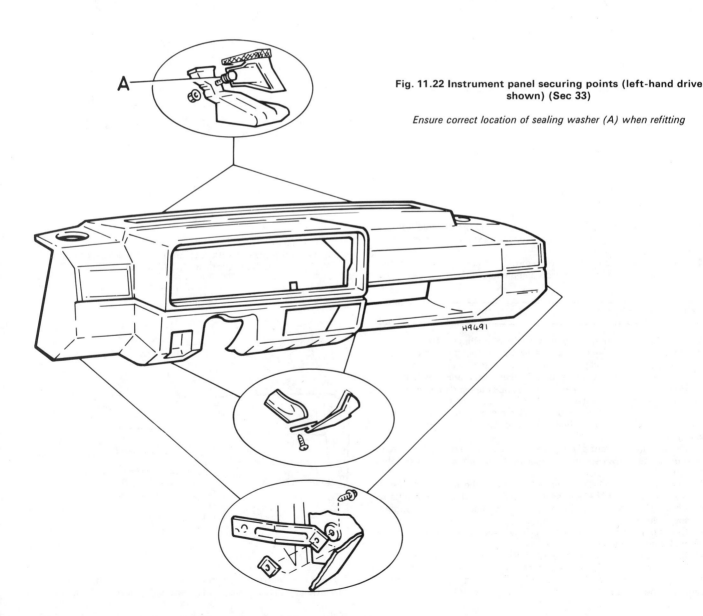

Fig. 11.22 Instrument panel securing points (left-hand drive shown) (Sec 33)

Ensure correct location of sealing washer (A) when refitting

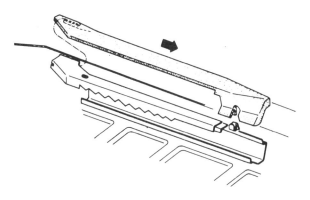

Fig. 11.23 Front seat upper runner cover removal (Sec 34)

Unclip cover and remove in direction arrowed

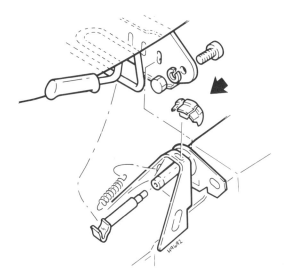

Fig. 11.24 Front seat securing rod and associated components (Sec 34)

Front slide arrowed

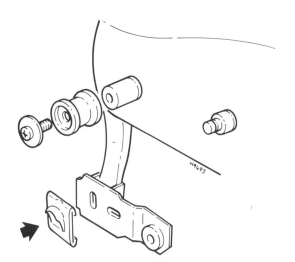

Fig. 11.25 Front seat rear slide (arrowed) – renew if worn (Sec 34)

Fig. 11.26 Rear seat cushion pressure points for removal – arrowed (Sec 35)

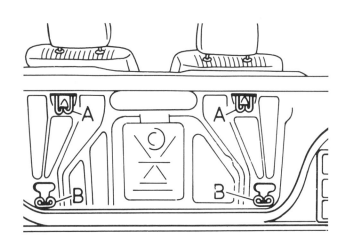

Fig. 11.27 Rear seat backrest retaining hook locations in luggage compartment – A and B (Jetta and Golf convertible) (Sec 35)

36 Seat belts – maintenance

1 Periodically check the belts for fraying or other damage. If evident, renew the belt.
2 If the belts become dirty, wipe them with a damp cloth using a little liquid detergent only.
3 Check the tightness of the anchor bolts and if they are ever disconnected, make quite sure that the original sequence of fitting of washers, bushes, and anchor plate is retained – See Figs. 11.28 to 11.33 inclusive.
4 Never modify the belt or alter its attachment point to the body.

37 Heater controls – removal and refitting

1 The control unit is located in the centre of the dashboard. It is accessible after the radio has been removed or, on cars without a radio, the cubby hole. Once the radio is extracted the control unit may be seen. Disconnect the battery earth lead.

314

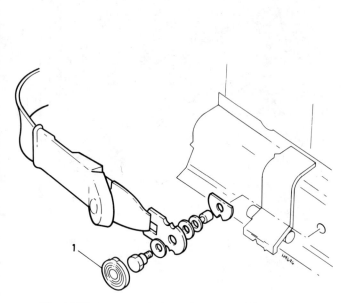

Fig. 11.28 Front seat belt anchorage to side-member (Sec 36)

Spring end (1) points to upper recess of belt link and is then tensioned 270° and hooked onto link pin

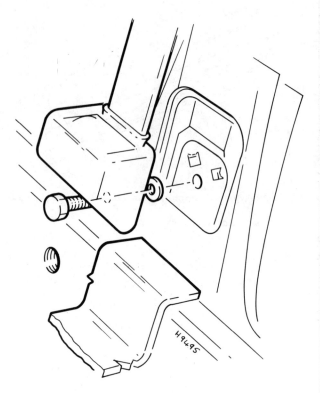

Fig. 11.29 Front seat belt anchorage to B pillar – lower (Sec 36)

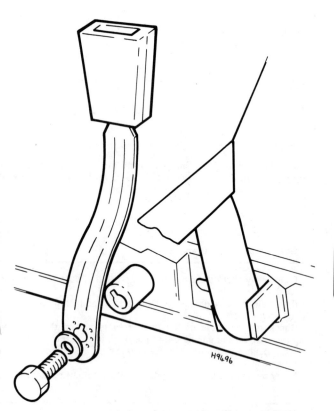

Fig. 11.30 Front seat frame anchorage (Sec 36)

Fig. 11.31 Front seat belt anchorage to B pillar – upper (Sec 36)

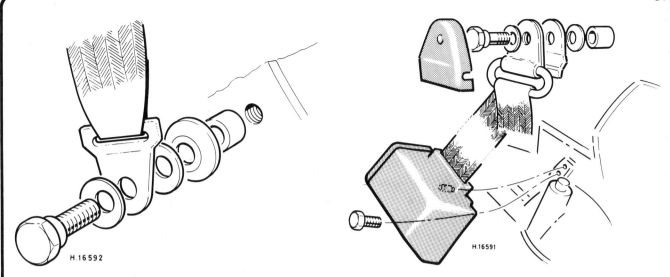

Fig. 11.32 Rear seat belt anchorage to floor (Sec 36)

Fig. 11.33 Rear seat belt anchorage to C pillar (Sec 36)

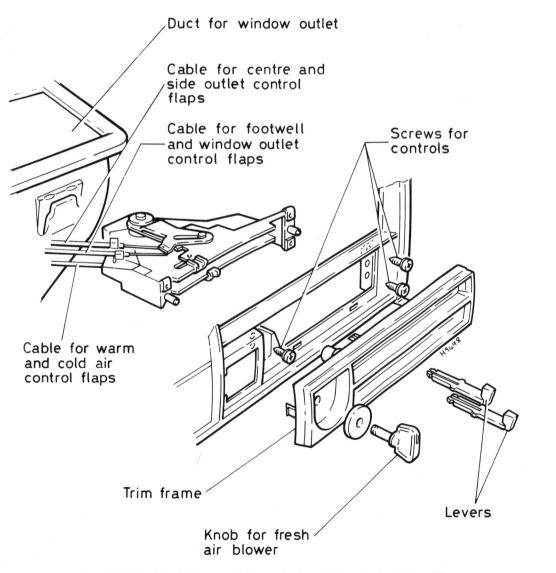

Duct for window outlet

Cable for centre and side outlet control flaps

Cable for footwell and window outlet control flaps

Screws for controls

Cable for warm and cold air control flaps

Trim frame

Knob for fresh air blower

Levers

Fig. 11.34 Exploded diagram of the heater/ventilation controls (Sec 37)

2   Pull off the control knobs and unclip the trim panel (photos).

3   Remove the three cross-head screws holding the control unit and it may be eased forward (photo).

4   The cables can now be unhooked from the control unit levers and their outer body unclipped from the control unit body.

5   If a cable is to be renewed, unhook it from the control flap at the other end and withdraw it. For access to the flap control valves it will be necessary to remove the lower parcel tray on the passenger side and also the insulation sheet (photos).

6   It is best to renew the heater cables completely if the inner cable snaps. In this way the exact length required is obtained. It is a good idea to fit new cable clamps too, as the old ones seem to distort when removed.

7   Refitting is a reversal of the removal procedure. Ensure that the cables are correctly routed with no sharp bends.

38 Heater and fresh air blower unit – removal and refitting

1   Disconnect the battery earth lead.

2   Remove the parcel shelf and insulation sheet on the underside of the instrument panel on the passenger side.

37.3 Detaching the control unit

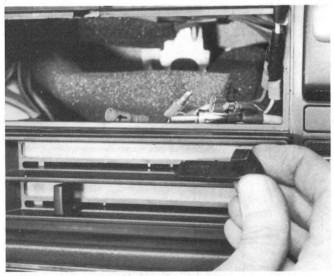

37.2A Pull free the heater/ventilation control knobs

37.5A Remove the parcel shelf ...

37.2B Unclip and withdraw the trim panel

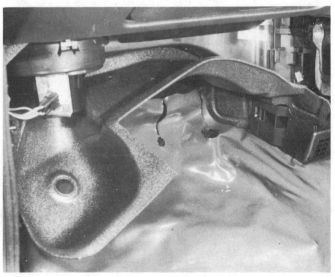

37.5B ... and insulation sheet

37.5C Control cable connections to flap valves at heater distribution box unit (arrowed)

38.3 Blower unit and wiring connection

38.4 Blower unit withdrawal from housing

3 The blower unit is mounted in the left-hand corner. Disconnect the wiring multi-connector (photo).
4 Release the retaining tab (carefully) then twist the blower unit in a clockwise direction and withdraw it from the housing (photo).
5 The wiring connection plate on the blower can be levered free by inserting a screwdriver blade under the retaining tab at the top.
6 If an ohmmeter is available the thermo cut-out can be checked as shown.
7 Check that the blower wheel runs freely and that the air ducts are not blocked up.
8 Refitting is a reversal of the removal procedure.

Fig. 11.35 Checking the blower unit thermo cut-out (Sec 38)

Zero ohms reading: OK
Infinity reading: Defective

39 Heat exchanger/fresh air box – removal and refitting

1 Disconnect the battery earth lead.
2 Remove the centre console (Section 32).
3 Remove the parcel shelf and insulator panel on the passenger side.
4 Drain the engine coolant (heater on) – Chapter 2.
5 Disconnect the heater coolant hoses at the bulkhead on the engine compartment side (Fig. 11.36).
6 Undo the retaining nuts and withdraw the outlet distributor from the fresh air box, disconnecting the distributor from the left and right-hand air ducts as it is withdrawn. Remove the gasket.

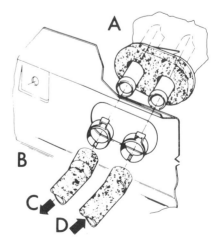

Fig. 11.36 Bulkhead coolant hose connections (Sec 39)

A Passenger compartment   C Return hose
B Engine compartment   D Supply hose

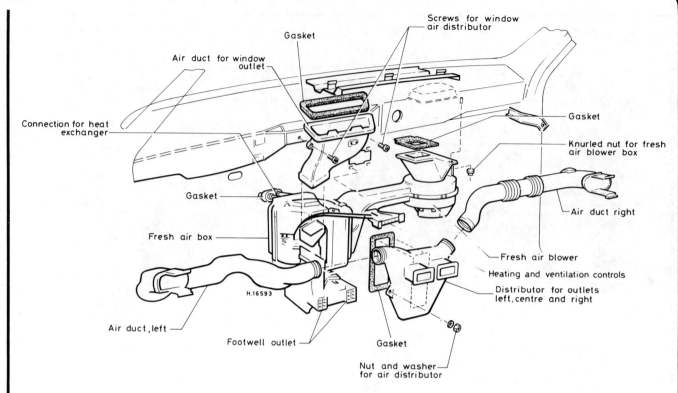

Fig. 11.37 Exploded view of the heater and ventilation system (Sec 39)

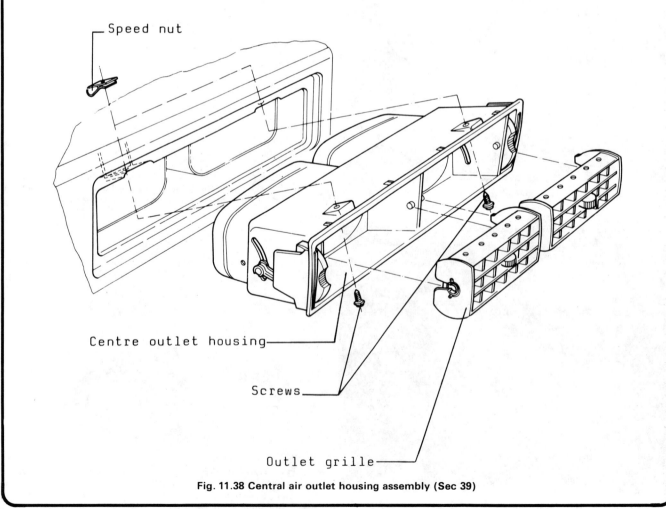

Fig. 11.38 Central air outlet housing assembly (Sec 39)

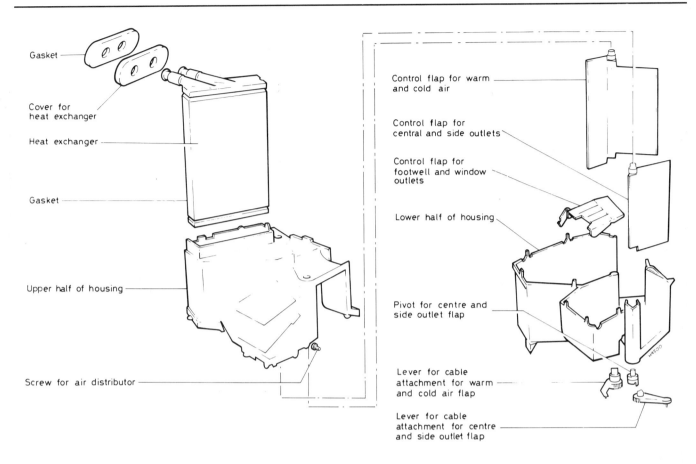

Fig. 11.39 Heater air box components (Sec 39)

7 Disconnect the control cables at the fresh air box end.
8 Loosen the dash securing screws enough to enable the fresh air box to be withdrawn and removed.
9 Release the clips and withdraw the heat exchanger unit from the fresh air box unit, but allow for further coolant drainage from the inlet and outlet pipes.
10 The housing upper and lower housing halves can be separated by

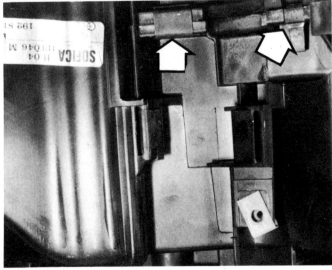

39.10 Upper-to-lower housing retaining clips (arrowed)

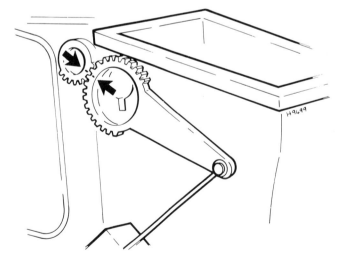

Fig. 11.40 Align marks to set the centre and side outlet flap positions (Sec 39)

releasing the securing clips (photo). Once separated the flap valves can be removed. **Note:** take care not to split or crack the housings.
11 Refitting is a reversal of the removal procedure. When engaging the control cable levers, align the index markings on the outer faces of the segments (Fig. 11.40). Renew the heat exchanger cover gasket and ensure that the hose connections are securely made.

12 Before refitting the parcel shelf, top up the cooling system and run the engine up to its normal operating temperature. Operate the heater and check for any signs of leaks from the heat exchanger hose connections. Check that the controls operate in a satisfactory manner.

40 Air conditioning system – general

1 The unit works on exactly the same principle as a domestic refrigerator, having a compressor, a condenser and an evaporator. The condenser is attached to the car radiator system. The compressor, belt-driven from the crankshaft pulley, is installed on a bracket on the engine. The evaporator is installed in a housing under the dashboard which takes the place of the normal fresh air housing. The housing also contains a normal heat exchanger unit for warming the intake air. The evaporator has a blower motor to circulate cold air as required.
2 The system is controlled by a unit on the dashboard similar to the normal heater control in appearance.

3 The refrigerant used is difluorodichloromethane (CF_2Cl_2) more commonly known as Frigen F12 or Freon F12. It is a dangerous substance in unskilled hands. As a liquid it is very cold and if it touches the skin there will be cold burns and frostbite. As a gas it is colourless and has no odour. Heavier than air, it displaces oxygen and can cause asphyxiation if pockets of it collect in pits or similar workplaces. It does not burn, but even a lighted cigarette causes it to break down into constituent gases, some of which are poisonous to the extent of being fatal. So if you have an air-conditioner and your car catches fire, you have an additional problem.
4 We strongly recommend that even trained refrigeration mechanics do not adjust the system unless they have had instruction by VW. We suggest that the system is left entirely alone, except for the adjustment of the compressor/drivebelt, which should have 5 to 10 mm (0.2 to 0.4 in) deflection in the centre when depressed by the thumb. See Section 41 for adjustment procedures.
5 Removal and refitting of the air conditioner compressor is straight-forward, as can be seen from Fig. 11.41 but the refrigerant

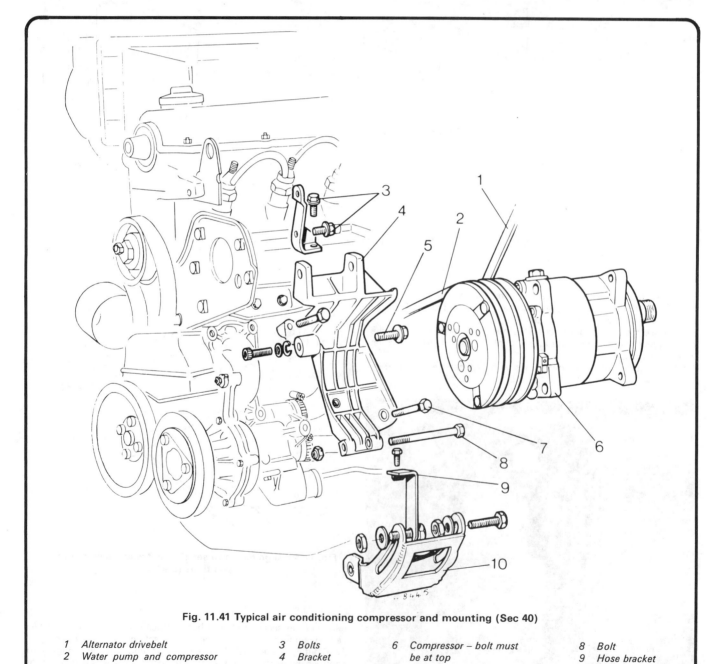

Fig. 11.41 Typical air conditioning compressor and mounting (Sec 40)

1	Alternator drivebelt	3	Bolts	6	Compressor – bolt must
2	Water pump and compressor	4	Bracket		be at top
	drivebelt	5	Bolt	7	Bolt

8	Bolt
9	Hose bracket
10	Tensioner

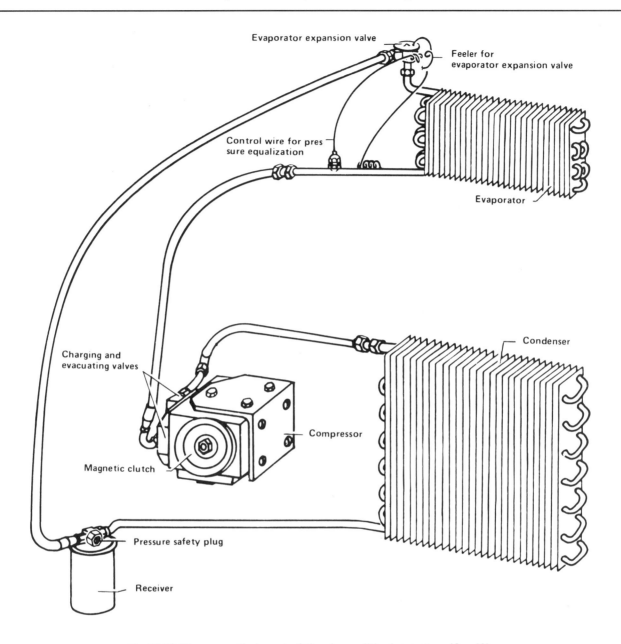

Fig. 11.42 Diagrammatic layout of the air conditioning system (Sec 40)

circuit **must not be opened**. The compressor must be placed on the side of the engine compartment when removing the engine, but only move it to the point where the flexible refrigerant hoses are in no danger of being stretched.

6   When a situation arises which calls for the removal of one of the air conditioning system components, have the system discharged by your VW agent or a qualified refrigeration engineer. Similarly have the system recharged by him on completion.

7   During the winter period operate the air conditioner for a few minutes each week to keep the system in good order.

8   Periodically, clean the condenser of dirt and insects, either by washing with a cold water hose or by air pressure. Use a soft bristle brush to assist removal of dirt jammed in the condenser fins.

41 Drivebelt – air conditioning system

1   Drivebelt tension is adjusted by adding or subtracting shims from between the halves of the compressor pulley.

2   When correctly adjusted the belt should give a deflection of 5 to 10 mm (0.2 to 0.4 in) on its longest run.

Chapter 12 Supplement:
Revisions and information on later models

Contents

1 Introduction

This Supplement contains information which has become available since the manual was first written. This includes the introduction of hydraulic bucket tappets, the Digifant fuel injection system, the 16-valve engine fitted to the GTI, additional carburettors, the fully

electronic ignition system (FEI), the 085 five-speed gearbox, and several other minor modifications and revisions.

In order to use the Supplement to the best advantage it is suggested that it is referred to before the main Chapters of the manual. This will ensure that any relevant information can be noted and incorporated within the procedures given in Chapters 1 to 11. Time and cost will therefore be saved and the particular job will be completed correctly.

2 Specifications

The Specifications below are revisions of, or supplementary to, those at the beginning of the preceding Chapters

Engine (1.05 and 1.3 litre) – 1986-on
General

Code letters:
  1.05 litre .... HZ
  1.3 litre .... MH
Bore:
  1.05 litre .... 75 mm (2.95 in)
  1.3 litre .... 75 mm (2.95 in)
Stroke:
  1.05 litre .... 59 mm (2.33 in)
  1.3 litre .... 72 mm (2.84 in)
Compression ratio:
  1.05 litre 9.5:1
  1.3 litre 9.5:1
Output:
  1.05 litre .... 37 kW (50 bhp) at 5900 rpm
  1.3 litre .... 40 kW (54 bhp) at 5200 rpm
Torque (max):
  1.05 litre .... 74 Nm at 3600 rpm
  1.3 litre .... 96 Nm at 3400 rpm

Cylinder head
Minimum dimension after machining (skimming) .... 135.6 mm (5.34 in)

Camshaft
Run-out (max) .... 0.01 mm (0.0004 in)
Radial play (max) .... 0.1 mm (0.004 in)

Valves
Head diameter:
  Inlet .... 36 mm (1.42 in)
  Exhaust .... 29 mm (1.14 in)
Valve length:
  Inlet .... 98.9 mm (3.897 in)
  Exhaust .... 99.1 mm (3.905 in)
Seat width (max) .... 2.2 mm (0.087 in)

Hydraulic tappets
Free travel (max) .... 0.1 mm (0.004 in)

Valve timing
(at 1.0 mm/0.04 in valve lift, zero valve clearance)

	HZ	MH
Inlet opens	12°ATDC	5° ATDC
Inlet closes	28° ABDC	29°ABDC
Exhaust opens	25° BBDC	33° BBDC
Exhaust closes	9° BTDC	9°BTDC

Lubrication system
Capacity:

Without filter change .... 3.0 litres (5.3 pints)
With filter change .... 3.5 lires (6.2 pints)
Dipstick MIN to MAX .... 1 litre (1.8 pints)
Oil pump:

Gear teeth backlash:

New .... 0.05 mm (0.002 in)
Wear limit .... 0.20 mm (0.008 in)
Gear teeth axial play (wear limit) .... 0.15 mm (0.006 in)
Chain drive deflection .... 1.5 to 2.5 mm (0.059 to 0.10 in)

Torque wrench settings

	Nm	lbf ft
Camshaft sprocket bolt	80	59.0
Timing belt cover:		
Upper bolt	10	7.3
Lower bolt	20	14.7
Camshaft bearing cap nuts:		
Stage 1	6	4.4
Stage 2	Tighten by further 90°	
Number 5 cap screws	10	7.3
Cylinder head bolts:		
Stage 1	40	29.5
Stage 2	60	44.3
Stage 3	Tighten by further 180° (or 2 turns of 90°)	
Oil pump bolts	20	14.7
Stay bracket bolts	10	7.3
Strainer assembly to pump body	10	7.3
Socket-headed bolts in sump (new)	8	5.9
Crankshaft sprocket bolt (oiled) – 1986-on:		
Stage 1	90	66
Stage 2	Tighten by a further 180°	
Flywheel bolt (with shoulder)	100	74

General

Engine (1.6 and 1.8 litre)
Code letters:

1.8 litre, GTI 16V .... KR
1.8 litre, GTI 8V (January 1987 on) .... PB
Compression ratio:

Engine codes KR and PB .... 10.0 : 1

Piston rings
End gap (new) – except 16V:

Oil scraper ring (2 part) .... 0.25 to 0.45 mm (0.010 to 0.018 in)
Oil scraper ring (3 part) .... 0.25 to 0.50 mm (0.010 to 0.020 in)
End gap (max) – all engines .... 1.0 mm (0.040 in)

Cylinder head
Minimum height:

Except 16V .... 132.6 mm (5.221 in)
16V .... 118.1 mm (4.650 in) measured through cylinder head bolt hole

Valves
Head diameter (16V):

Inlet .... 32.0 mm (1.260 in)
Exhaust .... 28.0 mm (1.102 in)
Stem diameter (16V):

Inlet .... 6.97 mm (0.274 in)
Exhaust .... 6.94 mm (0.273 in)
Overall length (hydraulic tappet engines):

Except 16V:

Inlet .... 91.0 mm (3.583 in)
Exhaust .... 90.8 mm (3.575 in)

16V:
    Inlet .... 95.5 mm (3.760 in)
    Exhaust .... 98.2 mm (3.866 in)

Valve timing

(At 1.0 mm/0.04 in valve lift):	KR engine	PB engine
Inlet opens	3° ATDC	3° ATDC
Inlet closes	35° ABDC	43° ABDC
Exhaust opens	43° BBDC	37° BBDC
Exhaust closes	3° BTDC	3° ATDC

Lubrication

Oil capacity (all engines from August 1985):
    With filter change .... 4.0 litre (7.0 Imp pint)
    Without filter change .... 3.5 litre (6.2 Imp pint)

Torque wrench settings

16V 1.8 litre engine (code KR):	Nm	lbf ft
Vibration damper	20	15
Intermediate shaft sprocket bolt	65	48
Valve cover	10	7
Oil cooler	25	19
Camshaft sprocket bolt	65	48
Camshaft bearing caps	15	11
Oil temperature sender	10	7
Oil pump cover	10	7
Oil pump mounting bolts	20	15
Oil jet	10	7
Crankshaft sprocket bolt (oiled)	180	133

Cooling system

Thermostat

1.05 and 1.3 litre bucket tappet engines:
    Opening temperature .... 87°C (189°F)
    Fully open temperature .... 102°C (216°F)
    Minimum stroke .... 7.0 mm (0.276 in)

Cooling fan thermo-switch (in radiator)

Fuel injection engines:
    Switch-on temperature (single speed and lst stage of twin
    speed) .... 92° to 97°C (198° to 207°F)
    Switch-off temperature (single speed and 1st stage of twin
    speed) .... 84° to 91°C (183° to 196°F)
    Switch-on temperature (2nd stage of twin speed) .... 99° to 105°C (210° to 221°F)
    Switch-off temperature (2nd stage of twin speed) .... 91° to 98°C (196° to 208°F)

Cooling fan thermo-switch (for injector cooling)

Switch-on temperature .... 110°C (230°F)
Switch-off temperature .... 103°C (217°F)

Torque wrench settings

	Nm	lbf ft
Radiator	10	7
Thermo-switch (radiator)	25	19

Fuel and exhaust systems

Carburettor (1.05 litre) – Pierburg 1B3

Venturi	23 mm
Main jet	105
Air correction jet	57.5
Idling fuel/air jet	50/130
Pump injection tube	32.5/150
Needle valve	1.5
Pump capacity (cc/stroke)	1.0 ± 0.15
Choke valve gap	1.8 ± 0.2 mm
Fast idle speed	2000 ± 100 rpm
Idling speed	800 ± 50 rpm
CO content	2.0 ± 0.5%

Carburettor (1.05 litre) – Weber 32 TLA

Venturi .... 22 mm
Main jet:
    Code 030 129 016 105
    Code 030 129 016 D 102
Air correction jet:
    Code 030 129 016 80
    Code 030 129 016 D 100

Emulsion tube	F96
Idling fuel jet	47
Idling air jet:	
Code 030 129 016	110
Code 030 129 016D	145
Auxiliary fuel jet (code 030 129 016D)	30
Auxiliary air jet (code 030 129 016D)	170
Pump injection tube	0.35/0.35
Needle valve	1.75
Needle valve washer thickness	0.75 mm
Pump capacity (cc/stroke)	1.05 ± 0.15
Choke valve gap (pull-down):	
Without vacuum	2.5 ± 0.2 mm
With 300 mbar vacuum	2.0 ± 0.2 mm
Choke valve gap (wide open kick):	
Code 030 129 016	2.0 ± 0.5 mm
Code 030 129 016D	2.3 ± 0.5 mm
Float setting	28.0 ± 1.0 mm
Fast idle speed	2000 ± 100 rpm
Idling speed	800 ± 50 rpm
CO content	2.0 ± 0.5%

Fuel injection system

K-Jetronic:	
System pressure – from March 1986	5.2 to 5.9 bar (75 to 86 lbf/in²)
Idle speed – from September 1984 (except 16V)	900 ± 100 rpm
Idle speed (16V)	950 + 50 rpm
Digifant II (1.8 engine, code PB):	
Idling speed	800 ± 50 rpm
CO content	1.0 ± 0.5%
System pressure – at idling speed:	
On	Approximately 2.5 bar
Off	Approximately 3.0 bar
Holding (10 minutes after switching off ignition)	2.0 bar minimum

Torque wrench settings

	Nm	lbf ft
16V engine:		
Injector insert	20	15
Thermo-time switch	30	22
Inlet manifold nuts/bolts	20	15
1.8 engine, code PB:		
Throttle valve housing	20	15
Inlet manifold	25	19
Fuel pressure regulator	15	11
Injector insert	20	15

Ignition system

Ignition coil – from August 1987

Primary winding resistance	0.6 to 0.8 ohm
Secondary winding resistance	6900 to 8500 ohm

Distributor

Rotor cut-out speed:	
1.05 and 1.3 litre (transistorized)*	6600 to 7000 rpm
1.6 and 1.8 litre (transistorized)**	6150 to 6450 rpm

* Discontinued from 1986 models
** Only on engine without hydraulic tappets

Ignition timing

1.8 engine, code PB with Digifant fuel injection system	6° ± 1° BTDC at between 2000 and 2500 rpm, with temperature sender disconnected

Spark plugs

Electrode gap:	
1.8 litre (16V and PB)	0.7 to 0.9 mm (0.028 to 0.035 in)
1.05 and 1.3 litre – from August 1987	0.7 to 0.8 mm (0.028 to 0.032 in)
Type – from September 1985:	
1.3 litre	Champion N7BYC, Beru 14-7DTU, or Bosch W7DTC
1.6 litre	Champion N9BYC
1.8 litre (except 16V and PB)	Champion C6BYC, or Bosch F5DTC
1.8 litre (16V)	Champion C6BYC, or Bosch F6DTC
1.8 litre (PB)	Champion N7YCX, Bosch W6DTC, or Beru 14-6DTU
Type – from August 1987:	
1.05 and 1.3 litre	Champion N7YCX, Beru 14-7DU, or Bosch W7DCO

Torque wrench settings

	Nm	lbf ft
Knock sensor (1.8 engine, code PB)	20	15

Clutch
General
Clutch friction disc diameter (085 gearbox)	190 mm (7.48 in)
Pressure plate maximum inward taper (085 gearbox)	0.3 mm (0.012 in)
Friction disc maximum run-out – measured 2.5 mm (0.099 in) from outer edge (085 gearbox)	0.4 mm (0.016 in)

Torque wrench settings
	Nm	lbf ft
Flywheel (085 gearbox):		
Bolt with collar	100	74
Bolt without collar	75	55
Guide sleeve (085 gearbox)	18	13
Pressure plate (085 gearbox)	25	18

Manual gearbox
Identification code
Five-speed (1.3 litre)	085 (8N)

Lubrication
Oil capacity (085 gearbox)	3.1 litre (5.5 Imp pint)
Lubricant type (085)	Gear oil, viscosity SAE 80 (Duckhams Hypoid 80)

Ratios (085)
1st	3.455 : 1
2nd	1.958 : 1
3rd	1.250 : 1
4th	0.891 : 1
5th	0.740 : 1
Reverse	3.384 : 1
Final drive	4.267 : 1

Torque wrench settings (085 gearbox)
	Nm	lbf ft
End cover bolt	8	6
Gear lever bracket (inside gearbox)	16	12
Selector arm pinch bolt	25	19

Electrical system
Fuses (Jetta models)
Fuse number	Component	Rating (amps)
3	Boot light	15

Suspension and steering
Front wheel alignment
Camber (in straight-ahead position):	
Golf GTI and Jetta GT	– 35′ ± 20′
Golf GTI 16V	– 40′ ± 20
Castor:	
Golf GTI and Jetta GT	1° 33′ ± 30′

Wheels
Size:	
Golf GTI 16V	6J x 14

Tyres
Size:	
Golf GTI 16V	185/60 VR 14

Torque wrench setting
	Nm	lbf ft
Rear suspension mounting bracket (1988 models on)	70	52

3 Routine maintenance

The Routine Maintenance intervals for models manufactured from August 1985 (ie 1986 models) are changed as follows:

Every 12 months

Check operation of all lights, direction indicators and horns (Chapter 9)

Check operation of washer system and top up levels if necessary (Chapter 9)

Check clutch pedal play and adjust where applicable (Chapter 5)

Check battery electrolyte level and top up with distilled water if necessary (Chapter 9)

Check engine for oil, fuel and coolant leaks (Chapters 1, 2 and 3)

Check antifreeze strength and adjust if necessary (Chapter 3)

Grease door check straps (Chapter 11)

Change engine oil and filter (Chapter 1)

Check brake hydraulic lines for leaks and damage (Chapter 8)

Check underbody sealant and re-seal where necessary (Chapter 11)

Check exhaust system for leaks and damage (Chapter 3)

Check steering tie-rod balljoints for wear and damage (Chapter 10)

Check front suspension lower balljoints for wear and damage (Chapter 10)

Check gearbox/transmission for oil leaks and damage (Chapter 6)

Check driveshaft boots for leaks and damage (Chapter 7)

Check front and rear brake linings for wear (Chapter 8)

Check all tyres for wear and damage (Chapter 10)

Check brake fluid level and top up if necessary (Chapter 8)

Check power steering fluid level and top up if necessary (Chapter 10)

Check automatic transmission fluid level and top up if necessary (Chapter 6)
Check and adjust idling speed and mixture (Chapter 3)
Check headlight beam alignment and adjust if necessary (Chapter 9)

Every 10 000 miles (15 000 km) if completing more than 10 000 miles (15 000 km) per annum

Change engine oil and filter (Chapter 1)
Check disc pad linings for wear

Every 20 000 miles (30 000 km)

Check drivebelt(s) for wear and damage and adjust tension if necessary (Chapter 9)
Renew the spark plugs (Chapter 4)
Renew air cleaner element and clean housing (Chapter 3)
Renew fuel filter where applicable (Chapter 3)
Renew automatic transmission fluid, clean sump and filter screen (Chapter 6)
Clean sunroof guide rails (where applicable) and lubricate with silicone spray

Every 2 years

Renew the brake fluid

Every 40 000 miles (60 000 km)

Renew the timing belt (Chapter 1)

4 Engine (1.05 and 1.3 litre with hydraulic tappets)

General description
1 The 1.05 litre and 1.3 litre engines, code letters HZ and MH, produced since August 1985 have a redesigned cylinder head incorporating hydraulic 'bucket' type tappets in place of the previous rocker finger tappets, and a redesigned engine oil pump, driven by chain from the crankshaft.
2 Additionally, different ancillary components are fitted, such as carburettor and distributor. Where differences to the servicing procedure described in the relevant Chapters of this book occur, they will be found in this Supplement.

Cylinder head – removal
3 The procedure for removing the cylinder head on engines with hydraulic tappets is basically the same as described in Chapter 1, but the following points should be borne in mind.

4 The valve cover is different, being held in place by three bolts (photo).
5 There is a plastic oil shield located at the distributor end of the engine (photo).
6 The fuel and coolant pipes differ, depending on model.
7 Spring type re-usable hose clips may be fitted. These are removed by punching the ends together to expand the clip and then sliding it down the hose.
8 The clips on the fuel hoses are designed to be used only once, so obtain new ones or replace them with screw type clips.

Camshaft – removal and inspection
Removal
9 Refer to Chapter 1, Section 11, all paragraphs up to number 4 (inclusive).
10 Devise a method to prevent the camshaft turning, and remove the sprocket bolt (photo). Remove the camshaft sprocket and where applicable the Woodruff key.
11 The camshaft bearing caps must be refitted in the same places from which they were removed, and the same way round. They are usually numbered, but centre-punch marks on them, if necessary, to ensure correct refitting.
12 Remove bearing caps 5, 1 and 3 in that order. Now undo the nuts holding 2 and 4 in a diagonal pattern and the camshaft will lift them up as the pressure of the valve springs is exerted. When they are free, lift the caps off.
13 If the caps are stuck, give them a sharp tap with a hide-faced mallet to loosen them. Do not try to lever them off with a screwdriver.
14 Lift out the camshaft, then oil seal will come with it.
Inspection
15 Clean the camshaft in petrol, then inspect the journals and cam peaks for pitting, scoring, cracking and wear.
16 The camshaft bearings are machined directly into the cylinder head and the bearing caps.
17 Radial play in the bearings can be measured using the Plastigage method. Compare the results with the dimension in the Specifications.
18 If wear is evident, consult your VAG dealer.

Camshaft oil seal – renewal
19 This is straightforward if the camshaft is removed, but it is possible to renew the oil seal without removing the camshaft.
20 A VAG special tool exists for this job, but if it is not available the old seal will have to be removed by securing suitable screws into it and pulling it out with pliers. Note which way round it is fitted.
21 Whichever method is used, the timing cover and camshaft sprocket will have to be removed. Slacken the water pump bolts to release the tension in the timing belt.
22 Lightly oil a new seal and slide it onto the camshaft – the same way round as the one which was removed. Use a suitable socket and a bolt in the end of the shaft to press the new seal home. Push it in as far as it will go.

4.4 New type valve cover

4.5 Plastic oil shield

4.10 Using two lengths of metal as a pair of scissors to prevent the camshaft turning

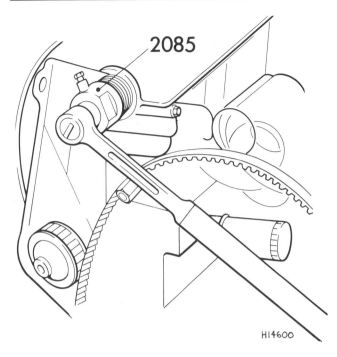

Fig. 12.1 Renewing the camshaft oil seal with the VAG special tool (Sec 4)

Camshaft endfloat
23 To check the camshaft endfloat, remove the camshaft and all the tappets.
24 Refit the camshaft using only number 3 bearing cap.
25 Set up a dial test indicator or use feeler gauges (photo) to measure

the endfloat (see the Specifications in Chapter 1). If the endfloat is greater than specified, consult your VAG dealer.

Camshaft – refitting
26 Oil the bucket tappets, the camshaft journals and the camshaft liberally with clean engine oil.
27 Place the camshaft in position on the cylinder head (photo).
28 Fit a new camshaft oil seal (photo).
29 Refit the bearing caps, ensuring they are the right way and in their correct position (they are numbered 1 to 5 and these numbers should be readable from the exhaust manifold side of the head).
30 Thread on the cap retaining nuts loosely, then tighten the nuts on number 2 and 4 caps in a diagonal sequence to the Stage 1 torque figure given in the Specifications (photo).
31 Tighten the nuts on caps 1, 3 and 5 to the Stage 1 torque.
32 Once all nuts have been tightened to the Stage 1 torque, tighten all nuts a further 90° (Stage 2). Fit and tighten No 5 cap screws to the correct torque.
33 Refit the Woodruff key into its slot in the camshaft where applicable, fit the camshaft sprocket and tighten the bolt to the specified torque (photo).
34 If the cylinder head is in the car, follow the procedure given in Chapter 1, Section 37, paragraphs 9 to 18.
35 Ignore any reference to the oil spray tube, and be sure to refit the oil shield at the distributor end of the camshaft before the valve cover is refitted.
36 If the cylinder head is out of the car it will obviously have to be refitted before the timing belt can be reconnected. Refitting the cylinder head is described later in this Section.

Cylinder head – inspection
37 If, on examination, the valve seats are badly pitted or eroded they can be reworked, but this is a specialist job best left to your dealer or local engine overhaul specialists.
38 Similarly, the cylinder head surfaces can be skimmed, again by specialist engineers, if the head is warped.
39 On inspection, if it is found that there are cracks from the valve seats or valve seat inserts to the spark plug threads the cylinder head may still be serviceable. Consult your VAG dealer.

4.25 Measuring camshaft endfloat with a feeler gauge

4.27 Refitting the camshaft

4.28 Camshaft oil seal

4.30 Tightening a camshaft bearing cap nut

4.33 Fitting the camshaft sprocket bolt

Hydraulic bucket tappets – removal, inspection and refitting

40 Remove the camshaft, as previously described.
41 Lift out the tappets one by one (photo), ensuring they are kept in their correct order and so are replaced in their original positions.
42 Place them, face down (cam contact surface), on a clean sheet of paper as they are removed.
43 Inspect the tappets for wear, indicated by ridging on the clean surface, pitting and cracks.
44 Tappets cannot be repaired, and if found worn must be renewed.
45 Before fitting the tappets, oil all parts liberally and slip the tappets back into their original bore.

Caution: *If new tappets are fitted, the engine must not be started after fitting for approximately 30 minutes, or the valves will strike the pistons.*

Hydraulic bucket tappets – checking free travel

46 Start the engine and run it until the radiator cooling fan has switched on once.
47 Increase engine speed to about 2500 rpm for about 2 minutes.
48 Irregular noises are normal when starting, but should become quiet after a few minutes running.
49 If the valves are still noisy carry out the following check to identify worn tappets.
50 Stop the engine and remove the valve cover from the cylinder head.
51 Turn the crankshaft clockwise, using a wrench on the crankshaft pulley securing bolt, until the cam of the tappet to be checked is facing upward, and is not exerting any pressure on the tappet.
52 Press the tappet down using a wooden or plastic wedge.
53 If free travel of the tappet exceeds that given in the Specifications the tappet must be renewed.

Inlet and exhaust valves – removal, inspection and refitting

54 Remove the cylinder head, camshaft and tappets, as described previously.
55 Using a valve spring compressor with a deep reach, compress the valve springs, remove the two cotters and release the compressor and springs.

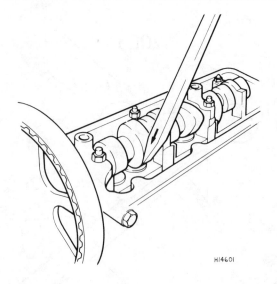

HI4601

Fig. 12.2 Checking the hydraulic tappet free travel (Sec 4)

56 Lift out the upper spring seat (photo).
57 Remove the outer and inner valve springs (photo).
58 Lift out the valve (photo).
59 The valves should be inspected as described in Chapter 1, Section 12.
60 Valves cannot be reworked, but must be renewed if they are worn. They should be ground in the normal manner.
61 If possible, check the valve spring lengths against new ones. Renew the whole set if any are too short.
62 Refitting is a reversal of removal.

4.41 Removing the bucket tappets

4.56 Remove the upper spring seat ...

4.57A ... the outer spring ...

4.57B ... and inner spring ...

4.58 ... then lift out the valve

Valve stem oil seals – renewal

63 The valve stem oil seals should be renewed whenever the valves are removed, by prising them from the ends of the valve guides (photo). With the oil seals removed the lower spring seats can also be lifted out for cleaning. Press the new oil seals onto the ends of the valve guides.

Cylinder head – refitting

64 Clean all traces of old gasket from the cylinder block and cylinder head faces.

65 Using a new gasket, fit the inlet manifold (photos).

66 If they have been removed, refit the oil pressure switches, using new copper sealing washers (photo).

67 Refit the thermostat housing using a new O-ring seal (photo).

68 Refit the coolant hoses, ensuring they are connected up in their positions (photo).

69 Lubricate the fuel pump plunger with clean engine oil and slip it into its housing in the cylinder head (photo).

70 Refit the fuel pump (photo) and fit and tighten the bolts, not forgetting the lifting eye (photo).

71 Slide the distributor into position and ensure that it goes fully home (photo). Hand-tighten the retaining bolts.

72 Fit the distributor rotor arm (photo).

73 Fit the distributor cap and connect up the earth lead (photo).

74 Check the timing marks on the cylinder head and camshaft sprocket are lined up.

75 The pistons in the cylinder block **must not** be at TDC when refitting the cylinder head.

76 Position a new cylinder head gasket on the cylinder block (photo).

77 Lower the cylinder head gently into position. Special guides are used by Volkswagen both to line up the gasket and guide the cylinder head into position, but this can be done using suitable sized rods inserted in two cylinder head bolt holes.

78 Refer to Chapter 1 and refit the cylinder head bolts in the sequence given in Fig. 1.11, but use the torque figures and stages given in the Specifications section of this Supplement.

4.63 A valve stem oil seal

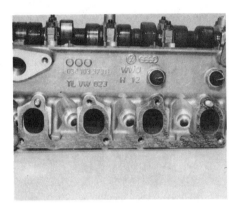

4.65A Fitting a new inlet manifold gasket

4.65B Fitting the inlet manifold complete with carburettor

4.66 Refitting an oil pressure switch

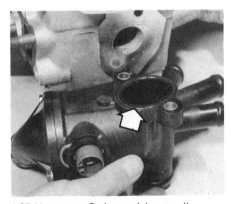

4.67 Use a new O-ring seal (arrowed) when refitting the thermostat housing

4.68 Coolant hoses in position

4.69 Fitting the fuel pump plunger (arrowed)

4.70A Fitting the fuel pump ...

4.70B ... not forgetting the lifting eye

4.71 Refitting the distributor ...

4.72 ... rotor arm ...

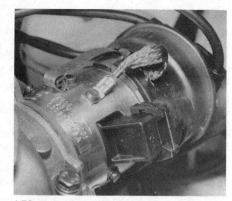
4.73 ... cap and earth lead

4.76 Fitting the new cylinder head gasket

4.80 Refit the plastic oil shield

4.81 Locating dowel for valve cover gasket

4.82 Fitting a new exhaust manifold gasket

4.83A Exhaust manifold bolted into position

4.83B Fitting the hot air shroud

79 It is not necessary to retighten the bolts after a period of service, as is normally the case.

80 Refit the plastic oil shield (photo).

81 Using a new rubber sealing gasket, properly located over the dowels, refit the valve cover (photo).

82 Fit a new gasket to the exhaust manifold (photo).

83 Fit the exhaust manifold, do up the nuts (photo), and fit the hot air shroud (photo).

84 Connect up the exhaust downpipe and any other exhaust brackets loosened during removal.

85 Refit all remaining hoses of the cooling system and fuel system, referring to the relevant Chapter where necessary.

86 Refit all electrical connections disturbed during dismantling (distributor, carburettor, oil pressure and coolant temperature switches, inlet manifold preheater etc). Do not forget the earth lead under the inlet manifold nut (photos).

87 Refit the distributor vacuum hose.

88 With reference to Chapter 1, Section 39, refit the timing belt and covers.

89 Refer to Chapter 3 and refit the throttle cable.

90 Refit the spark plugs, air cleaner and associated pipework and electrical leads.

91 Check oil and coolant levels, refilling as necessary, then adjust the ignition timing with reference to Chapter 4.

Oil pump

General description

92 The oil pump fitted to engines produced since August 1985 has been changed from the crescent type to a gear type pump, driven by chain from the engine crankshaft.

93 Only the oil pump has been changed, the rest of the lubrication system remains as before.

Removal and inspection

94 The oil pump can be removed with the engine still in the vehicle.

4.86A Distributor electrical connection

4.86B Coolant temperature sender electrical connection

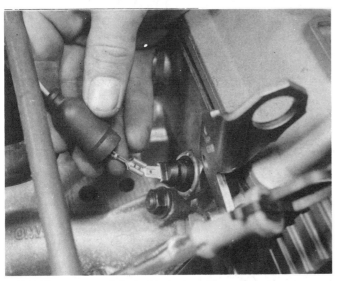

4.86C Oil pressure switch electrical connection

4.86D The earth lead under the inlet manifold nut

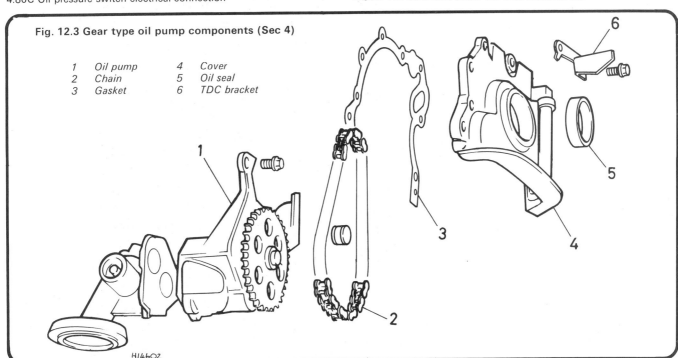

Fig. 12.3 Gear type oil pump components (Sec 4)

1   Oil pump   4   Cover
2   Chain   5   Oil seal
3   Gasket   6   TDC bracket

H14602

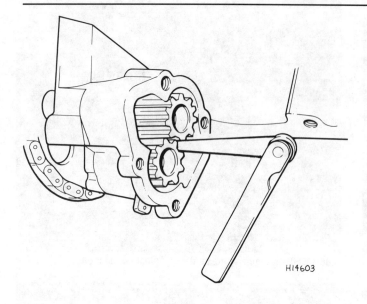

Fig. 12.4 Checking the oil pump gear backlash (Sec 4)

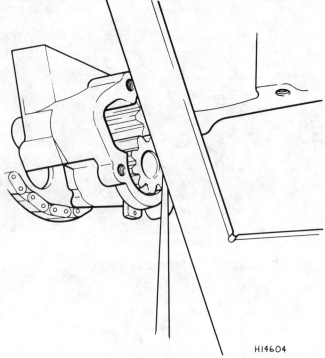

Fig. 12.5 Checking the oil pump gear axial play (Sec 4)

95 Drain the oil from the sump.
96 Refer to the relevant Chapters and disconnect the exhaust downpipe and the inboard end of the right-hand driveshaft to give room to remove the sump.
97 Remove the sump.
98 If it is only desired to check backlash in the gears this can be done by removing the oil pump cover and strainer assembly from the back of the pump.
99 Refer to Figs. 12.4 and 12.5 and check backlash and axial play against the tolerances in the Specifications.
100 If the tolerances are exceeded then the oil pump should be renewed, as follows:
101 Refer to the relevant Chapters and remove:

   (a) Camshaft drivebelt (timing belt)
   (b) Alternator drivebelt
   (c) Crankshaft pulley
   (d) Lower timing belt cover
   (e) Front cover and TDC setting bracket

102 If they are still in position remove the bolts holding the rear stay bracket.
103 Remove the two bolts holding the oil pump to the cylinder block.
104 This will release the tension on the chain and allow the pump to be removed.
105 If sufficient slack in the chain cannot be achieved by this method, then slide the pump, chain and crankshaft drive sprocket forward together.
106 Check the chain and teeth of the drive sprockets and renew any parts which are worn.
107 If a new pump is being fitted, it would be as well to renew all other parts at the same time.

Refitting
108 Refitting is a reversal of removal, but bear in mind the following points.
109 Use new gaskets on all components.
110 Oil all new parts liberally.
111 If the small plug in the front cover is at all damaged replace it.
112 Similarly, fit a new crankshaft oil seal to the cover. The old seal can be prised out and a new one pressed fully home.
113 The chain is tensioned by moving the pump housing against its mounting bolts.
114 With light finger pressure exerted on the chain, deflection should be as given in the Specifications.
115 Whenever the sump is removed with the engine *in situ,* the two hexagon screws in the sealing flange at the flywheel end should be replaced by socket-headed screws and spring washers, and tightened to the figure given in the Specifications.

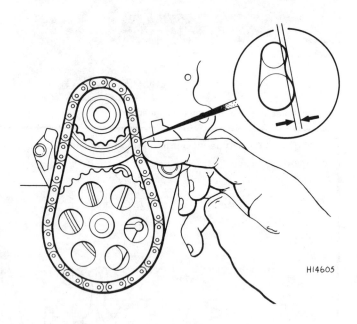

Fig. 12.6 Checking the oil pump drive chain tension (Sec 4)

Crankshaft sprocket – modification
116 As from August 1986 the crankshaft sprocket incorporates a lug for engagement with the groove in the crankshaft, and the Woodruff key has been discontinued.
117 When tightening the crankshaft sprocket bolt on the new sprocket observe the stages given in the Specifications.

5 Engine (1.6 and 1.8 litre)

Engine front mounting – modification

1 As from December 1984 the engine front mounting is changed from the bonded rubber type to a 'hydro' type with damping action. Refer to Fig. 12.7 – the tightening torques of the nuts and bolts with letters are given in the Specifications section of Chapter 1.

Camshaft and cylinder head – examination and renovation

2 On exchange engines or cylinder heads the camshaft is supplied with bearing shells instead of running directly in the head and bearing caps. Exchange units supplied by VW may have an undersized camshaft with corresponding bearing shells, and where this is the case the camshaft will have a yellow paint spot on it and the journal diameter will be 25.75 mm (1.014 in). An unmarked camshaft supplied with bearing shells will be of standard size with a journal diameter of 26.00 mm (1.024 in).

Hydraulic bucket tappets – description

3 All 1986-on engines are fitted with a redesigned cylinder head incorporating hydraulic bucket tappets in place of the previous shim bucket tappets. Camshaft bearing No. 4 is deleted on all single camshaft engines, and in order to identify the type of tappets fitted a sticker is normally affixed to the valve cover indicating that valve clearance adjustment is not necessary or possible.

4 All the relevant procedures given in Section 3 apply also to 1.6 and 1.8 litre engines. In particular note that the valves should not be re-cut as this will adversely affect the operation of the hydraulic tappets. Regrinding is permissible but if the valves are deeply pitted they should be renewed.

Sump – modification

5 As from August 1985 a larger sump is fitted and the oil capacity is increased as given in the Specifications.

Oil cooler – renewal

6 The oil cooler fitted to fuel injection engines should be renewed if the engine oil has been contaminated with metal particles following total or partial engine seizure. Renew it also if it is likely to contain any other harmful contaminant.

16-valve (16V) engine – general description

7 The 16-valve engine fitted to GTI models from October 1986 incorporates double overhead camshafts (DOHC), one operating the exhaust valves and the other the inlet valves, with four valves per cylinder. The valves operate in pairs simultaneously and provide the engine with a much improved breathing capability resulting in greater power output. A single camshaft sprocket is attached to the exhaust camshaft, and a chain and sprocket at the opposite end of the cylinder head is used to drive the inlet camshaft.

8 Apart from the obvious differences mentioned in paragraph 7, most work procedures for the 16-valve engine are basically the same as those for the 8-valve engine. The following paragraphs describe procedures which are different.

Timing belt (16V engine) – removal and refitting

9 Besides the timing mark on the camshaft sprocket shown in Chapter 1, Fig. 1.15, an additional timing mark is provided on the outside of the camshaft sprocket (Fig. 12.9) which aligns with a mark on the valve cover. This means that if the timing belt alone is being renewed it is not necessary to remove the valve cover in order to check the alignment marks.

10 When fitting the timing belt it is recommended that VW tool 210 is used to set the tension accurately as this is more critical with the double camshaft arrangement. Using this tool the tension should be set to record a reading of between 13 and 14 on the scale. The tool can be obtained from a VAG dealer.

Camshafts (16V engine) – removal and refitting

11 Remove the cover from the camshaft sprocket.

12 Unbolt and remove the upper section of the inlet manifold.

13 Unbolt and remove the valve cover after disconnecting the HT leads from the spark plugs. Remove the main gasket and the central gasket from around the spark plug locations.

14 Align the timing marks with reference to Chapter 1, then check also

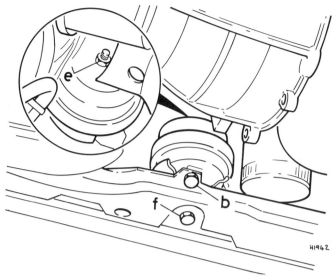

Fig. 12.7 'Hydro' type front engine mounting (Sec 5)

Refer to Chapter 1 for tightening torques

that the marks on the chain sprockets are aligned (Fig. 12.11).

15 Remove the timing belt and camshaft sprocket with reference to Chapter 1.

16 Note the fitted positions of the camshaft bearing caps, if necessary marking them to ensure correct refitment. Refer to Fig. 12.12.

17 Progressively unscrew the nuts and bolts from the end caps and bearing caps 1 and 3 on the exhaust camshaft.

18 Progressively unscrew the bolts from bearing caps 2 and 4; the exhaust valve springs will force the exhaust camshaft up as the bolts are loosened. Remove the bearing caps keeping them identified for position.

19 Working on the inlet camshaft, progressively unscrew the nuts and bolts from the end cap and bearing caps 5 and 7.

20 Progressively unscrew the bolts from bearing caps 6 and 8, then remove all the caps keeping them identified for position.

21 Lift both camshafts from the cylinder head, then release them from the drive chain.

22 If necessary remove the hydraulic bucket tappets with reference to paragraph 3 of this Section and the relevant paragraphs in Section 3. Check the camshafts and drive chain for wear referring also to Section 3.

23 Oil all the bucket tappets and the camshaft journals, then insert the tappets in their original locations.

24 Locate the drive chain on the camshaft sprockets so that the timing marks can be aligned as shown in Fig. 12.11, then lower the camshafts into position on the cylinder head. Recheck the timing mark alignment.

25 Fit a new oil seal to the front end of the exhaust camshaft.

26 When refitting the bearing caps make sure that they are located the correct way round. They are numbered as shown in Fig. 12.12 and the numbers must be readable from the inlet manifold side of the head. The recessed corners of the caps must also face the inlet manifold side of the head.

27 Refit bearing caps 6 and 8, then progressively tighten the bolts to the specified torque.

28 Refit the inlet camshaft end cap and bearing caps 5 and 7, then progressively tighten the nuts and bolts to the specified torque.

29 Refit bearing caps 2 and 4, then progressively tighten the bolts to the specified torque.

30 Refit the exhaust camshaft end caps and bearing caps 1 and 3, then progressively tighten the nuts and bolts to the specified torque.

31 Refit the camshaft sprocket and timing belt with reference to Chapter 1, and paragraphs 9 and 10 of this Section. Check that all the timing marks including the drive chain sprocket marks are aligned.

32 Refit the valve cover together with new gaskets and reconnect the spark plug HT leads.

33 Refit the inlet manifold upper section and the camshaft sprocket cover.

34 *If new hydraulic tappets have been fitted do not start the engine before 30 minutes have elapsed, otherwise the valves may strike the pistons.*

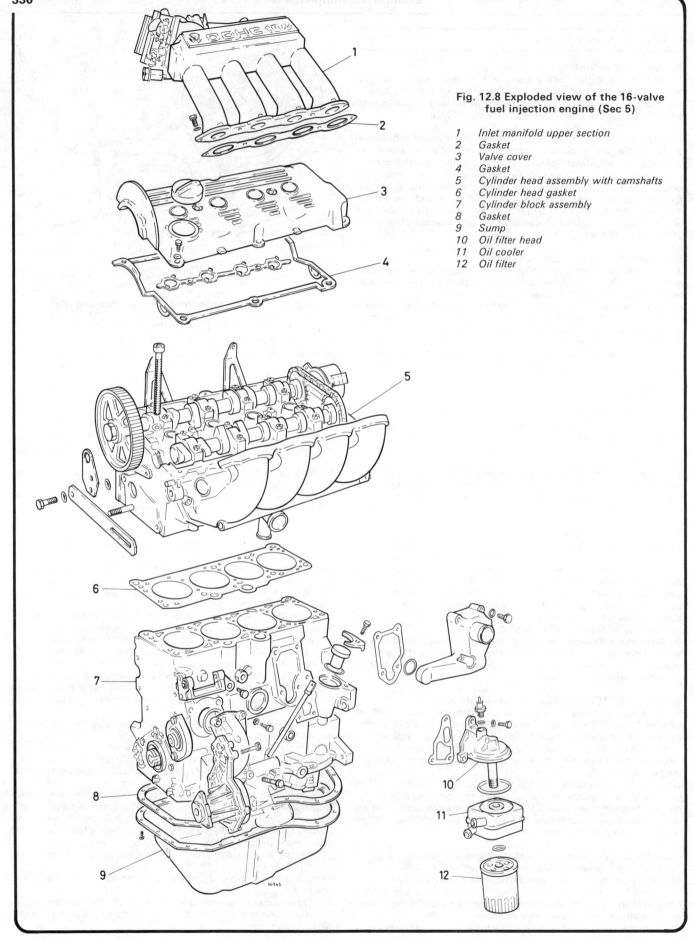

Fig. 12.8 Exploded view of the 16-valve fuel injection engine (Sec 5)

1   Inlet manifold upper section
2   Gasket
3   Valve cover
4   Gasket
5   Cylinder head assembly with camshafts
6   Cylinder head gasket
7   Cylinder block assembly
8   Gasket
9   Sump
10 Oil filter head
11 Oil cooler
12 Oil filter

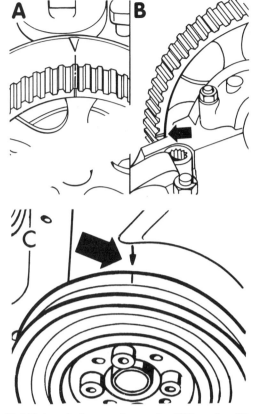

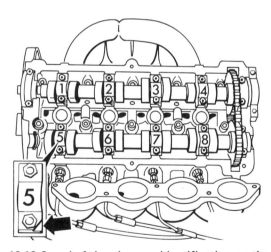

Fig. 12.9 Valve timing marks on the 16V engine (Sec 5)

A   Outer camshaft sprocket marks
B   Inner camshaft sprocket mark
C   Crankshaft vibration damper marks

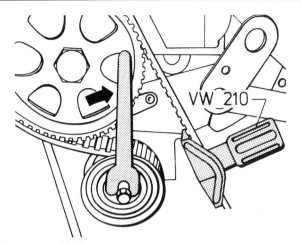

Fig. 12.10 Adjusting the timing belt tension using the special tool VW 210 (Sec 5)

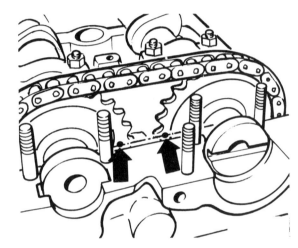

Fig. 12.11 TDC timing mark alignment on the camshaft drive chain sprockets (Sec 5)

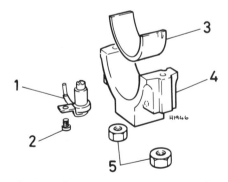

Fig. 12.12 Camshaft bearing cap identification on the 16V engine (Sec 5)

Insert shows recessed corner position

Fig. 12.13 Big-end cap components on the 16V engine (Sec 5)

1   Oil jet   4   Cap
2   Screw   5   Nuts
3   Bearing shell

Exhaust valves (16V engine) – description

35 Exhaust valves on the 16V engine are filled with sodium to provide improved heat dissipation, and special precautions are necessary when disposing of this type of valve, particularly where recycling of scrap metal is concerned.
36 To render the valve safe it should be wiped dry, then cut through the stem with a hacksaw. Throw the valve into a bucket of water keeping well away from it until the chemical reaction has subsided.

Big-end caps (16V engine) – description

37 The big-end caps on the 16V engine are fitted with oil jets which direct a stream of oil to the underside of the pistons mainly for cooling purposes.
38 The oil jets are secured to the caps by small screws which must be coated with thread locking fluid before inserting them and tightening them to the specified torque.

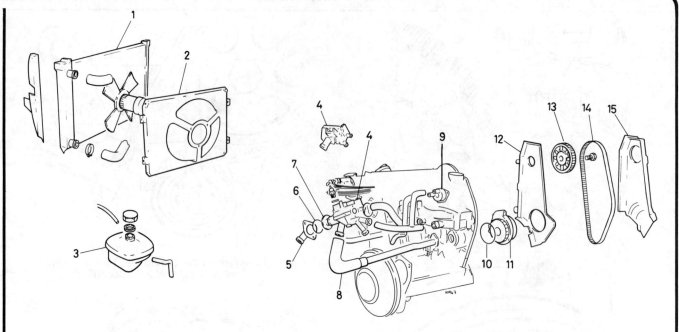

Fig. 12.14 Cooling system components for the 1.05 and 1.3 litre engines with bucket tappets (Sec 6)

1	Radiator	5	Cover	9	Automatic choke	13	Camshaft sprocket
2	Fan ring	6	O-ring	10	O-ring	14	Timing belt
3	Expansion tank	7	Thermostat	11	Water pump	15	Outer timing cover
4	Thermostat housing	8	Hose	12	Inner timing cover		

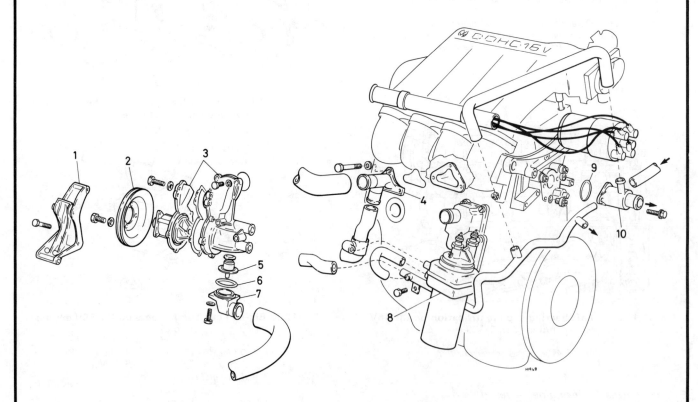

Fig. 12.15 Cooling system components for the 1.8 16V engine (Sec 6)

1	Alternator bracket	4	Outlet elbow	7	Cover	9	O-ring
2	Pulley	5	Thermostat	8	Oil cooler	10	Outlet elbow
3	Water pump assembly	6	O-ring				

6 Cooling system

Thermostat housing (1.05 and 1.3 litre engines) – modification

1 The carburettor on 1.05 and 1.3 litre bucket tappet engines incorporates a coolant-operated automatic choke, and the coolant supply and return hoses are routed from the thermostat housing. The modified components are shown in Fig. 12.14; however, the removal and refitting procedures remain basically as given in Chapter 2.

Water pump (1.05 and 1.3 litre engines) – removal and refitting

2 When fitting a water pump which has been reconditioned by VW a check should be made to see if the sealing ring groove has been reworked. If it has, the figure '5' will be stamped on the·pump mounting flange indicating that a 5 mm diameter sealing ring should be fitted instead of the normal 4 mm diameter ring.

Cooling fan and motor – removal and refitting

3 As from January 1986 the wiring on all new cooling fan motors obtained from VW incorporates a standardised connector. Where necessary, the old connector must be cut from the main harness and the standardised part fitted instead. The relevant parts are obtainable from a VW dealer.

Electric cooling fan (fuel injection engines) – modifications

4 As from September 1985, on fuel injection engines (except 16V) the cooling fan motor thermo-switch in the bottom of the radiator is of 3-pin type replacing the previous 2-pin type. The new switch has two operating temperature ranges (see Specifications) – the first range operates the cooling fan at normal speed and the second range operates the fan at boost speed.

5 The cooling fan fitted to 16V engines is of 6-blade type; however, on other engines it may be of 4 or 6-blade type.

6 As from March 1986 the electric cooling fan is also controlled by a temperature sensor located between the injectors for numbers 1 and 2 cylinders, in order to cool the injectors and injector pipes. A time relay is also incorporated in the wiring circuit to keep the system functional for up to ten to twelve minutes after switching off the ignition.

7 To prevent personal injury do not work near the cooling fan blades on a warm engine within the time relay operating period given in paragraph 6. Where possible disconnect the battery negative lead when working in this area of the engine.

Temperature sender (16V engine) – description

8 On the 16V engine the temperature sender is located on the flywheel end of the cylinder block below the outlet elbow. It controls the temperature gauge.

7 Fuel and exhaust systems

Carburettor (32 TLA and 1B3) – description

1 From March 1985, 1.05 litre engines are fitted with a Weber 32 TLA carburettor, although from July 1985 they may also be fitted with a Pierburg 1B3 carburettor. Since the 1.05 litre engine was discontinued in September 1985 parts for these carburettors may be hard to obtain.

Carburettor (32 TLA and 1B3) cleaning – general

2 Wash the exterior of the carburettor with a suitable solvent and allow to dry.

3 Dismantle the carburettor with reference to the relevant Figs. Before dismantling, obtain a set of gaskets. Be sure to mark the relationship of the automatic choke to the carburettor body before separating them.

4 Clean the internal components with a suitable solvent. **Do not** probe any jets or orifices with wire or similar to remove dirt; blow them through with an air line.

5 **Do not** alter or remove the full throttle stop, or adjust the Stage II throttle valve screw settings (if applicable).

6 Reassembly is a reversal of dismantling, but renew all gaskets and rubber rings. Refer to the following sub-sections for checks and adjustments.

Pierburg 1B3 carburettor – servicing and adjustment

7 Before undertaking any carburettor adjustments, be sure all jets, etc, are clean.

8 When inserting the accelerator pump piston seal, press it towards the opposite side of the vent drilling. The piston retaining ring must be pressed flush into the carburettor body.

General

9 All checks and adjustments are as described for the Pierburg 2E3 carburettor in Chapter 3, with the following additions.

Enrichment tube

10 With the choke valve closed, the bottom of the enrichment tube should be 1.0 mm (0.039 in) from the valve (see Fig. 12.18).

Idle speed and mixture

11 Before making any adjustment, make sure that the automatic choke is fully open, otherwise the throttle valve linkage may still be on the fast idle cam.

Idle speed boost valve

12 The idle speed adjustment screw incorporates a vacuum-operated valve which opens if the idle speed drops below 700 rpm in order to increase the idle speed. The valve is itself controlled by a two-way valve and further control unit. The control unit monitors the engine speed and activates the two-way valve which applies vacuum to the idle valve.

13 To test the system, run the engine at idling speed, then slowly reduce the engine speed by manually closing the choke valve. At 700 rpm there should be vacuum at the hose on the idle valve.

Fast idle speed

14 With the engine at normal operating temperature and switched off, connect a tachometer and remove the air cleaner.

15 Fully open the throttle valve, then turn the fast idle cam and release the throttle valve so that the adjustment screw is positioned on the second highest part of the cam.

16 Without touching the accelerator pedal, start the engine and check that the fast idling speed is as given in the Specifications. If not, turn the adjustment screw on the linkage as necessary. If a tamperproof cap is fitted renew it after making the adjustment.

Choke valve gap

17 With the engine cold, fully open the throttle valve, then turn the fast idle cam and release the throttle valve so that the adjustment screw is positioned on the highest part of the cam.

18 Press the choke operating rod as far as possible towards the pull-down unit.

19 Using the shank of a twist drill, check that the distance from the choke valve to the carburettor wall is as given in the Specifications. If not, adjust the screw behind the automatic choke.

Accelerator pump capacity

20 Hold the carburettor over a funnel and measuring glass.

21 Turn the fast idle cam so that the adjusting screw is off the cam. Hold the cam in this position during the following procedure.

22 Fully open the throttle ten times, allowing at least three seconds per stroke. Divide the total quantity by ten and check that the resultant injection capacity is as given in the Specifications. If not, refer to Fig. 12.21 and loosen the cross-head screw, turn the cam plate as required, and tighten the screw.

23 If difficulty is experienced in making the adjustment, check the pump seal and make sure that the return check valve and injection tube are clear.

Idle cut-off solenoid

24 When the ignition is switched on the solenoid should be heard to click, indicating that the idle circuit has been opened. If the solenoid is removed for testing, the plunger must first be depressed by 3.0 to 4.0 mm (0.118 to 0.158 in) before switching on the unit.

Weber 32 TLA carburettor – servicing and adjustment

25 Before undertaking any carburettor adjustments, be sure all jets, etc, are clean.

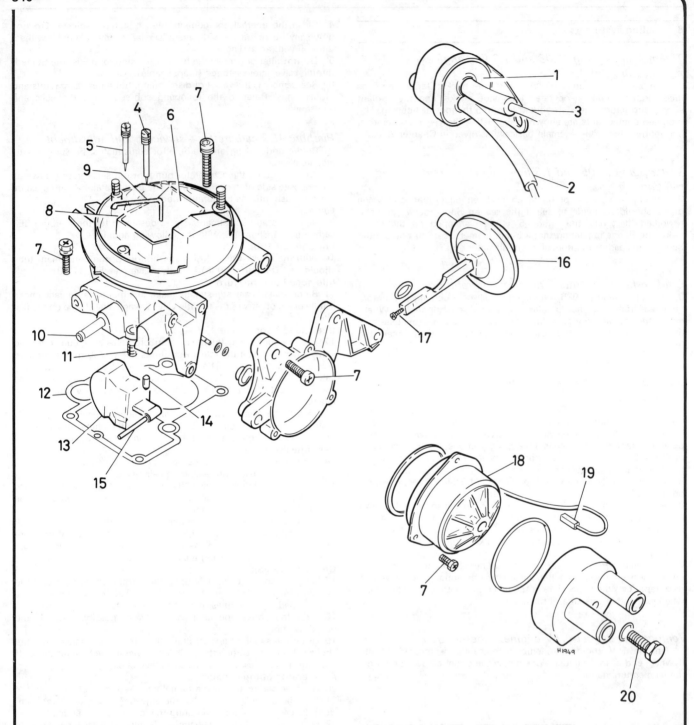

Fig. 12.16 Exploded view of the Pierburg 1B3 carburettor cover assembly (Sec 7)

1	Idle speed boost two-way valve	7	Screw	14	Needle valve
2	To idle adjustment screws	8	Cover	15	Pivot pin
3	To vacuum line and brake servo	9	Enrichment tube	16	Pull-down unit
4	Idling fuel/air jet	10	Fuel supply	17	Adjustment screw
5	Auxiliary fuel/air jet	11	Main jet	18	Automatic choke
6	Choke valve	12	Gasket	19	Wiring connector
		13	Float	20	Screw

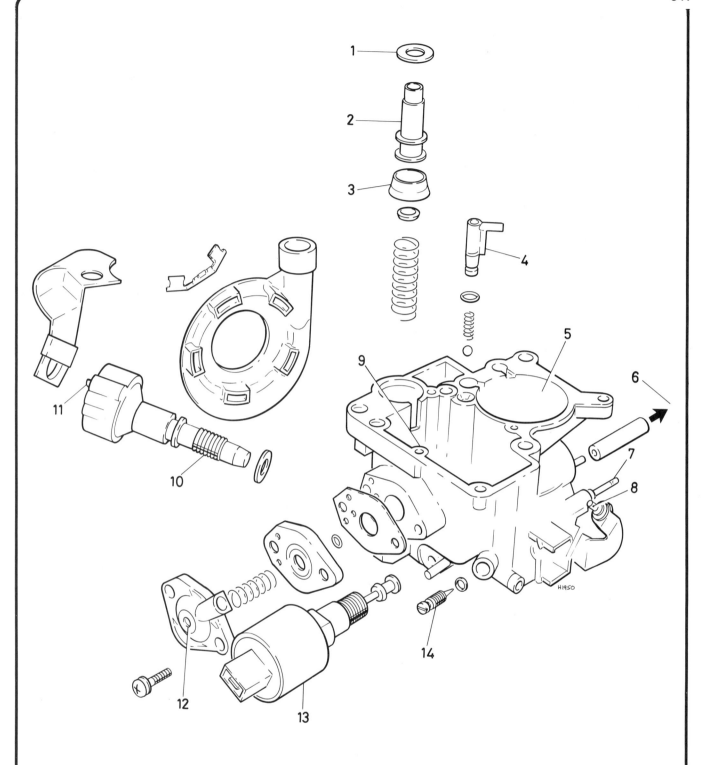

Fig. 12.17 Exploded view of the Pierburg 1B3 carburettor main body assembly (Sec 7)

1	Bearing ring	7	To air cleaner vacuum control	11	To two-way valve
2	Pump plunger	8	Fast idle adjustment screw	12	Part throttle enrichment valve
3	Seal	9	Part throttle enrichment jet	13	Idle cut-off solenoid
4	Injection tube	10	Idle speed adjustment screw	14	Mixture adjustment screw
5	Main body				
6	To pull-down unit				

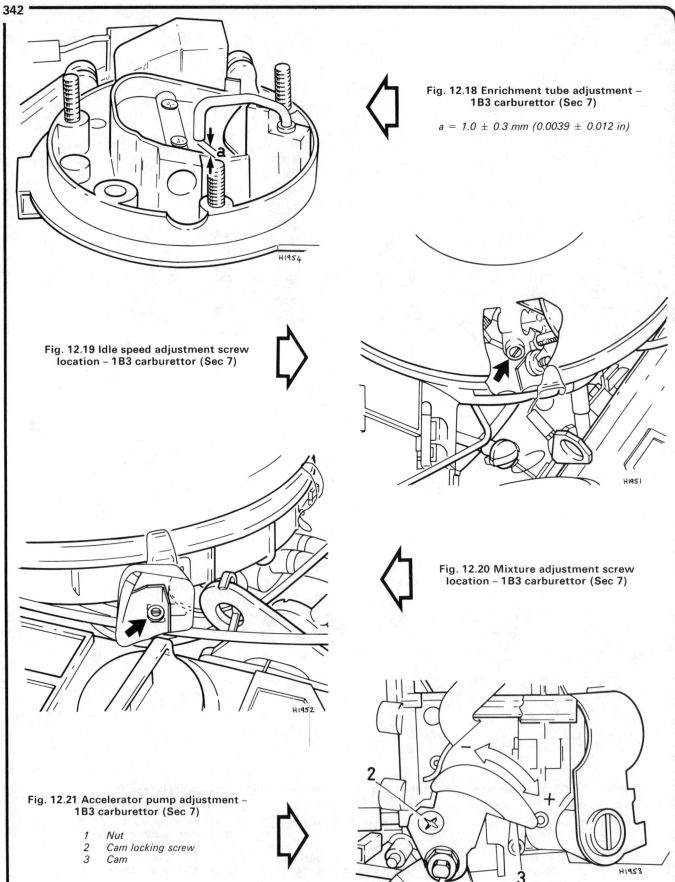

Fig. 12.18 Enrichment tube adjustment –
1B3 carburettor (Sec 7)

$a = 1.0 \pm 0.3\ mm\ (0.0039 \pm 0.012\ in)$

Fig. 12.19 Idle speed adjustment screw
location – 1B3 carburettor (Sec 7)

Fig. 12.20 Mixture adjustment screw
location – 1B3 carburettor (Sec 7)

Fig. 12.21 Accelerator pump adjustment –
1B3 carburettor (Sec 7)

1 Nut
2 Cam locking screw
3 Cam

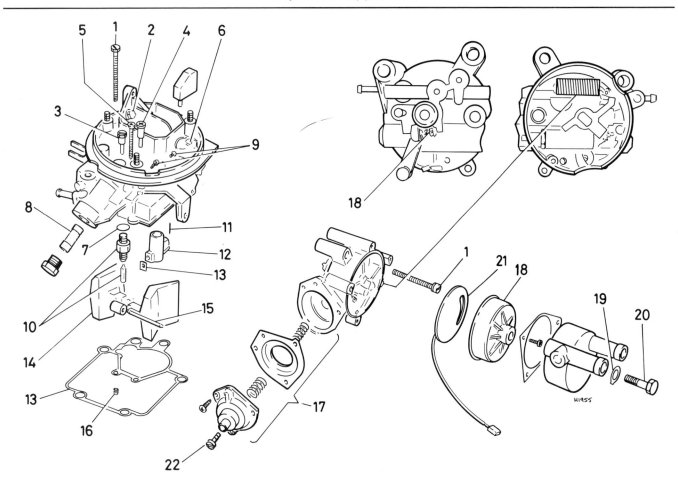

Fig. 12.22 Exploded view of the Weber 32 TLA carburettor cover assembly (Sec 7)

1	Screw	8	Gauze filter	16	Main jet
2	Air correction jet	9	Plugs	17	Pull-down unit
3	Auxiliary fuel jet (if applicable)	10	Needle valve	18	Automatic choke
4	Idling fuel jet	11	Pin	19	Sealing ring
5	Emulsion tube	12	Atomizer	20	Screw
6	Choke valve and lever	13	Gasket	21	Heater plate
7	Washer	14	Float	22	Adjusting screw
		15	Pin		

Float level

26 With the upper part of the carburettor inverted and held at an angle of approximately 45°, the measurement 'a' in Fig. 12.24 should be as shown. The ball of the float needle should not be pressed in against the spring when making the measurement.

Idle speed and mixture

27 The procedure for checking and adjusting the idling speed and CO content are basically the same as given in Chapter 3, Section 17. However, refer to Figs 12.25, 12.26 and 12.27 for the location of adjustment screws and to the Specifications in this Supplement for settings.

Idle speed boost valve

28 The idle speed boost valve is identical to the unit on the Pierburg 1B3 carburettor described in paragraphs 12 and 13.

Choke valve gap (pull-down)

29 Remove the choke cover.

30 Place the cold idling speed adjusting screw on the highest step of the cam (Fig. 12.28). The manufacturer's original instruction was to press the pullrod in the direction of the arrow in Fig. 12.28, then to check that the choke flap gap is 2.5 ± 0.2 mm. As from April 1987 however, this instruction is revised and it is now necessary to use a vacuum pump to apply 300 mbar vacuum on the pull-down unit. The choke flap gap in this case must be 2.0 ± 0.2 mm.

31 Adjustment is made on the screw at the end of the pulldown device. Ensure that the spring (2 in Fig. 12.29) is not compressed when making the check.

Idle cut-off valve

32 To check the cut-off valve, apply battery voltage. The valve must be heard to click when voltage is applied.

Fast idle speed

33 Before carrying out this check, ensure that ignition timing and manual idling adjustments are correct. The engine should be at normal operating temperature.

34 Remove the air cleaner.

35 Plug the temperature regulator connection.

36 Connect up a rev counter.

37 Remove the choke cover and set the fast idle speed adjusting screw on the second highest step on the cam (Fig. 12.30).

38 Tension the operating lever with a rubber band so that the choke flap is fully open.

39 Without touching the accelerator pedal, start the engine, which should run at the fast idle speed given in the Specifications.

40 Adjust on the screw as necessary.

Choke valve gap (wide open kick)

41 Remove the air cleaner.

42 Fully open the throttle and hold it in this position.

43 Refer to Fig. 12.31 and press the lever (1) upwards.

44 Check the gap with a twist drill which should be as given in the Specifications. Adjust by bending the lever (Fig. 12.32).

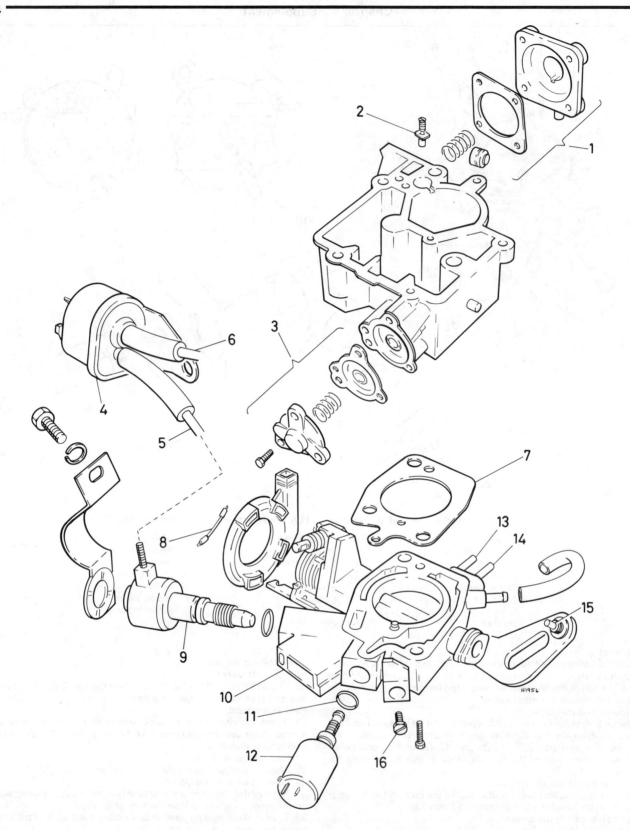

Fig. 12.23 Exploded view of the Weber 32 TLA carburettor main body assembly (Sec 7)

1	Accelerator pump	5	To idle adjusting screw	9	Idle speed adjustment screw	13	To air cleaner
2	Injection pipe	6	To vacuum line and brake servo	10	Throttle housing	14	To distributor
3	Part throttle enrichment valve	7	Gasket	11	Sealing ring	15	Fast idle adjustment screw
4	Idle speed boost two-way valve	8	Clip	12	Idle cut-off solenoid	16	Mixture adjustment screw

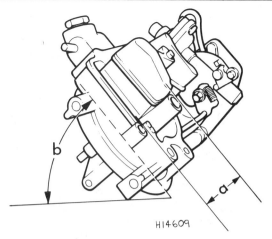

Fig. 12.24 Checking float level – 32 TLA carburettor
(Sec 7)

$a = 28 \pm 1.0\ mm$ $\qquad$ $b = 45°$

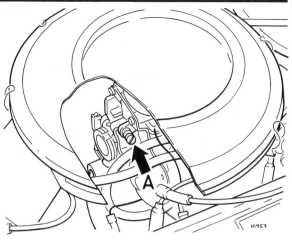

Fig. 12.25 Idle speed adjusting screw (A) for models up
to June 1985 –
32 TLA carburettor (Sec 7)

Fig. 12.26 Idle speed adjusting screw (A) for models
from July 1985 onwards –
32 TLA carburettor (Sec 7)

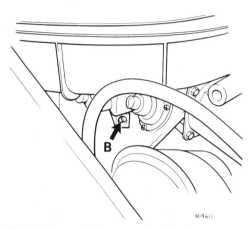

Fig. 12.27 Mixture (CO content) adjusting screw (B) –
32 TLA carburettor (Sec 7)

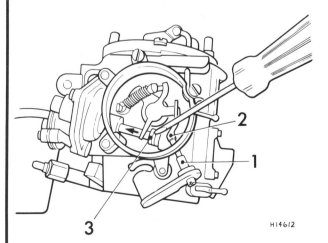

Fig. 12.28 Choke valve gap adjustment – 32 TLA
carburettor (Sec 7)

1   Fast idle adjusting screw
2   Cam
3   Pullrod

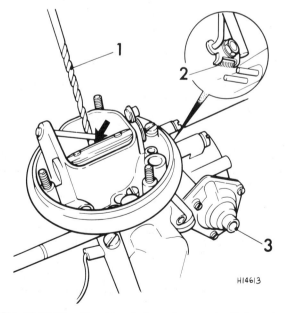

Fig. 12.29 Checking the choke valve gap (pull down) –
32 TLA carburettor (Sec 7)

1   Twist drill   3   Adjusting screw
2   Spring

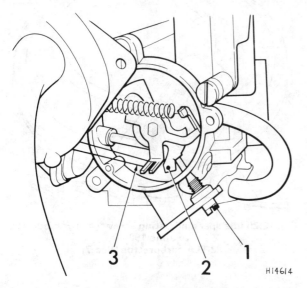

Fig. 12.30 Fast idle speed adjustment – 32 TLA carburettor
(Sec 7)

1   Fast idle adjusting screw   2   Cam
                                     3   Rubber band

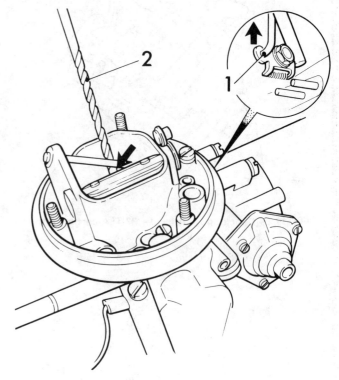

Fig. 12.31 Checking the choke valve gap (wide open kick) –
32 TLA carburettor (Sec 7)

1   Press upwards   2   Twist drill

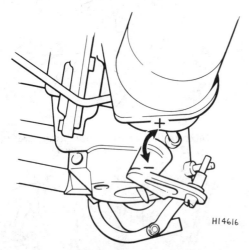

Fig. 12.32 Adjusting the choke valve gap (wide open kick) –
32 TLA carburettor (Sec 7)

Bend the lever as required

Accelerator pump capacity

45 This can be checked by following the procedure in chapter 3,
Section 16 with the following differences.
46 Open the throttle valve quickly when operating the pump (ie 1
second per stroke, with pauses of 3 seconds between strokes).
47 The amount of fuel injected can be altered, but only very slightly, as
follows:
48 Take the accelerator cable cam off the throttle valve lever.
49 Secure the cam for the accelerator pump with an M4 screw (Fig.
12.33).
50 Loosen the locknut on the cam securing screw. Loosen the screw
and turn the cam with a screwdriver – clockwise to decrease injected
fuel and anti-clockwise to increase injected fuel. Tighten the screw
and locknut and recheck the injection capacity.

Carburettor (2E2) – choke gap (wide open kick) adjustment

51 Remove the automatic choke cover and fit a rubber band to the
operating pin, so that the choke valve is held in the closed position.
52 Hold the primary throttle valve open 45°. To do this, temporarily

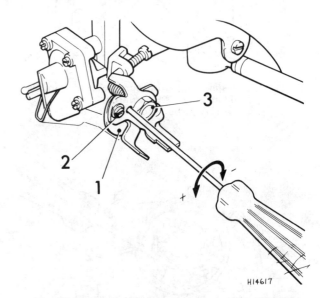

Fig. 12.33 Accelerator pump adjustment – 32 TLA
carburettor (Sec 7)

1   Cam   3   Cam locking nut
2   M4 screw securing cam

insert a 10 mm nut between the fast idling adjustment screw and the
vacuum unit plunger.
53 Using a twist drill, check that the gap between the choke valve and
carburettor wall is 6.3 + 0.3 mm (0.248 + 0.012 in). If not, bend the
choke operating lever as required.

54 After making an adjustment, check and adjust the choke pull-down unit as described in Chapter 3.

Carburettor (2E2) choke pull-down unit – modification

55 As of February 1987, the choke pull-down unit is both temperature and time-controlled by a thermotime valve. When the valve is open (starting a cold engine) the vacuum to the pull-down unit is reduced, and the choke valve will open by a small amount. After between 1 and 6 seconds (depending on ambient temperature), the valve heats up (to approximately 20 to 30°C) and closes. This allows more vacuum to reach the pull-down unit, and the choke valve will open by a larger amount. The choke is of course fully released by the heat of the engine coolant and the electric heater acting on the automatic choke bi-metallic spring.

Carburettor (2E2) three/four point unit – checking

56 The method described in Chapter 3, Section 20 requires the use of a vacuum pump, whereas the following method uses engine vacuum.
57 Run the engine to normal operating temperature then switch it off, remove the air cleaner, and close the vacuum line from the carburettor to the temperature regulator.
58 With the engine stopped, check that the diaphragm rod (A in Fig. 3.27) is fully extended to approximately 14.5 mm (0.571 in).
59 Start the engine and let it idle. The diaphragm rod must now be extended approximately 8.5 mm (0.335 in) for the three-point unit, or 9.5 mm (0.374 in) for the four-point unit, and must just contact the fast idling adjustment screw.
60 On models with air conditioning, switch on the air conditioner with the blower on maximum speed. The diaphragm rod dimension should be approximately 12.0 mm (0.472 in).
61 To check the overrun cut-off point, run the engine at idle speed.
62 On the four-point unit, disconnect and plug the pink-coloured hose at the control valve.
63 Using a screwdriver, hold the primary throttle valve fully closed to prevent it moving to the overrun cut-off point.
64 Disconnect the plug from the idling/overrun control valve, then check that the diaphragm rod dimension is approximately 1.5 mm (0.059 in).
65 To check the unit for leaks, first, on the three-point unit only, pinch the hose between the unit and Y-piece.
66 Stop the engine by disconnecting the coil terminal 15, and check that the diaphragm rod remains in the overrun/cut-off position for a minimum of 5 seconds.
67 Reconnect the coil wiring, control valve plug and hose where applicable, and refit the air cleaner.

K-Jetronic fuel injection system (except PB and 16V engines) – modifications

68 As from September 1984, the components associated with the inlet manifold were modified as shown in Fig. 12.34. All work procedures remain as described in Chapter 3, Part B.
69 As from March 1986, a temperature sensor is located between injectors 1 and 2. This switches on the electric cooling fan when the temperature of the cylinder head exceeds 110°C (230°F) after switching off the ignition. A time relay is incorporated in the circuit, to switch off the function between 10 and 12 minutes after switching off the ignition.

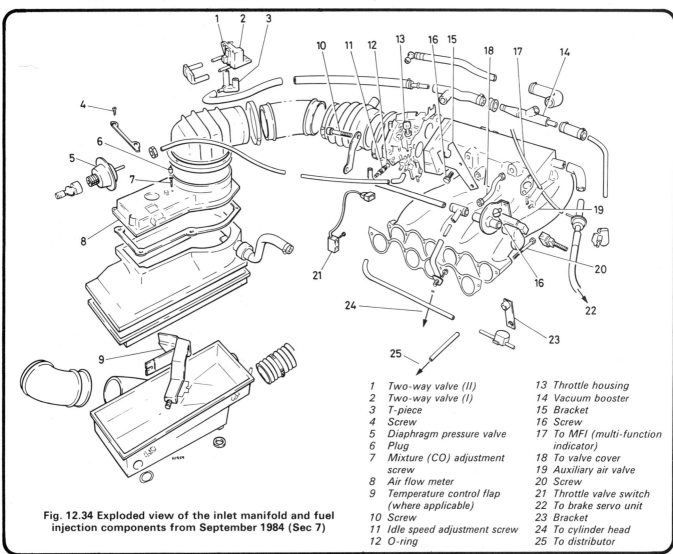

Fig. 12.34 Exploded view of the inlet manifold and fuel injection components from September 1984 (Sec 7)

1 Two-way valve (II)	13 Throttle housing
2 Two-way valve (I)	14 Vacuum booster
3 T-piece	15 Bracket
4 Screw	16 Screw
5 Diaphragm pressure valve	17 To MFI (multi-function indicator)
6 Plug	18 To valve cover
7 Mixture (CO) adjustment screw	19 Auxiliary air valve
8 Air flow meter	20 Screw
9 Temperature control flap (where applicable)	21 Throttle valve switch
10 Screw	22 To brake servo unit
11 Idle speed adjustment screw	23 Bracket
12 O-ring	24 To cylinder head
	25 To distributor

Digifant fuel injection system (1.8 engine, code PB) – description and precautions

70 The Digifant fuel injection system is a fully electronic and computerised version of the K-Jetronic system described in Chapter 3.

71 The main components include a computerised control unit, electronic injectors and various sensors to monitor engine temperature and speed, induction air flow and throttle position. The control unit determines the opening period of the injectors, and also continuously adjusts the ignition timing according to engine speed, load and temperature.

72 When working on the system, take extra care to prevent dust and dirt entering the various components. It is recommended not to use compressed air or fluffy cloths for cleaning purposes.

73 Switch off the ignition before disconnecting any relevant wiring or when washing the engine.

74 Boost-charging the battery is only permissible for 1 minute at 16.5 volts maximum.

75 Disconnect both battery leads before carrying out any electric welding.

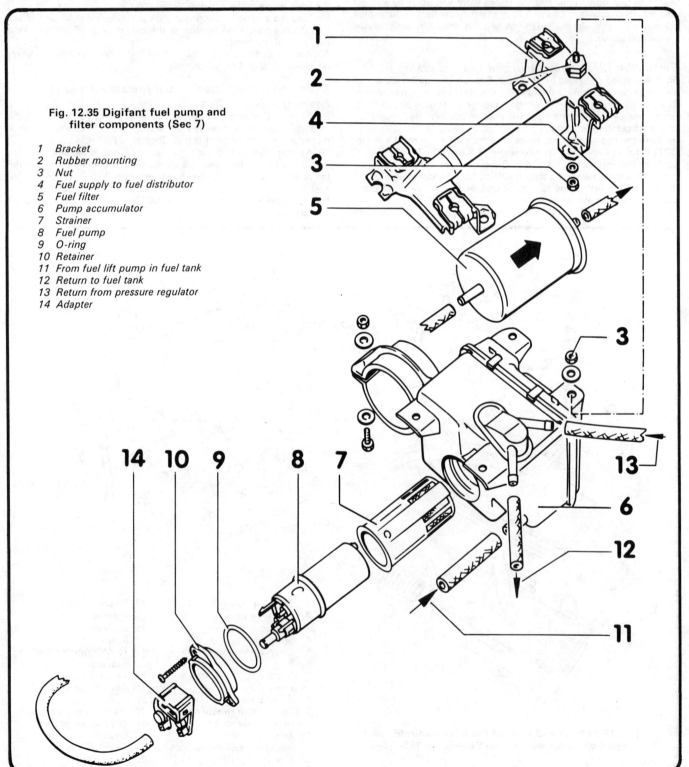

Fig. 12.35 Digifant fuel pump and filter components (Sec 7)

1   Bracket
2   Rubber mounting
3   Nut
4   Fuel supply to fuel distributor
5   Fuel filter
6   Pump accumulator
7   Strainer
8   Fuel pump
9   O-ring
10 Retainer
11 From fuel lift pump in fuel tank
12 Return to fuel tank
13 Return from pressure regulator
14 Adapter

Digifant fuel injection system (1.8 engine, code PB) – checks and adjustments

76 The following paragraphs describe checking and adjustment procedures for the fuel injection system. Information applicable to the ignition system is given in Section 8 of this Supplement.

Fuel pumps – checking

77 The main fuel pump is located in the accumulator housing beneath the rear of the car, and an additional lift pump is located in the fuel tank, together with the fuel gauge sender.

78 With the engine stopped, have an assistant switch on the ignition.

It should be possible to hear both pumps running for a short period. If not, check fuse 5 for continuity, and also check all wiring connections.

79 With the ignition on, disconnect each wire connector from the pumps and check that there is a 12 volt supply using a voltmeter.

80 Should there be no voltage at the pumps with the ignition switched on, the fuel pump relay (No 2 on fusebox) may be faulty. This is best checked by substituting a new relay.

Air flow meter – checking

81 Refer to Fig. 12.36 and disconnect the wiring plug from the airflow meter.

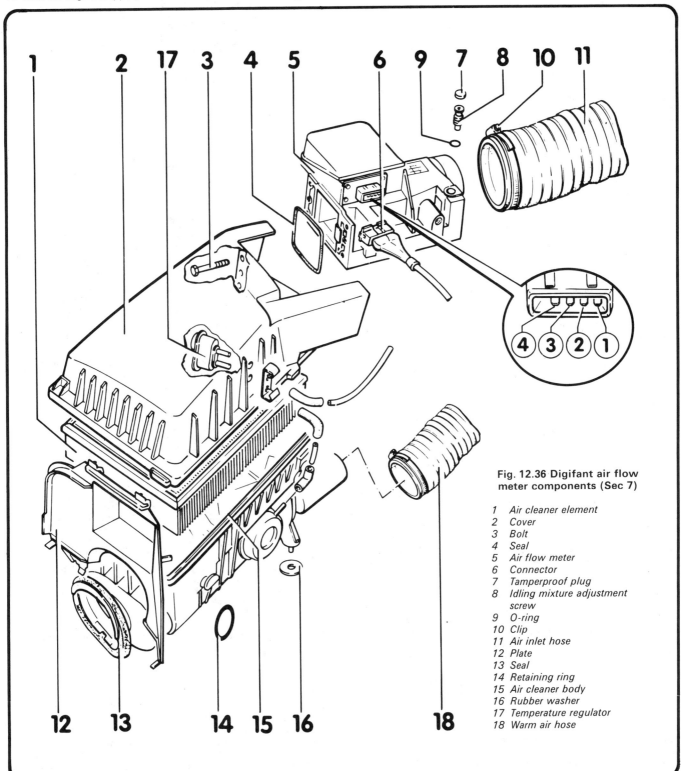

Fig. 12.36 Digifant air flow meter components (Sec 7)

1 Air cleaner element
2 Cover
3 Bolt
4 Seal
5 Air flow meter
6 Connector
7 Tamperproof plug
8 Idling mixture adjustment screw
9 O-ring
10 Clip
11 Air inlet hose
12 Plate
13 Seal
14 Retaining ring
15 Air cleaner body
16 Rubber washer
17 Temperature regulator
18 Warm air hose

82 Connect an ohmmeter between terminals 1 and 4 and check that the resistance of the intake air temperature sender is as shown in Fig. 12.37, according to the ambient air temperature.

83 Connect the ohmmeter between terminals 3 and 4 and check that the resistance of the potentiometer is between 0.5 k and 1.0 k ohms.

84 Connect the ohmmeter between terminals 2 and 3, and check that the resistance fluctuates as the air flow meter plate is moved.

Idle speed and mixture adjustment

85 Run the engine until the oil temperature is at least 80°C (176°F) – this should correspond to normal operating temperature.

86 Switch off all electrical components, including the air conditioner where fitted. Note that the radiator fan must also be stationary during the adjustment procedure.

87 For accurate adjustment, the throttle valve switch and idling stabilisation control valve must be functioning correctly, and the ignition timing must be correct.

88 With the engine stopped, connect a tachometer to the engine. Plug one of the exhaust tail pipes, and position the probe of an exhaust gas analyser in the remaining tail pipe.

89 Disconnect the crankcase ventilation hose from the pressure regulating valve on the valve cover, and plug the hose.

90 Run the engine at idle speed, then, after approximately 1 minute, disconnect the wire from the temperature sender (Fig. 12.38), and quickly increase the engine speed to 3000 rpm three times.

91 With the engine idling, check the idle speed and CO content. If necessary, adjust the screws shown in Fig. 12.39. The CO adjustment screw is fitted with a tamperproof plug at the factory, and should be prised out before making an adjustment.

92 Reconnect the temperature sender wire, and again quickly increase the engine speed to 3000 rpm three times. With the engine idling, the idle speed and CO content should be as specified, but if necessary make any small corrections required.

93 Fit a new tamperproof plug.

94 Reconnect the crankcase ventilation hose. Note that if this increases the CO content, do not alter the adjustment. The cause is fuel dilution of the engine oil due to frequent stop/start use, and a long fast drive should reduce the CO content to the correct level again. Alternatively, an oil change will achieve the same objective.

Automatic air cleaner temperature control – checking

95 Disconnect the hose from the vacuum unit, then remove the air cleaner cover and element.

96 Check that the flap in the lower body is closing the warm air inlet.

97 Suck on the vacuum hose, and check that the flap moves freely to close the cold air inlet.

98 The flap operation may be checked with the engine idling by extending the vacuum hose and positioning a thermometer by the temperature regulator. Below 20°C (68°F) the cold air inlet must be closed, above 30°C (86°F) the warm air inlet must be closed, and between 20 and 30°C (68 and 86°F), the flap should be positioned midway so that both inlets are open.

99 Refit the air cleaner element and cover, and reconnect the hose.

Throttle valve switches – checking and adjusting

100 There are two throttle valve switches. Switch 1 monitors the throttle valve closed position, and switch 2 monitors the throttle valve fully open position.

101 Disconnect the supply plug from switch 2 and check that approximately 5 volts is available across the two terminals with the ignition switched on. If not check the wiring from the control unit.

102 Connect an ohmmeter across the terminals of switch 2, then slowly open the throttle valve until the switch points close. The gap at the throttle lever stop must be 0.20 to 0.60 mm (0.008 to 0.024 in) when the points close. If necessary adjust the position of switch 1.

103 A piece of card marked with 10° is required to check switch 2. Attach the card to the first stage throttle valve shaft.

104 Fully open the throttle and align a datum with 0° on the card. Close the throttle by approximately 20°, then slowly open it until switch 2 points close. This should occur at 10° ± 2° before full throttle. If necessary adjust the position of switch 2. Note that the throttle valve lever roller must contact the sloping part of switch 2.

Throttle stop – adjustment

105 The throttle stop adjustment is initially set at the factory, and should not be tampered with. However if it is accidentally loosened, proceed as follows.

106 Back off the adjustment screw until a gap exists between the carrier lever and stop lever (Fig. 12.41).

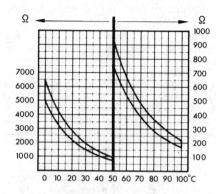

Fig. 12.37 Digifant intake air temperature sender resistance graph (Sec 7)

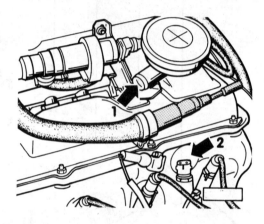

Fig. 12.38 Digifant crankcase ventilation pressure regulating valve (1) and temperature sender (2) (Sec 7)

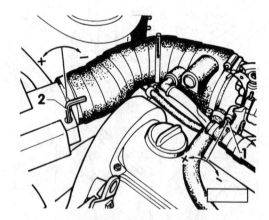

Fig. 12.39 Digifant idle speed adjusting screw (1) and CO adjusting screw (2) (Sec 7)

107 Turn the adjustment screw until the two levers just make contact, then continue to turn it a further half-turn. Tighten the locknut.

108 After making an adjustment, readjust the throttle valve switches, and the idle speed and mixture.

Idling speed stabilization system – checking

109 Check that the stabilization control valve buzzes when the ignition is switched on. If not, use an ohmmeter to check the valve continuity after pulling off the connector (Fig. 12.42).

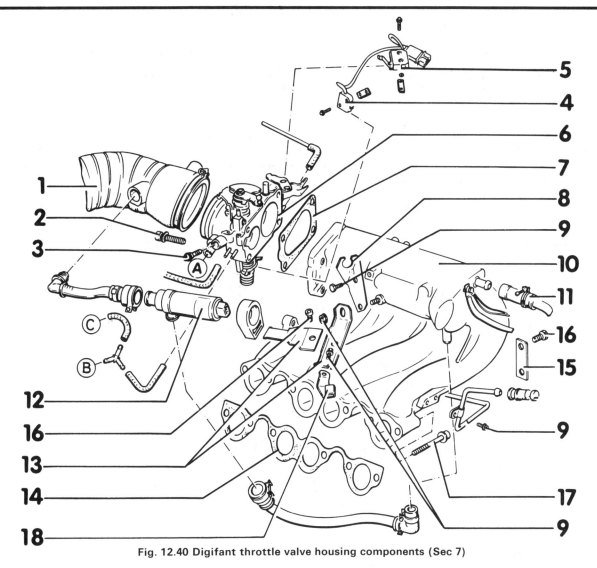

Fig. 12.40 Digifant throttle valve housing components (Sec 7)

A From crankcase ventilation valve
B Vacuum hose connection from fuel pressure regulator
C Vacuum hose from air cleaner temperature regulator
1 Air inlet hose
2 Bolt
3 Idling speed adjustment screw

4 Throttle valve switch 1
5 Throttle valve switch 2
6 Throttle valve housing
7 Gasket
8 Bracket
9 Bolt
10 Inlet manifold
11 Vacuum hose to brake servo unit

12 Idling speed stabilization control valve
13 Support
14 Gasket
15 Support
16 Bolt
17 Bolt
18 Bracket

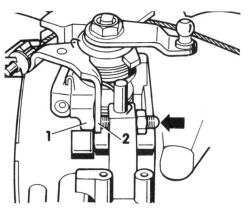

Fig. 12.41 Digifant throttle stop adjustment (Sec 7)

1 Carrier lever   2 Stop lever
Arrow indicates adjustment screw

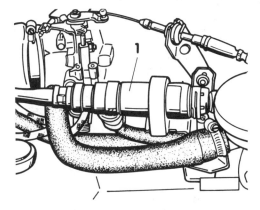

Fig. 12.42 Digifant idling speed stabilization control valve (1) (Sec 7)

110 Run the engine until the oil temperature is at least 80°C (176°F).
111 Connect a multi-meter to the stabilization control valve in series with the existing wiring.
112 Run the engine at idle speed, then, after approximately 1 minute, quickly increase the engine speed to 3000 rpm three times. At idling speed, the control current should be approximately 420 ± 30 mA and *fluctuating*. With the temperature sender plug disconnected, the current should be approximately 420 ± 30 mA but *constant*. All electrical components must be switched off during the check, and power steering (where fitted) centralised.

Fuel pressure regulator – checking
113 An accurate pressure gauge and adapter is required for the work, and as these will not normally be available to the home mechanic, it is recommended that a VW garage carry out the check.
Fuel injectors – checking
114 Refer to Chapter 3, Section 37, paragraphs 1 to 3, but in addition, carry out the following electrical tests.
115 Disconnect the wiring plug from the conduit next to the injectors, and connect an ohmmeter across the terminals on the conduit. The resistance of all four injectors should be 3.7 to 5.0 ohms. If one injector

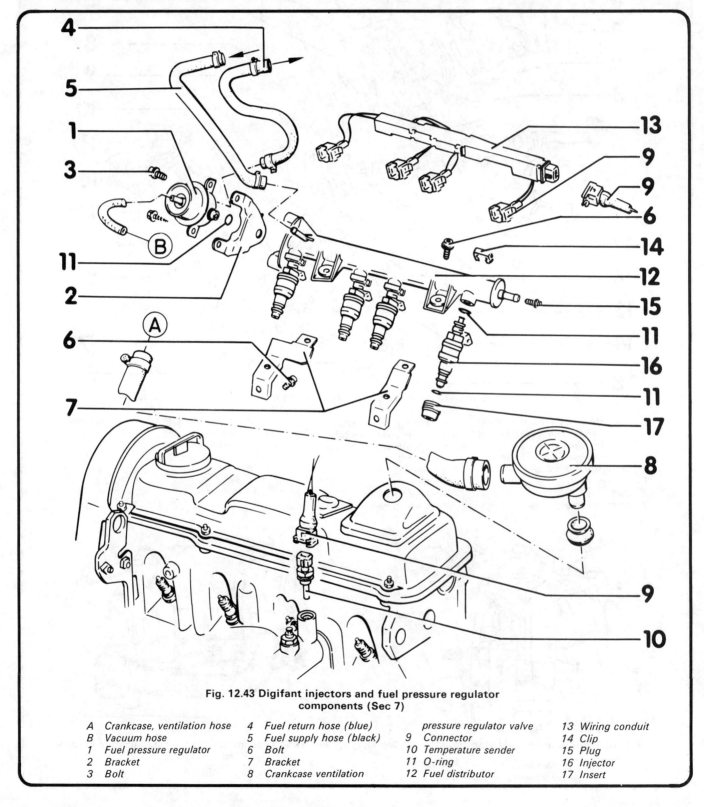

Fig. 12.43 Digifant injectors and fuel pressure regulator components (Sec 7)

A Crankcase, ventilation hose	4 Fuel return hose (blue)	*pressure regulator valve*
B Vacuum hose	5 Fuel supply hose (black)	9 Connector
1 Fuel pressure regulator	6 Bolt	10 Temperature sender
2 Bracket	7 Bracket	11 O-ring
3 Bolt	8 Crankcase ventilation	12 Fuel distributor

13 Wiring conduit
14 Clip
15 Plug
16 Injector
17 Insert

is open-circuit, the resistance will be 5.0 to 6.7 ohms, two injectors open-circuit 7.5 to 10.0 ohms, or three injectors open-circuit 15.0 to 20.0 ohms. If necessary, prise off the conduit and check that each individual injector has a resistance of 15.0 to 20.0 ohms.

116 Checking the injector spray patterns cannot be performed as described in Chapter 3, due to the position of the fuel distributor. However, the injectors may be removed together with the fuel distributor and wiring conduit, and the engine turned on the starter for a few seconds. Use a suitable container to catch the fuel.

Control unit – general

117 The control unit is located on the left-hand side of the bulkhead. The ignition must always be switched off before disconnecting the plug.

118 It is not possible to check the control unit without using the VW test appliances, so if a fault is suspected, it should be taken to a VW garage.

Overrun cut-off and full throttle enrichment – checking

119 Run the engine until the oil temperature is at least 80°C (176°F) – normal operating temperature – then let the engine idle.

120 Manually close the full throttle switch (No 2) and hold it closed. Open the throttle until the engine speed is approximately 2000 rpm, and check that the engine speed surges, indicating that the overrun cut-off is functioning.

121 If the engine does not surge, disconnect the wiring from the temperature sender and connect a bridging wire between the two contacts on the plug.

122 Repeat the procedure in paragraph 116. If the engine now surges, the temperature sender is proved faulty. However, if it still refuses to surge, check the associated wiring and throttle valve switch 2. If no fault is found, renew the control unit.

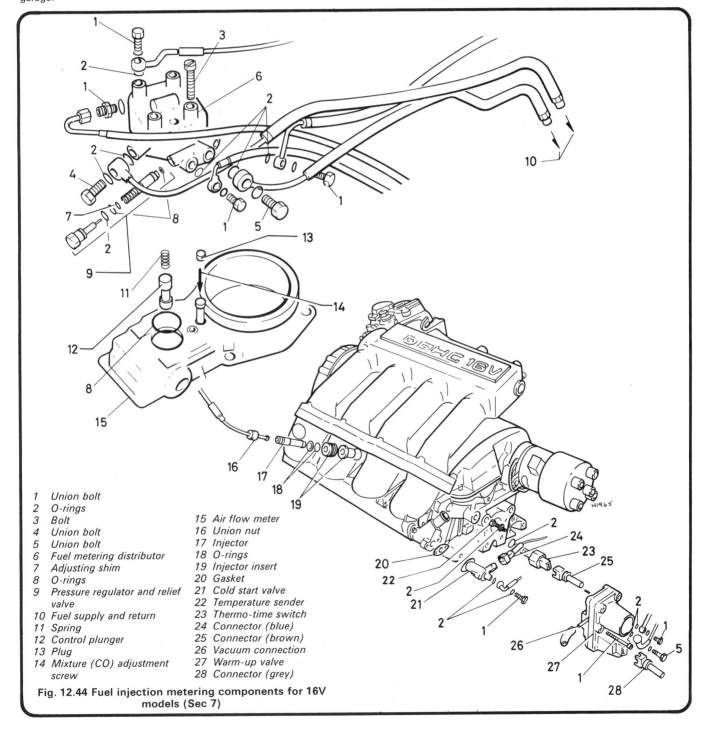

1 Union bolt
2 O-rings
3 Bolt
4 Union bolt
5 Union bolt
6 Fuel metering distributor
7 Adjusting shim
8 O-rings
9 Pressure regulator and relief valve
10 Fuel supply and return
11 Spring
12 Control plunger
13 Plug
14 Mixture (CO) adjustment screw
15 Air flow meter
16 Union nut
17 Injector
18 O-rings
19 Injector insert
20 Gasket
21 Cold start valve
22 Temperature sender
23 Thermo-time switch
24 Connector (blue)
25 Connector (brown)
26 Vacuum connection
27 Warm-up valve
28 Connector (grey)

Fig. 12.44 Fuel injection metering components for 16V models (Sec 7)

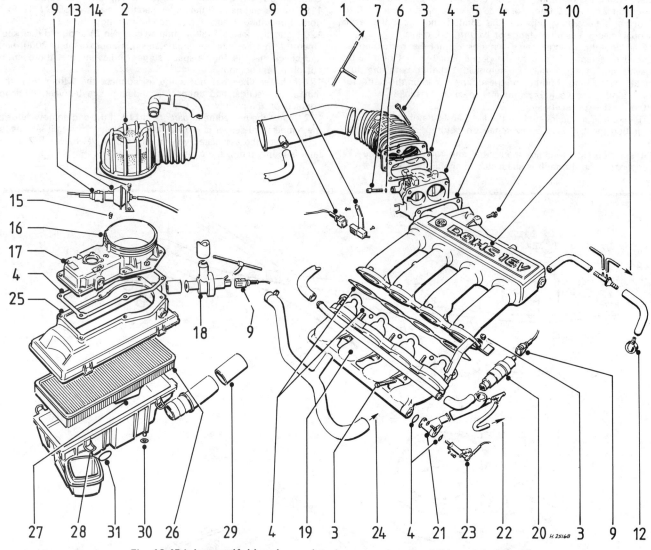

Fig. 12.45 Inlet manifold and associated components for 16V models (Sec 7)

1 To ignition control unit	10 Upper section of inlet manifold	16 Mixture (CO) adjustment screw
2 Intake elbow	11 To MFI (multi-function indicator)	17 Air flow meter
3 Screw	12 To brake servo unit	18 Overrun cut-off valve
4 Gaskets	13 Diaphragm pressure valve	19 Lower section of inlet manifold
5 Throttle valve housing	14 Screw	20 Idle stabilization control valve
6 O-ring	15 Plug	21 Elbow
7 Idle speed adjustment screw		22 To warm-up valve
8 Throttle valve switch		23 Cold start valve
9 Connector		24 To crankcase breather
		25 Upper air cleaner
		26 Air cleaner element
		27 Temperature control flap
		28 Lower air cleaner
		29 Warm air hose
		30 Washer
		31 Retaining ring

K-Jetronic fuel injection system (16V engine) – checks and adjustments

123 The fuel injection components for the 16V engine are shown in Figs. 12.44 and 12.45. Procedures are the same as described in Chapter 3, Part B except as given in the following paragraphs.

Idle speed (16V) – adjustment

124 Run the engine to normal operating temperature, then check that all electrical components are switched off. Note that the electric cooling fan must not be running during the adjustment procedure.
125 Disconnect the crankcase ventilation hose (Fig. 12.46).
126 Connect a tachometer and an exhaust gas analyser to the engine.
127 If the injector pipes have been removed and refitted just prior to making the adjustment, run the engine to 3000 rpm several times, then allow it to idle for at least two minutes.
128 Check that when the ignition is switched on the idling stabilization control valve is heard to buzz. If not, check the system with reference to paragraphs 63 to 66.

129 Disconnect the wiring plug for the idle stabilization system located near the ignition coil (Fig. 12.47).
130 Allow the engine to idle, then check that the idling speed is 1000 ± 50 rpm. If necessary remove the cap and turn the idle speed adjustment screw as required (Fig. 12.48).
131 Check that the idling CO reading is as given in the Specifications – temporarily block off the exhaust tailpipe not fitted with the analyser probe while making the check. If necessary, turn the CO adjustment screw as required after removing the cap. A special key is necessary in order to turn the screw, but a suitable substitute tool may be used as an alternative. Note that the adjustment screw must not be depressed or lifted and that the engine must not be revved with the tool in position.
132 Refit the crankcase ventilation hose. If the CO reading increases, refer to Chapter 3, Section 31, paragraph 9.
133 Reconnect the wiring plug and remove the test instruments. Note that after reconnecting the wiring plug, the stabilization system will return the idling to the specified speed (950 + 50 rpm).

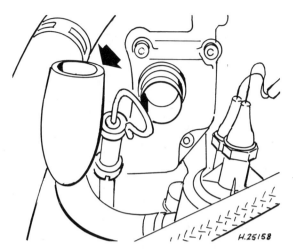

Fig. 12.46 Disconnecting the crankcase ventilation hose – 16V engine (Sec 7)

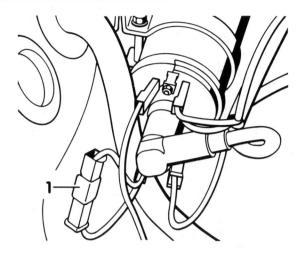

Fig. 12.47 Idle stabilization wiring plug (1) – 16V engine (Sec 7)

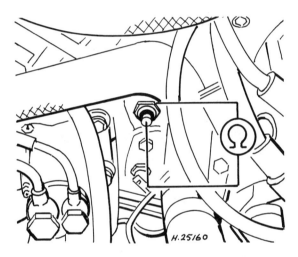

Fig. 12.48 Idling speed (A) and mixture (B) adjustment screw locations – 16V engine (Sec 7)

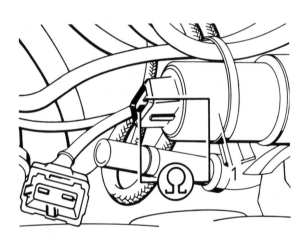

Fig. 12.49 Checking the wiring continuity of the idling stabilization control valve – 16V engine (Sec 7)

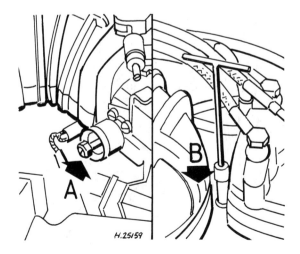

Fig. 12.50 Checking the resistance of the temperature sender – 16V engine (Sec 7)

Idling speed stabilization system (16V) – checking

134 Check that the stabilization control valve buzzes when the ignition is switched on. If not, use an ohmmeter to check the valve continuity after pulling off the connector (Fig. 12.49).

135 Similarly check the system temperature sender (Fig. 12.50). At 20°C (68°F) its resistance should be approximately 1000 ohms, at 60°C (140°F) the resistance should be approximately 250 ohms, and at 100°C (212°F) it should be approximately 75 ohms.

136 If the system fault cannot be traced using the previous test, check all the associated wiring and finally, if necessary, renew the control unit located behind the centre console.

137 The operations of the control valve may be checked by connecting a multi-meter to it. With a tachometer connected, run the engine (hot) at idling speed and note the control current. Now pinch the hose shown in Fig. 12.51 and check that the current rises. Release the hose, increase the engine speed to 1300 rpm, and actuate the throttle valve switch. The control current should drop below 430 mA. With the wiring disconnected as described in paragraph 129 the control current should be constant between 415 and 445 mA.

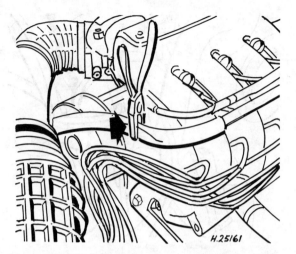

Fig. 12.51 Pinch hose (arrowed) when checking the idling stabilization control valve – 16V engine (Sec 7)

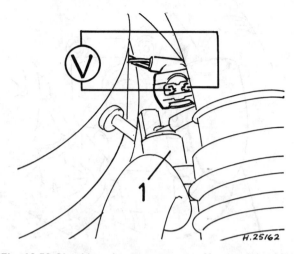

Fig. 12.52 Checking the overrun cut-off valve (1) – 16V engine (Sec 7)

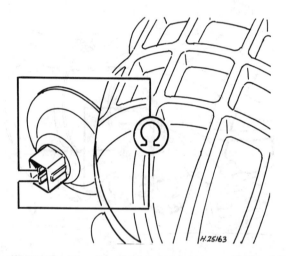

Fig. 12.53 Checking the diaphragm pressure switch – 16V engine (Sec 7)

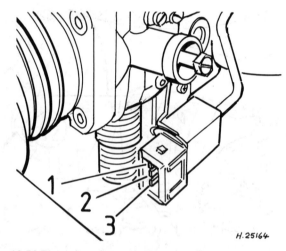

Fig. 12.54 Throttle valve switch connector terminals – 16V engine (Sec 7)

Overrun cut-off valve (16V) – checking

138 With a tachometer connected, run the engine (hot) at 2500 rpm, then operate the throttle switch and check that the engine hunts (ie speed fluctuates). If not, let the engine idle, disconnect the valve wiring and connect a voltmeter to the terminals (Fig. 12.52). Zero volts should be registered.

139 Increase the engine speed to 4000 rpm, then quickly close the throttle. At 1400 rpm battery voltage should be indicated.

140 If necessary renew the control unit located behind the centre console.

Diaphragm pressure switch (16V) – checking

141 Pull the wiring connector from the switch, then connect an ohmmeter to the switch terminals (Fig. 12.53). With the engine idling, the reading should be infinity. Quickly open and close the throttle and check that the resistance drops briefly then rises to infinity.

Throttle valve switch (16V) – checking

142 Pull the wiring connector from the throttle valve switch.

143 Refer to Fig. 12.54, then using an ohmmeter check that with the throttle closed there is zero resistance between terminals 1 and 2, but a reading of infinity between terminals 2 and 3. With the throttle open the readings should be reversed.

144 To adjust the switch, insert a 0.10 mm (0.004 in) feeler blade between the throttle lever and stop (Fig. 12.55), then loosen the

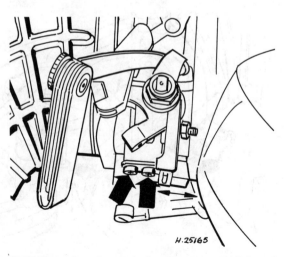

Fig. 12.55 Throttle valve switch adjustment – 16V engine (Sec 7)

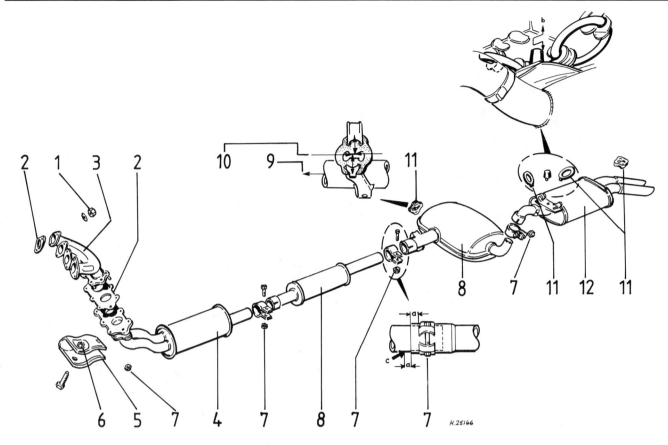

Fig. 12.56 Exhaust system for the 16V engine (Sec 7)

1 Nut
2 Gaskets
3 Exhaust manifold
4 Downpipe and front silencer
5 Heatshield
6 and 7 Nuts

8 Intermediate silencers
9 Front of car
10 Preload dimension – 5.0 mm
    (0.197 in)
11 Rubber mounting

12 Rear silencer
a = 5.0 mm (0.197 in)
b = 12.0 mm (0.472 in)
c = marks (S) – refer to Chapter 3, Fig. 3.36

screws and move the switch towards the lever until the contacts are heard to click. Tighten the screws on completion and remove the feeler blade.

Inlet manifold (16V) – removal and refitting

145 The inlet manifold is in two sections. When refitting the upper section, fully tighten the nuts securing it to the lower section first before attaching it to the rear support bracket.

Exhaust system (fuel injection models) – description

146 The exhaust system for the 16V engine is shown in Fig. 12.56. It incorporates four silencers together with twin downpipes and tailpipes. The manifold/downpipe flange is of standard type with a gasket. Refer to Chapter 3, Section 24 for the relevant procedures.

147 Non-16V models manufactured from August 1985 are also fitted with a manifold/downpipe flange incorporating a gasket instead of spring clips.

8 Ignition system

Ignition system (1.05 and 1.3 with hydraulic tappets) – description

1 With the introduction of hydraulic tappets on 1.05 and 1.3 litre engines the ignition system was changed from the contact breaker type to the transistorized type. Refer to Chapter 4 for the relevant Sections describing the function and precautions for the system, and note that as from late 1986, the rotor arm is not fitted with a speed limiter.

2 Test procedures for the switch unit and Hall sender are as described in Chapter 4. Distributor removal and refitting is basically as for the contact breaker type, and overhaul procedures as for the transistorized

type with reference also to Fig. 12.58 and the following paragraphs 3 and 4.

3 The distributor shaft is supported by a bearing plate which is removed by loosening the two screws securing it to the tensioning ring. Before removing the ring make a mark on the rim of the distributor body in line with the guide lug.

4 Shims are provided above and below the Hall sender and these should be selected to eliminate axial clearance and to provide for movement by the vacuum unit.

Ignition system (1.6 with automatic transmission) – description

5 On automatic transmission models fitted with the 1.6 litre engine a thermo-pneumatic valve and non-return valve are fitted in the vacuum line between the carburettor and distributor. This effectively retains the ignition vacuum advance when the engine is cold even during acceleration. At normal engine temperature vacuum advance is not effective during acceleration.

6 To test the thermo-pneumatic valve blow through it with the unit in heated water. It should be closed under 30°C (86°F) and open above 46°C (115°F). Check also that the non-return valve is only open in one direction.

Digifant ignition system (1.8 engine, code PB) – description and precautions

7 The Digifant ignition system uses the TC1-H ignition described in Chapter 4, but in addition it incorporates a knock sensor, which senses the onset of pre-ignition and retards the ignition timing accordingly. Normal ignition timing is automatically adjusted by the computerised control unit, which also controls the fuel injection system, and because of this, there are no centrifugal advance weights in the distributor.

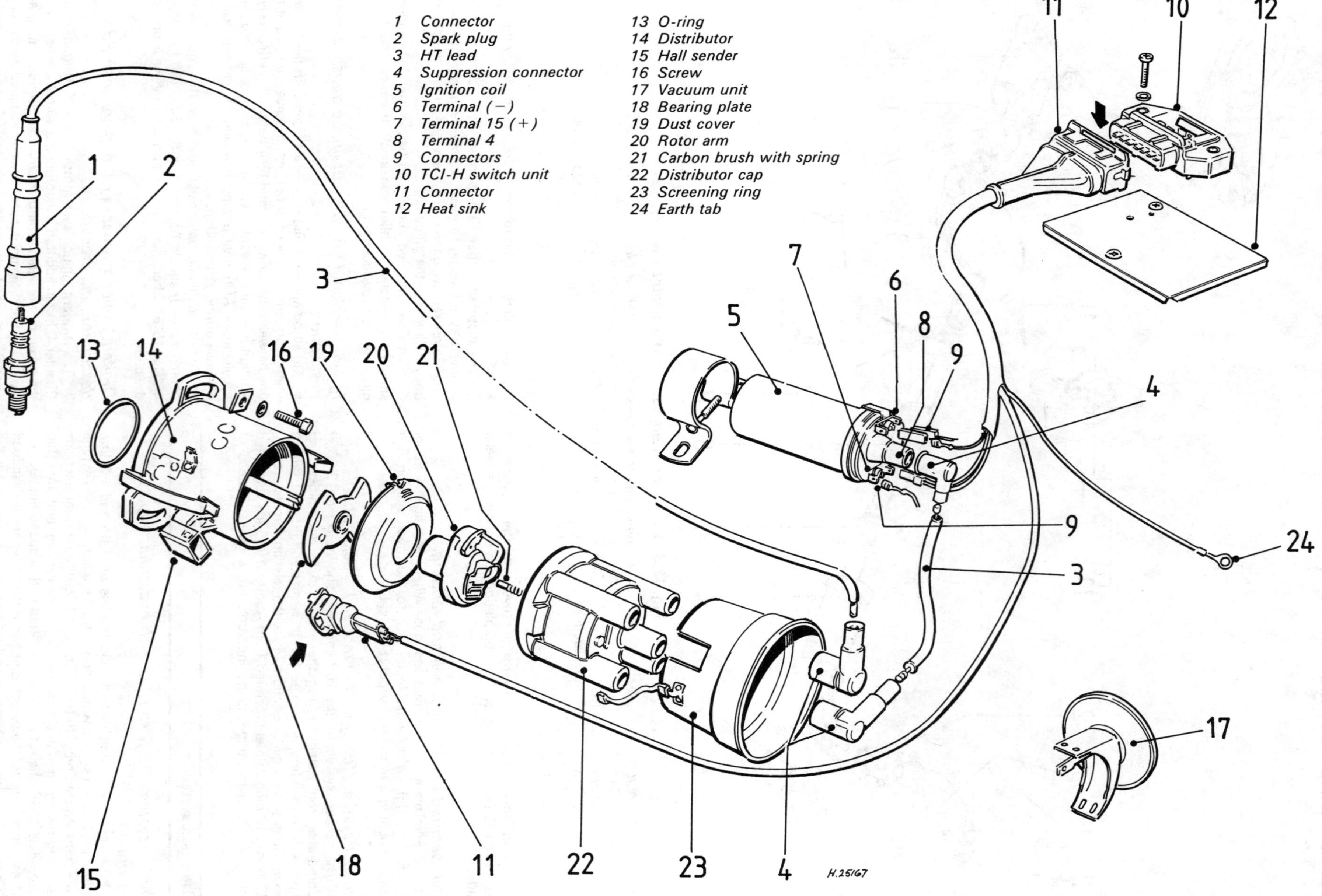

358

Fig. 12.57 Transistorized ignition system for 1.05 and 1.3
litre engines (Sec 8)

1 Connector		13 O-ring
2 Spark plug		14 Distributor
3 HT lead		15 Hall sender
4 Suppression connector		16 Screw
5 Ignition coil		17 Vacuum unit
6 Terminal (−)		18 Bearing plate
7 Terminal 15 (+)		19 Dust cover
8 Terminal 4		20 Rotor arm
9 Connectors		21 Carbon brush with spring
10 TCI-H switch unit		22 Distributor cap
11 Connector		23 Screening ring
12 Heat sink		24 Earth tab

H.25/67

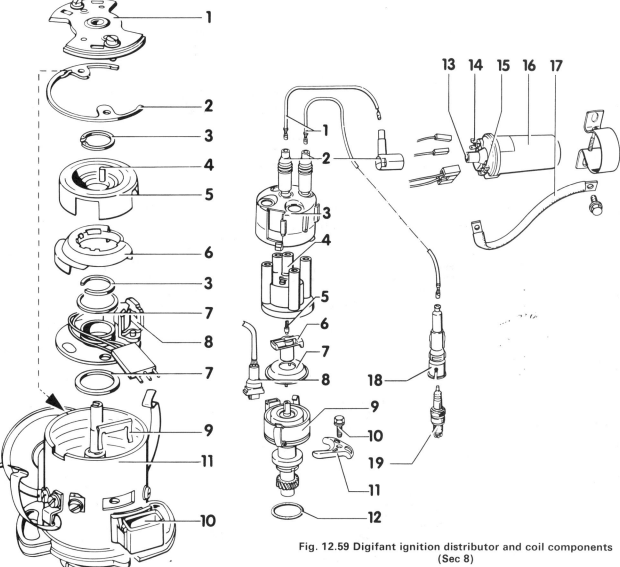

Fig. 12.58 Exploded view of the transistorized ignition distributor for 1.05 and 1.3 litre engines (Sec 8)

1	Bearing plate	7	Shims
2	Tensioning ring	8	Hall sender
3	Circlip	9	Clip
4	Pin	10	Connector
5	Rotor	11	Main body
6	Cover		

Fig. 12.59 Digifant ignition distributor and coil components (Sec 8)

1	HT leads	11	Clamp
2	Suppression connectors	12	O-ring
3	Screen	13	Coil terminal 4
4	Distributor cap	14	Coil terminal 15 (+)
5	Carbon brush and spring	15	Coil terminal 1 (−)
6	Rotor arm	16	Coil
7	Cover	17	Earth strap
8	Connector	18	Spark plug connector
9	Distributor	19	Spark plug
10	Bolt		

8 Components of the system are shown in Figs. 12.59 and 12.60. Work procedures are basically as given in Chapter 4, except for those described in the following paragraphs.

Digifant ignition timing (1.8 engine, code PB) – checking and adjustment

9 Run the engine to normal operating temperature, then switch off the ignition.
10 Connect a stroboscopic timing light to the engine.
11 Run the engine at idling speed.
12 Disconnect the wiring from the temperature sender (Fig. 12.61).
13 Increase the engine speed to between 2000 and 2500 rpm, then point the timing light at the aperture over the flywheel. The timing marks should be aligned (Chapter 4, Fig. 4.12), but if not, loosen the

clamp bolt, turn the distributor as required, and retighten the bolt.
14 While checking the ignition timing, the opportunity should be taken to check the temperature and knock sensor controls.
15 With the temperature sender wiring disconnected, increase the engine speed to 2300 rpm and note the exact ignition timing. Hold the engine speed at 2300 rpm, then reconnect the wiring and check that the ignition timing advances by 30° ± 3° from the previously noted value.
16 If the ignition timing only advances about 20°, slacken the knock sensor securing bolt, retighten to 20 Nm (15 lbf ft) and repeat the test. If there is no difference, check the associated wiring for an open-circuit, or as a last resort, renew the knock sensor.
17 If there is no increase in ignition timing, check the temperature sender wiring for an open-circuit. A fault is indicated in the Digifant control unit if there is no open-circuit.

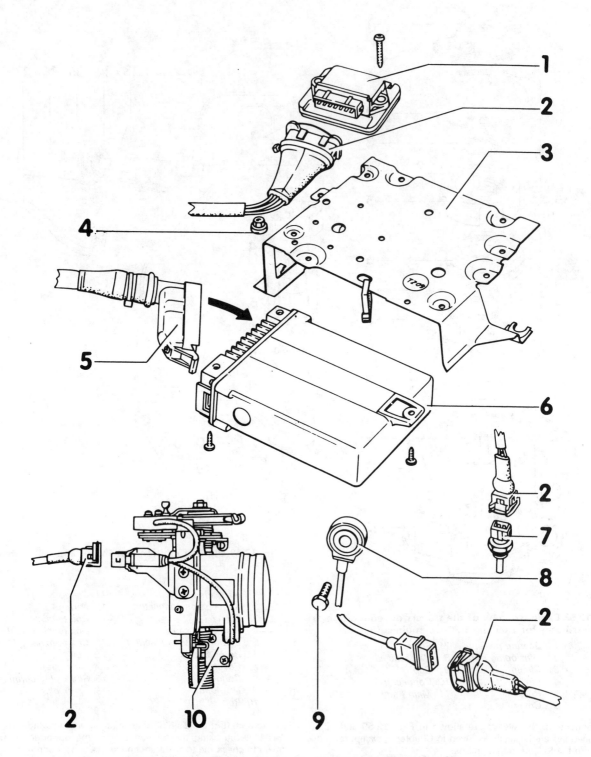

Fig. 12.60 Digifant ignition control unit components (Sec 8)

1	TC1-H switch unit	6	Digifant control unit
2	Connector	7	Temperature sender
3	Plate	8	Knock sensor
5	Nut	9	Bolt
5	Connector	10	Throttle valve switch 1

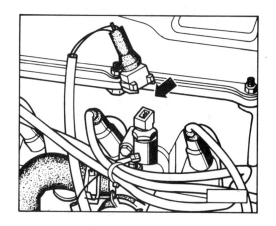

Fig. 12.61 Disconnecting the temperature sender wiring (Sec 8)

Ignition system (16V engine) – description and precautions

18 The 16V engine is fitted with a Fully Electronic Ignition (FEI) system as shown in Fig. 12.62. It functions in a similar manner to the transistorized system described in Chapter 4, but in addition it incorporates an electronic control unit which adjusts the ignition timing electronically according to engine speed, load, and temperature. The distributor is not fitted with centrifugal and vacuum advance mechanisms.

19 The precautions given in Chapter 4, Section 7 apply also to the FEI system.

20 Note that a digital multi-meter should be used for testing purposes otherwise the readings may be inaccurate. **Do not** under any circumstances use a testlamp as this will damage the electronic components of the system. When using the multi-meter **do not** switch between ranges during the test as this also may damage the components.

Distributor (16V engine) – removal and refitting

21 This is basically as described in Chapter 4, Section 10, but ignore the reference to the vacuum pipe and renew the O-ring if necessary.

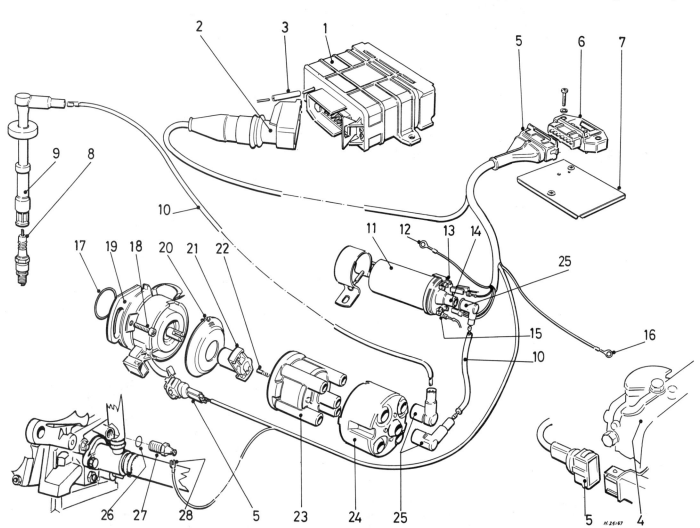

Fig. 12.62 Fully Electronic Ignition (FEI) system – 16V engine (Sec 8)

1 FEI control unit	8 Spark plug	15 Terminal 15 (+)	22 Carbon brush
2 Connector	9 Connector	16 Earth lead	23 Distributor cap
3 Vacuum line	10 HT lead	17 O-ring	24 Suppression cap
4 Throttle valve switch	11 Ignition coil	18 Screw	25 Suppression connector
5 Connector	12 Earth lead	19 Distributor	26 Washer
6 TCI-H switch unit	13 Terminal 1 (–)	20 Dust cover	27 Temperature sender
7 Heat sink	14 Terminal 4	21 Rotor arm	28 Connector

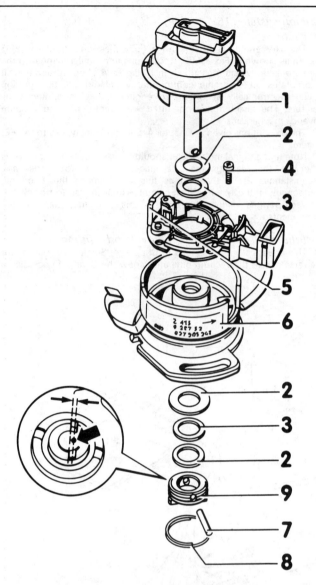

Fig. 12.63 Exploded view of the FEI distributor for the 16V engine (Sec 8)

1	Shaft	6	Main body
2	Shims	7	Roll pin
3	Plastic washers	8	Circlip
4	Screw	9	Drive coupling
5	Hall sender		

Distributor (16V engine) – overhaul

22 The only work likely to be necessary on the distributor is the renewal of the Hall sender, and this is obtainable in kit form including a drive coupling, pin and circlip.

23 If the rotor arm is defective it must be removed by crushing with pliers, as it is permanently fixed to the shaft with strong adhesive. Clean the shaft and secure the new rotor arm with adhesive obtained from a VW dealer.

24 To renew the Hall sender, first note the position of the drive coupling offset in relation to the rotor arm.

25 Support the drive coupling in a vice, then drive out the roll pin after removing the circlip.

26 Remove the coupling followed by the shims and plastic washer.

27 Remove the shaft complete with rotor arm, followed by the plastic dust cover, shim and plastic washer.

28 Remove the screws and lift the Hall sender from inside the distributor body.

29 Clean all the components, then fit the new Hall sender using a reversal of the removal procedure, but lubricate the shaft with a little grease.

Transistorized ignition switch unit (16V engine) – testing

30 The switch unit is located in the left-hand side of the plenum chamber beneath a plastic cover. The ignition coil should be in good condition before making this test.

31 Depress the wire clip and pull the connector from the switch unit.

32 Connect a voltmeter between terminals 4 and 2 on the connector, then switch on the ignition and check that battery voltage is available. Switch off the ignition.

33 Using an ohmmeter, check that there is continuity between terminal 1 on the connector and terminal 1 on the coil.

34 Refit the connector to the switch unit, then connect a voltmeter across the low tension terminals on the coil (Fig. 12.65).

35 Release the spring and pull the connector from the control unit, then switch on the ignition. Check that initially a reading of 2 volts is registered on the voltmeter, dropping to zero after 1 to 2 seconds. If this is not the case, renew the switch unit and also if necessary the ignition coil.

36 Using a temporary length of wire, briefly earth terminal 12 on the connector. The voltage should rise to at least 2 volts. If this is not the case, renew the switch unit.

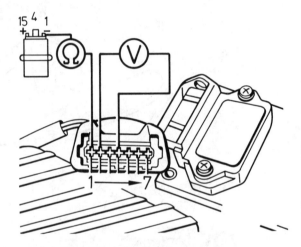

Fig. 12.64 Testing the FEI switch unit (Sec 8)

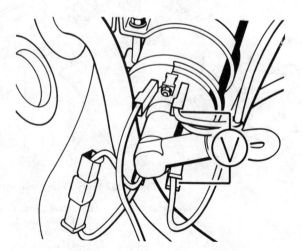

Fig. 12.65 Voltmeter connection on the ignition coil when testing the switch unit (Sec 8)

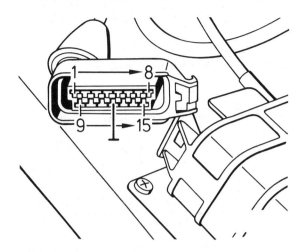

Fig. 12.66 FEI control unit connector terminals (Sec 8)

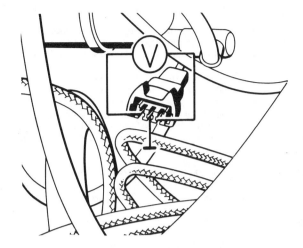

Fig. 12.67 Testing Hall sender connector on the side of the distributor (Sec 8)

FEI control unit (16V engine) – testing
37 Check the switch unit as previously described before checking the control unit.
38 Release the spring and pull the connector from the control unit located in the right-hand side of the plenum chamber.
39 Switch on the ignition, then use a voltmeter to check that battery voltage is available between terminals 3 and 5 on the connector (see Fig. 12.66).
40 Check also that battery voltage is available between terminals 6 and 3, then operate the throttle valve switch and check that the voltage drops to zero. Switch off the ignition.
41 Using an ohmmeter, measure the resistance between the connector terminals 1 and 3. These are the temperature sender terminals and the resistance varies according to the coolant temperature, as described in Section 7, paragraph 64.
42 Press the clip and pull the connector from the side of the distributor. Connect the voltmeter to the two outer terminals of the connector, then switch on the ignition. A reading of 5 volts should be registered. Switch off the ignition.
43 Connect a voltmeter across the low tension terminals of the ignition coil. Switch on the ignition.
44 Using a temporary length of wire, briefly earth the centre terminal of the distributor connector. The voltage should rise to at least 2 volts and the fuel pump should be heard to operate. if this is not the case, renew the control unit and if necessary check the fuel pump relay.

Hall sender unit (16V engine) – testing
45 Depress the wire clip and pull the connector from the switch unit.
46 A diode-type voltage tester must now be connected across terminals 2 and 6.
47 Spin the engine on the starter motor and check that the tester diode flickers indicating a fluctuating voltage. If not, renew the Hall sender unit. **Do not** use a bulb-type tester, as this may damage the electronic components.

Ignition timing (16V engine) – checking and adjustment
48 The procedure is as described in Chapter 4, Section 12, using the stroboscopic timing light method. The operation of the control unit can also be checked as follows.
49 Run the engine at idling speed and note the basic ignition timing. Pull the vacuum hose from the control unit, then increase the engine speed to 4600 rpm and read off the ignition advance. Deduct the basic advance and the resultant value should be 18°, this being the advance attributable to engine speed.
50 Reconnect the vacuum hose, then run the engine to 4600 rpm. Note the ignition timing. Pull off the vacuum hose and again increase the engine speed to 4600 rpm. The ignition timing should be approximately 20° retarded from the previously noted figure. This amount indicates the advance attributable to engine vacuum.

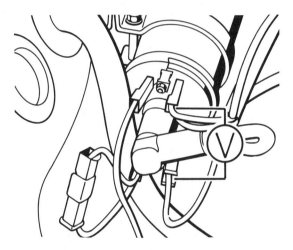

Fig. 12.68 Using a diode voltage tester at the switch unit connector to test the Hall sender (Sec 8)

Spark plugs – removal and refitting
51 Where applicable remove the air cleaner.
52 Pull the HT lead and fittings from the spark plugs, identifying them for location if necessary. On the 16V engine the end fittings incorporate extensions, as the plugs are deeply recessed in the cylinder head.
53 Using compressed air or a vacuum cleaner, remove any debris from around the spark plugs.
54 Unscrew the plugs using a plug socket, preferably with a rubber insert to grip the plug.
55 Refitting is a reversal of removal, but tighten the spark plugs to the specified torque.

Spark plugs and coil – general
56 From August 1987, single earth electrode spark plugs are fitted, together with a modified ignition coil as given in the Specifications. The coil is identified by a grey sticker instead of the previous green sticker.
57 Note that it is not permissible to use the new plugs with the old coil, or *vice-versa*.

9 Clutch

Clutch cable (with automatic adjuster on pedal) – renewal
1 Depress the clutch pedal fully several times.

2   Release the cable at the gearbox end by compressing the spring beneath the bellows.

3   Inside the car, unhook the cable from the clutch pedal.

4   Withdraw the cable from the engine compartment.

5   To fit the new cable, insert it through the bulkhead and hook it onto the pedal.

6   Have an assistant depress the clutch pedal by hand and at the same time pull the inner cable out at the gearbox end. This action will release the automatic adjustment mechanism and enable the cable to be attached to the release lever after compressing the spring.

7   Depress the clutch pedal several times to set the adjustment mechanism.. Note that the mechanism should not be dismantled, as there are loose balls inside.

Clutch (085 gearbox) – description

8   The clutch fitted with the 085 gearbox is similar to the 084 gearbox version described in Chapter 5. Most of the work procedures are as given in Chapter 5, but refer also to the information given in the following paragraphs.

Clutch cable (085 self-adjusting) – renewal

9   Some models equipped with the 085 five-speed gearbox are fitted with a self-adjusting clutch cable. Before removing the cable it must be pre-tensioned to allow sufficient clearance for disconnecting the end

Fig. 12.69 Clutch cable self-adjusting mechanism fitted with the 085 five-speed gearbox (Sec 9)

fittings. If the special VW tool No. 3151 is not available a suitable substitute tool will have to be made. Apart from this the renewal procedure is the same as for the 084 gearbox.

Flywheel bolt (085 gearbox) – tightening

10   The threads of the flywheel bolts should be coated with locking fluid before inserting and tightening them. Bolts with a collar have a different tightening torque to those without (see Specifications).

Clutch release mechanism (085 gearbox) – removal and refitting

11   The clutch release mechanism on the 085 gearbox is shown in Fig. 12.70. It differs from the 084 version by having a release lever splined

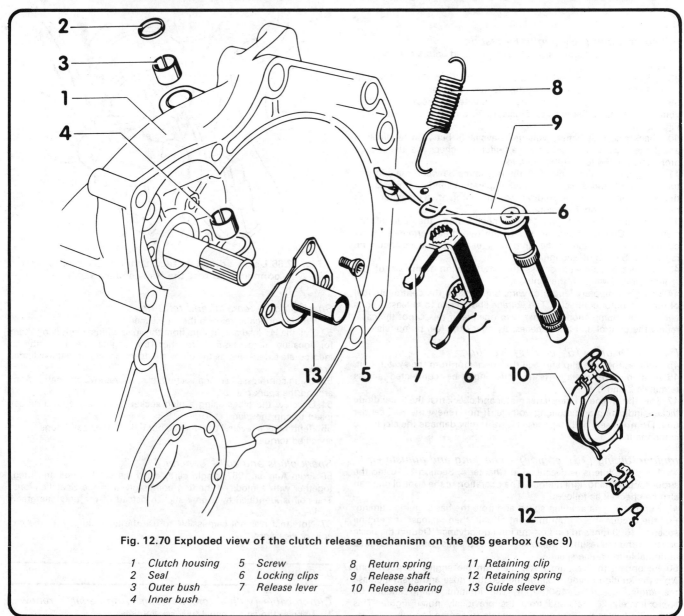

Fig. 12.70 Exploded view of the clutch release mechanism on the 085 gearbox (Sec 9)

1 Clutch housing	5 Screw	8 Return spring	11 Retaining clip
2 Seal	6 Locking clips	9 Release shaft	12 Retaining spring
3 Outer bush	7 Release lever	10 Release bearing	13 Guide sleeve
4 Inner bush			

to the release shaft. This enables the shaft to be removed without first removing the guide sleeve.

12 To remove the release shaft, prise out the two locking clips, then slide out the shaft and withdraw the release lever.

13 The bushes may be driven from the clutch housing with a suitable drift, although special VW tools may be required for the removal and fitting of the inner bush (consult a VW dealer if in doubt). The outer bush should be installed to allow flush fitting of the seal.

14 Refit the release shaft using a reversal of the removal procedure. A master spline is incorporated on the shaft and release lever to ensure correct assembly. Lubricate the bearing surfaces with a molybdenum disulphide based grease.

15 All other clutch release mechanism procedures are as given in Chapter 5, Section 7.

Clutch disc and pressure plate – anti-corrosion protection

16 Both the friction disc and pressure plate are treated with anti-corrosion grease during manufacture in order to prolong the service life of the components. The grease must only be removed from the contact surface of the pressure plate and **must** be left intact on all the remaining areas.

10 Manual gearbox

Gearbox oil level (084) – checking

1 The oil filler plug on the 084 gearbox is difficult to reach using the normal hexagon key and it will be found much easier to use a nut and bolt as shown in Fig. 12.71, together with a normal spanner. Instead of

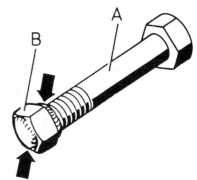

Fig. 12.71 Nut and bolt for removing the oil level plug on the 084 gearbox (Sec 10)

A *Bolt M10 X 100 mm*   B *Nut welded as arrowed*

welding a single nut on the bolt, two nuts may be tightened against each other using thread locking fluid.

Manual gearbox (085) – general description

2 Certain models may be fitted with the 085 manual gearbox which is a five-speed version of the 084 gearbox. Although the construction of the 085 gearbox appears similar to the 084, there are major differences which make most procedures different. Where necessary however reference is made to Chapter 6 in the following paragraphs. Note that special tools are required for certain procedures, therefore the complete sub-section should be read prior to commencing work.

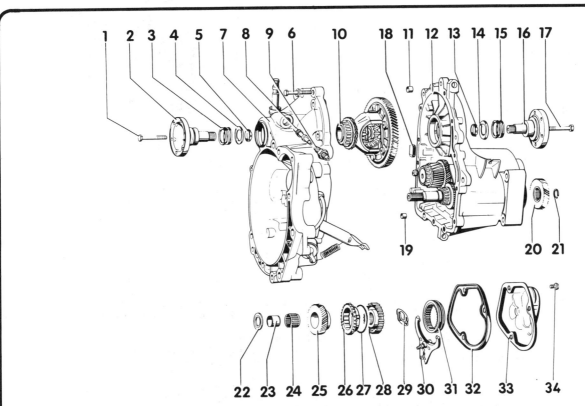

Fig. 12.72 Exploded view of 085 casings and 5th speed components (Sec 10)

1 Bolt	10 Differential	19 Dowel	27 Spring
2 Flange	11 Dowel	20 5th speed driving gear	28 5th gear synchro hub
3 Spring	12 Gearbox housing	21 Circlip	29 Locking clip
4 Thrust washer	12 Tapered ring	22 Thrust washer	30 5th gear selector fork
5 Tapered ring	14 Thrust washer	23 Sleeve	31 5th gear synchro sleeve
6 Bolt	15 Spring	24 Needle bearing	32 Gasket
7 Clutch housing	16 Flange	25 5th speed driven gear	33 Cover
8 Speedometer pinion	17 Bolt	26 5th gear synchro ring	34 Bolt
9 Bush	18 Magnet		

Manual gearbox (085) – removal and refitting
3 Refer to Chapter 6, Section 3. Before refitting the gearbox make sure that the location dowels are correctly inserted in the cylinder block.

Manual gearbox (085) – dismantling into major assemblies
4 Follow the procedure given in Chapter 6, Section 4, paragraphs 1 to 10, but note the following difference. Remove the clutch release bearing and shaft as described in Section 9 of this Chapter.
5 The input and output shafts are supported in taper roller bearings instead of ball bearings. First unbolt the gearbox housing end cover and remove the gasket.
6 Loosen the locknut, then unscrew the ball-head bolt securing the 5th gear selector fork.
7 Mark the 5th gear synchro hub and sleeve in relation to each other, then slide off the sleeve together with the selector fork from the selector rod.
8 Extract the locking clip from the end of the output shaft. If necessary this can be replaced by a normal circlip at reassembly.
9 Using a suitable puller, remove both the 5th gear synchro hub and the 5th speed gear from the output shaft together with the synchro ring.
10 Remove the needle roller cage from the output shaft, then lever off the inner shaft and 5th speed thrust washer together.
11 Extract the circlip from the end of the input shaft, then lever off the 5th speed driving gear.
12 Extract the plug covering the selector shaft.
13 Using a suitable drift from inside the gearbox housing drive out the selector shaft.
14 Remove the selector finger.
15 Unbolt and remove the gear lever bracket, noting the location of the bush.
16 Unscrew the three cross-head bolts from the front of the gearbox housing using a cross-head screwdriver.
17 Remove the 5th gear selector fork locking clip from the end of the selector rod by compressing it.
18 Withdraw both the 5th gear and reverse selector rods together with the reverse relay lever.
19 Using a suitable drift, tap out the reverse gear shaft from the gearbox housing.
20 As an assembly withdraw the input and output shafts together with the 1st/2nd and 3rd/4th selector rods and forks. Separate the components on the bench. Remove also the reverse idler gear and shaft.

Clutch housing (085) – overhaul
21 Clean and examine the clutch housing for damage and cracks. If evident renew the housing, but note that this will necessitate adjusting the bearing preload of the input shaft, output shaft and differential bearings.
22 Prise the seal from the inner shift lever. If the lever is not being removed, smear the lip of the new seal with grease, then drive it squarely into the housing until flush with the rim of the bush. To remove the lever, first mark the exact position of the selector arm on the shift lever, then unscrew the pinch bolt, slide out the lever and remove the detent.
23 Using a soft metal drift, drive out the lever bush. Drive the new bush into position, then smear the lever with molybdenum disulphide grease and slide it into the housing, through the selector arm and into the detent.
24 Position the selector arm on the lever as previously noted, then tighten the pinch bolt. Note that if any of the following components are renewed the position of the selector arm must be determined using a special VW gauge.

Selector finger
Selector arm
Clutch housing
Gearbox housing
Inner shaft lever
Inner shaft lever detent

The complete gearbox should be taken to a VW dealer or gearbox specialist for the adjustment. Briefly the procedure consists of fitting the gauge to the gearbox housing in order to determine the neutral

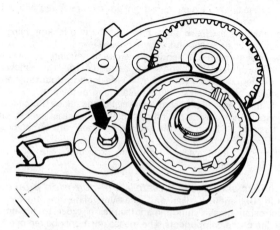

Fig. 12.73 Ball head bolt securing the 5th gear selector fork – 085 gearbox (Sec 10)

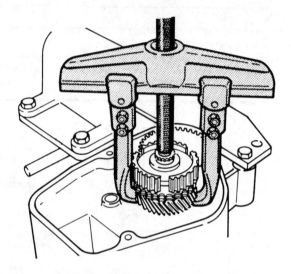

Fig. 12.74 Removing the 5th speed driven gear and synchro hub from the output shaft – 085 gearbox (Sec 10)

position of the selector finger. A dummy finger is then locked on the gauge and the gauge transferred to the clutch housing. The selector arm pinch bolt is then tightened with the inner shift lever in neutral.
25 Unscrew the speedometer pinion bush and withdraw the pinion. Examine the components for wear and renew them if necessary. Insert the pinion then tighten the bush.
26 Check the starter bush in the housing. If necessary remove it with VW tools 2046 and 2286, then drive in the new bush with a soft metal drift.
27 Prise out the driveshaft seal and if necessary the seal sleeve. Drive in the new sleeve squarely and press in the new seal.
28 Examine the outer tracks of the input and output shaft bearings and differential bearing for wear. If the bearings are renewed the outer tracks must be driven out, but note the shims fitted as these determine the bearing preload. The preload adjustment is described in paragraphs 36 to 45.

Gearbox housing (085) – overhaul
29 Clean and examine the gearbox housing for damage and cracks. If evident renew the housing, but note that the input and output shaft and differential bearing preloads must be adjusted as described in paragraphs 36 to 45.
30 Check the reverse idler gear, shaft, and relay lever for wear and damage and renew them if necessary.
31 Check the selector rods, finger and bracket and renew if necessary.
32 Examine the outer tracks of the input and output shaft bearings and differential bearing for wear. Refer to paragraph 28.

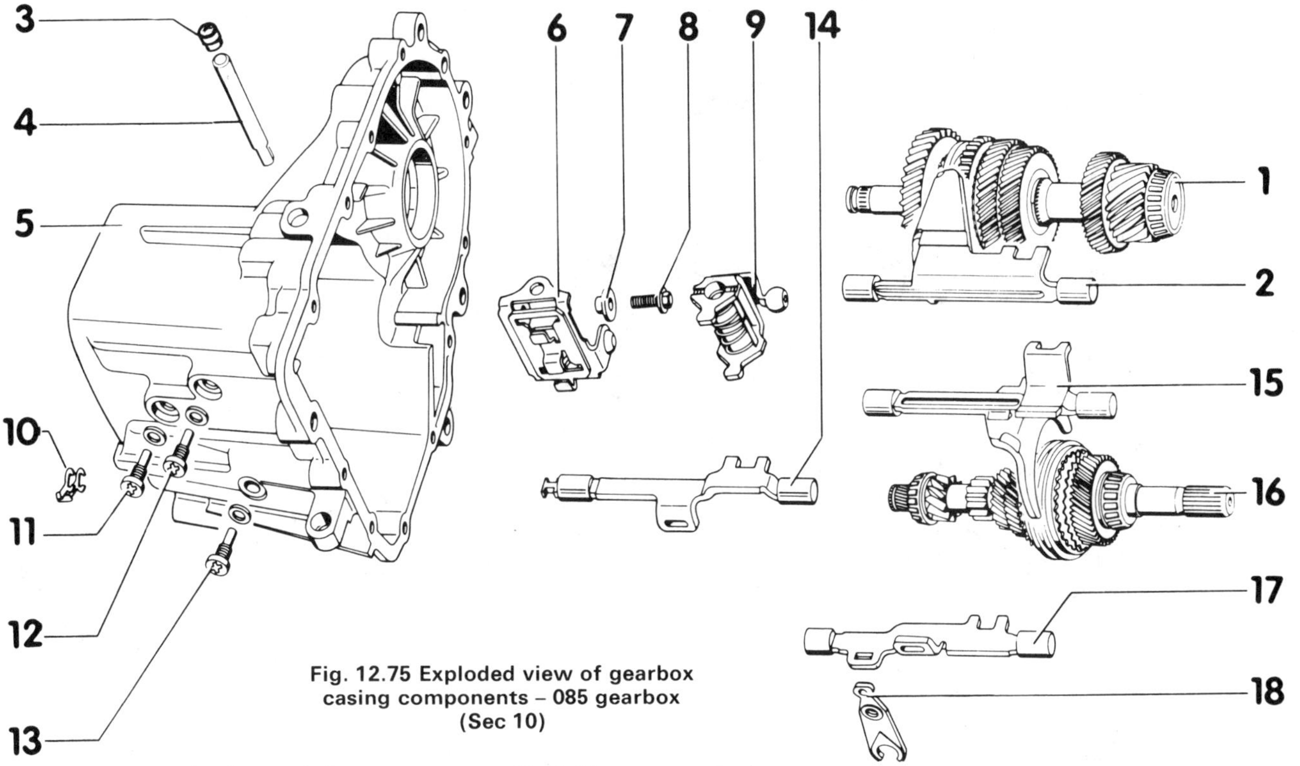

Fig. 12.75 Exploded view of gearbox casing components – 085 gearbox (Sec 10)

1 Output shaft
2 1st/2nd selector rod and fork
3 Plug
4 Selector shaft
5 Gearbox housing
6 Gear lever bracket
7 Bush
8 Bolt
9 Selector finger
10 5th selector fork locking clip
11 Bolt for reverse relay lever
12 Bolt for 5th/reverse selector rods
13 Bolt for reverse gear shaft
14 5th selector rod
15 3rd/4th selector rod and fork
16 Input shaft
17 Reverse selector rod
18 Reverse relay lever
19 Reverse idler gear
20 Reverse gear shaft

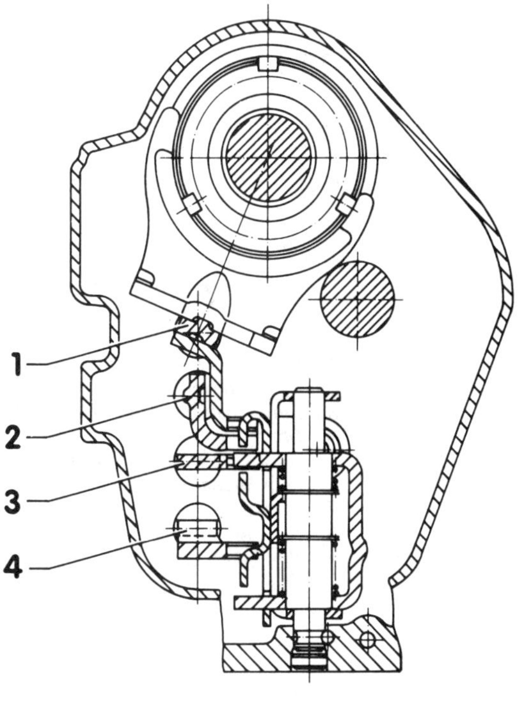

Fig. 12.76 Cross-section of the selector rods – 085 gearbox (Sec 10)

1 3rd/4th selector rod
2 1st/2nd selector rod
3 Reverse selector rod
4 5th selector rod

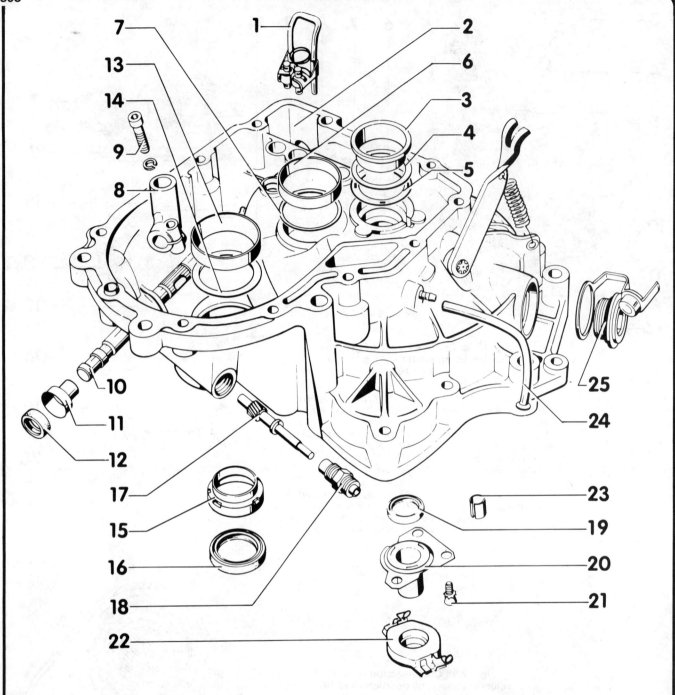

Fig. 12.77 Clutch housing components – 085 gearbox (Sec 10)

1 Inner shift lever detent	10 Inner shift lever	18 Bush
2 Clutch housing	11 Bush	19 Seal
3 Input shaft bearing outer track	12 Seal	20 Guide sleeve
4 Shim	13 Differential bearing outer track	21 Bolt
5 Washer (no longer fitted)	14 Shim	22 Release bearing
6 Output shaft bearing outer track	15 Sleeve	23 Starter bush
7 Shim	16 Seal	24 Breather pipe
8 Selector arm	17 Speedometer pinion	25 Plug
9 Pinch bolt		

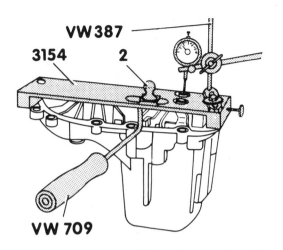

Fig. 12.78 Using the special VW tools to set the selector arm position on the inner shift lever (Sec 10)

Input shaft (085 gearbox) – servicing
33 The procedure is similar to that described in Chapter 6, Section 5 but with reference to Figs. 12.79 and 12.80.

Output shaft (085 gearbox) – servicing
34 The procedure is similar to that described in Chapter 6, Section 5, but with reference to Figs. 12.81 and 12.82. The gears do not require heating before fitting. Note that removal of the bearing from the pinion end of the shaft renders the bearing unfit for further use.

Synchro units (085 gearbox) – servicing
35 Refer to Chapter 6, Section 6.

Differential unit (085 gearbox) – servicing
36 Refer to Chapter 6, Section 7.

Input shaft bearing clearance (085 gearbox) – adjusting
37 Press the bearing outer track into the clutch housing **without** a shim. Also press the outer track into the gearbox housing.
38 Locate the input shaft in the clutch housing, then fit the gearbox housing and tighten the bolts to the specified torque.
39 Attach a dial gauge to the gearbox housing, then move the input shaft up and down to determine the total clearance. The shaft should

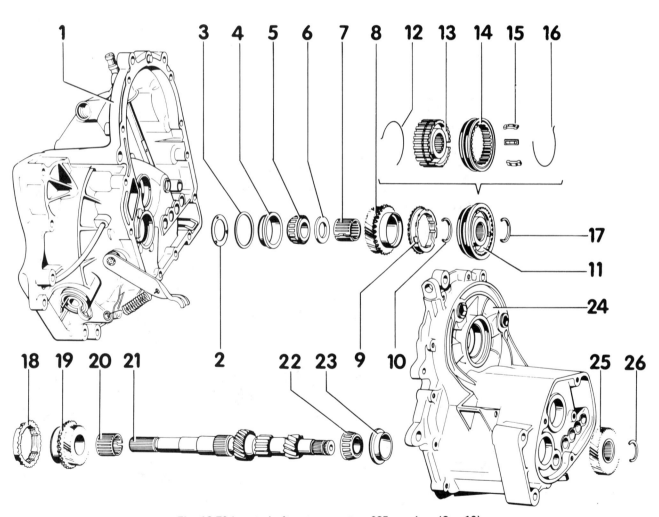

Fig. 12.79 Input shaft components – 085 gearbox (Sec 10)

1 Clutch housing	7 Needle bearing	14 Synchro sleeve	21 Input shaft
2 Washer (no longer fitted)	8 4th speed gear	15 Locking key	22 Bearing inner track and
3 Shim	9 4th gear synchro ring	16 Spring	roller bearing
4 Bearing outer track	10 Circlip	17 Circlip	23 Bearing outer track
5 Bearing inner track and	11 3rd/4th synchro unit	18 3rd gear synchro ring	24 Gearbox housing
roller bearing	12 Spring	19 3rd speed gear	25 5th speed driving gear
6 Thrust washer	13 Synchro hub	20 Needle bearing	26 Circlip

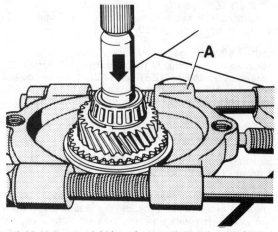

Fig. 12.80 Using tool (A) and a press to remove the taper roller bearing, 4th speed gear, thrust washer, 4th gear synchro ring, and 3rd/4th synchro sleeve (Sec 10)

Fig. 12.81 Output shaft components – 085 gearbox (Sec 10)

1 Clutch housing	19 Bearing inner track and roller bearing
2 Shim	20 Bearing outer track
3 Bearing outer track	21 Gearbox housing
4 Bearing inner track and roller bearing	22 Spring
5 Output shaft	23 Locking key
6 4th speed gear	24 Synchro hub
7 Circlip	25 Synchro sleeve
8 Circlip	26 Spring
9 3rd speed gear	27 Thrust washer
10 Needle bearing	28 Sleeve
11 2nd speed gear	29 Needle bearing
12 2nd gear synchro ring	30 5th speed gear
13 1st/2nd synchro unit	31 5th gear synchro ring
14 Circlip	32 Spring
15 Needle bearing	33 5th gear synchro hub
16 1st gear synchro ring	34 5th gear synchro sleeve
17 1st speed gear	35 Locking clip
18 Thrust washer	

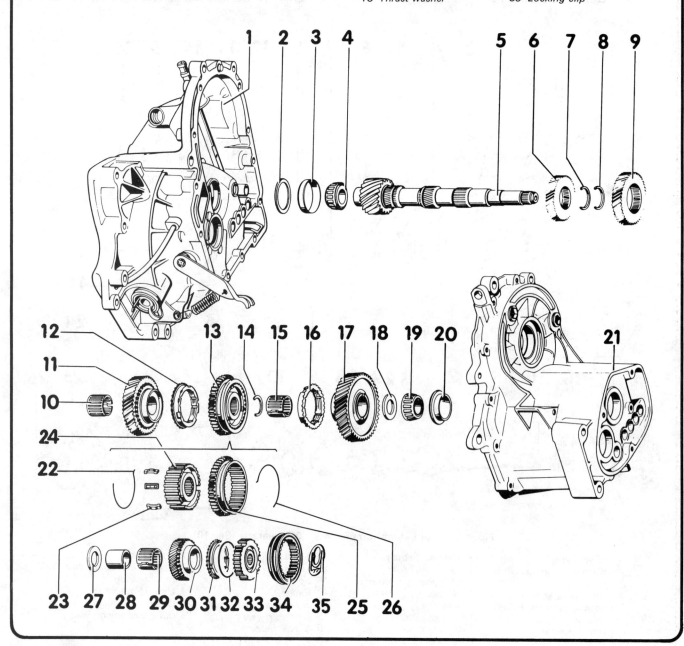

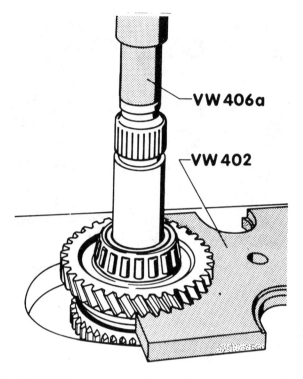

Fig. 12.82 Using a support plate and press to remove the bearing inner race and 1st speed gear (Sec 10)

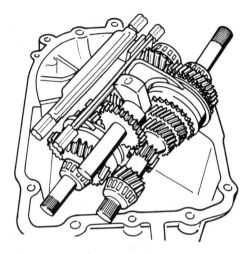

Fig. 12.83 Gear assembly ready to be fitted in the gearbox housing (Sec 10)

be turned prior to setting the dial gauge to ensure the bearings are settled.
40 Select a shim to provide between 0.01 and 0.12 mm (0.0004 and 0.0047 in) clearance, then fit the shim beneath the outer track in the clutch housing. The input shaft should turn freely without noticeable resistance.

Output shaft bearing preload (085 gearbox) – adjusting
41 Locate a 0.65 mm (0.256 in) shim in the clutch housing, then press in the bearing outer track. Also press the outer track into the gearbox housing.
42 Locate the output shaft in the clutch housing, then fit the gearbox housing and tighten the bolts to the specified torque.
43 Attach a dial gauge to the gearbox housing, then move the output shaft up and down to determine the total clearance. Turn the shaft prior to setting the dial gauge to ensure the bearings are settled.
44 Select a shim to provide a preload value of 0.20 mm (0.0079 in), but take into consideration the 0.65 mm (0.0256 in) shim already fitted.

Example:

Fitted shim	0.65 mm
Plus measured clearance	0.30 mm
Plus preload value	0.20 mm
Final shim thickness	1.15 mm

45 Fit the selected shim beneath the outer track in the clutch housing in place of the 0.65 mm shim.

Manual gearbox (085) – reassembly
46 Make sure that all components are clean and during reassembly lubricate all bearings with gear oil.
47 Engage the 1st/2nd and 3rd/4th selector forks in the corresponding synchro sleeves, then mesh the input and output shafts together.
48 Locate the reverse idler gear on its shaft, then position this together with the input and output shafts (Fig. 12.83).
49 Lower the complete assembly into the gearbox housing and check that all components are correctly positioned.
50 Tap the reverse gear shaft into the housing.

51 Insert the reverse selector rod together with the relay lever and locate the jaws of the lever on the reverse idler gear while fitting the gear.
52 Insert the 5th gear selector rod and fit the locking clip.
53 Align the reverse relay lever, then insert and tighten the cross-head pivot bolt together with the washer.
54 Align the 5th and reverse selector rods, then insert and tighten the cross-head stop bolt together with the washer.
55 Align the reverse gear shaft, then insert and tighten the cross-head bolt together with the washer.
56 Fit the gear lever bracket and bush, and tighten the bolt.
57 Locate the selector finger in position and drive in the selector shaft. Tap the plug over the shaft.
58 Locate the 5th speed driving gear on the end of the input shaft with the chamfer towards the taper roller bearing, then fit the circlip.
59 On the output shaft locate the 5th speed thrust washer followed by the needle roller cage and inner sleeve.
60 Locate the 5th speed gear on the needle rollers followed by the synchro ring.
61 Tap on the 5th synchro hub, but take care to align the synchro ring with the cut-outs.
62 Fit the circlip next to the synchro hub.
63 Push the 5th selector rod into 5th gear position.
64 Clean the threads of the ball-head bolt on the 5th gear selector fork and coat them with locking fluid.
65 Locate the 5th gear synchro sleeve on the hub referring also to Chapter 6, Section 6.
66 Engage the 5th selector fork with the sleeve and selector rod, push the sleeve into 5th position and screw in the ball-head bolt.
67 Refit the clutch housing to the gearbox housing by referring to Chapter 6, Section 8, paragraphs 23 to 29, then adjust the 5th selector fork as follows.
68 With all the selector rods in neutral, turn the ball-head bolt until the synchro sleeve is flush with the hub. Now engage 5th gear and screw in the bolt until the clearance between the selector fork and the sleeve groove is just eliminated. Back off the bolt an eighth of a turn, then lock by tightening the locknut.
69 Refit the end cover together with a new gasket and tighten the bolts.
70 Refit the clutch release bearing and shaft (Section 8).
71 Refill the gearbox with oil after fitting it to the engine.

Gearshift mechanism (085) – removal, refitting and adjustment
72 Refer to Chapter 6, Section 9.

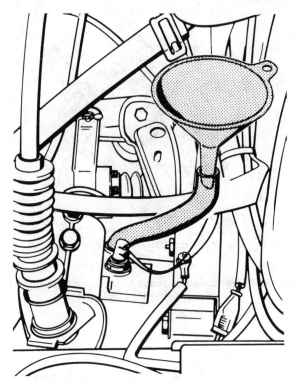

Fig. 12.84 Method of filling the gearbox through the speedometer drive shaft hole (Sec 10)

Gearbox oil level (020 5-speed) – checking
73 If there are no apparent oil leaks from the gearbox it is not necessary to check the oil level. However, if there is any doubt, a check should be made considering also the following points.
74 The 020 5-speed gearbox was originally designed for an engine/gearbox assembly without any inclination. When fitted to models in this manual a 2° inclination to the left exists, therefore an accurate check cannot be made with the car on ground level. Level checks on gearboxes removed from the car present no problem, as the specified amount of oil can be added from dry, or the gearbox can be positioned horizontally.
75 When checking the oil level with the car on level ground, unscrew the level plug and if there is a thick flow of oil immediately refit the plug. If there is no flow, first top up to the bottom of the hole, refit the plug, then add a further 0.5 litre (0.9 pint) through the speedometer drive shaft hole (Fig.12.84).

11 Electrical system

Oil pressure warning system – description
1 Some models are equipped with an optical and acoustic oil pressure warning system. The system incorporates two oil pressure switches, a 0.3 bar switch with brown insulation on the cylinder head and a 1.8 bar switch with white insulation on the oil filter head.
2 On starting the engine, as soon as the oil pressure rises above 0.3 bar, the oil pressure warning light will go out. At engine speeds above 2000 rpm the high pressure switch comes into operation, and should the oil pressure drop below 1.8 bar, the oil warning light will come on and the buzzer will sound.
3 Apart from changing the oil pressure switches, little can be done by way of maintenance, and your VAG dealer should be consulted if the system malfunctions.

Alternator drivebelt – adjustment
4 From early 1985 some models are fitted with a rack type alternator adjustment link. To adjust the drivebelt tension where this is fitted, first fully loosen the adjustment pinch bolt, the link pivot bolt and the alternator pivot bolt, so that the alternator falls to one side under its own weight.

Fig. 12.85 Rack type alternator adjusting link (A) and adjustment nut (B) (Sec 11)

5 Using a socket and torque wrench on the large adjustment nut apply a torque of 8 Nm (6 lbf ft) for a new drivebelt, or 4 Nm (3 lbf ft) for a used drivebelt.
6 If the special VW tool is being used the adjustment bolt can now be tightened, but if not, tighten the pivot bolt then remove the socket and immediately tighten the adjustment bolt, making sure that the alternator does not move.
7 Tighten the remaining nut/bolt.

Multi-function indicator (MFI) – description
8 Some models are equipped with a multi-function indicator consisting of an electronic processor and a digital display unit. With the ignition switched on the following information can be accessed by repeatedly pressing the MFA recall button on the end of the windscreen wiper control stalk.

Current time
Driving time
Distance driven
Average speed
Average fuel consumption
Engine oil temperature
Ambient temperature

9 Should a fault occur in the system the associated wiring should be checked for security and damage, particularly where it connects to the various sensors. Further checks should be made by a VW dealer using the special test instruments necessary.

Windscreen and rear window washer system – modifications
10 As from early 1986 the washer system described in Chapter 9, Section 41 is modified. The new system has a single reservoir and pump located in the engine compartment, with a plastic tube to the rear window incorporated in the rear wiring loom.
11 The wiper switch incorporates two sets of contacts which energise the pump with opposite polarities, causing rotation of the pump vane in two alternative directions. Using in-line non-return valves, the water is directed either to the windscreen or rear window according to which direction the pump is rotating

Headlamps (twin) – alignment
12 On models with twin headlamps, the inner lamps are adjusted laterally with the *lower* adjustment screw, and vertically with the *upper* screw.

12 Suspension and steering

Front syspension camber adjustment – general
1 On early models, front suspension camber adjustment was possible

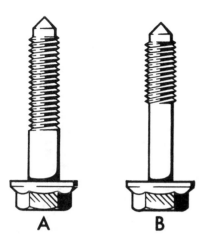

Fig. 12.86 Front suspension strut-to-wheel bearing housing bolts (Sec 12)

A *Standard 12.0 mm diameter bolt*

B *Special 11.0 mm diameter bolt*

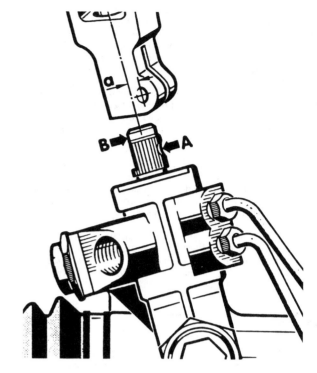

Fig. 12.87 Power steering gear pinion modification (Sec 12)

a *Dimension reduced from 12.1 mm to 11.0 mm*

A *Notch depth increased*

B *Flat for identification purposes*

by loosening the two bolts securing the strut to the wheel bearing housing, then turning the eccentric top bolt as required. Where this arrangement is fitted, the position of the eccentric bolt must be accurately marked before removing it, otherwise the camber adjustment will have to be reset.

2 On later models no adjustment was possible as the assembly tolerances were reduced sufficiently to make any adjustment unnecessary. However, in isolated instances it may be found that even on later models slight correction of the camber angle within 1° or 2° is required. In this case a special bolt, part number N 903-334-01 can be obtained from a VW dealer. The bolt shank is of 11 mm diameter instead of the standard 12 mm diameter and allows a small amount of adjustment to be made.

3 The special bolt should first be fitted in the top bolt position, but if this does not provide sufficient adjustment, the lower bolt should also be changed for the special type. No attempt should be made to reduce the diameter of the original bolts.

Front suspension camber adjustment – general

4 On 1988 models, the rear suspension mounting bracket bolts incorporate a modified shoulder, and the tightening torque is reduced to that given in the Specifications.

Power steering gear pinion – modification

5 As from May 1985 the pinch bolt clamping the intermediate shaft to the steering gear pinion is located approximately 1.0 mm (0.040 in) nearer the centre line of the pinion. To identify the modified pinion a flat is cut opposite the pinch bolt location.

6 When renewing either of the components separately it may be necessary to increase the depth of the pinch bolt recess in the pinion by 1.0 mm (0.040 in) so that the two components match. **Do not** alter the hole in the intermediate shaft.

Wheels and tyres – general care and maintenance

7 Wheels and tyres should give no real problems in use provided that a close eye is kept on them with regard to excessive wear or damage. To this end, the following points should be noted.

8 Ensure that tyre pressures are checked regularly and maintained correctly. Checking should be carried out with the tyres cold and not immediately after the vehicle has been in use. If the pressures are checked with the tyres hot, an apparently high reading will be obtained owing to heat expansion. Under no circumstances should an attempt be made to reduce the pressures to the quoted cold reading in this instance, or effective underinflation will result.

9 Underinflation will cause overheating of the tyre owing to excessive flexing of the casing, and the tread will not sit correctly on the road surface. This will cause a consequent loss of adhesion and excessive wear, not to mention the danger of sudden tyre failure due to heat build-up.

10 Overinflation will cause rapid wear of the centre part of the tyre tread coupled with reduced adhesion, harsher ride, and the danger of shock damage occurring in the tyre casing.

11 Regularly check the tyres for damage in the form of cuts or bulges, especially in the sidewalls. Remove any nails or stones embedded in the tread before they penetrate the tyre to cause deflation. If removal of a nail *does* reveal that the tyre has been punctured, refit the nail so that its point of penetration is marked. Then immediately change the wheel and have the tyre repaired by a tyre dealer. Do *not* drive on a tyre in such a condition. In many cases a puncture can be simply repaired by the use of an inner tube of the correct size and type. If in any doubt as to the possible consequences of any damage found, consult your local tyre dealer for advice.

12 Periodically remove the wheels and clean any dirt or mud from the inside and outside surfaces. Examine the wheel rims for signs of rusting, corrosion or other damage. Light alloy wheels are easily damaged by 'kerbing' whilst parking, and similarly steel wheels may become dented or buckled. Renewal of the wheel is very often the only course of remedial action possible.

13 The balance of each wheel and tyre assembly should be maintained to avoid excessive wear, not only to the tyres but also to the steering and suspension components. Wheel imbalance is normally signified by vibration through the vehicle's bodyshell, although in many cases it is particularly noticeable through the steering wheel. Conversely, it should be noted that wear or damage in suspension or steering components may cause excessive tyre wear. Out-of-round or out-of-true tyres, damaged wheels and wheel bearing wear/maladjustment also fall into this category. Balancing will not usually cure vibration caused by such wear.

14 Wheel balancing may be carried out with the wheel either on or off the vehicle. If balanced on the vehicle, ensure that the wheel-to-hub relationship is marked in some way prior to subsequent wheel removal so that it may be refitted in its original position.

15 General tyre wear is influenced to a large degree by driving style –

harsh braking and acceleration or fast cornering will all produce more rapid tyre wear. Interchanging of tyres may result in more even wear, but this should only be carried out where there is no mix of tyre types on the vehicle. However, it is worth bearing in mind that if this is completely effective, the added expense of replacing a complete set of tyres simultaneously is incurred, which may prove financially restrictive for many owners.

16 Front tyres may wear unevenly as a result of wheel misalignment. The front wheels should always be correctly aligned according to the settings specified by the vehicle manufacturer.

17 Legal restrictions apply to the mixing of tyre types on a vehicle. Basically this means that a vehicle must not have tyres of differing construction on the same axle. Although it is not recommended to mix tyre types between front axle and rear axle, the only legally permissible combination is crossply at the front and radial at the rear. When mixing radial ply tyres, textile braced radials must always go on the front axle, with steel braced radials at the rear. An obvious disadvantage of such mixing is the necessity to carry two spare tyres to avoid contravening the law in the event of a puncture.

18 In the UK, the Motor Vehicles Construction and Use Regulations apply to many aspects of tyre fitting and usage. It is suggested that a copy of these regulations is obtained from your local police if in doubt as to the current legal requirements with regard to tyre condition, minimum tread depth, etc.

13 Bodywork and fittings

Minor body damage – repair of plastic components

1 With the use of more and more plastic body components by the vehicle manufacturers (eg bumpers, spoilers, and in some cases major body panels), rectification of damage to such items has become a matter of either entrusting repair work to a specialist in this field, or renewing complete components. Repair by the DIY owner is not really feasible owing to the cost of the equipment and materials required for effecting such repairs. The basic technique involves making a groove along the line of the crack in the plastic using a rotary burr in a power drill. The damaged part is then welded back together by using a hot air gun to heat up and fuse a plastic filler rod into the groove. Any excess plastic is then removed and the area rubbed down to a smooth finish. It is important that a filler rod of the correct plastic is used, as body components can be made of a variety of different types (eg polycarbonate, ABS, polypropylene).

2 If the owner is renewing a complete component himself, he will be left with the problem of finding a suitable paint for finishing which is compatible with the type of plastic used. At one time the use of a universal paint was not possible owing to the complex range of plastics encountered in body component applications. Standard paints, generally speaking, will not bond to plastic or rubber satisfactorily. However, it is now possible to obtain a plastic body parts finishing kit which consists of a pre-primer treatment, a primer and coloured top coat. Full instuctions are normally supplied with a kit, but basically the method of use is to first apply the pre-primer to the component concerned and allow it to dry for up to 30 minutes. Then the primer is applied and left to dry for about an hour before finally applying the special coloured top coat. The result is a correctly coloured component where the paint will flex with the plastic or rubber, a property that standard paint does not normally possess.

Seat belts with height adjustment – description

3 As from early 1986 some models are fitted with front seat belts incorporating height adjustment of the 'B' pillar. The components involved are shown in Fig. 12.88.

4 The adjustable seat belts can be fitted to any model having a chassis number later than 16/19 G 054 900, but a new 'B' pillar trim must also be fitted.

Central locking system – description

5 The central locking system fitted to some models comprises a pressure/vacuum pump, control element (on the driver's door), shift elements (on the remaining doors and fuel tank flap), and interconnecting tubing.

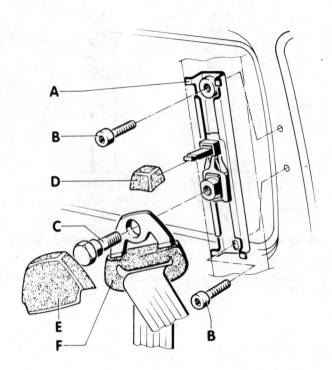

Fig. 12.88 Height adjustable seat belt components (Sec 13)

A	Adjuster bracket	D	Release knob
B	Socket head screw	E	Cap
C	Pivot bolt	F	Relay link

Central locking system components – removal and refitting

6 To remove the pressure/vacuum pump, release the rubber strap in the luggage compartment, remove the cover, then withdraw the pump and disconnect the wiring and tube.

7 To remove a control or shift element, first remove the door, tailgate, or luggage compartment trim panel as appropriate. On door elements, carefully peel back the protective foil. Remove the element mounting screws and disconnect the tubing. On the driver's door only, disconnect the wiring. Disconnect the operating rod (except on the the fuel tank flap) and withdraw the element.

8 Refitting is a reversal of removal, but make sure that the door protective foil is firmly stuck to prevent water penetration. Use double-sided tape to secure it if necessary.

Front door (1988 models) – dismantling and reassembly

9 The front door components for 1988 models are shown in Fig. 12.90. Dismantling and reassembly procedures are basically the same as for earlier models.

Exterior mirror (1988 models) – removal and refitting

10 On 1988 models, the exterior mirrors are mounted in the triangular area in front of the window glass.

11 The removal and refitting procedures are basically the same as for earlier models. Note that the mirror glass is clipped in position and may be removed by carefully levering out the bottom edge, then the top edge, using a plastic or wooden tool. When refitting the glass, align the guide pins and use a wad of cloth, pressing only on the middle of the glass.

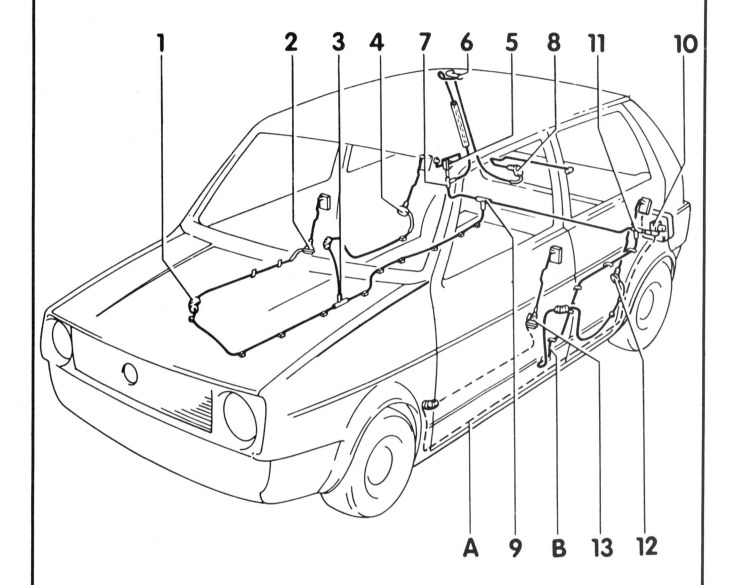

Fig. 12.89 Central locking system on LHD model (Sec 13)

1 Bellows
2 Front door shift element (or control element on RHD)
3 Connector
4 Rear door shift element
5 Fuel tank flap shift element
6 Grommet
7 Connector
8 Tailgate shift element
9 Connector
10 Pressure/vacuum pump
11 Connector
12 Rear door shift element
13 Front door control element (or shift element on RHD)
A Wiring
B Tubing

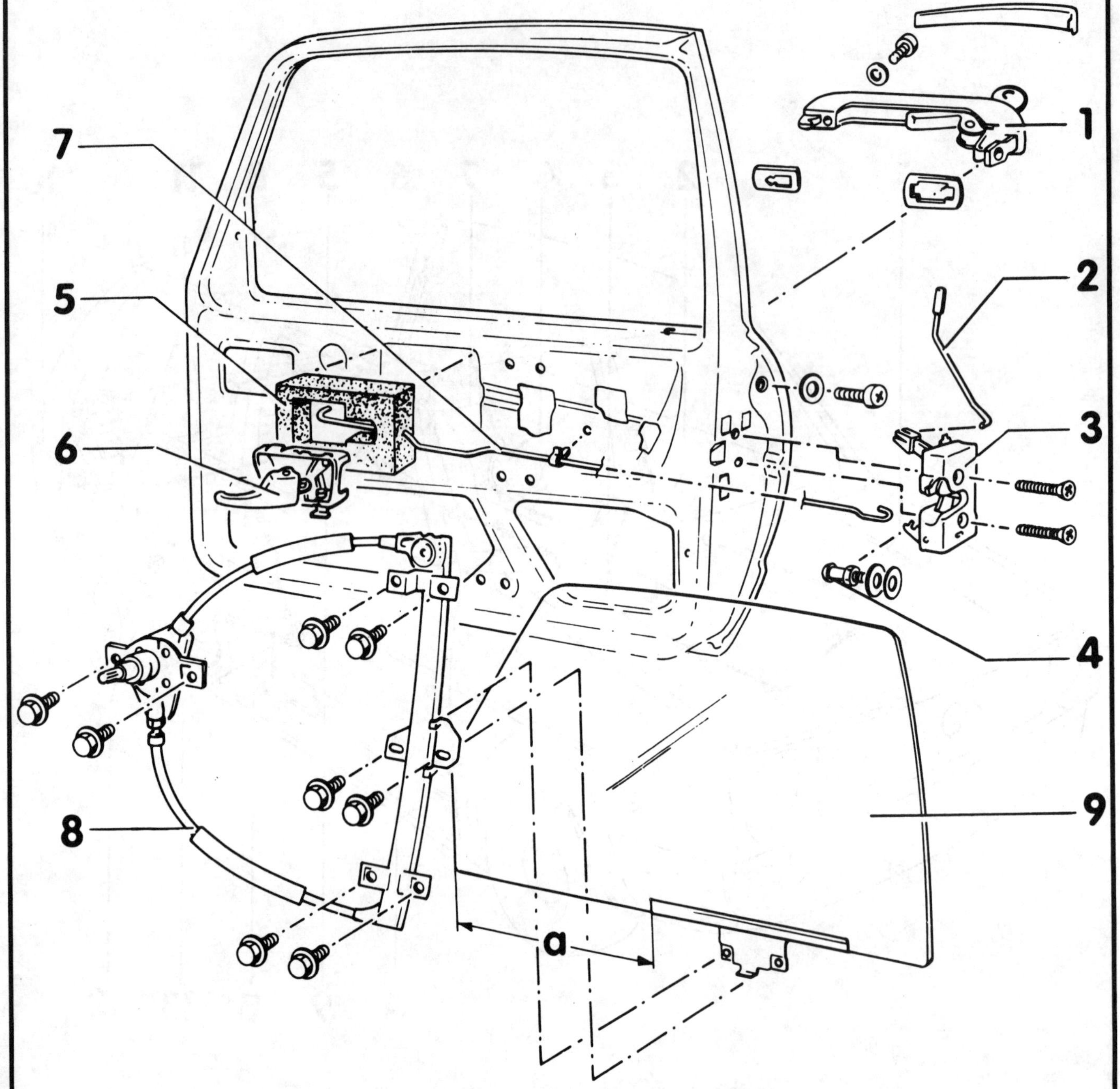

7

5

6

8

1

2

3

4

9

a

Fig. 12.90 Front door components for 1988 models (Sec 13)

1   *Exterior handle*
2   *Locking rod*
3   *Door lock*
4   *Locking pin*
5   *Seal*
6   *Internal remote control*
7   *Pull rod*
8   *Window regulator*
9   *Window glass*
a = *310 mm (12.2 in)*

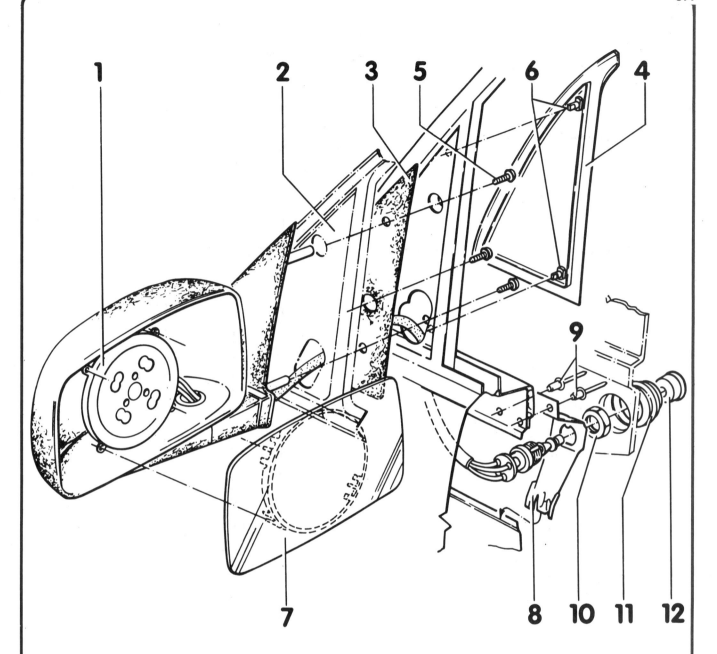

**Fig. 12.91 Exterior mirror components for 1988 models
(Sec 13)**

1	Body	7	Glass
2	Trim	8	Bracket
3	Packing	9	Pop-rivets
4	Inner trim	10	Nut
5	Screw	11	Bellows
6	Clip	12	Adjusting knob

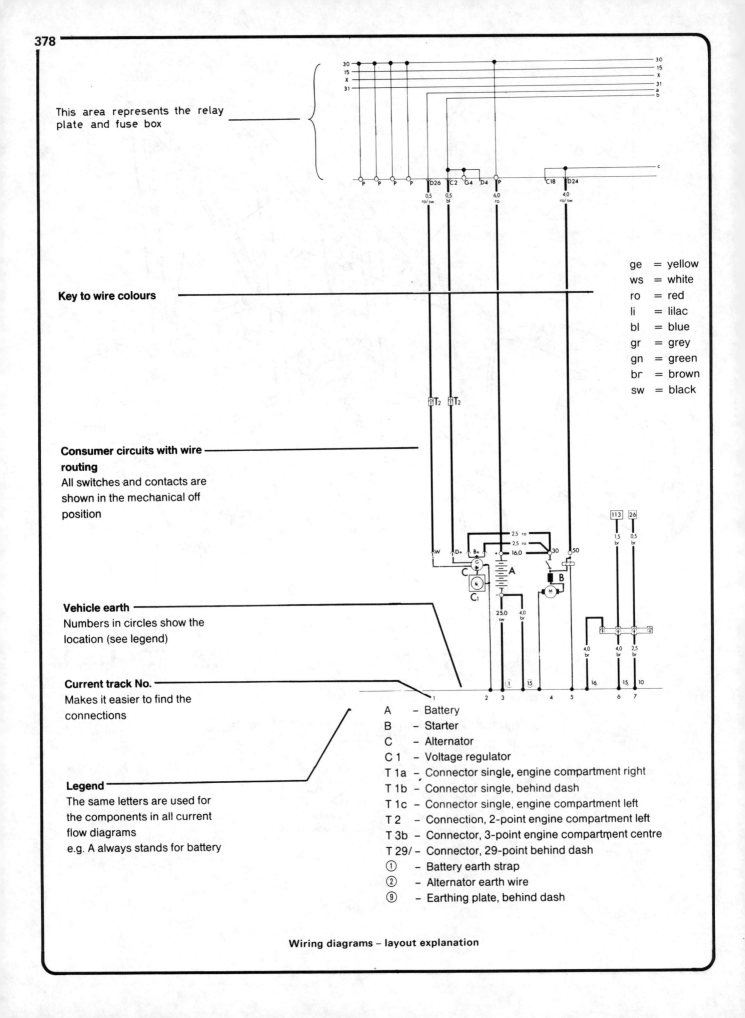

This area represents the relay
plate and fuse box

Key to wire colours

ge = yellow
ws = white
ro = red
li = lilac
bl = blue
gr = grey
gn = green
br = brown
sw = black

**Consumer circuits with wire
routing**
All switches and contacts are
shown in the mechanical off
position

Vehicle earth
Numbers in circles show the
location (see legend)

Current track No.
Makes it easier to find the
connections

Legend
The same letters are used for
the components in all current
flow diagrams
e.g. A always stands for battery

A – Battery
B – Starter
C – Alternator
C 1 – Voltage regulator
T 1a – Connector single, engine compartment right
T 1b – Connector single, behind dash
T 1c – Connector single, engine compartment left
T 2 – Connection, 2-point engine compartment left
T 3b – Connector, 3-point engine compartment centre
T 29/ – Connector, 29-point behind dash
① – Battery earth strap
② – Alternator earth wire
⑨ – Earthing plate, behind dash

Wiring diagrams – layout explanation

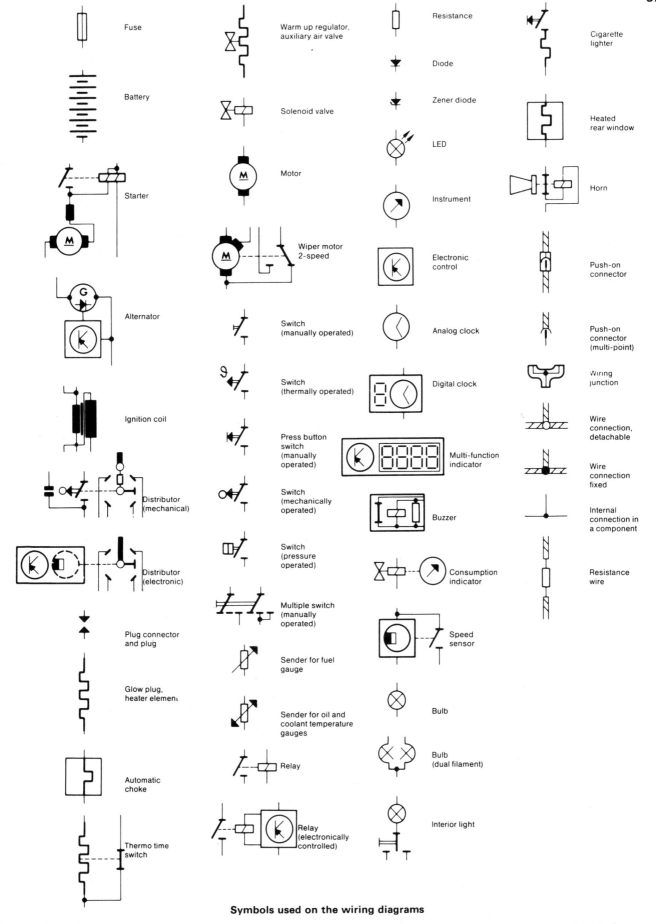

Fuse

Battery

Starter

Alternator

Ignition coil

Distributor (mechanical)

Distributor (electronic)

Plug connector and plug

Glow plug, heater element

Automatic choke

Thermo time switch

Warm up regulator, auxiliary air valve

Solenoid valve

Motor

Wiper motor 2-speed

Switch (manually operated)

Switch (thermally operated)

Press button switch (manually operated)

Switch (mechanically operated)

Switch (pressure operated)

Multiple switch (manually operated)

Sender for fuel gauge

Sender for oil and coolant temperature gauges

Relay

Relay (electronically controlled)

Resistance

Diode

Zener diode

LED

Instrument

Electronic control

Analog clock

Digital clock

Multi-function indicator

Buzzer

Consumption indicator

Speed sensor

Bulb

Bulb (dual filament)

Interior light

Cigarette lighter

Heated rear window

Horn

Push-on connector

Push-on connector (multi-point)

Wiring junction

Wire connection, detachable

Wire connection fixed

Internal connection in a component

Resistance wire

Symbols used on the wiring diagrams

Relay locations

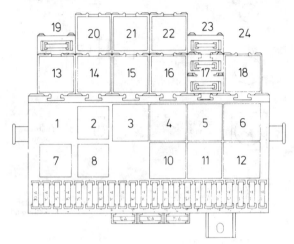

Connections

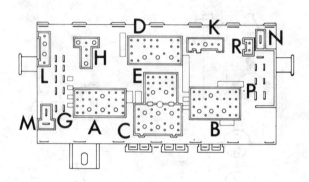

Relays and connections – all models

Relays (typical)

1 Vacant
2 Intake manifold preheating relay (carburettor models) or fuel pump relay (injection models)
3 Seat belt warning system relay
4 Gearshift indicator control unit
5 Air conditioner relay
6 Dual tone horn relay
7 Relay for foglights and rear foglight
8 Relief relay for X contact
10 Intermittent wash/wipe relay
11 Rear window wiper relay
12 Turn signal flasher or trailer towing warning relay
13 Seat belt warning system (interlock) or rear window, driving lights and oil pressure warning relay
14 Window lift or seat belt warning system relay
15 Headlight washer relay
16 Control unit for idling speed increase
17 Fuse for rear foglight
18 Control unit for coolant shortage indicator
19 Thermo fuse for window lifters
20 Switch unit for heated driver's seat
21 Switch unit for heated passenger's seat
22 Switch unit for overrun cut-off
23 Vacant
24 Vacant

Relays are symbolised as a number in a black box

Not all relays are fitted to all models

Connections

A Multi-pin connector (blue) for dash panel loom
B Multi-pin connector (red) for dash panel loom
C Multi-pin connector (yellow) for engine compartment loom left
D Multi-pin connector (white) for engine compartment loom right
E Multi-pin connector (black) for rear wiring loom
G Single connector
H Multi-pin connector (brown) for air conditioner or wiring loom
K Multi-pin connector (transparent) for seat belt warning system loom
L Multi-pin connector (black) for lighting switch terminal 56 and dip and flasher switch terminal 56b (carburettor models) or multi-pin connector (grey) for dual tone horn (injection models)
M Multi-pin connector (black) for lighting switch terminal 56 and dip and flasher switch terminal 56b (injection models)
N Single connector for separate fuse (manifold heater element)
P Single connector (terminal 30)
R Not in use

Fuse colours

Blue	15A
Green	30A
Red	10A
Yellow	20A

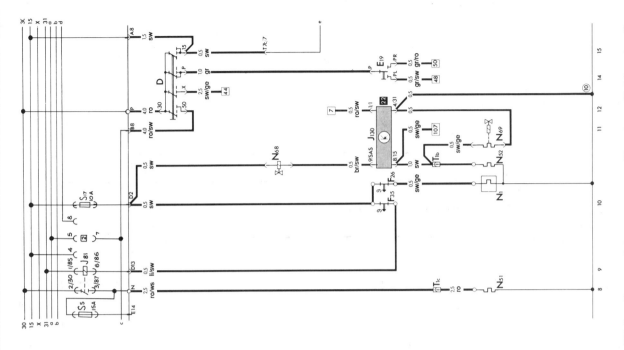

Wiring diagram for overrun cut-off and manifold preheating
1.6 models up to July 1987

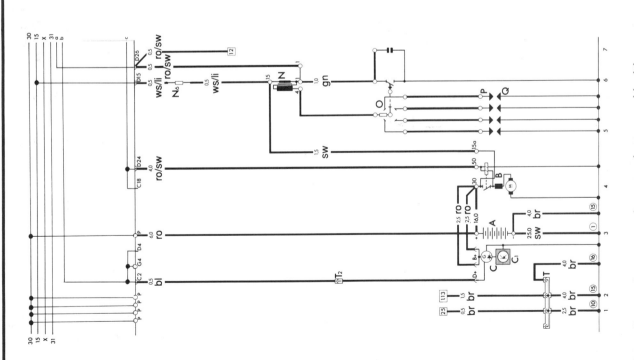

Wiring diagram for starter, alternator, battery and ignition system
1.05, 1.3 and 1.6 models up to July 1985

Wiring diagram for dash insert and dynamic oil pressure warning sender
1.05, 1.3 and 1.6 models up to July 1987

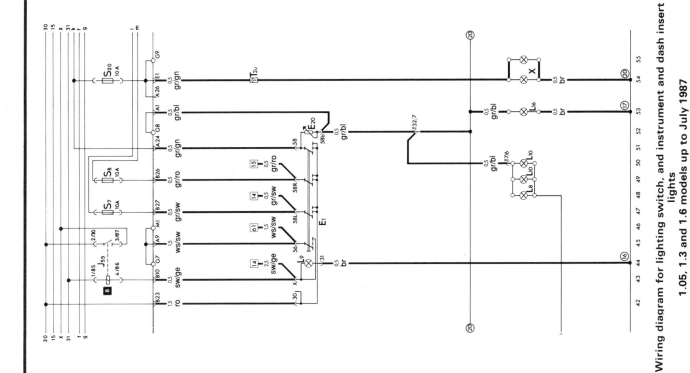

Wiring diagram for lighting switch, and instrument and dash insert
lights
1.05, 1.3 and 1.6 models up to July 1987

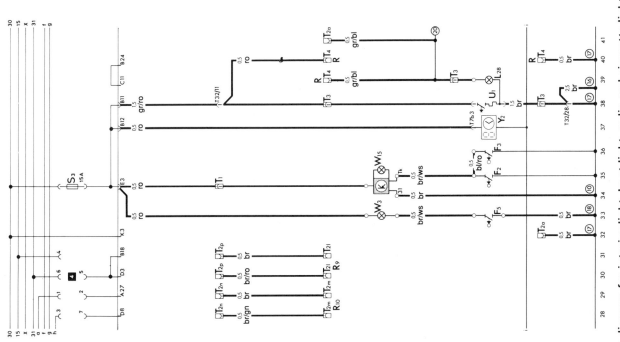

Wiring diagram for interior light, boot light, radio and cigarette lighter
1.05, 1.3 and 1.6 models up to July 1987

384

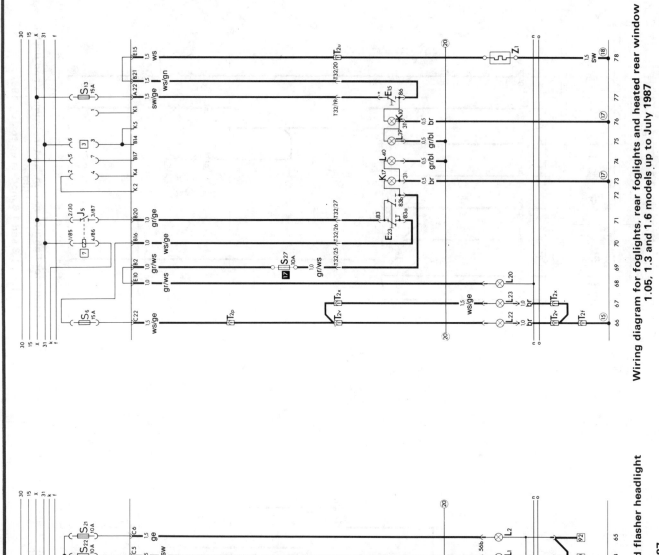

**Wiring diagram for foglights, rear foglights and heated rear window
1.05, 1.3 and 1.6 models up to July 1987**

**Wiring diagram for headlights, tail lights, and dip and flasher headlight
switch
1.05, 1.3 and 1.6 models up to July 1987**

385

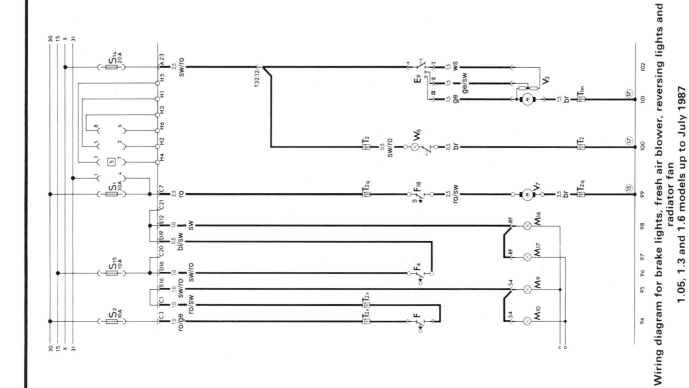

Wiring diagram for brake lights, fresh air blower, reversing lights and radiator fan
1.05, 1.3 and 1.6 models up to July 1987

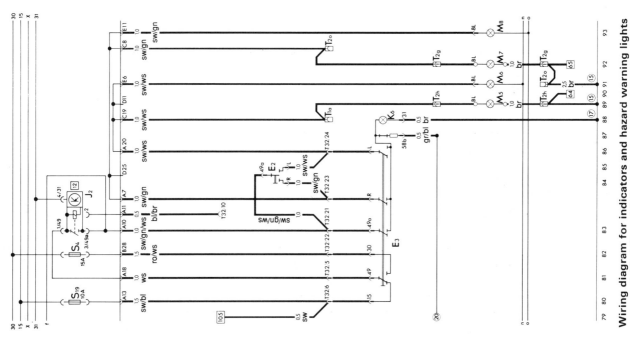

Wiring diagram for indicators and hazard warning lights
1.05, 1.3, and 1.6 models up to July 1987

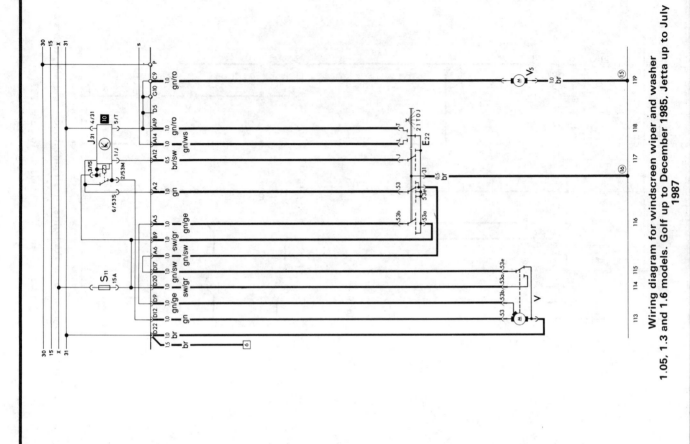

Wiring diagram for windscreen wiper and washer
1.05, 1.3 and 1.6 models. Golf up to December 1985. Jetta up to July 1987

Wiring diagram for dual tone horn, and handbrake and brake fluid level warning
1.05, 1.3 and 1.6 models up to July 1987

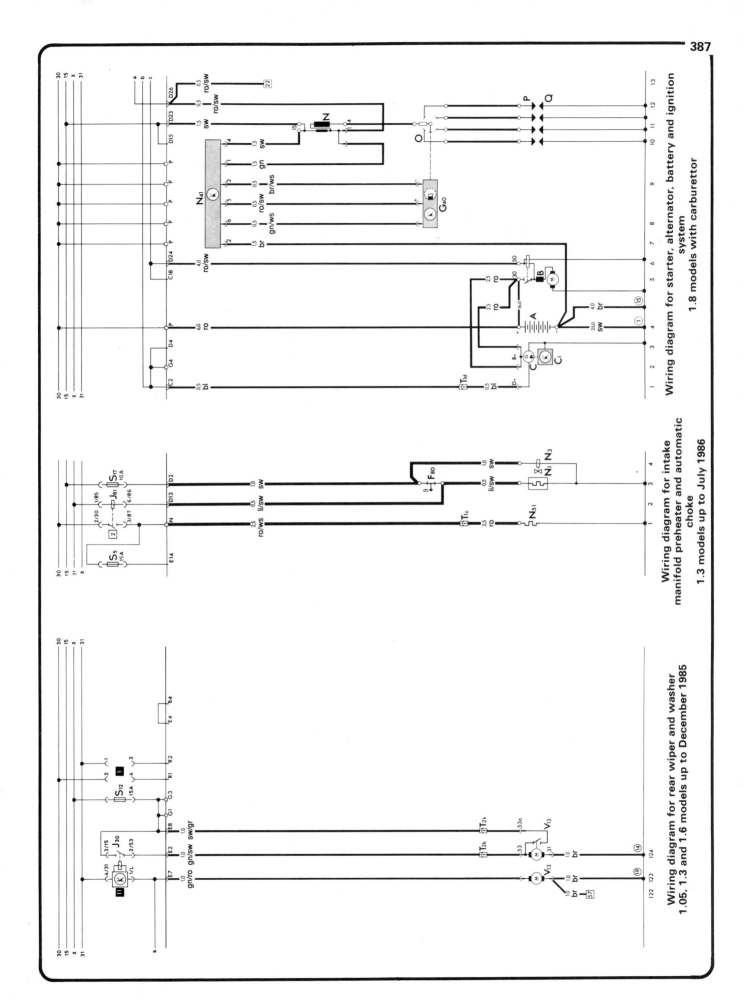

Wiring diagram for starter, alternator, battery and ignition system
1.8 models with carburettor

Wiring diagram for intake manifold preheater and automatic choke
1.3 models up to July 1986

Wiring diagram for rear wiper and washer
1.05, 1.3 and 1.6 models up to December 1985

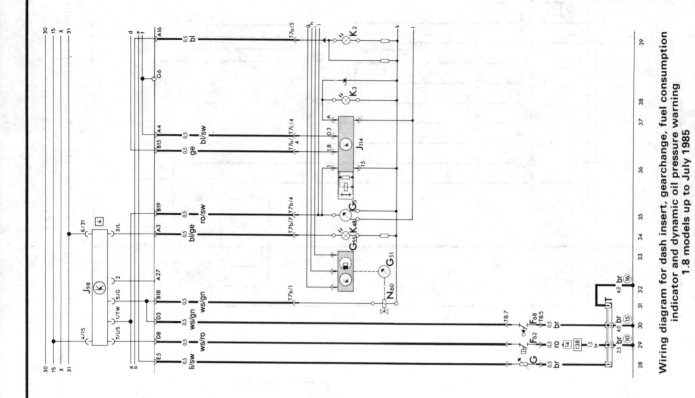

Wiring diagram for dash insert, gearchange, fuel consumption indicator and dynamic oil pressure warning
1.8 models up to July 1985

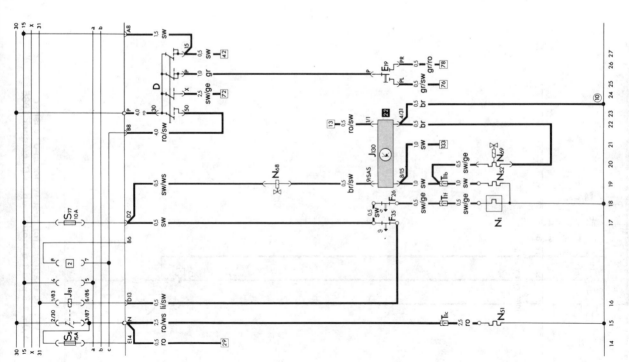

Wiring diagram for overrun cut-off and intake preheating
1.8 models with carburettor up to July 1987

388

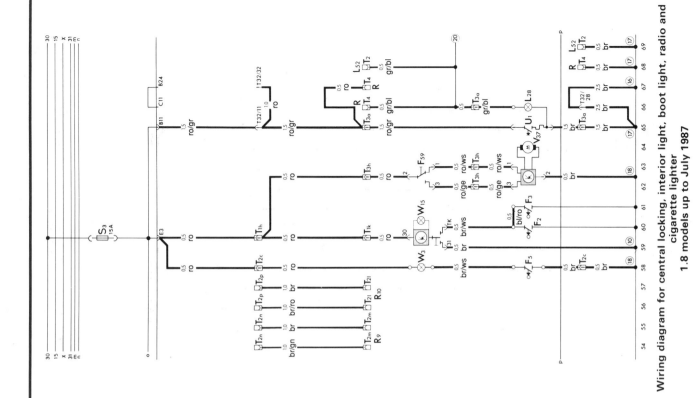

Wiring diagram for central locking, interior light, boot light, radio and cigarette lighter
1.8 models up to July 1987

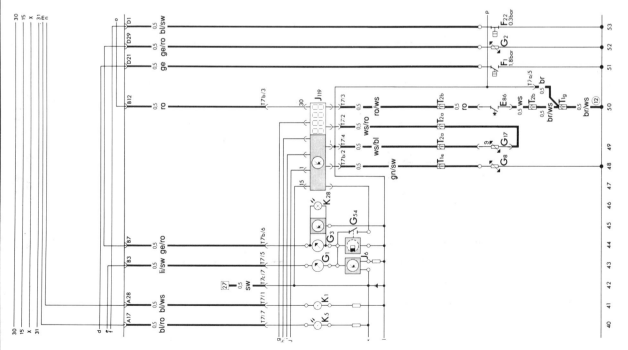

Wiring diagram for dash insert and multi-function indicator
1.8 models up to July 1985

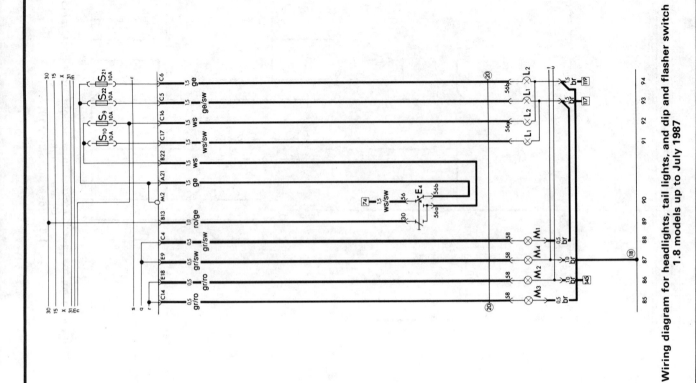

**Wiring diagram for headlights, tail lights, and dip and flasher switch
1.8 models up to July 1987**

**Wiring diagram for lighting switch, and instrument and dash lights
1.8 models up to July 1987**

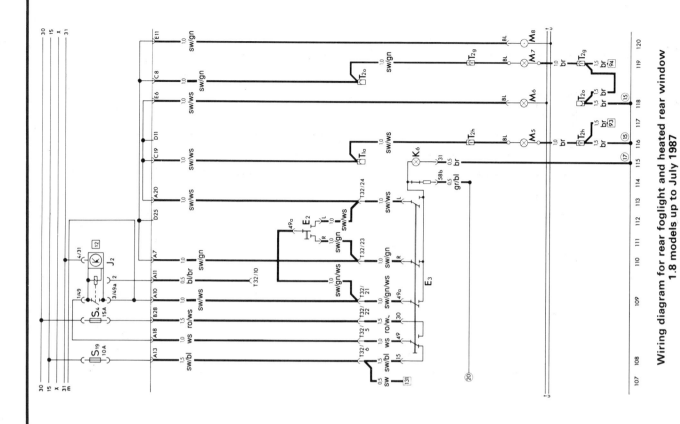

Wiring diagram for rear foglight and heated rear window
1.8 models up to July 1987

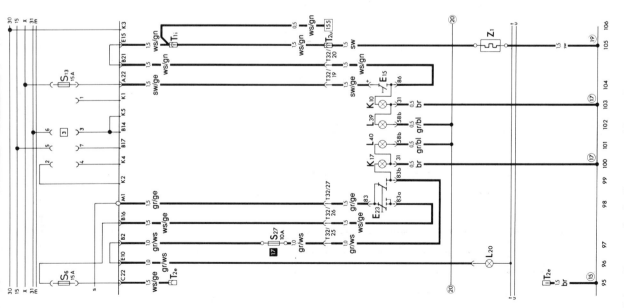

Wiring diagram for indicators and hazard warning lights
1.8 models up to July 1987

392

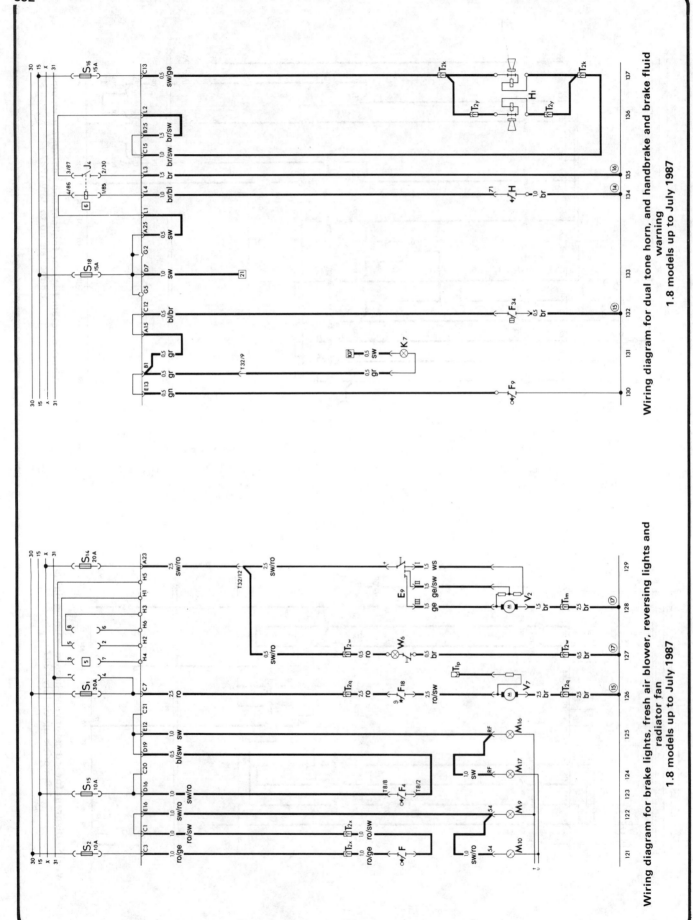

Wiring diagram for dual tone horn, and handbrake and brake fluid
warning
1.8 models up to July 1987

Wiring diagram for brake lights, fresh air blower, reversing lights and
radiator fan
1.8 models up to July 1987

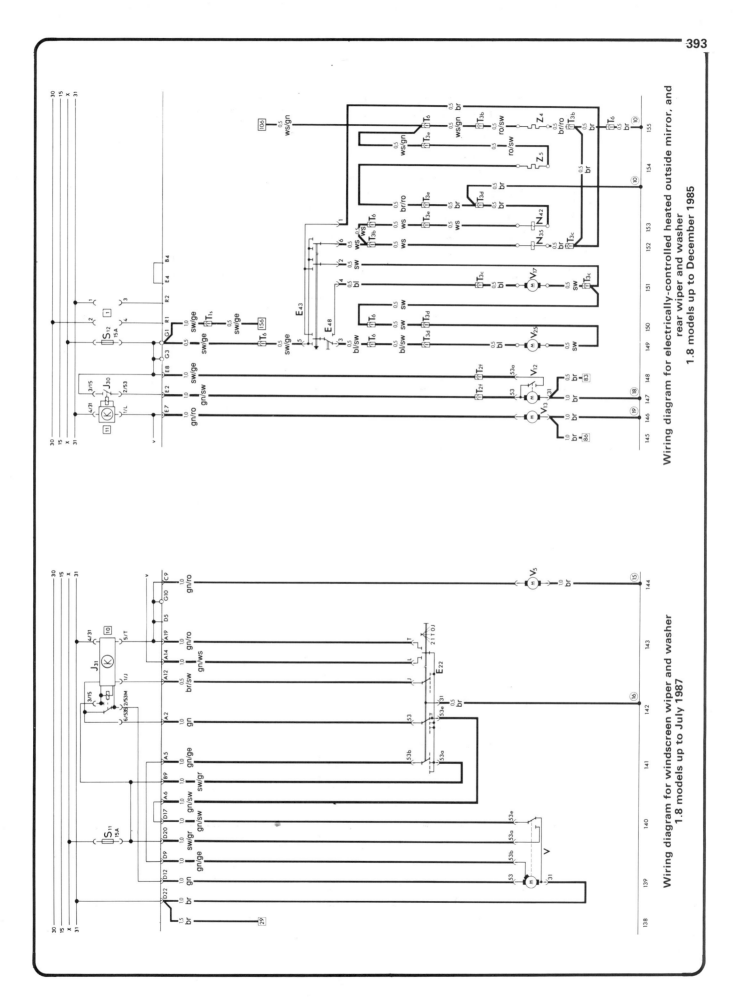

Wiring diagram for electrically-controlled heated outside mirror, and rear wiper and washer 1.8 models up to December 1985

Wiring diagram for windscreen wiper and washer 1.8 models up to July 1987

Wiring diagram for starter, alternator, battery and ignition system
1.8 models with fuel injection up to July 1984

Wiring diagram for electric windows
1.8 models with carburettor up to July 1987

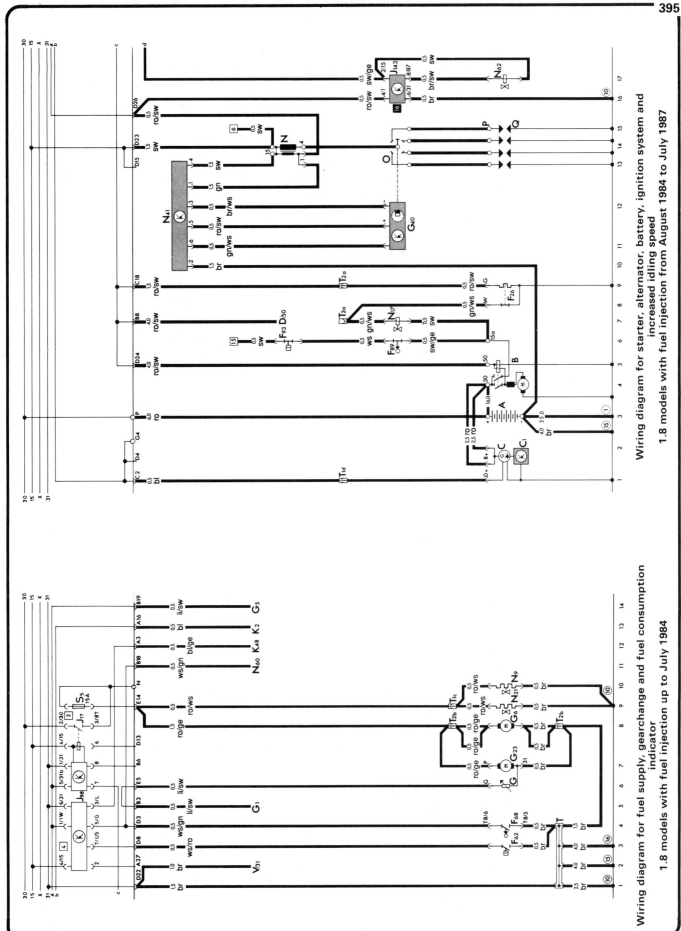

Wiring diagram for starter, alternator, battery, ignition system and increased idling speed
1.8 models with fuel injection from August 1984 to July 1987

Wiring diagram for fuel supply, gearchange and fuel consumption indicator
1.8 models with fuel injection up to July 1984

Wiring diagram for headlight washer
All models

Wiring diagram for fuel system, gearchange, and fuel consumption and
coolant shortage indicators
1.8 models with fuel injection from August 1984 to July 1987

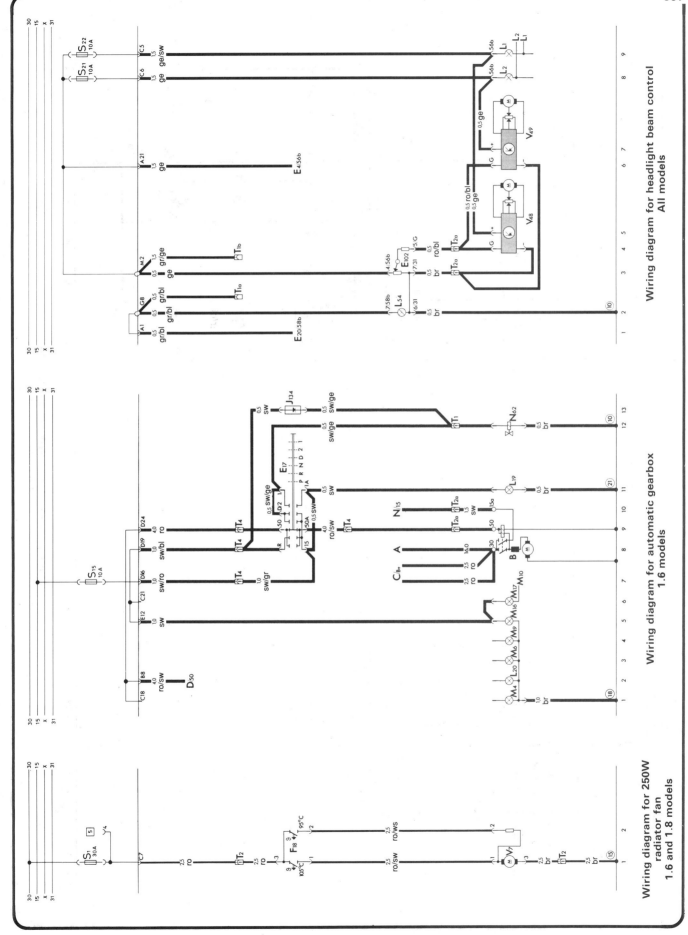

Wiring diagram for headlight beam control
All models

Wiring diagram for automatic gearbox
1.6 models

Wiring diagram for 250W radiator fan
1.6 and 1.8 models

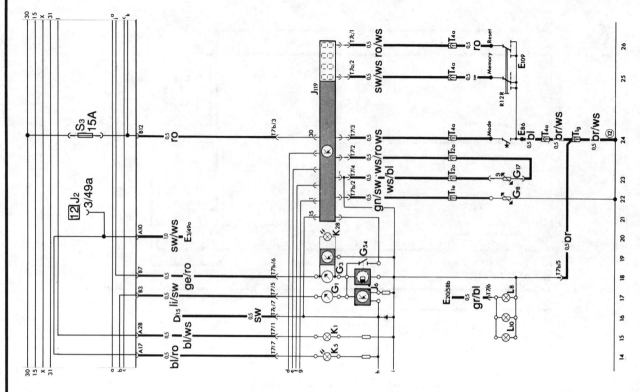

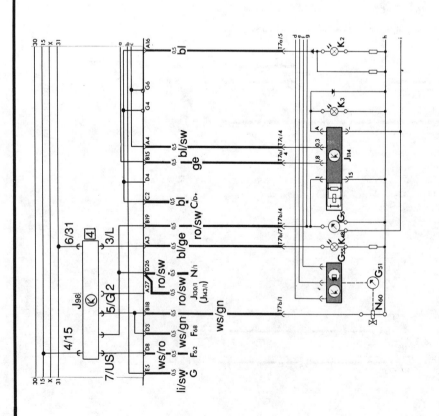

Wiring diagram for multi-function indicator 1.8 models

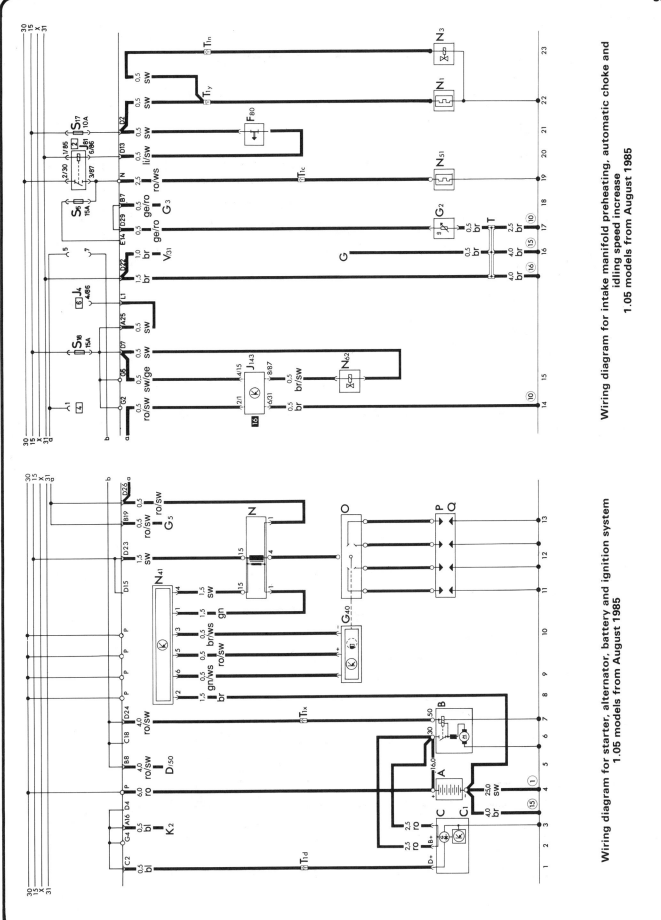

Wiring diagram for intake manifold preheating, automatic choke and idling speed increase
1.05 models from August 1985

Wiring diagram for starter, alternator, battery and ignition system
1.05 models from August 1985

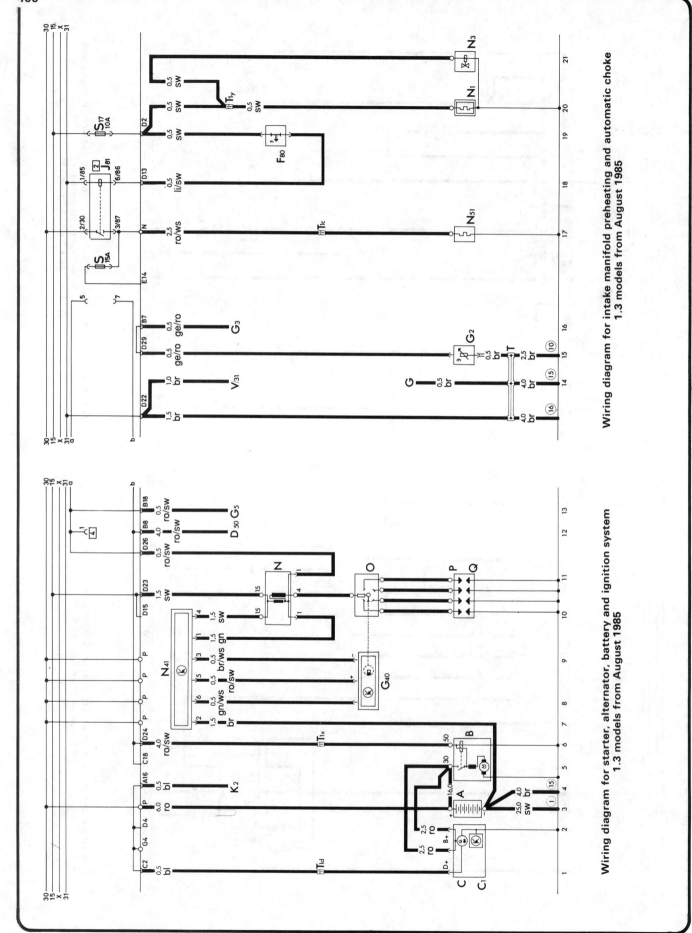

Wiring diagram for intake manifold preheating and automatic choke
1.3 models from August 1985

Wiring diagram for starter, alternator, battery and ignition system
1.3 models from August 1985

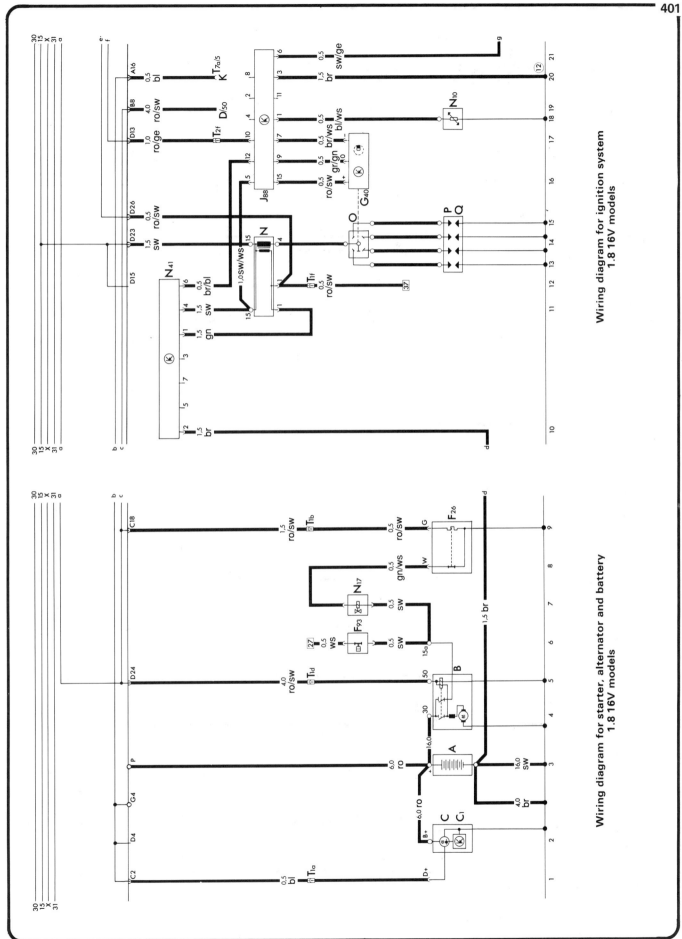

Wiring diagram for ignition system
1.8 16V models

Wiring diagram for starter, alternator and battery
1.8 16V models

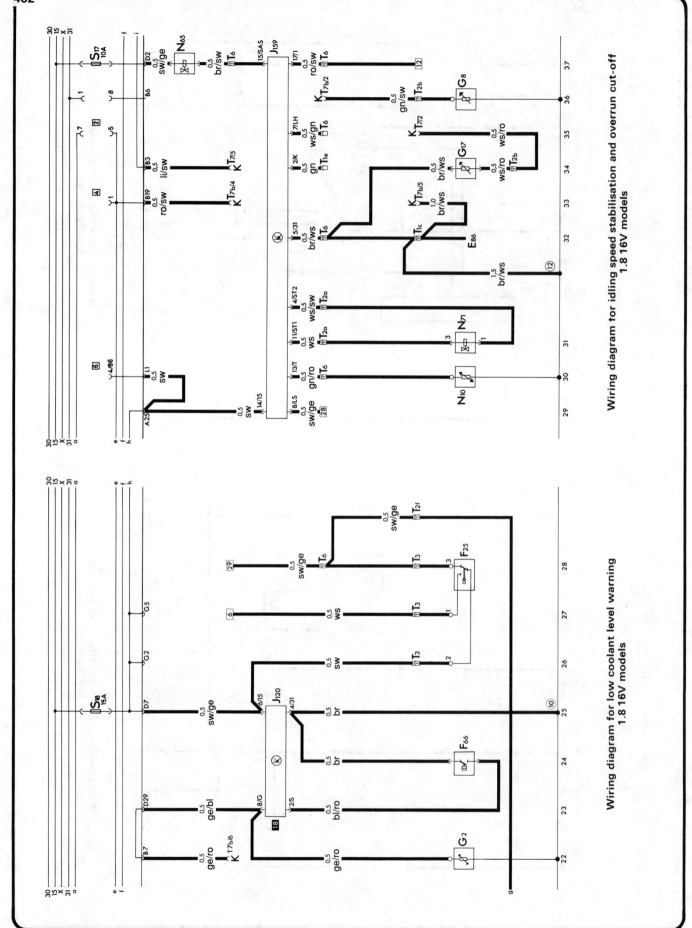

Wiring diagram for idling speed stabilisation and overrun cut-off 1.8 16V models

Wiring diagram for low coolant level warning 1.8 16V models

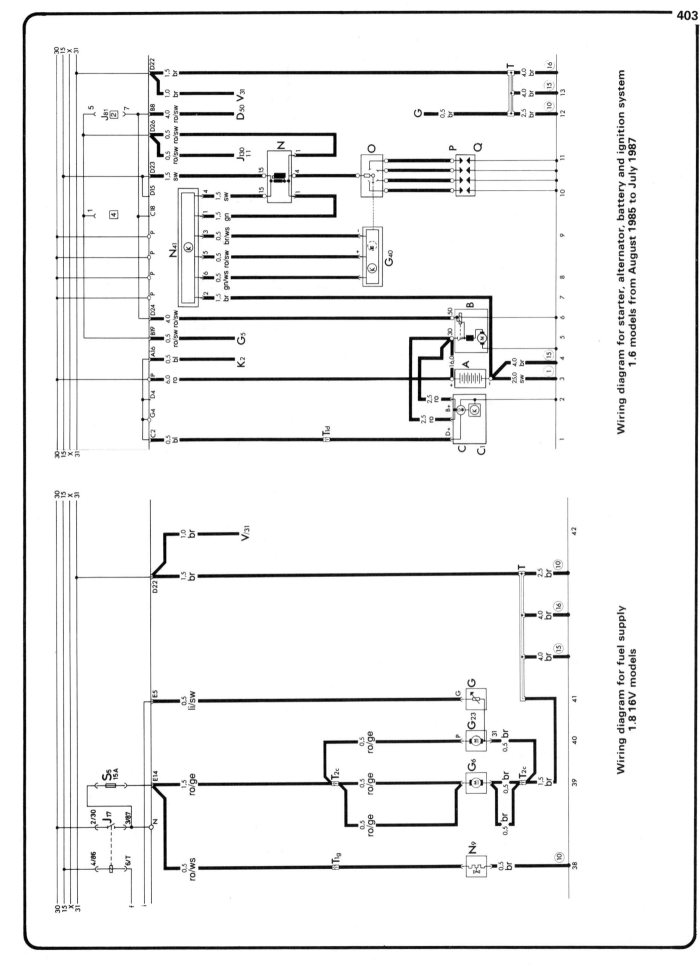

Wiring diagram for starter, alternator, battery and ignition system
1.6 models from August 1985 to July 1987

Wiring diagram for fuel supply
1.8 16V models

Wiring diagram for windscreen wiper
All Golf models from January 1986 to July 1987

Wiring diagram for radiator fan run-on
1.6 and 1.8 models from March 1986 to July 1987

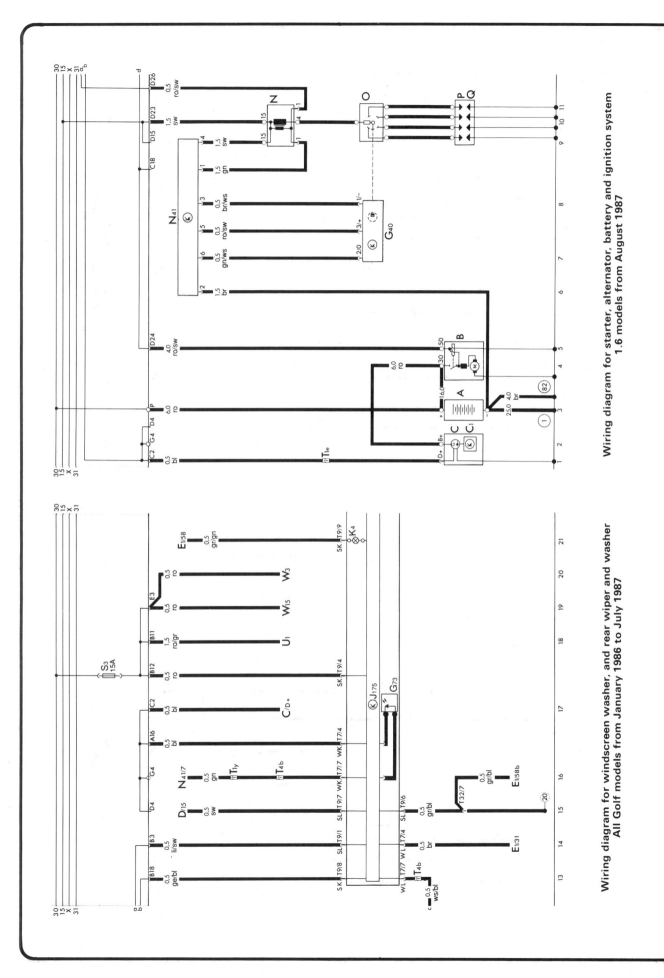

Wiring diagram for starter, alternator, battery and ignition system
1.6 models from August 1987

Wiring diagram for windscreen washer, and rear wiper and washer
All Golf models from January 1986 to July 1987

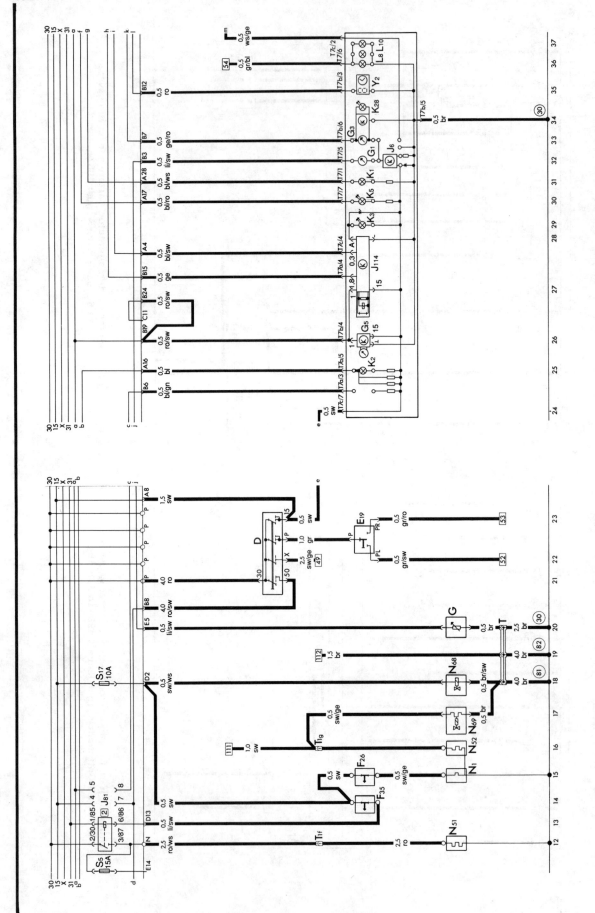

Wiring diagram for dash panel insert, optical and acoustic oil pressure warning, and rev counter
All models from August 1987

Wiring diagram for inlet manifold preheating and automatic choke
1.6 models from August 1987

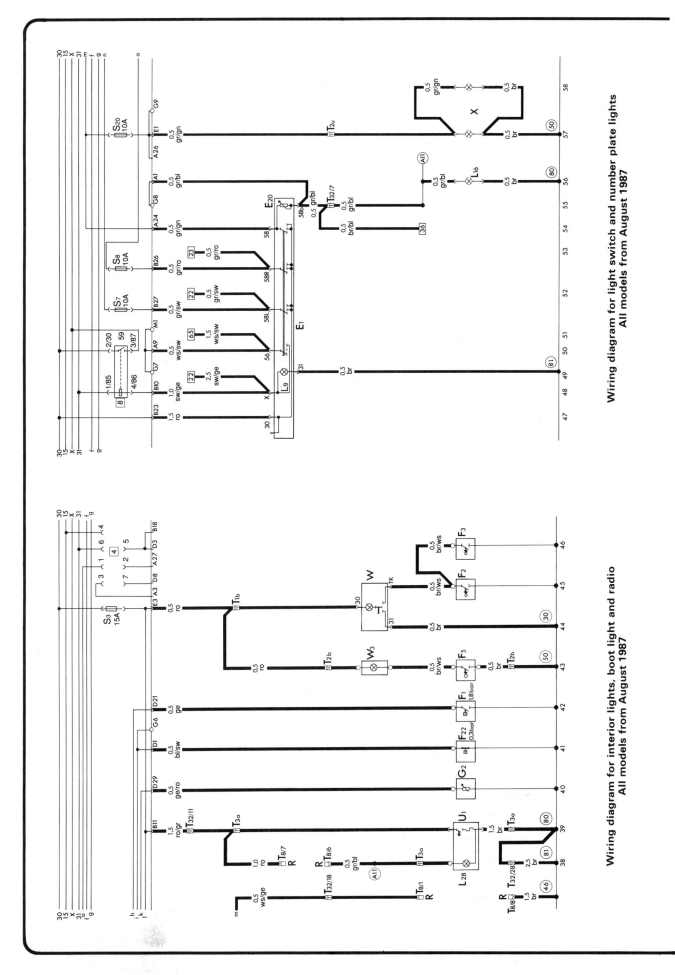

Wiring diagram for light switch and number plate lights
All models from August 1987

Wiring diagram for interior lights, boot light and radio
All models from August 1987

408

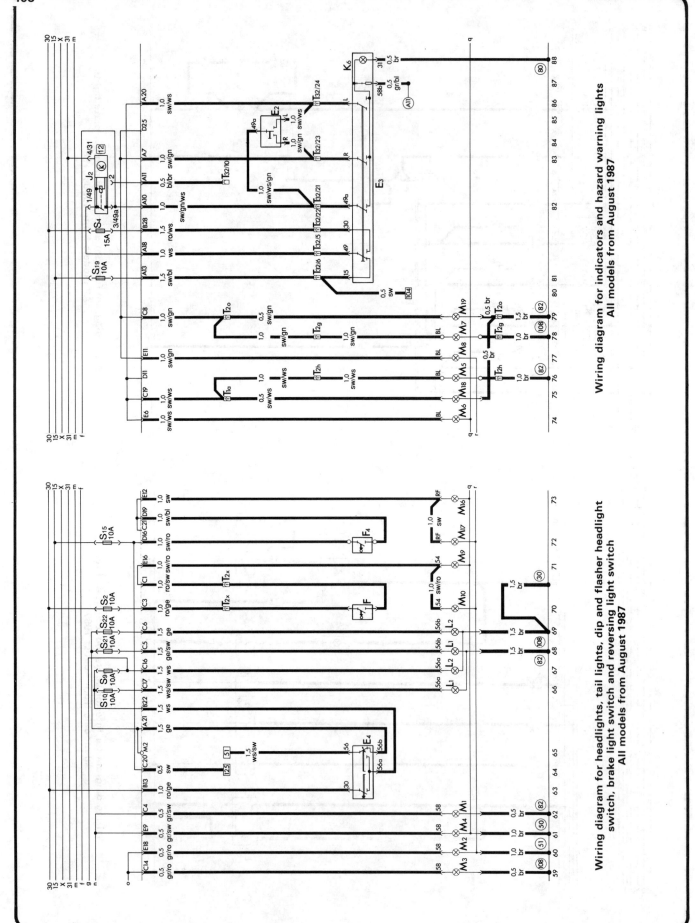

Wiring diagram for indicators and hazard warning lights
All models from August 1987

Wiring diagram for headlights, tail lights, dip and flasher headlight
switch, brake light switch and reversing light switch
All models from August 1987

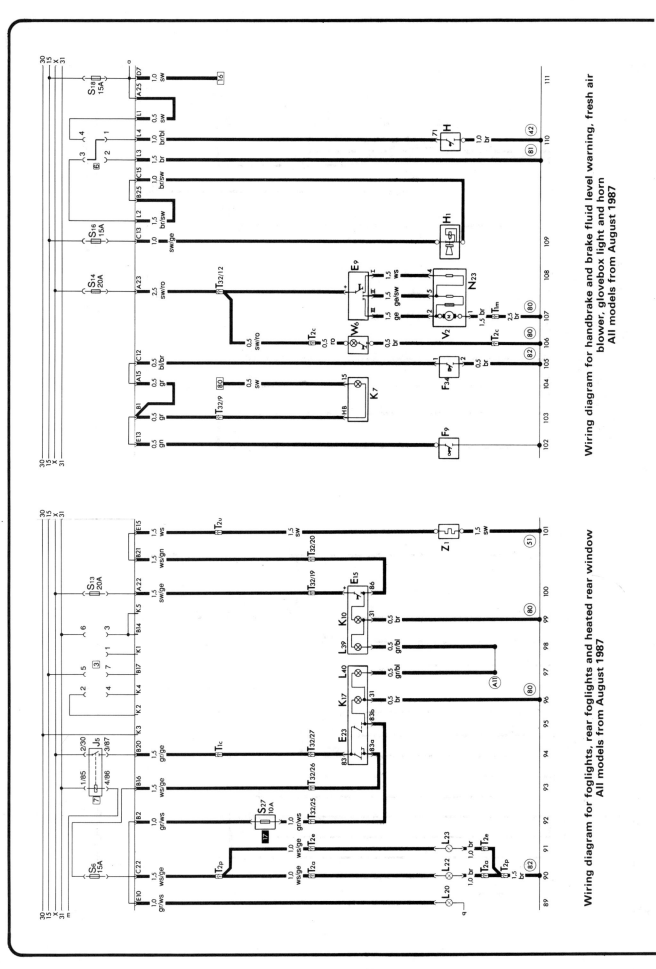

Wiring diagram for handbrake and brake fluid level warning, fresh air blower, glovebox light and horn
All models from August 1987

Wiring diagram for foglights, rear foglights and heated rear window
All models from August 1987

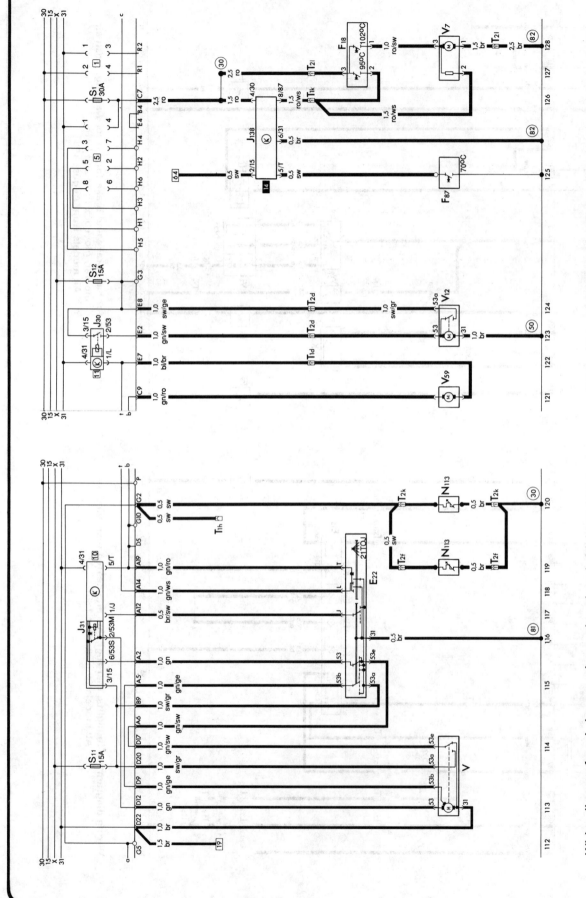

Wiring diagram for rear window wiper and radiator fan run-on 1.6 and 1.8 carburettor models from August 1987

Wiring diagram for windscreen wiper and washers (with heated jets) All models from August 1987

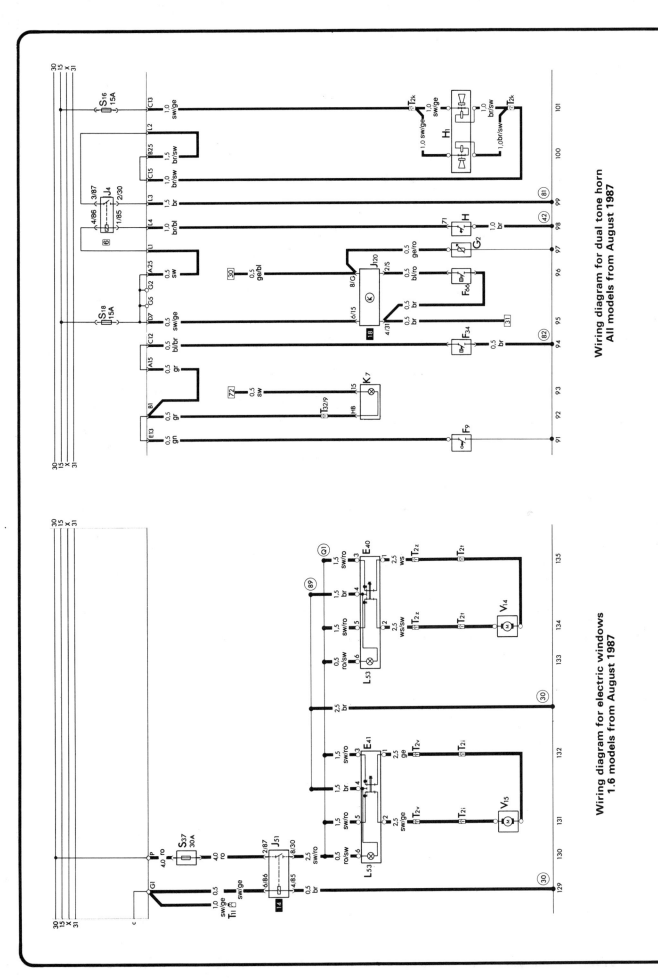

Wiring diagram for dual tone horn
All models from August 1987

Wiring diagram for electric windows
1.6 models from August 1987

412

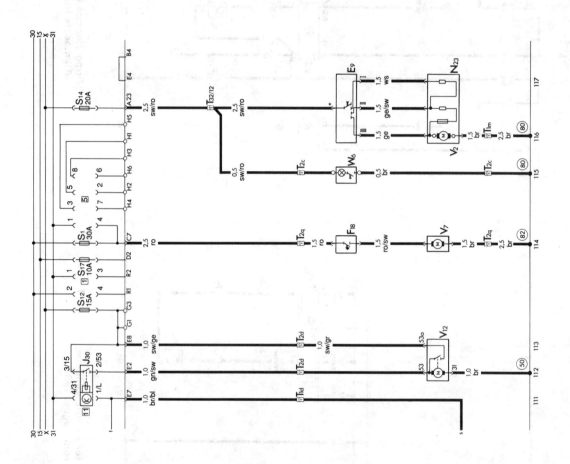

**Wiring diagram for rear window wiper and radiator fan
1.05, 1.3 and 1.8 fuel injection models from August 1987**

Key for all wiring diagrams

A	Battery		G2	Coolant temperature sender
B	Starter		G3	Coolant temperature gauge
C	Alternator		G5	Rev counter
C1	Voltage regulator		G6	Fuel pump
D	Ignition switch		G8	Oil temperature sender
E1	Lighting switch		G17	Feeler for outside temperature
E2	Indicator switch		G23	Electric fuel pump II
E3	Hazard warning light switch		G40	Hall sender
E4	Headlight dip and flasher switch		G51	Consumption indicator
E9	Fresh air blower switch		G54	Speed sensor for multi-function indicator
E15	Heated rear window switch		G55	Vacuum sensor for multi-function indicator
E17	Starter/inhibitor and reversing light switch		G114	Switch unit for oil pressure warning
E19	Parking light switch		H	Horn control
E20	Instrument/dash insert lighting control		H1	Dual tone horn
E22	Intermittent wiper switch		J2	Indicators flasher relay
E23	Foglight and rear foglight switch		J4	Dual tone horn relay
E39	Electric window switch		J5	Foglight relay
E40	Electric window switch, left		J6	Voltage stabiliser
E41	Electric window switch, right		J17	Fuel pump relay
E43	Mirror adjustment switch		J30	Rear wash/wipe relay
E48	Mirror adjustment changeover switch		J31	Intermittent wash/wipe relay
E52	Electric window switch, rear left, in door		J51	Electric window relay
E53	Electric window switch, rear left, in console		J59	Relief valve (for X contact)
E54	Electric window switch, rear right, in door		J81	Intake preheating relay
E55	Electric window switch, rear right, in console		J86	Electronic ignition control unit
E102	Headlight beam adjuster		J98	Gearchange indicator switch unit
E109	Memory switch for MFI		J114	Oil pressure monitor switch unit
F	Brake light switch		J119	Multi-function indicator
F1	Oil pressure switch (1.8 bar)		J120	Switch unit for low coolant indicator
F2	Door contact switch, front left		J130	Switch unit for overrun cut-off valve
F3	Door contact switch, front right		J134	Diode
F4	Reversing light switch		J138	Control unit for radiator fan run-on
F5	Boot light		J143	Switch unit for speed increase
F9	Handbrake warning switch		J159	Control unit for idle speed stabiliser and overrun cut-off
F10	Thermo-switch for radiator fan			
F22	Oil pressure switch (0.3 bar)		K	Dash insert
F25	Throttle valve switch		K1	High beam warning lamp
F26	Thermo-switch for choke		K2	Alternator warning lamp
F34	Brake fluid level warning contact		K3	Oil pressure warning lamp
F35	Thermo-switch for intake preheating		K5	Indicators warning lamp
F59	Central locking system switch		K6	Warning lamp for hazard lights
F62	Gearchange indicator vacuum switch		K7	Dual circuit and handbrake warning lamp
F66	Low level coolant switch		K10	Heated rear window warning lamp
F68	Switch for gearchange and consumption indicator		K17	Foglight warning lamp
F80	Thermo-switch for N52		K28	Coolant temperature warning lamp (too hot, red)
F87	Thermo-switch for radiator from run-on		K48	Gearchange indicator warning lamp
F89	Switch for accelerator enrichment		L1	Twin filament headlight bulb, left
F93	Vacuum timeswitch		L2	Twin filament headlight bulb, right
G	Fuel gauge sender		L8	Clock light bulb
G1	Fuel gauge		L9	Lighting switch bulb

Key for all wiring diagrams (continued)

L10	Dash insert bulb	R9	Loudspeaker, front left
L16	Fresh air control bulb	R10	Loudspeaker, front right
L19	Gear selector bulb	S27	Separate fuse for rear foglight
L20	Rear foglight bulb	S37	Fuse for electric windows
L22	Foglight bulb	T	Connector, behind relay plate
L23	Foglight bulb, right	T1	Single connector, various locations
L28	Cigarette lighter bulb	T1a	Single connector, various locations
L39	Heated rear window switch bulb	T1b	Single connector, left of engine compartment or behind relay plate
L40	Foglight switch bulb		
L52	Connection for fader control unit	T1c	Single connector, various locations
L53	Electric window switch light	T1d	Single connector, various locations
L54	Headlight beam adjuster bulb	T1e	Single connector, right of engine compartment or behind relay plate
M1	Parking light bulb, left		
M2	Tail light bulb, right	T1f	Single connector, near carburettor or coil
M3	Parking light bulb, right	T1g	Single connector, various locations
M4	Tail light bulb, left	T1h	Single connector, behind relay plate
M5	Indicator bulb, front left	T1i	Single connector, behind relay plate
M6	Indicator bulb, rear left	T1k	Single connector, behind relay plate or on radiator cowl
M7	Indicator bulb, front right		
M8	Indicator bulb, rear right	T1l	Single connector, behind relay plate
M9	Brake light bulb, left	T1m	Single connector, behind dash ·
M10	Brake light bulb, right	T1n	Single connector, behind relay plate or near carburettor
M16	Reversing light bulb, left		
M17	Reversing light bulb, right	T1p	Single connector, on radiator cowl
M18	Side indicator bulb, left	T1s	Single connector, behind relay plate
M19	Side indicator bulb, right	T1x	Single connector, near coil
N	Ignition coil	T1y	Single connector, near carburettor or behind relay plate
N1	Automatic choke		
N3	Bypass cut-off valve	T2	2-pin connector, various locations
N6	Resistance wire	T2a	2-pin connector, various locations
N9	Warm-up valve	T2b	2-pin connector, various locations
N10	Temperature sensor (NTC resistance)	T2c	2-pin connector, left of boot or behind dash
N17	Cold start valve	T2d	2-pin connector, left of boot or behind dash
N21	Auxiliary air valve	T2e	2-pin connector, left of engine compartment
N23	Series resistance for fresh air blower	T2f	2-pin connector, various locations
N35	Mirror adjustment solenoid, driver's	T2g	2-pin connector, right of engine compartment
N41	TCI control unit	T2h	2-pin connector, left of engine compartment
N42	Mirror adjustment solenoid, passenger's	T2i	2-pin connector, behind door trim
N51	Heater element for manifold preheating	T2k	2-pin connector, various locations
N52	Heater element for carburettor throttle passage	T2l	2-pin connector, behind dash or front of engine compartment
N60	Solenoid valve for consumption indicator	T2m	2-pin connector, behind dash
N62	Idling speed – acceleration valve	T2n	2-pin connector, behind dash
N65	Overrun cut-off valve	T2o	2-pin connector, right of engine compartment
N68	Idling – overrun cut-off valve	T2p	2-pin connector, various locations
N69	Thermotime valve for overrun cut-off	T2q	2-pin connector, right of engine compartment
N71	Control valve for idling stabilisation	T2r	2-pin connector, behind door trim
N113	Heater resistance for washer jets	T2s	2-pin connector, behind door trim
O	Distributor	T2t	2-pin connector, behind door trim
P	Spark plug connector	T2u	2-pin connector, left of boot
Q	Spark plug	T2v	2-pin connector, behind right A-pillar trim or in engine compartment
R	Connection for radio		

Key for all wiring diagrams (continued)

T2w	2-pin connector, behind dash		W3	Boot light
T2x	2-pin connector, front of engine compartment or behind dash		W6	Glovebox light
T2y	2-pin connector, front of engine compartment		W15	Delayed interior light
T2z	2-pin connector, behind left A-pillar trim		X	Number plate light
T3	3-pin connector, on throttle valve housing or behind relay plate		Y2	Digital clock
T3a	3-pin connector, behind relay plate		Z1	Heated rear window
T3b	3-pin connector, behind door trim		Z4	Heated mirror, driver's
T3c	3-pin connector, behind door trim		Z5	Heated mirror, passenger's
T3d	3-pin connector, behind door trim			
T3e	3-pin connector, behind door trim			

Earth connections

T3f	3-pin connector, behind right B-pillar trim		1	Battery earth strap
T3g	3-pin connector, behind left B-pillar trim		10	Near relay plate
T3h	3-pin connector, behind relay plate		12	On cylinder head cover or distributor
T4	4-pin connector, behind dash		14	Near steering column or in tailgate
T4a	4-pin connector, behind steering column trim		15	In front loom
T6	6-pin connector, behind relay plate		16	In instrument loom
T7	7-pin connector, on dash insert or behind steering column trim		17	In instrument loom
T7a	7-pin connector, on dash insert		19	In boot on right
T7b	7-pin connector, on dash insert		20	On front seat crossmember, in tailgate or in instrument loom
T7c	7-pin connector, on dash insert		21	In electric window loom
T8	8-pin connector, on gearbox or behind dash		22	In electric window loom
T32	32-pin connector, behind dash		23	In electric window loom
U1	Cigarette lighter		30	In front loom or next to relay plate
V	Windscreen wiper motor		42	Next to steering column
V2	Fresh air blower		46	Next to relay plate
V5	Windscreen washer pump		50	In boot on left
V7	Radiator fan		51	In boot on right
V12	Wiper motor		80	In instrument loom
V13	Washer pump motor		81	In instrument loom
V14	Window motor, left		82	In front loom
V15	Window motor, right		89	In electric window loom
V17	Mirror adjustment motor, driver's		108	In front loom
V25	Mirror adjustment motor, passenger's		A11	In instrument loom
V26	Window motor, rear left		Q1	In electric window loom
V27	Window motor, rear right			
V37	Central locking motor			
V48	Headlight motor, left			
V49	Headlight motor, right			
V59	Washer pump			
W	Interior light, front			

Index